AF897670

Franchise Law Compliance
MANUAL

Third Edition

Elizabeth S. Dillon and James A. Goniea
EDITORS

AMERICAN BAR ASSOCIATION
Forum on Franchising

Cover design by Jill Tedhams/ABA Design

Printed in the United States of America.

25 24 23 22 5 4 3 2

A catalog record for this book is available from the Library of Congress.

Summary of Contents

Contents

Foreword

The *Franchise Law Compliance Manual* was originally conceived in the mid-1990s. It came to fruition under the steady hands of Steve Goldman and Bret Lowell with significant assistance from then-Chair of the Corporate Counsel Division Jeff Brimer. When first published, the *Franchise Law Compliance Manual* immediately joined other Forum on Franchising publications as a must-have addition to the library of any serious franchise law practitioner. The first edition of the *Manual* focused on both legal and practical compliance issues facing virtually every company engaged in franchising. The second edition, edited by Jeff Brimer and published in 2011, went even further. Not only did it rework, reorganize, and provide significant updates, but it also added an entirely new chapter on international franchising.

Much has happened in the world of franchising and franchise compliance since 2011. In its third edition, editors Elizabeth (Liz) Dillon and James (Jim) Goniea, and 16 chapter authors (a number of whom are new contributors) have reworked and updated the contents of the *Franchise Law Compliance Manual* to reflect those developments. Their collective efforts, drawing upon groundwork laid by previous authors and their own deep experience in franchising, have resulted in a book that builds upon and exceeds the scope and content of the earlier editions. In addition to capturing material developments from the past decade, the third edition adds a new chapter on data privacy, an area that was in its infancy at the time of the publication of the second edition but now should be top of mind for franchise law practitioners.

On behalf of the Forum on Franchising, I want to express gratitude to Liz and Jim and each of the chapter authors for all of the hard work they put in to this fine publication. This book is an important contribution to existing scholarship surrounding franchising and franchise law and a gift to franchise law practitioners both in the United States and around the world. I am confident that the practical and legal advice contained in this volume will be useful to all those interested in franchise law and compliance and will be especially appreciated by those charged with developing and implementing franchise compliance programs.

Will K. Woods
Chair
American Bar Association Forum on Franchising (2019–2021)

Acknowledgments

As the editors of this third edition of the *Franchise Law Compliance Manual*, we would like to recognize the numerous individuals who contributed to the earlier editions and those that contributed to the present edition of the *Manual*. Without their efforts, the present edition of the *Manual* would not have been possible. First, we want to recognize Steven M. Goldman and Bret Lowell, who served as editors for the first edition of the *Manual*, and Jeffrey A. Brimer, who served as editor of the second edition. They set the bar high and produced publications that are among the mostly widely used in the Forum's history.

Like many multi-edition books, the *Manual* builds upon the work of earlier chapter authors by updating and adding additional information to make the subject matter of the chapters timely and relevant. Accordingly, it is appropriate to recognize the contributions of the previous chapter authors whose work has provided the foundation for the present publication. The following persons served as authors of the first edition of the *Manual*:

Chapter 1: William A. Finkelstein and Anthony M. Stiegler
Chapter 2: Mark B. Forseth and Grover C. Outland
Chapter 3: Charles B. Cannon, Jerry L. Lovejoy, and Ken R. Minami
Chapter 4: Donnell J. McCormack and Sheri A. Young
Chapter 5: Raymond L. Miolla and Andrew C. Selden
Chapter 6: Lisa Pender Morse and Ronald T. Coleman, Jr.

The following persons served as authors of the second edition of the *Manual*:

Chapter 1: William A. Finkelstein and Sherin Sakr
Chapter 2: Leslie D. Curran, Mark B. Forseth, and Karen Spencer
Chapter 3: Brian H. Cole, John M. Richardson, Andra J. Terrell, and Sandra J. Wall
Chapter 4: Victoria Blackwell and Andrew C. Selden
Chapter 5: James A. Goniea and Jeffrey S. Haff
Chapter 6: Kevin P. Hein and Ted P. Pearce
Chapter 7: Robert A. Lauer and Alison C. McElroy

In addition, of course, the present chapter authors, whose hard work is primarily responsible for the third edition, are worthy of special thanks. Those authors are:

Chapter 1: Elisa Edlund and Sherin Sakr
Chapter 2: Leslie D. Curran, David Oppenheim, and Max Schott
Chapter 3: Brian H. Cole and Susan Sheely
Chapter 4: Eric Karp
Chapter 5: Jeffrey S. Haff and Susan Tegt

Chapter 6: Kevin P. Hein and Ted P. Pearce
Chapter 7: Robert A. Lauer and Alison C. McElroy
Chapter 8: Brian Hengesbaugh and Mark Melodia

We would also like to recognize Nicole Micklich, who was our liaison to the Publications Committee of the Forum, and David Oppenheim and Gary Batenhorst, who served as Publication Officers of the Forum while this book was being written. Each of them helped keep us on task and provided valuable insight and advice in connection with the development of the chapters. Of course, this book would have never happened without the hard work of Sarah Forbes Orwig and the rest of the ABA Publications Staff, Courtney Coffman, and Yolanda Muhammad, the Director of the Forum on Franchising.

Liz Dillon
Jim Goniea
Editors, Third Edition

Introduction

The third edition of the *Franchise Law Compliance Manual* continues the tradition of providing a "practical, comprehensive guide to establishing and maintaining a successful corporate compliance program." It is a valuable resource to outside counsel as well. Each chapter in this third edition attempts to provide a comprehensive guide to an important area of franchise compliance, and each includes key updates from the second edition. In addition, a new chapter on data privacy has been added because data privacy compliance has become an integral part of every franchisor's business. Many of the authors from the second edition have returned, and we have added a few new authors, including in-house and outside counsel.

Chapter 1, Intellectual Property Rights, provides franchisors with an overview of many important intellectual property matters and includes several helpful forms and checklists. Several notable updates have been made to chapter 1 to address developments in trade secret law and, in addition, the forms and checklists have been refreshed. Sherin Sakr has returned as one of the authors of chapter 1, bringing with her many years of in-house experience. She is joined in this edition by Elisa Edlund, who has tremendous experience managing the international trademark portfolio of an iconic franchisor.

Chapter 2, Franchise Disclosure and Sales Compliance, provides an overview of the franchise registration and disclosure process. Chapter 2 had the most substantial updates as compared to the second edition of this book because of significant developments including new guidance from the North American Securities Administrators Association (NASAA) on multi-unit franchising, state cover pages, and financial performance representations. Leslie Curran continues to author this important chapter, and she is joined in this edition by David Oppenheim and Max Schott, who both bring decades of registration and disclosure experience.

As with chapter 2, chapter 3, Franchise System Operational Issues, went through significant revisions for this third edition. Importantly, this chapter includes a comprehensive discussion on vicarious liability, including agency and joint employer theories, reflecting the rapid changes in this area of the law and the impact on franchise operations. Chapter 3 also includes updates to reflect the importance of social media to franchise systems and the impact of the Telephone Consumer Protection Act (TCPA). Brian Cole is back as an author, contributing his in-house and outside counsel perspectives, and is joined in this edition by Susan Sheely, an in-house attorney who addresses franchise system operational issues on a daily basis.

Chapter 4, Franchise Relationship Management, focuses on the importance of the relationship between franchisors and franchisees. It provides key considerations and practical solutions for franchisors in achieving and maintaining good relationships with the franchise system, including communication and methods of interaction. Eric Karp is the author of chapter 4 and brings extensive experience working on the relationships between franchisors and franchisees as counsel for many franchisee associations.

Chapter 5, Termination, Nonrenewal, and Transfer, is authored by Susan Tegt, an experienced litigator representing franchisors, and veteran franchisee lawyer Jeff Haff and provides us with a balanced and comprehensive review of the termination, nonrenewal, and transfer process. Readers can use this chapter to review these important issues and will find comprehensive checklists and forms for use in their own practices.

Chapter 6, Mergers and Acquisitions in the Franchise System, provides a comprehensive guide to the mergers and acquisition process for a franchise system. Both Kevin Hein and Ted Pearce continued as authors of chapter 6 and contributed their significant franchise experience to the examination of this issue. In addition to important tax updates, the authors of this chapter added a section on acquisitions of distressed franchise systems out of bankruptcy to reflect the uncertainty coming out of the COVID-19 pandemic.

Chapter 7, International Franchising, is an overview of issues and considerations for franchisors who are expanding internationally. Franchising has continued to grow as a way of doing business internationally, and international franchise laws and regulations have increased to reflect that growth. Chapter 7 contains important developments on these international franchise registration and disclosure laws. It also provides useful checklists and resources. Both Ali McElroy and Rob Lauer are back as authors and provide important in-house and outside counsel perspectives.

Chapter 8, Data Privacy, is a new chapter that reflects the growing importance of data privacy as a compliance issue in franchise systems. We are lucky that Brian Hengesbaugh and Mark Melodia agreed to take on this endeavor. They have provided readers with a guide to relevant considerations and potential minefields for franchisors in the areas of data ownership and control, data breaches, the California Consumer Privacy Act, and the EU General Data Protection Regulation (GDPR). In chapter 8, the authors provide practical steps that franchisors can take to limit risks and comply with this complicated and emerging area of the law.

The second edition of the *Franchise Law Compliance Manual* was one of the books that we took home from our offices when the COVID-19 pandemic hit. It was a great resource for both of us at our home offices, especially when it was a little harder to drop in on a colleague to help analyze an issue. We hope that you find the third edition of this book just as helpful in your practice.

Jim Goniea and Elizabeth (Liz) Dillon
Editors, Third Edition

CHAPTER 1

Intellectual Property Rights

Elisa Edlund and Sherin Sakr

Contents

1-1. Introduction: Intellectual Property and Franchising

Intellectual property—primarily trademarks, trade names, trade dress, copyrights, patents, and trade secrets—is the cornerstone of the franchising concept. A franchisor's intellectual property is often its primary asset and includes items such as brand names, logos, symbols, construction designs, graphic designs, slogans, artistic and linguistic creations, inventions, know-how, formulas, recipes, and methods of doing business. The legal exclusivity that intellectual property rights afford a franchisor and its franchisees quite often offers the competitive advantage that is essential to a successful franchising business. As proprietary rights in intellectual property are generally protected legally only under certain conditions and limitations, a corporate compliance program is key to ensuring protection of these assets.

Since the impact of failing to manage a company's intellectual property assets properly can be substantial—from a business perspective, it can cause wasted investment, lost opportunity, or diminished or lost profits, and from a legal perspective, it may lead to uncertainty, unnecessary legal expenses, and litigation—this chapter provides an overview of the types of intellectual property and the steps to implement a compliance program to protect them.

1-2. Types of Intellectual Property

In a typical franchise business, trademarks are most likely to be the primary asset, followed by trade secret rights, which might cover methods of doing business and technical know-how such as recipes and formulas. Copyright rights will be implicated in works such as advertising and other promotional and marketing materials, software, websites, and operations manuals. In certain franchise systems, patents can be important as well. For example, utility patents might cover a proprietary piece of machinery or a software-based system, and design patents might cover a building design. Although the focus of this chapter is on trademarks, it briefly discusses the other types of intellectual property since they are often essential to the franchise system.

(a) Trademarks

In most franchising situations, trademarks represent the single most dominant element and the focal point of the franchise package. Trademarks can be any word or symbol used to identify one's goods or services to distinguish them from those sold or offered by others. Trademarks can be designs, words, pictures, slogans, colors, configurations, three-dimensional manifestations of the site where the business is located, sounds, or combinations of any of those, which sometimes are termed "trade dress." A trademark prevents consumer confusion between businesses and allows a franchisor to build brand recognition.

In the United States, trademark rights arise from use and are confirmed by federal registration, which provides substantial and procedural benefits.[1] Trademark protection, unlike most other forms of intellectual property, continues indefinitely as long as the mark is sufficiently protected, is not abandoned, and is used properly so that it does not become a victim of genericide. Genericide is when a trademark becomes a generic word for the product category, rather than an identifier for a specific branded product within the product category.[2] Examples of some famous words that were originally trademarks are aspirin, thermos, and zipper.

"Trade name" is a term originally used to mean trademark but now generally refers to the business or corporate name of the franchisor, or its d/b/a, which may or may not contain a trademark of the company. Trade names are a creature of state and local statutes, and rights in them can be enforced against confusingly similar trade names and trademarks under trademark principles.

A franchisor's website address, or its domain name, is generally not protected as intellectual property but may be protectable if it contains a trademark or if it comprises the name of the business. Domain names will be protected as trademarks only if they meet all the standard requirements for a trademark, particularly distinctiveness, exclusivity, and direct use in connection with the offering and/or sale of goods or services and not just as an Internet address. Domain names are becoming an increasingly important asset to businesses and deserve consideration in the franchisor's global protection strategy.

(i) Creation and Selection

The first step in protecting a trademark is to select a strong and distinctive mark, which makes it easier to protect the trademark. Unfortunately, many start-up franchisors select trademarks based on a marketing objective to describe a quality or characteristic of the goods or services. While this makes sense in the short term to help a consumer understand what the new business is selling, in the long term it

1. Certain of these benefits are included at 15 U.S.C. § 1111-18 (2016).

2. *See, e.g.*, 15 U.S.C. § 1064(3) (providing for cancellation of registered marks that have become generic).

makes protecting the trademarks more difficult and expensive. Selecting a strong and distinctive trademark will make searching and clearance smoother and more certain, registration easier, and protection more manageable and less costly. The best result of selecting strong trademarks is that very little litigation should occur.

We recommend involving experienced trademark counsel early in the trademark selection process, to help guide the franchisor toward trademarks that are both commercially viable and legally protectable, and to ensure sufficient time for the trademark clearance process.

(ii) Trademark Clearance

In order to forestall issues down the road, a trademark clearance search should be performed by experienced trademark counsel prior to adoption of a new trademark. To conduct the trademark clearance, the franchisor's marketing team should provide trademark counsel with information relating to the nature of the goods or services, the intended use, the competitive marketplace, and any industry-specific generic or descriptive terminology. This information is used by trademark counsel to understand how the mark fits into the business environment so that a comprehensive analysis can be conducted. Checklist 1-3 provides an example of how this information may be gathered and transmitted to trademark counsel.

We recommend that new trademarks not be used before the trademark clearance is complete since using a trademark before determining its availability could result in litigation, bad publicity, or lost investment. In the franchise context, failure to properly clear a trademark before use could result in claims by franchisees for breach of contractual representations or for rescission of the franchise agreement. Courts addressing the duty to search and clear trademarks have characterized the failure to do so adequately as "willful ignorance" and "bad faith," leading to adverse judgments. In *International Star Class Yacht Racing Ass'n v. Tommy Hilfiger U.S.A., Inc.*,[3] the Second Circuit found that Hilfiger could be found to have acted in bad faith by conducting only a simple trademark search, which was limited to federal registrations in a single class of goods and excluded state registrations and common law uses, because Hilfiger ignored its attorneys' advice to conduct a full trademark search. The court stated that "willful ignorance should not provide a means by which Hilfiger can evade its obligations under trademark law."[4]

Since conducting a comprehensive search is an experience- and expertise-based skill, sufficient lead time is necessary for completion of the process. A full trademark clearance search typically takes about 10 business days to complete, although expediting is generally available for an additional cost. A proper trademark search involves not only an analysis of the search results but also an investigation of potential prior rights holders. If there are other marks with a potential conflict, the franchisor will need to decide whether to approach the prior rights holder for consent, a license or purchase, or potentially to challenge the mark, such as through a non-use cancellation, or on the basis of prior use as explained in further detail below.

3. 80 F.3d 749 (2d Cir. 1996).
4. *Id.* at 754.

(iii) Perfecting Trademark Rights: Registration

Once a potential new trademark has been cleared for use, application for federal registration should be filed as soon as possible. Under U.S. law, priority rights are established by either the first use of a mark or the filing date of a federal application based on "intent to use." If based on "intent to use," the application filing date establishes a priority "constructive use" date that accrues once actual use of the mark is made and a registration issues.[5]

While trademarks without a federal registration (i.e., based on use alone) can be protectable under common law, these rights are limited and so a federal trademark registration is preferable. Federal registration of a trademark confers a presumption of the right to exclusive nationwide use and ownership of the mark and provides constructive notice to all other parties.[6] On the other hand, use-based rights extend only to the geographic area of use, reputation, and natural expansion. Therefore, to preserve the possibility of future expansion, federal registration is highly recommended, especially for a new, slow-growing franchise business that has a limited number of locations. Otherwise, the first party to use a mark in a particular area prior to a federal application will likely have superior rights that could block the franchisor's expansion into that area.

Under U.S. law, if a franchisor has not commenced use of a mark prior to filing a federal application, it can file an intent-to-use application based on a bona fide intent to use the mark in commerce.[7] Within six months after the date the mark is approved for registration by the United States Patent and Trademark Office (USPTO), the applicant must either provide evidence that it has begun use of the mark or pay for additional six-month extensions, for up to three years, as long as the applicant can provide proof to the USPTO that it has a continued bona fide intention to use the mark in commerce.[8] It is important for the franchisor to document the bona fide intent at the time it files its intent-to-use application, because a registration that issues from an intent-to-use application where the facts do not support the original bona fide intent could be invalidated. See checklist 1-4 for assistance with determining and substantiating a bona fide intent.

(iv) Maintaining Trademark Rights

Obtaining a federal registration is only the beginning of the ongoing protection and maintenance of a company's trademark. Procedurally, in order to maintain a U.S. trademark registration, the company must file an affidavit of use during the fifth year after registration, which should be filed as soon as possible in order to attain "incontestability" status.[9] Then, every 10 years after registration, the company must file a renewal application with an affidavit of use showing continued use of the trademark.

5. 15 U.S.C. § 1057(c).
6. 15 U.S.C. §§ 1115, 1072.
7. 15 U.S.C. § 1051(b).
8. 15 U.S.C. § 1051(d).
9. 15 U.S.C. § 1065.

Since a trademark can be lost if not used properly, it is important to establish guidelines for use to be distributed to employees, franchisees, agencies, and others who develop materials using the marks. The guidelines should include notification of the trademark registration and instructions on how to use the trademark properly. Instructions should include three basic concepts for proper trademark use: (1) using the proper trademark symbol after the trademark—either the ™ prior to registration or the ® symbol after registration; (2) distinguishing the trademark from the surrounding text, such as by putting it in *italics*, ALL CAPS, or a different **FONT**; and (3) a reminder that a trademark is an identifier of the source of goods and should always be used as an adjective and never in the plural or possessive. Aspirin, dry ice, escalator, and linoleum were all trademarks that were lost because they were incorrectly used as generic terms.

In addition, the franchisor should establish a process for legal review of all materials with the trademarks prior to dissemination. This should be supplemented with ongoing education in trademark protection, trademark clearance, and trademark use for new hires and existing personnel.

All these maintenance activities should be supported by an administrative infrastructure including a filing and tracking system for managing pertinent information about the company's trademark portfolio, including licenses, agreements, and conflicts with other parties. This system should incorporate functionality to maintain deadlines for renewals and other filings necessary to maintain the trademark registrations. See checklist 1-5 for a list of items that should be tracked in a portfolio management system. We recommend tracking this information at the inception of the franchise, as recreating it after the fact can be difficult and time intensive. While there is specialized software developed for tracking this type of information, which is helpful for the ability to generate automatic reminders, the franchisor could use something as simple as a spreadsheet.

(v) International Protection of Trademarks

U.S.-based franchisors frequently ignore international considerations such as language and culture when adopting new marks. Moreover, they often delay seeking protection for their marks in other countries. They then discover that their key marks are unacceptable or unregisterable, or that they have already been registered by another party, either coincidentally or with infringing intent. It is important to note (1) the need in most cases to register marks country-by-country; (2) the variability of laws, regulations, and standards for both registration (although use prior to registration is not required in most countries) and enforcement; (3) the different laws and regulations regarding licensing; and (4) the substantial burdens of administration and expense in implementing an international trademark protection program.

Keep in mind some general principles when considering an international trademark strategy. Never assume that an extensively used and successful U.S. trademark will be suitable for use in other countries. Since a franchisor often must weigh limited resources against uncertain future expansion, we recommend that the franchisor coordinate between marketing, operations, and legal to prioritize which trademarks to protect internationally and which countries to prioritize, and to brainstorm solutions that work across cultural and linguistic boundaries for things such as translations, transliterations, and logos.

We recommend filing early and as widespread as possible, for as broad a range of goods and services as possible, since trademark rights are strictly territorial. They must be perfected on a country-by-country basis (with the major exceptions of the European Union and two intellectual property organizations, OAPI and ARIPO, that register trademarks for a large number of African nations) and the sooner the better since trademark piracy is an international fact of life. In most jurisdictions, the first party to file places itself in a superior position.[10] Overcoming the prior registration of one's own mark by another party merely on proof of prior use or reputation is difficult and uncertain. In addition, clearance searches in each country prior to entering into franchise arrangements are essential to avoid inadvertent infringement of a third party's prior right or to discover piracy of one's own mark.

(A) Use Requirements

When registering in countries where the franchisor currently does not have locations, the franchisor should be aware of non-use vulnerability. Most countries have a non-use time period that constitutes a basis for invalidating a trademark registration.[11] Therefore, if the trademark is registered but then not used (many countries set this time period at three years), a third party can move to have the trademark canceled. It can be difficult to overcome an allegation of non-use, and the definition and extent of use needed to maintain a registration vary between countries. For countries where the trademark is being used, we recommend anticipating proof of use requirements and setting up a system to capture and retain use documentation in advance. For countries where the trademark is not being used, the franchisor may want to consider filing new applications to restart the non-use time period for key marks.[12] While this may help to maintain the trademark, it comes at an additional expense and may cause loss of a priority date.

---

10. While trademark rights in the United States generally belong to the first to *use* a mark, in many jurisdictions the right to a trademark may belong to the first to *file* an application to register the mark. *See Don't Sit and Wait: Stopping Trademark Squatters*, United States Patent and Trademark Office (Feb. 2013), https://www.uspto.gov/learning-and-resources/newsletter/inventors-eye/dont-sit-and-wait-stopping-trademark-squatters (discussing bad faith filings by trademark squatters in first-to-file jurisdictions).

11. For example, in the United States the presumptive period is three years. 15 U.S.C. §§ 1064(3), 1127 ("Nonuse for 3 consecutive years shall be prima facie evidence of abandonment."). In the European Union the period is five years, and in Canada the period is three years. Council Regulation 2017/1001 of 14 June 2017 on the European Union trade mark, art. 18; Trademarks Act, R.S.C. 1985, c. T-13, § 45(1).

12. This approach may not be effective in all jurisdictions, as some jurisdictions view such re-filings as demonstrating possible bad faith. We recommend consulting with local counsel prior to re-filing. *See* Case R 1785/2008-4, *Anja Holzapfel v. José Domingo López-Palacios González.*

Maintaining a registration can be a challenge when use of the trademark is only through a franchisee. Registrations can be inadvertently lost even when the mark is in use, and franchisors should ensure their franchise agreement requires franchisee cooperation with whatever filings are necessary. The franchise agreement should also provide that the agreement does not automatically lapse if a registration is temporarily lost.

(B) Enforcement of Rights

Pursuing infringers varies by jurisdiction, and swift and broad civil relief for trademark infringement can be difficult to obtain in many jurisdictions. It can be difficult to enforce a registration against similar or identical marks used in connection with different goods or services in a different class. In addition, initiating offensive litigation when one's registration may be vulnerable due to non-use is not recommended unless the situation is so grievous that it is a chance worth taking. Trademark opposition and cancellation actions can be crucial in depriving the other party of the ability to use a registration as a defensive shield.

(C) Licensing

Franchisors seeking to expand to international markets should obtain advance advice as to the applicability of any local laws or regulations controlling the licensing of trademarks, as some countries require recording the license with a government entity.[13] The trademark owner should analyze how the goods are made and marketed, or the services performed, to determine which entities in the franchise system qualify as users that need to be recorded. A trademark license is the best indication that recording is needed, but related corporate entities without a formal license and joint ventures are among those users that sometimes escape attention. Registered user requirements are most often merely routine, burdensome, and costly, but they can be a technical trap if not properly completed. We recommend the franchisor consult local counsel to determine the need and method for compliance with license recordal requirements. Actively enforced license recordal requirements cannot be ignored due to the potentially disastrous consequences to trademark ownership and the validity of the license supporting a franchising structure in a particular country.

(D) Madrid Protocol

There is no easy or inexpensive way to achieve worldwide international trademark rights, but the Madrid Protocol is one way to reduce the cost of filing in multiple countries.[14] The Madrid Protocol requires a trademark registration in

13. For example, China and Russia both require recordal of a trademark license. *See* Lanning G. Bryer, *International Trademark Protection*, International Trademark Association (2018), at p. 94.

14. *Madrid—The International Trademark System*, World Intellectual Property Organization (last visited Mar. 12, 2020), https://www.wipo.int/madrid/en/.

your home country before filing an international application.[15] The international application is forwarded to the World Intellectual Property Organization (WIPO), which notifies each country where the franchisor has requested trademark protection. The Madrid Protocol is beneficial because it preserves the priority date of the original home country trademark, but the downside is that each individual country has the ability to refuse to protect the trademark.[16] Therefore, trademark protection is not ensured through the Madrid Protocol. In addition, not all countries belong to the Madrid Protocol, which limits its usefulness.

(E) European Union Trademark System

Another way to reduce the cost of filing international trademarks is through the European Union trademark system. The European Union (EU) has a registration and protection system that issues a single registration that gives the trademark owner an exclusive right in all the member states of the EU.[17] It covers all present members of the EU and automatically extends to all new member countries at the time they join the EU. The system provides for one filing in a central office, and once registered, can be enforced against infringements by court action in any country. Use in any one country will support the registration and keep it from being canceled for non-use; this is significant for franchisors that may have franchisees in only one EU country. Perhaps most important, the cost of obtaining an EU registration is low,[18] especially considering the number of countries covered and the commercial importance of Europe.

(b) Trade Dress

Trade dress, a subcategory of trademarks, is generally protected under trademark law principles. Trade dress is the term given to a combination of elements that together represent the overall image of a product or business, and it can be a valuable proprietary element of a franchise business.[19] For products, it can include the shape, layout, and color combination of packaging or labeling, or the shape of the product. For services, it can include the shape of a building or specific architectural features, or the interior decor of a service establishment as well as signs, advertising, equipment, and uniforms.

Trade dress protection does not extend to vague images, themes, or concepts. Trade dress protection will be granted only to distinctive combinations of discreet characteristics that can serve to identify a particular business. However, this does

15. *How the Madrid System Works*, World Intellectual Property Organization (last visited Mar. 12, 2020), https://www.wipo.int/madrid/en/how_madrid_works.html.

16. *Id.*

17. Council Regulation 2017/1001 of 14 June 2017 on the European Union trade mark, art. 1(2), 9(1).

18. *EU Trade Mark Regulation Fees*, EUIPO (Feb. 13, 2017), *available at* https://euipo.europa.eu/ohimportal/en/eu-trade-mark-regulation-fees.

19. *Trademark Manual of Examining Procedure*, United States Patent and Trademark Office (Oct. 2018), § 1202.02 [hereinafter TMEP].

not prevent competitors from using individual public domain elements that may be part of the protectable trade dress combination. The premise of trade dress protection is to protect and reward investment in unique and original identifying features, which, taken as a whole, are nonfunctional.[20] To be protectable, trade dress must be either inherently distinctive or subject to proof that it has acquired secondary meaning through extensive use, advertising, and promotion so that consumers recognize it as an identifier of the business.[21]

If properly developed, nurtured, and protected, trade dress can become a valuable asset in the franchise mix that is worth the extensive work necessary to achieve legal protection. See checklist 1-6 for a list of how to develop protectable trade dress and how to implement a program to protect it.

(c) Copyrights

Copyright law protects original, fixed works of authorship that are capable of being tangibly expressed, as opposed to a mere idea or concept.[22] A copyright owner has the exclusive right to reproduce the work, to distribute copies to the public, and to publicly perform and display the work. In a franchise system, copyrightable material might include the operations manual, computer software programs, the website, advertising (print, television, radio, or Internet), architectural blueprints, and building designs.

(i) Creation and Work for Hire

Creation and authorship are the key concepts in copyright law. When potentially copyrightable materials are created, by employees, outside agencies, or contractors, the franchisor should ensure that these have been independently created. The Internet makes it very easy to copy images, photos, artwork, music, and other material from various third-party sources, and sometimes it is difficult to determine if such material is in the public domain since copyright notices are not always included. When in doubt, it is safest to assume that someone owns the copyright and to seek permission to use it.

In the United States, copyrightable work created by employees within the scope of their employment automatically belongs to the employer by law.[23] However, when a franchisor (or franchisee) hires a third party to create materials such as a logo, artwork, advertising, software, or website, it is important to have a written agreement in place granting the franchisor an assignment of the third party's copyright rights in the created material. The requirements for assignment of a copyright as a "work made for hire" are narrow and may not apply, and even if they do, a written agreement is recommended and may be required in some

20. Protection is not available for trade dress that is functional, as it is incapable of serving as a trademark. 15 U.S.C. §§ 1052(e)(5), 1052(f), 1091(c).

21. TMEP § 1202.02(b).

22. 17 U.S.C. § 102.

23. 17 U.S.C. §§ 101, 201(b).

instances.[24] If the franchisor does not provide for the written assignment of the rights in the created materials, technically the franchisor does not own them. The creator of the work could demand additional fees or a license with ongoing fees. To ensure the franchisor owns all of its copyrightable materials, it should educate any employee who may employ outside agencies or contractors about this facet of copyright law and then put in place a process to ensure a contract is signed prior to any creative materials being created. See form 1-7 for a form of agreement that can be modified for use with a contractor to ensure franchisor ownership.

Internationally, each country treats work made for hire differently, some requiring that franchisees or even employees be compensated for any copyrightable work created during the duration of the franchise agreement or their employment. Therefore, franchisors should be cautious and consult with local counsel about adding or modifying existing language in the franchise agreements regarding copyright rights in materials created by franchisees.

(ii) Registration and Enforcement

Copyright arises at the moment of creation, with no requirement for registration. However, under U.S. law, a work must be registered with the U.S. Copyright Office prior to filing a lawsuit in federal court in order to recover damages. The Supreme Court recently ruled in *Fourth Estate Pub. Benefit Corp. v. Wall-Street.com LLC*[25] that the work must be registered prior to filing a lawsuit; it is not sufficient to merely have filed an application. In addition, attorneys' fees and statutory damages (beneficial due to the difficulty in proving actual damages) are allowed only if the infringement started after registration.[26] However, there is a grace period if registration is made within three months after first publication.[27] Registration is easy and inexpensive, although backlogs at the U.S. Copyright Office can be substantial.

Internationally, a few other countries have copyright offices, but all countries that belong to the Berne Convention (including the United States) will enforce copyrights originating in any one of the Berne Convention countries without need of registration.

Additionally, filing copyrights internationally can potentially be used to bolster a franchisor's trademark rights. For example, filing a copyright for the franchisor's logo can provide greater rights protect against infringers who may be copying the general shape, colors, or elements of the logo.

---

24. Works made for hire defined under part (2) of the definition in 17 U.S.C. § 101 (applying to specific types of works such as contributions to collective works) require a written instrument. Even if the work made for hire appears to fall under part (1), works prepared by an employee in the scope of his or her employment, a written agreement is recommended.

25. No. 139 S. Ct. 881 (2019).

26. 17 U.S.C. § 412. See https://www.copyright.gov/circs/circ01.pdf for more benefits of registration.

27. 17 U.S.C. § 412.

(iii) Notice

Before the United States joined the Berne Convention, under U.S. law it was mandatory to use a copyright notice with publication of the work or the copyright was lost to the public domain. Since 1989, use of a notice is optional but necessary to overcome an innocent user defense.[28] Also, the United States belongs to another treaty, the Universal Copyright Convention, which requires a notice in order to gain automatic protection,[29] and there are countries that belong to it but not Berne.[30] Therefore, use of a notice is highly recommended in a reasonably prominent location within or on the work. The notice consists of the symbol ©, the year of first publication, and the name of the copyright owner, which can be a recognized abbreviation of that name. Since the © symbol is the abbreviation of the word "copyright," there should be a space between the symbol and the year. An example of a copyright notice would be: © 2021 Widget Corp. The owner's name should reflect the current owner's name, not the original author, if the author has assigned the rights. In the United States, the year may be omitted if the work is a "useful" article, such as a menu or giveaway toy.[31]

(iv) Term

Under U.S. law, the length of copyright protection for works created after January 1, 1978, is the life of the author plus 70 years, irrespective of registration.[32] If the work is a "work for hire," the term is the shorter of 95 years from first publication or 120 years from the year of first creation, irrespective of registration.[33] Even if registered, no renewals are allowed.

(d) Patents

A patent gives the owner exclusive rights over the patented invention for a limited period of time, including the right to exclude others from making, using, selling, or importing it.[34] The most useful patents incorporated into a franchise system are utility, design, or business method patents. Utility patents cover new and useful processes and machines, design patents cover new and original ornamental designs for articles of manufacture, and business method patents cover a new method of doing business. While patent protection generally is not a major factor in franchise businesses, it can occasionally provide an advantage over the

28. 17 U.S.C. § 401 *et seq.*

29. Universal Copyright Convention as revised at Paris on 24 July 1971, art. II § 1, art. III § 1.

30. Compare signatories to Universal Copyright Convention, available at http://portal.unesco.org/en/ev.php-URL_ID=15241&URL_DO=DO_TOPIC&URL_SECTION=201.html, to Berne signatories, available at https://www.wipo.int/treaties/en/ShowResults.jsp?lang=en&treaty_id=15.

31. 17 U.S.C. § 401(b)(2).

32. 17 U.S.C. § 302(a).

33. 17 U.S.C. § 302(b).

34. 35 U.S.C. § 154(a).

short term. Since there are precise procedures and technical requirements for obtaining patents, a compliance program should be implemented to ensure the franchisor maintains their rights to the patent. For example, since publicly using an invention for more than a year eliminates the ability to obtain a patent, regular technology reviews and a docketing system should be used to ensure the franchisor does not inadvertently relinquish their rights to obtain a patent.[35] The review process should include the decision to treat a new invention as patentable or to retain it as a trade secret. Once the patent route is chosen, the invention will be disclosed to the public and the owner's protection will expire after a certain number of years.[36] Trade secret protection, on the other hand, can result in indefinite protection and often is a vital, long-term element of a successful franchise business.

(e) Trade Secrets

Trade secret law protects the owner's right to control and protect proprietary information. A franchise business often has the types of material that are subject to trade secret protection, such as a secret recipe, a proprietary cooking process, a unique method of doing business (such as a special method for teaching speed-reading or ballroom dancing), customer lists, marketing and research information, or accounting and inventory management techniques. To be considered a trade secret, the information must derive independent economic value from not generally being known to the public, and reasonable measures must be taken to maintain its secrecy.[37]

A version of the Uniform Trade Secrets Act (UTSA) has been adopted in most states. For example, under California Civil Code § 3426.1(d), a plaintiff must establish that the information at issue "(1) derives independent economic value, actual or potential, from not being generally known to the public or to other persons who can obtain economic value from its disclosure or use; and (2) is the subject of efforts that are reasonable under the circumstances to maintain its secrecy." While useful for protecting trade secrets, the UTSA has its limitations since it has not been adopted in every state, differs from state to state, and is dependent on action in state court.

In 2016, the Defend Trade Secrets Act (DTSA) was passed, which allows a U.S. employer to seek federal action for seizure of property to prevent

35. 35 U.S.C. § 102(b)(1).

36. 35 U.S.C. §§ 154(a), 173.

37. Defend Trade Secrets Act, 18 U.S.C. § 1839. *See, e.g.*, I Can't Believe It's Yogurt v. Gunn, 1997 WL 599391 (D. Colo. Apr. 15, 1997) (Holding that the plaintiff franchisor failed to prove that its operational procedures were sufficiently different and unique to constitute a trade secret in an action against a former yogurt store franchisee who continued to operate a yogurt shop after the franchise agreement had been terminated. Further, the plaintiff failed to preserve the secrecy of the information, as much of the information claimed to be trade secrets was shared in a publication to its franchisees without any confidentiality warning.).

dissemination of a trade secret, along with an injunction and damages.[38] Since a state's UTSA may provide different relief than the DTSA, the franchisor may want to consider bringing concurrent state and federal trade secret claims.

One advantage of a trade secret over patent protection is that the standards of inventiveness and nonobviousness are not as high. Also, there is no time limitation for protection of a trade secret, as long as the information continues to qualify as a trade secret. However, there can be risk in the decision not to seek patent protection if a corporate compliance program is not properly executed, since a trade secret can easily be lost if it no longer is considered a secret. While loss of a trade secret from independent discovery or reverse engineering is out of the owner's control, a trade secret owner can take steps to prevent accidental or intentional disclosure by the business's employees (or about-to-be ex-employees), franchisees, outside suppliers, and other third parties.

To maintain the trade secret, the owner should ensure it has signed nondisclosure agreements before disclosing the trade secret. However, it is important to understand that the DTSA provides immunity for whistleblowers and requires employers to provide notice of the DTSA's immunity clauses "in any contract or agreement with an employee that governs the use of a trade secret or other confidential information."[39] The DTSA defines an employee to include both employees and independent contractors, but it arguably does not include franchisees. Furthermore, a franchisor would not want to include a whistleblower notice intended for employees in its franchise agreement, as that may be used as evidence against the franchisor that the franchisee should be classified as an employee instead of a franchisee.

Other measures the franchisor can take to protect its trade secrets include establishing physical, administrative, and technological controls.[40] For example, the trade secret should be stored in a secure location with access limited on a need-to-know basis. The franchisor should consider encryption or password protection for any electronic copies of the trade secret. And providing access to vendors—for example, a vendor may need access to a recipe to manufacture a proprietary product—should be carefully considered to maximize protection of the trade secret.

1-3. Intellectual Property Compliance Program

(a) Corporate Commitment

The key to a successful intellectual property compliance program is having the franchisor's management fully support the creation of the compliance program

38. 18 U.S.C. § 1836.
39. 18 U.S.C.A. § 1833(b)(3)(A) (2016).
40. World Intellectual Property Organization et al., *Trade Secrets: Learning Points*, IP PANORAMA p. 4, https://www.wipo.int/sme/en/multimedia/ (recommending implementation of physical, administrative, and technical controls as part of an information security program).

policies and communicate their importance to the franchisor's employees, franchisees, advertising agencies, and vendors. Since routine matters such as legal review of materials are rendered ineffective if items are submitted at the last minute with no time for adequate scrutiny or corrections, management should commit to the compliance program by allocating sufficient financial resources and legal expertise, through either inside or outside counsel or both.

(b) Identifying Sources of Conflict

The focus of the legal function should be to put the intellectual property assets into a position where their value can be exploited and maximized by the business. This includes protecting the assets from legal challenge by others and injurious actions by others, such as adverse registration or use. This goal can be achieved by implementing a corporate compliance program that anticipates potential sources of litigation or conflict. Generally, these fall into two categories. First, the company needs to be able to successfully defend its right to obtain, register, and use its own intellectual property assets. Second, the franchisor must be able to take successful legal action against others who infringe rights, pirate assets, or seek to register adverse rights. Litigation arising in both categories, therefore, regularly reflects a common genesis: a failure to adequately or properly develop, maintain, and enforce strong, protectable rights. Unfortunately, this often is a result of an earlier failure to diligently implement an internal compliance program.

(c) Asset Inventory

The first step in structuring a corporate compliance program is conducting an audit of the company's intellectual property assets to identify all assets and those currently in use. The assets in use can then be compared to the protections in place. Once the gaps between use and protection have been identified, the company can begin the process of cleaning up the intellectual property portfolio with actions such as abandoning registrations that are no longer in use, filing registrations, and updating or creating guidelines for maintaining, protecting, and enforcing the company's intellectual property. See checklist 1-1 for a list of the steps to complete an asset inventory and to identify the gaps between protection and use.

(d) Intellectual Property and Franchise Agreements

A crucial part of a trademark protection program is controlling any license relationship involving the marks. Primarily this will be the franchise agreement, but it must be considered for any other license agreement as well, such as a license for branded merchandise. The license agreement must contain a valid and enforceable trademark license. Moreover, it is imperative that licensee not gain any rights in the marks by virtue of the licensed relationship and that the marks not be licensed without quality control, both in the documentation and in fact. See checklist 1-10 and form 1-3 for assistance with drafting and implementing trademark-related provisions in a franchise agreement.

The franchise agreement should also contain provisions covering the generation and ownership of copyrightable material and patentable inventions, policies and procedures for protecting the franchise system's trade secrets, and provisions governing a franchisee's use of trade names or domain names incorporating the franchisor's trademarks, including cancellation or transfer to the franchisor following termination of the franchise agreement.

(e) Acquisition of Trademark Portfolios

Proper and thorough legal due diligence before any acquisition as well as appropriate contractual provisions in the purchase documentation is crucial. This ensures that the trademark and related rights being acquired are what the company expected and that the company will be able to conduct the acquired business unimpeded by defects or gaps in its intellectual property portfolio or by threat of potential litigation (see checklist 1-11 and forms 1-4, 1-5, and 1-6). Subsequent to the acquisition, the franchisor should execute and promptly file assignment documentation with the appropriate government agencies. It is important to have a provision in the acquisition agreement requiring the seller's cooperation for a reasonable period of time after the sale to ensure that the franchisor obtains all necessary documentation for the transfer.

1-4. Enforcing Trademark Rights

(a) Infringements

The franchisor needs to protect its system's trademark and trade dress assets by taking vigorous and prompt action against the use and attempted registration of marks and trade dress that are confusingly similar to the franchisor's trademark and trade dress assets. The resulting consumer confusion could translate into lost sales and weakened marketing efforts, followed by franchisee dissatisfaction and possible legal recourse against the franchisor. Failure to prevent others from using or registering infringing marks and trade dress could result in a gradual diminution of the strength of the company's rights and potentially an eventual loss of exclusive rights. Court action can result in injunctive relief and the recovery of monetary damages or the defendant's profits and, in cases where intent can be proved, those damages can be multiplied and attorneys' fees recovered as well. It is important to note that the trademark owner must use a registration notice or provide actual notice to the infringer in order to recover damages.

(b) Opposition and Cancellation Proceedings

All jurisdictions provide for objecting to applications for trademark registration by others, by way of either an opposition proceeding before a mark is registered or a cancellation proceeding after registration, or both. The grounds for such proceedings are usually more limited than in a court action for infringement, and the proceedings are more restricted as well. In the United States, the proceedings, while truncated (there is no trial per se, for example), do provide for discovery and thus often take on much of the trappings of litigation, while in most international jurisdictions these can be no more involved than counsel filing a brief and evidence as needed.[41] It is important to note that in the United States or most other countries, such proceedings decide only the right to register, not the right to use a mark, so parallel or subsequent court action may be necessary for effective action against an infringing use for an injunction and damages.[42]

(c) Cybersquatting

If another party has obtained and is using a domain name that consists of or contains a trademark of the franchisor, it may be possible, depending on the mark and the location of the other party, to take two types of legal action. A prerequisite is that the mark must be subject to proof of prior trademark rights and must be distinctive. If the mark is a dictionary word—for example, "apple" or "united" —it can be difficult to sustain successful action absent other evidence.

If the other party is subject to the jurisdiction of a U.S. court, a civil action can be brought under the trademark statute if it can be proven that the domain name owner had a bad faith intent to profit from the mark and registers, traffics in, or uses a domain name confusingly similar to the franchisor's mark.[43] The court can order cancellation of the domain name or its transfer to the mark's owner in addition to any other available remedies.

A quicker and less expensive alternative to court action, and one available irrespective of the other party's domicile, is an administrative complaint proceeding filed under the Uniform Domain Name Dispute Resolution Policy (UDRP) promulgated by ICANN, the nonprofit body charged with administration of the Internet.[44] This is an online arbitration generally limited to one filing by each party. The only remedy possible is cancellation or transfer of the domain name. A complainant in a UDRP proceeding must establish three elements to succeed: (1) the domain name is identical or confusingly similar to a trademark or service mark in which the complainant has rights, (2) the domain name registrant does not have any rights or legitimate interests in the domain name, and (3) the registrant registered the domain name and is using it in bad faith.[45]

If either party is dissatisfied by a UDRP decision, it may challenge the decision in court.[46] If a trademark holder loses a UDRP proceeding, it may still bring

---

41. For example, in the European Union each of the parties may only need to make one filing of arguments and evidence. Council Regulation 2017/1001 of 14 June 2017 on the European Union trade mark, art. 46–47.

42. *Compare* 15 U.S.C. §§ 1063–64 (providing mechanisms for opposition to and cancellation of trademark registrations) *with* 15 U.S.C. § 1114 (providing remedies for infringement by use in commerce of a trademark).

43. 15 U.S.C. § 1125(d).

44. *See Uniform Domain-Name Dispute-Resolution Policy*, ICANN (Oct. 24, 1999), https://www.icann.org/resources/pages/policy-2012-02-25-en.

45. *Id.* § 4(a).

46. *Id.* § 4(k).

a lawsuit against the domain name registrant in court where the administrative panel's UDRP decision is not binding and can be overturned.[47] Conversely, if a domain name registrant loses a UDRP proceeding, it must file a lawsuit against the trademark holder within 10 days to prevent ICANN from transferring the domain name.[48]

(d) Enforcement Strategy

Once the franchisor's management decides to prioritize a protection strategy emphasizing key marks, trade dress, and jurisdictions, a policing system can be established for regular surveillance of applications for registration and monitoring the marketplace for infringements. A trademark watch service can be set up with a third party, and regular Internet searches will often turn up marketplace infringements since an Internet presence is nearly required in this day and age. See checklist 1-7 for establishing a strategy to police the franchisor's trademark rights and form 1-1 for a sample trademark infringement report. A trademark infringement report can be distributed to the franchisor's employees and franchisees as a way for them to report suspected infringement.

Analyzing whether to take action by opposing an application for registration or through a court action for infringement, unfair competition, or dilution is fact intensive and subjective. See checklist 1-8 for a process in assisting with deciding whether to oppose or litigate and checklist 1-9 to assist with preparing for trademark enforcement once the franchisor has decided to take action. Before proceeding with a cease-and-desist letter, the franchisor should answer several questions to ensure they are on solid legal ground and have clear objectives: Would the third-party use be considered fair use? Is the priority of rights clear? Are the company's rights vulnerable to counterattack? What are the chances of success? What are the company's goals in taking action? This last question is especially important when the opportunity for settlement arises.

(e) Settlement

Settlement agreements for trademark matters require careful drafting since they govern the ongoing and future activities of two different parties with similar marks and opposing interests. If the agreement proposes restrictions on the franchisor's use of its own marks, caution should be observed due to the difficulty in anticipating the future direction of marketing activities, especially decades in the future. A franchisor can use the settlement section of checklist 1-8 to guide the decision to settle and for considerations in structuring the settlement agreement. Form 1-2 provides a sample settlement agreement. Once a restriction is agreed to in a settlement agreement, the restriction should be added as an item to be tracked in the compliance program.

47. *Id.*
48. *Id.*

1-5. Conclusion

As the cornerstone of the franchise system, intellectual property rights must be closely guarded. Failure to effectively protect those rights can result not only in substantial financial losses for franchisors but also in diminished brand recognition. A corporate compliance program that focuses on properly developing, maintaining, and enforcing a company's intellectual property rights will enable franchisors to maximize the value of their corporate proprietary assets. A properly implemented program will also minimize the risk of legal challenge by other parties, and it will guard against injurious activities by others, such as infringement.

Checklist 1-1
Intellectual Property Asset Inventory

1. Trademarks
   - Inventory existing registrations and applications worldwide
   - Inventory and review all marks in use and compare with existing portfolio
     - Obtain current prioritization guidelines from management
     - Review current usage of trade dress requiring secondary meaning to determine present availability of protection
     - Identify slogans and other ostensibly short-term material to see if these have achieved longer-term status requiring registration protection
     - Review acquired portfolios to verify complete assimilation
     - Review franchisee use
   - Review status of assigned assets to verify assignment recordal and current status
   - Inventory and review all licenses
     - From the company
     - To the company
   - Internationally, review license recordal/registered user compliance where appropriate
   - Internationally, review new jurisdictions to verify appropriate applications
   - Inventory and review all pending conflicts
     - Claims—actual and potential
       - By others
       - Against others
     - Litigation
       - By others
       - Against others
     - Opposition/cancellation
       - By others
       - Against others
     - Confirm proper and timely notice to insurance companies
     - Inventory and review all agreements
       - Settlement of conflicts
       - Coexistence
       - Consents
     - Review insurance coverage and procedures
     - Review all policies and procedures regarding adoption and protection of trademark assets
       - Selection, clearance, and acquisition of trademarks
       - Applications for trademark registration
       - Maintenance of trademark registration portfolio
       - Proper use of marks
       - Monitoring and review of franchisor and franchisee activities involving use of marks
       - Insurance coverage
       - Protection and enforcement of trademark rights
       - Website domain names
       - International protection

2. Trade names and corporate names
   - Review usage vs. incorporations, qualifications, assumed names
   - Review proper usage
3. Copyrights
   - Identify copyrightable material in use
   - Identify primary sources of material
     - Employees
     - Agencies, consultants, outside contractors
     - Franchisees
     - Licensed
   - Review policies and procedures for protection
     - "Work for hire" versus assignment
     - Registration
     - Review of materials
   - Identify potential compliance/avoidance issues
     - Licensing agencies, for example, ASCAP, CCC
     - Rights of others
       - Copyright
       - Publicity/privacy
     - Remedy gaps and insufficiencies
     - Identify all conflicts—pending or incipient
4. Patents
   - Review existing portfolio
     - Time frames until expiration
     - Pending applications
     - Identify underutilized or unused patents
   - Identify new possibilities
   - Review procedures
     - Internal development
     - Licensed patents and know-how
     - Avoiding rights of others
   - Review policies
     - Patents versus know-how
     - Patenting versus trade secrets
     - Design patents/trade dress
   - Review enforcement policies and execution
   - Remedy insufficiencies
   - Dispose of unused patents
     - Sell, license, or abandon
   - Identify all conflicts—pending or incipient
5. Trade secrets
   - Identify protectable material in use
     - Does it qualify?
     - Has it already been properly protected?
     - Is patent protection available?
     - Is it publicly known?
     - Can it realistically be protected?

- Review procedures for protection
  - Notices and written confidentiality agreements
  - Employee agreements
  - Employee "exiting" procedures
  - Contractual relationships, for example, suppliers, contractors
  - Franchisee use
  - Franchise creation
- Remedy insufficiencies in protective measures or their execution
- Identify all conflicts—pending or incipient

6. Domain names
   - Identify all domain names registered and in use
   - Review portfolio to ascertain if all important trademarks are registered in all pertinent top level and country level domains
   - Verify and docket all expiration dates
   - Verify and update ownership and administrative contacts
   - Verify and consolidate registrar for all domain names

Checklist 1-2
Selection of New Trademarks

1. Develop a corporate policy and procedure for the selection and adoption of new marks
2. Determine the intended function of the mark
   - Primary brand or service identifier
   - Secondary mark
   - House mark
   - Same as corporate name
   - Logo or design
   - Trade dress
   - Slogan
3. Aim to adopt a strong, distinctive trademark
   - Determines scope of legal protection
   - Can be valuable marketing asset
   - Need varies with intended function for the mark
   - Determine business objectives—to be a distinctive identifier versus describing or suggesting a quality or characteristic of the goods or services and/or conveying information about the product or service to consumers
4. Avoid adoption of generic terminology
5. Avoid adoption of descriptive terminology
   - Note, however, that with exclusivity of extensive use and resulting consumer recognition, "secondary meaning" can be developed, leading to protectability
6. Avoid surnames and laudatory, geographic, and nonregisterable terminology
7. Choose a distinctive logotype or other presentation format
   - Important for marks that are not strong
   - Can develop independent significance apart from the word mark
   - Can be beneficial internationally
8. Analyze business attributes for protectable trade dress elements (see checklist 1-6)
   - Two-dimensional, for example, packaging or labels
   - Three-dimensional, for example, physical locations for service businesses
   - Can be a combination or overall "package" of otherwise unprotectable elements
   - Usually needs proof of secondary meaning for legal protection but can be inherently distinctive
   - Must be non-functional
   - Must not deprive competitors of public domain items
9. Adopt trademarks that can be both protected and commercially viable
   - Suggestive, fanciful, or arbitrary
   - Brief and easy to recall
   - Readable and speakable, if words; recognizable and pleasing, if design
   - Appropriate for use in advertising
   - No unpleasant or negative connotations
   - Suitable for the intended audience
   - Suitable for use in other countries
   - Appropriate for future expansion, both geographically and into new types of products or services

Checklist 1-3
Prior to Searching New Trademarks

1. Goods and services
   - What are the particular goods or services for which the mark will be used?
   - Is this for an existing product or service, or something new?
   - Is the product or service unique and, if so, what would the generic terminology be for the product or service?
2. Will this be a primary brand name, a house mark, a secondary mark, or is it intended solely for use in advertising and/or promotion, such as a slogan?
3. Line extensions of an existing mark
   - Need to check adequacy of current registrations
     - Modification of presentation format
     - Confirm the specification of goods or services is broad enough
     - Need to do current search, even if already registered
4. Meaning
   - Does the word mark have any meaning in any language?
   - If a design mark, is there an apt description of it?
5. In use
   - Is the mark already in use on this product or service or on a different product or service? If so, since when?
   - What is the approximate intended date of first use?
   - Is there an estimated duration for the usage, especially if it is a slogan?
6. Is the intended use for a limited geographic area, nationwide throughout the United States, or for other countries?
7. Type of use
   - Exactly how will it be used, for example, containers, labels, menus, signs, and so on?
   - Are there any particular channels of trade in which the mark will be used?
   - Could it be used as a domain name for a company website?
8. Nature of use
   - If a secondary mark, with what primary or house marks will it be used?
   - Will it be used with any design mark or logo?
   - If a design mark, with what word marks will it be used?
   - If a word mark, will it be used in a special format or logo?
   - Will there be any particular colors used, for the words or for any design?
9. Are any of the words or designs generic or descriptive with regard to the particular goods or services in this particular channel of trade or usage?
10. Are any of the words or designs very commonly used in the particular channel of trade?
11. Are there any competitors or others using any of the words or designs for similar or unrelated goods or services?

12. What is the origin of the generation of this mark—internal sources, outside agencies or consultants, focus groups, etc.?
13. Is there a strategy statement, proposed advertising theme or concept associated with the new mark?
14. Are there any internal company policies that might bar the proposed mark?

Checklist 1-4
"Bona Fide Intent" Requirements for U.S. Trademark Applications

1. When filing a new application, determine who generated the new mark.
   - Internal
   - External (ad agencies, name development houses, etc.)
2. Is this the exact mark that will be used?
3. Will the mark be used in a stylized form or with graphic design elements?
4. Does the product or service for which the mark is intended to be used presently exist?
5. If not, is there ongoing research and development?
6. Are there any intended additional goods or services for which the mark might be used?
7. What steps have been taken to launch the product or service?
   - Product/service development
   - Market research
   - Package design/testing
   - Development/approval of advertising
   - Test marketing
   - Surveys/studies regarding customer acceptance
   - Is there a budget for launching this product or service?
   - Is there a time frame for the launch?
   - Have suppliers (of ingredients, packaging, and so on) been contacted yet?
   - Have franchisees been advised?
   - Have proposals been made to customers?
   - Have sales materials been prepared or disseminated?
   - Any press releases or other press reports?
   - Is regulatory approval pending?
   - Any other steps to full-scale use?
8. Find and retain all documentation supporting the above items
9. Are there any other alternative proposed marks intended to be used for this product or service?
   - If so, have applications been filed or are such intended?
   - How many?
10. Was any application previously filed for this mark and then abandoned for any reason?
11. Once intent-to-use application is filed, when requesting extensions of time to file a Statement of Use, determine continued bona fide intent by reviewing all above points (especially "steps taken to launch the product or service") as applicable and consider the following additional points:
    - What progress has been made or obstacles encountered since the last claim of bona fide intent?

- If there were any contemporaneously filed intent-to-use applications for the same goods or services, how many (or what percentage)
  - Have proceeded to registration?
  - Are still pending?
  - Have been abandoned?
- Has the product or service for which this mark was originally intended been launched under a different mark?
- Have there been any decisions regarding narrowing the coverage of the goods or services?
- Have there been any decisions regarding the exact form of the display of the mark?

Checklist 1-5
Trademark Portfolio Management Systems

1. Trademark searches and clearances
2. Trademark applications and registrations
   - Mark description
   - Owner
   - Country
   - Class and goods
   - Dates (application and registration)
   - Status
   - Assignments
   - Renewal and other maintenance dates
   - Follow-up dates
3. Conflicts
   - Oppositions
   - Cancellations
   - Infringements
4. Agreements with other parties
   - Local
   - Worldwide
5. Franchise and license agreements
   - Links to other records
   - License recordal
   - Registered user
6. Miscellaneous
   - Report generation (regular and ad hoc)
   - Link to word processing and form generation
   - Graphic images
   - Budget expense tracking
   - Outside counsel roster
   - Country law file

Checklist 1-6
Trade Dress Protection

1. Development stages
   - Survey the competition to determine what elements are in the public domain
   - Encourage distinctiveness and uniqueness during the development stages
     - Focus the development of distinctive elements for items that are nonfunctional or merely incidentally functional
     - Analyze the core concept and draw the distinctive elements from it; do not depend on protecting the concept as a whole
     - Discourage copying; design away, not around
     - Narrow the protectable items to as many distinctive and as few nondistinctive elements as possible
     - If possible, coin a term referring to the distinctive features that could and will become associated with them, as well as being a marketing and advertising tool
     - Perform trademark searches
     - Seek the advice of expert counsel
2. Consumer-directed actions
   - Incorporate it in a two-dimensional logo that is extensively used
   - Develop and consistently use a term, for example, "The Golden Arches," for the design
   - Feature in advertising and call attention to it and its uniqueness
   - Display in business materials such as cards, stationery, invoices, manuals, trucks, telephone and other directories
   - Use on packaging and in promotions
   - Explain the derivation, uniqueness, and proprietary nature of it when possible, for example, on menus or table tents while customers are waiting to eat
   - License as a mark on ancillary items such as toys, clothing, pens, and the like
   - Use in a consistent and precise manner pursuant to a company trademark and trade identity policy
3. Legal activities
   - Seek prompt and comprehensive trademark registration protection
   - Secure copyright ownership for any materials developed by parties outside the company
   - Seek copyright protection for architectural plans, all written materials, advertising, menus, packaging, and so on
   - Post conspicuous notices, both registration (®) and copyright (©), and explanatory notices in narrative style
   - Take vigorous and prompt policing actions against third parties as well as ex-franchisees, choosing the circuit carefully
   - Draft specific protection and de-identification language and insist on insertion in all franchise agreements; use the preamble as an opportunity to obtain franchisee acknowledgment of your proprietary position

4. Other in-house compliance activities
   - Develop, disseminate, and implement policies for uniform and consistent materials, signs, buildings, and so on, throughout the system and deal carefully with the inevitable exceptions
   - Involve and monitor (a) franchise development personnel—they must insist on the proper language in the agreement; and (b) real estate personnel—they must insist on the proper lease language
   - Develop a de-identification policy and a post-term implementation kit
   - Create franchisee and employee awareness in manuals, newsletters, awards, uniforms, and so on
   - Solicit reports of possible third party infringing activity (see form 1-1)
   - Collect third party comments in periodicals, customer letters, and the like that indicate recognition
   - Look for and collect market research that may be used to prove secondary meaning
   - Be aware of the competition

Checklist 1-7
Policing Trademark Rights

1. Establish a protection strategy
   - Prioritize portfolio of marks
   - Prioritize geographic areas
   - Incorporate franchisee concerns and objectives
   - Execute strategic marketing goals and objectives
   - Budget balancing
2. Police promptly
   - Unreasonable delay could impede the issuance of injunctive relief and preclude an award of damages
   - Consumer confusion and weakening of marketing efforts
   - Dissatisfaction and/or lawsuits by franchisees
   - Dilution of the scope of legal protection
   - Reduction in scope and extent of rights against other parties
3. Surveillance of federal applications
   - Subscribe to service to uncover applications by others as soon as they are filed
   - Review Official Gazette for published applications
4. Surveillance of marketplace
   - Use franchisees, company employees, distributors (see form 1-1)
   - Trade publications and other advertising media
   - Investigators
   - Internet
   - Preventative advertising
5. Oppositions/cancellations
   - Need for extensive and careful investigation and analysis (see checklist 1-8)
   - Protect against registration of confusingly similar marks
   - Parallel action against currently infringing marks
   - Protect against incursions into scope of exclusivity
   - Protect against dilution
   - Prevent others from gaining rights in descriptive or generic terminology
6. Infringement/unfair competition/dilution
   - Need for extensive and careful investigation and analysis (see checklists 1-8 and 1-9)
   - Before taking action, establish with certainty the essential requirement of priority/superiority of rights
   - Cease and desist warning letters
   - Preliminary injunctive relief or temporary restraining orders
   - Ex parte seizure orders
   - Injunctive relief
   - Monetary damages
   - Destruction of infringing goods
   - Transfer of domain names
   - Attorneys' fees and costs

7. Other enforcement areas
   - Counterfeiting
   - U.S. Customs
   - Internet
   - Domain names
8. Action against franchisees
   - Expired or terminated "holdover" franchisee
   - Breakaway franchisee
   - Consider infringement action as more expedient than breach of contract
9. Settlement (see checklist 1-8)
   - Timing
   - Coexistence and other agreements (see form 1-2)
   - Alternative Dispute Resolution
10. Insurance
    - Obtain defensive coverage
    - General liability coverage
    - Advertising injury coverage
    - Obtain offensive (pursuit) coverage to fund enforcement
    - Notice issues—procedures in place
    - Element of litigation strategy

Checklist 1-8
Policing Trademark Rights—Deciding Whether to Litigate and/or Oppose

1. Identify objectives and develop strategy
   - Protection of marks generally
   - Protection of the specific mark
   - Business posture versus the competition
   - Business posture versus the applicant
   - Preserving the company's right, as well as the competition's, to use descriptive, generic, or commonly used terms or material
2. Gather and develop the facts
   - Verify priority (absolutely essential)
   - Identify the importance of the company's mark
   - Identify current and future business plans
   - Establish the mark's history and current posture
     - Origin—internal development or purchase
     - Protective and/or enforcement efforts—any past court or Trademark, Trial and Appeal Board decisions
     - Check for restrictions on use or registration by prior agreements with others
     - Obtain use information, sales figures, advertising, packaging, and so on
     - Confirm bona fide intent for intent-to-use applications
   - Verify the company's mark is up-to-date and defensible
     - Validly registered, subsisting, and renewed
     - Registration is not vulnerable to attack on the grounds of nonuse or abandonment
     - Goods or services description is accurate vis-à-vis current use
     - Presentation of the mark is accurate vis-à-vis current use
     - Chain of title up-to-date and properly recorded
     - Licenses, if any, accurate and up-to-date
     - License recordal and registered entries, if any, accurate and up-to-date
   - Confirm there are no limiting agreements with the applicant
   - Investigate the applicant in depth
     - Application file history
     - Was a citation of the company's mark or any other citation overcome during prosecution?
     - Were any descriptiveness or other objections overcome?
     - Does the other party own other registrations, especially those that may be for a slight variation of the applied-for mark?
     - Determine nature and extent of other party's business, e.g., channels of trade, sales volume, geographic scope, affiliated businesses, etc.
     - Obtain specific information about, and samples of, use of the applied-for mark, advertising, packaging, and so on
     - Compliance with license recordal
     - Look for any technical defects, for example, gap in title, improper assignment
     - Determine strategies and psychological profile of other party

3. Evaluate the likelihood of a successful outcome
   - Evaluate legal strength of the case
   - Evaluate other party's commitment
     - Application based upon proposed use or intent-to-use?
     - Application based upon foreign registration?
     - Is it a secondary type mark, a slogan, or other short-term material?
     - What is the extent and duration of use?
   - Assess company's motivation
     - Business issues
     - Keeping the register "clean" to guard the company's mark against future progressive encroachment from third parties
     - Keeping a competitor from gaining rights to material that is so descriptive, commonplace, or nondistinctive that competitors would be deprived
     - Protecting the mark from an "infringement"

4. Evaluating the merits of an opposition versus a court action
   - Advantages of opposition (or threatened opposition)
   - Less expense
   - Puts junior party on notice before its use commences or becomes extensive
   - Simpler, more focused legal issues
   - May achieve very simple goal, for example, obtaining narrowing of the goods description
   - May get junior party to bargaining table/settlement posture
   - Obtain a favorable decision that may influence a court
   - Could be dispositive in countries requiring a registration
   - Keeping the register "clean"
   - May turn out to be quicker result if interlocutory relief is not available and court dockets clogged
   - Disadvantages of opposition only
   - Only decides the right to register, not the right to use, depending on jurisdiction
   - Narrow legal issues, not all evidence relevant
   - Decision not binding on a court, depending on jurisdiction
   - Loss of time
   - Business effect—the junior mark has a chance to make its impact on the marketplace
   - Legal effect
     - Delay reduces the ability to get interlocutory relief in a court action for infringement
     - With the continued buildup of investment and goodwill, a court may be reluctant to ultimately enjoin the junior party
   - Both at once
     - Bring pressure on other party
     - Expense for both parties
     - Opens up discovery more quickly
     - Obtain interlocutory relief
     - Obtain damages
     - Obtain precedent
     - Publicity, that is, deterrence of other similar defendants

5. Settlement
   - Timing of approach to applicant/defendant
     - After filing of application but before use
     - After publication but during statutory or extended time to oppose (but note risk of applicant withdrawing application without prejudice)
     - After opposition filed
     - After cease and desist letter sent (but note danger of declaratory judgment action)
     - After lawsuit filed
     - Benefits of settlement to opposer/plaintiff
     - Certainty of outcome
     - Avoid further expenditure of time, effort, and resources
   - Protect business interests
     - Ability to make/proceed with business plans
     - Restrict activities of competitors
   - Protect legal interests
     - Avoid potential counterattacks on existing registrations
     - Avoid adverse precedential decision
     - Allowing multiple similar marks to be registered or used could indicate weakness of the senior mark
   - The opportunity to resolve a wider range of issues beyond the specific issue of the mark, for example, use, trade dress, other potential conflicts
   - Downsides to settlement
     - Eliminates the possibility of a complete victory
     - Applied-for mark may be allowed
     - Avoids decision indicating strength of senior mark
     - Avoids decision indicating weakness of junior mark
     - Psychological benefits vis-à-vis this competitor and others who will learn of a favorable decision
     - The need to agree to certain restrictions to which it was not previously subject
     - If the settlement includes allowance of registration and/or use by the junior party, it could dilute the senior party's position vis-à-vis present or future third parties
     - The inability to accurately predict the future—that the junior party's mark may become a significant competitive property

6. Settlement of opposition agreement (see form 1-2)
   - Structure of the relationship
     - Application withdrawn but use of the mark will be allowed subject to limitations
     - Application assigned to the senior party with license back to applicant but note issues of quality control and review, liability, effect on other licensees, dilution, goodwill, and reputation
     - Application will be allowed to proceed to registration
       - With the consent of the senior party
       - With restrictions on the registration to be issued
       - With restrictions on use/coexistence
     - Coexistence conditions
     - The presentation and display of the mark

- The exact spelling
- The exact manner or style
- The exact design or device
- The use of the word or design in combination with other words or designs (and then in a certain sequence)
- The use of the mark in combination with a house mark or trade name
- The precise trade dress
- The language
- The precise goods or services with which the mark can be used
- The precise channels of distribution or method of offering the services
- The methods of use: packaging, advertising, signage, Internet, etc.
- Restrictions on "nontrademark" use, for example, "style" or "type"
- Limitations on geographic areas of use or locations
- Restrictions on registration
  - Certain goods or services
  - Disclaimers of descriptive or generic terms
  - Generally track the use conditions
- Executional issues
- Providing for the future
  - Modifications of the mark
  - Changes in the goods or services, channels of distribution, and so on
  - New applications
- Covenants not to cancel or take other court action for infringement (but note distinction regarding abandonment or genericness)
- Effect of abandonment, failure to renew, sale of business or mark
- Assignability
- Cooperation regarding third-party applications or infringements

Checklist 1-9
Preparing for Trademark Enforcement

1. Analyze strength and scope of company's trademark rights
2. Analyze scope and strength of infringement
   - Similarity of marks
   - Consumer confusion
   - Dilution
   - Legitimate defenses
   - Infringer's market penetration and/or market share
   - Costs/benefits of litigation
   - Necessary to set example
   - Can the results be publicized to company's advantage?
3. Gather evidence of infringement
   - Purchase products bearing infringing marks
   - Develop paper trail of custody and sales records
   - Engage investigator
   - Trace some of the infringing products to original supplier or as high up the chain as possible
4. Prepare evidence of company's ownership, use, and strength of mark
   - How strong is the company's mark?
   - Secondary meaning
   - Affidavits and exhibits regarding duration of use, marketing dollars spent, revenues generated, and scope of consumer recognition of mark
5. Select venue
   - Home court favorable
   - Personal jurisdiction
   - Relative impact of costs on parties
   - Location of key witnesses and documents
6. Cease and desist letters
   - Gives notice
   - Achieve early settlement
   - May achieve results desired with minimal expense
   - Raises possibility of defensive "preemptive strike" in form of declaratory judgment action
7. U.S. Customs Service
   - Marks recorded with Customs
   - Customs provided with "enforcement notebooks" at key ports of entry
   - Photograph of actual goods, infringing goods, counterfeit goods
   - Customs provided with identities of suspected illegal importers
   - Trips made to key ports to educate import specialists and line officers

Checklist 1-10
Essential Trademark Provisions in Franchise Agreements

1. A valid and enforceable trademark license is an indispensable part of a franchise agreement (see Form 1-3)
   - To establish the rights and relationship of the franchisor and the franchisee
   - To establish the validity of the trademark license vis-à-vis third parties
   - To validate and support the franchisor's trademark rights
2. Quality control
   - The essential element and basis of the trademark license
   - The franchisor could lose its trademark rights if it fails to control the nature and quality or the goods and services sold by its franchisees
   - Quality control is mandatory so that the franchisor and franchisee can qualify as "related companies" under the Lanham Act
   - The mere recitation of a right to quality control is insufficient if not accompanied by actual exercise of this right
   - Franchisor has a duty to reasonably police its franchisees
   - Note the risk that the extent of the control could give rise to claims of vicarious liability and agency
   - Specific rights must be retained by franchisor to supervise and maintain quality control
     - Specific procedures and requirements
     - Reference to an operations manual
   - "Naked" licensing
     - Failure to adequately provide for, or to exercise, quality control can lead to abandonment of trademark rights
3. Preamble clauses
   - Establish the special nature of the rights and business being licensed
   - Act as basis for fees, royalty payments, and post-termination injunctive relief
4. Granting clause
   - Exclusive versus nonexclusive
     - Must be extremely specific
     - Must define any restriction upon the franchisor's activities, for example, channels of distribution, including the Internet
   - Right to sublicense
   - Specifying the marks versus blanket grant of all present and future marks within the system
   - The ability to add or delete marks in the future
   - The need to define proprietary trade dress in great detail
   - Identifying the goods or services in great specificity and/or defining the nature of the system being franchised
   - The precise geographic territory and/or location of site and any restrictions

5. Trademark relationship
   - Franchisee's acknowledgment that its use of the mark inures to the benefit of the franchisor
   - Franchisee's acknowledgment of the mark's validity, the franchisor's ownership, and its goodwill
   - Franchisee's acknowledgment that it acquires no rights in the mark or goodwill and will not contest the validity of the mark
6. Trademark use
   - Franchisee's acknowledgment to comply with franchisor's standards and guidelines
   - Franchisor's right to approve all materials and other uses of the mark
7. Trademark policing
   - Franchisor usually reserves the right to protect and defend the mark and control all enforcement decisions
   - Franchisee cooperation required
   - Assumption or allocation of costs and expenses
8. Rights upon termination and expiration
   - Immediate discontinuance of use of marks by franchisee
   - De-identification of proprietary trade dress at business sites
   - Transition provisions, such as changes to telephone directories
9. Miscellaneous provisions
   - Prohibitions or restrictions on assignments by franchisee
   - Indemnification by the franchisee
   - Prohibition against or restrictions on franchisee use of marks in franchisee trade names
   - Prohibition against or restrictions on franchisee use of marks in franchisee domain names
   - Franchisor's ability to change or modify marks upon notice
   - Indemnity by franchisor as to validity of the marks

Checklist 1-11
Trademark Portfolio Acquisition—Due Diligence

1. Determine the nature of the transaction
   - Acquisition or merger
   - Asset purchase (ownership will change)
   - Stock purchase (ownership need not change)
2. Identify and analyze the complete portfolio to be transferred
   - Obtain lists and files from seller
   - Verify key information by independent searches
3. Determine the scope of the acquired assets to make sure that the goodwill accompanies the trademarks
4. Verify ownership and status of registrations and applications
   - Closely examine chain of title and identify any gaps
   - Confirm that all renewals have been made and fees paid
5. Review all uses of marks by the seller
   - Confirm that appropriate protection has been secured for all marks in use or in pipeline
   - Identify registrations with vulnerability due to nonuse
6. Review enforcement history
7. Verify scope and strength in key jurisdictions
   - Focus on important business areas
   - Focus on jurisdictions where there may be nonuse vulnerability and therefore lack of past enforcement
8. Inventory and review all restrictions that could limit the buyer's rights or ability to use or expand use
   - Settlement agreements
   - Prior rights agreements
   - Consent agreements
   - License agreements
9. Identify jurisdictions of interest to the buyer where rights have not yet been protected by the seller
10. Identify jurisdictions where the coverage of goods or services by the registrations do not adequately encompass the buyer's business activities
11. Identify and review all jurisdictions with license recordal
    - Identify gaps and resulting contingent liabilities
    - Identify any impediments to obtaining transfer of such recordations
12. Identify and analyze any encumbrances, that is, security interests, liens, and so on
    - That could block a transfer or must be dealt with prior to transfer
    - That will survive the transfer

13. Identify and review any limitations on marks being used but not owned by the seller
    - Trademark licenses
    - Franchise agreements
    - Distribution agreements
    - Must consent be obtained prior to transfer?
    - If transferable, what effect do these have on the buyer's business?

14. Identify and analyze all pending conflicts
    - Claims, challenges to registration, and/or claims of infringement against the seller
    - Claims, challenges to registration, and/or claims of infringement by the seller against third parties

15. Draft appropriate warranties and representations for inclusion in the purchase agreement
    - Requisite language can vary
        - Asset purchase (see form 1-4)
        - Stock purchase (see form 1-5)

16. Assignments
    - One blanket assignment recommended (see form 1-6)
    - Blanket assignments will cover any unregistered assets
    - Specific assignments required for each jurisdiction
    - Special assignment form needed for intent-to-use applications in the United States, if a complete transfer of the business related to the trademarks is occurring; otherwise, these cannot be assigned without jeopardizing the validity of the assignment and any registration that thereafter will issue from the application
    - Identify those jurisdictions that will tax the value of the assets being assigned and assess the impact of the resulting contingent liability
    - Provide for (especially in an asset purchase situation) a postsale procedure for executing assignment documents

17. Arrange for prompt transfer from seller
    - Files
    - Computer print-outs
    - Outside counsel roster

Form 1-1
Trademark Infringement Report

1. Name, address, and telephone number of infringing business.
2. How did this matter come to our attention: from a fellow employee, a customer, newspaper, TV or radio ad, telephone listing, or other?
3. How long has this business been in operation?
4. How long has the infringement situation existed?
5. If a service business, are there other locations or branches? Is there a headquarters office?
6. Describe the nature, size, and scope of the infringing business.
7. Describe the infringement in detail, including which trademarks of the company are believed to be infringed.
8. Provide samples of the packaging and/or advertising or photographs of, for example, the signage or a building.
9. Is any connection known between the infringer's current management and our company or any of our former employees?
10. Please provide a copy of a yellow pages telephone book listing if available.
11. Does this business have a website? If so, please provide the domain name.

Form 1-2
Prototype Contested Application Settlement Agreement

Agreement effective as of the ________________ of ____________ , 20__, by ____________ Senior, Inc. _______________, located at ________________________ (hereinafter referred to as "S") and _________________ Junior, Inc. ________________, located at __________________ (hereinafter referred to as "J").

WHEREAS, S is using and is the owner of the trademark ___________ for "______" as well as the owner of Trademark Registration _______. [or Trademark Application ________] for that mark as applied to those goods or services. **WHEREAS, J** has adopted, subsequent to **S's** registration [application] [use] the trademark __________ for "_________."

WHEREAS, J has filed trademark application __________ in the Patent and Trademark Office (hereinafter referred to as "PTO") on ___________ 20__, to register its mark for "______"; and **S** has threatened to file [has filed] an opposition proceeding against **J's** application for registration [which opposition is presently pending].

[or] **WHEREAS, J** has filed trademark application _________ in the PTO on ______________, to register its mark for "_______"; and **S's** trademark as above was cited by the PTO as blocking said application.

WHEREAS, both parties are in agreement that there will be no confusion in the trade or in the marketplace by the concurrent use of their respective marks on their respective goods or services subject to the conditions and limitations set forth in this Agreement.

WHEREAS, the parties are desirous of settling this matter without further controversy.

NOW, THEREFORE, in consideration of the background stated above and the terms and conditions stated below, the parties hereby agree as follows:

1. (a) **J** agrees to promptly abandon its application _______ by expressly abandoning it and agrees not to use or refile to register this mark for the same goods or services. [or]

(b) **J** will file a new application for its mark as modified as set forth in exhibit A.

2. **S** agrees to the use [and registration] by **J** of its mark on the following conditions:

(a) that the use [and registration] of **J's** mark shall be restricted to _________.

(b) that **J's** mark shall not be used [or registered] in connection with _______.

(c) that the products sold under **J's** mark shall not be described as "_______";

(d) that clear and conspicuous use of the house mark _______________ [or the design/logo] be used in conjunction with **J's** mark in all packaging and promotional materials with the ________________ products or services;

(e) that **J's** mark shall not be displayed in any manner of fashion similar to the manner or fashion in which **S** uses or displays its mark, and in no way shall imply any connection or relation to **S**; and

(f) that the graphic display of **J's** mark shall always be as set forth in exhibit A.

3. **S** agrees to provide **J** in a form suitable for filing with the PTO an appropriate letter of consent to its application to register its mark for its goods as noted above and agrees to [refrain from filing opposition] [withdraw its pending opposition] against said application, refrain from taking any adverse action with respect to the validity of any registration that issues from the application, or taking any adverse action against the use of **J's** mark. [If the PTO fails to accept the consent, it shall not be considered a breach of this Agreement and **J's** obligations herein shall continue.]

4. **S** and **J** agree to avoid using their respective marks in a manner that might cause consumers to mistakenly believe that the goods or services of one emanate from, are sponsored by, or otherwise associated with the other.

5. **J** agrees to refrain from taking any adverse legal action against **S's** use of its mark or against any of **S's** registrations or subsequent applications for its mark.

6. Provided **J** complies with all the terms and conditions of this Agreement, **S** shall not object to **J's** use and registration of its mark for its goods and services.

7. This Agreement shall be without definite term, shall have effect throughout the [territory] and shall inure to the benefit of and shall be binding upon any related parties, subsidiaries, or affiliates owned or otherwise controlled by the parties and shall further be binding upon any successors in interest or assigns of the parties hereto. This Agreement constitutes the entire agreement between the parties and may be altered, modified, or amended only by an express declaration in writing signed by a duly authorized officer of each party and referring specifically to this agreement.

Senior, Inc.

By: ________________________

Title: ________________________

Junior, Inc.

By: ________________________

Title: ________________________

Form 1-3
Sample Trademark-Relevant Provisions in a Franchise Agreement

Recitals

1.1 Franchisor is the originator and owner of a unique, distinctive, and high-quality type of _______ (the "Product") for which it has developed methods of manufacturing, marketing, and sales distribution (the "System").

1.2 Franchisor has developed a unique, distinctive, and high-quality system of business operation (the "System") for performing _______ services (the "Services"), consisting of certain business techniques, methods and procedures, distinctive features and characteristics, distinctive building designs, advertising signs, specially designed equipment and equipment layout plans, secret formulas, certain patents and proprietary technology, certain original and copyrighted materials, and a proprietary and confidential operations manual (the "Manual").

1.3 Franchisor owns valuable trademarks, service marks, and trade names, the primary ones of which are set forth on the attached Schedule, as well as various trademarks, service marks, trade names, slogans, designs, insignias, emblems, symbols, package designs, distinctive building designs and other architectural features, logos, and other proprietary identifying characteristics used in connection with the primary trademarks, service marks, and trade names (collectively the "Marks") all used in relation to and in connection with the Products, the System, or both.

1.4 Franchisee recognizes the benefits of being associated with the System and being able to use the Marks and wishes to use the System and the Marks in the business of operating a franchise to manufacture, market, and sell the Products and perform the Services at one location in ________ (the "Territory").

Grant of License

2.1 *License.* Subject to the terms and conditions of this Agreement, Franchisor grants to Franchisee a nontransferable license to use the Marks solely upon and in connection with the manufacture, marketing, and sale of the Products and the performance of the Services.

2.2 *Nonexclusivity.* The License granted is nonexclusive, and Franchisor reserves the right to operate and license others to operate locations to perform the Services under the Marks adjacent to, or in the vicinity of, Franchisee's location.

Marks

3.1 *Ownership.* Franchisee must use the Marks only in connection with the System or Products. Franchisor is the owner of the Marks and the goodwill associated with the Marks, and Franchisor owns all goodwill created by Franchisee's use of the Marks. Franchisee will not contest the validity of the Marks. Apart from the right of Franchisee to use the Marks under this Agreement, Franchisee acquires no right, title, or interest of any kind or nature in or to the Marks or the goodwill associated with the Marks.

3.2 *Approval.* Franchisee must display the Marks only in the form and manner approved by Franchisor and, upon request by Franchisor, include the legends, markings, and notices of trademark registration, Franchisor ownership, or Franchisor-Franchisee relationship specified by Franchisor. Franchisor has the right to approve all advertising, displays, and other materials using the Marks prepared by Franchisee. Franchisee agrees to follow Franchisor's instructions regarding proper use of the Marks.

3.3 *Franchisee Contributions.* All artwork, graphics, layouts, slogans, names, titles, or similar materials created by the Franchisee or its subcontractors using the Marks, or relating to the Franchisee's franchise, become Franchisor's property, including any copyright rights. Franchisee agrees on behalf of itself, its employees, its subcontractors, and any other party with whom it may contract to create such materials, to promptly execute any and all appropriate documents to transfer ownership in these materials to the Franchisor.

3.4 *Protection and Defense.* Franchisor will protect and defend the Marks. Franchisee agrees to cooperate fully with Franchisor in the defense and protection of the Marks and will promptly notify Franchisor in writing of potentially infringing uses by others, or of any lawsuits brought or claims made against Franchisee involving the Marks. Franchisor has control over all decisions involving the protection and defense of the Marks, and Franchisee will take no action without Franchisor's express written permission.

3.5 *Franchisee Cooperation.* Franchisee agrees to cooperate with the Franchisor in any application to record Franchisee as a registered or permitted user of the Marks with a government agency. Upon termination or expiration of this Agreement, Franchisor may immediately apply to cancel Franchisee's status as a registered or permitted user, and Franchisee will cooperate with Franchisor to effect any cancellation petition. The Franchisor will bear the expense of any recording or cancellation.

3.6 *Restrictions on Marks and Trade Names.*

(a) Franchisee must not use any trademarks or other identifying characteristics in connection with the Products or System other than the Marks.

(b) Franchisee must not manufacture, market, or sell products or perform services under the Marks that are not approved by Franchisor.

(c) Franchisee must not use or register, in whole or in part, the Marks or Franchisor's name, or anything similar, as part of Franchisee's name or any business entity name.

(d) Franchisee must not use or register, in whole or in part, the Marks or Franchisor's name, or anything similar, as part of a domain name.

3.7 *Goodwill.* The Marks are valuable to the System, and Franchisee will not use the Marks in a manner to disparage Franchisor or its reputation, and will not take any action that will harm or jeopardize the Marks, or Franchisor's ownership in the Marks.

3.8 *Changes to Marks.* Franchisor has the right to periodically make changes to the Marks. The Franchisor will provide notice of any changes to Franchisee, and Franchisee must, as soon as reasonable under the circumstances, adopt and use any changes to the Marks.

Standards of Operation and Quality Control

4.1 In order to protect, preserve, and enhance the value of the Marks, the Products, and the System, the Franchisee must manufacture, market, and sell the Products, and perform the Services in strict accordance with the standards, specifications, requirements, instructions, procedures, and other standards of nature and quality specified by the Franchisor (including those in the Manual). The uniform application and implementation of the Franchisor's standards is important to the Franchisee, the Franchisor, and the collective success of all franchisees. Failure to adhere to Franchisor's standards is deemed a material breach of this Agreement.

4.2 All materials related to the marketing and sale of the Products or performance of the Services, including but not limited to packaging, advertising, and signs, must meet Franchisor's standards of nature and quality.

4.3 Franchisee must make sure that the Products and Services meet Franchisor's standards, and Franchisee must reasonably cooperate with Franchisor in enabling Franchisor to ascertain that the standards are being met. For example, (a) the Franchisor's employees and agents have the right to enter, at any reasonable time, any of Franchisee's premises where Products are being manufactured or offered for sale, or where Services are being performed, to determine whether Franchisee's business is conducted in accordance with this Agreement and Franchisor's standards; (b) Franchisor's employees and agents have the right to request reasonable quantities of samples of Products, at Franchisee's expense, for testing, inspection, and review; and (c) all advertising by Franchisee must be approved in advance by Franchisor.

4.4 [Include appropriate deficiency and cure provisions tailored to franchise here.]

4.5 Franchisee must fully comply with, adhere to, and abide by all rules, procedures, standards, specifications, and requirements published by the Franchisor, as amended, modified, or supplemented periodically, which may be published together as a Manual or individually (collectively included in the definition of "Manual"). Franchisee agrees to keep its copy of the Manual current. The Manual remains Franchisor's property; Franchisee will not reproduce the Manual and will immediately return the Manual to Franchisor upon termination or expiration of this Agreement.

4.6 Franchisee must observe high ethical standards of operation reasonably calculated to maintain the uniformity of image, public goodwill, and reputation attached to the System and the Marks, and must not engage in any activity that may harm Franchisor's reputation, the reputation of any other of Franchisor's franchisees, or the goodwill in the Marks.

4.7 Franchisee must comply with all laws, regulations, ordinances, governmental standards, and other requirements applicable to the manufacture, sale, distribution, promotion, and advertisement of the Products and the provision of the Services.

Proprietary Information

5.1 Franchisor may disclose to Franchisee confidential and proprietary information related to the Products, the System, or the franchise system (collectively "Confidential Information"), and Franchisee must not reveal or disclose any Confidential Information. The Manual, Franchisor's proprietary formulations and secret formulas, and the System are Franchisor's trade secrets and are designated as Confidential Information. No right is given to or acquired by Franchisee to disclose, duplicate, license, sell, or reveal any of Franchisor's trade secrets to any person, other than an employee needing access for purpose of the employee's job duties. Franchisee agrees to keep all Confidential Information secret, to obtain from each of its stockholders, directors, officers, employees, and agents an agreement to keep and respect such confidences, and to be responsible for compliance by such stockholders, directors, officers, employees, and agents with such agreements.

5.2 Franchisee and each of its officers individually must pay to Franchisor for each and every breach the sum of ____________ as liquidated damages and not as a penalty if either of the following situations occur: (a) Franchisee discloses any trade secrets to any person, or (b) one of the persons subject to Franchisee's control makes a disclosure as a result of the failure of Franchisee to use its best efforts to take the necessary precautions to prevent such disclosure. The parties acknowledge that the precise amount of Franchisor's actual damages would be extremely difficult to ascertain and that this sum represents a reasonable estimate of actual damages.

Copyrights

6.1 All copyrights to the Manual and to all promotional, advertising, and other materials, in whatever medium, are Franchisor's property. This includes advertising or materials related to the System created by Franchisee or its agents that are deemed works made-for-hire by Franchisee for Franchisor, or if the materials do not qualify as a works made-for-hire, Franchisee assigns its copyright rights in all such materials to Franchisor. Franchisee agrees to execute whatever assignment or other documents are requested by Franchisor to prove Franchisor's copyright ownership, or to assist Franchisor in obtaining copyright registration. Franchisee may use any copyrights or copyrightable material solely in connection with the promotion and sale of Products according to the System.

Termination or Expiration

7.1 Upon the termination or expiration of this Agreement, Franchisee must immediately discontinue the use of the System, Products, and Marks. All rights granted in this Agreement relating to the Marks revert to the Franchisor.

7.2 Franchisee must immediately remove the Marks from all buildings, signs, fixtures, and furnishings, and alter and paint all structures and other improvements maintained under this Agreement to a design and color that are fundamentally different from Franchisor's authorized building design and painting scheme. In addition, Franchisee must make the following building alterations: ____________________________.

7.3 If Franchisee fails to effect the necessary removal, alteration, or repainting within ____ days after written notice, then Franchisor or its authorized agent has the right to enter the site, without being deemed guilty of trespass or any other tort or civil wrong, and make the necessary removals, alterations, and repainting at Franchisee's expense, which Franchisee must pay to Franchisor upon demand.

7.4 Following termination or expiration, Franchisee must not use any trademark, trade name, service mark, logo, insignia, slogan, emblem, symbol, design, package design, distinctive building design or other architectural feature, or other identifying characteristic that is in any way associated with Franchisor or similar to the Marks, and Franchisee and those associated with Franchisee must not operate or do business under any name or in any manner that might tend to give the public the impression that Franchisee is or was associated with Franchisor.

7.5 Immediately upon termination or expiration of this Agreement, Franchisee must return to Franchisor all copies of the Manual received by Franchisee, together with any and all other materials containing trade secrets or other proprietary information.

7.6 Franchisee's failure to follow the termination provisions in this section 7 will result in irreparable harm to Franchisor and the System and that Franchisor's remedy at law for damages will be inadequate. Accordingly, upon any breach by Franchisee of these termination provisions, Franchisor is entitled to injunctive relief or specific performance in addition to any other remedies available at law or in equity.

Form 1-4
Sample Provisions—Asset Purchase Agreement

Seller possesses and agrees to convey all right, title, and interest in and to all of the Company's Marks, trade names, trade dress, labels, as well as the goodwill associated therewith, copyrights and patents and all registrations, renewals and applications therefor (the "Intellectual Property") owned by the Company and all licenses or agreements under which the Company has the right to use any of the Intellectual Property, each of which is listed and briefly described in Schedule [___], in addition to the secret or confidential information, techniques, formulas, recipes, processes and related ancillary, and incidental know-how, standards and specifications relating to or essential to the manufacture and sale of products of the same characteristics and quality as now sold by the Company under the Company's Marks, and Seller represents these are valid and subsisting, are free and clear of any liens or encumbrances of any type, and are satisfactory and sufficient for the proper conduct of the Company's business under the Company's Marks.

To the best knowledge of the Company, except as set forth in Schedule [___], there are no other persons with rights, or claims of rights, superior to or which restrict the right of the Company to use the Company's Marks or which may give rise to a claim of infringement against the Company nor are there any proceedings that have been instituted or are pending or threatened that challenge the validity of the ownership or the use by the Company of the Intellectual Property. Schedule [___] contains a list of all licenses or agreements pursuant to which the Company licenses anyone to use any of the Intellectual Property or any other technical know-how or other proprietary rights of the Company, or pursuant to which the Company has consented, based upon its rights in the Intellectual Property, to any other person's use of a trademark, trade name, copyright, or patent. Except as set forth in Schedule [___], Company has no knowledge of any use or any application for registration by any other person infringing any of the Company's Intellectual Property, and there is no pending litigation based upon such use or application.

Form 1-5
Sample Provisions—Stock Purchase Agreement

All trademarks, service marks, trade names, symbols, logos, trade dress, all goodwill associated therewith, copyrights, and patents (collectively the "Intellectual Property"), whether registered or unregistered, and applications and registrations therefor, owned by the Company are listed and described in Schedule [____]. The Company has good, valid, indefeasible, and marketable title to, and is the exclusive and unrestricted owner throughout the [territory] of, all the Intellectual Property listed on Schedule [___], free and clear of any liens, claims, charges, pledges, security interests, options to purchase, encumbrances, or equitable interests of any nature whatsoever.

All franchises, licenses, consents, approvals, or authorizations that relate to the Company and to any of the Intellectual Property, including but not limited to all licenses and agreements under which the Company has the right to use or grants to any third party the right to use any of the Intellectual Property, are described in Section [___].

No claim has been received by the Company claiming that the Company's use of any of the Intellectual Property violates the rights of third parties.

To the best knowledge of the Company after reasonable inquiry: (a) neither the Company nor its operation as presently conducted infringes any of the Intellectual Property of any third party; (b) none of the Intellectual Property or registration listed on Schedule [___] is void, invalid, or unenforceable; (c) there are no other persons with rights, or claims of rights, superior to, or that restrict the right of the Company to conduct its business as it is presently conducted or that may give rise to a claim of infringement against the Company, nor are there any proceedings that have been instituted or are pending or threatened that challenge the validity of the ownership or use by the Company of the Intellectual Property listed in Schedule [___] or the right to conduct its business as it is presently conducted; and (d) no third party by adverse use or application for registration is infringing the rights of the Company with respect to the use of the Intellectual Property listed on Schedule [___].

Schedule [ ]
Trademarks, Service Marks, Trade Names, Symbols, Logos
(each being referred to below as "Mark"):

Mark	U.S. Reg.	U.S. Reg. Date	U.S. App.	R.S. App. Date	State App. or Reg. and Date: Name of State	Check here if no app. or reg. no.

Description of trade dress:

Copyrights:

Patents:

Description of all franchises, licenses, consents, approvals, or authorizations that relate to the Company and to any of the Intellectual Property, including but not limited to all licenses and agreements under which the Company has the right to use or grants to any third party the right to use any of the Intellectual Property:

Form 1-6
Blanket Assignment

WHEREAS, ________________________, a corporation of the State of ________, with its principal place of business at ____, has created, obtained, adopted, and otherwise owns intellectual and/or industrial property in connection with its business (the "Intangibles");

WHEREAS,________________________________, a corporation of the State of ________, with its principal place of business at ______________, is desirous of acquiring all the said Intangibles;

NOW THEREFORE, for good and valuable consideration, the receipt of which is hereby acknowledged, ________________________ does hereby sell, transfer, convey, and assign to _______________ all right, title, and interest throughout the world in or relating directly or indirectly to all the said Intangibles including, by way of example and not limitation: trademarks, service marks, and trade names, together with (a) the various symbols, designs, devices, logos, labels, trade dress, slogans, and other distinctive material used in association with, (b) the goodwill of the business symbolized thereby, (c) the technology and trade secrets, including, but not limited to, formulas, recipes, know-how, processes, techniques, methods, and specifications related to the manufacture and sale of the products and provision of services under the service marks and trade names, and (d) all relevant trademark and service mark registrations and applications for trademark and service mark registration; patents and patent applications, inventions and designs; copyrights and applications for copyright registration; the right to secure renewals, extensions, continuations, and reissues to any of the foregoing, related rights arising out of license or other contracts with third parties; and all pending or inchoate causes of action or claims related to any of the foregoing, including the right to sue and recover for past infringement or breaches of contract.

[Assignor]

____

By:
Name:
Title:

STATE OF }
} ss.
COUNTY OF }

__________________________________ being duly sworn, deposes and says that he is _______________________ of ___________________________, and that he has executed the assignment for and on behalf of ___________________, being duly authorized to do so.

Subscribed and sworn to before me
this _______ day of _______________, 20__

____
Notary Public

Form 1-7
Independent Contractor/Work for Hire/ Assignment Agreement

______________________________("Contractor") located at

____

____

hereby agrees with ______________________________ ("Company") as follows.

1. Contractor agrees that, in consideration of its agreement to perform commissioned services for Company for good and valuable consideration, the receipt and sufficiency of which is hereby acknowledged, all works of authorship, work product, and materials in any format, including digital or written, that arise out of these services for Company including, without limitation, all graphics, artwork, drawings, music or other audio work, textual materials, and any related software and computer code, all versions, iterations, and modifications thereof that have been or are in the future created or prepared in any medium now known or unknown (the "Work"), was and is expressly agreed to be considered a "work made for hire" under U.S. copyright law, provided, however, that in the event the Work is deemed not to be a "work made for hire," Contractor hereby irrevocably assigns to Company all right, title, and interest in and to the Work worldwide, including the copyright and all renewals, that shall exclusively forever belong to Company that shall have the unlimited right to own, use, and convey the Work without limitation or additional compensation or other consideration to Contractor.

2. Contractor further hereby assigns to Company all worldwide intellectual property rights, title, and interest of any kind to all names, words, symbols, designs, innovations, inventions, know-how, developments, and ideas, whether or not copyrightable or patentable, including, but not limited to all trademarks, trade dress, and patents related to the Work arising from the services (the "Related Rights"), that shall exclusively forever belong to Company that shall have the unlimited right to own, use, and convey these rights, title, and interest without limitation or additional compensation or other consideration to Contractor.

3. Contractor agrees to execute any appropriate documents requested by Company sufficient to vest exclusive title and ownership of the Work and the Related Rights in Company. If Company is unable for any reason to secure such execution, Contractor hereby irrevocably designates and appoints Company and its duly authorized officers and agents as Contractor's agent and attorney in fact, to act for and on behalf of Contractor to execute and file any such documents, including assignments, and to do all other lawfully permitted acts to further the purposes hereunder.

[Individual Contractor Alternative] 4. Contractor warrants and represents that the Work, or his/her contribution to the Work, and the Related Rights, if any, are and shall be original, not copied from any previous work not already in the public domain, and not subject to any adverse claim by any other party, including, but not limited to, claims of ownership or infringement, and hereby indemnifies and holds Company harmless in this regard.

[Corporate Contractor Alternative] 4. Contractor warrants and represents that the Work, or its contribution to the Work, and the Related Rights, if any, are and shall be origi nal, not copied from any previous work not already in the public domain, and not subject to any adverse claim by any other party, including, but not limited to claims of ownership or infringement, and hereby indemnifies and holds Company harmless in this regard. Contractor warrants and represents that no person who is not its employee contributed or will contribute to the Work, or to the extent that any nonemployee does or will contribute, Contractor will secure the execution by such contributor of an agreement similar in content to this Agreement flowing to Company.

5. Contractor hereby waives any moral rights of any kind or nature in the Work and agrees not to (i) contest Company's ownership of the Work, (ii) claim any ownership in or to the Work, (iii) use or exploit the Work; and (iv) object to any exploitation or use of the Work by Company or to any changes, modifications, or revisions to the Work made by Company. Contractor acknowledges and agrees that nothing herein or by virtue of the services performed for Company shall be construed as conveying to Contractor any rights with respect to any of Company's intellectual property, including any copyrights, trademarks, trade names, or any related or derivative rights, or the goodwill associated therewith.

6. This Agreement shall be binding upon and inure to the benefit of the parties hereto, and their respective related or affiliated companies, heirs, successors, administrators, and assigns.

________________________________ ("Contractor")

By: ______________________________

Name: ______________________________

Date: ______________________________

Company, Inc.

By: ______________________________

Name: ______________________________

Date: ______________________________

CHAPTER 2

Franchise Disclosure and Sales Compliance

Leslie D. Curran, David W. Oppenheim, and Max J. Schott, II

Contents

2-1. Introduction

To manage franchise sales activity and the growth of a franchise system, a franchisor should establish internal policies and programs that facilitate compliance with federal and state laws and regulations applicable to the offer and sale of a franchise. To effectively implement such policies and programs, a franchisor should ensure that all of the franchisor's personnel who may interact with prospective franchisees understand basic franchise sales laws and how the legal and regulatory frameworks of those laws may impact the franchisor's (including its personnel's) dealings with prospective franchisees. While this chapter provides an overview of applicable franchise relationship laws in connection with state registration requirements and issues related to system expansion, a discussion of such relationship laws in other contexts is addressed in chapter 5.

From a business standpoint, the franchisor's implementation and adherence to an effective compliance program will help the franchisor create an organized internal franchise sales program, make it easier to on-board franchise sellers, provide a pipeline of information that can be used when it is necessary to update its franchise disclosure document, and often, may help facilitate prospective franchises through the sales process. From a legal standpoint, a carefully crafted and implemented franchise sales program will assess the application of the various franchise laws and put tools and resources in place that franchisor personnel can use to more effectively follow any relevant franchise sales laws. These policies and procedures should be memorialized in an internal compliance program, which is likely to assist the franchisor with minimizing risk exposure for violations of federal and state franchise sales laws. For example, the program may provide the basis for a highly credible defense should any franchise sales transaction be challenged, to the extent that the franchisor and its franchise sales personnel conducted the franchise sales activity and business dealings in a manner consistent with the established policies. The failure of the franchisor or its franchise sales personnel to comply with established policies and procedures, however, can be introduced as evidence to prove that the franchisor failed to meet its own minimum standards of conduct. Consequently, system policies should establish standards that are achievable by the franchisor and its franchise sales personnel yet provide sufficient flexibility to address a variety of circumstances the franchisor may face. In addition, these policies should be reviewed regularly and communicated to all of the franchisor's personnel who may have relevant contact with prospective franchisees. The franchisor should consider conducting franchise sales compliance training, even for seasoned franchise sales personnel. Upon the franchise sales personnel's receipt of the compliance procedures and completion of the training, the franchisor should consider obtaining a written statement that the materials were received and reviewed. Some franchisors also require franchise sales personnel to take a short quiz that measures understanding of the policies and training materials.

2-2. Overview of Franchise Registration and Disclosure Laws

The offer and sale of franchises are regulated under both federal and state law. Such laws specify, among other things, the form and content of the disclosures that a franchisor must make to prospective franchisees, the timing for delivery of the required disclosures, and who must receive the disclosures.

The Federal Trade Commission (FTC) promulgated the trade regulation rule entitled Disclosure Requirements and Prohibitions Concerning Franchising and Business Opportunity Ventures ("original FTC Rule") on December 21, 1978. The original FTC Rule became effective on October 21, 1979. After a review that covered more than a decade and involved multiple hearings and public comment periods, the FTC amended the original FTC Rule on March 30, 2007 ("FTC Rule" or "amended FTC Rule"), which became effective on July 1, 2007, and covers only franchises.[1] The FTC Rule, which applies in all 50 states and the U.S. territories,[2]

1. 16 C.F.R. § 436 (2007), Bus. Franchise Guide (CCH) ¶ 6000. Although the original FTC Rule applied to both franchises and business opportunities, the amended FTC Rule applies only to franchises. The offer and sale of business opportunities are now governed by 16 C.F.R. § 437 (2007), Bus. Franchise Guide (CCH) ¶ 6030.

2. 16 C.F.R. § 436.2 (2007), Bus. Franchise Guide (CCH) ¶ 6347.

requires delivery of a franchise disclosure document (FDD) with the required disclosures to prospective franchisees, in accordance with the FTC Rule's timing requirement, prior to the franchisor accepting any consideration or signing any binding agreement for the sale of a franchise. The FTC Rule does not require that the franchisor file or register the FDD with, or obtain approval of the FDD by, any federal agency.

In the context of the regulation of franchise sales, the FTC Rule does not supersede (or preempt) all state efforts. Instead, the FTC Rule only supersedes state laws that provide prospective franchisees less protection than the FTC Rule.[3] As a result, the states are free to enact more protective franchise sales laws, and 15 states have enacted such laws.[4]

On January 1, 1971—more than seven and a half years before the original FTC Rule was promulgated—California became the first state to adopt a law specifically regulating franchise sales activity by requiring registration and disclosure in connection with the offer and sale of a franchise.[5] The other 14 states followed suit. Generally, these state franchise laws require a franchisor to disclose certain required information in its FDD; register (or file), and in some instances obtain approval of, the FDD prior to the franchisor offering and selling a franchise (as defined by statute) in that state;[6] comply with standards for, and in some states submit filings of, certain franchise sales advertising; and, in a number of states, register its franchise sellers with the state.[7] Further, more than 26 states have business opportunity laws or seller-assisted marketing plan acts that may affect a franchisor's ability to offer and sell franchises in a particular state.[8]

Where possible, a franchisor may attempt to structure its franchise program to qualify for an exemption or exclusion from the FTC Rule and state disclosure requirements, as well as the registration and/or filing requirements of the state franchise statutes.[9] A franchisor should keep in mind that, among other differences, the criteria and filing requirements for each exemption and exclusion can vary significantly between the jurisdictions.[10]

---

3. 16 C.F.R. § 436.10(b) (2007), Bus. Franchise Guide (CCH) ¶ 6020.

4. *See* Bus. Franchise Guide (CCH) ¶¶ 3050 (Cal.), 3110 (Haw.), 3130 (Ill.), 3140 (Ind.), 3200 (Md.), 3220 (Mich.), 3230 (Minn.), 3320 (N.Y.), 3340 (N.D.), 3370 (Or.), 3390 (R.I.), 3410 (S.D.), 3460 (Va.), 3470 (Wash.), 3490 (Wis.).

5. *See* Bus. Franchise Guide (CCH) ¶ 3050.

6. Oregon and Michigan are the exceptions. Oregon's franchise law is similar to the FTC Rule, requiring only presale delivery of a disclosure document and including no filing requirement. *See* Bus. Franchise Guide (CCH) ¶ 5370. In addition, while Michigan's franchise law requires the submission of a filing before a franchisor may offer and sell franchises in the state, the franchisor is not required to include its FDD with the filing. *See* Bus. Franchise Guide (CCH) ¶ 5220.

7. This is a general statement, and the requirements vary somewhat from state to state, as described below.

8. *See infra* section 2-7.

9. *See infra* section 2-6.

10. For a detailed summary of exemptions and exclusions, *see* Leslie D. Curran & Beata Krakus eds., Exemptions and Exclusions Under Federal and State Franchise Registration and Disclosure Laws (ABA Forum on Franchising 2017).

If a franchisor does not qualify for an exemption (or is otherwise excluded from coverage of the statute), the franchisor will likely be required to register in accordance with the terms of such laws prior to any offer or sale of a franchise in that state. If the manner in which the franchisor offers its franchises falls within state statutory definitions of a business opportunity or a seller-assisted marketing plan, then the franchisor may face registration and disclosure obligations under these statutes that are similar to, or in addition to, those required under federal or state franchise laws.[11] For franchise sales personnel to understand the importance of compliance with laws, the franchisor should communicate to them that violations of any of these laws can result in significant civil and criminal liability to the franchisor, as well as to the individuals responsible for, or involved with, the actions that constitute a violation.[12]

2-3. What Is a Franchise?

To assess if franchise laws even apply, the first step is to examine whether the contemplated relationship satisfies the definition of a franchise under federal and state laws. Generally speaking, a business relationship qualifies as a "franchise"[13] if three elements are present:

1. The franchisee makes a required payment (which can be a fee, security deposit, equipment purchase, or most other types of payment) to the franchisor or its affiliates;[14]
2. The franchisor has the right to exert significant control over, or promises to provide significant assistance in, the franchisee's business;[15] and
3. The franchisor grants the franchisee the right to use a trademark associated with the business.

Although the precise terminology of the definitional elements varies among the FTC Rule and the various state statutes, as a practical matter, in most circumstances, a relationship that satisfies the "franchise" definition of one law will also satisfy the other laws as well.[16]

---

11. *See infra* section 2-7.

12. *See infra* section 2-11.

13. Some states and territories use the term "dealership" rather than "franchise." *See, e.g.,* Wisconsin Fair Dealership Law, Wis. Stat. §§ 135.01 *et seq.,* Bus. Franchise Guide (CCH) ¶ 4490.01.

14. Most federal and state statutes provide a minimum threshold for the franchise fee element, generally ranging from $100 to $570.

15. *See, e.g.,* 16 C.F.R. § 436.2(a)(1)–(2) (2007), Bus. Franchise Guide (CCH) ¶¶ 6161–6163. Of course, there must also be some form of agreement between the parties. Some states require a written agreement while others, such as Connecticut, permit an oral agreement.

16. 16 C.F.R. §§ 436.1 (2007) *et seq.*, Bus. Franchise Guide (CCH) ¶ 6080.

(a) The FTC Definition—The Federal Law

Under the FTC Rule, a franchise is defined as

> [a]ny continuing commercial relationship or arrangement, whatever it may be called, in which the terms of the offer or contract specify, or the franchise seller promises or represents, orally or in writing, that: (1) the franchisee will obtain the right to operate a business that is identified or associated with the franchisor's trademark, or to offer, sell, or distribute goods, services, or commodities that are identified or associated with the franchisor's trademark; (2) the franchisor will exert or has authority to exert a significant degree of control over the franchisee's method of operation, or provide significant assistance in the franchisee's method of operation; and (3) as a condition of obtaining or commencing operation of the franchise, the franchisee makes a required payment or commits to make a required payment to the franchisor or its affiliate.[17]

Note that, under this definition, regardless of what label the parties place on a business relationship or whether they even expressly disclaim that the relationship is a "franchise," if the relationship meets the definitional elements of a franchise, it is a franchise. In addition, if the franchisor represents that the relationship being offered has the characteristics of a franchise, the relationship is a franchise, even if the franchisor never performs as represented. Conversely, a relationship that does not satisfy each definitional element will not be covered by a franchise law, even if the relationship is styled as a "franchise." Finally, in order to determine whether a relationship is a franchise, regulators and courts will look beyond the four corners of the parties' agreement to determine if the definitional elements of a franchise are present.

(b) State Laws

The definitions of a "franchise" under the state franchise laws are similar to the definition in the FTC Rule, with slight variations, primarily in the second element (i.e., the element typically referred to as the control element). Where the FTC Rule definition focuses on the franchisor's authority to exert control over or to provide significant assistance to the franchisee's method of operation, all state franchise laws except for South Dakota[18] contain a "marketing plan" requirement or, alternatively, a "community of interest" requirement.

(i) Marketing Plan

Twelve states (California, Illinois, Indiana, Maryland, Michigan, New York,[19] North Dakota, Oregon, Rhode Island, Virginia, Washington, and Wisconsin) uti-

---

17. 16 C.F.R. § 436.1(h) (2007).

18. South Dakota amended its franchise laws in 2008 to mirror the definition of a franchise under the FTC Rule. S.D. Codified Laws § 37-5B-1, Bus. Franchise Guide (CCH) ¶ [3410.01].

19. Under New York law, a relationship is considered to be a franchise if it satisfies the franchise fee element and either the marketing plan element or the trademark element. *See*

lize the "marketing plan" approach to define what legally constitutes a franchise.[20] In these states, for the contemplated relationship to be a franchise, the franchisor must, in addition to requiring the payment of a franchise fee and granting use of a trademark to the franchisee, grant the franchisee the right to engage in the business of offering, selling, or distributing goods or services under a marketing plan or system prescribed in substantial part by the franchisor.[21]

(ii) Community of Interest

Two states (Hawaii and Minnesota) utilize a "community of interest" element[22] to determine whether a franchise exists. A franchise exists where the franchisor, in addition to requiring the payment of a franchise fee and granting use of a trademark to the franchisee, has a "community of interest" with the franchisee in the marketing of goods or services.[23]

(c) Understanding the Definitional Elements

(i) Payment of a Fee

Common to the federal and state definitions of a franchise is the requirement that a franchisee make a payment to the franchisor or its affiliates. This element is

---

N.Y. GEN. BUS. LAW § 681.3, Bus. Franchise Guide (CCH) ¶ 3320.02.

20. The franchise relationship laws of California, Connecticut, and Iowa also require a "marketing plan" element for a franchise to exist. *See* CAL. BUS. & PROF. CODE § 20001, Bus. Franchise Guide (CCH) ¶ 4050.02; CONN. GEN. STAT. § 42-133e(b), Bus. Franchise Guide (CCH) ¶ 4070.01; IOWA CODE § 523H.1.3, Bus. Franchise Guide (CCH) ¶ 4150.01. Connecticut, however, does not require payment of a franchise fee. *See* CONN. GEN. STAT. § 42-133e(b), Bus. Franchise Guide (CCH) ¶ 4070.01.

21. *See* CAL. CORP. CODE § 31005, Bus. Franchise Guide (CCH) ¶ 3050.07; 815 ILL. COMP. STAT. § 705/3(1), Bus. Franchise Guide (CCH) ¶ 3130.03; IND. CODE § 23-2-2.5-1(a), Bus. Franchise Guide (CCH) ¶ 3140.01; MD. CODE ANN., BUS. REG. § 14-201(e), Bus. Franchise Guide (CCH) ¶ 3200.01; MICH. COMP. LAWS § 445.1502(3), Bus. Franchise Guide (CCH) ¶ 3220.02; N.Y. GEN. BUS. LAW § 681.3, Bus. Franchise Guide (CCH) ¶ 3320.02; N.D. CENT. CODE § 51-19-02.5, Bus. Franchise Guide (CCH) ¶ 3340.02; OR. REV. STAT. § 650.005(4), Bus. Franchise Guide (CCH) ¶ 3370.01; R.I. GEN. LAWS § 19-28.1-3(g), Bus. Franchise Guide (CCH) ¶ 3390.03; VA. CODE ANN. § 13.1-559.A(b), Bus. Franchise Guide (CCH) ¶ 3460.03; WASH. REV. CODE § 19.100.010(4), Bus. Franchise Guide (CCH) ¶ 3470.01; WIS. STAT. § 553.03(4), Bus. Franchise Guide (CCH) ¶ 3490.02.

22. In addition, the franchise relationship laws of Mississippi, Missouri, Nebraska, New Jersey, and Wisconsin require a "community of interest" element for a franchise to exist. *See* MISS. CODE ANN. § 75-24-51(6), Bus. Franchise Guide (CCH) ¶ 4240.01; MO. REV. STAT. § 407.400(1), Bus. Franchise Guide (CCH) ¶ 4250.01; NEB. REV. STAT. § 87-402(1)(a), Bus. Franchise Guide (CCH) ¶ 4270.02; N.J. STAT. ANN. § 56:10-3.a, Bus. Franchise Guide (CCH) ¶ 4300.03; WIS. STAT. § 135.02(3), Bus. Franchise Guide (CCH) ¶ 4490.02. The relationship laws of Missouri, New Jersey, and Wisconsin, however, do not require the payment of a franchise fee, and the relationship law of Mississippi requires only "consideration." *See* MISS. CODE ANN. § 75-24-51(6), Bus. Franchise Guide (CCH) ¶ 4240.01; MO. REV. STAT. § 407.400(1), Bus. Franchise Guide (CCH) ¶ 4250.01; N.J. STAT. ANN. § 56:10-3.a, Bus. Franchise Guide (CCH) ¶ 4300.03; WIS. STAT. § 135.02(3), Bus. Franchise Guide (CCH) ¶ 4490.02.

23. *See* HAW. REV. STAT. § 482E-2, Bus. Franchise Guide (CCH) ¶ 3110.02 and MINN. STAT. § 80C.01, subdiv. 4, Bus. Franchise Guide (CCH) ¶ 3230.01.

interpreted broadly to include any and all monies or other consideration that the franchisee must pay to the franchisor or its affiliates as a condition of obtaining or commencing operation of the franchise.[24] The franchise fee can be anything from contractually required payments made directly to the franchisor to payments made by the franchisee due to practical necessity. Over the years, courts have interpreted the fee element broadly to include amounts that are labeled as other payments or fees and/or that are not structured as traditional franchise fees. For example, the fees can include royalty payments,[25] equipment purchases,[26] inventory purchases,[27] marketing and promotional materials,[28] training fees,[29] security deposits, escrow deposits, nonrefundable bookkeeping charges, and rent payments paid on behalf of a franchisor.[30] Further, the FTC's Franchise Rule Compliance Guide ("Compliance Guide") confirms that the fee element is to be interpreted very broadly and it is intended to capture any types of consideration that a franchisee must pay to a franchisor or its affiliate for the right to be associated with the franchisor.[31] These payments may include an initial franchise fee, rent to the franchisor or its affiliates, advertising assistance, promotional literature or training kits, equipment and supplies, required training, escrow and security deposits, administrative fees such as accounting or bookkeeping charges, and continuing royalties.[32]

---

24. 16 C.F.R. § 436.1(h)(3) (2007).

25. Intermark, Ltd. v. H.B. Smith Co., Inc., Bus. Franchise Guide (CCH) ¶ 9660 (W.D. Wash 1990) (royalties paid by a sublicensee constituted a "franchise fee" under the Washington Franchise Investment Protection Act).

26. DataCard Corp. v. Secure Data Sys., Inc., Bus. Franchise Guide (CCH) ¶ 10,154 (D.C. Minn. 1993) (excess paid above fair market value for a Mexican distributorship could be considered a "franchise fee" under the Minnesota Franchise Act).

27. Am. Parts Sys., Inc. v. T&T Auto., Inc., 358 N.W.2d 674 (Minn. Ct. App. 1984) (minimum inventory purchase requirement could constitute a franchise fee under Minnesota law, even if the inventory was purchased at fair prices, when the quantity exceeded the reasonable requirements of the business).

28. Boat & Motor Mart v. Sea Ray Boats, Inc., 825 F.2d 1285 (9th Cir. 1987) (extensive advertising required by the dealership agreement constituted indirect payments of fees for the manufacturer's benefit).

29. Metro All Snax, Inc. v. All Snax, Inc., Bus. Franchise Guide ¶ 10,885 (D.C. Minn. 1996) (snack distributor's payment of $34,500 for training and assistance provided in building up its distribution network constituted a franchise fee for purposes of the Minnesota disclosure/registration law).

30. An interpretive opinion from the California Commissioner of Corporations (which regulates franchising in California) has indicated that if a franchisor leases real estate from a third party and then subleases the real estate to the franchisee, with the franchisee paying rent directly to the prime landlord, the rent paid by the franchisee to the third-party landlord can be considered paid "on behalf of" the franchisor and therefore count as a franchise fee. *See* Gary Mendoza, Cal. Comm'r of Corps., *When Does an Agreement Constitute a "Franchise"?*, Comm. Op. No. 3-F (Revised), (June 22, 1994), *reprinted in* Bus. Franchise Guide (CCH) at ¶ 5050.45.

31. Fed. Trade Comm'n, Franchise Rule Compliance Guide at 5 (May 2008), https://www.ftc.gov/system/files/documents/plain-language/bus70-franchise-rule-compliance-guide.pdf (last visited Apr. 10, 2021); Bus. Franchise Guide (CCH) ¶ 6086 ("Compliance Guide").

32. *Id.*

Despite the seemingly expansive view of what constitutes a franchise fee, some definitional limitations exist. First, some jurisdictions include a minimum payment exclusion or exemption. If the total of all payments made by the franchisee to the franchisor and its affiliates at any time from before to within six months after commencing operation of the franchisee's business is less than a set amount, the relationship is excluded or exempted from the application of the franchise laws. Under the FTC Rule, the minimum amount is currently $615.[33] Some states (including Maryland, Michigan, and Wisconsin) permit a minimum amount in fees (ranging from $100 to $1,000) to be paid without finding that the "franchise fee"[34] element of the definition has been satisfied. Illinois has a similar, but stricter, standard—if a franchisee is required to pay less than $500 to the franchisor or its affiliates *over the entire life of the arrangement*, the fee element is not satisfied.[35] A franchisor may be able to avoid the franchise definition by charging less than the minimum amount or by deferring all payments until six months after the franchised business opens.[36]

In addition, all jurisdictions exclude from the fee element payments by the franchisee for a commercially reasonable quantity of inventory that does not exceed the bona fide wholesale price of the inventory that a franchisee is authorized to distribute. It does not apply to the purchase of raw materials required to manufacture the goods that are ultimately sold to the consumer. For example, an ice cream or yogurt franchisor that sells product mixes that are used by the licensee to manufacture the ice cream or yogurt sold to the consumer cannot claim that the sale of such mixes, at bona fide wholesale prices, does not qualify as a franchise fee because there is no market for the product mixes other than the existing franchisees. The Statement of Basis and Purpose for the FTC Rule expressly states that this exemption encompasses both start-up inventory purchased at the franchisee's option and inventory purchased as a matter of contractual or practical necessity.[37] At the state level, there are some limitations on this exclusion including that the exclusion applies only to a reasonable quantity of merchandise for which there is an actual market.[38]

---

33. 16 C.F.R. § 436.8(a)(1) (2007). Under the FTC Rule, the monetary thresholds for all exemptions under Section 436.8 of the FTC Rule, including the minimum required payment originally in the amount of $500, are increased every fourth year based on the Consumer Price Index. 16 C.F.R. § 436.8(b) (2007).

34. CAL. CODE REGS. tit. 10, § 310.011 (2005); N.Y. GEN. BUS. LAW § 681.7(e) (1996).

35. *See* To-Am Equip. Co. v. Mitsubishi Caterpillar Forklift Am., Inc., Bus. Franchise Guide (CCH) ¶ 11,456 (7th Cir. 1998), *aff'g* 953 F. Supp. 1987 (N.D. Ill. 1997) (holding that the required purchase of parts and service manuals with a value of $1,600, over a period of eight years, was sufficient to satisfy the "fee" element of the franchise definition for purposes of Illinois law).

36. 16 C.F.R. § 436.8(a)(1) (2007); *see also* FTC Informal Staff Advisory Op. 98-5 (June 24, 1998), http://www.ftc.gov/bcp/franchise/advops/advis98-5.shtm (last visited July 11, 2009).

37. Statement of Basis and Purpose for the Amended FTC Rule, 72 Fed. Reg. 15, 464–65 (Mar. 30, 2007), Bus. Franchise Guide (CCH) ¶ 6050.

38. *See, e.g.,* Cal. Comm. Op. Nos. 73/1F, 73/10F (advising that the bona fide wholesale price exception applies only if no obligation is imposed upon the purchaser to purchase or

(ii) Trademark

Under federal and state definitions, the term "trademark" is intended to have a broad definition and includes not only registered trademarks but also any service mark, trade name, or other commercial symbol.[39] Further, the franchisor is not required to actually own the mark, so long as the franchisor has the right to permit others to use the mark.[40] The trademark element is easily satisfied and is generally met when any of the following actions occur: (1) the goods or services distributed by the franchisee are associated with the franchisor's trademark, service mark, trade name, advertising, or other commercial symbol; or (2) the franchisee is required to conform to quality standards prescribed by the franchisor where the franchisee operates under a name that includes, in whole or in part, the franchisor's trademark, service mark, trade name, advertising, or other commercial symbol. If the franchisor wants to avoid the trademark element of the franchise definition, and no mark is involved in the relationship, the FTC has indicated that an express prohibition on the franchisee's use of all marks that belong to the franchisor will avoid application of the FTC Rule.[41] However, a franchisor could fall within the coverage of the FTC Rule if the franchisor prohibits use of the name and marks in the written agreement or if the agreement does not address the issue but, in practice, permits the franchisee to use the franchisor's name and marks or fails to enforce the contractual prohibition against use of the franchisor's name and marks.[42] However, contrary to what may be considered a plain meaning interpretation of this element, simply selling a trademarked product does not necessarily mean that the seller has the right to sell goods that are "substantially associated" with that trademark. There are many cases interpreting this element and finding that simply selling a product or services identified by a trademark may not be sufficient to satisfy the "trademark" element of a

pay for a quantity of such goods in excess of that which a reasonable businessperson would normally purchase by way of a starting inventory or supply, or to maintain a going inventory or supply); *see also* Flynn Beverage Inc. v. Joseph E. Seagram & Sons, Inc., 815 F. Supp. 1174, Bus. Franchise Guide (CCH) ¶ 10,237 (C.D. Ill. 1993) (franchisee found when distributor was required to buy $500 of new brand products for which there was no market).

39. Compliance Guide, *supra* note 31, at 2. The Compliance Guide replaced *The Interpretive Guides to the Original Rule* previously issued by the FTC. 44 Fed. Reg. 49,966 (Aug. 24, 1979); Bus. Franchise Guide (CCH) ¶ 6200.

40. *Id.*

41. *Id.*

42. Chicago Male Med. Clinic, LLC v. Ultimate Mgmt, Inc., 2014 U.S. Dist. LEXIS 174478 (C.D. Cal. Dec. 16, 2014) (awarding rescission to a franchisee under a consulting agreement that was not specific about trademark use but nonetheless finding the trademark element satisfied since the franchisee was listed on the franchisor's national website and was using the same font, style, and logo as the franchisor. C.f., Prim Ltd. Liab. Co. v. Pace-O-Matic, 2012 U.S. Dist. LEXIS 177203 (D. Hawaii Dec. 13, 2012) (finding a relationship was not a franchise under Hawaii's Franchise Investment Law, in part because there was no contractual right to use the licensor's trademark.) and Atchley v. Pepperidge Farms, Inc. 2012 US Dist. LEXIS 173974 (E.D. Wash. Dec. 6, 2012).

franchise.[43] This is the case particularly where a business sells products or services associated with many different trademarks owned by multiple, unaffiliated parties.[44]

(iii) The "Control" Element

The "control" element (i.e., whether the purported franchisor (1) exerts significant control over, or offers significant assistance to, the franchisee as required under the FTC Rule; (2) prescribes a substantial part of the marketing plan for the offer, sale, or distribution of goods and/or services as required under most state laws; or (3) creates a community of interest as required under a couple of state laws) is the most difficult element to analyze.

Under the FTC Rule, in addition to the franchise fee and trademark elements, the definition requires that the franchisor has authority to exert or exerts a significant degree of control over the franchisee's method of operation, or promises to provide significant assistance in the franchisee's method of operation. According to the Interpretive Guides to the FTC Rule, this element is intended to measure a franchisee's reliance on the franchisor's superior business expertise that reduces the franchisee's business risks and increases the franchisee's probability for success. A franchisor conveys its expertise by controlling how franchisees operate their business or by providing assistance to franchisees in connection with the operation of the business.[45]

The Interpretive Guides provide examples of conduct evidencing significant control or assistance elements. The term "significant" is defined by the degree to which the franchisee is dependent upon the franchisor's superior business expertise to reduce his or her business risk. Significant types of control over the franchisee by the franchisor include site approval for unestablished businesses; site design or site appearance requirements; control over hours of operation, production techniques, accounting practices, and/or personnel policies; promotional campaigns that require franchisee participation or financial contribution; restriction on what customers can be served; and approval of the location or area of operation.[46] Significant types of assistance include formal sales or business training programs; establishing accounting systems; furnishing management,

---

43. *See, e.g.*, Gabana Gulf Distrib., Ltd, v. GAP Int'l Sales, Inc., 343 F. App'x 258 (9th Cir. 2009) (finding that a non-exclusive distributor of GAP brand clothing was not operating a business substantially associated with the manufacturer's trademarks and thus not a franchise under the California Franchise Investment Law).

44. Hoosier Penn Oil Co. v. Ashland Oil Co., 934 F.2d 882 (7th Cir. 1991) (finding that a licensee's business as a whole was not substantially associated with an alleged franchisor's trademarks where the defendant's logo was not always used in the plaintiff's business correspondence; only one of nine of plaintiff's delivery trucks bore the defendant's logo; and, more importantly, the plaintiff sold 20 other brands of motor oil in competition with the defendant's brand, and only 10 percent of the plaintiff's overall sales volume was attributable to the sale of the defendant's products).

45. Bus. Franchise Guide (CCH) ¶¶ 5700 *et seq.*

46. Compliance Guide, *supra* note 31, at 2–4.

marketing, or personnel advice; selecting site locations; furnishing system-wide networks and websites; and furnishing a detailed operating manual.[47]

On the flip side, the FTC has determined some types of assistance or control that are insufficient to satisfy this element in the absence of additional forms of assistance or control. These include trademark controls that are designed solely to protect the trademark owner's rights to a mark, enforcement of health or safety restrictions required by federal and state law, assisting franchisees with obtaining financing, and assisting franchisees with promotional activities. Because the control or assistance must relate to the franchisee's entire business, controls or aid directed to the sale of a specific product and having only a marginal effect on a franchisee's entire business will not be deemed significant.[48]

In Advisory Opinion 05-2,[49] the FTC staff considered whether a company that had developed a patent-pending method designed to increase sales of staffing companies would be, under its proposed business arrangement, affecting significant control or assistance over its licensees' (the staffing companies') business operations. According to the company's letter, the selected licensees were established companies in the staffing industry whose day-to-day business operations would not be significantly controlled by the company's training and ongoing support. Such training and ongoing support would consist of a one-day training program accompanied by printed materials, advice, encouragement, and specialized instruction by telephone, e-mail, or web-based announcements.

The FTC staff concluded that the proposed business arrangement did not satisfy the "significant control or assistance" element for two reasons. First, the staff believed that the company was to provide support services that happened to be tailored to the staffing industry, as opposed to seeking to control or assist its licensees in operating a staffing service business. As such, any controls and assistance would not be over the licensees' entire method of operation. Second, the staff believed that the licensees would not be likely to place great reliance on the company in the operation of their businesses since licensees would be well-established businesses in the staffing field.

(iv) Marketing Plan Definition

In the states that have adopted the marketing plan approach to the control element, the franchisor must grant the franchisee a right to engage in the business of offering, selling, or distributing goods or services under a marketing plan prescribed in substantial part by the franchisor. The determination as to whether the marketing plan criterion is met is a function of not only the contractual language but also the course of dealing between the parties. A marketing plan has been found to exist where the franchisor provides advice and training regarding the operation of the franchised business. The Illinois, Rhode Island, and Washington statutes identify the following as relevant in determining whether a marketing

47. *Id.*
48. *See* FTC Interpretive Guides, Bus. Franchise Guide (CCH) ¶ 6206.
49. Bus. Franchise Guide (CCH) ¶ 6526 (Mar. 2, 2005).

plan is present: specification of price, special pricing systems, or discount plans; use of particular sales or display equipment or merchandising devices; use of specific sales techniques; use of advertising or promotional materials or cooperation in advertising efforts; formal operations or management training; and operational, managerial, technical, or financial guidelines or assistance.[50] California has cited the following as examples of a prescribed marketing plan: controlling resale prices, restrictions on use of advertising, detailed advice and explanations, assigning territories, limiting sale of competitive products, providing training or a manual, and providing trade secrets.[51]

(v) Community of Interest Definition

Minnesota and Hawaii require a "community of interest" between the franchisor and franchisee in the marketing of goods or services in order for their franchise registration and disclosure laws to apply. These states examine the interdependence of the parties (i.e., shared goals and cooperative efforts) and the continuing financial interest between the franchisor and the franchisee in the operation of the franchised business or the marketing of goods and services offered by the franchisee. Courts consider not only the contractual language but also the parties' actual dealings. Each state's perspective on this element varies to some extent and should be carefully reviewed on a state-by-state basis.

The Wisconsin franchise relationship law also contains a "community of interest" element.[52] In analyzing this element, the Wisconsin Supreme Court has identified several factors to determine whether the "community of interest"

---

50. *See* 815 Ill. Comp. Stat. § 705/3(18), Bus. Franchise Guide (CCH) ¶ 3130.03; R.I. Gen. Laws § 19-28.1-3(l), Bus. Franchise Guide (CCH) ¶ 3390.03; Wash. Rev. Code § 19.100.010(5), Bus. Franchise Guide (CCH) ¶ 3470.01. *See also* Petereit v. S.B. Thomas, Inc., 63 F.3d 1169, 1181, Bus. Franchise Guide (CCH) ¶ 10,741 (2d Cir. 1995) (marketing plan found to exist under Connecticut's franchise relationship law where manufacturer of baked goods maintained the books for distributors' stores, controlled product prices, required participation in promotions and discounts, controlled product placement, and set performance standards for out-of-date products); Vaughn v. Digit. Message Sys. Corp., 1997 WL 115821, Bus. Franchise Guide (CCH) ¶ 11,160 (E.D. Mich. Mar. 10, 1997) (marketing plan existed where seller of telephone programming systems provided training guidelines, marketing supplies, manuals, demonstration tapes, and supply order and price forms; designated specific market areas to the licensees; and required the purchase and sale of a minimum number of systems each year). Chicago Male Med. Clinic, LLC v. Ultimate Mgmt., Inc., 2014 U.S. Dist. LEXIS 174478 (C.D. Cal. Dec. 16, 2014) (finding a prescribed marketing plan existed where licensor provided training for handling calls and suggested advertisements to be aired over radio and in print). New Jersey, like Wisconsin, also requires a "community of interest" in order for its relationship law to apply. *See, e.g.*, Orologio of Short Hills, Inc. v. The Swatch Grp., 653 F. App'x 134 (3d Cir. 2016) (finding no community of interest where there was not excessive control and the parties were economically independent).

51. *See* Gary Mendoza, Cal. Comm'r of Corps., *When Does an Agreement Constitute a "Franchise"?*, Comm. Op. No. 3-F (Revised), (June 22, 1994), *reprinted in* Bus. Franchise Guide (CCH) at ¶ 5050.45.

52. The Wisconsin Fair Dealership Law, a franchise relationship law, applies to dealerships in which there is a "community of interest" between the manufacturer and the dealer. Wis. Stat. § 135.02(30(a).

element has been satisfied: the percent of gross proceeds or profits derived from the franchisor's products; the extent and nature of the franchisee's investment in inventory, facilities, and goodwill; the length of the relationship; the extent and nature of an exclusive territory; the extent and nature of obligations imposed on parties contractually; the percentage of time, revenue, and personnel allocated by the franchisee to the franchisor; the extent and nature of the use of proprietary marks; the amount spent on advertising or promotional expenditures; the extent and nature of supplementary services to consumers; and the provision of specialized equipment to customers.[53] The factors are analyzed collectively rather than individually. The existence of a high percentage of business attributable to the franchisor's products, though not dispositive, is strong evidence that there is a continuing financial interest between the parties.

2-4. Preparing the FDD

If the relationship satisfies the definition of a franchise, the franchisor should assess its obligations under federal and state laws, keeping in mind that these obligations may vary from jurisdiction to jurisdiction. To begin, unless an exemption or exclusion applies, the franchisor will need to prepare an FDD and deliver it to prospective franchisees prior to entering into a binding agreement or accepting any money.[54]

The original FTC Rule, enacted in 1979, included provisions that described the form and substance of the required disclosure document. This prescribed document differed modestly from the disclosure documents required by the various states that had enacted franchise laws. To deal with this lack of uniformity and to assist in obtaining approval from states with franchise registration requirements, many franchisors used the state-required formats for preparing offering circulars rather than the FTC format. In an effort to standardize the state disclosure requirements, on April 25, 1993, the North American Securities Administrators Association (NASAA)[55] adopted The Guidelines for Preparation of the

---

53. Case was remanded on reconsideration; no other citation available. Ziegler Co. v. Rexnord, Inc., 407 N.W.2d 873, 879–80, Bus. Franchise Guide (CCH) ¶ 8882 (Wis. 1987), *recon. on other grounds*, 433 N.W.2d 8 (Wis. 1988). *See also* Kelly Supply, Inc. v. Chr. Hansen, Inc., 812 N.W.2d 539 (Wis. Ct. App. 2012) (affirming *Ziegler* and finding that "community of interest" element was met).

54. FTC Rule, 16 C.F.R. § 436.2 (2007), Bus. Franchise Guide (CCH) ¶ 6010. *See, e.g.*, Bus. Franchise Guide (CCH) ¶¶ 3017 (Ala.), 3130 (Ill.), 3230 (Minn.), 3200 (Md.), 4300 (N.J.).

55. NASAA is the oldest international organization devoted to investor protection. NASAA is a voluntary association whose membership consists of 67 state, provincial, and territorial securities administrators in the 50 states, the District of Columbia, Puerto Rico, the U.S. Virgin Islands, Canada, and Mexico. NASAA's Franchise and Business Opportunity Project Group (a standing committee formed in the 1980s) proposes model laws, commentaries, and other initiatives regarding franchise disclosure in an effort to further its investor protection role and to promote uniformity among state franchise regulators and the FTC. While NASAA has no direct authority over franchising, the FTC and states that

Uniform Franchise Offering Circular and Related Documents ("UFOC Guidelines"), which most of the states accepted. To accommodate franchisors who were using the UFOC Guidelines, the FTC permitted franchisors to comply with the original FTC Rule's disclosure requirements by using the UFOC Guidelines to prepare their offering circulars.[56]

The amended FTC Rule, which became effective in July 2007, is based on the UFOC Guidelines but includes a number of significant modifications, including changing the name from "offering circular" to "franchise disclosure document" or "FDD." To help franchisors prepare FDDs that comply with the amended FTC Rule, the FTC released its Statement of Basis and Purpose[57] in early 2007 and issued its Compliance Guide in May 2008.[58] The FTC staff also periodically poses and answers frequently asked questions (FAQs) regarding the amended FTC Rule ("FTC FAQs") on the FTC's website (there were 38 as of April 2021)[59] and occasionally releases informal staff advisory opinions.[60]

On June 6, 2008, in response to the enactment of the amended FTC Rule, NASAA adopted the 2008 Franchise Registration and Disclosure Guidelines ("NASAA Guidelines")[61] as a model for states with franchise registration and disclosure laws. The NASAA Guidelines incorporated the new disclosure requirements under the amended FTC Rule and added a new state cover page, new filing instructions, and new application forms. Less than a year later, on April 27, 2009, NASAA adopted the Commentary on 2008 Franchise Registration and Disclosure Guidelines ("NASAA Commentary")[62] to provide franchisors with practical guidance about the disclosure requirements and instructions adopted under the NASAA Guidelines.

Following its adoption of the NASAA Guidelines and Commentary, NASAA has remained an active force in guiding, interpreting, and shaping franchise disclosure requirements at both the federal and state levels. Specifically, NASAA

---

regulate franchising have historically given great weight to the recommendations, commentaries, and policy initiatives of NASAA's Business Opportunity Project Group and, in many cases, states have specifically incorporated them into their franchise laws.

56. On December 30, 1993, the FTC approved the disclosure format under the UFOC Guidelines as an alternative to the original FTC Rule disclosure format. Bus. Franchise Guide (CCH) ¶ 5700.

57. 72 Fed. Reg. 15,444–15,492 (Mar. 30, 2007); Bus. Franchise Guide (CCH) ¶ 6050.

58. Compliance Guide, *supra* note 31.

59. Fed. Trade Comm'n, Amended Franchise Rule FAQs, 16 C.F.R. § 436 (2007), Bus. Franchise Guide (CCH) ¶ 6090, https://www.ftc.gov/tips-advice/business-center/guidance/amended-franchise-rule-faqs (last visited Apr. 10, 2021) ("FTC FAQs").

60. *See* 72 Fed. Reg. 15,456 n.96; 72 Fed. Reg. 15,463 n.183; 72 Fed. Reg. 15,530 n.878 (Mar. 30, 2007).

61. https://www.nasaa.org/wp-content/uploads/2011/08/6-2008UFOC.pdf (last visited Apr. 10, 2021); Bus. Franchise Guide (CCH) ¶ 5705 ("NASAA Guidelines").

62. http://www.nasaa.org/wp-content/uploads/2011/08/FranchiseCommentary_final.pdf (last visited Apr. 10, 2021); Bus. Franchise Guide (CCH) ¶ 5706 ("NASAA Commentary").

adopted the "Multi-Unit Commentary" on September 16, 2014,[63] the NASAA Commentary on Financial Performance Representations ("FPR Commentary") on May 8, 2017,[64] and new Instructions for Preparing State Cover Sheets and State Effective Date Page ("State Cover Sheet Instructions") for FDDs on May 19, 2019,[65] which became effective January 1, 2020.[66] Most recently, on June 10, 2020, NASAA released a new commentary titled "Disclosing Financial Performance Representations in the Time of COVID-19" ("COVID-19 FPR Commentary")[67] to provide franchisors with guidance regarding the use of historical financial performance representations (FPRs) in Item 19 of an FDD in light of the economic downturn due to COVID-19.

All of the materials described above, which are periodically supplemented, as well as any new material the FTC, NASAA, or the states issue or release relating to the FTC Rule or state franchise laws, should be consulted in connection with the preparation of FDDs.

(a) Information Required to Be Disclosed

The FDD must contain 23 required substantive categories of information commonly referred to as "items." The information in each item must follow the specific instructions for that item, including any formatting requirements (such as text that is required to be in bold), negative disclosures (i.e., statements that say information required to be disclosed does not apply or exist), and table headings. Generally, the disclosures fall into three categories—information about the franchised business, information about franchise agreements, and information about the franchisor—and are intended to enable the prospective franchisee to assess whether to enter into the franchise arrangement.

Before the specific items are reviewed, some general instructions for preparing the FDD are important to note. The FDD must be written in plain English, avoiding legalese. Drafters should use the active voice, rather than the passive

---

63. http://www.nasaa.org/wp-content/uploads/2011/08/Franchise-Multi-Unit-Commentary-effective-Adopted-Sept.-16-2014.pdf (last visited Apr. 10, 2021); Bus. Franchise Guide (CCH) ¶ 15,039 ("NASAA Multi-Unit Commentary").

64. http://www.nasaa.org/wp-content/uploads/2017/05/Financial-Performance-Representation-Commentary.pdf (last visited Apr. 10, 2021); Bus. Franchise Guide (CCH) ¶ 5707 ("NASAA FPR Commentary").

65. https://www.nasaa.org/wp-content/uploads/2019/06/New-Frachise-State-Cover-Sheets-Instructions.pdf (last visited Apr. 10, 2021); Bus. Franchise Guide (CCH) ¶ 5709 ("NASAA State Cover Sheet Instructions").

66. The NASAA Franchise and Business Opportunity Project Group recently published the *Franchise Disclosure Handbook—A Resource Guide for Preparing a Franchise Disclosure Document*, which is a compilation of existing guidance and commentary from NASAA and the FTC regarding franchise disclosure. North American Securities Administrators Association, Franchise Disclosure Document Handbook: A Resource Guide for Preparing a Franchise Disclosure Document (2020).

67. https://www.nasaa.org/wp-content/uploads/2020/06/FPRs-in-the-time-of-COVID-19.pdf (last visited Apr. 10, 2021); Bus. Franchise Guide (CCH) ¶ 16,670 ("NASAA COVID-19 FPR Commentary").

voice. FDDs should avoid repetitive and potentially inconsistent disclosures. Also, the FDD should not include any materials or information other than those specifically required or permitted by the FTC Rule or by state law not preempted by the FTC Rule.[68]

While the focus of the FTC Rule is on single-unit franchises, its disclosure obligations apply equally to the offer and sale of multi-unit franchises. In addition, a subfranchisor (or master franchisee) that is offering subfranchises is required to disclose not only information about itself in its FDD but also information about its franchisor.[69] To provide additional guidance for disclosing certain of the most-common multi-unit franchising arrangements, including subfranchising, NASAA issued its Multi-Unit Commentary.

For purposes of simplicity and clarity, the remainder of section 2-4(a) describes the general information a franchisor must include in its FDD, not taking into account the Multi-Unit Commentary. Section 2-4(b) below then builds on this information and specifically addresses some of the special disclosure requirements for multi-unit franchises described in the Multi-Unit Commentary.

(i) Cover Pages

The FTC Rule instructions for preparation of FDDs begin with the description of an FTC cover page titled "FRANCHISE DISCLOSURE DOCUMENT," which must be in capital letters and bold type.[70] This cover page must contain certain identifying information about the franchisor, including its full entity name, state of formation, type of entity, principal business address, phone number, e-mail address, website, and a sample of the primary business trademark a franchisee will use in its business.[71] The cover page also must include a simple description of the franchise offered, the range of the estimated initial investment from Item 7, and the range of initial fees that must or may be paid to the franchisor or its affiliates prior to opening from Item 5.[72] After this information, the franchisor must include a number of boilerplate disclosures, as well as the issuance date of its FDD.[73] Further, the FTC Rule specifically notes that franchisors may include additional disclosures on the FTC cover page, on a separate cover page, or addendum to comply with state pre-sale disclosure laws.[74]

Following the FTC cover page, as described in the State Cover Sheet Instructions, a franchisor must include three state cover sheets with text not less than

68. 16 C.F.R. § 436.6 (2007). *See, e.g.*, VA. CODE ANN. §§ 12.1-13, 13.1-572, Bus. Franchise Guide (CCH) ¶ 5460. While a franchisor may include scroll bars, internal links, and search features in an electronic version of an FDD for the sole purpose of enhancing the prospective franchisee's ability to maneuver through the document, "all other features (e.g., multimedia tools such as audio, video, animation, pop-up screens, or links to external information) are prohibited." 16 C.F.R. § 436.6(d) (2007).

69. 16 C.F.R. § 436.6(f) (2007).

70. 16 C.F.R. § 436.3(a) (2007).

71. 16 C.F.R. § 436.3(b) and (c) (2007).

72. 16 C.F.R. § 436.3(d) and (e) (2007).

73. 16 C.F.R. § 436.3(e) (2007).

74. 16 C.F.R. § 436.3(g) (2007).

13-point type. The first two cover sheets—titled "How to Use this Franchise Disclosure Document" and "What You Need to Know About Franchising *Generally*"—must immediately follow the FTC cover page.[75] The purpose of these cover sheets is to provide prospective franchisees with some direction as to how to use the FDD, and more general information about franchising and the franchise relationship. The third cover sheet—titled "Special Risk(s) to Consider about *This* Franchise"—replaced the previously required state cover page.[76] It includes one standard risk factor relating to out-of-state dispute resolution and allows states to require additional risk factors. However, to promote uniformity and reduce repetition, a franchisor may be allowed to include non-uniform risk factors required by a particular state in a state addendum to the FDD, rather than on the cover sheet, if acceptable to the state. Finally, the State Cover Sheet Instructions require a franchisor to include the state effective dates page at the end of the FDD, immediately before the receipt pages, if the franchisor is filing in more than one state.[77] Otherwise, the franchisor may insert the effective date information for the single state on the third cover sheet, provided the information will fit on a single page.

(ii) Items 1–23

The remainder of the FDD includes 23 substantive disclosure items, the key components of which are summarized below.

Item 1: "The Franchisor and Any Parents, Predecessors and Affiliates"[78]—This item requires the disclosure of:

- The name and principal business address of the franchisor, any parents, and any affiliates that offer franchises in any line of business or provide products or services to the franchisees of the franchisor. An "affiliate" is defined as "an entity controlled by, controlling, or under common control with another entity."[79] A "parent" is defined as "an entity that controls another entity directly, or indirectly through one or more subsidiaries."[80] FTC FAQ 16 calls attention to the fact that the definition of "parent" focuses on "control," not mere ownership, and notes that a parent that merely owns, but does not control, a franchise system is not a parent for purposes of any disclosure item. For example, an entity that directly or indirectly owns the franchisor may not be a parent for purposes of disclosure if it does not shape the franchisor's policies or control franchise sales or operations.[81] Also of note, the FTC Rule requires disclosure of all intermediate parents, not just the ultimate parent company.

75. NASAA State Cover Sheet Instructions, *supra* note 65, at 8–9.
76. *Id.*
77. *Id.*
78. 16 C.F.R. § 436.5(a) (2007).
79. 16 C.F.R. § 436.1(b) (2007).
80. 16 C.F.R. § 436.1(m) (2007).
81. FTC FAQs, *supra* note 59, FAQ #16.

- The name and principal business address of any predecessors during the 10-year period immediately before the close of the franchisor's most recent fiscal year. A "predecessor" is defined as any person or entity "from whom the franchisor acquired, directly or indirectly, the major portion of the franchisor's assets."[82]
- The following information about the franchisor: the name that the franchisor uses and any names it intends to use to conduct business, the identity and principal business address of the franchisor's agent for service of process, the type of business organization used by the franchisor (for example, corporation, limited liability company, partnership), and the state in which the entity was organized.
- The following information about the franchisor's business and the franchises offered: whether the franchisor operates businesses of the type being franchised, the franchisor's other business activities, a description of the franchised business, the general market for the franchised business, any laws or regulations specific to the industry in which the franchised business operates and the competition the franchised business will face.
- The prior business experience of the franchisor, any predecessors, and any affiliates that offer franchises in any line of business or provide products or services to the franchisees of the franchisor, including the length of time each has conducted the type of business the franchisee will operate and the length of time each has offered franchises providing the type of business the franchisee will operate and whether each has offered franchises in other lines of business.

Item 2: "Business Experience"[83]—This item focuses on the identity of the individuals who are managing the franchise system. In Item 2, a franchisor must disclose by name and position the franchisor's directors, trustees, general partners, principal officers, and any other individuals who will have management responsibility relating to the sale or operation of franchises. This disclosure must include, for each person, a summary of his or her principal positions and employers during the past five years, including each position's starting date, ending date, and location. Many executives want to go beyond the required five-year history or to include a narrative description of related activities, but this information should not be included. State examiners are likely to require the franchisor to delete the information from Item 2. Further, since disclosures in Items 3 (Litigation) and 4 (Bankruptcy) are tied to the individuals included in Item 2, the franchisor should carefully assess which individuals within its organization are included in Item 2.

Item 3: "Litigation"[84]—This item requires the disclosure of information concerning certain pertinent criminal and civil litigation matters that involved the franchisor, any predecessor, or any parent or affiliate who *induces* franchise sales

82. 16 C.F.R. § 436.1(p) (2007).
83. 16 C.F.R. § 436.5(b) (2007).
84. 16 C.F.R. § 436.5(c) (2007).

by promising to back the franchisor financially or otherwise guarantees the franchisor's performance; an affiliate who offers franchises under the franchisor's principal trademark; and any person identified in Item 2.

For pending matters, the franchisor must disclose any administrative, criminal, or material civil action alleging a violation of a franchise, antitrust, or securities law, or alleging fraud, unfair or deceptive practices, or comparable allegations; and any civil actions, other than ordinary routine litigation incidental to the business, which are material in the context of the number of franchisees and the size, nature, or financial condition of the franchise system or its business operations. In addition, the franchisor must disclose any material civil actions, to which the franchisor was a party and involving the franchise relationship, that were *filed* in the last fiscal year. Here, the term "franchise relationship" means the contractual obligations between the franchisor and franchisee directly relating to the operation of the franchised business (such as royalty payment and training obligations). There is no interim update requirement for the actions involving the franchise relationship, and the matters can be removed for the next annually updated FDD, unless they fall within one of the other disclosure categories.[85] For example, if a franchisee files a counterclaim alleging a violation of a franchise law in an action involving the franchise relationship, the matter may have to remain in the FDD longer than one year.

For concluded actions, the FDD must include any actions during the 10-year period immediately before the issuance date in which the identified individuals or entities have been convicted of or pleaded nolo contendere to a felony charge or have been held liable in a civil action involving an alleged violation of a franchise, antitrust, or securities law, or involving allegations of fraud, unfair or deceptive practices, or comparable allegations. "Held liable" means that, as a result of claims or counterclaims, the person must pay money or other consideration, must reduce an indebtedness by the amount of an award, cannot enforce its rights, or must take action adverse to its interests. If a person is not required to pay a material amount or its rights are not materially restricted, no disclosure is required.[86]

Item 3 also requires the disclosure of information concerning certain relevant government actions that involved the franchisor, a predecessor, or a parent or affiliate who guarantees the franchisor's performance; an affiliate who offers franchises in any line of business within the last 10 years; or any other person identified in Item 2. Specifically, the franchisor must disclose any currently effective injunctive or restrictive order or decree involving any of these parties that resulted from a pending or concluded action brought by a public agency and relating to the franchise or to a federal, state, or Canadian franchise, securities, antitrust, trade regulation, or trade practice law.

For each matter required to be included in Item 3, the franchisor must state the title, the case number, the initial filing date, the names of the parties, the forum, the relationship of the opposing party to the franchisor, and, except in

85. *See* FTC FAQs, *supra* note 59, FAQ #5.

86. NASAA Commentary, *supra* note 62, at 5.

limited circumstances, a summary of the legal and factual nature of each claim in the action, the relief sought or obtained, and any conclusions of law or fact. The item clarifies that the material terms of a settlement agreement, even if confidential, must be disclosed.

Item 4: "Bankruptcy"[87]—This item requires the disclosure of any U.S. or foreign bankruptcy filing in the 10 years prior to the issuance date of the FDD. This disclosure should be made for the franchisor; any parent, predecessor, affiliate, officer, or general partner of the franchisor; or any other individual who will have management responsibility relating to the sale or operation of franchises. For the franchisor's management team, this includes bankruptcies filed by other companies while that person was a principal officer or a general partner with that company or within one year after that person left the other company. For each bankruptcy required to be included in Item 4, the franchisor must state the current name, address, and principal place of business of the debtor; the relationship of the debtor to the franchisor (for example, affiliate, officer) if the debtor is not the franchisor; and the date of the original filing and the material facts, including the bankruptcy court, the case name and number and, if applicable, the debtor's discharge date or the date of confirmation of any plans of reorganization.

Item 5: "Initial Fees"[88]—This item requires the disclosure of any payments that the franchisee must or may make to the franchisor or its affiliates prior to opening the franchised business and whether any such fees are refundable. If the initial fees are not uniform for all franchisees, the franchisor must disclose the range or formula used to calculate the initial fees paid during the last fiscal year and factors used to calculate the fees. The term "initial fees" as used in Item 5 is broadly defined and means all fees and payments, or commitments to pay, for services or goods received from the franchisor or any affiliate before the franchisee's business opens, whether payable in lump sum or installments. It is critical to note that the fees in Item 5 are not simply limited to the initial franchise fee. Instead, Item 5 initial fees include any payments (such as preopening training, application fees, and computer set-up fees) that the franchisee must or may make to the franchisor or its affiliates prior to opening the unit for business.

Item 6: "Other Fees"[89]—This item summarizes the isolated or continuing fees that a franchisee is required to pay to the franchisor or its affiliates, or that the franchisor or its affiliates impose or collect for any third party after the opening of the franchised business. These fees are disclosed in tabular form, with the column headings type of fee, amount of fee, due date, and summary of remarks relating to the fee. The fees typically disclosed in Item 6 include royalty fees, advertising fees, ongoing training fees, transfer fees, and renewal fees. The disclosures relating to these fees should track the language in the franchise agreements. In addition, if the fees are subject to increase, the franchisor must disclose the formula that determines the increase or the maximum amount of the increase.

87. 16 C.F.R. § 436.5(d) (2007).
88. 16 C.F.R. § 436.5(e) (2007).
89. 16 C.F.R. § 436.5(f) (2007).

The franchisor should disclose the following information in the remarks column in the table: whether the fees are payable to the franchisor; whether the fees are imposed and collected by the franchisor; whether the fees are refundable and, if so, the circumstances when the fees are refundable; and whether the fees are uniformly imposed. If the remarks are too extensive, they can be placed in notes following the table. If the franchisor has cooperatives, the notes must describe the voting power of franchisor-owned outlets on any fees imposed by cooperatives.

Item 7: "Estimated Initial Investment"[90]—This item is the franchisor's estimate (in tabular form) of the entire initial investment that the franchisee must make to open the franchised business. This item includes the initial fees; the cost of purchasing or leasing the premises; construction, remodeling, improvement, and other "build out" costs; equipment; inventory; advertising; training; signs; legal and accounting fees; security deposits; insurance payments; utility bills; and working capital/additional funds. In the table, the franchisor must state the type of expenditure, the amount (which may be a high/low range), the required method of payment, when the payment is due, and to whom payment is to be made.

The notes to the table must state whether any payment under Item 7 is refundable. The table must include an "additional funds" category for any other required expenses the franchisee will incur before operations begin and during the initial period of operations. The initial period should cover at least three months or a reasonable period for the industry, and should describe in general terms the factors, basis, and experience that the franchisor considered or relied upon in formulating the amount required for additional funds. The franchisor should specify the types of costs included in and excluded from the additional funds range in the notes to the table. If the franchisor will finance any portion of the initial investment, the franchisor must disclose the terms of that financing in Item 6, although the franchisor can refer to Item 10 (Financing) for additional information.

The franchisor should use notes to include remarks, definitions, or caveats and assumptions that elaborate on the information in the Item 7 table. In addition, the franchisor may include multiple tables to show expenditure variations caused by differences such as in site location and premises size. This item is of particular importance to the franchisee and is becoming increasingly more important in connection with franchisee efforts to obtain financing.

Item 8: "Restrictions on Sources of Products and Services"[91]—This item includes a summary of the franchisee's obligations relating to required purchases or leases of goods, services, supplies, fixtures, equipment, inventory, computer hardware and software, real estate, or comparable items either (1) from the franchisor, its affiliates, designated suppliers, and approved suppliers or (2) in accordance with the franchisor's specifications. These obligations may arise under an agreement or as a matter of practice. For each obligation, the franchisor should disclose the good or service required to be purchased or leased and whether the

90. 16 C.F.R. § 436.5(g) (2007).
91. 16 C.F.R. § 436.5(h) (2007).

franchisor or its affiliates are approved suppliers or the only approved suppliers of that good or service. In addition, the franchisor should identify any supplier in which an officer of the franchisor owns an equity interest. Note that for this disclosure, there is an exception for a de minimis interest. Therefore, before disclosure of such information, the franchisor should assess whether the officer's interest is material. Since the disclosure is not required to include the name of the owner or supplier, the FTC FAQs suggest franchisors err on the side of including any such interest in the FDD.[92]

The franchisor's policies for granting and revoking approval of alternative suppliers and whether the franchisor issues specifications for approved suppliers also must be summarized. In addition, the franchisor is required to disclose whether it or its affiliates will or may derive revenue or other material consideration from required purchases or leases by franchisees; whether any supplier will make payments to the franchisor based upon franchisee purchases; and the amount of revenue the franchisor and its affiliates received during its last fiscal year from all required purchases and leases of products and services. In addition, Item 8 must describe the estimated proportion of required purchases and leases by the franchisee to all purchases and leases by the franchisee of goods and services in establishing and operating the franchised businesses; the existence of any purchasing or distribution cooperatives; whether the franchisor negotiates purchase arrangements with suppliers, including price terms, for the benefit of franchisees; and whether the franchisor provides material benefits to franchisees based upon the purchase of particular products or services, or the use of particular suppliers.

Item 9: "Franchisee's Obligations"[93]—This item lists, in a table, the franchisee's principal obligations under the franchise and related agreements with cross-references to particular items in the FDD and the agreements. If a particular obligation is not applicable, the franchisor should state "Not Applicable." This table must include the 24 mandatory categories of information. The franchisor may add additional categories, if it desires. This item must include the following mandatory boldfaced introductory paragraph:

This table lists your principal obligations under the franchise and other agreements. It will help you find more detailed information about your obligations in these agreements and in other items of this disclosure document.[94]

Item 10: "Financing"[95]—This item discloses information on financing arrangements, including leases and installment contracts, that the franchisor, its agents, or affiliates offer directly or indirectly to franchisees. An indirect offer of financing includes a written arrangement between the franchisor (or its affiliate) and a lender for the lender to offer financing to the franchisees, an arrangement where the franchisor (or its affiliate) receives a benefit from the lender based upon franchisee financing, or the franchisor's guarantee of a note, lease, or other obligation

92. FTC FAQs, *supra* note 59, FAQ #18.
93. 16 C.F.R. § 436.5(i) (2007).
94. Compliance Guide, *supra* note 31, at 57.
95. 16 C.F.R. § 436.5(j) (2007).

of a franchisee. The terms of any financing arrangement must be set forth in Item 10, including:

- what the financing covers (for example, the initial franchise fee, site acquisition, construction or remodeling, initial or replacement equipment or fixtures, opening or ongoing inventory or supplies, or other continuing expenses);
- the identity of the lender and its relationship to the franchisor;
- the amount of financing offered or, if the amount depends on an actual cost that may vary, the percentage of the cost that will be financed;
- the annual percentage rate of interest charged, plus any finance charges;
- the number of payments or the period of repayment;
- the nature of any security interest required by the lender;
- whether a person other than the franchisee must personally guarantee the debt;
- whether the debt can be prepaid and the nature of any prepayment penalty; and
- the franchisee's potential liabilities upon default, including any accelerated obligation to pay the entire amount due, any obligations to pay court costs and attorneys' fees incurred in collecting the debt, potential liabilities upon termination of the franchise, and liabilities from cross-defaults such as those resulting directly from nonpayment or indirectly from the loss of business property.

A specimen copy of the financing documents must be included as an exhibit to the FDD. For any loan agreement, the franchisor must disclose whether the franchisee is required to waive defenses or other legal rights (such as confession of judgment) or whether the franchisee is barred from asserting any defense against the lender.

If the franchisor makes the loan, the franchisor must disclose whether the franchisor's practice or intent is to sell, assign, or discount to a third party all or part of the financing arrangement. If the loans are made by a third-party lender, the franchisor must disclose any consideration paid to the franchisor as a result of placing the financing arrangement.

Item 11: "Franchisor's Assistance, Advertising, Computer Systems, and Training"[96]—This item is typically one of the lengthier items in the FDD. The franchisor must disclose the obligations that the franchisor is contractually required to fulfill prior to and after the opening of the franchised business. Disclosures include the franchisor's obligations relating to selecting, leasing, or approving the premises for the franchised business; developing the premises; purchasing or leasing equipment for the franchised business; installing furniture, signs, and fixtures at the franchised business; furnishing opening inventory, supplies, and related materials; training the franchisee; engaging in advertising activities; establishing and maintaining administrative, bookkeeping, accounting,

96. 16 C.F.R. § 436.5(k) (2007).

inventory control, or other general operating procedures; and the franchisor's utilization of an operating manual to assist franchisees and their employees in the operation of the franchised business. These disclosures must cite to the agreement section that sets forth the obligation. The franchisor must also include a summary of the site selection process and the typical length of time between signing the franchise agreement and opening the franchised business, factors that may affect this period, and the consequences for not locating a site or opening by the required deadline.

The operations manual for the franchise system, which includes confidential and proprietary information, will form the cornerstone of the operation of the franchised business. The franchisor must include the table of contents of the operations manual in the FDD and state the number of pages devoted to each subject, as well as the total number of pages in the operations manual. The franchisor can omit this disclosure if it allows prospects to review the operations manual prior to buying a franchise. As a best practices point, if the franchisor permits the franchisee to view the operations manual before purchasing, the franchisor should require the prospect to sign a confidentiality agreement and include a copy of that agreement as an exhibit to the FDD.

The franchisor must also include detailed descriptions of the franchisee's obligation to conduct advertising, including a summary of the advertising funds and cooperatives. With respect to any cooperatives, the franchisor must disclose how the area or membership of the cooperative is defined; how much the franchisee must contribute and whether other franchisees contribute a different rate; whether the franchisor-owned outlets contribute to the fund and, if so, whether those contributions are on the same basis as those for franchisees; who is responsible for administering the cooperative; whether the cooperative will operate from written governing documents and whether the documents are available for the franchisee to review; whether the cooperative must prepare annual or periodic financial statements and whether the statements are available for review by the franchisee; and whether the franchisor has the power to require cooperatives to be formed, changed, dissolved, or merged. With regard to other advertising funds created, the franchisor must disclose who contributes to the fund; the amount of the franchisee's contribution and whether other franchisees must contribute a different rate; whether franchisor-owned outlets must contribute to the fund and, if so, whether those contributions are on the same basis as franchisees; who administers the fund; whether and when the fund is audited and if financial statements of the fund are available for review by the franchisee; and how the monies in the funds were used in the most recently concluded fiscal year, including the percentages spent on production, media placement, administrative expenses, and a description of any other use. As a best practice, the franchisor should broadly describe how it intends to spend the advertising fund, including whether it reserves the right to use it to offset administrative costs and salaries relating to its advertising and marketing program and team. The franchisor also is obligated to disclose what happens if not all advertising funds are spent in the fiscal year in which they accrue, and the percentage of advertising funds, if any, the franchisor uses principally to solicit new franchise sales.

Further, the franchisor must disclose whether there is an advertising council composed of franchisees that advises the franchisor on advertising policies. If so, the franchisor must disclose how members of the council are selected; whether the council serves in an advisory capacity only or has operational or decision-making power; and whether the franchisor has the power to form, change, or dissolve the advertising council.

For the training programs, the franchisor will need to summarize its initial and ongoing training programs including, among other things, how often training programs are held and the nature of the location or facility where training is held; the nature of instructional materials and the instructor's experience;[97] any fees or charges payable by the franchisee for training and who must pay travel and living expenses of the training program enrollees; who may and who must attend training; and whether additional training programs or refresher courses are required. The FDD must include a general description of any required computer or point-of-sale components. That description should be nontechnical and summarize the types of data to be generated or stored in the systems, and state the cost of purchasing or leasing the systems; any obligation of the franchisor, any affiliate, or third party to provide ongoing maintenance, repairs, upgrades, or updates; the franchisee's obligations to upgrade any system during the term of the franchise and any contractual limitations on the frequency and cost of such obligation; the annual cost of any optional or required maintenance, updating, upgrading, or support contracts; and finally, whether the franchisor will have independent access to the information that will be generated or stored in the systems and any limitations on that access.

Item 12: "Territory"[98]—This item addresses the territorial rights (if any) that the franchisor grants to the franchisees under the franchise and other agreements. If no exclusive territorial rights are granted, the FDD must contain a prominent warning to the franchisee that the franchisor may compete directly with the franchisee through other outlets owned by the franchisor or other franchisees. A territory is considered exclusive if the "franchisor promises not to establish either a company-owned or franchised outlet selling the same or similar goods or services under the same or similar trademarks or service marks" within the territory.[99] A common practice among franchisors, however, is to reserve to themselves the right to establish company-owned and franchised outlets similar to the franchised outlets at "non-traditional venues" within a franchisee's territory, such as airports or other transportation terminals, sports arenas, stadiums and facilities, hospitals, schools, college and university campuses, corporate campuses, health clubs, military bases, casinos, convention centers, theme and amusement parks, hotels, mall kiosks or enclosed shopping centers, fairs or festivals, or other similar types of "captive" locations that have a restricted trade area. If a franchisor reserves to

97. The summary of the trainer's experience should include the length of experience in the field and with the franchisor and should only cover experience that is relevant to the subject taught and the franchisor's operations.

98. 16 C.F.R. § 436.5(l) (2007).

99. FTC FAQs, *supra* note 59, FAQ #25.

itself the right to establish company-owned and franchised outlets similar to the franchised outlets at non-traditional venues within a franchisee's territory, then the franchisee's territory is not considered exclusive for the purposes of Item 12.[100]

If a territory is granted, the FDD must include the typical scope or boundaries (i.e., city, metropolitan area, county, state, radius of specific distance, population, number of registered vehicles, or other variant) of such rights, a summary of the rights granted to the franchisee in that territory, any rights reserved to the franchisor within the territory (such as the right to sell products or services within the territory at other types of units or through alternative channels of distribution such as the Internet, catalog sales, or telemarketing), any quotas that the franchisee must achieve to maintain the territorial rights, and any rights the franchisor has to modify the territorial rights. This item should include a summary of any options, rights of first refusal, or similar rights granted to the franchisee for additional franchises. In addition, the franchisor must summarize the franchisee's relocation rights for the franchised business. The franchisor must disclose any plans of the franchisor or its affiliates to operate or franchise a business under a different name or mark selling products or services that are similar to the services or products sold by the franchised business. Finally, this item must disclose any restrictions imposed on the franchisee regarding soliciting sales or accepting orders from outside of the franchisee's defined territory.

Item 13: "Trademarks"[101] *and Item 14: "Patents, Copyrights, and Proprietary Information"*[102]—These items provide information about the principal trademarks, service marks, patents, and copyrights used in the franchised system and licensed to the franchisee and any limitations on the franchisee's use of those marks, patents, or copyrights. If the franchisor does not have a federally registered mark, the franchisor must include a specific disclaimer that warns the franchisee that without the registration the franchisor does not have certain presumptive legal rights. In addition, the franchisor must disclose material litigation; agreements; and infringement, opposition, or cancellation proceedings that may affect the franchisee's right to use the marks, patents, or copyrights. If the franchisor does not own the registration to a trademark, additional disclosures are required about the nature and extent of the franchisor's right to permit the franchisee to use the trademark and what happens if the franchisor loses these rights. Further, a franchisor must describe the franchisee's rights under the franchise agreement if the franchisor requires the franchisee to modify or discontinue using a trademark or the subject matter covered by a patent or copyright.

Item 15: "Obligation to Participate in the Actual Operation of the Franchised Business"[103]—This item discloses the franchisee's obligation to participate personally in the direct operation of the franchised business. If on-premises supervision is not required, the franchisor must disclose whether the franchisor

100. 16 C.F.R. § 436 (2007), Bus. Franchise Guide (CCH) ¶ 6090, FTC FAQs, *supra* note 59, FAQ #37.

101. 16 C.F.R. § 436.5(m) (2007).

102. 16 C.F.R. § 436.5(n) (2007).

103. 16 C.F.R. § 436.5(o) (2007).

recommends on-premises supervision by an individual franchisee, any limits on who the franchisee can hire to manage the franchised business, whether the supervisor must complete any training programs, and, if the franchisee is a business entity, whether the supervisor must own an equity interest in the franchisee entity. Finally, the franchisor must disclose any restrictions that the franchisee must place on its managers—such as obligations to maintain trade secrets and covenants not to compete.

Item 16: "Restrictions on What the Franchisee May Sell"[104]—This item discloses any franchisor-imposed restrictions or conditions on the goods or services that the franchisee may sell or that limit access to customers. This includes any obligation to sell only goods or services approved by the franchisor, any obligation to sell all goods or services authorized by the franchisor, and whether the franchisor has the right to change the types of goods or services that the franchisor authorizes the franchisee to sell.

Item 17: "Renewal, Termination, Transfer, and Dispute Resolution"[105]—This item includes a summary (in tabular form) of some of the key provisions included in the franchise and related agreements. The franchisor can use a separate table for each agreement;[106] however, each table must include the 23 required categories of information with references to the specific sections of the agreement that relate to each category. If a particular item is not applicable, state "Not Applicable." Also, if the franchise agreement is silent about one of the listed obligations, but the franchisor unilaterally offers to provide certain benefits or protections to franchisees as a matter of policy, the franchisor should use a footnote to describe the policy and state whether the policy is subject to change. The table should summarize the agreement sections concisely, including the term, renewal rights (and what the term "renewal" means), termination, transfer, option to purchase, right of first refusal, noncompetition restrictions, integration, choice of law, and choice of forum.

Item 18: "Public Figures"[107]—This item discloses any compensation or other benefit paid to a public figure for the use of the public figure in the franchise name or symbol, or in franchise sales advertising through an endorsement or recommendation. This item must include the extent to which the public figure is involved in management or control of the franchisor and the investment, if any, made by the public figure in the franchisor. For Item 18, a "public figure" means a person whose name or physical appearance is generally known to the public in the geographic area where the franchise will be located.

Item 19: "Financial Performance Representation"[108]—This item includes any information the franchisor wants to provide to prospective franchisees in the

---

104. 16 C.F.R. § 436.5(p) (2007).
105. 16 C.F.R. § 436.5(q) (2007).
106. FTC FAQs, *supra* note 59, FAQ #13 (noting that "The use of separate charts for different agreements fosters precision and clarity, consistent with the goal of full and accurate disclosure.").
107. 16 C.F.R. § 436.5(r) (2007).
108. 16 C.F.R. § 436.5(s) (2007).

franchise sales process about actual or potential sales, income, or profits of the franchised business. Financial performance representations or FPRs are broadly defined under the amended FTC Rule as "any representation, including any oral, written, or visual representation, to a prospective franchisee, including a representation in the general media, that states, expressly or by implication, a specific level or range of actual or potential sales, income, gross profits, or net profits. The term includes a chart, table, or mathematical calculation that shows possible results based on a combination of variables."[109]

While franchisors are not required to include a financial performance representation in their FDDs, around two-thirds of franchisors currently do so. If a franchisor chooses not to include a financial performance representation in Item 19 of its FDD, however, the franchisor cannot make any statements or representations to its prospects concerning past, current, or potential sales, income, or profits. For example, if no financial performance representation is made in the FDD, the franchisor cannot make the following claims: "you will earn a $10,000 profit" or "your sales volume will be $250,000." Also, the franchisor will be prohibited from giving data that suggests, or from which a prospective franchisee easily could infer, a specific level or range of income, sales, or profits, such as "earn enough money to buy a new Porsche"[110] or "100 percent return on investment within the first year of operation." Certain statements are considered puffery and may be permitted—such as that you will "make big money" or that this is the "opportunity of a lifetime." However, note that these puffery statements might be problematic under the antifraud provisions of the franchise sales laws. If a franchisor includes a financial performance representation in the FDD, prospective franchisees should be directed to that disclosure, and franchise sellers and franchisor personnel should be careful not to make any statements that are inconsistent with the FPRs included in Item 19 or go beyond such information.[111]

A financial performance representation can include historical or projected financial performance of franchised or company outlets. For historical statements, the franchisor should disclose:

- whether the representation relates to the performance of all of the existing outlets or only to a subset of outlets that share a particular set of characteristics (for example, geographic location, type of location (such as free-standing versus shopping center), degree of competition, length of time the outlets have operated, services or goods sold, services supplied by the franchisor, and whether the outlets are franchised or franchisor-owned or -operated);
- the dates when the reported level of financial performance was achieved;
- the total number of outlets that existed in the relevant period and, if different, the number of outlets that had the described characteristics;

109. 16 C.F.R. § 436.1(e) (2007).

110. FTC Informal Staff Advisory Op. 98-5 (June 24, 1998), http://www.ftc.gov/bcp/franchise/advops/advis98-5.shtm (last visited July 11, 2009).

111. *See* Stuart Hershman & Joyce Mazero eds., Financial Performance Representations: The New and Updated Earnings Claims (ABA Forum on Franchising 2008).

- the number of outlets with the described characteristics whose actual financial performance data were used in arriving at the representation;
- of those outlets whose data were used in arriving at the representation, the number and percent that actually attained or surpassed the stated results; and
- the characteristics of the included outlets that may differ materially from those of the outlet that may be offered to a prospective franchisee.[112]

If the representation is a forecast of future financial performance, the franchisor should state the material bases and assumptions on which the projection is based. These factors may include economic or market conditions that are basic to a franchisee's operation and encompass matters affecting, among other things, a franchisee's sales, the cost of goods or services sold, and operating expenses.[113]

While franchisors and their attorneys have a fair amount of latitude as to the form and content of FPRs, a franchisor must have a "reasonable basis" and "written substantiation" for each FPR at the time it is made.[114] The FTC Rule, however, provides little information as to what constitutes a "reasonable basis." The Compliance Guide states that "the quality and quantity of information constituting a reasonable basis [in support of an FPR] will vary from case to case," but that this information "must reasonably support the representation" and be "the sort of information upon which a prudent businessperson would rely on in making an investment decision."[115] To help fill the void and provide more guidance as to what amounts to a "reasonable basis," NASAA adopted the FPR Commentary in May 2017.[116] The FPR Commentary contains a series of questions and answers to help franchisors, franchise attorneys, and state examiners better understand what information must be included, what information may be not included, and how information must be presented in FPRs in order for them to have a "reasonable basis." Included below is a summary of some of the important guidelines described in the FPR Commentary.

Use of Data from Company-Owned Outlets—Once a franchisor has at least one "operational franchise outlet" (a franchised outlet that has been open for one full year or one full season, in the case of a seasonal franchise system), the franchisor may not make an FPR based on gross sales data from company-owned outlets alone.[117] In addition, in those cases where a franchisor is permitted to include gross sales, gross profit, or net profits data of company-owned outlets in an FPR, the franchisor also must include additional information or adjustments to reflect all actual and reasonably expected differences between company-owned

112. 16 C.F.R. § 436.5(s)(3)(ii) (2007).
113. 16 C.F.R. § 436.5(s)(3)(iii) (2007).
114. 16 C.F.R. § 436.5(s)(3).
115. Compliance Guide, *supra* note 31, at 135.
116. NASAA FPR Commentary, *supra* note 64. For a detailed discussion of the content and drafting of FPRs, *see* Dale Cantone, Eric Karp & Max Schott, II, *Advanced Drafting of Financial Performance Representations: A Reasonable Basis*, 39th Annual Forum on Franchising, W13 (2016).
117. NASAA FPR Commentary, *supra* note 64, at 19.8 and 19.9.

outlets and operational franchise outlets, such as adjusting expenses to account for the standard royalty rate.[118]

Merging Data from Both Franchise Outlets and Company-Owned Outlets—Generally, a franchisor making an FPR that includes data from both franchised outlets and company-owned outlets must disclose the data from each category of outlets separately.[119] However, a franchisor that separately discloses franchised outlets and company-owned outlets in an FPR may then elect to present the same data in a combined format.[120] In addition, "if a franchisor has such a small number of total franchisees that the identity of franchisee(s) whose data is being reported in Item 19 is discernible [presumably less than 10 franchisees], and the franchise and company-owned outlets have gross sales that are not materially different, the franchisor may merge the data in the FPR."[121]

Use of Subsets—Generally, a franchisor can make an FPR based on a subset of outlets that share a particular set of characteristics, provided the FPR "(a) has a reasonable basis, (b) is accurate, and (c) is not misleading."[122] However, the franchisor may not include a subset of its *best performing outlets* in an FPR without including the corresponding *lowest performing outlets*, even if the FPR also discloses system-wide performance information for all outlets.[123] It is presumed that a franchisor with less than 10 substantially similar company-owned outlets and franchise operational outlets as of the end of its last fiscal year has too few outlets to make an FPR based on a subset of those outlets.[124] Subject to the other limitations, geographic subsets may be included in FPRs as long as the franchisor describes why and how the subsets were selected, and the information regarding them is not misleading.[125]

Averages and Medians—A franchisor cannot include an average in an FPR without including the corresponding median, and vice versa, and whenever a franchisor discloses average and median gross sales, it also must disclose the highest and lowest numbers in the range for both.[126] Outlets (including both company-owned outlets and franchise outlets) that closed can be excluded from averages and medians, provided the franchisor discloses the number of outlets that closed during the measured time period and the number of outlets that closed during the same time period after being open less than 12 months.[127]

Use of Forecasts and Projections—While forecasts and projections are still allowed, the FPR Commentary significantly restricts the data franchisors may rely on in preparing them. Projections must be based on historical data and not on

118. *Id.* at 19.10.
119. *Id.* at 19.11.
120. *Id.*
121. *Id.*
122. *Id.* at 19.12.
123. *Id.* at 19.13.
124. *Id.* at 19.14.
125. *Id.* at 19.15.
126. *Id.* at 19.16 and 19.17.
127. *Id.* at 19.18.

"mere hypothetical situations or expectations."[128] A franchisor may adjust or supplement historical results based on changes in the market (such as to reflect higher or lower than historic rents), but "the projections still must be based on historical data from outlets substantially similar to the type of outlet offered in the Franchise Disclosure Document."[129] Further, "[a] projection must be based on a reasonable sample of the historic results of the brand offered to the prospective franchisee."[130] Specifically, "[a] projection may not be based on the results of other brands operated or licensed by the franchisor or its affiliates, or on the results of similar or competitive brands operated by others, or on industry reports."[131]

Admonitions; Disclaimers—While franchisors are required to include an "admonition" in Item 19 that warns prospective franchisees that their performance may differ from the stated level,[132] a franchisor is prohibited from including any other disclaimers that arguably negate a prospective franchisee's ability to rely on the information presented.[133] Under the FPR Commentary, the following are the only permitted disclaimers, which must be presented in a separate paragraph from the rest of the FPR and must be in bold type:

> For historical representations—**"Some [outlets] have [sold] [earned] this amount. Your individual results may differ. There is no assurance that you'll [sell] [earn] as much."**
>
> For projections—**"These figures are only estimates of what we think you may [sell] [earn]. Your individual results may differ. There is no assurance that you'll [sell] [earn] as much."**[134]

If a franchisor includes an FPR in Item 19 of its FDD, the franchisor must retain written substantiation for the representation, as well as include a statement in the FPR advising prospective franchisees that the franchisor will make substantiating information available upon reasonable request.[135] If no FPR is included in the FDD, the franchisor and its employees and franchise sellers are limited in what financial information they can provide to prospects, and the franchisor must include in Item 19 of its FDD a mandatory disclosure explicitly stating that no financial performance information is being provided.[136]

Although generally all FPRs must be included in a franchisor's Item 19, there are two primary exceptions to this requirement. First, if a franchisor is selling a company-owned outlet, the franchisor may provide the actual operating results

128. *Id.* at 19.19.
129. *Id.*
130. *Id.* at 19.20.
131. *Id.*
132. 16 C.F.R. § 436.5(s)(3)(iv); NASAA FPR Commentary, *supra* note 64, at 19.3.
133. NASAA FPR Commentary, *supra* note 64 at 19.3, 19.21, and 19.22.
134. *Id.*
135. 16 C.F.R. § 436.5(s)(3)(v) (2008).
136. 16 C.F.R. § 436.5(s)(3) (2008); Compliance Guide, *supra* note 31, at 86.

for that outlet without complying with Item 19 requirements.[137] The financial information should be given only to potential purchasers of the specific outlet. Typically, franchisors that provide this type of information include a "wrap-around disclosure" with the information to explain the data and any assumptions for the results.

Second, if the franchisor furnishes financial performance information in the FDD, the franchisor may deliver to a prospective franchisee a supplemental financial performance representation about a particular location or variation, apart from the FDD. A supplemental financial performance representation must be in writing, must explain the departure from the financial performance representation presented in Item 19, and must meet all of the same requirements for its preparation as if it were going to be included in Item 19.[138]

Notably, the definition of "financial performance representations" ordinarily does not include costs and expenses of operation.[139] Accordingly, the franchisor can share this information so long as the cost and expense information is not presented as a percentage of sales, profits, or another measure that would allow a prospective franchisee to calculate the potential income, sales, or profits of the franchise.[140] The FPR Commentary clarifies, however, that "[a]lthough a presentation of cost or expense data alone is not an FPR, a franchisor that makes an FPR disclosing gross sales alone may not separately provide cost or expense data outside the FPR from which a prospective franchisee could readily calculate average net profits."[141] While the FTC does not consider cost and expense information alone to be an FPR, the States of Illinois, Maryland, and New York still arguably prohibit the disclosure of cost information outside of Item 19.[142] In addition, Minnesota requires that "any estimated or projected franchisee earnings, proforma statements, or break even statements prepared for presentation to prospective franchisees" be included in the franchisor's FDD.[143]

If the franchisor includes a financial performance representation in Item 19, the franchisor can use the Item 19 information outside of the FDD; however, the franchisor should always carefully assess whether the financial information is consistent with what is included in the then-current FDD. The information can be included on the franchisor's website, in advertising, or in discussions with a prospective franchisee. FPRs used in advertising are referred to as "general media claims." "General media" includes all forms of advertising, such as television, radio, print (i.e., magazines, newspapers, and journals), billboards, and

137. 16 C.F.R. § 436.5(s)(4) (2008).

138. 16 C.F.R. § 436.5(s)(5) (2008).

139. Compliance Guide, *supra* note 31, at 131; NASAA Commentary, *supra* note 62, at 19.1.

140. *Id.*

141. NASAA FPR Commentary, *supra* note 64, at 19.1 and 19.9 n.8.

142. *See* Ill. Admin. Code tit. 14A, Appendix A, Illustration L; Md. Regs. Code tit. 2, § 02.02.08.16; N.Y. Comp. Codes R. & Regs. tit 13, § 200.2(c).

143. *See* Minn. R. § 2860.3500(14).

web-based advertisements.[144] Under the FTC Rule, the franchisor cannot make a general media claim unless (1) the franchisor has a reasonable basis for the information; (2) the franchisor has written substantiation for the representation at the time the franchisor makes the representation; and (3) the representation, including the material bases and assumptions, appears in Item 19 of the franchisor's most current FDD.[145] In addition, the franchisor must disclose (1) the number and percentage of outlets from which supporting data for the representation were gathered that actually attained or surpassed the represented level of financial performance, (2) the time period when the performance results were achieved, and (3) a clear and conspicuous admonition that a new franchisee's results may differ from the represented performance.[146] As a best practices point, if the franchisor pulls data from the then-current FDD to be used in an advertisement, the franchisor should include a disclaimer that cautions readers to "see Item 19 of our FDD for further details" so that the data used in the advertisement is not taken out of context. For general media claims, the franchisor "must furnish any prospective franchisees with the required Item 19 disclosures while the advertisement is running."[147] After the advertisement is pulled from circulation, the franchisor must continue to disclose the Item 19 information for a reasonable period of time not less than six months.[148]

Finally, as mentioned earlier, in June 2020, NASAA released its COVID-19 FPR Commentary to provide franchisors with guidance regarding the use of historical FPRs in the wake of the economic downturn caused by the COVID-19 pandemic.[149] Essentially, NASAA took the position that if the franchisor includes FPRs in its FDD that are based on historical data from 2019 or an earlier period ("Historical FPRs") and the franchisor's franchise system has been negatively impacted by COVID-19 in a material way, the franchisor must amend its FDD to either remove the Historical FPRs from Item 19 or add 2020 information to Item 19 to reflect how its system has been negatively impacted. Otherwise, NASAA noted that the existing Historical FPRs, even if accurate, would not have a reasonable basis and would be misleading because they omit material facts.[150] The State of Washington also issued a similar press release on June 17, 2020, titled "Notice Regarding Historical Financial Performance Representation During the COVID-19 Pandemic." The notice informed franchisors that Washington will be following NASAA's COVID-19 FPR Commentary and amendment filings should be submit-

144. Ordinarily, statements made in publicly filed information submitted to the Securities and Exchange Commission, as well as speeches, press releases, and bona fide news stories, are not considered "general media claims"—and, therefore, the heightened disclosure requirements applicable to such claims are inapplicable—unless the representations are specifically directed at members of the public interested in purchasing a franchise. *See Compliance Guide*, *supra* note 31, at 133.

145. 16 C.F.R. § 436.5(s)(3) (2008); Compliance Guide, *supra* note 31, at 133–35.

146. *Compliance Guide*, *supra* note 31, at 133.

147. *Id.* at 134.

148. *Id.*

149. NASAA COVID-19 FPR Commentary, *supra* note 67.

150. *Id.*

ted to the state to update the franchisor's Item 19 if the pandemic had materially impacted its system in 2020.[151]

Item 20: "Outlets and Franchisee Information"[152]—This item includes five required tables showing a three-year snapshot of the changes in the outlet counts and franchisee transfers for the franchised system.

- Table 1—a three-year system-wide summary of company-owned and franchised outlets showing the number of outlets open at the beginning and end of each year and the net change.
- Table 2—a three-year summary of the number of transfers by state from franchisees to new owners (but not including outlets that are transferred to the franchisor or its affiliates).
- Table 3—a three-year summary by state of the status of the franchised outlets including the number of outlets open at the beginning of each year; the number of outlets that have left the franchise system due to termination, nonrenewal, reacquisition by the franchisor, or some other reason; and the number of outlets open at the end of each year.

Supplementing the information appearing in Table 3, the franchisor must include, as exhibits to the FDD, three lists current as of the end of the franchisor's prior fiscal year (or, at the franchisor's option, a more recent date) showing: (1) open franchised outlets, either all outlets or at least 100 outlets, if state-specific lists are used (including, for each outlet, the franchisee's name, address, and telephone number); (2) franchisees who have signed franchise agreements but have not opened their franchised outlet (including each franchisee's name, address, and telephone number); and (3) former franchisees (including the franchisee's name, city and state, and current business telephone number, or if unknown, the last known home telephone number, or at the request of the former franchisee, a home address, post office address, or personal or business e-mail address). The list of former franchisees should include every franchisee who had an outlet terminated, canceled, not renewed, transferred, or who otherwise voluntarily or involuntarily ceased to do business under a franchise agreement (including any agreement for which an outlet never opened) during the most recently completed fiscal year or who has not communicated with the franchisor within 10 weeks of the FDD issuance date. In addition, in immediate conjunction with this information, the franchisor must include the following: "If you buy this franchise, your contact information may be disclosed to other buyers when you leave the franchise system."

- Table 4—a three-year summary by state of the status of the company-owned outlets including the number of outlets open at the beginning of each year, the number of outlets that have closed or been transferred to franchisees, and the number of outlets open at the end of each year.

151. https://dfi.wa.gov/sites/default/files/notice-nasaa-fpr-guidance.pdf (last visited Apr. 10, 2021).

152. 16 C.F.R. § 436.5(t) (2007).

- Table 5—projections, by state, for the franchisor's next fiscal year of franchised outlets to be opened, new franchised outlets to be sold, and company-owned outlets to be opened.

The franchisor can use notes to the tables to explain the information. In addition to the outlet information provided in the tables, the franchisor must disclose whether, during the last three fiscal years, any of its franchisees have signed a confidentiality clause to prohibit that franchisee from discussing its experiences relating to the franchise system with prospective franchisees. The franchisor must disclose all franchisee associations that the franchisor endorses or supports, as well as incorporated independent associations, that are specific to the franchise network at issue and submit a timely request to be included in the FDD. Finally, if a franchisor is selling a previously-owned franchised outlet now under its control, the franchisor must disclose certain additional information for that outlet for the last five fiscal years to potential purchasers. Interestingly, this information may either be attached as an addendum to the FDD, or, if disclosure has already been made, then in a supplement to the previously furnished FDD.

Item 21: "Financial Statements"[153]—This item includes the franchisor's financial statements, in tabular form, comparing the franchisor's balance sheet for the previous two fiscal year-ends before the FDD issuance date; and statements of operations, stockholders equity, and cash flows for each of the franchisor's previous three fiscal years. In the alternative, the franchisor may include financial statements of any affiliate if that affiliate's financial statements satisfy the requirements of this item, and the affiliate absolutely and unconditionally guarantees the franchisor's obligations to the franchisees. A copy of that guarantee must be attached to the FDD. If a parent commits to perform the franchisor's post-sale obligations that are for the direct benefit of the franchisees[154] or guarantees the franchisor's obligations, the parent's financials and a copy of the guarantee must be included in the FDD. The franchisor also is obligated to include audited financial statements of a parent if that parent is the "sole supplier of a good or service without which a franchise cannot be operated."[155]

The financial statements must be prepared according to U.S. generally accepted accounting principles, as revised by any future United States government mandated accounting principles, or as permitted by the Securities and Exchange Commission. Except as described below, the financial statements must be audited by an independent certified public accountant.[156] If the franchisor owns a direct or beneficial controlling financial interest in a subsidiary, the franchisor's financial statements must reflect the financial condition of the franchisor and the subsidiary.

Start-up franchisors that do not have audited financial statements may phase in the use of audited financial statements by providing, at a minimum, the

153. 16 C.F.R. § 436.5(u) (2007).

154. FTC FAQs, *supra* note 59, FAQ #16.

155. *Id.* at FAQ #30.

156. Research & Dev. Arrangements, Statement of Fin. Accounting Standards No. 68, § 32 (Fin. Accounting Standards Bd. 1982).

following statements at the indicated times: (1) franchisor's first partial or full fiscal year selling franchises, an unaudited opening balance sheet; (2) franchisor's second year selling franchises, audited balance sheet as of end of first partial or full year selling franchises; and (3) franchisor's third and subsequent years selling franchises, all required audited financial statements for the prior year plus any audited statements previously disclosed. This phase-in may be used if the franchisor prepares audited financial statements as soon as practicable, prepares unaudited statements in a format that conforms as closely as possible to audited statements, and includes one or more years of unaudited financial statements or clearly and conspicuously discloses in this section that the franchisor has not been in business for three or more years and cannot include all financial statements required. Start-up franchisors should carefully check the financial statement requirements in the state franchise laws because a number of states, including Minnesota, New York, and Virginia, require the franchisor to include audited financial statements,[157] California requires at least reviewed financial statements,[158] and Illinois requires the financial statements to be prepared by a CPA.[159]

Item 22: "Contracts"[160]—This item is a list of all agreements between the franchisor and the franchisee relating to the franchise offering—including not only the franchise agreement itself but also any financing agreements, lease agreements, option agreements, product purchase agreements, area development agreements, subfranchisor agreements (master franchise agreements), and area representative agreements. These agreements must also be attached as exhibits to the FDD.

Item 23: "Receipt"[161]—This item includes two detachable receipt pages that acknowledge the prospective franchisee's receipt of the FDD. The prospective franchisee retains one copy of the signed receipt for the franchisee's records and signs and returns the other copy to the franchisor.

For each franchise sale, the franchise sellers involved with the sale must be identified on the receipt pages. The FTC Rule defines a "franchise seller" as a person that offers for sale, sells, or arranges for the sale of a franchise.[162] The definition expressly includes the franchisor and the franchisor's employees, representatives, agents, subfranchisors, and third-party brokers who are involved in franchise sales activities, but it excludes existing franchisees who sell only their own outlet and who are otherwise not engaged in franchise sales on behalf of the franchisor.[163] The term "third-party broker" as used in the definition of a "franchise seller" is defined in the Statement of Basis and Purpose as "a person who:

157. Minn. Stat. Ann. § 80C.04; N.Y. Comp. Codes R. & Regs. tit. 13, § 200.2; 21 Va. Admin. Code 5-110-55.

158. Cal. Code Regs. tit. 10, § 310.112.2(d) (2005).

159. Ill. Admin. Code tit. 14, § 200.600(c).

160. 16 C.F.R. § 436.5(v) (2007).

161. 16 C.F.R. § 436.5(w) (2007).

162. 16 C.F.R. § 436.1(j) (2007).

163. *Id.*

(1) is under contract with the franchisor relating to the sale of franchises; (2) receives compensation from the franchisor related to the sale of franchises; and (3) arranges franchise sales by assisting prospective franchisees in the sales process." The Statement of Basis and Purpose goes on to state that the term "broker" is sufficiently narrow to exclude existing franchisees who may refer potential franchisees to the franchisor because such individuals are not "under contract with the franchisor to sell franchises."[164]

The franchisor should note that the FTC definition of a franchise seller is broad and somewhat ambiguous because it encompasses any person who "arranges for the sale of a franchise." Determining the types of activities that constitute arranging for the sale of a franchise is difficult and must be made on a case-by-case basis. As a general rule, the passive referral of a prospective franchisee to a franchisor will not create a "franchise seller" relationship. However, any activity that may be interpreted as encouraging, enticing, or persuading a prospective franchisee to purchase a particular franchise may reach the threshold of creating a franchise-seller relationship.

Any person who had significant contacts with the prospective franchisee during the franchise sales process must be identified on the receipt page as a franchise seller, including individuals who assisted the specific prospective franchisee in completing the application and other forms or who engaged in ongoing conversations with the specific prospective franchisee during the franchise sales process.[165] In its FTC FAQs, the FTC staff has specifically noted that any person who receives a sales commission and/or quota credit if the deal is consummated should be listed as a "franchise seller" on the receipt.[166]

Generally, the franchisor should list as franchise sellers on the receipt page those individuals who definitely will have significant contact with all prospects, such as its VP of Franchise Sales. For those individuals who may or may not have significant contact with a particular prospect during the sales process, the franchisor has several options. The franchisor can include an instruction in the receipt page that the prospective franchisee should write in the name of the franchise seller or any additional franchise seller before signing and returning the receipt page to the franchisor.[167] While allowed, the prospective franchisee may have a difficult time determining whom to note as a franchise seller and will likely not know all of the franchise sellers who may be involved in the sales process at the time of signing the receipt. In addition, the franchisor bears the burden of ensuring that each prospect has been disclosed with a list of all applicable franchise sellers before signing a franchise agreement.[168] As an alternative approach and probably the one most franchisors use, the franchisor can (1) attach to the previously signed receipt a statement, business card, or other document

164. 72 Fed. Reg. 15,462 n.169 (Mar. 30, 2007). *See also*, FTC FAQs, *supra* note 59, FAQ #7.

165. FTC FAQs, *supra* note 59, FAQs #12 and #23.

166. *Id.* at FAQ #12.

167. *Id.* at FAQs #12 and #23.

168. *Id.* at FAQ #23.

showing the name of the seller, or fill in the name of the seller in a blank included in the previously signed receipt for additional franchise sellers; and (2) send a copy of the amended receipt page with any attachments to the prospective franchisee so that the prospective franchisee has a copy of the completed receipt.[169] At that point, both the franchisor and prospective franchisee will each have a copy of the same receipt. The absence of an identifiable franchise seller at the time the franchisor provides disclosure should not force a delay in the prospective franchisee's ability to sign the receipt page, provided that the receipt page is updated once the identity of all sellers is known.[170] As a best practice, many franchisors include as part of their closing checklist for each franchise sale a review of the receipt page to ensure it was properly signed, includes all applicable franchise sellers, and was provided to the prospect. The franchisor also must retain copies of signed franchisee receipt pages for at least three years to demonstrate compliance.[171]

As stated in the Statement of Basis and Purpose for the amended FTC Rule, this disclosure provides prospective franchisees with contact information for any franchise seller with whom the franchisee was dealing and also may be helpful in a private litigation matter or a state enforcement action to help identify the individuals that may have furnished disclosures.[172]

(b) Special Disclosure Requirements for Multi-Unit Franchises

While single-unit franchises remain at the heart of franchising, for purposes of efficiency and the prospect of more rapid growth, many franchisors also rely on multi-unit franchising in expanding their systems. Multi-unit franchises represent separate offerings from single-unit franchises and, as mentioned above, are subject to the same disclosure obligations under the FTC Rule. In recognition of the growing popularity of multi-unit franchises and the lack of specific direction relating to the disclosure of these arrangements, in September 2014, NASAA adopted its Multi-Unit Commentary. Its stated purposes are to define the three most-common multi-unit franchising structures or arrangements, which are described as "area development," "subfranchise rights," and "area representation," and to provide guidance for the uniform disclosure of information about these structures in FDDs.[173] While franchisors are encouraged to use the terms adopted by NASAA, the principles and disclosure obligations relating to each arrangement apply regardless of what name the franchisor assigns to it.[174]

The Multi-Unit Commentary includes a series of questions and answers relating to the disclosure of each of the three defined multi-unit structures. Included

169. *Id.* at FAQs #12 and #23.
170. *Id.*
171. Compliance Guide, *supra* note 31, at 117; FTC FAQs, *supra* note 59, FAQ #12.
172. FTC FAQs, *supra* note 59, FAQ #12.
173. NASAA Multi-Unit Commentary, *supra* note 63, Introduction.
174. *Id.*

below is a brief definition of each structure, as well as a summary of the key disclosure requirements specific to that structure.[175]

(i) Area Development

Under an area development arrangement, the franchisor, in exchange for a development fee, enters into an "area development agreement" with an "area developer" for the development and operation of two or more unit franchises within a defined development area in accordance with a development schedule.[176] Typically, for each unit an area developer develops under the development agreement, the area developer (or in some cases its affiliate) must enter into a separate unit franchise agreement with the franchisor. An area developer may receive some level of territorial protection within its development area, although, in some instances, territorial protection, if any, is only granted through the unit franchise agreement. While the development fee is usually nonrefundable, the franchisor may allow a portion of it to be credited against the initial franchise fee due under each unit franchise agreement it enters into under the area development agreement. Area developers do not have the right to grant or sell unit franchises to third parties.

The Multi-Unit Commentary clarifies that a franchisor may offer area development franchises in the same FDD as it offers unit franchises, given that an area developer is essentially a unit franchisee with the right to operate more than one unit franchise and there is little risk for confusion.[177] For a franchisor that wants to include an area development franchise offering in its unit franchise FDD, the franchisor must comply with certain additional disclosure requirements relating to the area development structure, including those listed here:

- *Item 1*—Disclose whether an area developer will be required to sign the franchisor's then-current form of franchise agreement when it signs future unit franchise agreements under the area development agreement.[178]
- *Items 11 and 12*—When describing the franchisor's approval of the sites and any territories of unit franchises, disclose, if applicable, that the franchisor will determine or approve the location of future units and any territories for those units, and that its then-current standards for sites and territories will apply.[179]

---

175. For a detailed discussion of these multi-unit arrangements, *see* Dennis E. Wieczorek & Max J. Schott, II, *Chapter 2: Structuring the Franchise Relationship* in Rupert M. Barkoff, Joseph J. Fittante, Ronald K. Gardner, Jr. & Andrew C. Selden, eds. Fundamentals of Franchising (4th ed. ABA 2015).

176. NASAA Multi-Unit Commentary, *supra* note 63, Definitions, A. An "area development agreement" also may be referred to as a development agreement or multi-unit development agreement. In addition, an "area developer" also may be referred to as an area franchisee or operator, multi-unit developer or operator, regional developer or operator, and master franchisee. *Id.*

177. *Id.* at AD 0.1.

178. *Id.* at AD 1.0.

179. *Id.* at AD 11.0 and 12.0.

- *Item 17*—Describe in the table summaries for (e), (f), (g), and (h), as applicable, any cross-default provision in the area development agreement and unit franchise agreement that may result in the termination of the other agreement.[180]
- *Item 20*—Because the focus of the Item 20 tables is on the number of outlets actually opened and closed and the number of unit franchise agreements actually signed, a franchisor is not required or allowed to include in this item (i) the number of franchised outlets that area developers have agreed to open, (ii) separate tables for area developers, or (iii) separate charts or lists of outlets of area developers.[181] However, the franchisor is required to identify area developers in Item 20 lists of current and former franchisees.[182]

(ii) Subfranchise Rights

Under a subfranchise arrangement (also known as a master franchising arrangement), the franchisor grants the "subfranchisor" (master franchisee) the right to develop, and subfranchise to third parties the right to develop, units in a specific geographic territory.[183] This is a three-tiered arrangement: the franchisor enters into a "subfranchisor agreement" (master franchise agreement) with the subfranchisor, and, in turn, the subfranchisor enters into "unit franchise agreements" (subfranchisee agreements) with "unit franchisees" or "subfranchisees" for the operation of subfranchised units. Generally, there is no direct contractual relationship between the franchisor and the subfranchisee, although the franchisor will have certain third-party rights under the subfranchisee agreement.

The subfranchisor agreement is significantly different from a typical unit franchise agreement. Under the subfranchisor agreement, a franchisor grants the subfranchisor the right to use, and sublicense to third parties the right to use, the franchisor's marks and system. There is a development schedule included that requires the subfranchisor to develop a certain number of units within a specified period of time. In consideration for the rights granted under the subfranchisor agreement, the subfranchisor typically pays the franchisor a sizeable initial fee and a percentage of the ongoing fees it receives from subfranchisees. A subfranchisor agreement also contains the subfranchisor's obligation to develop and support its subfranchisees.

The subfranchisee agreement between the subfranchisor and its subfranchisees is similar to a unit franchise agreement, although, as mentioned above, it often grants the franchisor certain third-party rights, including the right to assume or assign the unit franchise agreement upon the termination of the subfranchisor agreement and the right to enforce certain provisions in the unit franchise

180. *Id.* at AD 17.0.

181. *Id.* at AD 20.0, AD 20.1, and AD 20.2.

182. *Id.* at AD 20.3.

183. *Id.* at Definitions, B. Other terms used to describe subfranchisors also include area franchisor and regional franchisor. *Id.*

agreement as a third-party beneficiary. Most often a franchisor will either provide the form subfranchisee agreement the subfranchisor must use or reserve the right to review and approve the form to be used. For those units within the territory that a subfranchisor (or its affiliate) will directly operate, the subfranchisor will either enter into a single-unit agreement with the franchisor or enter into a subfranchisee agreement with itself (or an affiliate).

The Multi-Unit Commentary divides it guidance relating to subfranchise rights into two sections. The first section (Section A), titled "Franchisor Offer of Subfranchise Rights," focuses on the FDD a franchisor must use to disclose its subfranchise arrangement and subfranchisor agreement to prospective subfranchisors.[184] Because the relationships and agreements for subfranchise offerings and unit franchise offerings are very different, a franchisor may not include both offerings in the same FDD.[185] This means that a franchisor will have to create a separate FDD for its subfranchise arrangement. In preparing this document, the franchisor must comply with certain additional disclosure requirements, including those listed here:

- *Item 1*—Because the unit franchise offer is a separate line of business from the subfranchise arrangement offer, the unit franchise offer must be disclosed in the subfranchise arrangement FDD, and the subfranchise arrangement must be disclosed in Item 1 of the unit franchise FDD.[186]
- *Item 20*—Given subfranchise rights are not substantially similar to unit franchise rights, only disclose information about current and former subfranchisors.[187]
- *Item 22*—If the franchisor requires the use of an agreement (i.e., a unit franchise agreement) in a form prescribed by the franchisor (even if subject to some modification by the subfranchisor), then attach the franchisor's then-current form either (i) as an exhibit to Item 22 or (ii) as an attachment to the agreement between the franchisor and subfranchisor with its location cross-referenced in Item 22.[188] Also, if a franchisor requires its subfranchisors to use the franchisor's form FDD for unit franchises, disclose this requirement in Item 22, but do not include the franchisor's form FDD as an exhibit.[189]

The second section (Section B) of the subfranchise rights guidance, titled "Subfranchisor Offer of Unit Franchise," addresses the FDD a subfranchisor must use to disclose its unit franchise arrangement and subfranchisee agreement to prospective subfranchisees.[190] Because a subfranchisor's rights to subfranchise flow from the franchisor, a subfranchisor must disclose not only information

184. *Id.* at Subfranchisors, A.
185. *Id.* at SF 0.1.
186. *Id.* at SF 1.0.
187. *Id.* at SF 20.0.
188. *Id.* at SF 22.0.
189. *Id.* at SF 22.1.
190. *Id.* at Subfranchisors, B.

about itself in its FDD but also information about the franchisor. This means that any material changes to information regarding the franchisor or the subfranchisor will trigger amendments and updates to the subfranchisor's FDD.[191] However, the subfranchisor is not required to disclose in its FDD its financial arrangement with the franchisor but may state in Item 6 that the subfranchisor and franchisor will share fees paid by subfranchisees.[192]

In preparing its FDD, a subfranchisor must comply with certain additional disclosure re-quirements, including those listed here:

- *Items 2–4*—Even though the subfranchisees will deal with the subfranchisor and not with the franchisor, disclose the franchisor's officers and directors in Item 2, lawsuits against the franchisor and individuals associated with the franchisor identified in Item 2 in Item 3, and any bankruptcies of the franchisor and individuals associated with the franchisor identified in Item 2 in Item 4. Information must be presented first for the subfranchisor and then for the franchisor.[193]
- *Item 8*—Disclose all means by which the franchisor, the subfranchisor, and any affiliates may derive revenue as a result of required purchases or leases of goods and services by subfranchisees.[194]
- *Item 13*—Disclose any currently effective agreements that limit the subfranchisor's rights to use or license the use of the marks, including the circumstances under which its subfranchise rights may be canceled, and the effect, if any, that cancellation may have on a subfranchisee's rights to continue to use the franchisor's marks. Also, disclose whether the subfranchisee can continue to use the marks if the subfranchisor agreement with the franchisor expires or is terminated, canceled, or not renewed.[195]
- *Item 20*—Disclose all franchised outlets (i.e., unit franchises) in the entire franchise system, in addition to the franchised outlets of the subfranchisor's subfranchisees. The first set of Item 20 tables 1–5 must include information for the subfranchisor, and the second set of Item 20 tables 1–5 must include information for the entire franchise system.[196] In addition, include two separate lists of current unit franchisees and the addresses and telephone numbers of their outlets in the following order: (1) a list of the subfranchisor's own current unit franchisees (its subfranchisees); and (2) a list of the current unit franchisees of the franchisor and its other subfranchisors operating under the same brand, although the subfranchisor has potential options for limiting these lists.[197]
- *Item 21*—Because the purchaser of a unit franchise from a subfranchisor relies on both the franchisor and the subfranchisor, disclose the financial

191. *Id.* at SF 0.3.
192. *Id.* at SF 0.2.
193. *Id.* at SF 3.0 and SF 4.0.
194. *Id.* at SF 8.0.
195. *Id.* at SF 13.0.
196. *Id.* at SF 20.1 and SF 20.2.
197. *Id.* at SF 20.3.

statements of both entities.[198] If the subfranchisor and the franchisor have different fiscal years, the subfranchisor must update its FDD within 120 days after the end of its fiscal year, include any material changes that have occurred to the franchisor's information, and thereafter update its FDD if there are any subsequent material changes to either party's financial information.[199]

(iii) Area Representation

Under an area representation arrangement, the franchisor, in exchange for an initial fee, enters into an "area representative agreement" with an "area representative" for the right to solicit or recruit unit franchisees to enter into unit franchise agreements with the franchisor within a defined geographic development area and/or to provide support services to unit franchisees entering into unit franchise agreements.[200] The area representative advertises and promotes the franchise opportunity to potential franchisees within the development area and, if the franchisor ultimately decides to award a unit franchise to the prospective unit franchisee, the area representative typically provides ongoing operational support and guidance to the unit franchisee. Unlike a subfranchise arrangement, the franchisor ultimately determines whether to award a unit franchise to a prospective unit franchisee the area representative introduces to the franchisor. If a unit franchise is granted, the franchisor (not the area representative) will enter into the unit franchise agreement with the unit franchisee. No direct contractual relationship exists between the area representative and unit franchisees.

A typical area representative agreement will include a development schedule outlining the number of unit franchisees the area representative must solicit and recruit in its designated development area within a prescribed period. The area representative agreement also will detail the area representative's post-sale support obligations including, for example, operational support, site selection assistance, and training. The area representative agreement also may require or allow the area representative to open and operate a certain number of unit franchises for its own account under a separate unit franchise agreement with the franchisor for each unit, which units will count toward its development obligation. In exchange for recruiting unit franchisees and providing ongoing operational support, the area representative will most likely receive a portion of the initial franchise fee and ongoing royalties paid by the unit franchisee.

---

198. *Id.* at SF 21.0.

199. *Id.* at SF 21.1.

200. *Id.* at Definitions, C. An area representative agreement also may be referred to as a development agent agreement, area/regional developer agreement, and area/regional director agreement. In addition, an "area representative" also may be referred to as a development agent, area/regional developer, and area/regional director. Further, "[u]nder some state franchise laws, the area representative may be considered to be a subfranchisor if it provides support services to third parties with unit franchise agreements, even though the area representative does not sign unit franchise agreements with third parties." *Id.*

Given that the relationships and agreements for area representative franchise offerings and unit franchise offerings are very different, a franchisor may not include both offerings in the same FDD. Accordingly, a franchisor will have to create a separate FDD for its area representative arrangement.[201] In preparing this document, the franchisor must comply with certain additional disclosure requirements, including those described here:

- *Item 1*—Disclose the unit franchise offer as it is a separate line of business from the area representative franchise offer.[202]
- *Item 20*—Because area representative franchises are not substantially similar to unit franchises, only disclose information about current and former area representatives.[203]

Apart from its area representative FDD, a franchisor also will have to disclose information about its area representatives in its unit franchise FDD if they will be involved in offering and selling unit franchises or providing support to unit franchisees. Specifically, the franchisor must comply with certain additional disclosure requirements in its unit franchise FDD, including those listed here:

- *Item 1*—Disclose the area representative franchise offer, although the franchisor is not required or permitted to disclose the financial arrangements it has with its area representatives.[204]
- *Item 2*—Disclose the business experience of individual area representatives who exercise "management responsibility relating to the sale or operation of franchises," with the understanding that this condition generally is met if a franchisor's area representatives will provide service or support to unit franchisees.[205] If the franchisor does not grant an area representative any management responsibility relating to the sale or operation of franchises and is not required to disclose that area representative in Item 2, the franchisor must disclose this fact in Item 1.[206]
- *Items 3 and 4*—Make disclosures in Items 3 and 4 about the litigation and bankruptcy history of an area representative required to be included in Item 2 and, if an area representative is an entity, any of its directors, officers and employees or agents that have management responsibility relating to the sale or operation of franchises.[207] If the franchisor does not grant an area representative any management responsibility relating to the sale or operation of franchises and disclosures regarding the area representative are not required to be included in Items 3 or 4, the franchisor must disclose this fact in Item 1.[208]

---

201. *Id.* at AR 0.1.
202. *Id.* at AR 1.0.
203. *Id.* at AR 20.0.
204. *Id.* at AR 0.2 and AR 1.0.
205. *Id.* at AR 2.0.
206. *Id.*
207. *Id.* at AR 3.0 and AR 4.0.
208. *Id.*

- *Item 8*—Disclose rebates received by the area representative or its affiliates, only to the extent the franchisor is aware of the rebates.[209]
- *Item 11*—Disclose the experience of any area representative instructors who will be providing training to unit franchisees.[210]
- *Item 20*—While the existence of area representative franchises that have been sold, transferred, or terminated does not need to be disclosed, if an area representative owns a unit franchise, information about the ownership and/or statistics related to that unit franchise must be disclosed.[211]

Because area representatives may only operate in certain geographic areas, the Multi-Unit Commentary expressly permits the franchisor to include required disclosures in its unit franchise FDD regarding its individual area representatives (including disclosures required in Items 2, 3, 4, and 11) either in the body of the FDD or in an addendum to the FDD, provided the franchisor is consistent in its approach (i.e., all disclosures must be either in the body of the FDD or in the addendum).[212] If the addendum approach is used, the Multi-Unit Commentary allows the franchisor to use state-specific addenda or include information for all area representatives in the system in a single addendum. The fact that litigation against a specific area representative may be included in an addendum, however, does not change the requirement to disclose the litigation in the body of the franchisor's unit franchise FDD if the franchisor is named as a party, and the claim against the franchisor is of a type required to be disclosed in Item 3.[213] If a franchisor uses area representatives, it must include on the receipt of its unit franchise FDD any individuals who participate in a franchise sale on behalf of an area representative, including any employees and officers of the area representative (if an entity).[214]

(c) Compiling the Information for the FDD

One of the most critical components of preparing an FDD is obtaining the necessary information from the franchisor, including its departments and employees. Not surprisingly, this can often be the most time-consuming phase of the FDD preparation process. The first step in gathering this information is the identification of a point person or persons within the franchisor's management team who will be responsible for collecting the information. Regardless of the size of the franchisor's organization, it is essential that the point person for each item of the FDD understands the legal significance of the franchisor's registration and disclosure obligations, is detail-oriented, and has access to all aspects of the franchisor's organization.

209. *Id.* at AR 8.0.
210. *Id.* at AR 11.0.
211. *Id.* at AR 20.0.
212. *Id.* at AR 0.3.
213. *Id.*
214. *Id.* at AR 23.0.

In collecting the information for the FDD, it is imperative that the inquiries be designed to elicit from the franchisor a complete and accurate response to the disclosure requirements for each item of the FDD. Generally, providing the franchisor with a questionnaire tailored to the franchisor and that follows the disclosure obligations, as set forth above, is a useful way to obtain this information. The point person should review the completed questionnaires carefully for completeness and accuracy. Extensive, and often aggressive, follow-up with the contact person and other individuals and departments may be necessary before the information-gathering process is complete. Exhibit 2-1 is a sample questionnaire for gathering necessary information to prepare the FDD.

The franchisor and the attorney preparing the FDD should retain copies of the completed questionnaires. Proper retention of this documentation will enable the franchisor to establish the appropriate legal defenses, if the franchisor is challenged regarding the accuracy of any of the disclosures in the FDD in the future. The franchisor must be able to prove that it made a reasonable inquiry concerning the accuracy of the information contained in the FDD in order to establish its due diligence defense.

(d) Using and Registering the Completed FDD

Since the FTC Rule does not require the franchisor to file or register the FDD with the FTC or any other federal agency, once the FDD has been prepared, the franchisor can begin using the FDD immediately to offer and sell franchises in the non-registration states. The franchisor must include an issuance date on the cover page, state effective dates page, and receipt pages before using the FDD. The issuance date is generally the date that the document is completed and ready for use by the franchisor.

In the 14 states that are commonly referred to as the "registration states," the franchisor must apply to the appropriate state agency to register the franchise before offering to sell franchises in the applicable state. See section 2.5 for a discussion of what constitutes an "offer" and a "sale" in a registration state. The registration states are California, Hawaii, Illinois, Indiana, Maryland, Michigan, Minnesota, New York, North Dakota, Rhode Island, South Dakota, Virginia, Washington, and Wisconsin.[215] In each state, an agency is designated to be in charge of reviewing and/or approving franchise applications.[216] The individuals at the state agencies who review franchise applications are commonly referred to as the state administrators or state franchise examiners. Franchise applications are not subject to a merit review—rather, the review is one to assess accuracy and compliance with the required disclosure obligations.

---

215. In Wisconsin, registration is required only before a sale is made. Wis. Stat. § 135.02(3), Bus. Franchise Guide (CCH) ¶ 4490.02. While Oregon does not require registration, its statute does mandate disclosure and certain record keeping requirements. Ore. Rev. Stat. §§ 650.005 *et seq.*, Bus. Franchise Guide (CCH) ¶ 3370.

216. A list of the websites for the various state agencies and administrators is attached as exhibit 2-7.

In the four registration states commonly referred to as the "notice states"—Indiana, Michigan, South Dakota, and Wisconsin[217]—registration is relatively simple. These four states require franchisors to submit an annual notice form and filing fee. Generally, the state administrators in the notice states do not review the contents of the FDD or comment on the substance of the FDD and exhibits; however, in some circumstances, the state administrators may conduct a review and require the franchisor to alter or amend the FDD. While a state administrator may issue a letter with an effective date, the filings in these states are typically deemed effective upon receipt.

The 10 other registration states—California, Hawaii, Illinois, Maryland, Minnesota, New York, North Dakota, Rhode Island, Virginia, and Washington[218]—require the franchisor to file various documents with a state agency, pay a filing fee, and obtain approval of the documents prior to conducting franchise sales activity in the state.

In Hawaii, the registration is effective seven days after filing of all required forms, documents, and the filing fee; however, the franchise examiners do have the right to review the franchise application and issue a stop order at any time. The state administrators in the other nine states will review the FDD, and if the state administrator determines that the FDD does not comply with the state's disclosure requirements, the state administrator will issue a deficiency or comment letter detailing the additional or modified information that must be included in the FDD before the state administrator will approve the FDD for use in the state. Comments are likely to relate to the financial condition of the franchisor, the franchisor's compliance with the disclosure requirements, and provisions in the agreements that are prohibited by the state's franchise relationship laws. If a state administrator issues comments, the franchisor must respond to each of the state administrator's comments and provide a redlined and a clean copy of the FDD. The redlined copy must show all of the changes between the original FDD filed with the state and the updated FDD submitted in response to the comment letter. Once the state administrator is satisfied that the FDD complies with the state's disclosure requirements, the state administrator will approve the FDD for use in the applicable state and issue an effective date. Particular attention should be paid to the time frame provided in the comment letter for responding because failure to submit a timely response will result in abandonment of the franchise application.

With a few exceptions, the registration states accept the uniform application forms included in the NASAA Guidelines. An application for registration consists of the FDD containing the applicable state-specific disclosures and the registration fee, together with the forms listed here:[219]

- The application or "facing" page, which identifies the nature of the application (i.e., initial registration, renewal, annual report, or amendment) and

217. *See* Bus. Franchise Guide (CCH) ¶¶ 5140.012 (Ind.), 5220 (Mich.), 5410.01 (S.D.), 5490 (Wis.).

218. *See* Bus. Franchise Guide (CCH) ¶¶ 5050 (Cal.), 5110 (Haw.), 5130 (Ill.), 5200 (Md.), 5230 (Minn.), 5320 (N.Y.), 5340 (N.D.), 5390 (R.I.), 5460 (Va.), 5470 (Wash.).

219. NASAA Guidelines, *supra* note 61.

sets forth basic information about the franchisor and the contact person for the application.

- The verification of application, which is executed by an authorized representative of the franchisor and verifies that the contents of the application (including the FDD) are true and correct.
- The consent to service of process, which is executed by a representative of the franchisor and designates the appropriate state officer as the franchisor's agent for service of legal or other documents. Typically, this form designates the Securities Commissioner, Attorney General, or Secretary of State for service of process. There is a uniform consent to service of process that is generally accepted by all of the registration states.
- The franchisor's costs and sources of funds form, which is required by several, but not all, registration states. This form requires the franchisor to estimate the cost of providing preopening support to the franchisee and the sources of those funds but excludes fixed costs such as salaries or rent.
- The franchise seller form, which provides general information about each franchise seller. Ten of the registration states (California, Hawaii, Illinois, Indiana, Maryland, Minnesota, New York, North Dakota, Rhode Island, and Washington) require franchisors to file this form to register their franchise sellers with the state. If the franchise seller is an outside sales broker rather than an employee of the franchisor, two states (New York and Washington) require the filing of more detailed information by the franchisor. In addition, these states require the broker to make a filing with the state prior to engaging in franchise sales activities in the state.
- A form of auditor's consent, which must be executed by the auditor who prepared the franchisor's financial statements included in Item 21 and which states that the auditor permits the disclosure and distribution of its financial report in the FDD. The majority of the registration states (California, Hawaii, Illinois, Maryland, Minnesota, New York, North Dakota, Rhode Island, Virginia, and Washington) require franchisors to obtain consent from the franchisor's auditors to include the financial statements in the FDD filed with the state. The auditor's consent must be on the auditor's letterhead and manually signed. The franchisor is permitted to file copies of the consent with each state. In connection with issuing this consent, some auditors undertake a detailed review of the FDD and its exhibits and may require the franchisor to make certain changes to the FDD. As a best practices point, franchisors should ensure that they have built in sufficient time for their auditors to undertake this review.

Certain states also require other forms to be filed. For example, California requires the franchisor to submit a "Customer Authorization of Disclosure of Financial Records," which permits California to examine the franchisor's financial records,[220] and Maryland requires the franchisor to submit quarterly sales reports to maintain its registration.[221]

220. Bus. Franchise Guide (CCH) ¶ 3050.30(b).
221. Bus. Franchise Guide (CCH) ¶ 5200.14.

(e) Capitalization Requirements

Under franchise statutes in registration states, state franchise administrators have the authority to and often do scrutinize the capitalization of franchisors.[222] The state franchise administrators can condition approval of a franchise registration on, among other things, their determination that the franchisor's current financial condition demonstrates that the franchisor has adequate financial resources to provide the stated pre-opening support to new franchisees. Despite the fact that this can be a significant hurdle for franchisors, there is no comprehensive explanation of the criteria used by the state franchise administrators to assess whether a franchisor is adequately capitalized.

State franchise administrators have advised franchise practitioners that they generally use one of the following three measures to determine if the franchisor is adequately capitalized: (1) positive net worth, (2) the ratio of current assets to current liabilities that is at least 1:1, or (3) an operating profit during the prior year. Administrators usually review the information included in the franchisor's most recent audited financial statements but also may, in some instances, review more recent unaudited statements included in the FDD and other information provided by the franchisor. The state franchise administrators in Washington often impose financial assurances on franchisors who begin franchising irrespective of the financial condition.

If a franchisor is asked to provide financial assurances, the options may include impound, escrow, fee deferral, capital infusion, guarantee, or surety bond.[223] The available options for any state may be limited by state-specific statutes, regulations, or even the practices and policies of the state franchise administrators. For each request, the best course of action may be to contact the state franchise administrator who requested the financial assurance to review the possible options that examiner will permit the franchisor to use.

The state administrator will require the franchisor to modify the FDD and agreements (usually, by way of the state-specific addenda) to reflect the financial assurance option selected. In addition, the state administrator may require the franchisor to insert a risk factor on the state cover sheet about the franchisor's financial condition. The franchisor should review the state requirements carefully to determine what, if any, state specific requirements are imposed for the financial assurance selected. For impound, escrow, or deferral options, the franchisor should assess which fees are subject to the condition. This analysis will be particularly important for development fees and franchisee purchases from the franchisor or its affiliates. The state franchise administrator who imposes the condition may request, in connection with the next state filing, that the franchisor

---

222. *See, e.g.*, Cal. Corp. Code §§ 31111, 31113; Minn. Stat. Ann. § 80C.05; Va. Code Ann. § 13.1-561(B); Wash. Rev. Code Ann. § 19.100.050; N.D. Cent. Code Ann. § 51-19-07 (2); 815 Ill. Comp. Stat. Ann. 705/15; Ind. Code Ann. § 23-2-2.5-12; N.Y. Gen. Bus. Law § 685; Md. Code Ann., Bus. Reg. § 14-217; Haw. Rev. Stat. Ann. § 482E-8(6); *see also* Dale E. Cantone, Susan Grueneberg, Patty Hagner, & Theresa Leets, Regulatory Update 12–13 (ABA Forum on Franchising Oct. 2019).

223. *See, e.g.*, Cal. Code Regs. tit. 10 § 310.113.

provide evidence of how fees were dealt with while the financial assurance condition is in place. Carefully maintained records of the fees subject to financial assurances will make responding to such requests less onerous.

The simplest financial assurance option, from a cost and administration standpoint, may be to defer payment of the initial fees until each franchised outlet is open for business. For this option, the franchise agreement is signed with an addendum deferring the initial franchise fee until opening. The franchisee then proceeds with developing and opening the business, and the initial fees are due to the franchisor upon opening. The franchisor faces the risk, however, that when the franchised outlet is ready to open for business, the franchisee may no longer have sufficient funds to pay the initial fees. The franchisor could, at that point, refuse to approve the opening until payment of the initial fees, but refusal to permit an opening that would deliver a revenue stream to the franchisee could cause further delays in payment of deferred fees or preclude payment altogether.

The escrow and impound financial assurance options are a bit more complicated but diminish the risk that the franchisor does not get paid the fees at opening for business. Under these options, when a franchise agreement is signed, the franchisee (or the franchisor on behalf of the franchisee) pays the initial fees to an escrow or impound agent who holds the fees until the franchised outlet opens for business. Then, upon opening, the fees are dispersed from the escrow or impound agent directly to the franchisor. This option sounds simple, but escrow and impound arrangements may be subject to a number of restrictions and requirements under the state statutes that can complicate the process. The agent who holds the account may need to be a national bank (or similar financial institution) and that agent may need to be located in the registration state that requested the financial assurance. In some instances, the state statutes or state procedures may prescribe forms of escrow or impound agreements that must be used for the accounts, which the agent will need to review and sign. The state statutes and regulations may also designate specific processes for the deposit and release of funds from the escrow or impound, which can include submitting various proofs to the state franchise administrator and requesting approval for release of the initial fees.[224]

Most franchise registration statutes also permit the franchisor to post a surety bond. The amount of the bond is usually determined by multiplying the number of outlets that the franchisor expects to open in the particular state in the coming year (reported in Table 5 of Item 20) by the total initial fees that are due for each outlet (disclosed in Item 5). The franchisor's existing insurance provider may be the best place to start when considering the surety bond option. With this financial assurance option, the franchisor and franchisee sign the franchise agreement and the franchisee pays the fees in the normal course. The franchisor has access to the initial fees as soon as those amounts are paid by the franchisee. If this

224. *See, e.g.*, Ill. Admin. Code tit. 14, § 200.503; Md. Code Regs. 02.02.08.08(E); N.Y. Comp. Codes R. & Regs. tit. 13, § 200.6; Bus. Franchise Guide (CCH) ¶ 5340.60; and 21 Va. Admin. Code § 5-110-65(E).

option is selected, for each registration period, the franchisor will need a separate surety bond for each state that imposes this condition, and that bond must remain in place until the outlets disclosed for that year in the FDD have been opened. This means that the surety bond may need to be renewed in subsequent years to cover that prior registration year. If the financial assurance is imposed for subsequent registration periods, the franchisor would need a bond for those periods in addition to renewing the bond for the prior year. The resulting accumulation of bonds can be cost prohibitive.

For the capital infusion financial assurance option, there is no "set" amount of capital that must be added that, without a doubt, will satisfy state franchise administrators. State franchise administrators tend to look at the amount of capital necessary to give the franchisor a positive net worth, plus sufficient excess to demonstrate that the franchisor has resources to support the projected openings for the respective state. Here again, the state franchise administrator may look to the number of projected openings for the specific state (Item 20, Table 5) multiplied by the initial fees for each outlet or the cost to the franchisor to open each outlet. If there are no projected franchised outlets listed in the particular state, the examiner often assumes that one outlet will be opened when assessing the adequacy of a capital infusion. The state franchise administrators may require documentation that the infusion was lawful and that it will not be repaid at will or reversed after the state approval is issued. Some states require unaudited "verified" financial statements reflecting the infusion and a bank statement showing the infusion deposit. Finally, the states may request a signed undertaking from the franchisor stating, among other things, that the capital will remain in the franchisor's account until the expiration of the current registration period.

A final financial assurance option is to have an affiliate guarantee the franchisor's performance under the franchise agreements. If selecting this option, the franchisor must submit the affiliate's audited financials and consent of accountant, and include a copy of the guarantee in the FDD, as required under the FTC Rule.[225] In most instances, additional documents are required, including (1) a resolution of the board of directors of the affiliate authorizing the guarantee, (2) a certificate by the affiliate's secretary for the resolution, (3) a consent to service of process, and (4) corporate acknowledgment by the affiliate. The affiliate's guarantee must remain in place during the entire term of any franchise agreements signed and cannot be revoked even if the franchisor's financial condition improves. With this option, the franchisor has access to the initial fees as soon as they are paid by the franchisee.

(f) Use of a Multistate FDD or Roll-Up FDD

Some states require franchisors to make substantive changes to the FDD and agreements as a matter of state law or public policy. Generally speaking, these states permit the required disclosures to be included in addenda to the FDD and

225. *See* NASAA Guidelines, *supra* note 61, at Form E–Guarantee of Performance.

agreements. Practitioners may differ on the manner in which state-specific disclosures are prepared for registration and delivery to prospective franchisees. Most franchise practitioners use a multistate or "roll-up" FDD in which all of the state-specific disclosures are included in separate state-specific addenda to the FDD. A franchisor utilizing this approach will use the same FDD in all registration and nonregistration states, thereby ensuring that all prospects receive the same disclosures. Franchisees in states that require changes to the agreements are required to sign the state-specific addenda along with the agreements. While it is no longer common practice, some franchise practitioners prepare and use a separate FDD for each registration state containing state-specific cover sheets, receipt pages, and substantive changes to the body of the FDD.

To avoid delays in the state franchise application approval process, it is important to review relevant state franchise registration and disclosure requirements, as well as state relationship laws, before filing to ensure that the FDD, the franchise agreements, and all other exhibits comply with state-specific requirements. Examples of some state-required changes to FDDs and agreements are attached as exhibit 2-2.

FDDs should be labeled carefully (either in the footers or on cover pages) to ensure that the franchisor and its personnel are using the correct version of the FDD. For example, the date of the FDD and, if state-specific FDDs are used, the state where the FDD can be used should be clearly identified.

(g) Filing of Franchise Sales Advertising

In addition, six states (California, Maryland, Minnesota, New York, North Dakota, and Washington) require that a franchisor file all franchise sales advertising with the state prior to use in that state. Advertising filed with these states is generally deemed approved unless the state objects within a specified time period. The definitions of "advertising" in these states are very broad and include any published communication directed to a prospective franchisee that discusses the sale of a franchise.[226] These definitions encompass electronic advertising targeting prospects in these states, such as e-mail blasts or drip campaigns, or other electronic communications with links to videos or other sales material. The prudent course is to file any form materials that are sent to prospective franchisees. Most states exempt Internet advertising from their franchise advertising filing requirements.[227] In addition, the states generally exempt "national" advertising in publications whose circulation is two-thirds or more outside the state from the filing

226. *See, e.g.*, Cal. Corp. Code § 31003, Bus. Franchise Guide (CCH) ¶ 3050.04; Md. Code Ann., Bus. Reg. § 14-201(b), Bus. Franchise Guide (CCH) ¶ 3200.01; N.Y. Gen. Bus. Law § 681(1), Bus. Franchise Guide (CCH) ¶ 3320.02; N.D. Cent. Code § 51-19-02(1), Bus. Franchise Guide (CCH) ¶ 3340.02; Wash. Rev. Code § 19.100.010(1), Bus. Franchise Guide (CCH) ¶ 3470.01.

227. *See, e.g.*, Cal. Admin. Code § 310.156.3, Bus. Franchise Guide (CCH) ¶ 5050.355.

requirements.[228] A summary of advertising filing requirements is attached as exhibit 2-3.

Most of these states also restrict the types of claims that franchisors can make in franchise advertisements. These restrictions include prohibitions on referring to the franchise as a safe investment or implying that state registration of the FDD constitutes state approval of the franchise and a requirement that, when a public figure is used in franchisee advertising, the franchisor must disclose whether the public figure is being compensated. Other states, including Illinois, do not require filing of advertising but restrict particular claims in franchise advertisements.[229]

The franchisor should require that the franchisor's in-house legal department or outside counsel approve all advertising or printed promotional material concerning franchise sales prior to use. In addition, the franchisor should maintain a schedule documenting the filing of all franchise sales advertising and promotional materials with the appropriate state agencies and maintain records of such filings.

(h) Effective Dates, Annual Renewal, and Interim Updating

(i) Annual Renewal

Once the FDD is prepared, under the FTC Rule it can be used to sell franchises until 120 days after the end of the franchisor's fiscal year,[230] subject to any required updates relating to material changes. The expiration date for the FDD will vary among the registration states, but it is usually tied to either the anniversary of the registration date or the franchisor's fiscal year end.[231] Exhibit 2-4 contains guidelines concerning expiration dates and renewal filing deadlines, which are generally 15 to 30 days prior to the expiration date. The FTC Rule also requires that all information in the FDD be current as of the close of the franchisor's last fiscal year.

Prior to the expiration date, the franchisor should update the information in the FDD to be current as of the franchisor's fiscal year end. To update the information, the franchisor should follow the process outlined for gathering information to prepare the FDD. See section 2.4(c).

In the registration states, if the franchisor does not file the updated FDD (along with the required forms and fees) and, if necessary, obtain approval from the state administrator prior to the expiration date, the franchisor will go "dark"

---

228. *See* Cal. Corp. Code § 31013, Bus. Franchise Guide (CCH) ¶ 3050.15; Md. Code Ann., Bus. Reg. § 14-203(b)(2), Bus. Franchise Guide (CCH) ¶ 3200.03; N.Y. Gen. Bus. Law § 681(12), Bus. Franchise Guide (CCH) ¶ 3320.02; N.D. Cent. Code §51-19-02.14(b)(3), Bus. Franchise Guide (CCH) ¶ 3340.02; R.I. Gen. Laws § 19-28.1-4(e), Bus. Franchise Guide (CCH) ¶ 3390.04; S.D. Codified Laws § 37-5A-7.2, Bus. Franchise Guide (CCH) ¶ 3410.072; Wash. Rev. Code § 19.100.020(4), Bus. Franchise Guide (CCH) ¶ 3470.02.

229. Ill. Code R. 200.300–.304, Bus. Franchise Guide (CCH) ¶ 4130.

230. 16 C.F.R. § 436.7 (2007).

231. See exhibit 2-4 for a summary of how the expiration should be determined for each state.

in that state. This means that the franchisor cannot offer or sell franchises in that state until the franchisor has refiled the franchise application and, if necessary, obtained approval from the state. If the prior registration has expired, the franchisor may need to file the franchise application as an initial application, a reinstatement application, or some other variation.

One of the most frequent delays with the annual FDD renewal process is obtaining the audited financials along with the auditor's consent for inclusion of the financials in the FDD. A franchisor should begin this process early and be sure the auditors understand that if the FDD renewal is delayed, the franchise sales process must stop.

Once the FDD has been updated, there are a variety of rules to understand and follow concerning its use.

- Nonregistration states—The franchisor should cease using the prior FDD in all nonregistration states and begin using the updated FDD.
- Indiana, Michigan, South Dakota, and Wisconsin—The franchise registration will be effective upon the state administrator's receipt of the necessary forms, fee, and (except for Michigan) updated FDD, and the franchisor can immediately use the updated FDD in these states.
- Illinois—The franchise registration will be effective upon the state administrator's receipt of the necessary forms, fee, and updated FDD, and the franchisor can immediately use the updated FDD in Illinois. Illinois reserves the right to issue a comment letter on the filing. In that event, after the franchisor addresses the comments and obtains approval of the FDD, the franchisor must redisclose any prospects with the revised FDD as approved by Illinois and may be required to offer rescission to any franchisee who purchased a franchise after the annual registration was submitted and is an Illinois resident or intends to locate the franchise in the state.
- Hawaii—The updated FDD is effective seven days after receipt, unless Hawaii provides notice to the contrary.
- Maryland, Minnesota, North Dakota, Virginia, and Washington—Until each of these states approves the updated FDD, the franchisor cannot use the updated FDD in the state. However, the franchisor can continue to use the prior FDD in the state until the prior state registration expires, provided that there have not been any material changes to the information disclosed in the prior FDD. Once the updated FDD is approved, the franchisor should redisclose anyone in the franchise sales pipeline.
- California—If the franchisor has already provided disclosure to a California prospect under the prior FDD, the franchisor may close that deal until the earlier of the date that California approves the new FDD or the date the prior FDD expires. With respect to new prospects, the franchisor may "offer" to sell franchises under the new FDD but may not close a deal under the new FDD until California approves the new FDD. If the franchisor provides a copy of the new FDD to a California prospect prior to state approval of the FDD, the franchisor should enclose a cover letter that

states that (1) the new FDD has been filed in California but is not effective, (2) the information in the new FDD and exhibits has not been reviewed by the California commissioner, and (3) the franchisor will deliver to the prospective franchisee an effective new FDD and a redlined copy of the FDD demonstrating the changes required by California at least 14 days prior to the earlier of the date the franchisee signs a binding agreement or pays any consideration.[232]

- New York—If the franchisor has a prospect in New York, the franchisor may provide a copy of the new FDD that has been filed with New York to the prospect. If the franchisor closes the deal prior to the date that New York approves the filing and registers the new FDD, then the franchisor must hold the initial fees in a separate bank account until 10 business days after the prospect received the registered copy of the new FDD as approved by New York. The prospect can rescind the sale at any time prior to its receipt of the registered new FDD or during the 10-business-day period following its receipt of the registered new FDD.[233]

(ii) Interim Updating Requirements

The federal and state franchise regulations require the franchisor to update the FDD during the period that it is effective. The first step is to determine if there has been a change that requires the FDD to be modified. To do this, the franchisor must have in place periodic auditing, or other monitoring systems, of the information contained in the FDD. As a best practices point, questionnaire forms could be circulated to appropriate franchisor personnel for their review and signature confirming the accuracy of the information contained in the FDD, and follow-up interviews and other checks by members of the legal department in connection with these required updates should be conducted.

Under the FTC Rule, the FDD must be updated quarterly. Within a reasonable amount of time after the close of each fiscal quarter, the franchisor should collect any changes to the FDD and prepare an attachment to its FDD to reflect any material change to the information in the FDD. Although the FTC elected not to define "material change" in the amended FTC Rule, the Compliance Guide states that "[m]aterial changes include such events as the recent filing of a bankruptcy petition or the filing against the franchisor of a legal action that may have a negative effect on its financial condition."[234] In addition, although superseded by the amended FTC Rule, as a point of reference, the original FTC Rule defined "material change" as "any fact, circumstance, or set of conditions which has a substantial likelihood of influencing a reasonable franchisee or a reasonable prospective franchisee in the making of a significant decision relating to a named franchised business or which has any significant financial impact on a franchisee or

232. Cal. Corp. Code § 31107.
233. N.Y. Gen. Bus. Law § 200.3(h)(3), Bus. Franchise Guide (CCH) ¶ 5320.
234. Compliance Guide, *supra* note 31, at 126.

prospective franchisee."[235] If there have been no material changes, a quarterly update is not necessary. If there are quarterly updates, the franchisor must provide each prospective franchisee with the FDD plus all quarterly updates. If the material change relates to the financial performance representations in Item 19 of the FDD, a franchisor must notify prospective franchisees of the change immediately, even if it falls between quarterly updates.[236] A franchisor can provide this notice in any reasonable manner, including telephone and e-mail, but the franchisor should make sure to retain proof of having given it.

The state laws require the FDD to be updated or amended during the registration period if a material change occurs. What constitutes a "material change" varies from state to state, but a franchisor should consider a "material change" to be anything significant that might influence a prospective franchisee in making his or her investment decision.[237] As a practical matter, materiality must be determined on a case-by-case basis. Areas that may rise to the level of a material change are changes in key management personnel; mergers and acquisitions involving the franchisor or its affiliates; new material litigation or arbitration or significant developments in existing cases required to be disclosed in Item 3; changes to material terms of the franchise agreement, fees, or franchise program; changes in existing franchisees (including unilateral terminations by franchisees); and adverse changes in the company's financial condition. Some state franchise laws specifically set forth events that constitute a material change in that state. For example, Indiana, Hawaii, Maryland, and Minnesota require the franchisor to amend the FDD if a certain number of units close within a designated period.

If there has been a material change, the franchisor must cease all franchise sales activity in the registration states until the franchisor updates the FDD. In certain of the registration states, the amended FDD must be filed with and approved by the state prior to use. The time frame for completing the amendment varies from state to state—including requirements to amend the FDD "promptly," "as soon as reasonably possible," "upon the occurrence" of any material change, and "as soon as reasonably possible and in any case before the further sale of any franchise."[238]

---

235. 16 C.F.R. § 436.2(n) (1979), Bus. Franchise Guide (CCH) ¶ 6190.

236. 16 C.F.R. § 436.7(d) (2007).

237. *See, e.g.*, Ill. Admin. Code § 14A.135.353, Bus. Franchise Guide (CCH) ¶ 5,138.07; Minn. Rules 2860, 2400, Bus. Franchise Guide (CCH) ¶ 5,320.18; Va. Admin. Code § 5-110-10, Bus. Franchise Guide (CCH) ¶ 5,460.01.

238. *See, e.g.*, Bus. Franchise Guide (CCH) ¶¶ 3050.42, 3050.44 (Cal.) ("promptly" after a material change in the information contained in the registered application, by application to amend; application to amend must contain specified disclosure); 3110.03 (Haw.) (if any material change occurs in the information contained in the FDD, the FDD must be amended before further sales of the franchise are made); 3130.11 (Ill.) ("within 90 days of the occurrence" of any material change in the facts required to be disclosed; redisclosure required if material changes relate to or affect franchisor or the franchisee; amendment not required if changes merely reflect negotiated changes); 3140.13.1 (Ind.) ("not later than thirty (30) days after the occurrence of any material change in the information set forth in the person's disclosure statement . . . notify the commissioner of the change by filing an amended copy of the disclosure statement"); 3200.20 (Md.) ("promptly" after

California, Illinois, New York, Virginia, and Wisconsin allow the franchisor to continue offering franchises pending effectiveness of an amendment.

If prospective franchisees in the franchise sales pipeline were given an FDD that is subsequently amended after a material change, the franchisor should give the prospect the amended FDD and allow the prospect the required time to review the FDD prior to signing any agreements or paying any consideration.

2-5. State Law Applicability

(a) Jurisdictional Requirements

The applicability of most state franchise statutes is triggered by specific business activity that takes place within the state's borders or that involves the state's residents. While the jurisdictional scope of such laws varies, the following is a list of some activities that may trigger application of a particular state's franchise law:

- The offer to sell a franchise originates in the state;
- The offer to sell a franchise is directed by the franchisor to the state and is received at the place to which the offer was directed;
- The offer to buy a franchise is accepted in the state;
- The offer or sale of a franchise is made to a franchisee domiciled in the state, and the franchise is or will be operated in the state;
- The franchise will be operated in the state;
- The offer or sale of a franchise is made to a resident of the state;
- The offer of a franchise is to a person domiciled in the state; and
- The franchise contemplates or requires the franchisee to establish or maintain a place of business in the state.

The foregoing are general statements only. Exhibit 2-5 provides an overview of state franchise law jurisdictional requirements. All franchise sellers should be trained to ask relevant questions early in the franchise sales process in order to identify key jurisdictional elements. Alternatively, the franchisor may consider using a standard information sheet to be completed by prospective franchisees

---

a material change in the information contained in the registered application, by application to amend); 3220.19 (Mich.) ("promptly" after any change in the information contained in the notice as originally submitted or amended); 3230.07 (Minn.) (within 30 days after the occurrence of any material change in the information on file with the commissioner, by application to amend); 3320.04, N.Y. Gen. Bus. Law § 683.9(a) (N.Y.) ("promptly" after any material change, by application to amend); 3340.07, N.D. Cent. Code § 51-19-07.6(a) (N.D.) ("promptly" after any material change, by application to amend); 3390.11 (R.I.) ("promptly" after any material change, by application to amend); 3410.40 (S.D.) (within 30 days after the occurrence of any material change in the information on file, by application to amend); 3470.07(3) (Wash.) ("as soon as reasonably possible" after a material change in the condition of the franchisor or subfranchisor and after a material change in the information contained in the FDD and in any case, before the further sale of any franchise, by application to amend); 3490.13(1) (Wis.) (within 30 days after the happening of any material event affecting a registered franchise, by application to amend).

that systematically collects relevant information. If the information gathered suggests the state franchise laws apply, the franchise seller will need to ensure various state law requirements are met and determine the appropriate disclosure document to provide (see section 2.4(e)).

Specific questions to ask prospective franchisees in order to obtain pertinent jurisdictional information, may include

- Where will the franchised business be operated?
- Who will be the franchisee of record (individuals, corporation, or other entity form)?
- Where is the franchisee's residence, principal place of business, and/or domicile (including all principal interest holders)? For an entity, where was the entity formed?
- Where will the franchise seller communicate with the prospective franchisee or its principals?
- Where is the prospective franchisee when communicating with the franchise seller?

If the answer to any of these questions involves a franchise registration and/or disclosure state, the franchise seller must consult with the franchisor's counsel or internal compliance officer to determine whether an offer or sale can be made.[239]

The franchisor should provide all franchise sellers with a summary of states in which the franchisor is authorized to sell franchises and the dates of expiration of effectiveness, as well as a list of those states, if any, in which offer and sales activity may not be conducted. When changes to the registration report occur, the updated list should be disseminated immediately. The report, the information included, and its importance from a franchise sales law compliance standpoint should be explained carefully to all franchisor personnel who will have contact with prospective franchisees.

An important concept in franchise sales regulation is the "offer" of a franchise. Applicability of virtually every state's franchise law is triggered by sales activity constituting an offer, as that term is defined by each state's franchise law. Central to this analysis is the fact that most states' franchise laws will apply to an offer made to or from, or accepted in, a state, even though the prospective franchisee is domiciled in another state and the business may be operated in another state. State laws generally define the offer of a franchise to include "every attempt to offer or dispose of, or solicitation of an offer to buy, a franchise or interest in a franchise for value."[240] This broad definition of offer will generally include

- Oral or written contact with a prospective franchisee who is physically in the state;

239. Franchise sellers should also determine whether a business opportunity law is involved. These states may require the franchisor to file or otherwise be exempt or excluded from registration before the offer or sale of a franchise within their jurisdiction.

240. Bus. Franchise Guide (CCH) ¶¶ 3340.01(14), 3130.03(c)(iii)(12).

- Telephone communication originating from or received in the state;
- Newspaper, magazine, radio, or television advertising offering a franchise; however, if two-thirds of the circulation is outside the state, then most states will exempt that advertisement from the definition of offer;[241] and
- Promotional brochures and other franchise sales literature originating from or received in the state.

In contrast, the "sale" of a franchise generally refers to the execution of a franchise agreement or other binding contract (such as a development agreement, option agreement, or letter of intent), or the payment of consideration by the prospective franchisee to purchase franchise rights.[242] These events are particularly important as they may dictate when the franchisor must provide disclosure.

A franchisor must handle all communications regarding the franchise offering with great care. Any telephonic or written communication detailing the franchise program is likely to constitute an offer of a franchise under state law, thus requiring registration prior to such communication. So, if the franchisor receives an inquiry from a prospective franchisee in or relating to a registration state where the franchisor is not yet registered, unless an exemption or exclusion is satisfied (see section 2-6), the franchisor's representatives should not discuss the franchise program in detail or send any franchise sales information or data to that person. The franchisor should advise the person inquiring that the franchisor has not yet registered to sell franchises within the state in question and that the person's name and telephone number are being retained in the franchisor's files until such time as the franchise may be offered lawfully in that state. The communication to the person inquiring should be in writing. Once the franchise offering is registered with a state, the franchisor must ensure that the franchise sales materials do not conflict in any way with the information in that state's registered FDD. Franchise sellers should be familiar with the FDD and any state-specific addenda to the FDD.

Timely delivery of the FDD to the prospect is also crucial for compliance with federal and state franchise laws (see discussion of delivery of FDD in section 2-5(c)). Improper presale communication and disclosure can result in sales that are subject to challenge (see section 2-13).

(b) Multistate Transactions

A franchisor may face situations where an entity or individual residing in one state desires to purchase a franchise that will be operated in another state. To complicate matters further, the franchisor may have made the offer to grant that franchise in yet a third state. When relevant states are registration states and the

241. 815 Ill. Comp. Stat. Ann. 705/3(19); Ind. Code Ann. § 23-2-2.5-2(b); Mich. Comp. Laws Ann. § 445.1504(4); N.Y. Gen. Bus. Law § 681(12)(c); N.D. Cent. Code Ann. § 51-19-02(14)(b)(3); 19 R.I. Gen. Laws Ann. § 19-28.1-4(e); S.D. Codified Laws § 37-5B-3; Wash. Rev. Code Ann. § 19.100.020(4); Cal. Corp. Code § 31013(c); and Md. Code Ann., Bus. Reg. § 14-203(b)(2).

242. Bus. Franchise Guide (CCH) ¶¶ 3140.01(d), 3130.03(c)(iii)(9).

jurisdictional requirements are satisfied, the offer of a franchise can legally be made only by delivering an FDD that has been properly registered with all relevant states. For example, the franchisor may be approached by representatives of an Indiana-based corporation interested in operating a franchise in Virginia, and prospect's representatives met with the franchise seller at a trade show or convention in Maryland. All three of these states potentially have some interest in the transaction: Maryland as the site of the offer, Indiana as the residence of the prospective franchisee, and Virginia as the location for the franchise.

Each franchise sale that involves touch points in multiple states requires analysis and review of the circumstances and the requirements of the state statutes. Some state laws include exemptions (for example, out-of-state sales are exempt in California and Maryland[243]) that may alleviate, to some degree, the burden of complying with multiple state franchise sales laws. As described earlier in section 2-4(f), franchisors often, where possible, use a multistate FDD (i.e., the disclosures required by the various states are included in one FDD with state-specific addenda included as an exhibit to the FDD). When agreements are drafted, the franchisor must assess which, if any, state-specific addenda to the agreement must be signed. If the jurisdictional requirements are satisfied for various states, the franchisor may need to include, for signature, the state-specific agreement addenda for multiple states.

(c) Delivery of FDD

Unless a franchisor is exempt or excluded from the disclosure requirements, the franchisor must comply with the applicable requirements of the FTC Rule and registration states for the delivery of the FDD to prospective franchisees (for further discussion of exemptions, see section 2-6). Under the FTC Rule, the FDD must be provided 14 calendar days prior to the earlier of (1) execution by the prospective franchisee of any franchise or other agreement (such as a development agreement or option agreement) that imposes a binding, legal obligation on the prospective franchisee; or (2) the payment of any consideration for a franchise by the prospective franchisee.[244] The franchisee can request an FDD at any time during the franchise sales process and, if the request is reasonable, the franchisor must provide the FDD.[245] To avoid confusion, the Statement of Basis and Purpose provides that the 14-day period commences on the day after the FDD is delivered to the prospective franchisee, and signing can take place once the full 14 days have elapsed (or 15 calendar days after the prospective franchisee's receipt of the FDD).[246] Despite persuasive arguments from excited prospective buyers, the 14-day period cannot be waived.

---

243. Cal. Corp. Code § 31105; Md. Code Ann., Bus. Reg. § 02.02.08.10.B.

244. 16 C.F.R. § 436.2.

245. 16 C.F.R. § 436.9(e). *See also* Bus. Franchise Guide (CCH) ¶ 6090 (14) and (24) for more information about providing FDD upon reasonable request.

246. Bus. Franchise Guide (CCH) ¶ 6061.

Because this delivery period was modified by the 2007 changes to the FTC Rule, some registration states may have delivery requirements for the FDD that are not consistent with the FTC Rule. Where the state law delivery requirement is more protective (i.e., provides the prospect with more time to review the FDD), franchisors must comply with the state delivery requirements. The following states require the franchisor to deliver the FDD earlier than the FTC Rule:

State	Delivery Requirement
Iowa	Earlier of 14 days or first personal meeting[247]
Michigan	10 business days[248]
New York	Earlier of 10 business days or first personal meeting[249]

Under the "first personal meeting" trigger in New York and Iowa, the need to disclose arises when there is an actual face-to-face, in-person meeting between a prospective franchisee and a franchise seller to discuss the sale or possible sale of a franchise.[250] Even when there is an actual face-to-face meeting, a franchisor will not run afoul of this delivery requirement if the franchisor makes it clear, at that time, that the franchisor is not in a position to discuss the sale of a franchise, and the franchisor does not engage in a detailed discussion of the franchise. To document compliance with this requirement, the franchisor should maintain records of the occurrence of any "first personal meetings" along with a summary of the discussions that took place.

Compliance with the delivery requirement for the FDD must be documented by use of a franchisee-executed receipt (Item 23 of the FDD), as well as the franchisor's maintenance of compliance records. In addition to documenting compliance with the delivery requirement, the franchisor should confirm that no misrepresentations or unauthorized financial performance representations were made to the prospect during the franchise sales process. The franchisor may consider use of a compliance questionnaire (see exhibit 2-6)[251] or videotaped or audiotaped closing procedures to further memorialize compliance with pertinent legal requirements. The franchisor should note, however, that, aside from the

247. Iowa is not a registration state, but it has a business opportunity law; to qualify for the exemption from the business opportunity law, a franchisor must satisfy these timing requirements for delivery of the disclosure document. Iowa Code Ann. § 551A.4(1)(b).

248. Mich. Comp. Laws Ann. § 445.1508.

249. N.Y. Gen. Bus. Law § 683(8).

250. *Id. and* Iowa Code Ann. § 551A.4(1)(b).

251. While many franchisors require a compliance questionnaire, note that franchise regulators in at least two registration states—California and Maryland—have recently begun to require franchisors to narrow the scope of the questionnaire and/or include a statement in the questionnaire to declare that nothing contained therein can be construed as a prospective franchisee's assent to a release, estoppel, or waiver of liability under the state's franchise laws.

notice of violation process in California,[252] the federal and state statutes do not include a process for curing a disclosure violation.[253]

(d) Delivery Methods—Electronic Disclosure

The franchisor may deliver the FDD to prospective franchisees for disclosure on paper or electronically. The paper format delivery is simple—the franchisor delivers the entire FDD as one complete hard copy document with all exhibits and receipt pages attached as the last two pages. If the franchisor chooses to disclose the FDD by electronic delivery (i.e., over the Internet, by e-mail, via DocuSign, or by other electronic means), the FDD must be delivered as a single, integrated document or file without any extraneous content beyond what is required or permitted by law; cannot not include any links to or from external documents or content; must be delivered in a form that enables the recipient to store, retrieve, and print the disclosure document; and must conform in content and format to the requirements of law.[254]The franchisor should use a method of delivery that permits the franchisor to prove that it delivered the disclosure document electronically in compliance with applicable laws and should maintain a record of the electronic delivery of the FDD.[255]

Before furnishing an electronic FDD, the franchisor must advise the prospect of the format in which the FDD is available, any prerequisites for obtaining the FDD in that format, and any conditions necessary for reviewing the FDD (such as downloading Adobe Reader to view a PDF document). If the FDD will be e-mailed, the franchisor should send an advance e-mail alerting the prospect that the franchisor will send the FDD in a separate e-mail and note the file format of the FDD. The advance e-mail message might look like this:

> We will send you the FDD as an attachment to a separate e-mail. Your e-mail account must be able to accept attachments larger than __ MB. If you do not have a high-speed Internet connection, it could take a long time to receive the FDD. You will also need a copy of Adobe Reader, which you may already have on your computer, or which you can download for free at www.adobe.com.

In order to have a record that the prospect received the e-mail, the franchisor can set up an auto-notification. Then, after the FDD is delivered, the franchisor must obtain a "signed" receipt for the FDD. If the franchisor sends the FDD electronically, it can include a link from Item 23 in the FDD to a receipt-only web page. The web page must be identical to the printed Item 23 receipt page and should provide fill-in boxes to identify the person submitting the e-receipt. No other links

---

252. Cal. Corp. Code § 31303 and Cal. Code Regs. tit. 10, § 310.303.

253. *But see* Cal. Corp. Code § 31303, Bus. Franchise Guide (CCH) ¶ 3050.64 (provides for cure of certain violations by providing a notice to the prospect that has been preapproved by the state).

254. 16 C.F.R. § 436.6 and Bus. Franchise Guide (CCH) ¶ 6090 (15).

255. Bus. Franchise Guide (CCH) ¶ 5705.

or materials can be accessible from the receipt-only web page (even a link to the franchisor's home page). Alternatively, the prospect can open the electronic FDD, print out the last two pages, fill in name of the franchisee (whether an individual or entity), sign and date the receipt, and return one copy to the franchisor.[256]

(e) Who Must Receive Disclosure?

The FDD must be provided to the "prospective franchisee." The FTC Rule defines a "prospective franchisee" as "any person (including any agent, representative, or employee) who approaches or is approached by a franchise seller to discuss the possible establishment of a franchise relationship."[257] The FTC Rule permits a franchisor to fulfill its disclosure obligation by furnishing the FDD to a franchisee's representative (such as an attorney, accountant, or other advisor) in lieu of providing disclosure to the actual prospective franchisee.

Where state franchise sales laws lack the broadly inclusive language of the FTC Rule and imply a stricter delivery requirement, the franchisor must provide the FDD to the actual prospective franchisees and not a representative.[258] To comply with these requirements, the franchisor must identify the actual prospective franchisee and provide disclosure to that individual or entity. If an individual will operate the franchise as a sole proprietor, then disclosure to the individual will satisfy the disclosure requirement. The disclosure requirement gets a bit tricky when the prospective franchisee is an entity. If the prospective franchisee is a general partnership, the best practice would be to provide the FDD to all partners. In the case of a limited partnership, disclosure to the general partner will almost always suffice. Finally, disclosure to a prospective "entity" franchisee (such as a corporation, limited liability company, or some other type of formal legal entity) must be made to an officer authorized and possessing the capacity to receive disclosure on behalf of the entity. It is recommended that disclosure is also made to (and signed receipt obtained from) each individual who will be a guarantor of the franchisee entity's obligations.

(f) Delivery of Franchise Agreements

The FTC Rule requires that the franchisor deliver the franchise agreement to the prospective franchisee along with the FDD prior to signing so that the prospective franchisee can review and understand all material terms and conditions.[259] If no

256. *Id.*

257. 16 C.F.R. § 436.1(r).

258. *Compare, e.g.*, S.D. Codified Laws § 37-5B-1(24) *and* Wash. Rev. Code. § 19.100.010 (adopting the Amended FTC Rule's broad definition of "prospective franchisee") *with* Cal. Corp. Code §§ 31000 *et seq. and* Mich. Comp. Laws § 445.1502 (omitting "prospective franchisee" from Franchise Investment Law definitions).

259. 16 C.F.R. § 436.2(b). The FTC Rule forms the baseline expectation for franchise transactions nationwide, including in states that have not enacted franchise statutes of their own and/or do not require registration.

substantive changes are made to the form of franchise agreement appearing in the FDD and the franchise agreement that the franchisee will sign, there is no additional disclosure obligation with respect to the execution copies of the agreement. But, under the FTC Rule,[260] if the franchisor has unilaterally and materially modified the terms of the franchise agreement attached to the FDD, then the franchisor is required to furnish "execution ready" copies of that agreement to the franchisee seven full calendar days prior to the franchisee's execution of the agreement.[261]

This delivery requirement will not be triggered by (1) changes to the standard franchise agreement that are made by the franchisor as a result of negotiations of the agreement with the prospective franchisee or (2) completion of non-substantive "fill-in-the-blank" provisions such as the date of the agreement and name and address of the franchisee.[262] In the Statement of Basis and Purpose, the FTC noted that the clause "fill-in-the-blank provisions" will be interpreted narrowly. Specifically, the FTC noted that "[t]o the extent that substantive contractual details—such as geographic area of a protected territory and interest rates—are not disclosed in the basic disclosure document or its attachments, then the completed document must be disclosed seven calendar days before signing."[263] Substantive terms of a franchise arrangement—such as fees, interest rate, and the parameters of a protected territory—must be disclosed in the agreement attached to the basic disclosure document, or the franchisor must afford the prospect seven days to review the terms before signing or paying a fee.

2-6. Exemptions and Exclusions from Franchise Laws

The FTC Rule and most of the state franchise laws provide exemptions or exclusions from the registration and/or disclosure requirements that may be available to qualifying transactions, franchisors, or franchisees. While the availability, nature, and terms of such exemptions and exclusions vary from jurisdiction to jurisdiction, they typically fall into three broad categories: (1) exemptions or exclusions based upon the nature of the offeror, (2) exemptions or exclusions based upon the nature of the offeree, and (3) exemptions or exclusions based upon the nature of the offer or transaction. Some exemptions and exclusions that may be available are based upon criteria such as the franchisor's net worth and

---

260. Under the original FTC Rule, franchisors were required to deliver execution-ready copies of the franchise agreements to the prospective franchisee five business days prior to the franchisee's execution of the franchise agreement.

261. States enact laws and regulations that purport to modify franchisors' temporal obligations under the FTC Rule: while state rules that could otherwise be interpreted as *reducing* the requirement (*see, e.g.*, Va. Code Ann. § 13.1-565) are preempted by the federal regulation, state rules that *increase* franchisors' disclosure obligation are enforceable in those states.

262. 16 C.F.R. § 436.2.(b) and Bus. Franchise Guide (CCH) ¶ 6061.

263. 72 Fed. Reg. 15,471 n.277 (Mar. 30, 2007).

experience, the existing franchise relationship, the prospect's net worth and experience, and the amount of the investment.

The laws vary in their treatment of exemptions and exclusions, both as to type of exemptions or exclusions granted and the specific qualifications for obtaining the exemption or exclusion. Determining whether the criteria for an exemption or exclusion applies in a particular jurisdiction depends upon the applicable law and the specific procedural prerequisites. It is the role of franchise counsel to review the company's franchise program and applicable laws and then to provide the franchisor with a summary of the statutory exemptions and exclusions from franchise laws that may be applicable to the franchise program.

By way of example, California, Illinois, Indiana, Maryland, New York, North Dakota, Rhode Island, Virginia, and Washington have exemptions based on the net worth and/or experience of the franchisor.[264] If a franchisor satisfies the criteria for this exemption, in order to rely on this exemption, the state statutes may require the franchisor to file certain forms and pay a required fee annually. While the state franchise administrators may review the FDD and financial statements to verify that the franchisor satisfies the exemption criteria, the examiners do not comment on the contents of the FDD. Since the review and comment period for a registration filing may take months to complete and require multiple rounds of changes to the FDD and its exhibits, applying for the exemption from registration is likely to save the franchisor a significant amount of time and money in this process. Franchisors who qualify for this exemption must still provide presale disclosures to prospective franchisees; however, in some states, these disclosures differ from those required of registered franchises.[265]

To qualify for an exemption based on net worth and/or experience, the franchisor (or the franchisor's parent)[266] must meet certain minimum requirements for each. The net worth requirement varies from state to state—$5 million (California, Illinois, Indiana, New York, and Washington),[267] $10 million (Maryland, North Dakota, and Rhode Island),[268] and $15 million (Virginia).[269] In California, Illinois, Indiana, Maryland, New York, North Dakota, Virginia, and Washington, the franchisor must have a minimum net worth of $1 million to rely on its

264. Cal. Corp. Code § 31101; Ill. Admin. Code tit. 14 § 200.202(e); Ind. Code § 23-2-2.5-3(a)–(b); Md. Code Regs. § 02.08.10(d); N.Y. Gen. Bus. Law § 684(2); N.D. Cent. Code § 51-19-04(1); R.I. Gen. Laws § 19-28.1-6(a); Wash. Rev. Code § 19.100.030(4)(b); 21 Va. Admin. Code § 5-110-75.

265. *See, e.g.,* Cal. Corp. Code § 31101; Ind. Code § 23-2-2.5-3(c); NY Gen. Bus. Law § 684(2)(c).

266. A parent is generally defined as a company that owns at least 80 percent of the franchisor. *See, e.g.,* Cal. Corp. Code § 31101(b).

267. Cal. Corp. Code § 31101; 815 Ill. Comp. Stat. Ann. 705/8(a)(2); Ind. Code Ann. § 23-2-2.5-3(a); N.Y. Gen. Bus. Law § 684(2)(a); and Wash. Rev. Code Ann. § 19.100.030(4)(b)(i)(A). New York also has a super-large franchisor exemption, which requires the franchisor to have a minimum net worth of $15 million. N.Y. Gen. Bus. Law § 684(3)(a).

268. Md. Code Regs. 02.02.08.10(D); N.D. Cent. Code Ann. § 51-19-04(1)(a); and 19 R.I. Gen. Laws Ann. § 19-28.1-6(1)(i).

269. 21 Va. Admin. Code § 5-110-75(4).

parent's financial statements.[270] If the franchisor relies upon its parent's audited financials in Maryland, Rhode Island, and Virginia,[271] the parent must unconditionally guarantee the franchisor's obligations to franchisees. With the exception of New York, all states include an experience prong for this exemption. Specifically, franchisors must have a minimum number of years of franchising, minimum number of franchisees, or minimum operational experience. The experience requirement varies from state to state. If a franchisor relies on its parent's experience, changes in the parent's ownership or organization may result in loss of the exemption.

The filings and disclosure required of a franchisor in any registration state in which the franchisor qualifies for an exemption vary depending on the particular state and type of exemption claimed. In some states, an annual filing of a notice claiming the exemption is required for certain types of exemptions and not others. In other states, the actual exempt disclosure document to be used in the state must be filed (although it is not substantively reviewed as in the registration process). Alternatively, some exemptions do not require a filing (for example, the very high net worth exemptions in Illinois and New York). Typically, in these states, the date of any exemption is the effective date of the FDD used in nonregistration states. If the franchisor does not perfect an exemption or exclusion under the laws of a particular jurisdiction, registration (if applicable) and disclosure will be required under that jurisdiction's laws.

Exemption from registration under the laws of one jurisdiction does not mean that the franchise is entitled to exempt status in any other registration state. As evidenced by the example above, counsel must review and consider exemptions and exclusions available under applicable law in each jurisdiction where the franchisor plans to pursue its franchising activities. A detailed analysis of all available exemptions is beyond the scope of this chapter. With regard to each exemption, the franchisor should assess whether the exemption applies to registration or registration and disclosure.[272] In addition, the substantive laws of the jurisdiction applicable to franchising (for example, antifraud and unfair practices) generally will continue to apply to each offering regardless of any exemption or exclusion perfected or relied on by the franchisor.

---

270. Cal. Corp. Code § 31101; 815 Ill. Comp. Stat. Ann. 705/8(a)(2); Ind. Code Ann. § 23-2-2.5-3(a); N.Y. Gen. Bus. Law § 684(2)(a); N.D. Cent. Code Ann. § 51-19-04(1)(a); Md. Code Regs. 02.02.08.10(D); 21 Va. Admin. Code § 5-110-75(4); and Wash. Rev. Code Ann. § 19.100.030(4)(b)(i)(A). If the franchisor relies on its parent's financials for the super-large franchisor exemption in New York, the franchisor must have a minimum net worth of $3 million. N.Y. Gen. Bus. Law § 684(3)(a)(i).

271. Md. Code Regs. § 02.08.10(D); R.I. Gen. Laws § 19-28.1-6(1)(i); 21 Va. Admin. Code § 5-110-75(4)(a)(1).

272. *See* Curran & Krakus, *supra* note 10.

2-7. State Business Opportunity Laws

In addition to the FTC Rule and the franchise laws of the registration states, the sale of a franchise may also be subject to state business opportunity laws and seller-assisted marketing plan laws. While state business opportunity laws vary, these laws usually define a business opportunity so broadly that the typical franchise is covered by the definition. Under such laws, it is generally unlawful to offer or sell business opportunities in the state without appropriate presale disclosure and (where required) registration.[273] Twenty-six states now have one of a variety of business opportunity statutes. These states are Alaska, Arizona, California, Connecticut, Florida, Georgia, Illinois, Indiana, Iowa, Kentucky, Louisiana, Maine, Maryland, Michigan, Missouri, Nebraska, New Hampshire, North Carolina, Ohio, Oklahoma, South Carolina, South Dakota, Texas, Utah, Virginia, and Washington.[274] Still others regulate business opportunities through their consumer protection statutes.[275]

Franchisors should be aware of these business opportunity laws, although most franchisors are exempt or excluded from such laws based on either of two exemptions or definitional exclusions: (1) offering a franchise in compliance with the FTC Rule or (2) offering a franchise in conjunction with the licensing of a registered trademark or service mark. Further, a franchisor that registers a franchise offering (or is exempt from such franchise registration) in a state that has both a franchise law and a business opportunity law usually will be exempt from any disclosure or registration provisions of the business opportunity statute. As with state franchise registration laws, an offering exempt from the registration and disclosure provisions of a business opportunity law will still be subject to

---

273. For a detailed description of business opportunity laws, *see* Beata Krakus & Alexander Tuneski, *Caught in the Web of Federal and State Opportunity Laws: Managing and Avoiding the Entanglement of Regulations*, *in* ABA 36th Annual Forum on Franchising, W7 (2013); Keith J. Kanouse & Christina M. Noyes, *The Proposed New Business Opportunity Rule and State Business Opportunity Laws*, *in* ABA 30th Annual Forum on Franchising, W3 (2007).

274. Alaska Stat. §§ 45.66.010–45.66.900; Ariz. Rev. Stat. Ann. §§ 44-1271–44-1282; Cal. Corp. Code §§ 1812.200–1812.221; Conn. Gen. Stat. §§ 36b-60–36b-80; Fla. Stat. §§ 559.80–559.815; Ga. Code Ann. §§ 10-1-410–10-1-417; 815 Ill. Comp. Stat 602/5-1–602/5-135; Ind. Code §§ 24-5-8-1–24-5-8-21; Iowa Code §§ 523B.1–523B.13; Ky. Rev. Stat. Ann. §§ 367.801–367.819, 367.990; La. Stat. Ann. §§ 51:1801–51:1804; Me. Stat. tit. 32, §§ 4691–4700-B; Md. Code Ann., Bus. Reg. §§ 14-101–14-129; Mich. Comp. Laws §§ 445.902, 445.903b; Mo. Rev. Stat. §§ 409.1000–409.1006; Neb. Rev. Stat. §§ 59-1701–59-1761; N.H. Rev. Stat. Ann. §§ 358E:1–358-E:6; N.C. Gen. Stat. §§ 66-94–66-100; Ohio Rev. Code Ann. §§ 1334.01–1334.15, 1334.99; Okla. Stat. tit. 71, §§ 801–829; S.C. Code Ann. §§ 39-57-10–39-57-80; S.D. Codified Laws §§ 37-25A-1–37-25A-54; Tex. Bus. & Com. Code Ann. §§ 41.001–41.303; Utah Code Ann. §§ 13-15-1–13-15-6; Va. Code Ann. §§ 59.1-262–59.1269; Wash. Rev. Code §§ 19.110.010–19.110.930.

275. *See, e.g.*, Ala. Code § 8-19-5(20) ("'seller-assisted marketing plan' includes any plan, scheme, or system in which for a consideration a buyer acquires goods or services, or both, together with a plan, scheme, or system for the resale of said goods or services, or both"); Tenn. Code Ann. § 47-18-103(3) (including "any person who purchases or to whom is offered for sale a . . . business opportunity" in the statutory definition of "consumer").

any antifraud or other substantive provisions of the law. However, if the franchisor's offering is excluded from the definition of a business opportunity based on the statutory requirements, typically none of the provisions of the law will apply.[276]

Under the Texas Business Opportunity Act[277] and the Nebraska Seller-Assisted Marketing Plan Act,[278] the typical franchise falls within the definition of a business opportunity. However, a franchisor offering a franchise in either state that materially complies with the disclosure requirements of the FTC Rule may claim an exemption from these business opportunity laws by filing a one-time notice of exemption with the appropriate state authorities and paying the requisite fee. The Kentucky Sale of Business Opportunities Act also requires franchisors to make a one-time filing to claim the exemption but does not require any filing fee.[279] In contrast, the Florida Business Opportunity Sales Act and the Utah Business Opportunity Disclosure Act each exempt franchisors from these laws based on the franchisor's compliance with the FTC Rule but require franchisors claiming the exemption to file an annual notice with the state and pay a fee.[280] Both the Florida and Utah Acts also specifically exclude from the definition of a business opportunity the sale of a marketing or sales program made in conjunction with the licensing of a registered trademark or service mark.[281] Therefore, if a franchisor has a registered trademark and does not meet the other elements of the respective business opportunity definition, it may not be required to submit an exemption notice filing in Florida or Utah. However, given the filing fee is only $100 in each state and the exemption notice filings can be easily submitted electronically, for peace on mind, most franchisors elect to submit these annual filings if they will be offering franchises in these states.

Franchisors should consult qualified franchise counsel regarding the applicability of particular business opportunity laws. Even where the franchisor complies with the FTC Rule or offers the franchise in connection with the licensing of a registered mark, the existence of certain franchise agreement provisions, such as those granting the franchisee the right to a partial or total refund of the initial franchise fee at the franchisee's discretion, or the right to compel the franchisor to "buy back" certain equipment or inventory, can trigger the applicability of state business opportunity laws. Examples of other business opportunity ventures include distributorships, rack jobbing, and vending machine routes.

276. *See, e.g.*, Alaska Stat. § 45.66.220(2) ("This chapter does not apply to a sale or an offer to sell: . . . a franchise under 16 C.F.R. 436.").

277. Tex. Bus. & Com. Code §§ 41.001–41.303.

278. Neb. Rev. Stat. §§ 59-1701–59-1761.

279. Ky. Rev. Stat. §§ 367.801–367.819, 367.990.

280. Fla. Stat. §§ 559.80–559.815; Utah Code Ann. §§ 13-15-1–13-15-6.

281. Fla. Stat. §§ 559.80–559.815; Utah Code Ann. §§ 13-15-1–13-15-6.

2-8. Document Use, Filing, and Control

For best practices and procedure, franchisors are encouraged to set up strict filing and control procedures that include these elements:

- All FDDs should indicate the jurisdictions where the FDD may be used and the issuance or effective date.
- When an updated FDD is prepared, all copies of the prior FDD must be removed from all franchisor personnel and destroyed or archived. This includes the prior forms of agreements if those are updated. Separate files should be maintained for each registration/disclosure or exempt state.
- The updated FDD and all ancillary documents should be forwarded to each person responsible for conducting franchise sales along with instructions for use of the documents. Each franchise seller should maintain adequate files so that the franchisor's current FDD and its exhibits are readily identifiable. The franchisor's legal department should monitor compliance with this practice.
- If there are any questions as to the appropriate FDD to be distributed at any time, the franchise seller should contact franchise counsel.
- A complete FDD (including all exhibits) should be given at the appropriate times to each prospective franchisee and each individual who will be a guarantor of the franchisee's obligations. If there is any question regarding which individuals should receive disclosure in any proposed sales transaction, the franchise seller should consult counsel.
- Upon delivery of each FDD, an executed receipt (Item 23) should be obtained from the prospective franchisee and each guarantor. A compliance tracking form should be prepared for each franchise sold. This form documents and tracks the various FDDs and completed agreements distributed to the franchisee and its principals, dates of distribution, and signed receipt forms by the franchisee and its principals for the FDD, as well as the completed agreements.
- The files of every franchise seller, or the central franchise sales file if all records are maintained by a department administrator, must show that appropriate disclosure was delivered. The liability for failing to disclose or delivering inappropriate disclosure is substantial. As discussed below, willful violations of federal and state franchise laws carry criminal penalties and/or civil fines, and they create causes of action by prospective franchisees for damages.
- There are currently software programs available for purchase that may be helpful in streamlining electronic disclosure and keeping records. However, users of these types of software programs should be aware of the limitations and potential data privacy implications of such use. Franchisors are responsible for ensuring the programs are configured to be in compliance with the law.

2-9. Permissible Representations

The FTC Rule and all state franchise laws prohibit the making of oral or written representations to a prospective franchisee that are inconsistent with the information and representations contained in the FDD, as well as any other document filed with the state franchise administrators. Any materially inconsistent representations may subject the franchisor, and its officers and franchise sellers to civil (and possibly criminal) liability and may permit a franchisee to recover substantial damages based on those misrepresentations. Accordingly, franchisor personnel and franchise sellers who will have direct contact with prospective franchisees must have a working knowledge of the representations and contractual provisions contained in the current FDD and all agreements, in all approved advertisements, brochures, and other promotional material, and in the operations manual. The franchisor should determine what methods may help their franchise sales personnel stay on track with these rules—periodic franchise sales law compliance training with short knowledge assessments, role playing sessions, short video clips of Q&A sessions, periodic open-forum calls with legal counsel to review questions, or other options. In addition, the franchisor should have a process in place to obtain acknowledgments from prospective franchisees, developers, and their principals that all statements made to them were consistent with the representations contained in the current FDD and agreements.

2-10. Negotiation with Prospective Franchisees

State franchise laws typically permit franchisors and prospective franchisees to negotiate franchise agreements; however, some of the laws impose certain procedural requirements that may hinder negotiations or, in some cases, make them impractical. California's approach to negotiated changes is unique among the franchise registration states and by far the most burdensome.

Essentially, a franchisor must amend its California FDD and registration to reflect any negotiated changes with California franchisees, unless it is able to rely on one of two exemptions. If a franchisor negotiates changes to its franchise agreement with a California prospect and meets certain criteria (including that the changes, on a whole, benefit the franchisee), then the franchisor may take advantage of the statutory exemption under Section 31109.1, which is the easier of the two exemptions to comply with.[282] Section 31109.1 requires that if a franchisor negotiates with a California prospect, it must disclose to that prospect any material negotiated terms it agreed to with other California franchisees during the past 12 months. However, if a franchisor does not negotiate with a California prospect, it is not obligated to disclose to that prospect any prior negotiated terms. When the franchisor renews its franchise registration, it must

282. Cal. Corp. Code § 31109.1.

certify to California that it has complied with these requirements.[283] Alternatively, if a franchisor negotiates changes to its franchise agreement with a California prospect and the changes, on a whole, do not necessarily benefit the prospect, the franchisor may only take advantage of the regulatory exemption under Section 310.100.2.[284] This section requires the franchisor to file notices for all negotiated changes with California and provide to each prospect in California (at the time it receives an FDD) a copy of all negotiated change notices filed with the state during the last 12 months.[285] While the purpose of these laws is to provide California prospects with more information and bargaining power, many franchisors, in the face of these requirements, simply elect not to negotiate with California franchisees.

In contrast, the Virginia Franchise Investment Law mandates that the franchisee be given an opportunity to negotiate the franchise agreement.[286] A franchisor also must consider the duty it may have to disclose those negotiated changes to future prospective franchisees, if statements made in the FDD might be construed as misleading as a result of the negotiated change. For example, in Items 5 and 6, the FTC Rule requires franchisors to disclose whether fees are uniformly imposed and, if the fees are not uniform, the franchisor must disclose the range of fees paid by the franchisees. A franchisor can build some flexibility into the FDD for certain terms that may be negotiated. For example, when addressing the potential geographical scope and duration of any territorial exclusivity that may be granted to the franchisee, the franchisor can disclose the relevant factors and basis the franchisor considers in determining the restrictions. If the franchisor negotiates the royalty fee, the franchisor could disclose the range within which it has negotiated the fee and the factors upon which it based that decision. Most franchisors communicate to franchisees that few, if any, amendments or clarifications to the agreements can be expected or will be permitted, in an attempt to maintain some level of uniformity in the terms of the franchises granted. Any such amendments should be considered by franchise counsel. In addition, franchisors should be aware that a number of registration states have laws that prohibit discrimination among franchisees without legitimate business reasons for doing so.[287]

283. *Id.* at § 31109.1(a)(3).

284. Cal. Corp. Regs. tit. 10, § 310.100.2.

285. *Id.*

286. Va. Code § 13.1-563(b), (e), Bus. Franchise Guide (CCH) ¶ 3460.08.

287. *See e.g.*, Haw. Rev. Stat. § 482E-6(2)(C), Bus. Franchise Guide (CCH) ¶ 4110.01; Ill. Comp. Stat § 705/18, Bus. Franchise Guide (CCH) ¶ 13130.18; Ind. Code § 2(5), Bus. Franchise Guide (CCH) ¶ 4140.02; Mich. Comp. Laws § 445.1527(e), Bus. Franchise Guide (CCH) ¶ 3220.27; Minn. Admin. Code § 2860.4400(B), Bus. Franchise Guide (CCH) ¶ 5230.31; Wash. Rev. Code § 19.100.180(2)(c), Bus. Franchise Guide (CCH) ¶ 4470.01.

2-11. Franchise Disclosure Violations

(a) Private Right of Action

If there is a violation of the franchise sales laws, most of the state statutes provide that a franchisee can commence certain legal actions, which are referred to as a private right of action. The franchisee can institute an action against a variety of parties as permitted by such laws and that may include the franchisor and its officers, directors, and employees (including the franchise sellers). Note that there is no direct private right of action under the FTC Rule. [288] However, state "Little FTC Acts" may provide for an indirect private right of action for a violation of the FTC Rule.

While there is no direct private right of action for a violation of the FTC Rule, the Federal Trade Commission may impose severe civil (and even criminal) penalties for a violation of the FTC Rule, including, the ones listed here:

- *Civil fines*—The fines can be up to $40,000 *per violation*, and it is common for a single sale in violation of the FTC Act as a result of a sale with the required disclosure to actually result in multiple violations for the same transaction.
- *Cease and desist orders*—Orders preventing franchisor and sales personnel from offering or selling franchises, temporarily or permanently.
- *Cost of investigation/administrative proceedings*—The costs and other administrative fees related to investigation or administrative proceedings.
- *Rescission*—Requiring the franchisor to cancel the franchise agreement and making the investors whole by returning their entire investment.

Most state franchise laws permit franchisees and purchasers of "business opportunities" to seek one or more of these remedies:

- *Actual damages*—All payments made to acquire and develop the franchise; may also include damages to a franchisee's reputation and lost past and future profits and earnings.
- *Injunctive relief*—An order preventing franchisor and sales personnel from offering or selling franchises, temporarily or permanently.
- *Attorneys' fees*—The fees that are incurred related to litigation.
- *Cost of litigation*—The court costs and other administrative fees related to litigation.
- *Treble damages*—Damages equal to three times a franchisee's actual damages.
- *Rescission*—Requiring the franchisor to cancel the franchise agreement, to relieve the franchisee from all liability under that agreement, and to return the franchisee to the position the franchisee would have been in had the agreement not been executed (for example, returning all initial franchise

288. FTC Rule, 16 C.F.R. § 436.1.

and royalty fees paid and compensating the franchisee for all losses and investment costs). Rescission, however, can be a difficult remedy to define when a franchise has operated for a number of years and the franchisee has derived revenue from the operation of the franchised business.[289] Rescission is handled differently by many states. Some states will focus on the initial investment without regard for any revenues or profits derived from the business while others, such as New York, will account for revenues generated by the business in calculating the amount due for rescission.

- *Other damages*—For example, punitive damages if permitted by statute.

(b) Administrative Liability under State Franchise Laws

In addition to private rights of action that can be brought by a franchisee, the federal and state franchise laws provide government administrators with powers to regulate the offer and sale of franchises and to pursue certain remedies for violations of the statutes.[290]

Most state franchise sales laws grant to their franchise administrators the power to issue stop orders prohibiting any franchise sales activities by individuals or entities who allegedly are violating the franchise statute in question, as well as the power to order the escrow or impoundment of franchise fees.[291] The franchise sales laws also grant the state administrators extremely broad investigative powers that can be used to assess potential violations of the laws.[292] Some state laws also confer remedial powers over and above the power to deny registration, including the ability to obtain injunctive relief and to issue cease and desist orders.[293]

In most instances, the statutes also empower the state administrators to institute civil proceedings to seek restitution on behalf of those injured by practices declared fraudulent and illegal, including the right to seek such remedies against a broad range of individuals (including freezing the assets of the companies and individuals violating such laws).[294] Administrators can also seek civil penalties ranging from $100 to $100,000 per violation. Finally, in circumstances involving a willful violation of the statutes, the statutes authorize the state administrators to pursue criminal liability (along with fines and imprisonment), including felony exposure in many states.[295]

---

289. Lake City Rental & Leasing, Inc. v. Madison Rental and Leasing, Inc., Bus. Franchise Guide (CCH) ¶ 10,902 (Wis. Ct. App. Mar. 28, 1996).

290. FTC Rule, 16 C.F.R. § 436, Bus. Franchise Guide (CCH) ¶ 6010.

291. *See, e.g.*, Cal. Corp. Code § 31408; Minn. Stat. § 80C.16-17; Va. Code § 13.1-567-571.

292. *See, e.g.*, Cal. Corp. Code § 31401; 815 Ill. Comp. Stat. 705/22(b); Md. Code Regs. § 14-208; Minn. Stat. § 80C.16-17; Va. Code § 13.1-567-571.

293. *See, e.g.*, Cal. Corp. Code § 31406; 815 Ill. Comp. Stat. 705/24; Md. Code Regs. § 14-210; Minn. Stat. § 80C.16-17; Va. Code § 13.1-567-571.

294. *See, e.g.*, Cal. Corp. Code § 31408; Md. Code Regs. § 14-210; Minn. Stat. § 80C.16-17; Va. Code § 13.1-567-571.

295. *See, e.g.*, Cal. Corp. Code § 31410; 815 Ill. Comp. Stat. 705/25; Md. Code Regs. § 14-211; Minn. Stat. § 80C.16-17; Va. Code § 13.1-567-571.

2-12. Implementing Sales Compliance Policies

The purpose of any franchise sales compliance program is to establish a practical system to oversee the franchisor's compliance with the FTC Rule and states' registration and disclosure laws. This, in turn, requires extensive cooperation between the franchisor's legal department and those employees having a connection to franchise sales. Several tensions are inherent in any implementation effort, including distilling complex due diligence and registration/disclosure considerations and terminology into a usable policy document and procedures readily understandable by any employee associated with the franchisee sales process. Also inherent are those tensions that exist by reason of the potential conflicting missions of the franchise sales department, and legal or other department responsible for franchise compliance within the franchisor entity.

An effectively implemented set of franchise sales compliance processes and procedures can balance these tensions and assist in the management of any conflicting objectives within the franchisor's departments to facilitate the sales process, while minimizing the franchisor's liability for violations of federal and state laws and regulations. The franchisor's future success, if not its continued existence, depends on proper implementation of compliance processes and procedures throughout all departments and at all levels of the company.

(a) Role of Counsel

At the outset, counsel must recognize the competing missions of the franchise sales and legal/compliance department staffs. The primary objective of the franchise sales department is to meet or exceed the company's growth goals through the execution of franchise agreements (and other commitments) to develop and/or convert other businesses to the franchisor's concept, and to generate revenue to the company in the form of initial franchise fees and continuing fees. Regardless of the size of the franchisor, it seeks to build, or improve upon, a base of franchisees for the collection of royalty fees and advertising contributions to enhance the franchisor's profitability, access to media and other marketing tools, and distribution points for customers, and to promote the franchisor's concept.

The in-house lawyer (or legal department, if there is more than one lawyer, which is generally not the case with a start-up franchisor) often has a conflicting mission. As with all corporate counsel (outside or in-house), and regardless of the financial strength and size of the franchisor, the goal is to assist in the creation and preservation of the financial strength of the franchisor, while being mindful of the franchisor's legal obligations. Counsel must communicate the need for realistic compliance measures and should take the lead to formulate and implement sales compliance processes and procedures.

No aspect of the franchisor's sales practices should be immune from counsel's scrutiny in the formulation and implementation process. Compliance programs should establish the routine tasks to be followed in selling franchises with due regard for the regulatory framework. Effective training and utilization of established compliance programs substantially reduce the in-house lawyer's need to review day-to-day details of the sales process.

(b) Internal Compliance Manual

One of the most effective means of communicating due diligence requirements and registration and disclosure laws to all of the franchisor's personnel is to draft and circulate an internal compliance "manual" among all franchisor employees who have contact with prospective franchisees. If the drafting or use of a manual is impractical, then, at a minimum, supervisory employees within the franchise sales department and franchise sellers should receive training on a routine basis and have a checklist, or series of checklists, available to them to assist in monitoring and documenting the process through which a prospective franchisee becomes a franchisee or an existing franchisee obtains an additional franchise.

The manual should summarize due diligence considerations and registration and disclosure requirements in the jurisdictions in which the franchisor offers or contemplates offering its franchises for sale. Careful instructions must be given if the franchisor is not registered to sell franchises in some of the registration states. The manual and any training materials should focus on the franchisor's personnel's need to complete and document a series of routine tasks before the prospective franchisee becomes a franchisee. Where possible, the franchisor should incorporate simple steps into the process, and the various conflicts or inconsistencies between federal and state laws should be consolidated, if possible, into a single compliance regime. Administrative employees need a system under which pursuing and checking off a series of regular assignments for each prospective franchisee will satisfy as many jurisdictions as possible. In this regard, as discussed earlier in section 2-4 on preparing the FDD, the franchisor and its counsel should give strong consideration to registering in all states (in which the franchisor has an interest in offering) and providing all prospects with a single roll-up or multistate FDD that is valid in all jurisdictions.

Unfortunately, having a manual does not immunize the franchisor from all potential liabilities related to the franchise sales process, and no such policies should remain static. In-house counsel must continually review the documentation as regulatory and due diligence requirements evolve based on, among other things, legislative action and judicial decisions. Furthermore, counsel must monitor the manner in which franchise sales personnel adhere to sales compliance policies. The sales compliance training should emphasize the need to educate sales personnel regarding the applicable regulatory framework.

(c) Sales Compliance Training

The in-house practitioner should stress to officers and senior executives of the franchisor the relative cost-effectiveness of thorough, proactive training of the franchise sales force and administrative personnel versus the expense of litigating claims from franchisees or responding to complaints from franchise enforcement officials. The franchisor also should offer separate training for the person charged with administering the franchise program, if such position exists, and any administrative staff in the franchise sales department. Officers and senior executives of the franchisor should also be encouraged to attend, in order to buttress their understanding of the regulatory environment in which they do business and to demonstrate their commitment to and support for the compliance program.

The sales training can take a variety of approaches, depending on the needs of the company and experience of the sales and franchise administrative staff. Counsel preparation (particularly new counsel to a franchisor) for the training should include reviewing the most recent FDDs (including franchise agreement provisions), drafting or revising the manual, reviewing franchise sales brochures and other materials used in the sales process (e.g., PowerPoint presentations, website pages, social media postings), and possibly attending a few franchise sales presentations to prospective franchisees. Initial training of salespersons needs to include a thorough familiarization with the FDD, particularly Items 1, 5, 6, 7, 8, 11, 12, and 19 and the form agreements. The franchise agreement is the most important of the exhibits to the FDD, and substantial time should be dedicated to reviewing the franchisor's approach to the underlying business, as reflected in the franchise agreement. Sales compliance training does not end when the new sales employee completes the initial compliance program offered by the franchisor; however, the franchisor should offer, and require, "refresher" training for existing franchise salespersons on a regular basis.

If there are points in the franchise agreement that the franchisor is willing to clarify, or negotiate, then these should be reviewed at the outset, first between in-house counsel and the franchisor's executives, and then as part of the training for franchise salespersons. Most franchisors choose not to negotiate (or to substantially limit negotiations) for various legal and business reasons. Counsel should advise the franchisor's management that any changes regularly negotiated by the franchisor should be disclosed as part of the FDD, because once the FDD and any applicable franchise agreements have been filed with the appropriate state regulator, the scope of permissible negotiation narrows in terms of provisions that the franchisor may uniformly change per request by any prospective franchisee.[296] This narrowing does not prohibit the franchisor from addressing a point raised by a prospect or from clarifying an agreement to reflect the particulars of a prospect's situation. The administrative burden placed on disclosure of the terms of the negotiation (by California[297] in particular—including the negotiated sales notice filing requirements) should be kept in mind.

If the franchisor is willing to consider either negotiating or clarifying the franchise agreement, then a senior management individual should be designated as a point of contact for such discussions (recognizing the other internal tension in franchise companies—franchise sales wants to close a deal, operations must live with the negotiated contract, and legal must comply with any disclosure or similar obligations). Counsel must also keep in mind the level of delegated corporate approval and whether the changes are so material that a committee must approve them. In any event, the franchisor's policies on the negotiation and clarification of franchise agreement provisions should be reviewed in detail as part of initial

296. *See* Bus. Franchise Guide (CCH) ¶ 3055.
297. *Id.*

and refresher sales compliance training so that the sales agents clearly understand the scope of their authority with respect to negotiation before commencing the sales process.

Counsel (or at least an experienced paralegal) should participate in the actual training of new franchise salespersons. The use of audio/visual materials and abstracts from the franchisor's actual documents, coupled with detailed review of manual procedures, should be included in all compliance training. From an administrative standpoint, the legal department representative in attendance should, prior to the end of the initial training, obtain from each franchise salesperson a statement of attendance. The franchisor may also consider giving a short quiz to assess if the program materials were understood by the participants.

A franchisor may consider offering refresher training to franchise salespersons contemporaneously with the annual renewal/updating process for the FDD each franchisor undergoes pursuant to the FTC Rule and applicable state laws following the end of the franchisor's fiscal year. If the opportunity for live refresher training is not available during this period, then, at a minimum, the franchisor should circulate a memorandum describing changes in the FDD and other franchise documents among existing sales staff, together with a discussion of any other policy changes the franchisor intends to implement in the coming year. If in-person attendance at a refresher course is not feasible, then the memorandum and a certificate to be signed can be circulated and collected from salespersons in order to document the receipt of information on FDD changes and the fact that the franchise salespersons have reviewed such information.

(d) Internal Auditing and Monitoring Compliance

The drafting and circulation of a manual and the formulation and holding of sales compliance training sessions will provide limited value to the franchisor if the effectiveness of these tools is not monitored or otherwise evaluated. The franchisor should strongly consider spot auditing sales presentations in order to confirm adherence to compliance procedures. A senior franchise sales executive or legal department employee can monitor all or part of such a sales presentation and then provide feedback to the salesperson with any business or legal points.

As a result of these review programs, or in connection with franchisee complaints or litigation, the in-house attorney will from time to time become aware of a need or opportunity to counsel a salesperson directly on a specific issue. The opportunity may arise based on counsel's general observations or monitoring of a sales presentation. On the other hand, the assertion by a franchisee of allegations that applicable laws have been violated demands immediate attention. Even if counsel's investigation of the facts produces no corroboration of the franchisee's claims, and the franchisor's management decides not to discipline the salesperson in question, the in-house practitioner should insist whenever possible on specific retraining or counseling in compliance procedures for the salesperson against whom such allegations are lodged, particularly where the salesperson has previously been the subject of similar complaints. In the event of complaints in the future or state enforcement action results, such steps can be useful in establishing that such action is not condoned and mitigate the perceived need for action by federal or state regulators.

The opportunity for internal auditing of administrative personnel within the franchise sales department should occur at least once per year during the update of the FDD. For example, for each franchise sold during the preceding fiscal year, the first page and signature page of each franchise agreement, together with a copy of the receipt for the franchise documents signed by the then-prospective franchisee, could be reviewed as part of the franchisor's annual update to confirm compliance with timing obligations (although a closing checklist should be used to eliminate any potential mistakes in this area). The franchisor could audit sales 30–60 days prior to fiscal year end in order to determine whether certain documents are missing from the file or additional documents are needed to complete the company's records of the transaction. If the volume of transactions prohibits a review of all files, minimally, a select number of transactions in each region (or market area, depending on how the company allocates its resources) could be audited to ensure that either the manual or compliance checklist(s) are being followed by the appropriate personnel. Deficiencies found in any franchisee's file should be addressed with the administrator of the franchise sales department in order to determine the cause and prevent recurrence. Such an audit would help verify specific disclosures in the FDD.

(e) Curing Franchise Sales Law Compliance Violations

The likelihood of franchise sales law violations will be substantially reduced by the establishment of, and adherence to, internal compliance procedures. Nevertheless, instances of noncompliance may inadvertently occur even in the best-run systems.

For example, consider the following scenario: the franchisor has properly disclosed to a prospective franchisee the terms of development of a unit that will be operated in a registration state with the franchisor's then-current effective FDD. In the four months subsequent to the initial disclosure, the franchisor's salespersons have had ongoing conversations with the prospective franchisee concerning the terms of the franchise agreement, and the franchisee has been reviewing proposed sites for the unit. Also during that time, the franchisor is involved in litigation with another franchisee to collect royalties, and that franchisee files a counterclaim alleging fraud and state franchise law violations subject to disclosure in Item 3 of the FDD and seeking substantial damages. Given the financial condition of the franchisor, an adverse judgment for fraud may make it difficult for the franchisor to meet its obligations to its franchisees. Upon the filing of this counterclaim, the franchisor's legal department assesses whether the action is a material change, determines that it is, and promptly files its amended FDD with the appropriate state agencies. Because of the length of time the parties have been negotiating, the franchisor's salesperson forgets to redisclose the prospective franchisee with the amended FDD and that sale closes. One week later the compliance coordinator is organizing the franchisee's files and reviewing the closing binder, or even auditing the files as discussed in the preceding section, and notices that there is a signed receipt for the earlier FDD in the file but not one for the currently effective FDD.

For purposes of our example, the franchise is to be operated in the state of Illinois and the franchisee's principal place of business (and domicile) is Ohio, and all correspondence and contact with the prospective franchisee have taken place either in the franchisor's home state (Virginia) or in the state of Ohio. The first step is to determine the jurisdictional scope and applicability of state franchise laws to the transaction to determine which, if any, state law(s) has been violated. Section 705/10 of the Illinois Franchise Disclosure Act states that no franchisor may sell or offer to sell a franchise in Illinois if (1) the franchisee is domiciled in Illinois or (2) the offer of the franchise is made or accepted in Illinois and the franchise business is or will be located in Illinois.[298] Furthermore, the statute provides that an offer to sell is made in the State of Illinois when the offer either originates from the state or is directed by the offer or to the state and received at the place to which it is directed. In contrast, section 13.1-599 B of the Virginia Retail Franchising Act provides that the act applies only to a franchise where the performance of which contemplates or requires the franchisee to establish a location or maintain a place of business within the Commonwealth of Virginia.[299]

In this circumstance, although there was contact with two registration states, there is no violation of the registration and disclosure laws of either state because neither the conduct of the franchisor and franchisee nor their domiciliary status or development plans trigger jurisdiction of the laws. But consider changing one variable of the scenario: Franchisor and franchisee negotiate and execute the final documents at a meeting in Illinois approving the site for the franchised unit. In this case, the Illinois Franchise Disclosure Act applies, and the franchisor has therefore violated the law.

In the first scenario, once in-house counsel has determined that no violation of a specific state franchise registration and disclosure law has occurred, the franchisor must determine whether there are any other sources of liability resulting from the franchisor's failure to provide the appropriate FDDs (such as violation of the FTC Rule or state Little FTC Acts). If there is an applicable Little FTC Act on which a franchisee could rely to bring an action for the alleged failure to comply with the FTC Rule, the franchisor has, depending on the provisions of the state law, a variety of options to attempt to reduce or eliminate future liability concerning such claims. The franchisor may do nothing and simply wait for the statute of limitations to run for a claim under the state's Little FTC Act; however, such statutes of limitation typically run three to four years.[300] Further, it is better to attempt to limit liability early on while the relationship between the franchisor and franchisee is still in its honeymoon period. At this stage, the franchisor

---

298. *See* Bus. Franchise Guide (CCH) ¶ 3120.
299. *See* Bus. Franchise Guide (CCH) ¶ 3465.
300. *See, e.g.*, 1 Bus. Franchise Guide (CCH) ¶¶ 3017 (Ala.), 3447 (Utah), 3517 (D.C.).

should consider taking a more aggressive approach and either notify the franchisee of the inadvertent omission and provide the franchisee with the additional disclosure to review, or provide the additional disclosure and offer the franchisee rescission at this stage when the franchisee is least likely to accept it. Under common law, once the franchisee has notice of the violation or receives an offer of rescission, and fails to act within a reasonable period, the franchisee's causes of action may be barred.[301]

In the second scenario, in which the final documents are executed at a meeting in Illinois, the circumstances are somewhat more complicated because the inadvertent violation involves the registration and disclosure laws of a state where the franchisor is subject to registration. The approaches to cure will vary depending upon the state, its regulatory requirements, and even the administrator with whom the franchisor attempts to cure the breach. As in the nonregistration state where there was an applicable Little FTC Act, the franchisor has the option of doing nothing and waiting for the statute of limitations to expire. Most state franchise laws provide for a three- to four-year statute of limitation for civil liability.[302]

Failure to act poses the additional risk that the state administrator may become aware of the franchisor's violation through means other than those that the franchisor controls (for example, later the franchisee becomes aware of the violation and complains to the state agency, or at renewal time the state agency inquires about the date of sale because of the timing of the amendment). Assuming the franchisor makes the decision to address the situation while there is no other dispute between the franchisor and the franchisee, the franchisor would generally notify the state agency in writing of the inadvertent omission and provide a copy of a letter notifying the franchisee of such omission. If the violation were in Illinois, as in the example, the franchisor must give notice in the specified format for issuing a notice of violation.[303] If the violation involves California law, the franchisor will not have to offer rescission but merely provide a notice of violation. Section 31303 of the California Franchise Investment Law provides that no action may be maintained under the civil liability section of the law unless brought within 90 days after delivery to the franchisee of a written notice disclosing any violation of sections 31201 or 31202 of the law.[304] The form of notice of violation is prescribed by the California Department of Corporations.[305] In the other states, the franchisor will generally have some flexibility with the content of any notice.

For minor inadvertent infractions of the type described above, if brought to the state administrator's attention by the franchisor, the state administrator may be willing to permit the matter to be informally resolved between the franchisor

301. *See* Bagel Enter. v. Baskin & Sears, 467 A.2d 533, 541 (Md. Ct. Spec. App. 1983).

302. *See, e.g.*, Bus. Franchise Guide (CCH) ¶¶ 3050.725 (Cal.), 3130.24 (Ill.), 3140.30 (Ind.).

303. *See* 815 Ill. Comp. Stat. 705/27, Bus. Franchise Guide (CCH) ¶ 3130.27.

304. *See* Bus. Franchise Guide (CCH) ¶ 3050.64.

305. *See* Bus. Franchise Guide (CCH) ¶ 5050.37.

and franchisee, in lieu of a direct regulator involvement. Some administrators may, however, demand that the franchisor enter into a consent order that must be disclosed in the FDD, regardless of the inadvertence or technicality of the violation.

If an alleged violation is brought to the attention of franchise regulators, an investigation by federal and state agencies can take a variety of forms depending on the authority of the agency, the alleged conduct on the part of the franchisor, and the perceived threat of future consumer injury. Such action may range from a telephone call or a letter inquiring about the alleged conduct to a civil investigative demand or subpoena accompanied by an order requiring the franchisor to cease and desist selling franchises or engaging in other specific conduct that is alleged to be in violation of a particular law (see sections 2-11(b), Administrative Remedies under State Franchise, and 2.11(a), Private Rights of Action).

2-13. Granting the Franchise

(a) Legal Considerations

Before execution of any binding franchise or related agreement by franchisor, the legal department (or franchise administration staff) should confirm compliance with all applicable franchise registration and disclosure laws. The franchisor should not deliver any agreement for final execution by the authorized franchisor executive unless (1) the prospective franchisee and its principals have been given all FDDs in accordance with the FTC Rule and state law, if applicable; (2) the franchisor has received the fully executed receipt of the applicable FDD from the franchisee named in the agreement (if the disclosure was sent and receipt signed prior to formation of the franchisee—consider what additional documentation may be required to evidence authorization and proper compliance); (3) the appropriate time has passed between the date of the prospective franchisee's receipt of the FDD and the date set for the agreement's execution; (4) the time period has passed for the franchisee to have held the final franchise agreement with all material terms filled in prior to execution; and (5) all due diligence on the franchisee and required franchisee signatories (e.g., guarantors) have been received.

Some franchisors, as part of their due diligence process, require that the franchisee and all of the franchisee's principals complete and sign a summary of acknowledgments form in which they acknowledge that the franchisor has complied with its disclosure obligations (a sample of which is attached as exhibit 2-6).[306] While not a release of claims, these forms provide evidence of compliance. The franchisor must review all pages of the franchise and related agreements prior to signature to determine that no changes or modifications have been made by the franchisee. Since many franchise agreements are now signed using electronic means, agreements should be checked for all relevant signatures, to ensure documents have not been altered and to determine what date signatures are received. Fees are also being paid by electronic means, and the date of receipt should be checked.

306. See *supra* note 251.

(b) Business Considerations

Business realities often overshadow the legal considerations in the granting of a franchise. Because of state licensing requirements, certain franchisors may be compelled to require that the franchisee, or a majority owner of the franchisee, hold a valid state license for the business conducted under the franchisor's system. For example, real estate agency franchisors typically must require that the franchisee have a valid real estate broker's license in the state in which the franchisee intends to do business, and a pharmacy franchisor may require the franchisee to be a licensed pharmacist in the state where the pharmacy franchise is to be established. Even if strict licensing requirements do not exist in a particular industry, the franchisor, depending on the business it franchises, may require its franchisees to have a substantial experience and background in its industry, or at least a demonstrated skill level in that type of business. On the other hand, some franchisors take the position that their franchisees do not have to be the chef or the cook; their criteria for potential success as a franchisee often include success in a business endeavor in another industry or in middle-management, where systems or procedures must be followed in order to achieve business objectives.

Financial considerations are often an essential qualification of granting a franchise, including access to both equity and financing. If the franchisor has negotiated financing programs for its franchisees through third-party lenders, then the franchisor must strictly follow the lenders' criteria. Accordingly, a franchisee with substantial cash flow and little home equity or other collateral may be a candidate for an equipment leasing program, whereas a prospect with the minimum amount of cash required and substantial equity in assets such as homes and other real estate may fit the profile of a U.S. Small Business Administration–guaranteed loan applicant. Challenges most often arise from the standpoint of business considerations when the franchisor is presented with a candidate with marginal financial qualifications.

The franchisor should follow established procedures when processing the franchisee's application, whether it appears qualified or not. Administrative personnel in the franchise sales department should approach this process with the same care and standards and procedures they do in assuring compliance with the disclosure and registration laws. One franchisor employee can be assigned the routine task of ordering credit, reference checks, or background checks, including those for compliance with the requirements of the U.S. Treasury Office of Foreign Assets Control. In order to meet compliance obligations, franchisors must have a process in place for obtaining and running background checks on material investors in any franchisee, and confirmation that at the time of entering into the franchise agreement none of such investors is on the Specially Designated Nationals list of persons with whom U.S. companies are prohibited from doing business.[307]

307. U.S. Treas. Dep't, Office of Foreign Assets Control, https://home.treasury.gov/policy-issues/office-of-foreign-assets-control-sanctions-programs-and-information (last visited June 13, 2021).

A candidate with minimal assets (according to a balance sheet and income statement) who has an acceptable credit report and a positive employment history may well be financeable under one or more of the franchisee financing programs. On the other hand, a franchisor must consider the underlying creditworthiness of the franchisee entity and the equity and debt structure of the project and its principals (or any parent company or guarantors) in doing its underwriting of any franchise project. The franchisor may be relying on that financial underwriting to ensure support for ongoing operations and to fund anticipated future capital requirements.

To summarize the business considerations in granting the franchise, the franchisor must have established procedures, similar to the sales compliance policies, for evaluating the prospective franchisees' financial and business needs. If the franchisor fails to organize itself in weighing business considerations in the grant of the franchise, then it runs the risk of having many of its new franchisees fail, damaging the goodwill associated with its marks, and damaging its reputation with consumers of its products in connection with such store closures. Moreover, numerous franchisee failures may jeopardize the continuation of the financing programs that the franchisor has worked hard to establish if lenders consider the endeavor too risky. Business consultants also may play a significant role in designing standards, operating manuals, and business practices and procedures to coordinate the business operations with the compliance obligations of the franchisor and related franchising activities.

2-14. Conclusion

Managing the franchise sales activity and growth of a franchise system is a continuing challenge for legal counsel, as the methods through which systems expand continue to multiply and evolve. Internal policies and programs that facilitate compliance with regulatory requirements, promote the management of system expansion, and foster sound relationships with franchisees are necessary for the continued long-term health of any franchise system. A well-designed and -implemented franchise compliance program, organized and executed according to the best practices set forth in this chapter, should contribute significantly to the well-being of the franchise system, while minimizing areas of potential conflict.

Exhibit 2-1
Excerpts from FDD Questionnaire to Gather Information

Initial Questionnaire*

Please answer *all* questions and respond to *all* requests for information as fully as possible. Please note that sections of this Initial Questionnaire correspond to the numbered Items of the Franchise Disclosure Document (the "FDD"). Attach additional sheets as necessary. Use "N/A" or "None" where applicable.

FDD Cover Page and State Cover Page

A. General Information

Please provide:

1. General business e-mail address for franchise inquiries: ____________________
2. Primary web page address: ____________________

B. Electronic Disclosure

You may (but are not required to) make the FDD available to prospective franchisees by electronic means (for example, CD Rom, e-mail, or website access). If you wish to offer this option, then certain statements and information must be included on the cover page of the FDD. Please check as applicable:

1. [ ] YES, we want to be able to make the FDD available in formats other than the traditional paper format, and would like to discuss our options with you.

   If YES, please provide the following information for use by the prospective franchisee in contacting you to inquire about the alternative option(s):

   Name of individual or office to contact: ____________________

   Address of contact: ____________________

   Telephone number of contact: ____________________

2. [ ] NO, we do NOT want to make the FDD available in formats other than the traditional paper format.

C. Brokers

1. Does your Company currently use or intend to use any individual, corporation, partnership, or other entity (whether referred to as a broker, area representative, sales representative, or otherwise), *other than employees of the franchisor* (each a "Broker") and to whom you will pay a fee to help your Company in the offer and/or sell franchises?

   Yes ____ No ____

2. If the answer to C.1 is "Yes," please complete appendix A and appendix B for each broker and, if the Broker is not an individual, each of the Broker's directors, officers, and employees with management responsibility.

---

*Certain Items have been intentionally deleted. This is not a complete questionnaire. For renewal and amendments, a similar questionnaire can be utilized.

3. Please note that separate registrations and special disclosure forms are required for *brokers* in certain states. Please confirm that the Broker has made the required filings.

I. Item 1: The Franchisor and Any Parents, Predecessors, and Affiliates

A. 1. Please note that completion of the franchisor's basic disclosure document (the FDD) will allow the franchisor to offer and sell franchises in all states *except* the "registration" or business opportunity states listed below. These states require filing, registration, or special disclosure *before* the offer or sale of franchises.

For the states listed below, please:

(1) Check the states below in which you would like to be able to offer and sell franchises

California	New York
Hawaii	North Dakota
Illinois	Rhode Island
Indiana	South Dakota
Kentucky	Texas
Maryland	Utah
Michigan	Virginia
Minnesota	Washington
Nebraska	Wisconsin

* If the franchisor does not have a federally registered trademark, additional filings may be required in certain states with applicable business opportunity laws.

2. Does the franchisor have a logo (primary trademark or service mark under which the franchisee will conduct business)?

Yes _____ No _____

If answer to I.A.7. is "Yes," please attach a clear copy of the logo, preferably no larger than 2"× 2". Also, please provide a copy in electronic form (preferably in TIFF format) so that we may add the logo to the cover page of the FDD.

3. Will advertising (including brochures and pamphlets) be used in the offer or sale of franchises?

Yes _____ No _____

If answer to I.A.8. is "Yes," please provide us with two copies of each piece of advertising that you want to file with the required states. If the advertising is not yet finalized and available, by what date do you expect it to be available?

B. Identification

1. Full legal name of the entity that will be the franchisor:

____

2. Name under which the franchisor does business (or intends to do business):

____

3. Business form of the franchisor (corporation, partnership, sole proprietorship, etc.): _______________________________________

4. Date of incorporation/partnership: ______________________________
   (if a corporation/partnership)
5. State of incorporation/partnership: ______________________________
   (if a corporation/partnership)
6. Franchisor's principal business address:

   ____
7. Franchisor's phone number at that address:

   ____
8. Will the franchisor maintain a sales organization in any state other than the state in which the principal place of business is located?

   Yes _____ No _____

   If answer to I.B.8. is "Yes," please give:

   a. Address: ______________________________

   b. Telephone Number: ______________________________
9. Please provide us with the *full legal names* and *principal business addresses* of any affiliates that are controlled by, controlling, or under common control with another entity and that are offering franchises in any line of business:
10. Please provide us with the *full legal names* and *principal business addresses* of any affiliates that are controlled by, controlling, or under common control with another entity and that are providing or will provide products or services to franchisees of the franchisor:
11. Has the franchisor acquired the major portion of its own assets from another company, partnership, or individual?

    Yes _____ No _____

    If the answer to I.B.11. is "Yes," please give the following information for the other company(ies) during the 10-year period immediately before the close of the franchisor's most recent fiscal year:

    a. Name: ______________________________

    b. Most recent principal business address:

    c. If a corporation:
       1. State of incorporation: ______________________________
       2. Date of incorporation: ______________________________
12. Are there any "parent" company or companies (these companies may be direct owners or in the chain of ownership through one or more subsidiaries) that "controls" the franchisor by effectively exercising control over the policies and direction of the franchisor and franchise system?

    Yes _____ No _____

    If "Yes," please provide the names and principal addresses for any "parent" entities that "control" the franchisor or franchise system.

    ____

C. History of the Franchisor, and Its Predecessors, Parents, and Affiliates

1. Have any of the companies, partnerships, or individuals listed in I.B.9.–I.B.12. ever offered franchises?

   Yes _____ No _____

If the answer to I.C.1. is "Yes," please give the following information:

a. The exact years in which the company, partnership, or individual offered franchises:

b. Type of franchises offered:

c. Number of franchises sold: ______________________________

d. Description of franchise program:

2. Have any of the companies listed in I.B.9–I.B.12. conducted a business similar to the business that will be conducted by franchisees of the franchisor?

Yes _____ No _____

If the answer to I.C.2 is "Yes," for how long was the business conducted? (give starting and ending dates by month):

____

D. The Franchisor's Business

1. Does the franchisor engage in another business or other business activities, in addition to the granting and servicing of franchises?

Yes _____ No _____

If the answer to I.D.1. is "Yes," please describe the other business or business activities of the franchisor:

2. Does the franchisor operate company-owned units similar to the franchises offered?

Yes _____ No _____

If the answer to I.D.2. is "Yes," please give starting date (month and year) when the franchisor began operation of such units:

3. Has the franchisor ever offered franchises in any other line of business?

Yes _____ No _____

If the answer to I.D.3 is "Yes," please give the following information:

a. The type of franchise: ______________________________

b. The length of time that the franchisor offered such franchises (give starting and ending dates by month): ______________________________

c. Number of franchises sold: ______________________________

E. The Franchise to Be Offered

1. Describe, in detail, the business that the franchisee will conduct:

2. Describe the market and competition for the goods and services to be offered by the franchisee:

3. Describe, in general terms, any *proposed* federal, state, and local laws or regulations that are specific to the industry in which the franchised business operates and that (a) are likely to become law; and (b) if enacted, would have a significant effect upon the franchised business (it is not necessary to include laws or regulations that apply to businesses generally): ______________________________

II. Item 2: Business Experience

A. Directors and Officers of Franchisor and Certain Other Personnel

1. How many directors are there of the franchisor? _____

   Please state the full names of all directors of the franchisor.

2. How many officers are there of the franchisor? _____

   Please state the full names of the principal officers of the franchisor (e.g. President, Vice President, Secretary, Treasurer, etc.):

3. Please state the full names of other persons* who will have management responsibility in connection with the sale or operation of the franchises offered (e.g., Director of Training, Store Opening Supervisor) (if there are none, please indicate "N/A" below):

   [*Note: This is not limited to your employees. It also includes persons who work for your affiliates or parent companies if those persons will have management responsibility in connection with the sale or operation of the franchises offered.]

B. Appendix A—Questionnaire for Directors, Officers, Sales Personnel of the Franchisor and Certain Other Personnel (Attached)

Must be completed by:

1. Each individual listed in II.1, 2, and 3 of this Initial Questionnaire.
2. Each other individual who is an employee of the Company who will offer and sell franchises.

III. Item 3: Litigation

Appendix B—Questionnaire for Litigation and Arbitration History (Attached)

Must be completed by the following:

1. The franchisor;
2. Each person or entity listed in I.B.11. (a "predecessor") and II.1, 2, and 3 of this Initial Questionnaire;
3. Each other individual who is an employee of the Company who will offer and sell franchises;
4. Each affiliate of the franchisor who (a) offers franchises under the franchisor's principal trademark; (b) has offered or sold franchises in any line of business during the last 10 years; and/or (c) guarantees the franchisor's performance or promises to back the franchisor financially as part of the franchisor's franchise sales or other activities;

   Are there any such parent or affiliates?

   Yes___ No____

5. Any parent guaranteeing the franchisor's performance or promising to back the franchisor financially as part of the franchisor's franchise sales or other activities.

   Are there any such parents?

   Yes___ No____

6. Each principal of the franchisor and any entity that owns more than 80 percent of the franchisor (if such parties do not otherwise fall under the categories above), only if the franchisor would like to be able to offer and sell franchises in the state of New York.

* * * * *

V. Item 5: Initial Fees

A. Will the initial franchise fee be a fixed amount?

Yes _____ No _____

If yes, what is the amount? __________

B. If the answer to V.A. is "No," give the range within which the fee will vary:

from $__________ to $__________

C. If the initial franchise/development fee is not uniform for all franchisees/developers (as evidenced by variations in the initial fee during the prior fiscal year), please complete *either* (1) or (2) below.

1. State the formula used to calculate the amount of the initial fee.
2. Indicate the highest and lowest initial franchise/development fees actually paid during the franchisor's last complete fiscal year.

   Highest: $__________ Lowest: $__________

   Please list the factors that were used to determine the amounts of the initial franchise fees charged to franchisees during the last fiscal year (e.g., negotiation with the franchisee, size of territory, demographic factors).

VI. Item 6: Other Fees

Please estimate the cost to the *franchisee* of obtaining the following services. Note that the estimates in this item will ordinarily be for fees or payments that the franchisee must pay to the franchisor, its affiliates, or that the franchisor or its affiliates impose or collect in whole or in part on behalf of a third party. If a listed service will not be required for the franchise you will offer, or if a more precise description of the service can be provided, please feel free to revise the listed services. For *each fee*, please specify whether the fee is nonrefundable, or, if applicable, the circumstances under which the fee may be refunded. If a single estimate is difficult to make, please feel free to furnish an estimated *range* of costs, instead:

Cost/Fee	Amount or Range
Required local advertising expenditures, including cost to obtain white/yellow page ads	
Additional on-site inspection(s) by the franchisor	
Attend initial training	
Attend additional training and/or refresher courses	

VII. Item 7: Your Estimated Initial Investment

On the chart that follows this page, please furnish us with the franchisor's estimate of expenses to be incurred by franchisees during the "initial period" of operating the franchised business. The categories and other information now furnished on the chart are *suggestions only*. Please delete nonrelevant categories and information and add other categories and information that are necessary to make the chart complete and accurate. For *each payment*, please specify whether the payment is nonrefundable, or (if applicable), the circumstances under which the payment may be refunded.

Type of Expenditure	**Estimated Amount**	**Method of Payment**	**When Due**	**To Whom Payment Is to Be Made**
Initial Franchise Fee 1/	$_____	_____	_____	Franchisor
Real Property 2/	$_____ to $_____	Monthly, nonrefundable	As arranged	Lessor, Seller
Leasehold, Contractor Improvements; Construction Costs 3/	$_____ to $_____	Progress payments, nonrefundable	As arranged	_____
Equipment 4/	$_____ to $_____	As arranged	As incurred	Suppliers
Opening Advertising 5/	$_____ to $_____	As arranged	As incurred	Suppliers
Initial Training 6/	$_____ to $_____	As arranged	As arranged	Suppliers of transportation, food, and lodging
Start-up Supplies/ inventory 7/	$_____ to $_____	As arranged	As incurred	Suppliers
Utility Deposits 8/	$_____ to $_____	Lump sum	As incurred	Utility Companies
Business Licenses 9/	$_____ to $_____	Lump sum	As incurred	Governmental Authorities
Additional Funds 10/	$_____ to $_____	__________	__________	__________
Insurance 11/	$_____ to $_____	As arranged	As incurred	Insurers
TOTAL	**$_____ to $_____**			

VIII. Item 8: Restrictions on Sources of Products and Services

A. Please identify below all products and services that the franchisee is, or will be, obligated to purchase or lease (a) from the franchisor or its affiliate; (b) from a specific source designated by the franchisor; (c) from suppliers approved by the franchisor; (d) in accordance with the franchisor's specifications (specifications may include a brand specified or approved by the franchisor, or a generic description of product qualities). A description of the categories or types of products and services, rather than a list of individual products and services, is all that is necessary. These categories should include all goods, services, supplies, fixtures, equipment, inventory, computer hardware and software, and real estate that relate to establishing or operating the franchised business. Please note that these Franchisee Purchase/Lease Requirements should include obligations imposed both by written agreement and by the practice of the franchisor.

B. Please identify for which of the categories of goods and services listed above the franchisor or its affiliates are, or will be, (a) an approved supplier; and (b) the only approved supplier. Please indicate the name of the affiliate for each category of goods or services provided by an affiliate:

C. For the franchisor's most recent fiscal year, provide the following information. This information should be taken from the statement of operations (i.e., profit and loss statement) in the franchisor's most recent audited financial statement, which will be attached to the disclosure document. If not apparent in that statement, identify the source of the information used in computing revenues.

1. Total revenues: $______________.
2. Revenues from products and services purchased or leased by franchisees (including any income the franchisor received based on franchisees' purchases or leases from third parties): $______________.
3. Revenues in (b) stated as a percentage of total revenues: ______________%.

   The source of the foregoing information was (check applicable):

   The Franchisor's audited financial statements; or

   Other (please describe): ______________

D. For the franchisor's most recent fiscal year, provide the amount of revenue that the franchisor's *affiliates* derived from franchisee purchase/lease requirements: $______________.

1. Was the information about affiliate revenues obtained from audited financial statements?

   Yes _____ No _____
2. If so, which financial statements?
3. If not, how was the answer to question VIII.D obtained or computed?

E. Provide an estimate of the percentage of the franchisee's purchases and leases under VIII.A(a)–(d) in relation to *all* purchases and leases of products and services that the franchisee will make in:

1. Establishing the franchised business: ______________%
2. Operating the franchised business: ______________%

   If you wish, please feel free to provide these percentages separately for specific purchasing requirements (e.g., if insurance must be purchased in accordance with specifications, the cost of insurance as a percent of start-up costs and ongoing operating costs). Use separate pages if necessary.

F. Does/will the franchisor negotiate purchasing arrangements with suppliers (including any arrangements involving price terms) for the benefit of franchisees?

   Yes _____ No _____

1. Provide an estimate of the number of such purchasing arrangements currently in existence:

2. If any of such purchasing arrangements involve price terms, provide a range of the discount off standard pricing that the franchisor has been able to obtain for the benefit of franchisees:

3. Please describe the types of products or services for which the franchisor negotiates or will negotiate arrangements with suppliers:

G. Does/will the franchisor or its affiliates receive payments, rebates, or other consideration from suppliers who sell to franchisees?

Yes _____ No _____

1. Are such payments related to the suppliers' sales to franchisees?

   Yes _____ No _____

2. Describe the basis for each such payment, including the percentage formula or flat amount used to determine each payment:

3. Does/will the franchisor purchase goods or services from suppliers at lower prices than the prices available to franchisees?

   Yes _____ No _____

4. If so, provide details of each such arrangement covered by (c), including, if known, (i) the price differences involved, (ii) whether such price differences are attributable to volume discounts, and (iii) whether the franchisor performs services related to the distribution of the goods that the franchisees do not perform (e.g., negotiation of supply arrangements, warehousing and/or shipment of products, central order-taking, billing of franchisees, collection from franchisees, guaranteeing of franchisee payments).

H. Does the franchisor own any interest (includes ownership or other financial interest) in any supplier?

Yes _____ No _____

If "Yes," identify the supplier(s):

I. Does any officer of the franchisor own any interest (includes ownership or other financial interest) in any supplier?

Yes _____ No _____

If "Yes," identify the officer(s) and supplier(s).

J. Describe the way in which any specifications and standards are/will be issued to franchisees and suppliers, including how any specifications and standards are formulated and modified: _______________

K. Identify all purchasing and distribution cooperatives that serve or will serve the franchise system, including the categories of products and services involved:

L. State whether the franchisor offers or will offer inducements to, or confers benefits on, franchisees who purchase from approved or designated sources (e.g., renewal rights, additional franchises, a larger territory)?

Yes _____ No _____ If so, provide details of such inducements or benefits:

* * * * *

X. Item 10: Financing

1. Will the franchisor or any of its affiliates provide financing for the establishment or operation of the franchised business? (Please note that the term "financing arrange-

ment" includes loans, leases, and installment contracts.) If more than one financing program will be provided, please photocopy Item X of this questionnaire and complete for each financing program.

Yes _____ No _____

XI. Item 11: Franchisor's Assistance, Advertising, Computer Systems, and Training

Site Selection

1. Please describe the franchisor's practices with regard to site selection:

____

Time between Signing the Agreement and Opening the Franchised Business

2. a. What is the typical time range between signing the franchise agreement and opening the franchised business?

   b. Please list the factors that might affect the time estimated above (such as ability to obtain a lease; financing or building permits; zoning and local ordinances; weather conditions; shortages; or delayed installation of equipment, fixtures, and signs):

Training

3. Please present the following information with respect to the franchisor's *initial* training program. If the franchisor offers training *after* the initial phase of operations, please also describe the following information for such program on a photocopy of the following chart.

Subject	Number of Hours of Classroom Training	Number of Hours of On-the-Job Training	Location

4. Is enrollment in the initial training program mandatory for certain individuals?

   Yes _____ No _____

   If "No," what percentage of new franchisees enrolled in the initial training program during the past year? _____%

5. Who is *required* to attend the initial training program?
6. Who *may* attend the initial training program, but is not required to attend?
7. How often are training classes held and what is the nature of the location or facility where training is held (for example: company headquarters, home, office, company-owned unit, or franchisee operated unit)?
8. Will franchisees be required to pay a training fee for initial training?

   Yes _____ No _____

9. If the answer to XI.8. is yes, please provide the amount of the initial training fee:

   $_______________

10. Who will be responsible for transportation costs and living expenses of the initial trainees?
11. Will the franchisor have a formal training staff?

    Yes _____ No _____

    If the answer to IX.11. is "Yes," identify each staff member and provide the following information:

Staff Member	Position or Title	Principal Duties	Previous Experience Relevant to Training Program

12. Is there a specified time period in which the initial training must be complete (for example, within a certain time following signing the franchise agreement, or a minimum time period before the opening of the unit)?

    Yes _____ No _____

    If "Yes," please describe the timing requirement:
13. Does the franchisor plan to offer additional training and/or refresher courses?

    Yes _____ No _____
14. If the answer to XI.13. is "Yes," please provide the following information:
    a. Will such training be optional or required?
       i. Optional __________
       ii. Required __________

       If it is required, please provide details about these programs.
    b. Will franchisees be required to pay a training fee for additional training and/or refresher courses?

       Yes _____ No _____
    c. If the answer to XI.14.b. is "Yes," please provide the franchisor's best estimate of the training fee:
    d. Who will be responsible for transportation costs and living expenses of the trainees who will receive additional training?
15. Please describe the general nature of the training and instructional materials.

Advertising

16. Does the franchisor plan to offer any services to its franchisees (either free of charge, or for which the franchisor will impose a fee) relating to advertising?

    Yes _____ No _____
17. If the answer to XI.16. is "Yes," please provide the following information:
    a. The media in which the advertising may be disseminated (for example, print, radio, or television).
    b. The scope of media coverage (i.e. local, regional, or national).

c. The source of the advertising (for example, in-house advertising department, a national or regional advertising agency).

d. If there is an advertising council composed of franchisees that advise the franchisor on advertising policies:

e. If the franchisee must participate in a local or regional advertising cooperative:

   i. How the area or membership of the cooperative is defined:

   ii. How the franchisee's contribution to the cooperative is calculated (may reference Item VI).

   iii. Who is responsible for administration of the cooperative (for example, franchisor, franchisees, or advertising agency).

   iv. Whether cooperatives may operate from written governing documents and whether the documents are available for review by the franchisee. Please attach a copy of the cooperative bylaws or other governing documents.

   v. Whether cooperatives must prepare annual or periodic financial statements and whether the statements are available for review by the franchisee.

   vi. Whether the franchisor has the power to require cooperatives to be formed, changed, dissolved, or merged.

f. If applicable, for each advertising fund not described in subpart e, above:

   i. Who contributes to each fund (for example, franchisees, franchisor, franchisor-owned units, outside vendors or suppliers):

   ii. Whether the franchisor-owned units must contribute to the fund and, if so, whether it is on the same basis as franchisees.

   iii. How much the franchisee must contribute to the advertising fund(s) and whether other franchisees are required to contribute at a different rate (it is not necessary to disclose the specific rates).

   iv. Who administers the fund(s). Whether the fund is audited and when, and whether financial statements of the fund are available for review by the franchisee.

   v. Use of the fund(s) in the most recently concluded fiscal year, specifically the percentages spent on:

Type of Expenditure	**Percentage (These need to total 100%)**
Production	
Media Placement	
Administrative expenses	
Other (describe below)	

   Description of "Other": ______________

   vi. Whether the franchisor or an affiliate receives any payment for providing goods or services to an advertising fund.

g. Whether the franchisor is required to spend any amount on advertising in the area or territory where the franchisee is located.

h. If all advertising fees are not spent in the fiscal year in which they accrue, explain how the franchisor uses the remaining amounts: ______________

i. Will franchisees receive a periodic accounting of how advertising fees are spent? If so, how often will the accounting be provided?

j. The percentage of advertising funds, if any, used for advertising that is principally a solicitation for the sale of franchises.

Cash Registers and/or Computer Systems

18. Does the franchisor require franchisees to buy or use electronic cash registers or computer systems?

Yes _____ No _____

If the answer to XI.18. is "Yes":

a. Please describe the electronic cash registers and/or computer systems in nontechnical language:

b. What is the estimated cost to the franchisee of purchasing or leasing any required computer systems and/or electronic cash registers? $_______________

c. Is (i) the franchisor, (ii) the franchisor's affiliate, or (iii) any third party, obligated to provide ongoing maintenance, repairs, upgrades, or updates to electronic cash registers or computer systems?

Yes _____ No _____

If "Yes," please provide details about any such obligations.

d. State whether the franchisee has any contractual obligation to upgrade or update any hardware component or software program during the term of the franchise, and, if so, whether there are any contractual limitations on the frequency and cost of the obligation.

e. What is the estimated annual cost of any optional or required computer and POS system maintenance, updating, upgrading, or support contracts or services?

$_______ _______ Not applicable

f. i. For each electronic cash register system or software program, describe how it will be used in the franchisee's business, and the types of business information or data that will be collected, generated, and stored.

ii. State whether the franchisor will have independent access to the information and data, and if so, whether there are any contractual limitations on the franchisor's right to access the information and data.

Manual—Table of Contents

19. Will you arrange for prospective franchisees to view the operating manual before purchasing the franchise?

Yes _____ No _____

20. If the answer to Question XI.19 is "No," please attach the table of contents of the operating manual(s). The table of contents needs to indicate the total number of pages devoted to each subject and the total number of pages in the manual.

21. If the answer to Question XI.19 is "Yes," will you require the prospective franchisee to sign a Confidentiality Agreement before viewing the Manual?

Yes _____ No _____

XII. Item 12: Territory

1. Do you grant any form of territorial protection to a franchisee?

Yes _____ No _____ If "No," please skip the remaining questions in this Item and go to Item XIII of this Questionnaire.

2. Within the protected territory, do you have the right to offer or sell goods and services using the Proprietary Marks?

   Yes _____ No _____ Please skip to question XII.4.

3. Within the territory, are there restrictions on your ability to offer and sell goods and services using (check all that apply):

   a. franchised units?

      Yes _____ No _____

   b. company or affiliate owned units?

      Yes _____ No _____

   c. other channels of distribution, such as catalogs, supermarkets, Internet, telemarketing, other direct marketing, etc.?

      Yes _____ No _____ If "Yes," what other distribution channels?

4. Does the continuation of a franchisee's territorial protection depend on its achievement of a certain sales volume, market penetration, or other contingency?

   Yes _____ No _____ If "Yes," what are these contingencies and how will they affect a franchisee's protected rights?

5. Other than as described in response to XII.4., do you have the right to modify any protected territorial rights that you initially grant to a franchisee?

   Yes _____ No _____

   If "Yes," describe the circumstances under which a modification can occur, and the likely consequences to the franchisee that would result from the modification:

6. Does the franchisee have any options, rights of first refusal, or similar rights to acquire additional franchises within the protected territory or contiguous territory?

   Yes _____ No _____ If "Yes," what rights does the franchisee have?

7. Are you (or an affiliate) restricted from soliciting or accepting orders, or selling products or services using any trademarks (regardless of whether the trademarks are used *by* the franchise system), from consumers inside a franchise's territory, including those secured from other distribution channels, such as Internet, catalogues, telemarketing, or other direct marketing sales?

   Yes _____ No _____ If "Yes," describe the restrictions.

8. Do you or an affiliate currently engage in, or have reserved the right to engage in, the activities described in question 7?

   Yes _____ No _______

9. Is the franchisee restricted in any way from soliciting or accepting orders, or selling products or services from consumers outside a franchise's territory, including those secured from other distribution channels, such as Internet, catalogues, telemarketing, or other direct marketing sales?

   Yes _____ No _____ If "Yes," describe the restrictions.

XIII. Item 13: Trademarks

Note: Please provide the information in response to the following questions relating *only* to the *principal* marks that will be licensed to the franchisee:

1. Please identify the entity that owns the trademarks or service marks that will be licensed to the franchisee:
2. Please identify the *principal* or *primary* marks that will be licensed to the franchisee and the goods or services for which the marks are used:

Mark	Goods or Services

3. *Federal Registrations:*
   a. If any of the marks listed in 2 above are registered in the U.S. Patent and Trademark Office, please provide the following information:

Mark	Registration No.	Registration Date	Principal or Supplemental Register	Goods or Services Covered

   b. Have all required affidavits (of use, incontestability, etc.) regarding the above registrations been filed?

   Yes _____ No _______
4. *Federal Applications:*
   a. If any of the marks listed in 2 above are not registered, but have been applied for in the U.S. Patent and Trademark Office, please provide the following information:

Mark	Serial No.	Application Date	Principal or Supplemental Register	Goods or Services Covered

   b. Have all required affidavits (of use, incontestability, etc.) regarding the above registrations been filed?

   Yes _____ No _______
5. Is there any effective determination of the U.S. Patent and Trademark Office, Trademark Trial and Appeal Board, the trademark administrator of any state, or any court; or any pending interference, opposition, or cancellation proceeding; or any pending material litigation involving any of these marks?

   Yes _____ No _______
6. If the franchisor does not own the trademarks or service marks, is there an agreement authorizing their use by the franchisor?

   Yes _____ No _______

   If the answer to XIII.7. is "Yes," please attach a copy of the agreement.

7. Are there any other agreements currently in effect that limit the rights of the franchisor to use or license the use of any of these marks?

   Yes _____ No _______

   If the answer to XIII.8. is "Yes," please attach a copy of the agreement.

8. Are there any infringing uses actually known to the franchisor that could materially affect the franchisee's use of these marks in any state?

   Yes _____ No _______

XIV. Item 14: Patents, Copyrights, and Proprietary Information

1. Does the franchisor own any rights in or to any patents (including pending applications for patents) or copyrights that are material to the franchise?

   Yes _____ No _______

2. If the answer to XIV.1. is "Yes," please provide the following information:

   a. *Patents:*

Patent No.	Issue Date	Title	Type (Mechanical, Process, Design, etc.)

   b. *Patent Applications:*

Serial No.	Filing Date	Title	Type (Mechanical, Process, Design, etc.)

   c. *Copyrights:*

Copyright	Registration No.	Date

   d. Describe the manner in which, and term for which, the franchisee may use each patent or copyright:

   e. Is there any effective determination of the Patent and Trademark Office, Copyright Office, or any court, with respect to a registered patent or copyright?

      Yes _____ No _______

   f. If the answer to XIV.2.e. is "Yes," please provide details:

   g. Are there any agreements currently in effect that will limit the franchisor's use of any of the patents or copyrights?

      Yes _____ No _______

   h. If the answer to XIV.2.g. is "Yes," please provide details:

3. Does the Franchisor claim rights in any proprietary information (e.g., formula, recipe, trade secret, or other confidential information) that will be communicated to the franchisee?

   Yes _____ No _______

4. If the answer to XIV.3.i. is "Yes," please provide a general description of the proprietary information:

5. If the answer to XIV.3.i is "Yes," please describe the terms and conditions that attach to the franchisee receiving the proprietary information.

XV. Item 15: Obligation to Participate in the Actual Operation of the Franchise Business

1. Describe franchisee obligations to participate personally in the franchised business that arise from any written agreement (include identification of the agreement, e.g., personal guarantee, confidentiality agreement, or noncompetition agreement):

2. Describe franchisee obligations to participate personally in the franchised business that arise from the franchisor's practice:

   If none, does the franchisor nevertheless recommend such participation?

   Yes _____ No _______

3. If the franchisee's personal "on-premises" supervision is not required, please provide the following information:

   a. Are there any *limitations* on whom the franchisee can hire as an on-premises supervisor?

      Yes _____ No _______

   b. If the answer to XV.3.a. is "Yes," please provide details: ____________________

   c. Must the on-premises supervisor successfully complete the training program?

      Yes _____ No _______

4. Is the on-premises supervisor required to have an equity interest in the business?

   Yes _____ No _______

5. If the answer to Question XV.4. is "Yes," what is the amount of equity interest the supervisor must have?

6. Are there any *restrictions* in agreements or otherwise (e.g., manuals) that the franchisee must place on its managers?

   Yes _____ No _______

XVI. Item 16: Restrictions on What the Franchisee May Sell

1. Are there any restrictions as to the customers to whom the franchisee may sell goods and services?

   Yes _____ No _______

2. If the answer to XVI.1. is "Yes," please provide details:

3. Does the franchisor impose any sales quotas or other measure of market penetration that the franchisee is required to meet?

   Yes _____ No _______

4. If the answer to XVI.3. is "Yes," please provide details:
5. Is the franchisee obligated to sell or provide *all* the goods and services authorized by the franchisor?

   Yes _____ No _______
6. If the answer to XVI.5. is "No," please provide details:
7. State whether the franchisor has the right to change the types of goods and services that the franchisee is authorized to sell, if such right is not or will not be contained within the franchise agreement (i.e., the operating manual provides the franchisee with the right to change the goods or services that the franchisee is authorized to sell):

   Yes _____ No _______
8. State whether there are or will be any limits on the franchisor's right to change the types of goods and services that the franchisee is authorized to sell, and, if so, describe such limits:

* * * * *

XVIII. Item 18: Public Figures

Note: A "public figure" is a person whose name or physical appearance is generally known to the public in the geographic area where the franchise will be located.

1. Is any compensation or other benefit given or promised to a public figure arising from:
   a. The use of the public figure in the franchise name or symbol?

      Yes _____ No _______
   b. The endorsement or recommendation of the franchise to prospective franchisees?

      Yes _____ No _______
2. If the answer to either part of XVIII.1. is "Yes," please provide the following information:
   a. Is there any charge to franchisees for the right to use the name or likeness of the public figure?

      Yes _____ No _______
   b. If the answer to XVIII.2.a. is "Yes," please provide details:
   c. Is there any compensation or other benefit promised to the public figure for the endorsement or use of his/her name?

      Yes _____ No _______
   d. If the answer to XVIII.2.c. is "Yes," please provide details:
3. Are there are public figures in the actual management or control of the franchisor?

   Yes _____ No _______
4. If the answer to XVIII.3. is "Yes," please provide the following information:
   a. Describe the position and duties of the public figure:
   b. Has the public figure made any investment in the franchisor, and, if so, what is the nature of the investment? Describe the extent of the amount contributed in services performed or to be performed and state the type of investment (e.g., common stock, promissory note).

* * * * *

XX. Item 20: Outlets and Franchise Information

1. There are five tables that must be included. These are:
   - Table 1—Systemwide Outlet Summary for Years 2019–2021
   - Table 2—Transfers of Outlets from Franchisees to New Owners (other than the Franchisor) for Years 2019–2021
   - Table 3—Status of Franchised Outlets for Years 2019–2021
   - Table 4—Status of Company-Owned Outlets for Years 2019–2021
   - Table 5—Projected Openings for 2022

   Do you currently have any franchisees?

   Yes _____ No _______

   If you do not currently have any franchisees, then only Tables 3 and 5 will apply.
2. Table 1: Please provide the total number of franchised and company-owned outlets for the last three fiscal years, by completing the chart that follows. For this section, "outlet" includes outlets of a type substantially similar to the franchises currently being offered or to be offered. If you need to explain any information contained in the chart, please use the space that follows the chart.

Table 1
Systemwide Outlet Summary for Years 2019–2021

Outlet Type	Year	Outlets at the Start of the Year	Outlets at the End of the Year	Net Change
Franchised	2019			
	2020			
	2021			
Company-Owned	2019			
	2020			
	2021			
Total Outlets	**2019**			
	2020			
	2021			

3. Table 2: Please provide the total number of franchised outlets transferred in each state during each of the Company's last three fiscal years, by completing the chart that follows. For purposes of this section, "transfer" means the acquisition of a controlling interest in a franchised outlet, during its term, by a person other than the Company or an affiliate.

Table 2
Transfers of Outlets from Franchisees to New Owners (other than the Franchisor) for Years 2019–2021

State	Year	Number of Transfers
STATE	2019	
	2020	
	2021	
Total	**2019**	
	2020	
	2021	

4. Table 3: Please provide in the following table the status of franchisee-owned outlets located in each state for each of the Company's last three fiscal years.

Table 3
Status of Franchised Outlets for Years 2019–2021

State	Year	Outlets at Start of Year	Outlets Opened	Terminations	Nonrenewals	Reacquired by Franchisor	Ceased Operations Other Reasons	Outlets at End of the Year
State	2019							
	2020							
	2021							
Totals	**2019**							
	2020							
	2021							

5. Table 4: Please provide in the following table the status of Company-owned outlets located in each state for each of the Company's last three fiscal years.

Table 4
Status of Company-Owned Outlets for Years 2019–2021

State	Year	Outlets at Start of the Year	Outlets Opened	Outlets Reacquired from Franchisee	Outlets Closed	Outlets Sold to Franchisee	Outlets at End of the Year	Outlets at End of the Year
State	2019							
	2020							
	2021							
Totals	**2019**							
	2020							
	2021							

6. Table 5: Please provide in the following table projected new franchised and company-owned outlets.

Table 5
Projected Openings for 2022

State	Franchise Agreements Signed but Outlet Not Opened	Projected New Franchised Outlets in 2022	Projected New Company-Owned Outlets in 2022
STATE			
Total			

List of Franchisees: Please provide a list of all franchisees.

List of Former Franchisees: Please provide a list of former franchisees.

XXI. Item 21: Financial Statements

1. Are comparative audited financial statements (including at least a balance sheet, statement of operations, of stockholders equity, and of cash flows) available for the franchisor for the franchisor's last three fiscal years?

   Yes _____ No _______

Attachment A to FDD Questionnaire: Employment History

FOR DIRECTORS, OFFICERS, SALES PERSONNEL OF THE FRANCHISOR AND CERTAIN OTHER PERSONNEL AND BROKERS

1. Name: ____________________________________
2. List all positions held with the franchisor and the starting and ending dates (month/year) of service

   (a) Title ____________________ Start / End Dates ____________________

   (b) Title ____________________ Start / End Dates ____________________

   (c) Title ____________________ Start / End Dates ____________________

   A full five-year employment history is required. If you have been associated with the franchisor for fewer than five full years or if you have been employed by others concurrently with your association with the franchisor during the past five years, please provide the following information about your other employment until a full five-year period is covered. Include employment by an affiliate or independent entity as well as self-employment or nonemployment.

   a. Employer ____________________

      Title ____________________ City / State of Employment ____________
      Start and end dates of employment ____________________

   b. Employer ____________________

      Title ____________________ City / State of Employment ____________
      Start and end dates of employment ____________________

   c. Employer ____________________

      Title ____________________ City / State of Employment ____________
      Start and end dates of employment ____________________

Pending Litigation and Arbitrations

Table 1
Pending Litigation and Arbitrations (Part 1)

Are you at the present time:	**Check the appropriate box**	
	Yes	**No**
A defendant in a pending criminal action?		
A defendant, or a defendant to a counterclaim, cross-claim, or third-party complaint, in any pending civil matter, e.g., an action in a federal or state court?		
A party to a pending administrative action?		
A party to a pending arbitration proceeding?		

Table 2
Pending Litigation and Arbitrations (Part 2)

If you answered yes to any question in Table 1, then please complete this table. **Do any of the matters to which you answered "yes" in Table 1 involve an allegation that you violated or engaged in any of the following:**	**Check the appropriate box**	
	Yes	**No**
Any franchise law?		
Any securities law?		
Fraud?		
Embezzlement?		
Any antitrust law?		
Other allegations?		

Concluded Litigation and Arbitrations

Table 3
Concluded Litigation and Arbitrations (Part 1)

Within the past ten years, have you ever:	**Check the appropriate box**	
	Yes	**No**
Been convicted of any felony?		
Pleaded nolo contendere to any felony?		
Been convicted of a misdemeanor?		
Pleaded nolo contendere to a misdemeanor?		
Been held liable in a civil action by final judgment?		
Been held liable in any material arbitration proceeding?		
Been the subject of a material complaint?		
Been the subject of other legal proceedings?		

Table 4
Concluded Litigation and Arbitrations (Part 2)

If you answered "yes" to any of the questions in Table 3, then please complete this table with respect to each such "yes" answer.	**Check the appropriate box**	
	Yes	**No**
Any franchise law?		
Any securities law?		
Fraud?		
Embezzlement?		
Any antitrust law?		
Misappropriation of property?		
Unfair or deceptive practices?		
Fraudulent conversion?		
Comparable allegations?		

Details of Any Pending or Concluded Litigation and Arbitrations

A. Please complete Table 5 for *each litigation* referenced in Tables 2 or 4. If you need more space, or have more than one case for which the answer is yes, please make additional copies of Table 5.

Table 5

Case name and number:	
Court in which action filed:	
Date of filing:	
General nature of claims asserted:	
Were you employed by or associated with another defendant in this action, such as an employee, supplier, etc. If so, how?	
For pending actions, current status:	
For actions no longer pending, the disposition of the case, including the specific terms of settlement. Please indicate whether the settlement is a matter of public record:	
Please also send us a copy of the complaint, as well as any judgment or settlement agreement.	

B. Please complete Table 6 *for each material arbitration or administrative proceeding* referenced in Table 2 or 4. If you need more space, or have more than one case for which the answer is yes, please make additional copies of Table 6.

Table 6
Arbitration or Administrative Proceedings

Case name and number:	
Arbitration or other public agency office in which action filed:	
Date of filing:	
General nature of claims asserted:	
Were you employed by or associated with another defendant in this action, such as an employee, supplier, etc. If so, how?	
For pending actions, current status:	
For actions no longer pending, the disposition of the case, including the specific terms of settlement. Please also indicate whether the settlement is a matter of public record:	
Please also send us a copy of the complaint, as well as any judgment or settlement agreement.	

a. The number of such pending and/or concluded material arbitration proceedings: __________

b. The number of material arbitration proceedings initiated by the franchisor: __________

c. The number of material arbitration proceedings initiated by franchisees: __________

Currently Effective Administrative Orders

a. Are you at the present time:

   i. Subject to any currently effective injunctive or restrictive order or decree relating to franchises:

   Yes _____ No _______

   ii. Subject to any currently effective injunctive or restrictive order or decree under any federal, state, or Canadian franchise, securities, antitrust, trade regulation, or trade practice law as a result of a concluded or pending action or proceeding brought by a public agency?

   Yes _____ No _______

   iii. Subject to any currently effective order of any national securities association or national securities exchange (as defined in the Securities and Exchange Act of 1934) suspending or expelling you from membership in such association or exchange?

   Yes _____ No _______

b. For any "Yes" answers, please provide the following information:

   i. The public agency or court: ______________________________

   ii. A summary of the allegations or facts found by the court or agency: __________

   iii. The date of the order or decree: ______________________________

   iv. Nature, terms, and conditions of the order or decree: ____________________

   ____

   ____

   ____

To Be Completed Only by the Franchisor or an Affiliate

During your most recently completed fiscal year, did you initiate any arbitration or judicial proceedings against a franchisee that involved a contractual dispute that is directly related to the operation of the franchised business (such as royalty payments, training, or operations)? Please disregard actions involving suppliers or other third parties or indemnification for tort liability.

Yes _____ No _______

Please complete Table 7 for each arbitration or judicial proceeding. *Make additional copies of Table 7 as needed.*

Table 7

Case name and number:	
Court or arbitration office in which action filed:	
Date of filing:	
Concise description of claim, such as "royalty collection suit," "termination," "noncompete," etc.	
Case name and number:	
Court or arbitration office in which action filed:	
Date of filing:	
Concise description of claim, such as "royalty collection suit," "termination," "noncompete," etc.	
Case name and number:	
Court or arbitration office in which action filed:	
Date of filing:	
Concise description of claim, such as "royalty collection suit," "termination," "noncompete," etc.	

1. During the past ten years, did you:
   a. File as a debtor (or have filed against you) a petition to start an action under the U.S. Bankruptcy Code or the equivalent law of another country?

      Yes _____ No _______

   b. Obtain a discharge of debts under the bankruptcy code or the equivalent law of another country?

      Yes _____ No _______

   c. Were you a principal officer of any company or a general partner in any partnership that, during the time you held (or currently hold) such a position, or during the one-year period before you held such position (a) filed as a debtor (or had filed against it) a petition to start an action under the U.S. Bankruptcy Code or the equivalent law of another country; (b) obtained a discharge of its debts under the U.S. Bankruptcy Code or the equivalent law of another country?

      Yes _____ No _______

2. If you answered "Yes" to any portion of question 1, please provide the following information:
   a. The name of the proceeding:
   b. Name the party that is/was the debtor in the bankruptcy proceedings and explain its relationship to you or the franchisor: _______________________

c. Date of filing (if pending): ______________________________

d. Date of judgment (if discharged): ______________________________

e. Court:

f. Docket or case number:

g. Any other material facts or circumstances: ______________________________

I certify that I have completely and accurately answered all of the questions in this Questionnaire.

____
Signature

____
Print Name

____
Date

Exhibit 2-2
Examples of State-Required Changes to FDDs and Agreements

This list is not meant to be all inclusive. These are some examples of changes that may be required in state addenda. Review various state resources and statutes when drafting FDDs and state-specific addenda.

California

State FDD Differences:	Disclose each item that may be negotiated or has been negotiated within the 12 months immediately preceding the FDD's effective date. Item 3 must include currently effective order of any national securities association or national securities exchange, suspending or expelling such persons from membership in such association or exchange. California Corporations Code, Section 31125 requires the franchisor to give the franchisee a disclosure document, approved by the Department of Corporations prior to a solicitation of a proposed material modification of an existing franchise. Item 17 – California law provides franchisees with additional rights concerning termination and non-renewal. If the Franchise Agreement is inconsistent with the law, the law will control. Provisions requiring waiver of compliance with the franchise law are void. Forum selection and choice of law provisions may not be enforceable. Termination upon the bankruptcy of the franchisee may not be enforceable. Liquidated damage provisions may be restricted or prohibited. Section 31125 of the California Corporations Code requires us to give you a disclosure document approved by the Commissioner of Corporations before we ask you to consider a material modification of your franchise agreement. The Franchise Agreement contains a waiver of punitive damages and jury trial provision. These provisions may not be enforceable. Prospective franchisees are encouraged to consult private legal counsel to determine the applicability of California and federal laws (such as Business and Professions Code Section 20040.5, Code of Civil Procedures Section 1281, and the Federal Arbitration Act) to any provisions of a franchise agreement restricting venue to a forum outside the State of California. FRANCHISOR'S WEBSITE HAS NOT BEEN REVIEWED OR APPROVED BY THE CALIFORNIA DEPARTMENT OF CORPORATIONS. ANY COMPLAINTS CONCERNING THE CONTENTS OF THIS WEBSITE MAY BE DIRECTED TO THE CALIFORNIA DEPARTMENT OF CORPORATIONS AT WWW.CORP.CA.GOV.

Hawaii

State FDD Differences:	THESE FRANCHISES WILL BE/HAVE BEEN FILED UNDER THE FRANCHISE INVESTMENT LAW OF THE STATE OF HAWAII. FILING DOES NOT CONSTITUTE APPROVAL, RECOMMENDATION OR ENDORSEMENT BY THE DIRECTOR OF COMMERCE AND CONSUMER AFFAIRS OR A FINDING BY THE DIRECTOR OF COMMERCE AND CONSUMER AFFAIRS THAT THE INFORMATION PROVIDED HEREIN IS TRUE, COMPLETE AND NOT MISLEADING. THE FRANCHISE INVESTMENT LAW MAKES IT UNLAWFUL TO OFFER OR SELL ANY FRANCHISE IN THIS STATE WITHOUT FIRST PROVIDING TO THE PROSPECTIVE FRANCHISEE, OR SUBFRANCHISOR, AT LEAST SEVEN DAYS PRIOR TO THE EXECUTION BY THE PROSPECTIVE FRANCHISEE, OF ANY BINDING FRANCHISE OR OTHER AGREEMENT, OR AT LEAST SEVEN DAYS PRIOR TO THE PAYMENT OF ANY CONSIDERATION BY THE FRANCHISEE, OR SUBFRANCHISOR, WHICHEVER OCCURS FIRST, A COPY OF THE DISCLOSURE DOCUMENT, TOGETHER WITH A COPY OF ALL PROPOSED AGREEMENTS RELATING TO THE SALE OF THE FRANCHISE. THIS DISCLOSURE DOCUMENT CONTAINS A SUMMARY ONLY OF CERTAIN MATERIAL PROVISIONS OF THE FRANCHISE AGREEMENT. THE CONTRACT OR AGREEMENT SHOULD BE REFERRED TO FOR A STATEMENT OF ALL RIGHTS, CONDITIONS, RESTRICTIONS AND OBLIGATIONS OF BOTH THE FRANCHISOR AND THE FRANCHISEE.

Illinois

State FDD Differences:	Item 17: Governing law, venue, and jurisdictional requirements are subject to the Illinois act, and waiver of same are ineffective, except that arbitration outside Illinois is allowed. In addition, Illinois law will govern the Franchise Agreement to the extent required by the Illinois Franchise Disclosure Laws. Conditions under which franchise can be terminated and rights upon non-renewal may be affected by Illinois law, 815 ILCS 705/19 and 705/20.

Maryland

State FDD Differences:	Item 17: Termination for bankruptcy filing may not be enforceable; general release required as a condition to renewal, sale or consent to assignment/transfer shall not apply to any liability under the Maryland Law; franchisee may sue in Maryland for claims under the Maryland Law; claims under Maryland must be brought within three years after grant of franchise.

Michigan

State FDD Differences:	Include specific "Notice Mandated by Section 8 of Michigan Franchise Investment Act", regarding right to join associations; restriction on releases, etc., restrictions on termination without good cause and opportunity to cure; failure to renew without fairly compensating franchisee under certain circumstances; discrimination on renewal; arbitration or litigation outside Michigan; restrictions on transfer rights without good cause; restrictions on requirements to resell items not uniquely identified with franchisor; restrictions on franchisor's transfer of its contractual obligations.

Minnesota

State FDD Differences:	Item 13: Provisions pertaining to protection of franchisee's rights to use trademarks. Item 17: Restrictions of choice of law and forum selection or abrogation of rights under Minnesota franchise law; given 90 days notice of termination (with 60 days to cure) and 180 days notice for non-renewal of the Agreement; restrictions on requirement release of claims as condition of renewal or assignment, or release or waiver of rights under Minnesota franchise law.

New York

State FDD Differences:	Item 3: No time limitation on disclosure of felony or nolo contendere plea; disclosure of misdemeanor or nolo contendere plea for last 10 years. Item 12: Disclose franchisee rights to rescind or amend the franchise agreement if franchisor exercise a right to establish another franchise that will be allowed to use the franchisor's trade name or trademark within an exclusive territory of the franchisee. Item 17: Permits franchisee to terminate on ground available by law; no assignment by franchisor unless assignee is willing and able to assume obligations of franchisor; choice of law other than New York does not limit franchisee's or franchisor's rights under New York franchise law.

North Dakota

State FDD Differences:	Item 17: Forum selection outside North Dakota; waiver of punitive damages; jury trial waiver; North Dakota law governs claims arising out of franchise law; liquidated damages, limitation of claims and contractual statute of limitations; requirement to sign release not enforceable; prevailing party entitled to attorney's fees.

Rhode Island

State FDD Differences:	Item 17: Claims enforceable under the Rhode Island Franchise Act are not subject to forum selection and choice of law.

Virginia

State FDD Differences:	Item 17: Unlawful for a franchisor to cancel a franchise without reasonable cause. Provisions to the contrary in franchise agreement may not be enforceable.

Washington

State FDD Differences:	Item 17: Washington Law may supersede the Franchise Agreement, including the areas of termination and renewal; Washington Law applies in event of conflict of laws; release or waiver of rights shall not include rights under Washington Franchise Protection Act, unless part of a negotiated settlement with counsel; provisions such as those which unreasonably restrict or limit the statute of limitation period for claims under the Act, rights or remedies under the Act, such as rights to jury trial might not be enforceable. Item 17: Transfer fee collectible only to the extent they reflect our reasonable estimated or actual costs in effecting a transfer.

Exhibit 2-3
State Advertising Filing Requirements

State*	Requirement	Examiner
California	Unless the examiner has any comments, the advertisement is automatically approved 3 business days after it is filed. The following **disclaimer** is required on the advertisement filed in California: **THESE FRANCHISES HAVE BEEN REGISTERED UNDER THE FRANCHISE INVESTMENT LAW OF THE STATE OF CALIFORNIA. SUCH REGISTRATION DOES NOT CONSTITUTE APPROVAL, RECOMMENDATION, OR ENDORSEMENT BY THE COMMISSIONER OF FINANCIAL PROTECTION AND INNOVATION NOR A FINDING BY THE COMMISSIONER THAT THE INFORMATION PROVIDED HEREIN IS TRUE, COMPLETE, AND NOT MISLEADING.**	Department of Financial Protection and Innovation One Sansome Street Suite 600 San Francisco, CA 94104-2980
Maryland	The advertisement must be filed at least 5 days before its anticipated initial use. **The franchisor's name, address, and phone number must appear on the advertisement.**	Franchise Examiner Maryland Division of Securities Office of the Attorney General 200 St. Paul Place Baltimore, MD 21202-2020
Minnesota	Unless the examiner has any comments, the advertisement is automatically approved 5 business days after it is filed. **The franchisor's name, address, telephone number, and state registration number must appear on the advertisement.**	Franchise Examiner Minnesota Department of Commerce Securities Section 85 7th Place E., Suite 280 St. Paul, MN 55101

*If the franchisor has secured a large franchisor exemption filing in California, Maryland, New York, North Dakota, and Washington, then advertising registration filing is not required.

State*	**Requirement**	**Examiner**
New York	Unless the examiner has any comments, the advertisement is automatically approved 7 days after it is filed. The franchisor must submit a signed, notarized verification page with the advertisement verifying that the advertising materials are consistent with its FDD. A **disclaimer** is required on the advertisement as follows. **DISCLAIMER for small ad** (print ad under 5-inch long and not more than one column wide, or that are broadcast for 30 seconds or less)—"THIS OFFERING IS MADE BY PROSPECTUS ONLY." **DISCLAIMER for long ad**—"THIS ADVERTISEMENT IS NOT AN OFFERING. AN OFFERING CAN ONLY BE MADE BY A PROSPECTUS FILED FIRST WITH THE DEPARTMENT OF LAW OF THE STATE OF NEW YORK. SUCH FILING DOES NOT CONSTITUTE APPROVAL BY THE DEPARTMENT OF LAW."	Franchise Examiner New York State Department of Law Investment Protection Bureau 28 Liberty Street New York, New York 10005
North Dakota	Unless the examiner has any comments, the advertisement is automatically approved 5 business days after it is filed.	Franchise Examiner North Dakota Securities Department State Capitol, 5th Floor 600 East Blvd, Bismarck, ND 58505
Washington	Unless the examiner has any comments, the advertisement is automatically approved 7 days after it is filed.	Franchise Examiner Securities Administrator Dep't of Financial Institutions Securities Division 150 Israel Street, S.W. Tumwater, Washington 98501

Exhibit 2-4
List of States' Expiration Dates for Registration Filings (initial and renewal)

(For dates regarding large franchisor exemptions, see the notes in italics.)

STATE	EFFECTIVE DATE	EXPIRATION DATE	DEADLINE FILING DATE
California	Assigned by examiner *Exemption: effective upon receipt*	110 days after fiscal year end *Exemption: expires on 15-month calendar basis; file prior to fiscal year end date*	15 business days prior to expiration date *Exemption: file any time after July 1 to qualify for the following fiscal year exemption*
Florida	Initial filing: assigned by examiner Renewal filing: typically the same date as the previous year *No large franchisor exemption available*	One year from effective date	Same as expiration date
Hawaii	7 days after receipt of app. and/or follow-up materials; subject to further review by examiner *No large franchisor exemption available*	90 days after fiscal year end	Same as expiration date
Illinois	Initial filing: assigned by examiner Renewal filing: upon receipt; subject to further review by examiner *Exemption: effective date assigned by examiner* *Jumbo exemption: no filing required; effective automatic*	120 days after fiscal year end *Exemption: expires 120 days after fiscal year end*	1 day prior to expiration date
Indiana	Initial filing: upon receipt (however, processing takes some time; call examiner to find out exact date) Renewal filing: typically the same date as the previous year *Exemption: no filing required; effective automatic*	One year from effective date *Exemption: expires 120 days after fiscal year end*	Same as expiration date

STATE	EFFECTIVE DATE	EXPIRATION DATE	DEADLINE FILING DATE
Kentucky	Assigned by examiner *No large franchisor exemption available*	N/A: one time filing	N/A
Maryland	Assigned by examiner *Exemption: effective date assigned by examiner, but typically effective within 10 business days*	One year from effective date *Exemption: one year from effective date*	15 business days prior to expiration date *Exemption: 10 business days prior to expiration date*
Michigan	Upon receipt *No large franchisor exemption available*	One year from effective date	N/A
Minnesota	Assigned by examiner *No large franchisor exemption available*	120 days after fiscal year end	Same as expiration date
Nebraska	Assigned by examiner: typically effective upon receipt *No large franchisor exemption available*	N/A: one time filing	N/A
New York	Assigned by examiner *Exemption: effective date assigned by examiner* *Jumbo exemption: no filing required; effective automatic*	120 days after fiscal year end *Exemption: expires 120 days after fiscal year end*	Same as expiration date
North Dakota	Assigned by examiner *Exemption: effective date assigned by examiner*	One year from effective date *Exemption: expires 120 days after fiscal year end*	15 business days prior to expiration date (examiner notes that, regardless of the expiration date, an amendment or renewal filing must be submitted within 120 days after the franchisor's fiscal year end to include updated audited financial statements) *Exemption: same as registration above*

STATE	EFFECTIVE DATE	EXPIRATION DATE	DEADLINE FILING DATE
Rhode Island	Assigned by examiner *Exemption: effective date assigned by examiner*	120 days after fiscal year end *Exemption: expires 120 days after fiscal year end*	30 days prior to expiration date *Exemption: same as registration above*
South Dakota	Upon receipt *No large franchisor exemption available*	One year from effective date	Same as expiration date
Texas	Upon receipt *No large franchisor Exemption available*	N/A: one time filing	N/A
Utah	Initial filing: upon receipt (however, processing takes some time; call examiner to find out exact date) Renewal filing: typically the same date as the previous year *No large franchisor exemption available*	One year from effective date	Same as expiration date
Virginia	Initial filing: assigned by examiner Renewal filing: same date as the previous year, but examiner assigns new "amendment" date *Exemption: effective date assigned by examiner*	One year from effective date *Exemption: same as registration above*	30 days prior to expiration date *Exemption: same as registration above*
Washington	Assigned by examiner *Exemption: effective date assigned by examiner*	One year from effective date *Exemption: same as registration above*	15 business days prior to expiration date *Exemption: same as registration above*
Wisconsin	Upon receipt *No large franchisor exemption available*	One year from effective date	Same as expiration date

Exhibit 2-5
Chart of State Franchise Law Jurisdictional Requirements

Jurisdictional Requirements Summary

State	Franchisee Domiciled in State	Franchised Business to Be Located in State	Offer to Sell Franchise Made in State	Offer to Sell Franchise Directed to State and Received in State	Offer to Buy Franchise Accepted in State
California	X	X (and franchisee domiciled in state)	X	X	X
Hawaii	X	X	X	X	
Illinois	X	X (and offer to sell franchise is made or accepted in Illinois if they are not a resident of Illinois)	X	X	X
Indiana	X	X			
Maryland	X	X	X	X	X
Michigan	X	X (and franchisee domiciled in state)	X	X	X
Minnesota		X	X	X	X
New York	X	X (and franchisee domiciled in state)	X	X	X
North Dakota	X	X (and franchisee domiciled in state)	X	X	X
Oregon	X	X (and franchisee domiciled in state)	X	X	X

State	Franchisee Domiciled in State	Franchised Business to Be Located in State	Offer to Sell Franchise Made in State	Offer to Sell Franchise Directed to State and Received in State	Offer to Buy Franchise Accepted in State
Rhode Island	X (and franchised business to be located in state)	X (and franchisee domiciled in state)	X	X	X
South Dakota	X (and franchised business to be located in state)	X (and franchisee domiciled in state)	X	X	X
Virginia		X			
Washington	X	X	X (and the offer violates the franchise law of the state to which the offer is directed)	X	X
Wisconsin			X	X	X

In the table, the existence of one factor is enough to evoke application of the state's franchise registration and/or disclosure law *unless* the table indicates that the factor requires that factor *and* another factor as set forth in the parenthetical.

Exhibit 2-6
Sample Franchisee Compliance Questionnaire

As you know, you and XYZ, Inc. (the **"Franchisor"**) are preparing to enter into a Franchise Agreement for the establishment and operation of an "**XYZ**" franchised business (an "**XYZ Business**"). The purpose of this Questionnaire is to determine whether any statements or promises were made to you that the Franchisor has not authorized and that may be untrue, inaccurate, or misleading. Please review each of the following questions and statements carefully and provide honest and complete responses to each.

1. The following dates and information are true and correct:

a. _____________, 20__ Initials ____________	The date of my first face-to-face meeting with any person to discuss the possible purchase of an XYZ Business franchise.
b. _____________, 20__ Initials ____________	The date on which I received Franchisor's Franchise Disclosure Document ("FDD").
c. _____________, 20__ Initials ____________	The date when I received a fully completed copy (other than signatures) of the Franchise Agreement and Addenda (if any) and all other documents I later signed.
d. _____________, 20__ Initials ____________	The date on which I signed the Franchise Agreement.

2. Have you received and personally reviewed the Franchise Agreement and each Addendum and related agreement attached to it?

   Yes _____ No _____

3. Do you understand all of the information contained in the Franchise Agreement, each Addendum, and/or related agreement provided to you?

   Yes _____ No _____

   If no, what parts of the Franchise Agreement, Addendum, and/or related agreement do you not understand? (Attach additional pages, as needed.)

   ____

   ____

   ____

   ____

4. Have you received and personally reviewed the FDD that was provided to you?

   Yes _____ No _____

5. Did you sign a receipt for the FDD indicating the date you received it?

   Yes _____ No _____

6. Do you understand all of the information contained in the FDD and any state-specific Addendum to the FDD?

   Yes _____ No _____

   If No, what parts of the FDD and/or Addendum do you not understand? (Attach additional pages, as needed.)

   ____

   ____

   ____

   ____

7. Have you discussed the benefits and risks of establishing and operating an XYZ Business with an attorney, accountant, or other professional advisor?

   Yes _____ No _____

   Have you had the FDD and Franchise Agreement reviewed by an attorney, accountant, or other professional advisor?

   Yes _____ No _____

   If No to either question, do you wish to have more time to do so?

   Yes _____ No _____

8. Do you understand that the success or failure of your XYZ Business will depend in large part upon your skills and abilities, competition from other businesses, interest rates, inflation, labor and supply costs, lease terms, and other economic and business factors?

   Yes _____ No _____

9. Do you understand that no agreement or addendum is effective until it is also signed and dated by the Franchisor?

   Yes _____ No _____

10. Do you understand that there are no promises, representations (other than in the franchise disclosure document), agreements, "side deals," or other arrangements, written or oral, that are not in the Franchise Agreement?

    Yes _____ No _____

11. If you have answered "No" to any one of questions 8–10, please provide a full explanation of each No answer in the following blank lines. (Attach additional pages, as needed, and refer to them below.) If you have answered "Yes" to each of questions 8–10, please leave the following lines blank.

____
____
____
____

12. Has any employee or other person speaking for the Franchisor made any statement or promise concerning the revenues, profits, or operating costs of an XYZ Business operated by the Franchisor or its franchisees that is contrary to the information contained in the FDD?

    Yes _____ No _____

13. Has any employee or other person speaking for the Franchisor made any statement or promise regarding the amount of money you may earn in operating the XYZ Business that is contrary to the information contained in the FDD?

    Yes _____ No _____

14. Has any employee or other person speaking for the Franchisor made any statement or promise concerning the total amount of revenue the XYZ Business will generate that is contrary to the information contained in the FDD?

    Yes _____ No _____

15. Has any employee or other person speaking for the Franchisor made any statement or promise regarding the costs you may incur in operating the XYZ Business that is contrary to or different from the information contained in the FDD?

    Yes _____ No _____

16. Has any employee or other person speaking for the Franchisor made any statement or promise concerning the likelihood of success that you should or might expect to achieve from operating an XYZ Business that is contrary to or different from the information contained in the FDD?

    Yes _____ No _____

17. Has any employee or other person speaking for the Franchisor made any statement, promise, or agreement concerning the advertising, marketing, training, support service, or assistance that the Franchisor will furnish to you that is contrary to or different from the information contained in the FDD?

    Yes _____ No _____

18. Have you entered into any binding agreement with the Franchisor concerning the purchase of this franchise before today?

    Yes _____ No _____

19. Have you paid any money to the Franchisor concerning the purchase of this franchise before today?

    Yes _____ No _____

20. If you have answered "Yes" to any one of questions 12–19, please provide a full explanation of each Yes answer in the following blank lines. (Attach additional pages, as needed, and refer to them below.) If you have answered "No" to each of questions 12–19, please leave the following lines blank.

    ____

    ____

    ____

    ____

21. Do you understand that all disputes and claims you may have under the Franchise Agreement and the Personal Guarantee must be heard in the courts of ______________ (if they cannot be informally resolved or by mediation)?

    Yes _____ No _____

22. Do you understand that the Franchise Agreement and the Personal Guarantee provide that you can only collect compensatory damages on any claim under or related to the Franchise Agreement and not any consequential or punitive damages?

    Yes _____ No _____

23. Do you understand that the Franchise Agreement and the Personal Guarantee both include a waiver of jury trials?

    Yes _____ No _____

24. I have spoken with current and former XYZ Business franchisees, and I chose which franchisees, and how many franchisees, to speak with.

    Yes _____ No _____

25. During my negotiations and evaluations leading up to my decision to buy an XYZ franchise business, I communicated with the following individuals from XYZ, Inc. or its affiliates or independent brokers:

Name Address

1. ____
2. ____
3. ____
4. ____

[Insert additional names and addresses below if needed.]

By signing this Questionnaire, you are representing to us that you have responded honestly, accurately, and completely to each of the above questions.

FRANCHISE APPLICANT

____

Signed

____

Printed Name

_______________, 20____

Date

Exhibit 2-7
List of State Websites

State	Franchise Registration or Business Opportunity State Website
California	https://dfpi.ca.gov/franchise-investment-law/
Connecticut	http://www.ct.gov/dob/cwp/view.asp?a=2230&q=297810&dobNAV_GID=1662
Florida	https://www.fdacs.gov/Business-Services/Sellers-of-Business-Franchises
Georgia	https://consumer.georgia.gov/business-compliance/required-filings/multilevel-distribution-business-opportunity-consent-service
Hawaii	http://hawaii.gov/dcca/sec/registration_forms/franchise_filings/
Illinois	http://illinoisattorneygeneral.gov/consumers/franchise.html
Indiana	https://securities.sos.in.gov/general-information/franchise/
Kentucky	https://ag.ky.gov/Priorities/Protecting-Kentuckians/business/Pages/forms.aspx
Maine	http://www.maine.gov/pfr/securities/business_opp.htm
Maryland	http://www.oag.state.md.us/Securities/about.htm#franch
Michigan	https://www.michigan.gov/ag/0,4534,7-359-81903_83221-198444--,00.html
Minnesota	https://mn.gov/commerce/industries/securities/franchises/
Nebraska	http://www.ndbf.ne.gov/busopp/index.shtml
New York	https://ag.ny.gov/franchisors-franchisees
North Carolina	https://www.sosnc.gov/divisions/business_opportunity_sales
North Dakota	https://www.nd.gov/securities/franchise-registration
Rhode Island	https://dbr.ri.gov/divisions/securities/franchising.php
South Carolina	https://sos.sc.gov/services-and-filings/business-opportunities
South Dakota	https://dlr.sd.gov/securities/franchise_registration.aspx
Texas	http://www.sos.state.tx.us/statdoc/faqs2700.shtml https://www.sos.state.tx.us/other/forms.shtml#BOAF
Utah	http://consumerprotection.utah.gov/registrations/businessopps.html
Virginia	http://www.scc.virginia.gov/srf/index.aspx
Washington	http://www.dfi.wa.gov/sd/franchise.htm
Wisconsin	http://www.wdfi.org/fi/securities/franchise/bdgerreg.htm http://www.wdfi.org/fi/securities/franchise/default.htm

CHAPTER 3

Franchise System Operational Issues

Brian Cole and Susan Sheely

Contents

3-1. Introduction

Franchisors dedicate significant time and energy to developing and delivering particular products and services to the ultimate customer. Of potentially equal importance to the long-term success of the business, however, are the structure and operations of the franchise system. Does the franchisor have the right tools in place to manage the system successfully, and has it communicated its expectations adequately to its franchisees? This chapter gives practical advice for structuring franchise system operations—drafting operations manuals; formulating advertising programs; avoiding common liability issues; and creating records management, purchasing, and compliance and audit programs.

3-2. Operations Manuals

As a matter of trademark law, a franchisor (or, for that matter, any owner of a trademark) must control the nature and quality of the goods and services used with the mark if it licenses another to use the mark. No franchise law in the United States specifically obligates a franchisor to exercise these controls through an operations manual, but the general assumption is that all franchisors will provide an operations manual. One of the requirements for preparing Item 11 of a franchise disclosure document (FDD) is that the franchisor either disclose the table of contents of the franchisor's operations manual in the FDD or make the operations manual available for review before the prospective franchisee buys the franchise.[1] No explicit exception is made for a franchisor that does not have an operations manual.

The assumption that all franchisors have an operations manual is consistent with the legal definition of "franchise," which (for example, under the Federal Trade Commission (FTC) Rule[2]) makes the existence of a franchise dependent upon the franchisor exerting significant controls or providing significant assistance.[3] While it is possible to meet the definition of a franchise without providing an operations manual, an operations manual serves multiple purposes. Among other things, an operations manual can be used as the primary source document for the franchisor's training program and can provide assurance to the franchisees that the controls exercised by the franchisor are applied consistently. A well-drafted and well-organized operations manual can also save the franchisor (and its personnel) substantial time, as franchisees can (be directed to) refer to the operations manual to refresh the franchisee's recollection of matters taught in the training program.

Despite this assumption about the existence of operations manuals, there have not been many cases addressing the need for an operations manual. One of the few is *Kohr v. Gropp & Lehman Enterprises, Inc.*[4] In *Kohr*, the franchisee complained about the inadequacy of the training and the informality of the operations manual (which consisted of "a few typewritten pages for waitresses, bus boys and supervisors, a set of Gropps' secret recipes, some supply lists, and inventory order forms"). The trial court found that even though the "Operations Procedure Manual was crude, the plaintiffs were not misled as to what it contained or the fact of its existence." The court also stated that "the plaintiffs were well aware of the fact that they were doing business with a less established [franchisor] and at a better price." Ultimately, the court found that the defendants did not make any untrue statements of material fact, and did not breach the franchise agreement, but had failed to register the franchise with the State of Michigan. As a result of

---

1. There are two (overlapping) sets of requirements for preparing FDDs. The first is part of the Federal Trade Commission's "Franchise Rule" (formally, "Disclosure Requirements and Prohibitions Concerning Franchising," 16 C.F.R. part 436)—specifically 16 C.F.R. § 436.5(k)(6). The second is part of the "2008 Franchise Registration and Disclosure Guidelines," published by the North American Securities Administrators Association (NASAA), *available at* https://www.nasaa.org/wp-content/uploads/2011/08/6-2008UFOC.pdf (last accessed Oct. 9, 2019). Although the NASAA guidelines have different provisions for cover pages and application pages, the disclosure "requirements are substantively equivalent to the requirements adopted under the Amended FTC Franchise Rule, . . . although the format, style, and some references have been revised for the readers' convenience." Chapter 2 of this book contains a more extensive discussion of the disclosure requirements of the FTC Rule and NASAA's FDD Guidelines.

2. See *supra* note 1.

3. 16 C.F.R. § 436.1(h)(2).

4. Bus. Franchise Guide (CCH) ¶ 8123 (D. Mich. 1981); *aff'd mem.* 718 F.2d 1099 (6th Cir. 1983).

this failure, the plaintiffs were awarded a return of their $15,000 initial fee plus interest and attorneys' fees, but no further damages.

(a) Getting Started

Preparing an effective operations manual is a significant undertaking. For a company new to franchising, it is best to prepare the operations manual before the first franchise is sold. This forces the franchisor to document the important aspects of its system and provides a format for assuring that the franchisees implement the system consistently. It also allows all franchisees to be introduced to the operations manual from the very beginning. The majority of this discussion is geared to an existing franchisor that is considering revising its operations manual, although much of the discussion would also apply to a company first getting into franchising and producing its initial operations manual. Anyone preparing or revising an operations manual will need to identify the fundamental elements of the business to be covered by the manual (in the case of revisions, some or all of the issues may already be covered by the existing manual). The drafter(s) may also want to enlist the assistance of subject matter experts to develop portions of the manual. In a larger company, representatives from various functional areas within the company may be able to provide some of this functional expertise, but there may still be a need for consultation with outside experts. Specialists in preparing operations manuals can also provide valuable guidance on the format and structure of the manual to enhance its readability and comprehension by franchisees. It may also relieve some of the pressure on the drafters to consider that the operations manual does not need to be a static document; it is likely to continue to be revised as the needs of the franchise system change.

An operations manual will likely address two different categories of information. The first category consists of mandatory standards of the franchise system that a franchisee must follow to comply with its franchise obligations. These mandatory standards should set forth *what* a franchisee must do to maintain its operations, not *how* to conduct its operations. For example, a standard could require a franchisee's employees to greet customers in a courteous and friendly manner, but it is preferable not to mandate exactly what the franchisee's employees say. Similarly, an appropriate standard may require a franchisee to provide reasonable security for its premises but without dictating specific security measures that must be taken (see the discussion of *Martin v McDonald's Corp.*, below, in which a franchisor incurred direct liability by providing overly detailed guidance on security[5]).

It is worth remembering that personal injury plaintiffs attempt to use an operations manual against franchisors in almost every lawsuit. The "what, not how" approach helps protect against a plaintiff's claim that a franchisor controls a franchisee sufficiently to establish actual agency or a claim of independent negligence by the franchisor. Thoughtful drafting of standards—to place clear

5. Martin v. McDonalds Corp., 213 Ill. App. 3d 487, 492–93 (Ill. App. Ct. 1991).

responsibility for operations on the franchisee—can help avoid franchisor liability and the attendant costs. (See the discussion of vicarious liability and direct liability in sections 3-5 and 3-6 of this chapter.)

The other category of information in the manual will consist of suggested, but not required, procedures that the franchisee may follow to improve business and more closely meet the standards of the franchisor. For example, the franchisor may *require* as a standard that the franchisee have an adequate number of competent and fully trained employees. An operations manual may contain *suggested* procedures for employee hiring and retention that the franchisee may, in its discretion, decide to follow.

These suggested procedures should answer for the franchisee the questions of "what," "how," "who," "where," "when," and "why." If the franchisee decides to follow the procedures, it will then have a clear understanding of what the franchisor is suggesting. The franchisor might also recommend tools to assist in following the procedures.

Some franchisors delineate in the operations manual the functional areas that consist of mandatory standards as opposed to those that consist of suggested procedures. For example, the introduction to the operations manual may provide that the sections on equipment, products, and services are mandatory, while the sections on building design/layout, security, and employee relations are optional. There may also be sections that incorporate some of each. For instance, in the accounting section, the descriptions on charts of accounts may be optional, but the requirements for weekly reporting of sales (including format of reports) may be mandatory. The franchisor may also wish to specify within each standard or procedure whether the standard or procedure is mandatory for franchisees or is just suggested.

(b) Establishing the Basics

The operations manual should set forth the standards and procedures related to the various fundamental areas of the franchised business—such as operations, marketing, accounting, sales planning, franchise development, and legal. In a larger organization, one of the better ways to approach drafting or revisions of an operations manual to assure incorporation of the standards and procedures of these various fundamental areas is through the use of a committee that incorporates representatives of these various functional groups. A committee of this type requires the full endorsement of the senior management because significant resources in time, personnel, and costs will be required to complete the project and to address franchisee concerns. If a manual committee of this type is used to draft the operations manual, then smaller working teams of the committee may be used to determine the standards and procedures for the manual related to the various fundamental areas of the franchised business identified by the committee. The work teams may suggest further refinement of these areas as the manual develops.

If more than one person is involved in drafting the operations manual (and especially if there is a manual committee with smaller working teams), it is wise to develop an agreed process for creation and communication of the manual, as well as the format for the manual and the individual standards and procedures. These processes can help to enhance consistency and efficiency, and ideally they should be used over the life of the franchise to incorporate, and subsequently to communicate, changes to the operations manual.

Form 3-1 is a format for updating manual standards and procedures. This format includes a section to describe the policy reason for the standard or procedure (or for the changes to the standard or procedure). The policy statement will help the franchisee understand the reason for and accept the standard or procedure. The standard or procedure will then inform the franchisee how the policy objective is expected to be or can be accomplished. The format in form 3-1 also directs the franchisee to related topics in the manual and informs the franchisee which job functions will find the information useful. The format also provides for a reference number, date, and other information to guide the reader.

Exhibit 3-1 is a sample of how this form would be completed if a revised policy has been issued dealing with inventory accounting.

(c) Developing and Revising Standards and Procedures

The persons developing (or revising) standards will need to follow a consistent process to develop and revise standards and procedures—especially if more than one person is involved in the process. Although the same general approach is applicable for initial development of standards and procedures, the following is a summary of suggested general steps for revising an operations manual:

1. Determine what niche and image the franchisor wants for the franchise system. For example, does the franchisor want to project the best service or the best value?
2. Determine if the franchised system is operating in accordance with the franchisor's vision. If not, review whether the franchisor's vision is realistic. If the franchisor's vision is realistic, determine the root causes of any circumstances that are preventing the franchised system from operating in accordance with the franchisor's vision.
3. Determine the current standards and procedures—what is in writing, what is understood, and what is really being practiced at both franchised and company locations?
4. Evaluate these current standards and procedures—what is problematic, relevant, effective, efficient, competitive, practical, and best practice?
5. As necessary, develop revised standards and procedures. New or revised standards are particularly likely to be needed if there are discrepancies between the franchisor's vision and the actual performance of the franchised system. Develop standards that are repeatable, measurable, and realistic.
6. The franchisor should only implement standards that it is prepared to justify and enforce in a nondiscriminatory manner. Psychologists and economists (as well as practical experience) confirm that humans tend to

optimize any behavior that is measured—especially if that behavior is rewarded. As a result, some people suggest that "If you are going to count it, make sure it counts."

7. Develop measurements and measurement tools for assuring that each operator (whether a franchisee or a company employee) follows the prescribed standards and procedures. This should include the development of a standards checklist that will measure whether the standard or procedure is being followed correctly. The standards checklist should mirror the operations manual and should be updated when the operations manual is updated. As with all standards and procedures, standards checklists should be monitored to ensure consistency in format and content.
8. Identify any technology, marketing program, modernization program, and other system changes that may be required to perform the standards and procedures. Confirm the ability of the franchisor to make these changes (both contractual and practical) and evaluate the ability of the franchisees to comply before issuing the standards and procedures.
9. Document the new standards and procedures.
10. Test the new standards and procedures and revise as necessary. The franchisor will get the greatest benefit from a test if it is conducted in operating units with varying characteristics (first with company-owned units and, if successful, with franchised units) that will challenge the standard or procedure. Also, testing in one or more franchisee locations may ultimately give the standard or procedure more credibility.
11. Communicate the new standards and procedures. A communications action plan should be established to ensure that interested parties are informed about the progress of the project and any critical issues that may arise. Interested parties will include the franchisor's senior management, the franchise department, the franchisee advisory committee or franchisee association, and the franchisees. Obtaining everyone's agreement and support in the order listed above should help with obtaining the support of the successive group.

The work teams should agree on the steps above and how to maintain their files so that the work can be readily reviewed and accessed. For example, the work teams may agree that all their files should include the following subfiles:

- Current practice on Standard "X"
- Interview notes on Standard "X"
- Measurement of Standard "X"
- Drafts of Standard "X"
- Comments on Standard "X"
- Changes to Standard "X"
- Final Standard "X"
- Issued updates to Standard "X"
- Quality inspection checklist for Standard "X"

(d) Team Membership

Membership on the working teams should be carefully considered to ensure the best product and the least resistance to the changes. Each working team will require a highly organized leader and a detailed action plan identifying (1) the key objective, (2) the actions to be taken to meet the objective, (3) the responsible parties, (4) the date by which the action must be completed, (5) the current status of the project, and (6) whether the status has been communicated to the proper parties.

Using working teams with members from different functional areas will help minimize the likelihood that a standard or procedure will have an unexpected detrimental effect on the business. In addition, if the franchisor has an independent franchisee association or a franchisee advisory committee (FAC), it is wise to invite representatives of the independent franchisee association or the FAC to work closely with the franchisor's manual committee. In fact, it may even be helpful, and even more efficient, to have a franchisee member on each of the working teams. The franchisee members of the working team can report to the franchisee association or FAC on the progress of updating the operations manual and obtain suggestions regarding particular issues. This process should allow for the raising of troublesome issues along the way, so that when the franchisor is ready to publish revisions to the manual, it will already have addressed any material issues with the franchisees and, hopefully, have achieved franchisee acceptance of the revisions.

Note: If the franchisor is involved in or anticipates any litigation that relates to policies or other information in the operations manual, the franchisor should be careful to preserve the attorney-client privilege regarding documents and communications that involve adoption or modification of any standard or procedure that relates to the pending or anticipated litigation. A lawyer should coordinate the team's communications regarding all matters that are (or are anticipated to be) involved in litigation.

As sections of the manual are completed, the working teams should deliver their proposed manual sections to the manual committee. All of the working teams' standards and procedures should be reviewed by the manual committee to ensure that the standards and procedures are consistent, complete, and accurate.

The manual committee should maintain a copy of all revisions to the manual dated as they occur. The level of detail should be such that the manual committee should be able to recreate quickly the version of the manual in existence on any particular date in the past.

(e) Tips on the Creation and Organization of the Manual

1. Use a structure that is user friendly.
2. Write in plain English.
3. Use short, concise sentences written in the active voice.

4. Only use abbreviations, acronyms, or industry terms if a glossary is provided.
5. Do not use clichés.
6. Before the operations manual is first distributed, consider how updates will be handled (see subsection (f), below).
7. If the operations manual will have multiple parts for separate topics, clearly label each as part of the manual and identify what portion of the overall operations manual is contained in each part.
8. For each separate portion of the operations manual, use a table of contents and provide an index for the entire operations manual.
9. Limit the number of typefaces and sizes on each page or screen.
10. Use the same format on each page or screen so the reader can easily find the needed information.
11. Use subheadings and an outline form to facilitate ease in information retrieval and a better understanding of the relationships among the information provided.
12. Use clearly understandable charts as a reference tool, but also explain the charts in plain language.
13. Date each page and give each topic a series number.
14. Distinguish between required standards and suggested procedures; for example, separate sections or parts of the operations manual may be devoted to required standards and to suggested procedures; alternatively, there may be other cues (such as different colors) to distinguish the two.
15. If the operations manual will be distributed electronically, consider the appearance of the materials on a computer screen, where some fonts are easier to read than others.

(f) Distribution of Operations Manual

The operations manual can be distributed either in physical form or electronically (or both). Some franchisors may distribute copies of the operations manual on a thumb drive or one or more CDs, but more commonly now many franchisors make their operations manual available electronically on a secure section of the franchisor's website (sometimes known as an "extranet") or on the company's internal site (an "intranet"). Properly implemented, methods of this type can assure that all franchisees have access to the most up-to-date version of the operations manual at all times and can decrease the cost of distribution. E-mail and other methods of electronic communication can be used to notify franchisees when modifications are made to sections of the operations manual. When the manual is distributed over the Internet, the technology also exists to be able to determine when and for how long each franchisee views sections of the manual. Among other things, this can be useful as a way to prove that the franchisee was on notice of a new or revised standard or procedure.

No matter how copies of the manual are distributed, an original "master version" of the manual should stay at the franchisor's headquarters—especially when copies of the manual are distributed in print. The franchise agreement should have a provision that states that in the event of any disputes about the contents of the manual, the master version of the manual maintained at the franchisor's headquarters will be considered the governing manual.

If the franchisor distributes physical copies of the manual to its franchisees, it is advisable to number each copy and obtain a receipt for the manual from the recipient. Preferably, the receipt should include an acknowledgment by the franchisee that all right, title, and interest in the manual are owned by the franchisor; that the manual is a confidential document; and that the franchisee will not disclose the information in the manual to persons other than those who need to know the information to operate the franchised business and will not use it for any purpose other than to conduct the franchised business. In addition, franchisees should be advised that the operations manual is copyrighted and that franchisees are not to make copies of any portions of the operations manual without the franchisor's consent.

The person or department within the franchisor that is responsible for distributing copies of the operations manual (typically, either the franchise sales department, the training department, or the franchise operations department) should maintain a distribution log for copies of the operations manual along with the receipts. The distribution log should reflect (at a minimum) the serial number of the manual distributed to each franchisee and the date and contents of each update sent to the franchisee.

If the franchisor distributes the operations manual online, on a thumb drive or on CDs, the franchisor should consider using an appropriate digital rights management (DRM) program. DRM programs can accomplish such goals as keeping the thumb drive or CDs from being copied and making the thumb drive or CDs unusable after a specified date. Use of thumb drives or CDs protected by DRM programs can ease some of the difficulties of tracking copies of the manual, but similar security procedures should still be implemented.

When a franchisee transfers its franchise, the transfer document signed by the transferee should contain an acknowledgment of receipt of the manual. Copies of this transfer document should be kept with the distribution log, and the distribution log should be updated to reflect the identity of the new franchisee.

(g) Updating the Manual

One of the better ways to approach revisions of an operations manual is through the use of a committee that incorporates representatives of a variety of functional groups within the organization—such as operations, marketing, accounting, sales, planning, franchise, development, and legal. A committee of this type requires the full endorsement of the senior management because significant resources in time, personnel, and costs will be required to complete the project and to address franchisee concerns.

A procedure should be developed for incorporating changes into the operations manual on a periodic basis, such as semiannually (or more often if there is a critical need). The manual committee should distribute the various sections of the manual to the assigned working teams with the request that the teams review the sections and identify any changes, additions, or deletions that need to occur. The same method for approving original standards and procedures should be used to evaluate and include changes, unless the change is not material.

At the time of distribution, updates should be made easily recognizable by presentation with either different colored cover pages or pages with, for example, "updates" printed across the cover page in bold, large print. A cover page that explains the updates or provides a redlined version of changes will help the reader identify and understand the change quickly.

As franchisors propose changes to the franchise system (through updates to the operations manual), franchisees occasionally feel sufficiently attached to the old ways of doing business that they attack the changes—either actively (by bringing suit) or passively (by refusing to make the required changes). When the franchisees challenge the changes, the courts have generally upheld the franchisor's ability to require franchisees to make changes to the franchise system, provided that the changes are reasonable and are implemented for reasonable business purposes.

For instance, in *Huang v. Holiday Inns, Inc.*,[6] the franchisor changed its inspection method. After one informal and two formal inspections that resulted in "unacceptable" ratings, the franchisee was given a default notice and allowed to cure. The franchisee did not dispute that its hotel was in violation of the franchisor's quality standards, but it contended that termination would cause it severe hardship. The court permitted the changes to the inspection method and upheld the termination, saying that changes in policies were objectionable only where used by the franchisor to extort additional profits for the franchisor at the franchisee's expense.

The franchisor's power to make changes is not unlimited, however; in *Bird Hotel Corporation v. Super 8 Motels, Inc.*,[7] the court held that the franchisor could not increase advertising fees despite franchisee's obligations in the franchise agreement to comply with franchisor's system rules, which were subject to change.

Cassidy Podell Lynch, Inc. v. Snyder General Corp.[8] involved a distributor of air-conditioning equipment. The distributorship agreement required compliance with the "then current sales manual." Among other things, the sales manual required payment for all orders within 30 days after delivery (although the distributor consistently delayed payment until 90 days after delivery), and it limited the size of each invoice to $15,000. The distributor entered into a contract to sell air-conditioning equipment with a total value of $350,000 but divided the sale into a series of contracts, each for less than $15,000. After the distributor had taken delivery of (and installed) the bulk of the equipment, the manufacturer

6. 549 F. Supp. 352, 358 (C.D. Cal. 1984).
7. 2010 U.S. Dist. LEXIS 14124 (D.S.D. Feb. 16, 2010).
8. 944 F.3d 1131, 1136 (3d Cir. 1991).

refused to ship the final shipments unless the distributor paid cash on delivery. Ultimately, the court held that the manufacturer could change the terms of the sales manual (including enforcing or changing the "net 30" payment terms) but could not make that change in the middle of a single contract (finding that the series of related contracts constituted an "installment sales contract" for purposes of the Uniform Commercial Code, which governed the transaction).

Another interesting case is *Economou v. Physicians Weight Loss Centers.*[9] In *Economou*, news reports of medical problems with the franchisor's diet plans initially caused the franchisor to require franchisees to distribute to customers information sheets concerning the risks of the diet; later, the franchisor modified the diet plan. A franchisee went out of business as a franchised location and then went into competition with the franchisor. When the franchisor sued for violation of the covenant against competition, the franchisee claimed as a defense that the franchisor had first violated the contract (by changing the operations manual). The court held, however, that there was no breach of contract because the franchisor had reserved the right to change the methods of operations and the manuals.

The result is generally no different if the franchisee has a specialized reason for resisting the change proposed. For instance, *In re Sizzler Restaurants International, Inc.*[10] involved the decision by Sizzler Restaurants to abandon the "buffet court and grill" concept that had been the primary sales driver (but only a minor profit source) for many years. A franchisee (Triple S Restaurants, Inc.), owned in part by two former executives of Sizzler who had been involved in developing and promoting the buffet court and grill concept, argued that Sizzler could not reorient the concept in this way. The court interpreted this argument as an assertion that the covenant of good faith and fair dealing did not allow Sizzler to make changes in the concept unless Sizzler was willing to ensure that no franchisee that followed Sizzler's methods would fail. After reviewing several franchise-related cases on the duty of good faith and fair dealing,[11] the court disagreed, stating that the duty of good faith required only that Sizzler act honestly or within accepted commercial practices, and the court further declined to second-guess the result reached as long as the process was appropriate by that measure. Because Triple S "failed to establish that there exists a triable issue of fact as to

---

9. Bus. Franchise Guide (CCH) ¶ 9771 (N.D. Ohio 1991).

10. 225 B.R. 466 (Bankr. C.D. Cal. 1998).

11. Among the cases cited by the court were *Svela v Union Oil Co of California*, 807 F.2d 1494, 1501 (9th Cir 1987) (court cannot second-guess franchisor's economic decisions if made in good faith); *Burger King v Agad*, 941 F. Supp. 1217, 1222 (N.D. Ga. 1996) (implied covenant of good faith and fair dealing cannot be used to second-guess franchisor's legitimate business decisions); *Vasco v Mobil Oil Corp.*, 698 F. Supp. 102 104 (D. Md. 1988) ("'Good faith' has been uniformly interpreted as meaning subjective good faith, that is an honest evaluation of the franchisor's economic decisions"); Clark v America's Favorite Chicken Co., 110 F.3d 295, 297–99 (5th Cir. 1997) (no breach of the implied covenant of good faith and fair dealing despite fact that franchisor's national marketing strategy and concept made individual franchisee less competitive and resulted in loss of business); and *Vaughn v General Foods Corp.*, 797 F.2d 1403, 1413 (7th Cir. 1986) (no protection against dissatisfaction of franchisee with the degree of success it achieved as a result of franchisor's attempts to create a viable franchise system).

whether Sizzler acted in breach of the implied covenant of good faith and fair dealing in deciding to reorient the emphasis" of the franchised business, Sizzler was "entitled to judgment as a matter of law on the claim that it breached the implied covenant of good faith and fair dealing with regard to its decisions concerning the buffet court and grill marketing concept."

Sometimes the changes proposed by the franchisor are not entirely voluntary. In *Bonfield v. AAMCO Transmissions, Inc.*,[12] the franchisor entered into "stipulated final judgments" with the attorneys general of 14 states that required AAMCO (and, by extension, its franchisees) to modify the way it did business, by eliminating what the court described as "sharp practices." Bonfield objected, asserting that the changes violated the duty of good faith and were "in callous disregard of AAMCO's commitment to help its licensees achieve success." Bonfield also asserted that AAMCO's actions violated a fiduciary duty and constituted economic duress. The only claim that survived AAMCO's motion to dismiss was for breach of the covenant of good faith and fair dealing, and there, the court indicated that Bonfield would need to show that AAMCO had not acted reasonably and with proper notice in requiring the changes.

A similar case arising out of the same changes is *Layton v. AAMCO Transmission, Inc.*,[13] in which the court held that a decision by AAMCO to extend the effect of the consent decrees in 14 states to franchisees in other states was "entirely reasonable on its face" and not a breach of the duty of good faith.

A similar instance of externally imposed changes appears in *DFO, Inc. v. Northeast Inn of Meridian, Inc.*,[14] involving the Denny's chain. Following a number of highly publicized allegations of racial discrimination, DFO (the franchisor of Denny's) entered into a consent decree with the federal government requiring changes to avoid further discrimination; among other things, DFO changed its operations manual to prohibit discrimination. Northeast Inn refused to implement the changes, so DFO terminated the franchise. After losing a fight over the proper venue and governing law for the case (Mississippi or California), the franchisee stipulated to the termination.

(h) Monitoring and Enforcement

The manual will have limited value if the franchisor fails to ensure that the members of the franchise system comply with the manual. Three steps should be taken to ensure that franchisees comply with the manual.

First, the franchisor should communicate with franchisees about the purpose, importance, and content of the manual through mailings and meetings.

Second, the franchisor should provide training on the manual's content, in both initial training/orientation and retraining. For each standard and procedure, the franchisor should identify any tools that may help the franchisee meet the

12. 708 F. Supp. 867 (E.D. Ill. 1989).

13. 717 F. Supp. 368 (D. Md. 1989).

14. Bus. Franchise Guide (CCH) ¶ 11,552 (C.D. Cal. 1998); Bus. Franchise Guide (CCH) ¶ 11,662 (C.D. Cal. 1999).

standard or follow the procedure. Further tools, such as software programs, may need to be developed by the franchisor for the franchisee to comply. Additionally, the franchisor may need to train its franchisees on how to use the tools.

Third, the franchisor should monitor and enforce compliance. While some franchise companies are moving toward statistics-based quality evaluations, on-site quality inspections are vital in defending tort claims and minimizing exposure to punitive damages. To ensure objective enforcement of standards, it is preferable that a group in the franchisor company that is separate from the franchise sales group should be responsible for monitoring the franchisee operations. Quality inspectors should have a good understanding of the business so they can more quickly identify problems of, and solutions for, the franchisee. A franchisor's staff member who has successfully operated company stores is a good candidate for the inspector position because he or she has more credibility with franchisees. For further information on this topic, see section 3-8, Compliance Programs and Support.

3-3. Advertising

(a) Overview

Franchisors have options for how they establish, fund, and carry out their advertising programs. They can require franchisees to contribute either a percentage of sales or a flat sum on a periodic basis to a fund for the purpose of marketing, either national or local, for the brand. Monies can be contributed to the fund solely from the franchisees or from a combination of franchisees, the franchisor, and the units owned and operated by the franchisor. Franchisors can also require each franchisee to spend a specified amount (again, either a percentage of sales or a flat amount of money) on a periodic basis. Each of these approaches is discussed below.

With respect to most national advertising funds, the franchisor will solely control administration of the fund and placement of advertising, or may do so in conjunction with a designated or elected group of franchisees. Occasionally, a national advertising fund is controlled by the franchisees, and input from the franchisor is limited to proper trademark usage. This is not a recommended solution, as it can be seen as an abdication of the franchisor's responsibility to set the direction of the brand, but there are a few franchise systems that operate in this manner.

In addition to national advertising funds, franchisors may also create local or regional advertising cooperatives (local advertising funds). The purpose of a local advertising fund is to create advertising tailored to regional or local market variations. Local advertising funds contain a subset of franchisees, instead of the entire franchise system. Local advertising funds may be administered by the franchisees, the franchisees with the franchisor's assistance, or solely by the franchisor. Depending upon how the fund is administered, franchisees may vote on how the local advertising funds are allocated among expenses, as well as the specific advertising and marketing activities. Advertising funds managed by franchisors, and the use of advertising dollars paid into those funds, can be a frequent source of litigation. In *Broussard v. Meineke Discount Muffler Shops, Inc.*,[15] the Meineke franchisees alleged that a fiduciary relationship was created through the advertising fund and that the franchisor had a fiduciary duty to spend its marketing dollars to the benefit of the franchisees. The district court denied the franchisor summary judgment in holding that the question of whether a franchisor was a fiduciary in relation to franchisee payments to the advertising fund was fact intensive. A fiduciary relationship would place the highest standard of care on the franchisor to protect the franchisee's interests in the handling of advertising funds and how those funds are used. On appeal, the Fourth Circuit Court of Appeals rejected this view, holding that no North Carolina court had ever ruled that a fiduciary relationship existed between franchisor and franchisee.[16] "Only when one party figuratively holds all the cards—all the financial power or technical information, for example—have . . . courts found that the 'special circumstance' of a fiduciary relationship has arisen."[17] Other courts agree with the Sixth Circuit that administering an advertising fund does not create a fiduciary duty from franchisor to franchisee, especially if the franchise agreement specifically dissuades that no fiduciary relationship exists between the parties.[18]

In *Gregory v. Popeyes Famous Fried Chicken and Biscuits, Inc.*,[19] the franchisor reserved sole discretion in the administration of an advertising fund, including timing, selection, and placement of advertising. One franchisee complained that Popeyes failed to commit funds to advertising in its local market when the franchisee's location initially opened and that Popeyes failed to provide adequate advertising in its local market. The franchisee did not allege or prove complete failure by Popeyes to provide advertising and promotional materials in breach of contract, but rather alleged that Popeyes did not provide as much assistance as the franchisee "believed was necessary to give it the 'help' needed."[20] When Popeyes moved for summary judgment after trial, the trial court dismissed the franchisee's claims, declining to write into the parties' franchise agreement that Popeyes had "undertaken the duty to please individual franchisees . . . by selecting advertising that specifically benefitted a particular market or a particular store."[21] The Sixth Circuit affirmed, and other courts have agreed with this

15. 945 F. Supp. 901 (W.D.N.C. 1996).

16. Broussard v. Meineke Muffler, 155 F.3d 331, 349 (4th Cir. 1998).

17. *Id.* at 348.

18. *See, e.g.*, Prince Heaton Enterprises, Inc. v. Buffalo's Franchise Concepts, Inc., 111 F. Supp. 2d 1357, 1365 (N.D. Ga. 2000); *see also* Domed Stadium Hotel, Inc. v. Holiday Inns, Inc., 732 F.2d 480, 485 (5th Cir. 1984); O'Neal v. Burger Chef Systems, Inc., 860 F.2d 1341, 1349 n.4 (6th Cir. 1988); Rajala v. Allied Corp., 919 F.2d 610, 623 (10th Cir. 1990), *cert. denied*, 500 U.S. 905, 111 S. Ct. 1685, 114 L. Ed. 2d 80 (1991); Camp Creek Hospitality Inns, Inc. v. Sheraton Franchise Corp., 139 F.3d 1396, 1408 (11th Cir. 1998).

19. 857 F.2d 1474 (6th Cir. 1988).

20. *Id.*

21. *Id.*

result.[22] While the franchisor creates a contractual duty to deposit advertising fees collected from franchisees into the intended advertising fund,[23] courts widely agree that control of an advertising fund does not create a special or fiduciary relationship between franchisor and franchisee.

Even before *Meineke*, many franchisors expressly stated in their contracts that the advertising fund does not create a special trust or fiduciary relationship. Since *Meineke*, however, that practice has become almost universal. Franchisors need to document how monies from the fund are spent. When drafting the franchise agreement, franchisors should be careful when including provisions in the franchise agreement that restrict how the advertising funds will be spent and should consider including provisions allowing the allocation of funds toward the franchisor's administrative expenses. Generally, advertising funds involve more than just the cost of the advertisement itself, but also development, research, testing, marketing, and administration. A well-drafted franchise agreement will allow the franchisor to deduct monies from the fund to cover its administrative costs (sometimes with a cap on the portion of the fund that can go to these expenses). Some franchise agreements specify that the franchisor will audit the fund on a periodic basis and provide copies of the audit results to the franchisee either upon demand or on a periodic basis. In the event a provision establishing an audit requirement is included, defining what the franchisor means by "audit" is very important. Does it mean an audit certified by an independent accountant according to generally accepted accounting principles, or merely that a financial statement will be produced? Can the franchisor tie-out all invoices to the fund's financial statements?

Franchisors should also be aware that a catch-all provision in an existing franchise agreement requiring franchisees to abide by the general rules of the franchisor's system, including the franchisor's right to make revisions or amendments to such system, does not necessarily give them discretion to increase fees. In *Bird Hotel Corporation v. Super 8 Motels, Inc.*,[24] Super 8 Motels sought to implement a new customer rewards program that required franchisees to pay a new fee equal to 5 percent of the gross room sales paid by customers enrolled in the program. The new fees were to be used to fund the issuance of customer rewards, advertising, and administration of the program.[25] Bird Hotel argued that while Super 8 had the right to revise the customer loyalty program, it did not have the right to increase advertising fees over what was explicitly provided for in the franchise agreement.[26] The court agreed and held that the imposition of additional fees was a "unilateral revision of the terms of the contract."[27] As a

22. *See, e.g.*, Khorchid v. 7-Eleven, Inc., *slip copy*, Civ. Action No. 18-8525, 2018 WL 5149643, at *7 (D.N.J. Oct. 22, 2018) (no duty to benefit any franchisee when franchise agreement retains "sole and absolute right to determine how Advertising Fees will be spent . . . .").

23. Moghaddam v. Dunkin Donuts, Inc., 295 F. Supp. 2d 136 (D. Mass. 2003).

24. 2010 WL 572741, No. CIV 06-4073 (D.S.D. Feb. 16, 2010).

25. *Id.* at *4.

26. *Id.* at *8.

27. *Id.*

general practice, franchisors should include in the franchise agreement the high end of any fees that may be imposed and/or specifically state whether the fees may increase over time, if an increase may be anticipated.

Start-up franchisors may not wish to establish an advertising fund at all until they are certain they will have an adequate number of units to effectively fund the program. In that situation, the franchisor may instead require the franchisee to spend a specified amount within a given period of time on specified types of advertising in their local market, also referred to as a local advertising spend requirement. Money the franchisee spends locally can be credited, in whole or in part, against the franchisee's required payments to the fund, or it can be an additional advertising spend requirement. Because markets and advertising costs vary, it is recommended that any local advertising spend requirements take into account variations, such as population density, in the markets in which franchisees are operating. The amount of any local spend requirement must be identified in the FDD and the franchise agreement. The franchisor should also have an audit mechanism in place to ensure compliance and identify the remedy for noncompliance (for example, an obligation to pay the difference between the required amount and actual amount spent into the local or national advertising fund).

Use of a local advertising spend requirement is a tactic often employed by international franchisors to address variations in the markets and regulations of the countries in which they operate. If the franchisor chooses this route, it is important to establish in the franchise agreement not only what amount the franchisee must spend but also how often and whether the franchisor may audit the franchisee's expenditures to determine whether the franchisee is spending the required amounts on appropriate activities. Finally, the start-up franchisor must also look to the future; if the franchisor believes that in the future it will want to establish a fund, it should expressly reserve the right to do so in the franchise agreement and require the franchisee's participation when it reaches a certain size. To avoid future conflict, the franchisor should give some guidance of how much it will require the franchisee to contribute. For example, the franchisor should state whether the franchisee will need to contribute a higher amount to the fund than it is currently spending on advertising and, if so, the additional amount. If the franchise agreement allows the franchisee (or a group of franchisees, such as a local advertising co-op) to create its own advertising, the franchisor must have the right to review and approve or reject the advertising prior to use in order to preserve the integrity of its trademark. This allows the franchisor to avoid conflicting messages or images in the media. If the franchisor has the right to review the advertising, it will also want to consider stating how long it can take to review the materials and whether there are any other process restrictions on the franchisee's ability to advertise.

The use of social networks such as Facebook, Instagram, Snapchat, and Twitter to advertise the brand has grown exponentially in the past few years. Leveraging these technologies and platforms allows franchisees and franchisors greater opportunities to connect and interact directly with their customers and the public at large. These online platforms deliver significant benefits and connect with far more people in a far more economical manner than television, print, and radio, but with the expanded reach and informal nature of the communications comes increased risk. Many of the same issues that exist when a franchisee creates its own advertising exist here, and because content can be user generated as well as generated quickly and easily by franchisees, the need for monitoring is significant. The franchisor should retain the right to review the content and the type of messaging and, if permitted by the terms of the franchise agreement, should consider creating and pushing corporate content to social media platforms and directly onto the franchisees' branded social media pages. With the ability for franchisees and customers to very quickly create and post brand-related social media content, and the need for franchisees and franchisors to timely respond to public comments, franchisors should have a very nimble process in place for the regular review of locally generated content.

It is important to remember that the FTC has issued guidance[28] on advertising that requires full disclosure practices for social media influencers, bloggers, and reviewers of products and services any time there is a "material connection" between the social media influencer and the advertiser (which is a broader standard than payment of consideration). As a result, it is necessary to set legal and ethical guidelines for the use of paid reviews, blogs, or other content by social media influencers. Social media promotions (such as asking consumers to "share" a post or "tag a friend" to be entered to win a prize) are another area in which it is important to understand the applicable rules and regulations. In addition to FTC and state laws and regulations governing sweepstakes and promotions, many of the largest social media platforms (Facebook, Snapchat, Instagram, Twitter, and so on) have their own specific guidelines that must be followed when conducting promotions through their platforms.

What makes social media so interesting is its viral nature and, thus, the difficulty in controlling it. A franchisor or franchisee can create a website or social media page almost instantly, and those platforms can penetrate markets worldwide. If the franchisor wants to shut down the website, doing so is not always a simple task. In addition, advertising messages can be spread worldwide almost instantaneously, sometimes with bad results. For example, Burger King released a coupon on its Facebook page that allowed people to receive a free Whopper in exchange for deleting 10 friends from their Facebook page. Facebook asked Burger King to make modifications to the promotion, which prompted Burger King to end the program, but not before nearly 234,000 friends on Facebook were defriended, amounting to more than 23,000 coupons issued for free Whoppers.[29] The company said afterward that it had no plans to introduce the campaign on any other social networking sites.

---

28. Guides Concerning Use of Endorsements and Testimonials in Advertising, 16 C.F.R. § 255.198 (2009).

29. Jenna Wortham, *"Whopper Sacrifice" De-Friended on Facebook*, N.Y. Times, Jan. 15, 2009.

(b) Best Practices for National and Local Advertising Funds

Best practices for national and local advertising funds include the following:

- Make sure to include language in the franchise agreement that states that the establishment and administration of a national or local advertising fund does not create a fiduciary or trust relationship between the franchisor and franchisee.
- State that the fund will not be used solely for the benefit of any one franchise store but will be used to advertise all locations covered by the fund, and describe who determines how the money will be used (for example, that the franchisor has sole discretion and control of the fund).
- State when the franchisee must start making contributions, the amount the franchisee must contribute, and how often and whether local expenditures count toward the required expenditure amount.
- Outline how the advertising funds will be used, including administrative and other costs the franchisor may incur, including whether the franchisor may collect all of these costs from the fund, whether there is a maximum amount the franchisor may collect, and whether the amount may be increased during the term of the franchise agreement.
- Describe who must contribute to the fund (such as all stores in a particular area, or only franchised stores in an area). In particular, state whether the franchisor will contribute to the fund, and if so, how much and how often.
- State whether all of the funds collected during the fiscal or calendar year must be spent during the same year or whether some portion of the funds can be carried over to subsequent year(s).
- State whether the franchisee is entitled to any audited or unaudited reports on collections and expenditures relating to the fund, and if so, whether the franchisor will automatically release the report or the franchisee must request the report, as well as how often the report will be available.

(c) Best Practices for Individual Expenditures (Local Advertising Spend Requirements)

Best practices for national and local advertising funds and local advertising spend requirements include the following:

- State whether the franchisee must spend a certain amount of funds to advertise its franchise business, and if so, how often, in what amount, and what types of advertising are acceptable to the franchisor. Include whether grand opening expenditures are required, with respect to a new location.
- Include whether the franchisor will furnish the advertising or whether the franchisee can draft the advertising and use after approval by the franchisor.
- Allow for periodic auditing of the franchisee's expenditures, including requiring the franchisee to furnish copies of invoices and expenditures to the franchisor.

- If individual contribution or a local advertising spend requirement takes the place of contributing to a fund, reserve the right to require the franchisee to participate in a fund in the future upon notice from the franchisor, either in addition to or in the place of the individual contribution.
- Consider whether the required spend can be effectively (and efficiently) spent in the required period, especially for smaller amounts, and whether it is preferable to require a rolling average. For instance, if the required ad spend is 1 percent of sales monthly, and the best advertising vehicle in a particular market costs the equivalent of 3 percent of monthly sales, is the franchisee required to spend 1 percent of sales each month on a suboptimal advertising vehicle, allowed to purchase the optimal advertising vehicle every third month, or required to spend three times the minimum each month?

3-4. Liability of Franchisors for Events Occurring at Franchisee Locations

In most contexts, each person is responsible for the person's own legal faults but is not responsible for the acts of others—at least in the absence of the first person's own fault. However, because franchisors (generally) are perceived to have "deeper pockets" (that is, more nonexempt assets) than their franchisees, plaintiffs (in various contexts) have tried to find ways to reach those deeper pockets. Sometimes, those efforts have consisted of attempts to make the franchisor solely responsible for events occurring (or losses incurred) at franchisee locations, and sometimes the goal has been to make the franchisor jointly and severally liable (along with the franchisee) for those events or losses.

There are multiple potential ways to categorize these cases, depending on factors such as the relationship of the plaintiff to the franchisee (for example, a customer, an employee, or an unrelated third party), the nature of the claim or the loss (personal injury or economic damage), and the relief sought (such as money damages or an order that multiple entities should be considered the "employer" of a group of persons for purposes of union organization). Despite this variety of contexts and issues, the cases do not always draw fine distinctions, and a case addressing one context may cite or rely on cases from an unrelated context in support of its reasoning. As an example, one can argue that a person injured in an automobile accident with a delivery driver (a tort claimant seeking money damages, who did not "choose" to be injured by a franchisee employee) may be in a very different situation than a customer who purchased from a franchised location because of the franchisor's trademarks on the sign (and attendant reputation), and that both of them may be in very different situations than a union seeking a declaration that employees who work at multiple franchised locations should be declared part of a single bargaining unit. But until such time as the courts and the cases definitively hold that these sorts of differing circumstances should necessarily lead to different analyses (or even different outcomes), it is wise for lawyers to be aware of all of the approaches used and all of the outcomes generated in these various types of cases.

Depending upon the context, the most-common efforts to impose liability on franchisors for events occurring at franchised locations have been attempts to impose "vicarious liability" on the franchisor (that is, making the franchisor jointly and severally liable for the acts of the franchisee or the franchisee's employees, often on the theory of respondeat superior), and claims of "direct liability" (that is, assertions that a franchisor was independently liable for injuries caused by a franchisee or the franchisee's employees because of some action that the franchisor itself took or failed to take).

An additional theory (almost a blend of vicarious and direct liability) is that two separate entities should be treated as one for purposes of liability. In a variety of employment-related contexts (including labor law/union organization and payment of wages/overtime), claims have been asserted that the franchisor had "jointly employed" the franchisee's employees or that the franchisor and the franchisee constituted a "single employer" of the franchisee's employees. In the context of the Americans with Disabilities Act, claims have been asserted that a franchisor and its franchisee(s) "jointly operated" a facility, or that they jointly designed and constructed the facility. Although many of the cases applying this theory have their genesis in some specialized situations/statutes, some lawyers have expressed concerns that the same approach could be applied more broadly in contexts beyond those in which it arose.

3-5. Vicarious Liability

Vicarious liability (often known as respondeat superior) is most often used in situations in which the liability of the franchisee has been established, but the plaintiff is trying to reach beyond the franchisee to find the franchisor (also) liable. Vicarious liability is often asserted in situations in which a third party (such as a customer of the franchisee) is trying to assert that the franchisor is liable, or in cases in which an unrelated party is injured by actions of an employee of the franchisee (such as an automobile accident involving an employee of a franchisee).

As noted above, the general rule is that each person is responsible for the person's own legal faults but is not responsible for the acts of others in the absence of the first person's own fault. To a greater or lesser extent, the common law has recognized an exception to this rule in the doctrine of respondeat superior. In this case, some "employers" are jointly and severally responsible (along with the tortfeasor employee) for the torts of some classes of "employees" (as discussed below, this doctrine has also been extended in some cases to franchisor/franchisee relationships as well as employer/employee relationships). Some commentators (and a few cases on third-party liability) draw distinctions for purposes of vicarious liability, depending on the exact nature of the work done (and therefore the relationship involved).[30] In this approach, the relationship

30. D. Dobbs, The Law of Torts § 333, at 905 (West 2001).

known as "principal/agent" is one in which the agent is expected to enter into contracts on behalf of the principal; in this case, the principal is normally liable for the contracts entered into by the agent but *not* for the agent's torts. In the relationship known as "master/servant," the "servant" is expected to carry out physical tasks instead of (or in addition to) negotiating contracts for the "master"; in this type of relationship, the master generally is held liable for torts committed within the course and scope of the servant's employment. Finally, in the relationship known as "employer/independent contractor," the employer has a decreased level of control over its independent contractor and is not generally liable for either the contracts or the torts of the independent contractor. In the franchise context, the first two categories are frequently lumped together as "employer/employee," and the distinction between that category and employer/independent contractor generally depends on the level (and type) of control exercised by the franchisor.

The attributes that make a franchise system strong (and valuable) to various constituencies are the same attributes that make it vulnerable to vicarious liability claims. For the franchisor, a franchise system enables the franchisor to increase distribution and grow its brand more rapidly than it could through company-owned outlets. For the franchisee, one of the fundamental sources of value is the investment in a business with a recognized name and a pretested and established product (or service) and operating method. For the public, the value lies in being able to readily identify and obtain a product (or service) with a consistent character and quality. All of these interests compel the franchisor to establish and monitor system standards and procedures (typically through the operations manual and other support systems discussed in this chapter).

The trademarks, service marks, logos, trade names, and associated goodwill collectively constitute one of the two primary elements of a franchise. The second primary element consists of the "system"—the operating method and standards for delivering a consistent product or service to the public. Collectively, these constitute the franchisor's intellectual property. Among a franchisor's primary activities should be defining, protecting, and enhancing this intellectual property. There are typically three parts to this process. First, the franchisor must create an appropriate franchise agreement. Second, the franchisor must create an appropriate operations manual.[31] Third, the franchisor must establish various types of support systems to enforce the franchise agreement and the operations manual. These three parts must be coordinated, and the franchisor must otherwise act in a manner consistent with the franchise agreement and the operations manual.

While each franchisor can customize the manner of carrying out these duties, the franchisor has no choice but to create and enforce standards. Trademark law (including the Lanham Act at the federal level) requires the owner of a trademark or service mark that is licensed to third parties must protect that trademark or service mark by controlling the nature and quality of the goods and services identified with the licensed mark. Trademark law and the interests of the franchisor,

31. See, generally, section 3-2 of this chapter.

franchisees, and the public are all in sync in this regard. The franchisor wants to ensure that its system is followed. By carefully describing the requirements of its system to franchisees (typically in an operations manual), the franchisor protects and enhances its intellectual property and the system. The franchisees want to know the specific criteria by which their performance will be evaluated. If the franchisor has articulated clear standards, that provides franchisees with the specific criteria they desire and leads to consistency in the way all franchisees perform and are treated. The public gains from this consistency because they understand what the trademark represents. This understanding promotes public confidence in the business, which returns to benefit the franchisor and franchisees by increasing consumption, revenue, and market share. Thus, the requirement of trademark law to control the use of the franchisor's intellectual property has significant and essential benefits for the franchisor, franchisees, and the public.

The description and exercise of this right to control a franchisee's activities is not without challenges and risks. For example, drafting an operations manual that accurately describes the franchise system is challenging and time-consuming. As further discussed in the section above on the operations manual, the franchisor should impose requirements only to the extent necessary to protect the intellectual property and system belonging to the franchisor. Extending beyond this level of control may create a basis for a claim that the franchisee is the franchisor's agent. If a court concludes that the franchisee is the franchisor's agent, the franchisor is at greater risk of being held liable for third-party claims arising from the franchisee's actions. Since the reality is that the franchisor is not at the franchisee's location making the day-to-day decisions regarding the franchised business, this creates an unknowable and untenable risk to the franchisor. Federal case law states clearly that the "control" required by the Lanham Act does not create a federal law of agency. "It does not automatically saddle the licensor with the responsibilities under state law of a principal for his agent."[32] The franchisor needs to ensure, however, that by its own actions it does not create an agency relationship that would not otherwise exist.

The challenge for a franchisor is that doing the things that are necessary to establish and monitor performance by franchisees could make the independent franchisee's locations appear to be owned and operated by the franchisor. In turn, that appearance of centralized control can increase the likelihood that persons injured at a franchised location will sue the franchisor, thus increasing the franchisor's exposure to vicarious liability claims. To limit this exposure, the franchisor should circumscribe the requirements imposed on the franchisee to reflect that the franchised business is owned and operated by the franchise owner, not the franchisor. In this way, while assuring that the franchised units operate properly, the franchisor can simultaneously take steps to protect itself from liability under respondeat superior and similar theories.

Two things are worth noting about respondeat superior. First, this doctrine is one of *vicarious* liability—that is, liability for the tortious acts of another without

32. Oberlin v. Marlin Am. Corp., 596 F.2d 1322, 1327 (7th Cir. 1979).

fault of the person sought to be held liable. In the case of respondeat superior, the plaintiff seeks to hold the "superior" (the employer or the franchisor) liable for the tortious acts of a person working "under" the superior (the employee or franchisee), without regard to the fault of the superior. Of course, there can also be instances in which the plaintiff simultaneously seeks to hold the superior liable for its *own* faults (for instance, for negligent hiring, negligent training, negligent supervision, or negligent entrustment with a dangerous instrumentality).[33] Second, although more frequently pursued in the franchise context than in the employment context, the superior that is held vicariously liable has a right of indemnity under common law for the torts committed by the franchisee or employee (in the franchise context, this is often supplemented by a contractual indemnity provision). In many cases, however, there is insurance that protects both parties (typically purchased by the franchisee in the franchise context, or by the employer in the true employment context); when this insurance protects both parties (such as through an "additional insured" endorsement), the insurance company that actually paid the loss cannot seek to recover from its own (additional) insured.

As noted above, the law of respondeat superior has frequently distinguished between liability of a master for acts of its servant (or liability of a principal for acts of its agent), and the liability of a principal/employer for acts of an independent contractor. Absent the employer's own fault, the general rule is that employers are not vicariously liable for the wrongful acts of independent contractors. Of course, that general rule is "riddled with exceptions."[34] Even where there is agreement on the general rule, however, it can be difficult to determine for certain whether a person is an employee or an independent contractor.

Under Section 220 of the *Restatement (Second) of Agency*, there were 10 separate factors to consider in trying to determine whether a person acting for another is a servant or an independent contractor.[35] Those factors include the extent of control, the level of skill required, who supplies the tools and place of work, whether the work is part of the regular business of the employer, and whether the parties believe they are creating a master/servant relationship.

When the *Restatement (Third) of Agency* was promulgated, much of this guidance distinguishing between employees and independent contractors was eliminated. Instead, the *Third Restatement* simply defines an employee as "an agent whose principal controls or has the right to control the manner and means of the agent's performance of work."[36] Within this context, an employer is subject to liability under respondeat superior for "torts committed by employees while acting within the scope of their employment,"[37] which includes "performing

33. This form of liability is discussed more fully in section 3-6 of this chapter on direct liability.

34. Gordon v. Sanders, 692 So. 2d 939, 941 (Fla. App. 1997).

35. Restatement (Second) of Agency § 220, ALI (1958).

36. Restatement (Third) of Agency § 7.07(3)(a), ALI (2006).

37. Restatement (Third) of Agency § 2.04.

work assigned by the employer or engaging in a course of conduct subject to the employer's control."[38]

Many of the reported cases in which a plaintiff is trying to impose respondeat superior liability on a franchisor involve a situation in which the plaintiff was struck by a franchisee employee who was making a delivery. Often, the courts simply focus on the extent of the control exercised by the franchisor and determine whether the degree of control is sufficient to find the franchisor liable in respondeat superior. For example, in *Martinez v. Higher Powered Pizza, Inc.*,[39] the court held that the franchisor's rights to enforce standards, perform inspections, and audit compliance were "typical" of most franchise agreements and that the franchisor was not liable to plaintiff who was struck by an employee of the franchisee making a delivery. Compare this case to *Parker v. Domino's Pizza, Inc.*,[40] in which the court stated that the franchisor retained the right to control the store operations—"the manual literally leaves nothing to chance"—and, therefore, the court held that a jury should decide whether the franchisor exercised sufficient control over the franchisee delivery driver who injured plaintiffs.

Even where a person clearly is an independent contractor, doctrines have been developed that limit the ability of the employer to disclaim vicarious liability for the acts of the independent contractor. One of these doctrines is that of nondelegable duties. In a sense, this doctrine reflects a policy decision by the courts that a business enterprise should not be able to escape liability for certain matters by pursuing its work through independent contractors. This may occur, for example, with activities that the courts consider inherently or intrinsically dangerous (whether or not abnormally dangerous or ultrahazardous). Activities that have been construed to fall within this doctrine are such things as crop dusting, use of poisons, and handling of explosives.[41] In the franchise context, this doctrine has been applied to cases of door-to-door vacuum salesmen, who were in a position to commit sexual assault once they were admitted to a customer's home.[42]

The other major situation in which an employer can be held vicariously liable for the acts of an independent contractor is a doctrine that goes (variously) by the names of "apparent authority," "ostensible authority," "apparent agency," or "agency by estoppel." Specifically, where a person creates an appearance that an independent contractor is, in fact, the agent of the person, and a plaintiff is justifiably induced to make a detrimental change in position because the transaction is believed to be on the person's account, then the person can be held responsible in some cases for the appearances that the person has created.[43]

---

38. Restatement (Third) of Agency § 7.07(2).

39. 841 N.Y.S.2d 526 (N.Y. App. Div. 2007).

40. 629 So. 2d 1026, 1029 (Fla. Dist. Ct. App. 1993).

41. Dobbs, *supra* note 30, § 337.

42. McLean v. Kirby Co., 490 N.W.2d 229 (N.D. 1992); Read v. Scott Fetzer Co., 990 S.W.2d 732 (Tex. 1998).

43. Restatement (Third) of Agency § 2.05. The person is subject to liability to the plaintiff if the person intentionally or carelessly caused the plaintiff's belief or, alternatively, if the

To pursue a defendant on an apparent authority basis, the rule articulated in the *Restatement (Third) of Agency* requires the plaintiff to show a *reasonable belief* that the services were being rendered by the defendant (or the defendant's employee). The *Restatement (Third) of Agency* defines apparent authority as the "power held by an agent or other actor to affect a principal's legal relations with third parties when a third party reasonably believes the actor has authority to act on behalf of the principal and that belief is traceable to the principal's manifestations."[44]

The consequence of the actual reliance doctrine can be seen in *Frey v. PepsiCo, Inc.*[45] The plaintiffs brought suit against PepsiCo, Inc., among others, to recover for injuries caused by a bottler's delivery truck. PepsiCo's motion for summary judgment was granted, and the plaintiffs appealed. Before getting to the issue of apparent agency, the court first addressed actual agency. The court found that PepsiCo retained control over the bottler's manufacturing and packaging but had not "retained or exercised any supervisory control over the hiring and firing of the bottler's route salesman or over the time, manner, and method of their performance."[46] The fact that the bottler's trucks and employee uniforms bore the PepsiCo trademark and that the trucks carried only PepsiCo products was not sufficient to find actual agency. After disposing of the claim of actual agency, the court also concluded that the plaintiff could not succeed on an apparent agency claim, stating, "[u]nless the appellants chose to be hit by the bottler's truck, that doctrine has no application under the present circumstances, inasmuch as it requires reliance on the apparent agency relationship."[47]

The most common response of franchisors to the apparent authority doctrine has been to require their franchisees to post notices that the location is "independently owned and operated" or is "operated by [the franchisee's name] under a franchise from [the franchisor]." The purpose of these signs is to block an injured party from claiming that the franchisee's use of the trademark induced the plaintiff to actually rely on a belief that the franchisee was a servant of the franchisor. Even if an injured plaintiff demonstrates that it actually relied on a belief that the franchisee was the agent of the franchisor and was not on notice that the franchisee was an independent operator, a court may still require the plaintiff to prove that the injury was caused by the plaintiff's belief that the franchisee was the servant of the franchisor. In *Little v. Howard Johnson Co.*,[48] the plaintiff was injured when she slipped on ice outside a franchised Howard Johnson's restaurant. The court denied plaintiff's apparent agency claim, stating that the plaintiff's

person had notice of the plaintiff's belief and that it might induce others to change their positions but did not take reasonable steps to notify the others of the facts.

44. Restatement (Third) of Agency § 2.03. Interestingly, the rule articulated in the *Restatement (Second) of Agency* was that the plaintiff must show *actual reliance* on the understanding that the person with whom the plaintiff is dealing is either the person subsequently sued or the servant of the person.

45. 382 S.E.2d 648 (Ga. App. 1989).

46. *Id.* at 650.

47. *Id.* at 650–51.

48. 455 N.W.2d 390 (Mich. Ct. App. 1990).

belief that Howard Johnson (the franchisor) operated the restaurant could not have reasonably led her to expect that the sidewalk outside the restaurant would be free of ice and snow.

(a) Sample Cases

(i) Reasonable Reliance

In *McDonald v. Century 21 Real Estate Corp.*,[49] the appellate court concluded that the evidence regarding whether the plaintiff had reasonably relied on the appearance of agency was subject to conflicting interpretations, which required reversal of the grant of a motion for summary judgment for the defendant/franchisor.

The court noted the following facts: a plaintiff claimed that he had seen commercials that represented that Century 21 was the largest real estate company in the country with a nationwide referral service and "neighborhood professionals" to assist consumers; the franchisee real estate company displayed the Century 21 logo on signs and forms, and "advertised as a business containing a 'neighborhood professional' belonging to a nationwide organization that more people have put their trust in."

In contrast, the franchisee's signs and printed materials contained the statement "Each office is independently owned and operated," and the Century 21 warranty form that the plaintiff signed contained three statements that the franchisee was an independent operator. The plaintiff explained that he thought that the language "independently owned and operated" referred to that particular office's responsibility for a particular territory but generally believed that he was dealing with a real estate broker who was part of a national company. From this combination of evidence, the court concluded that apparent agency may have existed. This case indicates that franchisors should require clear disclosure of the franchise relationship in national advertising in addition to a franchisee's individual signs and forms. Ensuring proper disclosure in one aspect of a franchisee's business, while ignoring other aspects of the business, leaves the franchisor vulnerable to losing summary judgment motions and (potentially) to findings of liability to the franchisee's customers.[50]

In some cases, courts have concluded that injured plaintiffs have presented sufficient showings of reliance upon apparent authority. In *Crinkley v. Holiday Inns, Inc.*,[51] the plaintiffs, who were robbed and beaten in their hotel room, brought suit against the franchisor, Holiday Inns. Their claim of apparent agency was supported by the manner in which they booked their room. The plaintiffs were attending a function in Charlotte, North Carolina, and initially attempted to book a room at the Charlotte Holiday Inn. When they learned there was no room

49. 111 Wis. 2d 600, 331 N.W.2d 606 (1983).

50. *See also* Sprague v. Andrews, 2010 Wis. App. LEXIS 683, at *4 (citing *McDonald v. Century 21 Real Estate Corp.*) ("When a third party reasonably believes, based on the principal's actions, that an agent has authority to act in a particular transaction, the principal is bound by the agent's acts within the scope of his or her apparent authority.").

51. 844 F.2d 156 (4th Cir. 1988).

at that hotel, they consulted a Holiday Inn directory and booked a room in the Concord Holiday Inn, 20 miles away. The plaintiffs testified that they had previously stayed at Holiday Inns, were familiar with the system's national advertising, and "would be greatly surprised to find out that Holiday Inns was not involved in the operation of the Holiday Inn-Concord."[52] On that evidence, the court upheld submission of apparent authority to the jury, which held for the Crinkleys.

A similar holding in *Holiday Inns, Inc. v. Shelburne*[53] noted that the franchisee was allowed to use the Holiday Inns reservation center, logo, and signs "in order to draw customers through name recognition."[54] The court concluded that the testimony demonstrated "Holiday Inns, Inc.'s extensive efforts to have its franchisee recognized by the public as part of its system," from which the jury could find reliance.[55] This case has had disturbing implications for franchisors, which commonly seek to draw the public to their franchisees' locations through the franchisors' name recognition, including at reservation centers.

The Florida appellate court later modified its *Shelburne* opinion in *Dalia v. Electronic Realty Associates, Inc.*[56] In *Dalia*, Electronic Realty Associates, Inc. (ERA) was the franchisor and Northgate Realty, Inc., was its franchisee. Their franchise agreement required the franchisee to hold itself out as an independently owned and operated business. The franchisee did business as Northgate Realty, Inc. In *Dalia*, the court decided that the *Shelburne* opinion applied to franchisors that required use of a single trade name throughout their chains so that the public might assume that all properties were operated by the same organization.[57] In contrast, the court found no evidence of this approach by ERA and therefore a lack of reasonable reliance on the plaintiff's part. Summary judgment for the franchisor was affirmed.[58]

Because a strict interpretation of *Shelburne* would unfairly impose sweeping liability upon a franchisor, when it has little ability to affect the event from which a claim arises, courts likely will find that the *Shelburne* opinion is limited to its specific facts. Nevertheless, franchisors that want to minimize the chances of being held vicariously liable should establish and enforce standards that require clear and conspicuous identification of the franchise relationship to the public in all instances to avoid liability for the acts of franchisees. The holding of *Dalia* assists franchisors that use a common trademark to identify their franchisees to defeat a claim of apparent agency if they follow such a practice.

52. *Id.* at 168.
53. 576 So. 2d 322 (Fla. App. 1991).
54. *Id.* at 334.
55. *Id.*
56. 629 So. 2d 1075 (Fla. App. 1994).
57. *Id.* at 1075.
58. *Id.*

(ii) Conspicuous Identification

An example of the consequences for a franchisor that did not require its franchisees to emphasize their independence in a sufficiently conspicuous manner is found in *Beck v. Arthur Murray, Inc.*[59] The appellate court affirmed the trial court's finding that the plaintiff, a purchaser of dance classes, reasonably believed that the dance studio franchisee was an agent of its franchisor. The plaintiff presented evidence of a collection of phone calls, mailings, signs, and cards, all of which referred to "Arthur Murray" or "Arthur Murray Dance Studio." The court found that these communications misled the plaintiff to believe that the franchisor, Arthur Murray, Inc., was the operator of the dance studio rather than merely the franchisor of the true operator. The contract between the dance studio and the plaintiff was also misleading, as it identified the dance studio contracting party as "Arthur Murray School of Dancing."[60]

None of the representations by the dance studio included a word such as "dealer" to indicate to the plaintiff that the dance studio was independently owned. In fact, the plaintiff testified that she focused completely on the trade name and that no one informed her that the particular dance studio was owned by someone other than Arthur Murray.

Arthur Murray, Inc., contractually required its franchisee to display a conspicuous sign identifying itself as a separate entity. The disclaimer sign used by the franchisee, however, was inconspicuous and was not brought to the plaintiff's attention. The court concluded that apparent authority existed and suggested that the franchisor "could have easily protected itself by requiring that its franchisee inform the public of his franchisee status in more effective ways than the one inconspicuous sign that was in fact required."[61]

(iii) Agency Relationship

A case with a thorough discussion of the differences between franchising and other vicarious liability cases is *Patterson v Domino's Pizza LLC*,[62] decided by the California Supreme Court. In *Patterson*, the court noted that "using traditional 'agency' terminology, [courts] have reached various results on whether a franchisor should be held liable for torts committed by a franchisee or its employees in the course of the franchisee's business. In analyzing these questions, the . . . courts have focused on the degree to which a particular franchisor exercised general 'control' over the 'means and manner' of the franchisee's operations."[63] The court went on to note that this traditional analysis is not sufficient because "Analysis of the franchise relationship for vicarious liability purposes must accommodate [the] contemporary realities [of the franchise relationship]. The imposition and enforcement of a uniform marketing and operational plan cannot

59. 54 Cal. Rptr. 328 (Ct. App. 1966).
60. *Id.* at 330.
61. *Id.* at 331.
62. 60 Cal. 4th 474, 333 P.3d 723 (2014).
63. *Id.* at 478, 333 P.3d at 735–39

automatically saddle the franchisor with responsibility for employees of the franchisee who injure each other on the job."[64]

In *Patterson*, the plaintiff alleged that she had been sexually harassed by a fellow (supervisory) employee of the franchisee and that she did not receive a satisfactory resolution even after her father complained to the franchisor's "corporate office" (specifically, her father called the 1-800 number provided by the franchisor for customers to complain about their food or service). She contended that the franchisor was vicariously liable for the actions (or inactions) of its franchisee. The franchisor sought summary judgment on the basis that it could not be held vicariously liable for its franchisee.

The court reviewed the franchise agreement, as well as the issues that the employee claimed supported her claim (such as control over hiring, training, and supervision of employees). Ultimately, the court determined that the franchisor provided guidance on how the franchisee produced products but did not direct how the franchisee dealt with its employees. Even though representatives of the franchisor advised the franchisee to terminate the employee accused of sexually harassing the plaintiff, the franchisee disregarded that advice and did not terminate the supervisor (although the supervisor later resigned on his own). The court upheld summary judgment in favor of the franchisor on the basis that the franchisor did not have day-to-day control over the activities of the franchisor and therefore was not in a principal/agent relationship that would make it liable for the actions (or inactions) of the franchisee.

Similarly, in a Telephone Consumer Protection Act (TCPA) case affirmed by the Ninth Circuit, the court found that the franchisor, Taco Bell Corp., was not vicariously liable for alleged TCPA violations made by an advertising agency hired directly by Taco Bell franchisees to conduct an independent marketing campaign.[65] The court found that Taco Bell Corp. was not vicariously liable as it did not have actual control over the marketing campaign and the campaign decisions were made by the Taco Bell franchisees and the advertising agency.[66] However, the court indicated that if a plaintiff could show that the telemarketer had apparent authority from the franchisor, and that the franchisor ratified the telemarketer's conduct, then a franchisor could be held vicariously liable for TCPA violations by franchisees conducting independent marketing campaigns.[67] This case portends that a franchisor that controls, or has the right to control, franchisee marketing campaigns could be held vicariously liable for TCPA violations.

(iv) Constructive Termination

When an employee of franchisee argues that its employer is an agent of the franchisor, that argument requires a careful analysis of the facts and is less likely to be dismissed with a summary judgment motion, except in constructive

64. *Id.*
65. Thomas v. Taco Bell Corp., 582 F. App'x 678 (9th Cir. 2014).
66. *Id.* at 679 (quoting Thomas v. Taco Bell Corp., 879 F. Supp. 2d 1079, 1084 (C.D. Cal. 2012)).
67. *Id.* at 680.

termination cases. A successful claim of constructive termination requires a finding that the employer "intentionally created or knowingly permitted working conditions that were so intolerable or aggravated" that the employee was compelled to resign.[68] A third party, including a franchisor, who is not an employer of the employee cannot generally be held liable for constructive termination, even if the franchisee-employer is found to be the franchisor's agent.

As the court in *Garcia v. Midas* explained:

> [Plaintiff] ignores the differences between an agency relationship and the employment relationship. They are not synonymous. While it is true that an employment relationship ordinarily creates a principal-agent relationship between the employer and employee, the converse does not apply: agency does not necessarily create an employer-employee relationship.[69]

The court noted that while a principal is usually responsible for its agent's tortious acts, this rule does not apply to the tort of constructive termination. For a franchisee's employee to win a constructive termination claim against a franchisor, the employee has to prove that the franchisor is also an employer.

(b) Practice Tips

There are numerous methods by which a franchisor can improve its chances of avoiding vicarious liability, many of which are reflected in the cases discussed above. The following sections summarize some of these methods from a practitioner's perspective.

(i) The Franchise Agreement

The franchise agreement and operations manual are the first documents that the franchisor's attorney will offer to the court as evidence that the franchisor has reserved the right to exert control over the method by which the franchisee conducts its business in excess of the control required (and therefore allowable) under applicable trademark laws. While oral statements and conduct may also be considered in a vicarious liability action, the franchise agreement is of particular significance and should, therefore, be drafted carefully to avoid findings of too much control. The franchise agreement should state that the franchisee shall have no authority, express or implied, to act as an agent of the franchisor or any of its affiliates for any purpose and that franchisee is, and shall remain, an independent contractor responsible for all obligations and liabilities of the franchise.

(ii) Disclaim Agency

As noted above, the franchise agreement should explicitly state that the franchisee is not an agent of the franchisor but, instead, is an independent contractor.

68. Garcia v. Midas Int'l Corp., Bus. Franchise Guide (CCH) ¶ 11,149 (Cal. App. 1997) (opinion not for publication.).

69. *Id.*

Although the stated contractual characterization of the parties' relationship is not considered determinative of whether agency has been created, its absence may be. In addition, the franchisor has to decide on the restrictions or reservations of control to be placed in the franchise agreement. The goal is to achieve consistency among the various businesses using the franchisor's marks and to protect the mark's goodwill, while avoiding excessive controls over daily operations, particularly employee hiring, firing, and supervision.

(iii) Require Conspicuous Franchisee Disclosure of Independent Status

In all instances, the franchisor should require and ensure that all franchisees have conspicuously displayed signs and conspicuously displayed statements in all forms, advertisements, and other documents exposed to the public (including on the Internet) that clearly identify the franchises as independently owned and operated businesses (often under a different corporate name). This is especially important on any document a customer signs, such as bills of sale, or other documents confirming a transaction. The courts are often not sympathetic to franchisors that do not avail themselves of this simple protection.

(iv) State-Only Standards or Rights the Franchisor Intends to Enforce

The franchise agreement should contain a statement requiring the franchisee to comply with the manual and making noncompliance a default under the agreement. If a franchisor does not intend to exercise a right or enforce a particular standard, it should not be mentioned in the franchise agreement or operations manual. Similarly, if the franchisor does not intend to enforce compliance with a particular method of operation, the franchisor should not retain a right to do so.

(v) Require Indemnification from Franchisee

The franchise agreement should contain a specific provision requiring the franchisee to indemnify and defend the franchisor and any parent, subsidiary, affiliates, and their respective officers, directors, employees, agents, successors, and assigns. These parties are often sued when the franchisor is sued in addition to the franchisee. Preferably, the provision should allow the franchisor to retain its own counsel and conduct its own defense if the franchisor considers it appropriate. The indemnification provision should state further that the franchisor is entitled to indemnity, even when punitive damages are allowed or awarded against the franchisor. Some insurance policies prohibit coverage for punitive damages but may make exceptions if the protection is required by the franchise agreement.

(vi) Require Insurance

The franchise agreement should also contain a provision requiring types of insurance in sufficient amounts to cover all potential claims. The franchisor and its affiliates should all be included as additional named insureds on the franchisee's commercial general liability policy, using "Grantor of Franchise Form CG2029" or an insurer's comparable form,[70] which can usually be done for little to no cost to the franchisee. The protection of an insurance policy overlaps the protection of an indemnification clause but also protects against additional (and different) risks.

For example, in *Murray v. Wilbur Curtis Co.*,[71] the franchisee's insurance agent failed to obtain an endorsement adding the franchisor (Burger King) as an additional insured. When Burger King was sued, it tendered defense and liability to the franchisee under the indemnity because there was no insurance protecting it. The franchisee had declined the tender on the grounds that Burger King had acted negligently in designating defective equipment, relying on a provision of the franchise agreement that required indemnity unless Burger King was negligent. Despite this, the court held for Burger King, determining that the comprehensive general liability policy would have covered "all liability arising out of the activities contemplated by the agreement, including liability based upon [Burger King's] own alleged negligence."[72]

3-6. Direct Liability

In addition to facing claims for vicarious liability, franchisors also remain (directly) liable for their own actions. Direct liability involves an assertion that the acts (or failures to act) by the franchisor make the franchisor independently liable to a plaintiff for injuries caused by a franchisee or by the franchisee's employees. As an example, the franchisor may be accused of negligent selection or negligent training of the franchisee, or it may be asserted that some action that the franchisor took (or failed to take) caused an injury for which the franchisor is liable.

Although vicarious liability and direct liability are distinct claims, the level of the franchisor's control over the franchisee's day-to-day operations is largely the dispositive factor for courts in connection with tort claims based on either theory. The key to avoiding litigation for direct tort liability is to distinguish the franchisor's control over the end product (i.e., control over its intellectual property, marketing, brand identity, and business methods) from the franchisor's control over the day-to-day operations of the franchisee's business. In direct tort liability cases, courts are assessing the franchisor's level of control over the injury-causing activity.

---

70. This form provides protection to the franchisor for all liability as grantor of the franchise. It is superior to the typical additional insured form (CG2010), which limits coverage to ongoing operations only and excludes injury arising after all work has been completed (for example, the latter form may provide insurance against a claim by a patron of a franchised automotive repair business only so long as the patron's car is being serviced on the business's premises, but not if the work done by the franchisee causes the car to fail after all work is complete and the patron—and the car—have left the premises).

71. 592 N.Y. Supp. 2d 837, 189 A.D.2d 980 (App. Div. 1993).

72. *Id.* at 839.

As a practical matter, direct tort liability claims are more problematic for the franchisor because it may not be able to hand over the defense of that claim to the franchisee. The indemnity provision of the franchise agreement may not obligate the franchisee's insurance to defend a direct negligence action, which means the franchisor and its insurer become a deep pocket. Plaintiffs' counsels are more apt to include a direct liability claim with their vicarious liabilities claims for this precise reason.

Certain types of injuries lend themselves more easily to direct tort liability claims. As noted earlier, the theories on which franchisors can be alleged to be independently liable include negligent selection or negligent training of a franchisee. However, less obvious are situations in which a franchisor designs or constructs a franchisee's building. For instance, in *Vaughn v. Columbia Sussex Corp.*,[73] the court denied summary judgment to a hotel franchisor in a slip and fall case at a franchisee location because the franchise agreement had called for the franchisor to construct and inspect the hotel and participate in employer training. Similarly, in *Repeti v. McDonald's Corp.*,[74] the court denied summary judgment to the franchisor in a personal injury case involving a defendant who was severely injured by electronic doors at the entrance of a thruway rest site (not at the entrance of the restaurant) because it could not determine whether McDonald's "lacked the requisite control over the facility to form the basis of duty to the public users of the rest area."[75]

Courts have also imposed liability upon franchisors on negligence theories where the franchisor voluntarily undertook responsibility for aspects of a franchisee's business and then failed to fulfill its obligations. This theory has been applied, for example, where the franchisor set standards for, or actually controlled, security at franchised locations and failed to ensure the security standards were followed. In *Martin v. McDonald's Corp.*,[76] McDonald's appealed from an adverse judgment arising from a murder and robbery that took place at a franchised McDonald's location. The plaintiffs, who were the franchisee's employees, alleged that McDonald's voluntarily undertook to provide for the security of the employees at the McDonald's franchise and was negligent in providing security.

McDonald's had created a corporate branch to address franchisee security problems and prepared a security operations manual. It had also assigned a regional security manager to communicate security policies, check for franchisee security problems, correct problems, and follow up on implementation of recommended security procedures. McDonald's security program recommended that the back door of stores remain locked after dark. Store employees failed to keep the door locked at the franchisee crime scene, and an intruder gained access through the unlocked back door. The plaintiffs in the *Martin* case alleged that McDonald's security personnel failed to ensure compliance with the programs they recommended.

---

73. 1992 WL 18843 (S.D.N.Y. Jan. 28, 1992).
74. 2008 N.Y. App. Div. LEXIS 2693 (N.Y. App. Mar. 28, 2008).
75. *Id.* at *3.
76. 572 N.E.2d 1073 (Ill. App. 1991).

Although McDonald's asserted that it was only the franchisor and did not employ the injured employees of its franchisee, the court noted that "[n]o matter what legal relationships existed, it was McDonald's Corporation which undertook to provide security and protection to plaintiffs."[77] The McDonald's franchisee did not have its own security supervisor, relying instead on employees of McDonald's. From this, the court concluded:

> Once McDonald's Corporation assumed the duty to provide security and protection to plaintiffs, it had the obligation to perform this duty with due care and competence, and any failure to do so would lead to a finding of breach of duty.[78]

In the *Shelburne* case (discussed in the Reasonable Reliance section above), the appellate court also found that Holiday Inns was negligent in fulfilling duties it had undertaken to maintain security at the franchise location.

Holdings of negligent undertaking by franchisors also have occurred when franchisors have specified equipment for franchisees and failed to ensure the safety of the specified equipment or failed to change the specifications when safety issues arose. In *Papastathis v. Beall*,[79] the plaintiff brought a wrongful death action against Southland Corporation after the plaintiff's decedent had been struck by a soda can that fell from a soft drink rack in a franchised store. The decedent had reached into the cooler to make a selection just as the franchisee's employee was loading soft drink cans into the rack. The lower court found for the plaintiffs and the defendants appealed, with the appellate court affirming.

On appeal, Southland did not dispute that the franchisee's employee had been negligent but contested its vicarious liability. The facts demonstrated that Southland requested its franchisee's permission to allow Coca-Cola to install the racks, and Southland's regional manager chose the rack and did little to check the safety of the rack. Southland argued that it did not own or maintain the rack or require its franchisee to use the rack; that it did not know of any defect in the rack; and that, therefore, it had acted reasonably in offering the rack to its franchisee. Finding no Arizona case law on the issue, the court decided to follow the *Restatement (Second) of Torts*, which states:

> One who undertakes, gratuitously or for consideration, to render services to another which he should recognize as necessary for the protection of a third person or his things, is subject to liability to the third person for physical harm resulting from his failure to exercise reasonable care to protect his undertaking, if (a) his failure to exercise reasonable care increases the risk of such harm, or (b) he has undertaken to perform a duty owed by the other to the third person, or (c) the harm is suffered because of reliance of the other or third person upon the undertakings.[80]

77. *Id.* at 1077.
78. *Id.* at 1078 (citation omitted).
79. 723 P.2d 97 (Ariz. App. 1986).
80. Restatement (Second) of Torts § 324(A) (1986) (*quoted in Beall*, 723 P.2d at 100).

The court held Southland had negligently selected, recommended, and inspected the rack and, therefore, there was a jury issue as to Southland's negligence.

In *Whitten v. Kentucky Fried Chicken Corp.*,[81] an employee of a Kentucky Fried Chicken (KFC) franchisee brought suit against a number of persons, including the franchisor, for injuries he suffered while cleaning cooking equipment. The case against KFC was dismissed on summary judgment, but the judgment was reversed on appeal.

Before signing a franchise agreement with KFC, the franchisee purchased a large quantity of pressure fryers for its restaurants. The franchise agreement specifically required the franchisee to use equipment approved by KFC. The franchisee instructed its employees to clean the fryers by releasing the steam pressure through vents in the fryers. Apparently, the pressure had not been released when the plaintiff opened the lid of the fryer, and the plaintiff was severely burned. The court examined two potential bases for liability against the franchisor. The first was section 414 of the *Restatement (Second) of Torts* (1965), which provides:

> One who entrusts work to an independent contractor, but who retains the control of any part of the work, is subject to liability for physical harm to others for whose safety the employer owes a duty to exercise reasonable care, which is caused by his failure to exercise his control with reasonable care.[82]

The court of appeals found a question of fact as to the extent of KFC's ability to control the operations of the franchisee, noting that "[t]he amount of control sufficient to impose liability must consist of something more than a general right to make suggestions or recommendations or to order the work stopped or resumed."[83] The court found that because KFC acknowledged in its franchise agreement that some franchisees were using earlier model fryers, and because the renewal franchise agreement specifically required the franchisee to use approved equipment, KFC could have required new equipment as a condition of renewal. Thus, the court found that there were material issues of fact as to whether KFC could be held liable under section 414 of the *Restatement (Second) of Torts*.

The court also concluded, as in *Beall*,[84] that the jury could find under section 324A of the *Restatement (Second) of Torts* that

> KFC undertook to recommend or select a safe fryer for the use of the employees of its franchisees, and increased the risk to Whitten due to KFC's failure to exercise reasonable care. A jury could also find, pursuant to subsection (b) of the Restatement that KFC undertook to perform a duty owed by Wheeler to Whitten, *i.e.*, the recommendation or selection of safe equipment to be used by Wheeler's employees. In addition, the franchise contract provided for the right to inspect to determine compliance with

81. 570 N.E.2d 1353 (Ind. App. 1991).
82. Restatement (Second) of Torts § 414 (1965) (*quoted in Whitten*, 570 N.E.2d at 1356).
83. 570 N.E.2d at 1356.
84. *Beall*, 723 P.2d 97.

> the contract specifications. KFC admitted in its answer that it had exercised that right of inspection.[85]

Courts, however, are generally more forgiving where there is a "typical franchisor-franchisee relationship" at play. For example, in *Allen v. Greenville Hotel Partners, Inc.*,[86] the third-party plaintiffs, who suffered severe injuries (and, in some instances, death) in a fire at the hotel, argued that the hotel franchisor had a duty to require its franchisees to retrofit the hotel's sprinkler system at the same time that it required the franchisees to make other significant renovations before opening the facility as a Comfort Inn in 2003. Despite plaintiffs' argument that the hotel franchisor had assumed a duty to control by requiring compliance with system standards in the franchise agreement and operations manual, the court held that the franchisor had no duty to require a retrofit of the sprinkler system.[87] By requiring other renovations, Choice Hotels had "merely guarded its trademark by assuring uniform appearance and operations of hotels operating under the Comfort Inn mark."[88]

Many of the practical tips for avoiding vicarious liability (discussed earlier) apply to avoiding direct liability, such as disclaiming an agency relationship with the franchisee. For direct liability claims, however, the franchisor wants to be in the best position to argue at summary judgment that it does not owe a duty to the plaintiff as a matter of law and that the operating documents (and practices of headquarters) support this view. Franchisees should be reminded that they are in control of day-to-day operations, including in those areas that are frequently litigated, such as safety, security, cleanliness, parking lots, swimming pools, and common areas for special venue locations. Franchisors should inspect operations only for compliance with standards of quality and brand trust, and not micromanage issues such as security, safety, and employee relations, including hiring and firing.

3-7. "Joint Enterprise" or "Single Enterprise"

In addition to claims of vicarious liability or direct liability for tort claims, there has been an increase in recent years in claims that a franchisor and its franchisee(s) are portions of a single enterprise. When the claim is made by an employee, this is described as a "joint employer" or "single employer" situation. In other contexts, other terms may be used (for instance, in the context of the Americans with Disabilities Act, the franchisor and franchisee may be described as the "joint operator" of the facility (because the ADA imposes liability on all "operators" of a facility)). In any event, this form of liability is a hybrid of vicarious liability and direct liability, as it has features of both.

---

85. *Whitten*, 570 N.E.2d at 1357.
86. 409 F. Supp. 2d 672, 676 (D.S.C. 2006).
87. *Id.* at 677.
88. *Id.*

Much of this litigation in the employment area appears to be driven by employee unions because if a franchisor can be found to be the joint employer with its franchisees of all employees, then the unions can seek to organize all employees working for a franchisor and its franchisees in a market as part of a single bargaining unit. (Note that a similar strategy appears to underlie efforts to have franchisees declared employees of their franchisor—if the franchisees are all employees, then a union can try to organize them as a bargaining unit.)

Most of the reported cases have not (directly) involved union organizing activities but instead have focused on establishing that the franchisor is liable for wage and hour violations by its franchisees. One of the few situations directly involving union organizing is not a franchise case but is often cited in connection with franchising. That situation culminated in the case of *Browning-Ferris Industries of California, Inc. v. National Labor Relations Board*.[89] That case involved an operator of a recycling facility (Browning-Ferris Industries or BFI) that had its own employees but also contracted with an unrelated company to provide additional workers who were engaged in sorting materials and in maintaining the equipment at the facility. The union representing the employees of BFI sought to have the employees of the contractor included in the same bargaining unit, on the theory that BFI and the contractor were "joint employers" of all of the workers at the recycling facility.

Initially, the Regional Director of the National Labor Relations Board (NLRB) concluded that BFI and its contractor were not joint employers, and therefore their employees could not form part of the same bargaining unit. Upon appeal to the full NLRB, the NLRB decided (on a 3–2 vote) that if a party (here, BFI) possessed the authority to control the employees of its contractors, that party could be considered a joint employer of the employees, even if the party never exercised this reserved control.[90] After a change in administration (the election of Donald Trump) and a change in the membership of the NLRB, the NLRB issued a new decision expressly overruling its outcome in the *Browning-Ferris* case and holding that joint employer status required not merely reservation of the right to control employees but the actual exercise of that control.[91] That decision was vacated because of ethical issues,[92] which caused the D.C. Circuit to take up the case. The D.C. Circuit held that BFI had not merely *reserved* the right to exercise control over the employees of its contractor but in fact had *exercised* that control. Based upon that finding, the court held that both BFI and the contractor exercised control over individuals who were indisputably employees of the contractor and therefore that BFI and the contractor were joint employers of those employees. The court held that, on remand, the NLRB should focus on who sets the essential terms and conditions of employment of the employees and should ignore decisions that set objectives, basic ground rules, and expectations for the third-party contractor. As noted, this is not specifically a franchise case, but the language

89. 911 F.3d 1195 (D.C. Cir. 2018).
90. Browning-Ferris Indus. of Cal., Inc., 362 N.L.R.B. No. 186 (Aug. 27, 2015).
91. Hy-Brand Industrial Contractors, Ltd., 365 N.L.R.B. No. 156 (Dec. 14, 2017).
92. Hy-Brand Industrial Contractors, Ltd., 366 N.L.R.B. No. 26 (Feb. 26, 2018).

used in the opinion is close enough to the circumstances of franchising to cause concerns to franchisors.

While the proceedings were going on in the *Browning-Ferris* case, a case that clearly involved franchising was proceeding in the Southern District of New York.[93] That case (which is actually three separate cases that were consolidated), addressed whether a franchisor could be considered the "joint employer" with a group of franchisees who (together with related parties) owned 32 franchised restaurants. The employees of the franchisees claimed that the franchisor was liable as a "joint employer" for all wage and hour violations that occurred at the franchisees' locations. The employees relied on language in the Fair Labor Standards Act (FLSA)[94] (and the equivalent New York law) that defined an employer as "any person acting directly or indirectly in the interest of an employer in relation to an employee."[95] Existing case law from the Second Circuit provides that whether a person is an employer should be decided based upon economic reality rather than technical concepts, and that both formal control and functional control can be used to make this determination.

Initially, the court noted that no other court has determined that a franchisor is a "joint employer" for purposes of the FLSA (citing, among others, *Patterson v. Domino's Pizza, supra*[96]). Nonetheless, the court examined both the formal and functional control factors that had been previously identified. "To determine whether an entity exercised formal control over putative employees, courts consider 'whether the alleged employer (1) had the power to hire and fire the employees, (2) supervised and controlled employee work schedules or conditions of employment, (3) determined the rate and method of payment, and (4) maintained employment records.'"[97] The court determined that even if all factual inferences were in favor of the employees, there was insufficient evidence for a reasonable juror to conclude that the franchisor exercised formal control over the employees in this case.

Next, the court considered the issue of functional control. The court stated that functional control was measured by (1) whether the franchisor's premises and equipment were used for the employees' work, (2) whether the franchisees had a business that could or did shift as a unit from one putative joint employer to another, (3) the extent to which the employees performed a discrete line job that was integral to the franchisor's process of production, (4) whether responsibility under the contracts could pass from one franchisee to another without material changes, (5) the degree to which the franchisor or its agents supervised the employees' work, and (6) whether the employees worked exclusively or

93. *In re* Domino's Pizza Inc., No. 16-CV-2492, 2018 WL 4757944 (S.D.N.Y. Sept. 30, 2018).

94. 29 U.S.C. § 203

95. 29 U.S.C. § 203(d).

96. See text accompanying footnotes 62–64.

97. Irizarry v. Catsimatidis, 722 F.3d 99, 105 (2d Cir. 2013) (quoting Carter v. Dutchess Community College, 735 F.2d 8, 12 (2d Cir. 1084)).

predominantly for the franchisor and franchisee.[98] After drawing all factual inferences in favor of the employees, the court determined that the franchisor exercised only the oversight typical of a franchisor. As a result, the court determined that the franchisor was not a joint employer as a matter of law.

More recently, the employees of several McDonald's franchisees in California tried to establish that McDonald's was their "joint employer" (along with the franchisees for whom they worked).[99] The plaintiff employees brought a class action, alleging that they were denied overtime premiums, meal and rest breaks, and other benefits in violation of the California Labor Code. The District Court had entered summary judgment for McDonald's, and the Ninth Circuit affirmed, holding that McDonald's and its franchisees were not joint employers, nor were the franchisees ostensible agents of McDonald's; the employees' negligence claims against McDonald's were also rejected.

Under applicable California Wage Orders,[100] "an 'employer' is one 'who directly or indirectly, or through an agent or any other person, employs or exercises control over the wages, hours, or working conditions of any person.' In construing [the applicable Wage Order], the California Supreme Court has provided three alternative definitions for what it means for a person or entity to 'employ[]' someone: '(a) to exercise control over the wages, hours or working conditions, or (b) to suffer or permit to work, or (c) to engage, thereby creating a common law relationship.'"[101] After examining each of these standards, the court determined that McDonald's did not meet any of these criteria. Further, the court determined that McDonald's could not be held liable on an "ostensible agent" theory and that McDonald's was not liable in negligence for failure to prevent wage and hour violations by its franchisees.

(a) Special Cases Based upon Statutory Language

There are some cases where the normal rules of vicarious liability or direct liability are not applied. Included among these are cases in which an employee of a franchisee asserts that the franchisor is liable for discrimination, sexual harassment, or similar violations of civil rights laws, and cases under the Americans with Disabilities Act of 1990 (ADA)[102] and its state-law counterparts, in which the government or a private plaintiff asserts that the franchisor is liable for violations of the ADA by a franchisee. In these cases, rules have evolved that are slightly

98. *In re Domino's Pizza Inc.*, at Section III.A.2, quoting Olvera v. Bareburger Group LLC, 73 F. Supp. 3d 201, 205–206 (S.D.N.Y. 2014).

99. Salazar v McDonald's Corp., No. 17-15673 (9th Cir. Oct. 1, 2019).

100. In California, the Industrial Welfare Commission, part of the Department of Industrial Relations, is statutorily empowered to issue "Wage Orders" that explain and provide the wage, hour, and working condition requirements both in general and for specific industries. These Wage Orders address such matters as minimum wages, overtime qualifications, maintenance of records, and meal and rest breaks.

101. *Salazar*, No. 17-15673, quoting Martinez v. Combs, 231 P.3d 259, 277–79 (Cal. 2010).

102. 42 U.S.C. §§ 12101–12213 (1997).

different from the standards outlined in the sections on vicarious and direct liability, and more closely resemble the discussion of joint liability. Additionally, there is concern in the franchise community that the recently enacted Assembly Bill 5 (AB-5) in California (and potentially similar laws in other states) may also affect this area, once cases begin to be reported.

(i) Title VII of Civil Rights Act[103]

Employee-plaintiffs have sought recovery, based on civil rights claims such as discrimination and wrongful discharge, from franchisors due to the actions of the plaintiffs' employer (the franchisee). In some of these cases, the plaintiffs/employees claim that the franchisor is vicariously liable for the franchisee's actions because the franchisee is the franchisor's agent (as discussed in the section above about vicarious liability)—that is, that the franchisor has the means to control the methods of operation of the franchisee's business. A second argument (relevant here) is that the franchisor is actually the plaintiff's employer jointly with the franchisee.

The question of whether a franchisor is an employer of its franchisee's employee has been addressed in various Title VII cases. Title VII addresses unlawful employment practices of employers. Thus, a franchisee's employee must prove that he or she is also the employee of the franchisor as a threshold to a successful claim. As noted in *Lockard v. Pizza Hut*,[104] courts have used several different tests to determine whether an apparent third party is an employer.

In *Lockard*, where the plaintiff/employee of a franchisee brought a Title VII sexual harassment claim against the franchisor, the court identified three common tests to determine employer status. The common law agency test examines whether the defendant controls the "means and manner by which the work is accomplished." As noted above (in the section on vicarious liability), this test, if passed, will not be persuasive in constructive discharge cases. A second, hybrid test combines the first test with a look at the economic dependence of the person on the third party. The third test is the single employer or economic reality test. This test requires an examination of (1) the interrelation of the operations, (2) centralized control of labor relations, (3) common management, and (4) common ownership or financial control.

The *Lockard* court noted that the single employer or economic reality test is the most favorable to plaintiffs and the common law test is the most favorable to defendants. Under the single employer test, the plaintiff-employee must have a justified belief that the franchisor is jointly responsible with the franchisee for the franchisee's acts. According to the *Lockard* court, "The critical question is, [who] made the final decisions regarding employment matters related to the person claiming discrimination?" With respect to this question, the *Lockard* court held that the fact that the franchisor's policies were used at the franchisee company and even the fact that the franchisor had an ownership interest in the franchisee

103. 42 U.S.C. §§ 2000e, *et seq.*
104. 162 F.3d 1062 (10th Cir. 1998).

did not overcome the lack of evidence that the franchisor had a role in implementing the policies at the franchisee location.

A franchisor should be very careful when it receives notice that one of its franchisees has engaged in employment discrimination or other employment-related torts. For example, a creative plaintiff unsuccessfully asserted a claim that a franchisor should be held to have conspired with its franchisee's alleged race discrimination since the franchisor failed to terminate the franchisee upon learning of the alleged discrimination.[105] A person can be held liable for another party's Title VII civil rights violations if the person has actual knowledge that a civil rights violation is about to occur, can prevent the violation with reasonable diligence, fails to do so, and the violation occurs.[106]

The question of what constitutes actual knowledge arose in *Barnett v. Doctors Associates.*[107] The court held that "notice of isolated events or acts of discrimination is insufficient as a matter of law to impose liability."[108] The plaintiff's allegations that she made an anonymous telephone call and sent a letter to a company that provided franchise services to the franchisor failed to constitute sufficient notice of an ongoing civil rights conspiracy. However, if a franchisor has notice of ongoing discrimination activities and fails to investigate or take appropriate action based on the investigation results, it may place itself at risk of liability. Note that the term "ongoing" is important; a franchisor should not pursue franchise agreement default and termination procedures unless the default is material.

In *Barnett*, the court found that the franchisor could not have prevented the violation with reasonable diligence, in addition to concluding that there was no actual notice of the violation. The plaintiff asserted that the franchisor was part of a conspiracy to discriminate because it failed to terminate the franchise agreement following notice of the allegations. The court concluded that it would be unreasonable to require a franchisor to terminate a franchisee based only on complaints of discrimination. "[I]f Plaintiffs' theory were accepted, it would impose liability on any company that did not immediately terminate its contracts with other businesses based upon unsubstantiated allegations that those businesses are discriminating against their own employees."[109]

The discussion in *Barnett* also provides a sampling of the issues that arise in franchisee-employee claims against franchisors. Although the particular cases discussed were favorable to the franchisors, they emphasize the need for franchisors to structure their franchise systems to avoid an agency relationship with their franchisees and to be proactive when presented with complaints that their franchisees are violating employment law.[110]

---

105. *See* Barnett v. Doctors Assocs., Inc., Bus. Franchise Guide (CCH) ¶ 11,061 (S.D. Fla. 1996).

106. *See* 42 U.S.C. § 1986 (1996).

107. Bus. Franchise Guide (CCH) ¶ 11,061 (S.D. Fla. 1996).

108. *Barnett*, ¶ 11,061 at III.A., para. 6.

109. *Id.* at III.B., para. 3.

110. *See* Jeffrey A. Brimer & Brian C. Bacon, *Franchisor Liability for Gender Discrimination and Sexual Misconduct*, 20 ABA FRANCHISE L.J. 188 (Spring 2001).

(ii) Americans with Disabilities Act

A franchisor must give serious consideration to the ADA in developing and enforcing standards. Section 302 of the ADA generally requires all persons that "operate" places of public accommodation to comply with the ADA. Unfortunately, the ADA does not define what an "operator" is or whether (in the normal case) a franchisor is the "operator" of its franchisees' stores. To comply with federal law and the terms of the typical franchise agreement, a franchisee must comply with the ADA. However, the ADA is extremely vague in its requirements. The franchisor faces the dilemma of how to monitor compliance within its system without mandating activities that will subject the franchisor to direct or vicarious liability.

Since the passage of the act, disabilities' rights groups have vigorously pursued the act's enforcement through publicity and civil lawsuits. The U.S. Department of Justice (DOJ) has been equally aggressive. The DOJ even attempted to make a franchisor responsible directly for ADA compliance at its franchisees' premises but failed in its attempt. *Neff v. American Dairy Queen Corp.*[111] arose from an action wherein a wheelchair-bound customer complained of numerous barriers that made Dairy Queen stores in San Antonio, Texas, inaccessible to the disabled.[112] The district court granted summary judgment for American Dairy Queen Corp. (ADQC), concluding that ADQC only had the power to veto modification of the franchise store's facilities, and that this amount of control was insufficient to bring ADQC within the scope of the ADA as the "operator" of the franchisees' stores. Neff appealed on the ground that a question of fact existed in determining whether ADQC was the "operator" of its franchised stores for purposes of the ADA. The Fifth Circuit affirmed the order granting summary judgment to ADQC.[113]

The *Neff* court examined the ADQC franchise agreement in detail and held that the relevant inquiry was whether ADQC specifically controlled the modification of the franchised facilities to improve accessibility to the disabled.[114] The court pointed out the relevant provisions of the franchise agreement requiring the franchisee to establish, equip, and operate the stores as part of the franchise system; mandating that the store be constructed and equipped in accordance with ADQC's specifications and standards; requiring that modifications to the building or equipment must be approved by ADQC; requiring the building and equipment be maintained according to ADQC's standards; giving ADQC the right to inspect for compliance; and requiring that the franchisee use the ADQC management system as its continuing operational routine. The court found that such requirements demonstrate only that ADQC sets standards for buildings and equipment and for approving or disapproving structural changes. Such supervisory authority

111. 58 F.3d 1063 (5th Cir. 1995).
112. *Id.* at 1064.
113. *Id.* at 1070.
114. *Id.*

did not constitute sufficient control over the franchisee's business to conclude that ADQC operated the business within the meaning of the ADA.[115]

The *Neff* case dealt with a building that existed before passage of the ADA and involved an assertion by the DOJ that franchisors have an obligation to require modification of those (existing) buildings to comply with the ADA. Between the fact that the opinion of the *Neff* court was clear and reasonable and that, with the passage of time, there are fewer buildings that were built before the passage of the ADA that are still not in compliance with the ADA, the emphasis in the cases seems to be shifting to new construction and modification of existing buildings, and whether franchisors have an obligation to assure that their franchisees comply with the ADA in connection with construction or modification. Much of this litigation has involved Days Inn of America, Inc., and its then-parent company, Hospitality Franchise Systems.

The cases seem to fall into two categories. The first line of cases relies on the same language that was used in *Neff*, from section 302 of the ADA.[116] Since that language imposes liability on persons that own, lease, or operate places of public accommodation, and since the franchisors in those cases are not owners or lessors, the focus is on "operators" just as in *Neff*. Generally, the outcome has been the same as in *Neff*.

United States v. Days Inn of America, Inc.[117] (*Days Inn I*) involved modifications to a hotel constructed before enactment of the ADA. The court predicated its holding on language in the ADA that defined potentially liable parties as owners, operators, lessors, and lessees.[118] The court found that the license agreement, operations manual, training programs, and quality assurance inspections neither individually nor collectively made Days Inn an "operator" within the definition of the statute. In order to leave no doubt about the interpretation of its decision, the court stated that Congress did not intend to make franchisors such as Days Inn liable under the ADA. This court's reasoning is consistent with the practicalities of the franchise relationship.

The other line of cases focuses on section 303 of the ADA,[119] which defines discrimination as including "failure to design and construct facilities" in a manner that makes them compliant with the ADA. In the franchise context, these cases have focused on the right of the franchisor to review and approve the franchisee's building plans as grounds to impose liability on the franchisor. In *United States v. Days Inn of America, Inc.*[120] (*Days Inn II*), the court of appeals stated that the district court should defer to the interpretation of the ADA by the DOJ; according to the DOJ, even an architect or contractor can be held liable under the "design and construct" standard of the ADA if the party substantially participates

115. *Id.* at 1068, 1069.
116. 42 U.S.C. § 12182.
117. 22 F. Supp. 2d 612 (E.D. Ky. 1998).
118. *Id.* at 614.
119. 42 U.S.C. § 12183(a).
120. 151 F.3d 822 (8th Cir. 1998).

in the design and construction of the facility. According to the court, if a franchisor has the right to control the design and construction process (even if it does not exercise that control), the franchisor can be held liable under the ADA (at least if it has knowledge that its franchisee is not complying with the ADA).

United States v. Days Inn of America, Inc.[121] (*Days Inn III*) held that Days Inn, through its license agreements and manual, had a supervisory role in the design of the hotel and could be held liable for ADA violations. The outcome in the *Days Inn II* and *Days Inn III* cases (as well as in several cases imposing liability on architects) was criticized in *Lonberg v. Sanborn Theaters, Inc.* on the basis that the courts in those cases had "created a category of liability found nowhere in the text or legislative history of the ADA; namely, anyone possessing a 'significant degree of control over the final design and construction of a facility' is liable."[122]

Despite its broad reading of section 303 of the ADA in the context of new construction, the Eighth Circuit Court of Appeals has not read section 302 as broadly in the operational context. *Pona v. Cecil Whittaker's, Inc.*[123] involved a restaurant franchisee that required a disabled person to leave its premises because a service dog accompanied her. The plaintiff, Pona, made two arguments as to why the franchisor should be liable. First, she contended that the franchisee had called the franchisor's president for advice, and that the president said that allowing dogs in the restaurant did not look good. The court held that the franchisor was not the "operator" of the restaurant,[124] despite allegedly having given advice to the franchisee. Second, Pona argued that she believed that the franchisee had authority to act on behalf of the franchisor, and so the franchisor should be held liable. The court rejected the second argument on the basis that liability under the ADA turns on actual connection to the restaurant, rather than to the plaintiff's belief about that connection.

(iii) California AB-5 and Similar Laws

During its 2019 session, the California Legislature enacted a law known as Assembly Bill 5 (AB-5), which broadly adopted the "ABC" test to determine whether individuals are employees or independent contractors of the persons retaining them. The ABC test is similar to what has been used to make this determination in Massachusetts for some time.[125] Under the provisions of AB-5, "a person providing labor or services for remuneration shall be considered an employee rather than an independent contractor unless the hiring entity demonstrates that all of the following conditions are satisfied:

---

121. 997 F. Supp. 1080 (C.D. Ill. 1998).

122. 2001 U.S. App. Lexis 21065, at *14 (9th Cir. 2001) (citing U.S. v. Days Inn of Am., 151 F.3d 822, 826 (8th Cir. 1998)).

123. 155 F.3d 1034 (8th Cir. 1998).

124. *Id.* at 1036 (comparing Neff v. American Dairy Queen Corp., 58 F.3d 1063 (5th Cir. 1995)).

125. Mass. Gen. L. c151A, § 2.

(A) The person is free from the control and direction of the hiring entity in connection with the performance of the work, both under the contract for the performance of the work and in fact.
(B) The person performs work that is outside the usual course of the hiring entity's business.
(C) The person is customarily engaged in an independently established trade, occupation, or business of the same nature as that involved in the work performed.

As of the deadline for this chapter, there have been no reported (appellate) cases from California addressing how AB-5 applies to franchising, although the International Franchise Association has brought a declaratory judgment action seeking a ruling that franchising is not within the scope of AB-5.[126] There has, however, been a recent case from Massachusetts addressing whether franchisees are employees of their franchisor under the (similar) Massachusetts ABC Test.[127] In that case, the court granted summary judgment in favor of the defendant franchisor after finding a "direct conflict" between the FTC Franchise Rule and the Massachusetts Independent Contractor Law (which contains the Massachusetts ABC Test). Specifically, the court in the *Patel* case determined that the FTC Franchise Rule requires franchisors to exercise "substantial control" over their franchisees, and that this requirement is inconsistent with prong "A" of the ABC Test.

Although franchisors in Massachusetts seem safe (for now) from being held to be the employers of their franchisees, if AB-5 (or similar laws in states other than Massachusetts) is determined to apply to franchising/franchisees, then franchisees could be held to be the employees of their franchisors, entitled to minimum wages, mandatory work breaks, and other perquisites of employees (including unemployment compensation, disability insurance, and worker's comp coverage).

Additionally, if AB-5 applies to franchisees, there is an increased risk that a franchisor and its franchisees could be determined to be joint employers of the franchisee's workers (if the franchisees are employees of the franchisor, rather than independent contractors, then by extension the employees of the franchisee are also employees of the franchisor). A finding that all employees of the franchisees are employees of the franchisor makes the franchisor liable for the pay and benefits of all of those employees (in spite of any provisions of the franchise agreement that the franchisee is solely responsible for its employees). Further, if the employees of the franchisee are considered employees of the franchisor, this has implications for potential union organization efforts; if all employees of a franchisor's franchisees are employees of the franchisor, an argument can be made that a single bargaining unit can be established for all of the employees of all of the franchisees in a market.

---

126. Int'l Franchise Ass'n v California, Case No. 3:20-cv-02243-BAS-DEB (S.D. Cal., filed Nov. 17, 2020).

127. Patel v. 7-Eleven, Inc., 2020 WL 5440623 (D. Mass. Sept. 10, 2020).

Depending upon how franchisors and franchisees are treated, laws such as AB-5 could have the effect of making franchising no longer a viable business model. If franchisors must treat all of their franchisees (and all of their franchisees' employees) as employees, then franchisors may determine that it makes more sense to develop through company-owned facilities instead of franchises.

3.8. Records Management and Retention

The provisions of various statutes and regulations either explicitly or practically obligate U.S. companies to keep records of their business activities. Sometimes, these statutes and regulations identify specific records that companies must keep. Other times, the statutes and regulations provide that certain presumptions will apply unless the company can prove otherwise through adequate documentation. For example, the Internal Revenue Code requires every business to generate and retain tax records. The Securities Exchange Act requires that public companies create and preserve detailed corporate and financial records. The Immigration Reform and Control Act requires U.S. employers to obtain and preserve documentary evidence of their employees' nationalities. Examples of other statutory record-keeping requirements could fill an entire book. The FTC Franchise Rule requires franchisors to make available to the FTC upon request a sample copy of each materially different version of their FDD for three years after the close of the fiscal year when it was last used,[128] and, for each completed franchise sale, franchisors must retain a copy of the signed receipt for at least three years.[129]

Practical considerations also require companies to keep detailed records of their activities. Manufacturers can develop reliable production schedules only by knowing how many units they produced in the past and when customers wanted those units delivered. Sales representatives can keep track of their customers' buying habits only by developing customer profile databases. Franchise executives can determine which franchisees are complying with system standards only by referring to quality/service/cleanliness reports and notes of field representatives. People remember with their minds; corporations remember with their file folders and computer records.

No business can survive without records. But a business that continues to accumulate outdated, redundant, and other unnecessary records takes on ever-increasing risk, both from a business and legal perspective. To be used effectively and reliably, and to mitigate legal risk, records must not only be created, but they must also be managed properly.

Records management programs vary widely in complexity and sophistication. A company's size, organizational structure, the regulatory framework within which it operates, and sensitivity to record-keeping issues all contribute to the type of records management program it adopts.

128. 16 C.F.R. § 436.6(h).
129. 16 C.F.R. § 436.6(i).

Safekeeping of essential contracts, correspondence, and financial records, and sound administration of records retention policies lie at the heart of a records management program. These functions entail significant legal considerations, and many companies assign responsibility for the design and administration of their records management programs to their legal departments. This section examines the elements a franchise records management program should include and explores the issues a legal department should address when chosen to serve as architect and gatekeeper of a franchise company's records management program.

(a) Objectives of a Records Management Program

Some people describe a records management program as actually being a "records destruction program" because a fundamental part of any comprehensive records management program is a set of schedules that specify when particular records should be destroyed. A comprehensive franchise records management program is much more than that and accomplishes four objectives:

1. *The program expedites access to files and records by employees who need to use them.* For the sake of administrative efficiency, employees must be able to find the files they need speedily and with a minimum of effort.
2. *The program preserves and protects the files from unauthorized use or access and natural catastrophes.* Industrial espionage and data security concerns can present problems even for small franchisors. A single data breach can bankrupt a brand's credibility as well as its financial stability. Predatory competitors can wreck a company's fortunes by stealing secret recipes, proprietary formulae, and other trade secrets. Employees or contractors can leak the company's product development plans or sell its marketing strategy to a competitor. Fires and floods can create equally devastating consequences by destroying a company's records and erasing its institutional memory.

   Implementing data security measures that are appropriate and adequate for the type of data stored and retained is essential for mitigation of legal risk and maintaining compliance with applicable regulatory frameworks as well as local, state, federal and international data security standards and laws, such as the California Consumer Privacy Act (CCPA), the European Union General Data Protection Regulation (GDPR), and the Personal Information Protection and Electronic Documents Act (PIPEDA) in Canada. This is particularly important with respect to documents or data that includes personally identifiable information (PII), personal health information (PHI) and/or payment card information (PCI).
3. *The program ensures that records are preserved for an appropriate time but are purged and destroyed after the appropriate retention period ends.* Legal requirements and practical business considerations dictate that companies develop formal procedures to ensure that they maintain

appropriate records. Federal and state regulations require that businesses retain tax, personnel, and other records to assist government agencies in conducting audits and investigations. Companies must also preserve records they may need to prosecute claims against franchisees, suppliers, and other adversaries; to defend themselves against claims their adversaries may lodge; and to establish their compliance with various laws and regulations.

Creation and implementation of a document retention policy and a records retention schedule establishes necessary guidelines to determine when documents have reached the end of their useful and regulatory lives. When that occurs, procedures are necessary to ensure that these records are purged and effectively destroyed. When a company cannot produce a document in response to a discovery request or subpoena because the document was destroyed, it may be called upon to show that its document retention program was properly formulated and administered and that the document was not destroyed in anticipation of litigation. For proper risk mitigation, a company must be able to locate and destroy all copies and forms of a record (electronic as well as hard copy) when its retention period expires.

4. *The program conserves storage space.* The use of office and warehouse space to store paper that contains outdated, redundant, or otherwise useless information—the equivalent of trash—is an extravagant expense.

(b) Design and Administration of a Records Management Program

The heart of an effective and comprehensive records management program is a document retention policy (DRP). An effective DRP identifies and explains key concepts such as the importance of records management; explains the distinction between records that must be retained for business, legal, or regulatory purposes and those that are disposable; identifies who is responsible for managing the records management program; delineates employee responsibilities with respect to records management; and outlines the consequences for noncompliance.

In addition to a DRP, a records retention schedule is also an essential component of an effective records management program. A records retention schedule identifies categories of company records and instructs employees on how long such records must be retained. Typically, retention schedules take the form of a chart and retention time periods are based on a combination of business and legal factors. There are mandatory legal requirements that apply to a record's retention. For example, the franchise statutes of Minnesota, North Dakota, and South Dakota all require that a franchisor maintain disclosure document receipts for a period of three years.[130] Where these types of mandatory requirements exist, a company must satisfy them to avoid fines and penalties for failure to maintain the records long

130. Minn. Stat. § 80C.06, subdiv. 5 (2021); N.D. Franchise Investment Law § 51-19-08.6 (2021); S.D. Codified Laws § 37-5B-11 (2021).

enough. And, short of legal requirements, there are legal considerations that come into play with regard to retention periods—the offensive and defensive uses a company may have for a document in dispute resolution proceedings. When there are no mandatory requirements to retain records, these legal uses may be the guiding principle for records retention, but even when there are mandatory legal requirements to maintain records for certain minimum periods, a company should take these uses into account in deciding how much longer, if at all, a document should be retained beyond its mandatory retention period. When establishing retention periods, it is important to remember that there are some statutes and regulations that establish maximum time limits for the retention of documents. For example, some state employment laws require the destruction of job application data for those individuals who were not hired, after a specified period of time. A company's legal department should always have the responsibility for identifying a record's legal retention period. Proper discharge of this function depends on the ability to locate and interpret sometimes obscure or ambiguous statutes and regulations. To complicate matters, mandatory retention periods are frequently buried under generic or obscure captions. The Minnesota requirement for disclosure document receipts, for example, appears under the caption "Public Offering Statement." Unless a researcher knows of these kinds of requirements and pointedly searches for their source, he or she can easily overlook pertinent information. Fortunately, useful research materials are available. *Legal Requirements for Business Records*[131] contains an extensive survey of federal and state requirements that apply to various industries and types of records. CCH also publishes a useful resource called the *Guide to Record Retention Requirements.*[132] *A sample records retention schedule is attached as exhibit 3-2.*

A litigation hold policy is a third element of an effective records management program. If a business is involved in, or reasonably anticipates becoming involved in, a litigation, arbitration, government investigation, or audit matter, it has an affirmative obligation to ensure that relevant information is preserved and not deleted or destroyed. A litigation hold policy requires the suspension of the normal records destruction process (i.e., the application of the records retention policy) and the preservation of all affected records. A litigation hold policy may be included as part of the DRP or stand alone as a separate policy.

The Sedona Conference®[133] and ARMA International[134] are two of the leading authorities establishing best practices in information management and provide helpful information for the development of a DRP and an effective records management program generally.

---

131. D. Skupsky, Legal Requirements for Business Records: State Requirements, Info. Requirements Clearinghouse (currently out of print).

132. CCH, Inc., Guide to Records Retention Requirements, (2006 ed.).

133. The Sedona Conference® is a nonpartisan, nonprofit 501(c)(3) research and educational institute dedicated to the advanced study of law and policy in the areas of antitrust law, complex litigation, and intellectual property rights.

134. ARMA International is a not-for-profit professional association for records and information managers and related industry practitioners and vendors.

From a practical perspective, an effective records management program should (1) incorporate other policies that relate to records and information retention, such as Bring Your Own Device, social media, data privacy, and computer use policies; (2) instruct employees on how to integrate records retention processes and requirements into their daily work; (3) require mandatory employee compliance and provide for compliance audit and enforcement; (4) provide regularly scheduled training, educational materials, and easily accessible resources documenting records retention policies and procedures and identifying who at the company to contact with questions; and (5) update the DRP annually.

A carefully designed and administered records retention program reduces the risk that a company will be fined or sanctioned for failure to safe keep a required record or to produce it in response to a discovery request. A conscientiously administered program also reduces the risk that production of an informal, unofficial record, or a record that has outlived its legal and practical usefulness, can be compelled in response to a subpoena or discovery request. Last, but not least, a conscientiously administered archiving program can significantly increase employee efficiency and reduce a company's expenditures for storage space.

A franchise company can realize improved employee productivity and expense reduction, as well as reduce its legal risk, by implementing a comprehensive records management program. The earlier in its life a company becomes cognizant of these benefits and begins to incorporate records management considerations into its strategic planning, the greater the benefits it will derive.

3-9. Purchasing Requirements

Almost all franchise systems have a greater or lesser concern with purchasing. In product distribution franchises, the products to be distributed form the heart of the franchise, and much of the focus of the franchise agreement may be on the purchasing requirements. Examples of product distribution issues include whether the franchise agreement allows the franchisee to sell products other than those manufactured or distributed by the franchisor; what limits will be imposed on the franchisee purchases from sources other than the franchisor directly (that is, can the franchisee purchase and resell "gray market" goods that have been designated for sale outside the United States?); and, if the franchisee is allowed to sell products other than those manufactured or distributed by the franchisor, the limits that will be imposed on those other products (that is, can the products be competitive to the franchisor's products, or are only complementary products allowed?).

Purchasing requirements can lead to antitrust litigation for alleged "tying arrangements" when an agreement between franchisor and franchisee amounts to "an agreement by a party to sell one product on the condition that the buyer also purchases a different (or tied) product, or at least agrees that he will not purchase that product from any other supplier."[135] Such an arrangement may violate the

135. Burda v. Wendy's International, Inc., 659 F. Supp. 2d 928 (S.D. Ohio 2009) (quoting Eastman Kodak Company v. Image Technical Services, Inc., 504 U.S. 451, 112 S. Ct. 2072, 119 L. Ed. 2d 265 (1992)).

Sherman Act "if the seller has 'appreciable economic power' in the tying product market and if the arrangement affects a substantial volume of commerce in the tied market."[136] Market power may exist when a franchisee purchases a franchise and by doing so is thereafter locked in to buying another product because of the seller's rules.[137] Succeeding on a theory requires that the franchisee did not know prior to purchasing the franchise that it could be required to purchase the tied-in products—largely, that the franchisor either changed its rules after making the initial sale or concealed its rules from prospective franchisees until they are "locked in" through purchase of a franchise.[138]

In *Burda v. Wendy's International, Inc.*, franchisees alleged antitrust claims under a lock-in tying arrangement theory, claiming that they had no knowledge of a potential obligation to buy buns or food supplies from a specified supplier.[139] Reviewing the language in Wendy's franchise agreement, the court determined that potential franchisees were not put on notice that Wendy's would be able to eliminate all competition by naming an exclusive supplier or that they could impose a surcharge on approved suppliers.[140] Rather, the language suggested that supplier competition was welcome so long as prospective suppliers met Wendy's "standards and specifications."[141] The court decided this satisfied the "change of policy" requirement for a lock-in theory.[142] The court allowed the franchisees to proceed with their antitrust claim, finding that the franchisees had sufficiently pleaded market power, in spite of Wendy's argument that its "right to insist that [franchisees] purchase certain produces arose from contract, and not the assertion of market power. . . ."[143]

The *Burda* court readily distinguished the Wendy's franchisees' allegations from those in *Queen City Pizza, Inc. v. Dominos' Pizza Inc.*,[144] where that court dismissed the Domino's franchisees' antitrust claims. In *Queen City Pizza* the Domino's franchisees knew about the exclusivity purchasing requirements prior to becoming "locked-in" by the franchise agreement, and they knowingly chose to invest in a franchise arrangement that limited their choices.[145] Domino's standard franchise agreement provided that Domino's "may in our sole discretion require that ingredients, supplies and materials used in the preparation, packaging, and delivery of pizza be purchased exclusively from us or from approved suppliers or distributors."[146] Domino's was identified as the exclusive seller of approximately 90 percent of the ingredients and supplies used by Domino's fran-

136. PSI Repair Servs., Inc. v. Honeywell, Inc., 104 F.3d 811, 815 (6th Cir. 1997).
137. *Burda*, 659 F. Supp. 2d at 931.
138. Michigan Division–Monument Builders of North America v. Michigan Cemetery Ass'n, 524 F.3d 726, 737 (6th Cir. 2008).
139. *Burda*, 659 F. Supp. 2d at 935
140. *Id.*
141. *Id.* at 935–36.
142. *Id.* at 936.
143. *Id.*
144. Queen City Pizza, Inc. v. Domino's Pizza, Inc., 124 F.3d 430 (3rd Cir. 1997).
145. *Id.* at 440.
146. *Id.* at 433.

chisees.[147] The issue with purchasing requirements arises when, "[a]s a result of adverse information and switching costs, franchisees also may be locked in to a situation whereby franchisors are able to exercise their market power to cause franchisees to have to pay supracompetitive prices. . . ."[148]

In business format franchise systems, purchasing requirements tend to be focused more on quality control issues. By assuring that the inputs used meet the franchisor's quality control standards, it becomes easier to assure that the outputs also meet those standards.

These differences in purpose also lead to differences in related provisions. For example, a franchise agreement for a business format franchise is more likely to have provisions addressing the ability of franchisees to request approval of alternative suppliers. Occasionally, these provisions for approval of alternative suppliers lead to litigation when franchisees believe that the franchisor is not approving alternative suppliers in accordance with the standards of the franchise agreement. In *Bores v. Domino's Pizza, LLC*,[149] for example, the issue before the Eighth Circuit Court of Appeals was whether Domino's franchisees were required to purchase from the company a custom-designed integrated computer system (the PULSE system) created especially for Domino's units. Domino's was the only supplier of the computer software. Section 8.2 of the Domino's franchise agreement stated, "We will provide you with specifications for . . . computer hardware and software. . . . You may purchase items meeting our specifications *from any source*."[150] Franchisee plaintiffs argued the company had violated the "from any source" clause of the franchise agreement by mandating the purchase of the PULSE system from Domino's and not providing alternative sources. Plaintiffs maintained that Domino's specifically limited the available suppliers to generate additional revenues.[151] The court held that while the franchise agreement indeed allowed franchisees to purchase computer hardware and software meeting those specifications "from any source," and not solely from defendant, the "from any source" clause could not be interpreted to require multiple suppliers. If Domino's, therefore, was the only source for meeting the company's computer specifications, then franchisees had to comply.[152]

If franchisees believe that the franchisor is unduly profiting from the purchasing requirements, as was the case in *Bores*, they may agitate for establishment of purchasing cooperatives to hold costs down. By pooling their purchasing power,

147. *Id.* at 433–34.

148. Collins v. International Dairy Queen, Inc., 980 F. Supp. 1252, 1258 (M.D. Ga. 1997).

149. 530 F.3d 671 (8th Cir. 2008).

150. *Id.* at 673 (emphasis added).

151. *Id.*

152. *Id.* at 676. *See also* Queen City Pizza v. Domino's Pizza, 124 F.3d 430 (3d Cir. 1997), *cert. denied*, 523 U.S. 1059 (1998) (holding franchisor did not violate antitrust laws because requirement of buying products from Domino's Pizza was contractual and not due to Domino's market power over a unique product). *Cf.* Collins v. Int'l Dairy Queen, Inc., 939 F. Supp. 875 (M.D. Ga. 1996) (holding franchisor had monopoly power over franchisees because evidence of excessive costs to purchase another franchise locked them into the franchise in violation of the antitrust laws).

the franchisees in purchasing cooperatives are able to achieve economies of scale and cost savings that would not be possible on their own. Purchasing cooperatives might also provide a mechanism to work with franchisors to find alternative suppliers.

In general, purchasing cooperatives are owned and controlled by their members—that is, franchisees. While in some instances purchasing cooperatives are independently operated by franchisees without franchisor involvement, it is often a collaboration, although one in which the franchisor should maintain sufficient control to ensure standards are not compromised. A purchasing cooperative is commonly owned and democratically controlled by its members; provides products and services to its members only, including proprietary products required by the franchisor; and benefits its members by providing discounts on goods and services and returns any unused capital to members in the form of distributions known as patronage dividends.[153] In forming the cooperative, the franchisor must decide how it will participate—that is, whether company-owned units will have voting rights and own membership interests, and what products or services will be included. It is common for the cooperative to be owned by franchisees with the franchisor holding an ownership interest.[154]

The hallmark of the purchasing cooperative is its ability to achieve economies of scale and decrease costs. However, there are other benefits, including supply chain innovation and the creation of certain efficiencies; the ability to make a group request to the franchisor for alternative suppliers (potentially solving issues like the one discussed in *Bores* above through better planning and communication) and to provide feedback on existing suppliers; and systematic supply chain support (inventory controls, IT support), including supply chain professionals (consultants to the cooperative) whose expertise would otherwise be missing.[155]

To get started, any franchise system considering a purchasing cooperative should do its research. It should engage an expert to conduct a feasibility study and should examine what has worked for similar business models. Next, there should be representatives appointed by the franchisor and franchisees to work through the logistics of forming the cooperative. Discussions should focus on what support the franchisor can give (e.g., funding certain start-up costs or providing office space). The franchisee representatives should gauge interest among its membership and the willingness of franchisees to pay ongoing fees to keep the system running. Once a feasibility study has been conducted, representatives from each side should come to an agreement on the governing structure of the cooperative and outline a time frame for adoption of the cooperative governing documents.[156]

---

153. *See* Joyce Mazero & Suzie Loonam, *Purchasing Cooperatives: Leveraging a Supply Chain for Competitive Advantage*, 29 ABA Franchise L.J. 148 (Winter 2010).

154. Suzie Loonam, *Purchasing Cooperatives: Opportunities and Challenges*, Franchising World (IFA) (Apr. 2010).

155. Mazero & Loonam, *supra* note 153, at 148 n.5.

156. *Id.*

For further discussion of the benefits of pursuing a joint purchasing cooperative, see chapter 4, section 4-4(c)(ii)(A).[157]

3-10. Compliance Programs and Support

(a) Compliance Programs

There are many reasons to develop a comprehensive compliance program. First and foremost, as discussed previously, the Lanham Act imposes on a franchisor a legal duty to control the quality of the goods and services sold under its trademark. In addition, when the business falters, a good compliance program will deter franchisee claims that the franchisor is responsible for failing to uphold standards. Finally, enforcing system standards and maintaining brand integrity is good business. Franchisors can identify and grow with those franchisees that maintain and exceed the system's high standards.

Franchisors should make sure the compliance program treats the review and evaluation of franchisees with consistency. The process should be standardized, including the criteria upon which the franchisee is evaluated and the frequency with which the franchise is reviewed. There should be an organizational commitment to implement the program system wide.

"Check, coach, check, enforce" is one guiding principle for structuring a compliance program.[158] Franchisors recognize the commitment and significant investments franchisees have made, and they view the franchise relationship as a collaborative endeavor that emphasizes the need for training and consultation. A franchisor's first reaction to noncompliance should always be training and coaching, but franchisees must know that continued noncompliance will result in serious consequences.

(b) Franchise System Standards

A rigorous compliance program should have as its cornerstone a set of franchise standards—the criteria upon which franchisee performance is evaluated. The franchise agreement, and its references to compliance with the franchise system, is generally not sufficient to give form to the franchisor's expectations of performance. How can the franchisee reasonably be expected to meet standards that are not articulated by the franchisor? For example, what is the framework for evaluating the business's operational success? What does "adequate financial performance" mean? Is there adequate capital to handle the ups and downs of the yearly

---

157. For a comprehensive review of the challenges of establishing these programs, including issues revolving around the rights and duties of members; funding and cash flow; board considerations; and technical legal issues, such as securities and antitrust concerns, *see* Mazero & Loonam, *supra* note 153.

158. Joseph Schumacher, Edward Wood Dunham & G. Adam Schweickert III, *Retaining and Improving Brand Equity by Enforcing System Standards*, 24 ABA Franchise L.J. 10 (Summer 2004).

business cycle? When should reinvestments be made to the physical plant? What does a proper training program look like? Franchise system standards should be developed to answer these questions.

(c) Quality Inspectors

Once franchise system standards are articulated, the franchisor must decide who is going to evaluate the operation of the business. Regardless of whether the franchisor uses independent quality inspectors or has the inspection and enforcement role filled by franchise business representatives, it is best if all of the persons who will be handling the quality inspections are periodically trained together so that they learn the same approaches for interpreting and measuring standards, and assessing what is a material variance from a standard. It will also be beneficial for the persons handling the quality inspections to periodically audit different franchisees or regions. This can help to eliminate biases that may develop with particular franchisees and allow auditors to identify regional variances when evaluating a franchisee's compliance. Regular meetings to review questions of interpretation or evaluation will help ensure that the quality inspectors continue to approach inspections consistently. Mystery shoppers and customer surveys may also be helpful to add to the neutrality of the inspection results.

The main function of quality inspections is to ensure the franchisee is complying with franchise system standards and, if not, to identify deficiencies and bring the franchisee into compliance. A secondary benefit is that reports of on-site quality inspections will provide evidence of the condition of a franchisee's premises at the time of the most recent inspection if a lawsuit ever arises from an event at the franchised premises. If the person conducting the inspection performed a thorough job and objectively recorded the conditions of the unit, the franchisee addressed any deficiencies revealed in the inspection report, and the franchisor had no actual or imputed notice of a subsequent problem, then a court should find that the franchisor acted in a reasonable and prudent manner. Under those circumstances, the franchisor should be able to establish that it fulfilled the duties of a reasonable franchisor, and, thereby, increase its likelihood of defeating an asserted negligence claim and eliminate the potential for punitive damages based upon those claims.

A standard inspection report form should be developed to ensure that the same information is obtained for each inspection and is communicated uniformly. The persons conducting the inspection should avoid subjective comments, such as "the franchisee seems to be trying very hard" or "the franchisee is fighting hard against competition and therefore is doing. . . ." The first, and often overlooked, item on the checklist should be an examination of the permits and certificates required to keep the franchise property in operation. The inspection should note only whether the certificate appears on its face to be current and valid. Such certificates include verifications that the property has undergone governmental inspections of fire equipment, kitchens, elevators, and any other certification applicable to the franchisee's operation.

In addition to assuring compliance with the franchisor's system standards, the persons conducting inspections should have the common sense necessary to recognize obvious issues (and be in a position to notice obvious defects that might result in safety problems), even if they are not trained to conduct loss prevention surveys. Most franchise agreements require, at a minimum, that franchisees operate safe premises and comply with federal, state, and local laws. Language of this type is sufficient to justify inclusion in the inspection checklist of questions addressing blatant safety and security issues. For example, the quality inspector should note obvious safety issues such as water leaks, blatantly inadequate lighting, holes or tears in the floor covering, faulty doors or door locks, furniture in disrepair, and other issues that would be apparent to most people.

At the conclusion of the inspection, the inspector should try to obtain the signature of the franchisee (or, if the franchisee is not present, of the person in charge of the unit) on any report and should leave a copy with the franchisee (or at the unit, if the franchisee is not present). The inspector must be trained to decide whether a condition can be fixed so quickly (or presents such a large risk if not repaired immediately) that the inspector should require the franchisee to cure the problem immediately. If the inspector determines that an immediate cure is neither reasonable nor practical, then the franchisor should monitor the situation to make certain the franchisee makes the cure as soon as reasonably possible. One way to achieve this is to incorporate a review of inspection results in the regular business review conversations between the franchisee and franchisor. The franchisor may also want to designate a supervising employee to be available to answer questions and handle disputes between the inspector and the franchisee over any matters arising out of inspections; some of these disputes may even be of a type that should be resolved while the inspector is still at the franchised unit.

The inspector should send a copy of the report to the franchise department and any other department that is responsible for an area that may be violated. All reports issued and any responses should be maintained in the franchisor's files associated with that franchisee. Any action that a department agrees to take in relation to the franchisee—for example, that a particular department will review the issues with the franchisee—should be included in the report. If the franchisee fails to cure the problem by the required date, either a reasonable basis for extending the date should be recorded or the franchisor should issue an immediate default with an accelerated termination date. If appropriate, the franchisor should require the franchisee to post warnings of any hazards and restrict public access during the cure period or until the property is terminated from the system.

(d) Business Reviews

In addition to evaluating compliance with franchise system standards, the franchisor should also establish a process for evaluating the franchisee's success. One way to achieve this is through a regular business review, which provides management a regular opportunity to discuss with the franchisee any issues and, importantly, where opportunities exist to drive the business forward. The business review can be conducted once a year, or more or less frequently, depending on the franchisee's performance. Establishing a regular interval for assessing franchisee performance allows the franchisor the opportunity to review business operations reports and, if applicable, the inspection report, with the franchisee and to discuss any issues, all without making the franchisee feel it is being indiscriminately singled out for review. It also provides the franchisor an opportunity to give the franchisee a written report detailing any noncompliance with the franchising standards with clear instructions for remedying noncompliance, which may support the record in any future enforcement or collection action.

(e) Avoiding Waiver Claims

When a dispute arises, whether through the quality inspection or through some other manner, franchisees often allege that the pattern and practice of past dealings waives, modifies, or estops the franchisor from enforcing its franchise system standards.[159] Waiver occurs when one party voluntarily and intentionally relinquishes its rights in full knowledge that the other party has failed to perform.[160] However, while "[c]onduct may constitute waiver of a contract term, . . . an implied waiver must be demonstrated by clear evidence."[161]

While many courts impose a high standard for proving waiver, franchisors should be concerned about the precedent that can be set by ignoring offending conduct. For example, in *Terry International v. Dairy Queen, Inc.*,[162] plaintiffs filed an action seeking a declaration that their sales of nonfranchisor food products did not breach their license agreement but, if it did, that the franchisor had waived its rights to enforce the contract because it had failed to object. The court agreed: "The failure of the [l]icensor to object for a period of at least 25 years . . . surely constitutes a waiver of the requirement of written approval."[163]

Franchisors should consider adding a no-waiver clause in the franchise agreement that states that no waiver by the franchisor or any breach or series of breaches shall constitute a waiver of any subsequent breach. While some courts enforce these provisions, others do not, and it is prudent for franchisors to enforce their standards or, if a decision is made to provide temporary relief, to communicate with franchisees about the time period for compliance and the consequences for noncompliance as courts have waived compliance defaults for failure to enforce for shorter periods.[164]

---

159. *See* Kerry L. Bundy & Scott Ikeda, *How Waiver, Modification, and Estoppel May Alter Franchise Relationships*, 30 ABA Franchise L.J. 1 (Summer 2010).

160. *See, e.g.*, Burger King v. E-Z Eating 41 Corp., 572 F.3d 1306, 1315 (11th Cir. 2009).

161. *Id.*

162. 554 F. Supp. 1088 (N.D. Ind. 1983).

163. *Id.* at 1095. *See also* LaGuardia Assocs. v. Holiday Hospitality Franchising, 92 F. Supp. 2d 119, 130 (E.D.N.Y. 2000) (franchisor waived its right to terminate franchise for nonpayment by not enforcing its right to collect for nearly 10 months).

164. *See, e.g.*, LaGuardia Associates v. Holiday Hospitality Franchising, Inc., 92 F. Supp. 2d 119, 129–30 (E.D.N.Y. 2000) ("Holiday, by not terminating on the April 1999 default for nearly ten months, but instead essentially abandoning that right until February 2000,

(f) Support Models

Part and parcel of any compliance program is the support that franchisors provide to the system. Every franchisor will provide some level of support to its franchisees, although the amount of support varies widely. A strong support system will help franchisors to identify and remedy problems earlier. As a general proposition, there are two broad models for franchisee support. In the "traditional" model, the support provided to franchisees is completely independent from any company-owned operations of the franchisor and its affiliates. This means that the franchisor has one or more departments dedicated solely to support of franchisees. This department generally has some sort of field operations personnel (called "franchise business representatives" or similar) that contact franchisees and/or visit franchised units on a regular basis. Depending on the overall company organization, this department may also have a central training staff or other functions to support the franchisees.

A less common model is the "integrated" support model. In this model, the franchisees are treated very similarly to units operated by the company or its affiliates. In an integrated support model, the same people will support both franchised and company-owned units, and in the same manner. For instance, the number of unit visits will be roughly the same, and the inspections will be handled in the same manner. Depending on how far this model is carried, franchisees may even be able to call on other departments within the franchisor's organization (such as marketing or product development) for assistance with issues encountered by the franchisee. Franchisors that choose to use the "integrated" support model should be aware that there may be increased legal risks from that model because of the increased level of control over the franchisees assumed by the franchisor. (See section 3-4 above, discussing vicarious liability.)

(g) Business Representatives

One of the most common forms of support that franchisors provide to their franchisees is a person or group of persons that visits franchisee locations (and, in an integrated support model, also company-owned locations). These persons may be referred to by titles such as "franchise business representatives," "franchise operations supervisors," or "franchise support representatives." In most franchise systems, these personnel generally have multiple roles vis-à-vis the franchisees. The franchise business representatives will often serve as the main point of contact between the franchisee and the franchisor. They may act as a liaison between the franchisee and various persons or departments within the franchisor organization. They may also have other functions, such as providing training to the franchisees on new products or services, inspecting the franchisee's locations, and enforcing the franchisor's standards. In some franchise systems, the roles of

---

waived its right to rely on that default . . . as a basis for termination of the Agreements.") (determining that "[a] reasonable time for returning to strict compliance with the payment terms in the Agreement is required as a matter of equity.").

"teacher" and "police officer" are separated out, and there are independent quality inspectors who have no other support role. It is not uncommon, however, for the "teacher" and "police officer" roles to be combined, which presents the franchise business representatives with the difficult challenge of deciding when training and support has failed and when to enforce the franchisor's standards. Franchise business representatives should have a solid background in the functioning of the franchised business and should be acquainted with the persons and departments within the franchisor company who are responsible for various business functions.

(h) Cautions Regarding Giving Support

Even in franchise systems using an "integrated" support model, in which franchisees are given the same access to departments within the franchisor as are company-owned units, there is often a line drawn at the door of the legal department. The franchisor's legal department should not provide legal advice to franchisees. There are several reasons for this, including vicarious liability, legal malpractice, and avoiding conflicts of interest.

Some franchisors using an integrated support model will provide an intermediate level of assistance to franchisees. In this scenario, the legal department will not answer specific legal questions from the franchisees but will provide guidance on how company-owned stores address similar issues. When this approach is used, it is important to inform the franchisee, preferably in writing, that no legal advice is being given and that the franchisee's particular legal situation is not being addressed; rather, the legal department is providing general information concerning how the franchisor has applied a combination of legal advice, business decisions, and other factors to decide how to proceed.

An example of how this approach is applied can be seen in the advice provided to franchisees when the Americans with Disabilities Act took effect. Most franchisors that also operated company-owned units developed some level of plans to address the "readily achievable barrier removal" initially required by the ADA. Those plans typically incorporated knowledge of the franchisor's standard building designs, costs of various construction tasks, and legal advice about the meaning of the applicable provisions of the ADA. Many franchisors then provided copies of those plans to their franchisees, along with disclaimers that the plans were not to be considered legal advice and that the franchisees should consult their own attorneys for advice on how to comply with the law in their individual circumstances. This is a compromise between a strict policy of not providing any legal advice to franchisees and true analysis of the franchisees' individual situations to give "true" legal advice.

Another caution is that some franchisors sell or gratuitously provide their own form contracts (such as membership agreements) to franchisees and assume that the form will be properly adapted by the franchisee (by such steps as changing notice addresses and deleting the franchisor as a party). Experience indicates that franchisees do not always follow this practice. Occasionally, the franchisor's name is printed as the contracting party but the document is signed by the franchisee—or the franchisee inserts its name as an additional party and signs on behalf of both. Usually, the franchisee is not intending to commit fraud, but these types of sloppy practices create a risk that the franchisor will be found liable for permitting the franchisee to hold out the franchisor as a party to the transaction. Form contracts delivered to franchisees should delete the franchisor's name and contain a blank for the franchisee's name (or be printed with the franchisee's name only). However, while the franchisor entity name should be removed from contracts provided to franchisees for their use, there is minimal risk from leaving the franchisor's trademark on the form, since the franchisee is an authorized licensee of the trademark.

3-11. Audit Program and Techniques

Almost all franchise agreements grant the franchisor the right to "audit" the franchisee's business. While perhaps most commonly thought of as a verification of financial accounts, audits can be much broader than that and may best be thought of as any form of check or examination. In this broader sense, any inspection of the franchisee's operations can be considered an "audit." In this section we do not discuss general inspections of the franchisee's operations conducted by the company's quality inspectors or business representatives (which are covered in the section of this chapter dealing with compliance and support above) but instead focus on other types of reviews.

(a) Developing an Audit Program165

Broadly speaking, there are two types of audit programs—random and "for cause." While both types of audits can cause anxiety among franchisees—particularly an accusation that the franchisor does not trust the franchisees—this problem is particularly acute with respect to random audits. One issue, therefore, is explaining to franchisees the overall benefits of an audit program. Of course, one benefit is that audits assure that all franchisees are paying their fair share of the costs of operating the franchise (since royalties and advertising contributions fuel the business), but audits can also detect internal theft, weak internal controls, and out-of-line operational costs, which can be of direct benefit to the franchisee that is audited. By contrast, one of the principal benefits (to the franchisor) is the decreased likelihood that franchisees will under-report sales if they believe there is a chance (even a small one) of being audited.

For most franchisors, the prospect of auditing a franchisee is a difficult step. The franchisee may believe it is being singled out or has been unfairly selected

165. This section benefitted from the insights provided in Jim Marasco & Andrew Zappia, *Developing and Implementing Franchise Audits*, FRANCHISING WORLD MAG. (Jan. 2003) (*copy available at* https://stonebridgebp.com/library/uncategorized/developing-and-implementing-franchise-audits/; last accessed Oct. 14, 2019).

for review. However, an audit program that is properly planned, is fairly administered, and communicates the purpose of, and benefits to, the system should help dispel franchisees' apprehension. To that end, the franchisor would be well-advised to define and articulate its audit procedures, including how it selects its audit targets and any on-site review and how it will document any findings and enforce system standards. By articulating the process early on, franchisors can avoid claims of unfairness or inconsistency.

One factor to consider in developing an audit program is deciding what triggers an audit and whom to audit. Although it might be the easiest approach, it is advisable to include random audits and not to limit the audit to "problem" franchisees. The franchisor should find a way of selecting a cross-section of franchisees to review and establish a process that will fairly test the system as a whole. A "for cause" audit might be triggered by unusual results appearing in the quality inspections or by unusual financial results. The triggers should be defined but should not necessarily be communicated to franchisees. The program should also be flexible enough to allow for the review of franchisees who do not trigger other criteria.

The intent of the audit should be identified. For example, if detecting sales underreporting is the goal, the franchisor should decide if it intends to check governmental filings, review point-of-sale information and other computer register data, and review product usage and volume to gauge potential sales. The franchisor may also want to verify that the franchisee has spent the required percentage of gross revenues on advertising or that the franchisee is buying products for the business from approved suppliers. The franchisor may also want to verify compliance with a wide range of obligations.

Once a decision has been made about the scope of the review in a particular audit, the affected franchisee should be given formal notice of the time, place, and manner in which the audit will be conducted. The amount of advance notice to franchisees may be dictated by the franchise agreement; if not, it is generally preferable to give the franchisee long enough to gather the records to be reviewed but not long enough to fabricate evidence.

Depending on circumstances, the franchisor must decide whether to pursue a comprehensive financial audit or take a less formal approach. Many larger franchisors will have an internal audit department that conducts comprehensive reviews. Small franchisors may rely on an outside accounting firm (sometimes referred to as a "forensic accounting" firm) to conduct the audit, although many large franchisors also take this approach. A comprehensive audit is similar to the audits done by the Internal Revenue Service to determine if taxes have been properly paid, and by accountants to determine if a company's financial statements have been properly prepared. Many franchise agreements will require that several years of financial records be available for review. Comprehensive audits may include a review of those statements or anything else—cash register receipts, bank statements, inventory records, and sales and income tax returns—that might help to determine if the franchisee is properly reporting sales or complying with system standards. Franchisors should also decide whether they want to limit the scope of the initial financial audit to a portion of the records that must be retained (perhaps a year or six months), instead of reviewing several years of records. If discrepancies are found, additional periods can then be reviewed.

The cost and expense of a comprehensive audit (and the intrusion to the franchisee) might outweigh the benefits. After all, most franchisors are trying to grow their businesses and not unnecessarily scrutinize their franchisees. Franchisors might consider other techniques to verify whether standards are being met.

(b) Mystery Shoppers

There are numerous companies that provide independent "mystery shoppers" that will visit a franchisee's businesses to determine if the franchisee is complying with specified standards. A mystery shopper who remains in the publicly accessible areas of a franchised location and observes interactions between the franchisee (or the franchisee's employees) and customers (including the mystery shopper himself or herself) may be able to act without any explicit authorization in the franchise agreement.

In some franchise systems, however, the use of mystery shoppers is described in the franchise agreement. The franchisor may explicitly reserve the right to have the franchisee's operations observed by independent mystery shoppers. In some instances, the franchise agreements go further, and all franchisees agree not only to periodic investigations by mystery shoppers but also to paying a monthly charge to cover their share of system-wide mystery shoppers. Depending on details of the approach, the franchisee may be assured a specified number of visits by a mystery shopper each year (for instance, once a year or once a quarter) or may simply acknowledge that there may be one or more visits per year by a mystery shopper.

Generally, the scope of the investigation undertaken by a mystery shopper is agreed on between the franchisor and the mystery shopper. It is important that the mystery shoppers are objective, neutral third parties. The mystery shopper may be asked to call a franchised location and ask a series of questions or to visit a franchised location and purchase an agreed-upon selection of items. In either event, the mystery shopper typically fills out a report after the call or visit, describing such things as whether the staff was friendly, whether questions were answered properly, whether the total charge was calculated properly, whether the money was placed in the cash drawer, whether proper change was given, and other questions of interest to the franchisor. Sometimes these written reports are routinely shared with the affected franchisee, and other times there is no mention made of the report unless a problem is revealed.

At times, the difference between mystery shoppers and private investigators can get blurry. For example, one interesting use of mystery shoppers is to ferret out instances in which the franchisee (or the franchisee's employees) is not properly entering sales in the point-of-sale system or cash register. There have been cases in which a mystery shopper was tasked with inconspicuously "loitering" in a franchised location, watching the register over a period of time, and making a record of every sale actually made and what amount was entered into the cash register. If there is a discrepancy, the testimony of the mystery shopper can be used as evidence that the franchisee is not paying the proper amount of royalties.

(c) Auditing through the P.O.S. System

One of the easiest ways to audit financial matters is through access to the franchisee's point-of-sale (P.O.S.) system (the modern counterpart of an electronic cash register). Many franchise agreements grant explicit authority to the franchisor to obtain access to the franchisee's P.O.S. system at any time, without notice to or other consent from the franchisee. Other times, the franchisee uses a P.O.S. system that is integrated with the franchisor's computer systems (for inventory control, reordering, etc.), and the license agreement for the P.O.S. system allows the franchisor access to the franchisee's sales records, either explicitly or as part of the franchisor's ability to restock the franchisee's inventory. Whether or not the franchisee reports its sales and pays its royalties and advertising fees through the P.O.S. system, the franchisor's access to the franchisee's sales data allows the franchisor to cross-check the level of sales reported by the franchisee as compared to the sales recorded in the P.O.S. system. Franchisors should be aware that there are ways to evade P.O.S. systems, ranging from the low tech (failing to enter sales into the terminal) to the high tech (the use of "zappers"—software programs that can modify the records of electronic P.O.S. systems, often with an eye to evading taxes).[166]

(d) Purchasing Reviews

Franchisors that are predominantly distribution businesses have always been able to match up purchases of goods to reported sales—if a franchisee consistently purchases more of a product than it reports selling, that is almost an automatic audit flag. Many franchisors of service businesses have now developed similar measurements based on "key ingredients" purchased by franchisees. As an example, consider a coffee shop franchisor. There should be a rough correlation between the amount of coffee beans purchased and the amount of coffee sold. If a significant discrepancy exists between the reported sales of the franchisee and the amount of coffee purchased, the franchisor may wish to undertake a more in-depth audit. As an example, the franchisor's experience may be that franchisees report sales ranging from $35 to $42 per pound of coffee purchased; under those circumstances, a franchisee reporting revenues of $33 per pound may have control/waste issues, but a franchisee reporting revenues of $25 per pound is likely to have a more serious issue (not necessarily fraud, although that is a possibility).

166. *See generally*, Roy Furchgott, *With Software, Till Tampering Is Hard to Find*, N.Y. Times, Aug. 30, 2008 (*available at* https://www.nytimes.com/2008/08/30/technology/30zapper.html?searchResultPosition=1; last accessed Oct. 14, 2019) (stating that "even technologically illiterate restaurant and store owners can siphon cash from computer cash registers and cheat tax officials").

(e) Practical Advice

Once the audit is complete, if a problem has been discovered, the franchisor should document the issue in writing, whether found through a comprehensive audit or one of the techniques described above. The franchisor might consider whether meeting face-to-face is appropriate. A written report of any meetings should be prepared and sent to the franchisee. Franchisors should also recap any discussions—whether in person or by telephone—with franchisees in writing. If a legal dispute arises, the written file will serve an important role. As discussed previously, "Check, coach, check, enforce" may guide your enforcement process, but if the franchisor has not built its case in the written file, its ability to enforce standards will be significantly impaired. As legal counsel reviews the audit results, particular attention should be paid to the chronology of events, and there should be a continuing assessment of whether the record supports a finding of fairness and whether any waiver or modification claims may be countered.

The audit results also provide an opportunity to take an objective look at the business and may help the parties identify and correct any barriers to success. What level of financial success has been achieved? How can the business be more competitive? The audit gives the franchisor an opportunity to do more than just identify the underreporting of sales; it can serve as another tool to increase profitability and energize the business.

3-12. Conclusion

The long-term success of any franchise system is dependent on the care and precision with which the franchisor deals with issues related to franchise operations. Legal counsel should work with management to ensure a system is in place that takes advantage of the best practices described in this section for developing an operations manual, a records management program, and compliance and audit programs; structuring national or local advertising funds; and avoiding unnecessary litigation. While franchise systems are built on trust, the franchisor has both a legal and business obligation to create and structure an enforcement program—for both quality inspections and audit purposes—and to carry through on its commitments.

Form 3-1
Operations Manual Update

Subject: ______________________________ **Date:** ______________

No. _________ **Tab:** ____________________ **Replaces:** ____________

Other References: ____

____

Distribution: ____

____

____

Purpose: ____

To communicate: ____

Policy:

____

____

____.

Procedure:

____

____

____.

Contact for information and feedback: ______________________________________

Title of Contact: ______________________

Telephone: (xxx) yyy-zzzz

E-mail: ____

This policy is Mandatory for all company-owned units; for franchisees, this policy is: ____ **Mandatory** ___ **Suggested**; check with your franchise owner concerning implementation.

Exhibit 3-1
Sample Completed Operations Manual Update

Subject: Inventory Accounting (revised) **Date:** September 1, 2011

No. 2011-6 **Tab:** Chart of Accounts **Replaces:** 2003-5

Other References: Inventory Procedures; Accounting Maintenance

Distribution: Store Operations; Accounting Department; Accounts Payable; and Financial Analysis and Reporting

Purpose: To ensure consistency in month-end inventory reporting.

To communicate: New procedure for estimating month-end inventory.

Policy: All inventory will be reported to the nearest ¼ package.

Procedure: Effective with month-end inventory for September 2011, open packages will be counted to the nearest ¼ package. All packages that are past the "sell-by" date should be discarded (refer to policy ____ for procedures for writing off inventory). Once those packages have been discarded, all open packages should be identified. The person conducting inventory should estimate whether open packages are full, three-quarters full, half full, or one-quarter full. Packages that are between these amounts should be estimated as being closest to one of these levels. The inventory reporting forms should show the sum of full packages and partial packages.

Contact for information and feedback: ________________________________

Title of Contact: ____________________

Telephone: (xxx) yyy-zzzz

E-mail: ________________________________

This policy is Mandatory for all company-owned units; for franchisees, this policy is: ____ **Mandatory** ___ **Suggested**; check with your franchise owner concerning implementation.

Exhibit 3-2
Sample Records Retention Schedule

Overview

Following are excerpts from a sample "functional retention schedule" that covers the franchise documents a hypothetical franchise company might use. Rather than assigning individual records retention periods to thousands of record titles, this approach simplifies the process by grouping records into functional categories. In this example, the "functions" that particular records serve are designated as "franchise relations" and "sales compliance." Documents are listed by type under one of those two functions, and subheadings have been included to facilitate locating a particular record category.

The sample retention schedule is presented as a finished product. It assumes that senior management and departmental representatives have already decided how to combine legally required retention periods with practical business considerations to determine total retention periods. Decisions have also been made as to which department will maintain the records and serve as the office of record.

Information Fields

The Records Retention Schedule contains several fields of information. The titles and contents of these fields are as follows:

Record title: A brief label identifying the basic content of the record group.

Description: A brief label identifying the types of records in the record group.

Office: The period during which the records will be kept in a departmental or central storage area in the company's offices.

Records center: The period during which the records will be kept in an off-site storage facility.

Total: The total retention period for particular categories of official records.

Unofficial records: The period for retaining copies of unofficial records, including photocopies, microfilm, etc.

Office of record: The office or department responsible for maintaining particular categories of official records during the retention period.

Abbreviations

ACT: Active—retain record while matter is active or in force

P: Permanent—retain record indefinitely

S: Superseded—retain record until replaced by more current version (applicable to forms)

+ Plus. Some retention periods consist of two or more components. For example, records with the period ACT+3 should be kept while the matter is active, plus three years.

Retention Periods of Official Records

Record Title and Description	Office	Record Center	Total	Unofficial Records (duplicates)	Office of Record
		Franchise Relations			
CORE CONTRACTS	*ACT*	*4*	*ACT +4*	*ACT*	*Legal*
Master franchise agreements for U.S. master franchisees (subfranchisors)					
Development agreements for U.S. area developers					
Franchise agreements for traditional units or outlets in the United States					
Franchise agreements for special purpose/special venue units or outlets in the United States					
Master franchise agreements for foreign master franchisees					
Development agreements for foreign area developers					
Joint venture agreements for foreign venture partners					
Franchise agreements for units/ outlets operated outside the United States by franchisees or subfranchisees of foreign master franchisees					
Guaranties of payment/ performance by owners of domestic and international franchisees					
Alliance agreements governing co-branding alliances					
Trademark licenses for nontraditional units/ outlets					
Standard amendments and addenda to core contracts					

Record Title and Description	**Office**	**Record Center**	**Total**	**Unofficial Records (duplicates)**	**Office of Record**
ANCILLARY CONTRACTS	*ACT*	*4*	*ACT +4*	*ACT*	*Legal*
First refusal options					
Building leases and subleases					
Equipment leases					
Assignments of building and equipment leases					
Loan agreements					
Security agreements					
Promissory notes					
Software licenses					
Confidentiality agreements					
Product/service test agreements					
Advertising co-op agreements and bylaws					
Franchise broker and sales agent/representative contracts					
Standard amendments and addenda to ancillary contracts					
Site/location approval forms					
Construction document approval forms					
Required real estate lease provisions for U.S. franchisees					
UCC financing statements					
Financial reporting forms (royalty statements, P&Ls, and so on)					
Operations report forms (QSC evaluations, local area marketing reports, equity ownership reports, and so on)					
Preauthorized payment (direct debit) agreements					

Record Title and Description	**Office**	**Record Center**	**Total**	**Unofficial Records (duplicates)**	**Office of Record**
Assignments of telephone numbers					
Transfer approval forms					
Sales Compliance					
CURRENT DOCUMENTS	*S*	*4*	*S +4*	*S*	*Legal*
Franchise disclosure document (Federal Trade Commission version for nonregistration states)					
State-specific records					
Franchise disclosure document, w/state-specific addenda, for each state in which the program is registered					
Registration applications and orders					
Exemption notices					
Advertising copy and approvals					
Correspondence with administrators					
Disclosure statements for foreign transactions (Brazil, Canada, France, Mexico, and so on)					
Brochures and information kits					
Franchise application forms					
Financial performance representations backup for franchise disclosure document (questionnaires, calculations, projections, and so on)					
HISTORICAL DOCUMENT LIBRARY		*P*	*P*		
Core contracts—samples of all generations and versions					
Ancillary contracts and forms—samples of all generations and versions					

Record Title and Description	**Office**	**Record Center**	**Total**	**Unofficial Records (duplicates)**	**Office of Record**
Franchise disclosure documents—copies of prior year circulars for all jurisdictions					
Registration applications and orders—prior year documentation for all jurisdictions					
Exemption statements and orders—prior year documentation for all jurisdictions					
Operations manuals—samples of all generations and versions					
Bulletins, newsletters, and other communiqués—copies of all issues					

CHAPTER 4

Franchise Relationship Management

Eric H. Karp

Contents

4-1. Introduction

The integration clause in the typical franchise agreement recites that it constitutes the entire agreement between the parties and that nothing outside the four corners of the document has any binding effect. While the franchise agreement defines the legal relationship between the parties, it does not prescribe the business relationship that exists between a franchisor and its franchisees on a day-to-day basis.

Cheryl Bachelder, the highly successful CEO of Popeyes from 2007 to 2017 and a proponent of servant leadership, described that franchisor's decision to serve the franchise owners well as its first priority, summarizing her view of the franchise relationship as follows:

> As we looked at our options for who we would serve, we thought the franchise owners merited our immediate attention. They had made sizable investments and committed by contract to operate our brand. If they did not prosper, there was no chance Popeyes sales would go up (royalties) or franchise fees would increase (new openings). Either franchise owners would succeed or Popeyes would fail.[1]

In fact, this enlightened collaborative approach to the franchise relationship took a franchise system marked by a deeply dissatisfied franchise community and an anemic stock price to one that enjoyed steep increases in the number of franchised units and franchisor shareholder equity.[2]

No one builds a franchise system, or invests in a franchise, merely for the purpose of "having a good franchise relationship." Rather, the purpose is to achieve a desired business outcome—primarily to achieve a positive return on the investment. Good relationships between a franchisor and franchisees are a means to that end. But the extent to which positive and constructive relationships in a franchise system can drive success often depends in large measure on the culture of the franchise system, meaning the nature and quality of the business relationships that exist within the franchise organization, both bilaterally between the franchisor and individual franchisees, and more holistically within the system generally.

Assuming a successful franchisor is one with a profitable system, growing in units, sales, transactions, and market share, a good relationship requires more than strict compliance with laws and contracts. It also requires acknowledging that the franchisor/franchisee relationship is a unique long-term relationship in which the ultimate success of both parties depends upon mutual goals, cooperation, and a shared sense of responsibility.

Greg Nathan, a corporate psychologist and founder of the Franchise Relationships Institute, whose career involves having been both a franchisee and a senior executive for a franchisor, summarizes this elementary principle as follows:

> Cooperation, commitment and communication are the real building blocks of success in a franchise chain. These largely come, not from legal agreements, but from ethical dealings, strong leadership and the mutual respect of each party for the goals of the other.[3]

Mr. Nathan's thesis is that good relationships will make you money and prevent costly disputes. Accordingly, the goal of the franchisor should not be limited

---

1. Cheryl Bachelder, Dare to Serve—How to Drive Superior Results by Serving Others 21 (Berrett Koehler Publishers 2015). The benefits of this collaborative approach are not theoretical. From 2011 to 2015, Popeyes' revenue grew from $154 million to $259 million, and its net income grew from $24 million to $44 million. By 2014, average restaurant sales were up 25 percent. The result was that franchisees voted with their checkbooks by reinvesting in the brand, remodeling restaurants, and building new units.

2. *See* Erin E. Conway, Eric H. Karp & Brenda B. Trickey, Franchisee Associations to the Rescue—Using Associations and Advisory Councils to Avoid Joint Employer Risk and Enhance the Brand 14 (ABA Forum on Franchising 2017).

3. Greg Nathan, Profitable Partnerships 5 (Franchise Relationship Institute, 7th ed. 2007).

to ensuring that franchisees follow, and corporate employees enforce, the franchise agreement. It should also provide a framework for ensuring that franchisees and corporate employees alike are acting in accordance with the policies and values of the brand. This chapter explores the importance of good franchisor/franchisee relations and examines ways to build into the franchise system the foundation, institutions, processes, and guidelines necessary to exploit fully the power of an aligned, cooperative franchise system.

4-2. Why Good In-System Relationships Matter

(a) Interests of System Participants

Good in-system relations are much more than a moral objective. The objective of a franchise-based business is no different from any other: distinguishing the brand, outperforming the competition, anticipating and serving the customers' needs, and, most importantly, making money doing it. Good relations within a franchise organization are necessary, not simply desirable, because competing in a crowded and dynamic market segment requires the strategic vision and leadership of a franchisor combined with the practical knowledge and invested capital of franchisees applied toward a common goal. For most franchise systems, the best candidate for the next unit to be opened is an existing franchisee motivated to expand its investment in the brand and in the system. Disruption and internal strife distract the parties from focusing on the external competition and the changing market, as well as challenges that may result from regulatory or legislative initiatives, resulting in a confused message to the consumer, misdirected energy and resources, and lost opportunity.

Although franchisors and franchisees share this general economic interest, the structure of the traditional franchise relationship often sends them in different directions when they do not agree on the best method for achieving their goals. Traditional franchisors and franchisees both benefit from sharing a strong, competitive system, but they may also make their profit in different ways. The franchisor may run its own outlets; it may also be a brand licensor, a vendor, a service provider, a trainer, a lender, and/or a landlord. Product distribution and vertically integrated systems may prioritize profit on goods and services sold to franchisees. The form of ownership of the franchisor may also have a profound effect on its goals and objectives; the publicly held franchisor focused on quarterly earnings may approach the franchise relationship differently than a private equity owner. The franchisee is usually engaged in a retailing business and, relative to the franchisor, may be a buyer, a tenant, a borrower, and/or a brand licensee. The franchisor may tend to focus on the franchisee's top line sales because that is the source of its franchise royalty revenue stream.[4] But the franchisee is necessarily focused on its bottom line. These differing roles and objectives create an inherent conflict

4. One of the reasons courts struggle with restitution damages in franchise rescission cases is because the complexity of the relationship makes it difficult to untangle. *See* ERIC

of interest in even the best run and most cooperative franchise organizations. For a franchise-based business to function up to its full potential, this divergence of interest must be regularly managed and reconciled with the parties' common goal of a successful system.

Franchise organizations flourish when the franchisor and franchisees recognize the significant advantages to be derived from acknowledging their differences, learning from each other, and working together to create and execute a common plan to achieve their goals. Multigenerational franchise owners may have deep institutional knowledge and keen entrepreneurial instincts; franchisor executives with experience in other brands bring invaluable experience to the table. Franchise organizations that fail to take advantage of these resources will never realize their full potential. In those cases, shareholders of the franchisor will be every bit as frustrated and disappointed as will the franchisee/investors in the system.

Author Greg Nathan writes that through objective questionnaires, the Franchise Relationships Institute characterizes the following behaviors of healthy relationships in a franchise system:

- Franchisees and franchisor employees are glad of their decision to be involved in a network;
- There is collaboration and transparent sharing of information between franchisor and franchisees as well as between franchisees;
- Dealings between the parties are conducted with courtesy and respect;
- People give each other the benefit of the doubt; and
- People comply with their agreed obligations without coercion.[5]

What are the investment objectives of parties to a franchise-based business? From the perspective of the franchisee, the objectives include purchasing from the franchisor the know-how that would otherwise be developed at presumably greater cost through trial and error, combined with the (presumably favorable) goodwill associated with use of the franchisor's methods, trademarks, and advertising and marketing programs. The franchisee expects to use this leveraged capital and information base to run a successful business, to earn a positive return on its investment in the business, to achieve a level of personal satisfaction in doing so, and to harvest the value thus created. In pursuing these goals, franchisees certainly expect to have to function in a competitive and controlled environment; however, few, if any, genuinely expect their own franchisor to be a significant competitive threat in terms of sponsoring "encroaching" brick and mortar locations or Internet distribution, or requiring the purchase of unnecessarily expensive equipment, services, goods, or supplies. These expectations exist empirically and subjectively irrespective of the contents of the franchisor's franchise disclosure document (FDD). These are prime examples of areas in which a franchise

---

H. KARP & NATALMA M. MCKNEW, RESTORING THE STATUS QUO ANTE: RESCISSION AND RESTITUTION IN FRANCHISING (ABA Forum on Franchising 2007).

5. Greg Nathan, *How to Create Healthier Franchise Relationships and Happier Clients*, 13(1) THE FRANCHISE LAWYER (Winter 2010).

relationship can become strained when the two parties single-mindedly pursue their own individual goals without due regard for the interests of the other, or of the system as a whole.

The franchisor's objectives in building a franchise-based business organization also include capital leverage, but beyond that, particular objectives of individual franchisors vary globally. The franchisor most often undertakes a franchise-based form of business to recruit into the enterprise the capital, both financial and human, of the franchisee/investor. This leveraging allows for a more rapid expansion of the brand; facilitates penetration of distant or foreign markets; and, in some cases, allows more rapid accretion of market share than would otherwise be the case. Yet the franchisor's goals can be threatened, and the relationship strained, when franchisees resist a change in products, services or marketing approaches or deviate significantly from system requirements, perhaps by refusing to contribute to or participate in system marketing initiatives, cutting costs by purchasing substandard supplies, or deferring facility repairs.

If the franchisee perceives that the economic model in the franchise system does not permit an adequate return on invested capital, pressures may mount for the franchisee to cut corners in ways that may be detrimental to both parties to the franchise relationship. In his book *The Fissured Workplace*, Professor David Weil states that a variety of factors inherent in the franchise relationship provide company-owned units with a greater incentive to comply with applicable laws that affect consumer perception of the brand.[6] One of these factors, as noted above, is that the franchisor seeks to maximize sales while the franchisee seeks to maximize unit-level profit.

One issue where these competing interests are currently colliding is in the area of third-party delivery services.[7] Franchisors have entered into agreements with these third parties in an effort to keep up with evolving consumer desires for delivery to their homes and businesses. These arrangements frequently allow the third-party delivery services to take as much as 30 percent of the retail price off the top, but the franchisee is frequently required to pay royalties and advertising contributions on the full retail price, including revenue that it does not receive. As third-party delivery becomes more ubiquitous, efforts must be found to balance the competing interests of the franchisor and franchisee and to equitably share the economic results of these transactions.

The relationship roles that franchisors and franchisees undertake within the ongoing franchise are represented by a variety of more traditional common law relationship models. Franchising is not only a long-term relationship but also one that contains multiple components, representing an accumulation of relationships set forth in the franchise agreement and collateral contracts and filtered through traditional common law principles for interpreting and enforcing private

---

6. David Weil, The Fissured Workplace (Harvard University Press 2014).

7. According to *QSR Magazine*, the global food delivery mobile app market is expected to hit $16.6 billion by 2023, a compound annual growth rate of 27.9 percent. *See* Danny Klein, *Fighting for Share in the $16.6 Billion Delivery App Market*, QSR Magazine, June 2019.

contracts. The common law has yet to establish a fully satisfactory, single legal model for the combination of traditional business relationships embraced by most business format franchises. Thus, the challenge remains for parties and their lawyers to find workable solutions to system conflict arising from a variety of sources, without sacrificing the parties' respective investment objectives.

Within the component relationships of the franchise contracts are the seeds of dissension. Each of these component or subordinate relationships involves an element of adversarial relations. Certainly, a seller and a buyer have conflicting interests relative to price and terms of sale, as do a landlord and a tenant. If a franchise system devolves into only one of these relationships, the inherent adversarial character of that relationship is likely to come to the fore, damaging the prospects for cooperation and collaboration that drive success of a franchise-based business network, viewed as a whole. This is true even in cooperative or ideal circumstances because the friction of divergent or conflicting economic interests is intrinsic in these component relationships. Where either party to a franchise relationship exploits power or position in one of the component relationships to obtain opportunistic advantage, a breakdown in the franchise relationship is all but certain. This breakdown can not only impair the working relationship between the franchisor and that franchisee; the strain and collateral damage can also injure the entire system.

Thus, the success of the franchise-based enterprise, involving efforts of both the franchisor and the franchisees in a shared business enterprise, depends on identifying and exploiting the parties' shared interests in their common objectives. This usually involves competitive success of the system as a whole, appropriate research and development, marketing and advertising campaigns, adherence to system norms, fair allocations of growth opportunities, and reconciling sometimes divergent or conflicting partisan economic interests.[8]

Parties that act opportunistically in a franchise relationship to exploit their individual interests in the component or subordinate relationships usually end up doing so at the expense of undermining their ability to achieve success in the broader franchise enterprise. For example, franchisors that so exploit their franchise networks, perhaps through inappropriate sourcing restrictions,[9] unduly restrictive system governance procedures, or the like, certainly should not then wonder why franchisees do not respond enthusiastically to "company" marketing initiatives, or may even resist forcefully, in legal and even legislative channels,

8. Nathan, *supra* note 5. Mr. Nathan describes two franchise systems he has studied. Company A's franchisees make on average 30 percent more in profit than those of Company B. Company A is marked by authoritarian and confrontational leadership obsessed with control. Company B has leadership committed to collaboration, resolution of conflict through open discussion, positive two-way communication, and rewarding franchisees for good performance. Despite making less money, the franchisees of Company B were significantly more satisfied on a whole range of measures studied by Mr. Nathan. He concludes, "the point is that the corporate culture of a franchise network will have a significant impact on franchisee satisfaction. In some cases culture will be an even more important determinant of franchisee satisfaction than financial performance."

9. Queen City Pizza, Inc. v. Domino's Pizza, Inc., 124 F.3d 430 (3d Cir. 1997).

franchisor activities (such as encroachment or monopolization of sourcing) that franchisees perceive as threatening to their core investment interests.[10] Similarly, franchisees that consistently ignore system-wide marketing programs, or let the physical appearance of their outlets deteriorate, should not complain when their franchisor denies them expansion or renewal opportunities in favor of other franchisees that more fully embrace shared system initiatives and values.

Franchisees are increasingly sophisticated, well-educated, well-advised, well-capitalized, multi-generational, organized, and demanding in their franchise relationships. In recent years, there have been a number of franchise systems involved in high-profile legal disputes that have system-wide implications for them. These include disputes relating to material changes to the business format (Hot N'Now), hours of operation (Edible Arrangements), fixed dollar pricing policies (Great Clips), mandated deep discounting (Burger King), alternate channels of distribution (Carvel), and required point-of-sale computer systems (Domino's Pizza).[11] Win, lose, or draw, these cases illustrate the enormous distraction, reduction in franchisee morale, and misdirected economic resources devoted to these kinds of disputes.

Franchisors that fail to respect the symbiotic nature of the franchise relationship and the investment objectives of their franchisees (in the eyes of their franchisees, irrespective of what the parties' technical legal rights might be) should not wonder why their systems become unmanageable as increasingly experienced franchisees become alienated, resentful, and fearful. Franchisees, by the same token, should not wonder why their franchisor becomes alienated, hostile, and suspicious if they exploit opportunistically their relative individual advantage, perhaps by pursuing individual local business initiatives at the expense of system integrity or uniformity of brand development.

The growth of communications and information exchanges through the Internet and social networking and face-to-face interchange at various gatherings (increasingly including events sponsored by franchisee associations) have promoted and accelerated opportunities for issues and concerns to spread rapidly through entire systems.

(b) Public and Regulatory Perspective

Since franchising is an important economic force in the U.S. economy, it should be little wonder that public policy addresses itself to the franchise relationship.[12] Legislatures and even most administrative bureaucracies take seriously the public

10. *See* Siemer v. Quizno's Franchise Co., LLC, No. 07-cv-02170, 2008 WL 904874 (N.D. Ill. Mar. 31, 2008).

11. *See* Loehr v. Hot N' Now, Inc., No. 95-6253-cv-Gonzales (S.D. Fla. 1998); EA Independent Franchisee Association, LLC v. Edible Arrangements International, Inc., 2011 WL 2938077. (D. Conn. 2011); Great Clips Inc. v. Levine, 1991 WL 322974 (D. Minn. 1991); Carvel Corp. v. Noonan, 4 N.Y.3d 182, 818 N.E.2d 1100 (Court of Appeals of New York 2004); National Franchisee Assoc. v. Burger King Corp., 715 F. Supp. 2d 1232 (S.D. Fla. 2010); *and* Bores v. Domino's Pizza, Inc., 530 F.3d 671 (8th Cir. 2008).

12. *See* PricewaterhouseCoopers LLP, The Economic Impact of Franchised Businesses: Vol. IV (2016) http://www.franchise.org/franchiseesecondary.aspx?id=37842.

objectives of promoting economic stability, encouraging growth in employment, conserving judicial resources, pursuing efficiency of public agency operation and administration, and protecting the public from misrepresentation.

As many elected officials have learned, there are many more franchisees than there are franchisors. According to the most recent study of the franchise industry by the International Franchise Association, there are more than 801,000 franchised businesses in the United States employing more than 8.9 million people with a combined payroll of more than $351 billion.[13] Franchisees tend to be local small business owners, employers, and voters. Franchisors tend to be out-of-state or even off-shore corporations. Since "all politics is local,"[14] it should surprise no one that when state legislatures are motivated to investigate franchise relationships, the tendency is to protect the interests of the local investor, business owner, employer, and voter.

What most legislators hear about franchising seems to come more often from franchisees whose businesses have under-performed or failed for one reason or another. This incomplete factual understanding of franchising makes a volatile mix with the political environment in which those grievances are voiced. For franchisors that oppose public legislative intervention into franchise relationships, the imperative of maintaining good in-system relations is self-evident.

4-3. Role and Responsibilities of Franchise Lawyers

The rules of professional responsibility recite that a lawyer has a duty to be a zealous advocate of the lawyer's client's interests.[15] Every business lawyer knows that a lawyer's role in a business transaction is to provide the best advice possible, to seek to maximize the client's position in negotiations, and then to facilitate a closing.

The business lawyer is accustomed to dealing with distinct transactions, where the parties often will have little or no continuing relationship. If a bridge needs to be burned, it is a regrettable, but profitable, necessity. A trial attorney may be even less concerned with preserving a relationship between two combatants.

The problem with these traditional roles is that they seldom make sense in the franchisor/franchisee context. In most cases, the franchisor and franchisee will remain in business together long after the transaction or dispute is forgotten. For example, if the franchisor's lawyer adequately disclaims on paper an equipment warranty but does not ensure that the franchisee understands the existence or

13. PricewaterhouseCoopers LLP, The Economic Impact of Franchised Businesses: Vol. IV I-14 (2016).

14. While coined by others, this phrase was popularized by former Speaker of the U.S. House of Representatives, Thomas P. ("Tip") O'Neill (1912–1994).

15. *See* ABA, Modern Rules of Professional Conduct: Preamble and Scope, http://www.americanbar.org/groups/professional_responsibility/publications/model_rules_of_professional_conduct/model_rules_of_professional_conduct_preamble_scope.html.

meaning of the disclaimer, the lawyer has done his or her client no good service when the equipment fails. All the lawyer has done is left the franchisor with a frustrated, aggrieved business associate. Similarly, if a trial lawyer for a franchisee alienates the franchisor with baseless claims of "bad faith" in a lease dispute at one site, the franchisor is unlikely to be responsive to the franchisee's later attempt to find a "business solution" to an issue at another location.

This does not mean that franchisors or franchisees must stoically suffer abuse at the hands of each other. What it does mean is that lawyers (for either side) can add value and well represent their own client's best interests by tempering their approach, to remember at all times that the franchisor and franchisee will probably remain in business together at the conclusion of the transaction or dispute, and that both share an overriding interest in a healthy and productive system. Transactions can be an opportunity to build trust and cooperation if handled correctly, and disputes can be handled professionally and without personal recrimination in order to minimize the damage to the relationship and collateral damage to the system. The Alternate Dispute Resolution/Conflict Resolution section of this chapter focuses on how various procedures can further this goal.

The challenge to the lawyer representing the franchisor, the franchisee, or a group or association of franchisees is to observe that the client's interests in a franchise business, even in the event of a particular transaction or a dispute, include an overriding interest in the long-term success and growth of the system as a whole. This strategic interest of the client may cause the lawyer to adopt a strategy in advising and representing the client that differs from what "zealous advocacy" of partisan interest might call for outside of an ongoing business relationship. A lawyer must recognize that the client may have a material interest in acting in a manner consistent with the best interests of all stakeholders in the system.

4-4. How to Go About Achieving Good Relationships

(a) Methods of Identifying Common Ground

Good franchise relationships are an ongoing *process* more than a particular result.

Franchisors and their franchisees can employ an array of effective methods of identifying the common ground in each franchise system. Consistent, continuous, repetitive, transparent, substantive, professional, and copious communication is a necessary foundation. A full discussion of communication issues in franchise systems is found later in this chapter.

The first, easiest, and most important method of identifying common interests is to establish, collaboratively, the goals of the system. Certainly, in a start-up franchise organization this responsibility will fall entirely or disproportionately on the franchisor. But in a mature organization, system goals may never have been concretely articulated, may have changed, or may have become obsolete over time or in response to market conditions or other external challenges and developments. In those circumstances, there is every reason for a franchisor to work with its franchisees collaboratively to identify and articulate shared system goals. It does no good for a franchisor to dictate goals or strategies that its franchisees do not accept.

Different means can be employed to achieve these goals. If a franchisee association exists, the franchisor can ask it to form a task force to work with representatives of the franchisor to develop a mission statement. If there is no independent group representing the franchisee community, the franchisor can organize or use an existing franchisee advisory council or ask for help from successful franchisees who are respected by the franchisee community for their success and best practices.

Franchisee opinion and participation in this effort can also be pursued through the use of focus groups, surveys, or other recognized, objective methods of gathering opinion data. The franchisor, a franchise association, or an advisory council can organize and conduct these activities on its own or use third-party vendors, which may be able to obtain more objective responses. The franchisee association may also want to use surveys to make sure that they understand the goals and objectives of their constituent franchisees in dealing with the franchisor.

Participants in the process of articulating shared system objectives must all understand, recognize, and respect the investment interests of other parties to the system. Without reciprocal understanding and respect for the other participants' investment interest, this process cannot be successful.

In mature franchise systems, there have been a number of examples of successful system-wide negotiation of franchise agreements and other collateral agreements involving vital, important issues.[16] Give-and-take, collaboration, and negotiation between a franchisor and its franchisees can serve not only to resolve a particular point of contention between the parties but also to form the foundation for better relationships going forward, and in some cases, a turnaround of the franchise system itself.[17]

---

16. For five specific examples of collaboration between franchisee associations and the franchisor, see Erin E. Conway, Eric H. Karp & Brenda B. Trickey, Franchisee Associations to the Rescue-Using Associations and Advisory Councils to Avoid Joint Employer Risk and Enhance the Brand 8–15 (ABA Forum on Franchising 2017).

17. For example, the former CEO of Popeyes described the beginning of the turnaround of that company as follows:

> The pivotal moment in the turnaround came when we tried to sell our business plan to the franchisees. We met 10 franchise leaders in a windowless hotel conference room in Chicago. At that time, all Popeyes advertising was controlled locally, and each franchisee contributed 3% of sales to pay for ads. Our plan called for increasing that number to 4% and creating a national ad campaign, to coordinate the brand message and drive awareness. We brought in an outside expert who described the chain as being at an inflection point: The time was right to make the move from local to national advertising. The franchisees asked us to sit in the hallway while they debated the idea. When we came back in, they said they'd agree—if the company would invest $6 million to increase the number of weeks of advertising. That was a big ask. It would require board approval and would lower our earnings, disappointing Wall Street. But it was essential to gaining system wide franchise alignment. We committed the dollars and saw it through, even

Paramount in the articulation of shared objectives is the ongoing mutual responsibility of the various participants for the success of the system. This is an area that may be challenging for some lawyers, who may be more focused on preserving and enforcing the "rights" of their clients. The client, however, certainly did not invest in the franchise system to establish and exercise its "rights" but to achieve its business objectives. Both the franchisor, which solicited sales of franchises, and the franchisee, which by buying into the system became a brand stakeholder and a member of the team, share a business responsibility to their respective owners to work toward the success of that shared business enterprise. For a franchised business organization to flourish, both the franchisor and the franchisees—and their lawyers—must continuously ask, "What is best for the franchisor and the franchisees of the *system*?"

(b) Methods of Communication

(i) Methods of Communication between Franchisor and Franchisees

Good communication is key to a good franchisor/franchisee relationship. Successful or effective communication between the parties must be respectful, bi-directional, and marked by the sharing of relevant information behind the proposed choices. Too often, franchisors act paternalistically; rather than communicate the "why," thereby opening dialogue and creating understanding and alignment, the message is, "Because I said so," which often creates frustration, mistrust, and resentment.

For example, if the franchisor chooses to test a particular new product, it would be well advised to seek franchisee volunteers to participate in the test and commit to sharing the resulting data with the wider franchisee community. That way, if it proceeds with the new product, the franchisor will have a higher likelihood of achieving franchisee buy-in and reducing resistance.

Another traditional practice is polling or surveying franchisee support for various franchisor initiatives. For example, if a franchisor wants to initiate a national price-point product promotion, it can poll its franchisees to evaluate the level of franchisee support. Commercials advertising a $0.99 price-point product promotion will be counterproductive if two-thirds of the franchised outlets decline to participate in the promotion.

Still another traditional communication tool is training provided by the franchisor in the classroom, at the franchised outlet, or at national or regional meetings. Franchisors that approach training as a "police officer" miss an important opportunity to set a tone of cooperation and mutual investment. Approaching training and operations support as a teacher may not put the franchisor in the best position to take legal action against an isolated nonperforming franchisee, but it will maximize the performance of all of the other franchisees. The value of

---

when the economy went into recession in the fall of 2008. National advertising was the first critical step in driving the Popeyes turnaround.

Cheryl Bachelder, *The CEO of Popeyes on Treating Franchisees as the Most Important Customers* Harvard Bus. Rev., Oct. 2016.

maximizing the performance of the entire system vastly outweighs the extra effort required to prepare an isolated enforcement action.

Extranets, intranets, e-mail, blogs, texting, and social media can create a sense of integration and incorporation on both sides in real time, allowing the franchise system to be aligned as a brand and nimble against its competition. However, it also can create an easy conduit for dissension and debate among the parties, without the benefit of preparation or consideration.

The information and communications revolution brought about by the Internet has had an enormous impact on franchising. It has been a two-edged (or more) sword, and it continues to evolve. Franchise-specific sites such as www.bluemaumau.org and www.unhappyfranchisee.com provide unfiltered forums for the expression of opinions by franchisees, over which neither a franchisor nor a franchisee association has any control. In addition, a number of long-standing franchisee associations have their own websites that they use to communicate directly with franchisees and the outside world. These tools can help parties to a franchise system better align their understandings and behaviors. They can also be used by disaffected franchisees to organize resistance to franchisor initiatives. They leave trails of discoverable evidence, and they have rendered all but moot the notion of keeping things "secret." For purposes of this chapter, the Internet (and related channels of communication) has, if nothing else, underscored the vital importance of understanding, pursuing, and maintaining good business relations within franchise organizations.

(ii) Communication among Franchisees

Franchisees take full advantage of the opportunities to communicate among themselves for purposes of participating in system decision making and governance. Franchisors that attempt to ignore, limit, or manage franchisee communication lose the opportunity to understand the perspective and needs of their business partners. Franchisees who volunteer to serve in leadership capacities in a franchisee association or advisory council take on a somewhat anomalous position of responsibility for the success of the system, which sometimes has the practical effect of aligning them more with the franchisor than with the views of some individual franchisees. Franchisee leaders are no more omniscient or possessed of perfect foresight and judgment than are the franchisor's executives. Thus, franchisee leaders have both a practical and a political need to stay in close touch with the constituents they represent.

Communication among the franchisees must be constant, substantive, and informative. Association meetings must occur with sufficient frequency and with an opportunity for exchange of ideas to assure informed decision making within the franchisee ranks. In any relationship, constantly being talked at, rather than eliciting input, leaves one party unsatisfied. Newsletters, opinion surveys, and independent professional advice are all part of the process of informing franchisee leaders in their role in system governance.

Effective, responsible, and professional franchisee participation in system decision-making sometimes requires that franchisees engage, at their own expense, their own independent experts, whether legal, marketing, financial, or other, to inform them in areas that may be beyond their individual experience or competencies. There is nothing inappropriate about franchisees, for example, engaging expert legal counsel to advise them on the laws relating to the franchise relationship, or marketing experts to advise them on consumer preferences and advertising strategies. Some of this information may be shared within the franchisee community and some with the franchisor, and some of it may be kept confidential. Franchisee leaders must carefully consider with whom to share particular information. Nondisclosure agreements proposed by franchisors must carefully balance the need to keep sensitive competitive information out of the public domain with the equally compelling need of franchisee association leaders to communicate with and inform their constituent members. Franchisees often will find that hiring an expert consultant will refine and validate their opinions, as well as add great weight to their opinions when shared with the franchisor. Occasionally, expert advice may provide grounds for franchisees to reconsider their opinion on a matter, and franchisees must be open to that possibility. Good ideas do not depend upon where they originate.

Finally, it is every bit as incumbent on franchisees as it is on the franchisor to share information responsibly and appropriately within the system. This does not mean that franchisees have a legal or practical duty to share everything they know with their peers or with the franchisor, but it does mean that the franchisees should not withhold material information when disclosure to the franchisor would enhance system decision-making or business growth. The same is true for the franchisor.

(iii) Methods of Communication with External Audiences

In addition to communicating with each other, franchisors, franchisee associations, and individual franchisees must also communicate with external audiences who affect the franchisor/franchisee relationship. This highlights the need for the franchise system to have an agreed-upon mission and set of values. What is the brand, what does it stand for, and what do customers expect from the brand? If the system understands and embraces these basic characteristics, the communication to external audiences is more likely to be consistent and advance the interest of the system as a whole. The most obvious examples of external communications are with government officials and members of the media.

In the governmental arena, franchisors and franchisees will have some areas of common interest (for example, minimum wage legislation) and some areas with the potential for complete disagreement (for example, proposals for franchise relationship laws). Although lobbying activities typically are handled by professional and properly registered lobbyists, franchisors and franchisees can add value by identifying the areas where franchisors and franchisees have common interests. Combining their efforts in these areas can both build a spirit of cooperation and trust and also present a more effective case to government officials.

For franchisors and franchisees, communicating with one voice in the legislative and regulatory arenas is critical. It is the most sure-fire way to affect the outcome of important public policy issues successfully. Obviously, that means the franchisor and franchisees need to have the same (or largely similar) positions on the issue under consideration. However, on many commercial, tax, and regulatory issues, this consensus is not difficult to achieve.

Issues about which franchisors and franchisees tend to care most are those that affect the profitability of their businesses. For regulatory issues that affect the system as a whole, finding common ground in identifying and prioritizing issues is often surprisingly easy. In some cases, however, the nature of the franchisor-franchisee relationship makes achieving consensus more difficult. Franchise relationship legislation is a good example. However, if the legislation being considered would have the same impact on the franchise system as a whole, sometimes agreement can be reached even here.

Once both parties clearly understand the potential impact of proposed policy, they often find they share a common interest. Franchisors frequently have the resources to participate in organizations such as the International Franchise Association (IFA) and to analyze the impact of proposed policy, and they can involve franchisees in the analysis in order to help develop consensus. Franchisee organizations such as the Coalition of Franchisee Associations and the Asian American Hotel Owners Association also have the resources and expertise to participate in the political arena on behalf of franchisees. At the same time, individual franchisees can be excellent conduits of information to franchisors, particularly on state and local policy issues. They are the eyes and ears of the system throughout the country. There potentially are excellent synergies on policy issues to be realized in the franchise relationship.

Once issues are identified and prioritized, the focus turns to strategy to affect outcomes and orchestrating a tactical lobbying campaign accordingly. Again, franchisees can play a critical role. Legislators tend to focus intently on their reelection and having resources necessary to achieving that goal. Only their constituents can vote for them, and the constituents are therefore the ones they want most to please. Franchisees, who can emphasize the jobs they create and their roots in the community, are perfect contacts to do the grassroots lobbying, while franchisors are most often best at coordinating the political process. This is yet another example of potential franchise synergies.

Leadership responsibility in building and managing the brand's interactions with the media usually should fall to the franchisor. With this responsibility comes the hiring of a professional public relations advisor and incorporating franchisees into the process. Franchisees must, in turn, view the franchisor's public relations representative as an asset and ally, and must commit to working with that representative to ensure that the brand is presented in a way that is consistent with the system's marketing strategy. If both sides work collaboratively in public relations, rather than unilaterally, then the system as a whole is most likely to benefit.

Cooperation of the franchisor and franchisees in the area of public relations is especially important in crises involving public health[18] or allegations of wrongdoing, such as racial discrimination. The franchisor can facilitate cooperation and damage control in these instances by establishing a clear program for crisis management and ensuring that all franchisees have a clear understanding of which franchisor executive or system spokesperson should be contacted in case of such a crisis.

Franchise systems increasingly must interact with another external constituency: third-party interest groups. Whether those groups are devoted to combating discrimination, animal rights activists, health advocates, or disability rights organizations, it is in the entire system's interest that the brand be represented by one voice. From the franchisor's perspective, this will be possible only if the franchisees and their associations actively participate in initiatives of concern to the third-party interest groups. Again, the key is active collaboration between the franchisor and franchisees for the benefit of the system.

(c) Means of Interaction

(i) Councils and Associations

Each franchise system has its own idiosyncrasies concerning franchisor/franchisee interaction. However, one of the most effective and efficient means of interaction between franchisors and franchisees, both from the franchisees' perspective and from the perspective of the system as a whole, is the independent, autonomous franchisee association funded and operated by franchisees. A franchisee association is a trade association representing the interests of its members in a common area, in this case, franchise system governance and success. Another effective option for franchisor/franchisee interaction is the franchisor-sponsored, but franchisee-elected, advisory council. Usually unincorporated, the advisory council serves to provide a forum for bilateral communication between the franchisees and the franchisor. In addition, systems that are too young or too small to function effectively with an advisory council or autonomous association, or a larger or older system with a specialized need for one-time or issue-specific interaction, might form some type of ad hoc task force or advisory body with both franchisor and franchisee members to deal with a specific issue over a limited period of time.

In this regard, some systems use advisory groups or standing committees that are focused on specific issues, such as marketing or advertising, facility standards, unit-level operations, franchisee profitability, and the development and

18. For example, 73 Jack in the Box restaurants were involved in an outbreak of *E. coli* that caused 4 children to die and 700 people to become ill after eating contaminated Jack in the Box hamburgers; one family whose child was brain damaged received over $15 million in a settlement with Foodmaker, Inc., the parent company of Jack in the Box. U.S. Dep't of Agric., Economic Res. Service, AER-831, Food Safety Innovation in the United States (2004), https://www.ers.usda.gov/webdocs/publications/41634/18032_aer831.pdf?v=3628.1

distribution of new products or services. These groups or committees sometimes function over long periods of time or exist only for a limited period of time.

Franchisee associations themselves can exist in a variety of different forms: some may be a single national organization; others may be discrete local, state, or geographic regional associations; or there may be some combination of the two, with discrete regional organizations participating in and funding a national umbrella organization.[19] Associations often engage in a scope of activities that transcends interaction with their franchisor, such as sponsoring conventions and trade shows, organizing and operating purchasing co-ops, publishing advertising-supported magazines, tracking industry and regulatory developments that can affect franchisees, and engaging professional consultants. When the association is truly representative of its constituent franchisee community, and professionally run, it can be a real asset to the system and a benefit to the franchisor. An association does not, of course, eliminate or preclude problems or friction in the system, but it can go a long way to solve relational problems and business challenges in the system when they arise. In addition, franchisor-sponsored initiatives that the franchise community has helped to develop, understands the need for, and agrees with the implementation of will be adopted faster, more cheaply, and more effectively.[20]

The advantages of transparent communication with an established franchise organization are illustrated by the outcome of bankruptcy court litigation involving the Sizzler franchise system in 1998.[21] At that point, each restaurant in the system had a grill concept as well as a buffet court, each with different economic metrics, outcomes, and advantages. The franchisor believed that the best policy would be to orient its advertising and marketing investments toward the grill concept. Yet before doing so, the franchisor brought its proposal to the association, sharing marketing studies in support of the change. The association studied the proposal and later issued a written report supporting the change and giving specific reasons for doing so. A later claim by a franchisee that the change violated the implied covenant of good faith and fair dealing was turned away because the franchisor could not possibly have acted in bad faith given its consultation with the franchisee association and its concurrence with the proposal.

(ii) Special Function Bodies: Co-ops

(A) Purchasing Co-ops

In many business-format franchise systems, the franchisor is also a manufacturer and/or distributor of goods to the franchise system. This may be a function of the

19. For example, the National Coalition of Associations of 7-Eleven Franchisees, formed in 1973, is an umbrella organization of 41 franchise owners associations in 30 states. *See* www.ncasef.com/about-ncasef/who-we-are .

20. For a comprehensive treatment of the role of autonomous associations, and how to organize and manage them, *see* Gerald T. Aaron, et al., The Dynamics of Franchisee Associations (ABA Forum on Franchising 1991), and *Counseling Franchisees, in* Fundamentals of Franchising (Rupert M. Barkoff, Joseph J. Fittante, Ronald K. Gardner & Andrew Selden, eds., ABA 4th ed. 2015).

21. *In re* Sizzler Restaurants International Inc., BGF 11,408 (U.S. Bank. Court, C.D. Cal. 1998).

franchisor's desire to regulate the nature of the goods being used or sold at the franchised outlets and/or the need to maintain proprietary information. It may also reflect the franchisor's desire to develop a separate or different source of additional income.[22]

Franchisors sometimes receive secondary benefits from the supply and distribution channel, even if they are not the direct manufacturer or distributor. The franchisor may receive various types of fees, rebates, or allowances from suppliers or distributors. Such arrangements often distress franchisees, who see them as merely adding to their costs[23] and going straight to the franchisor's bottom line. On the other hand, franchisors may use these additional sources of funds to provide services to franchisees for which they would otherwise have to charge the franchisees. Alternatively, franchisors may contribute these funds to national or regional marketing programs.

These franchisor goals will sometimes conflict with the goals of the franchisee, which is interested in minimizing its cost of goods sold. This will create an inherent conflict and source of distrust if the franchisor is indeed seeking a second source of income, or if the franchisor simply cannot provide the goods at the lowest possible price. Some less obvious considerations can also come into play. Obtaining the lowest possible price is not the only goal of a supply and distribution system. A supply and distribution system must also ensure a continuous and reliable supply of goods that meet the specifications of the franchise system. These goals may require that franchisees compromise their attempts to obtain goods at the lowest possible price.

The idea of a joint purchasing cooperative for the entire system is sometimes the best way to balance a franchisor's need to assure system-wide reliability of delivery and quality against the franchisees' desire to obtain the lowest possible price.

A purchasing cooperative is the pooling of purchasing requirements by a group of individual businesses with common needs to achieve lower delivered costs and more favorable terms. Of course, skilled, professional management is usually necessary to achieve efficient volume purchasing. In a fast-food chain of 2,000 units, averaging $1 million of sales annually per unit and incurring food costs equal to 30 percent of revenues, total purchases for food items will be $600 million annually. If a 1 percent savings in food costs can be achieved, the system saves a staggering $6 million per year, which translates to $3,000 of additional profit per unit on average.

There is no precise formula for achieving this type of savings, but it is clear that volume purchasing and distribution open up many options. Even suppliers benefit from a system that purchases through cooperatives. Among other things, it allows suppliers to (1) plan production more effectively, thereby reducing

22. *See* Chapter 3, Section 3-7, Purchasing Co-ops.

23. For example, in *Queen City Pizza*, the plaintiff franchisees alleged that the franchisor had imposed sole-source requirements on ingredients and supplies purchased by franchisees of more than $450 million per year in the aggregate. They further alleged that these restrictive sourcing requirements increased costs for each franchised outlet by an amount ranging from $3,000 to $10,000 per year.

manufacturing costs; (2) purchase raw materials in larger quantities, which usually leads to better unit prices for those raw materials; (3) take advantage of volume freight rates and other distribution efficiencies; and (4) reduce credit risk and cost of sales.

All of this translates into lower cost for the supplier, which should in theory be passed on to the franchise system. Volume purchasing may also result in improved distribution methods and allow the system to coordinate and more effectively use marketing allowances.[24]

In summary, however, the basic decisions must take into account (1) the best form of legal structure for the organization, (2) federal income tax considerations, (3) securities law considerations, (4) antitrust law considerations, (5) sourcing restrictions in the franchise agreement, (6) trademark usage issues, and (7) vicarious liability considerations.

(B) Marketing Co-ops

Not surprisingly, one commentator points out that when franchisees are asked to name the most important aspect of their franchise system, most mentioned the brand and services related to marketing.[25]

In addition to cooperatives designed to purchase goods for use at the franchised outlet, franchise systems occasionally also include an arrangement whereby franchisees pool their efforts in advertising, promotion, and marketing activities through cooperative efforts or organizations, either on their own initiative or in a franchisor-sponsored program. Franchisors are often very reluctant to cede control over brand identity and brand development to the franchisees. The brand itself often is the most valuable asset owned by the franchisor, and its development and promotion are the principal activities of most franchisors.

In a typical franchisor-administered advertising program, the franchisor sets up the fund, collects franchisee and franchisor contributions, and controls expenditures. The franchisor usually retains total control over creative concepts and media allocation, but it may permit franchisees to participate in the decision making to some degree, perhaps by way of a franchisee advisory committee. The franchisor may or may not create a separate legal entity, such as a trust or nonprofit corporation, to administer the funds.

The franchisor may not have the resources to perform the advertising function effectively or may be required to share control of this activity in order to keep the franchise system alive. In some systems, the national advertising function is funded and controlled by franchisees or by a franchisee-dominated cooperative.

---

24. For a complete discussion of the technical legal issues relating to the establishment of a purchasing cooperative, *see* Andrew C. Selden & Rupert M. Barkoff, Franchise-Related Purchasing Cooperatives (15th ABA Forum on Franchising 1992). *See also* The Franchise Cooperative Handbook (Robert L. Perry ed., IFA 1998), *available at* http://www.franchise.org/uploadedFiles/Franchise_Industry/IFA_Store/FRANCHISE%20RELATIONS%20COOP%20HANDBOOK.pdf.

25. Greg Nathan, *How to Create Healthier Franchise Relationships and Happier Clients*, 13(1) The Franchise Lawyer 11 (Winter 2010).

Franchisees may wish to form a local advertising cooperative to coordinate local spending beyond that done by the franchisor, or even to form a national franchisee cooperative advertising program that is committed to national "investment spending" by the franchisees beyond their commitment to the franchisor.

Cooperative advertising programs such as these, in which franchisees pool their financial resources, sometimes with those of the franchisor, to promote the brand at a local, regional, or national level, allow franchisees to achieve economies of scale through coordination of franchisee advertising and promotion efforts. Participating franchisees benefit from the use of uniform, coordinated advertising and from access to more sophisticated research, creative, and production resources than would be available to individual owners, as well as the ability to afford to use broadcast media. The national advertising co-op functions in a way as a national purchasing co-op for advertising and can have the same systemic and relationship benefits (in addition to purchasing efficiencies) as a joint purchasing co-op.[26] In summary, the multilayered approach to advertising and promotion that results from these cooperative advertising programs benefits the entire franchise system because it builds brand awareness through channels that might not be used by the franchisor's more nationally geared advertising program.

(iii) External Trade Associations

Franchisors and their franchisees may occasionally interact through external trade associations, such as a state or local restaurant association (or similar industry association), a chamber of commerce, or a Better Business Bureau committee. Jointly sponsored political action committees exist in some organizations.[27] Some systems may jointly sponsor an off-shore, captive insurance organization. Still others may share ownership or participation in a purchasing and distribution cooperative or advertising cooperatives.

All of these "external" organizations afford opportunities for the franchisor and its franchisees to interact constructively, although usually on a specific topic, rather than on the broad range of issues affecting the franchise organization generally.

(iv) Resources

(A) Use of Experts

Conventional wisdom holds that few, if any, franchisors possess the level of perfect information, perfect foresight, and perfect judgment to enable them to act unilaterally with any effectiveness in managing the ongoing affairs of the franchise organization.

---

26. Organizing and operating an advertising cooperative raise many of the same legal and business issues and choices present when considering a more traditional purchasing cooperative. *See* Selden & Barkoff, *supra* note 23.

27. For example, the Asian American Hotel Owners Association established a political action committee in 1998 and since that time has raised more than $1 million. *See* www.aahoa.com/advocacy/aahoa-pac.

The same is true of franchisees. Franchisees often collectively have more experience than the franchisor in the day-to-day operation of the franchised business and therefore have a "street wisdom" that potentially transcends anything available at the franchisor's headquarters. This may be especially true in legacy franchise systems marked by multiple second-generation franchisee owners and multiple successive owners or managers of the franchisor. The other side of that coin, however, is that franchisee perspectives tend sometimes to be too parochial or short-term to be effective in system-wide decision making.

Both sides are well advised in many cases to engage the services of outside consultants or experts on any of a range of issues that the franchise system must deal with in order to succeed. Ideally, a franchisor and its franchisees will act jointly to engage the services of experts so that the result of the expertise can be shared by the collaborative decision-making mechanism in each system. Joint procurement of expert advice and information can often help maximize the efficiency and effectiveness of system advertising, marketing, procurement, and distribution functions. Those engagements should be jointly funded in most cases to reflect the joint benefit to be derived from the engagement.

Failing that, however, there is nothing inappropriate about either the franchisor or an independent franchisee association separately engaging experts to advise it and to assist in system decision making. If the results of such an engagement are shared with the other party for the benefit of the system, it is also not inappropriate to expect the other party then to reimburse a proportionate share of the expense of the engagement reflecting the benefit to the system.

The benefit lies in the efficient collection, sharing, and use of information. Decisions affecting system welfare cannot be made in a vacuum and should not be made on the basis of only one party's information and interests. It is to the advantage of all participants in a franchise organization that information concerning the performance of the system or the opportunities available to the system be collected and shared appropriately to facilitate collaborative decision making. Some franchisors control the availability and use of information to further a purely parochial interest in maintaining (at least the illusion of) control within the organization. The most successful franchisors understand that this sophisticated form of corporate "hide the bean" management is usually counterproductive. Franchisees also have a corresponding interest in sharing with the franchisor information they have that would be useful to system decision making.

(B) Codes of Behavior and Training

Certain external codes of behavior affect the interaction between franchisors and franchisees. Federal and state laws and regulations govern sales activities, franchise transfers, termination, and certain other activities. The 2007 revision to the FTC Rule[28] on franchise sales disclosure requires franchisors to include in their FDD basic identification and contact information for organized franchisee associations, under prescribed circumstances and upon an annual request. The

28. 16 C.F.R. § § 436 (2007), Bus. Franchise Guide (CCH) ¶ 6010.

existence of purchasing and advertising co-ops also should be disclosed in the FDD.[29]

Some professional and trade associations have their own codes. The most prominent is the IFA's Code of Principles and Standards of Conduct.[30] Although the IFA Code may not provide franchisees with a legal remedy, it must certainly be generally respected by franchisors that wish to maintain their IFA membership, avoid bad press, and maintain good relations with franchisees.

More effective than the IFA Code is a franchisor-initiated code of ethics for its own employees. Although franchisors are often painted as monolithic and controlling, the truth is that all large companies struggle to balance employee empowerment and minimum standards of conduct. A franchisor can help minimize problems created by individual conflict or misdeeds by clearly communicating to its employees the company's expectations regarding relations with franchisees. A good code of ethics will go beyond legal obligations relating to franchising and deal with a broader range of topics such as sexual harassment, conflict of interest, and limits of employee authority.

If such a code of ethics is to be most effective in regulating all parties, it should be countersigned by each employee and returned to the franchisor. A franchisor employee (often the general counsel) should be designated and available to answer questions and provide advice concerning the code. Beyond obtaining signatures and discussing such a code, however, the franchisor must take the extra steps necessary to create a culture that embodies the code and encourages the employees to consistently *follow* the code. Without such employee buy-in, the franchisor's efforts in establishing a code of ethics risk becoming futile.

Most franchisor employees want to be fair to franchisees and do the right thing. The more guidance they receive, the better equipped they are to avoid mistakes that will hurt the franchisor/franchisee relationship.

It is equally important to communicate clearly the expectations of conduct by the franchisees in a franchise system. In their business, among each other and during their interaction with representatives of the franchisor, communication founded in mutual respect and basic courtesy will be more productive. While it may be difficult to enforce a code of conduct without a specific requirement in the franchise agreement, leading by example with consistent behavior will improve the quality and effectiveness of the communication between franchisor and franchisees, maintain positive relationships, and improve the chances that the franchisees and their employees will ultimately foster a system-wide code of ethics.

Another important element of maintaining a good relationship with franchisees is employee training. Well-trained employees are respected and will communicate the brand's standards and initiatives, which ultimately adds more value to the system and contributes to better relations between the franchisor and

29. FED. TRADE COMM'N, FRANCHISE RULE 16 C.F.R. PART 436 COMPLIANCE GUIDE 51, 65 (2008) (franchisor must disclose the existence of purchasing co-ops under Item 8 and advertising co-ops under Item 11).

30. *See* https://www.franchise.org/about-us/mission-statement-vision-code-of-ethics#:~:text=PREFACE%3A,subscribe%20in%20their%20franchise%20relationships.

franchisees. In large franchise systems, however, the franchisor should not miss the opportunity to expand its employee training beyond the nuts and bolts of the franchise system. Courses in leadership, conflict resolution, negotiation, diversity, and so on will all help minimize conflict and enhance the franchisor/franchisee relationship. Finally, the franchisor can reinforce important topics through the use of pocket guides and other easy reference tools.

4-5. ADR/Conflict Resolution

Some form of conflict and dispute is inevitable in every franchise system.[31] Before resorting to any type of external conflict resolution, the franchisor should employ every means possible, both formal and informal, to understand the conflict fully. Much litigation or ongoing conflict between franchisors and franchisees occurs because the franchisees believe that the only way for them to be heard or to gain information they perceive as having been withheld is to institute some type of formal proceeding. Franchisors can avoid much conflict simply by listening and, if appropriate, taking responsibility and making reasonable business reparations for any wrongdoing.

Litigation is rarely a good tool for resolving disputes in a franchise system. It frequently takes much longer and costs much more than either party thinks it will at the outset. The time, expense, and scorched earth approach often found in the litigation arena are inconsistent with fostering an ongoing business relationship. Litigation potentially may continue for extended periods at exorbitant costs to both sides while the parties are still obligated to maintain a business relationship. It is also difficult to expect the parties to set aside their differences and focus on the ongoing business while simultaneously attending depositions, answering interrogatories, and engaging in other confrontational and distracting conduct. There is a point in all disputes, however, where an ongoing relationship diminishes in concern, in which case the well-developed body of law, rules of civil procedure, and appellate review make the outcome more predictable as well as provide a clear victor in the conflict.

Both sides should remember to keep conflict in context and find a way to resolve the dispute in the manner that does the least damage to the system generally and to the ongoing business relationship between the parties to the dispute. When the parties are acting with this perspective, franchise disputes can be well suited for the use of out-of-court procedures generally referred to as alternative dispute resolution (ADR). However, if the parties are so polarized that they can no longer discuss and negotiate without the assistance of an outside party, ADR may not be effective. Good communication, training, and adherence to company policies and procedures will always help to avoid disputes and minimize those that do occur.

31. *See* Chapter 5, Section 5-2.

To minimize or control disputes, a franchisor can (1) institute a formal system of objective measures, (2) provide a business process for franchisee appeals, and (3) establish a system of checks and balances before legal action is taken.

The task of establishing objective performance criteria will differ in each franchise system and is probably best viewed as a goal. Complete objectivity is seldom possible (for example, "How clean is clean?"), but if the franchisor strives to be as objective as possible in its standards (for example, "no rodents, no mold"), then the objectivity will benefit both franchisor and franchisee by clearly setting forth both duties and obligations. This will make both performance and enforcement easier.

Given the ongoing business relationship between franchisor and franchisee, it is also important that the franchisee understand the franchisor's organizational structure or chain of command so that "appeals" may be directed to the appropriate executive. This also benefits the franchisor, which does not want all disputes immediately escalating to the office of the chief executive. Indeed, some large franchisors have sought to protect the CEO from day-to-day disputes and give the franchisees a formal forum for complaints by establishing an ombudsman whose sole duty is to review franchisee/franchisor disputes. The ombudsman is usually a well-respected senior or retired executive of the franchisor.

All franchisors should undertake some formal legal review of disputes before deciding to take legal action against franchisees. This review should not be limited to an analysis of the legal rights of the franchisor. The franchisor's goal should not be to win a lawsuit; rather, it should be to solve a business issue and to protect the equity of the brand and the business of the system. Thus, the legal review should also ask whether the field staff has worked with the franchisee to solve the problem, whether the franchisee has any valid complaints of its own, and whether settlement options such as a buy-out, sale, or remediation plan have been explored.[32] If all of these measures fail to avoid or resolve the dispute, then ADR should be considered.

Traditional litigation can be especially destructive in a franchise environment. Courts are overburdened, parties are angry, litigation costs are astronomical, and franchise relationships are destroyed. The entire system can be affected adversely by an individual dispute that is not resolved quickly and fairly. The system may be distracted by waiting for an outcome or the cataclysmic effect of a resolution that may affect some or all of the franchisor's businesses and, possibly, fundamentally damage the system. Businesspeople can become frustrated with lawyers who are too busy addressing procedural issues, posturing, or foot-dragging. They can become angry with protracted negotiations, lengthy court-imposed schedules, and discovery processes that consume huge chunks of time and legal budgets. The appeal of ADR is that it can help resolve conflicts quickly and fairly and with the minimal possible damage to the franchise system and the franchise relationship.

ADR is not just arbitration; rather, it is a collection of strategies for resolving disputes outside the usual process of litigation and confrontational negotiations.

---

32. The checklist used by one national franchisor before taking legal action to terminate a franchisee is attached as form 4-1.

It can be formal or informal. The most common types of ADR are facilitated negotiation, mediation, and arbitration. There are dozens of variations including neutral evaluation, summary jury trial, minitrial, and judicially hosted settlement conferences. Indeed, one reason for ADR's attractiveness is its flexibility.

ADR is not always preferable to litigation. Litigation offers full discovery, the opportunity to establish precedent, transparency, and appellate review. Arbitration has many advantages, but its out-of-pocket costs for provider administration and arbitrator compensation cannot outweigh those advantages, particularly when the arbitration clause calls for three arbitrators. That said, ADR often has a number of significant advantages over traditional litigation, including the following:

- ADR often reduces legal costs. Pretrial settlement often occurs "on the courthouse steps" or in a judicial settlement conference held within weeks or days of trial. This occurs only after the parties have expended considerable sums of money and time on discovery and trial preparation. Since statistics show that most lawsuits tend to settle, ADR simply helps the parties to settle sooner and more economically.
- ADR can reduce the time spent on disputes. Many ADR processes involve summary or abbreviated procedures, and most ADR processes take less time than going to trial. For example, the American Arbitration Association's Rules for Expedited Commercial Arbitration provide for the arbitrator's award to be rendered within 30 days of his or her appointment.[33] Because ADR can operate outside the court system, a dispute does not need to wait its turn in an overcrowded court docket, a result that can lead to a prolonged period of poisoned or deteriorating relations between the franchisor and the franchisee.
- ADR allows the parties to control who decides the dispute. The parties can agree on a mediator or arbitrator who has expertise, either legal or business, in the franchising or particular industry sector. Judges hear a wide variety of cases and may have never seen or participated in any franchise-related matter until trying a franchisor-franchisee dispute.
- ADR allows for increased participation by business representatives. The constraints of typical courtroom procedures often reduce meaningful, problem-solving communication. ADR, on the other hand, allows for more informal communication. It also allows the business representatives to talk directly and bypass the escalation of hostilities often associated with U.S. trial lawyers.
- ADR facilitates creative communicative problem-solving. Courts can provide only a limited range of remedies, usually involving an exchange of money or issuing orders for injunctive relief. Often the business representatives have a continuing business relationship and can fashion a solution that revolves around a "win-win" proposition such as a commitment from

33. Am. Arbitration Ass'n, Commercial Arbitration Rules and Mediation Procedures, https://adr.org/sites/default/files/Commercial%20Rules.pdf. The Expedited Procedures section provides for the arbitrator's award to be rendered within 30 after confirmation of the arbitrator's appointment.

the franchisee to build additional units, or a commitment by the franchisor to deploy additional training or marketing resources, or to make changes in corporate policies or procedures. Courts have no power to order these types of solutions.

- ADR makes it easier to keep the dispute confidential, as almost all litigation is public to a great degree.
- ADR allows the parties to tailor their approach to the nature of the dispute. For example, they can agree to involve a third party, allow for a binding or nonbinding decision, limit discovery, relax evidence rules, or take whatever other steps they deem appropriate.
- ADR allows each party to fashion a settlement that will not only deal with the problem at hand but also improve relations going forward and avoid similar disputes. The usual "winner-take-all" results of litigation generally breed only resentment and bitterness, which can lead to additional conflict.

On the other hand, there are also some disadvantages to overcome when using ADR:

- Many business representatives are unfamiliar with ADR, and some shortsighted trial lawyers are reluctant to leave the familiar and remunerative courtroom environment.
- Many ADR facilitators are unfamiliar with franchising and its body of law, and they do not understand the systemic ramifications of a dispute between the franchisor and a particular franchisee.
- ADR works best where the parties have essentially equal bargaining power, which is often not the case in the franchisor/franchisee relationship. A neutral party, such as a judge, can provide some balance, but if one side can overwhelm the other, the weaker party may need the protection of a courtroom setting.
- ADR, while usually less expensive and quicker than litigation, is still costly and time-consuming. If the dispute is unlikely to be resolved in ADR, then use of ADR tools could actually add to the cost and time necessary to resolve the dispute.
- Most ADR proceedings require some minimum amount of cooperation and good faith effort—and a mutual desire—to resolve the dispute. If the franchisor/franchisee relationship is so poisoned that the two parties cannot speak to the other directly in a rational manner, then litigation may be the only workable solution.
- ADR is focused on compromise. The goal is to resolve the dispute, and rarely will an ADR facilitator opine wholly for one party on any issue that may be necessary to move the dispute from conflict to acceptable resolution.
- The very efficiency of ADR may encourage a party to a dispute to pursue additional claims against the other or resort to an adjudicative process too hastily.

- Appeal options are frequently extremely limited, if they exist at all, depending on the circumstances.

Determining the most appropriate form of ADR is necessary for the most efficient and least destructive resolution of a franchise dispute. The Center for Public Resources[34] (CPR) operates the Franchise Mediation Program, a franchise-specific mediation program that includes a panel of neutrals who purport to have franchise-related expertise.[35]

4-6. Conclusion

Good relationships underpin good business results. Sustained success for franchisors and franchisees alike requires good relations between the parties and generally within the system.

The keys to good relations and franchise success are a focus on shared interests of the participants; emphasis on what is good for the system as a whole; ample communication and collaboration; transparency; participation of franchisees in system governance and supply chain arrangements; leveraging system resources through franchisee associations, advisory councils, and outside experts; parties playing their appropriate roles in system operations; and appropriate use of ADR.

Finally, franchisors and their franchisees should seek to exploit their common interests and goals as a means to promote a partnership-like relationship so as to avoid conflict that naturally arises by virtue of each parties' respective, and often differing, role in the franchise system.

34. http://www.cpradr.org/.
35. *See* https://www.cpradr.org/resource-center/rules/mediation/franchise-procedure.

Form 4-1
Franchise Termination Checklist

*****Privileged and Confidential*****

*****In Anticipation of Legal Action*****

DATE: May 8, 2011

TO: V.P. Operations Name

cc: Attorney Name, Law Department

FROM: Finance Manager

SUBJECT: **Franchise Default/Termination Checklist—Franchisee Name**

We have discussed with (Attorney Name) of the Law Department the possibility of placing the above franchisee in default for reasons outlined below. At (Attorney's Name) request, in anticipation of the possibility of taking legal action, we are requesting certain information and approval from you as indicated below. Please complete and return to me, and I will follow up with the Law Department.

(Items 1–7 to be completed by Corporate)

1. Why is the franchise being reviewed for default and potential termination?
2. What is the personal financial strength of each franchisee/owner?
3. Why hasn't the franchisee paid?
4. Has repayment plan been implemented? Explain:
5. Detail financial viability of the business:
6. Has the franchisor guaranteed any loans for the franchisee? ___ Yes ___ No
   If yes, for what amount? ____________
7. Are there any loans outstanding through the FAC Finance Program? ___ Yes ___ No
   If yes, what is the total amount of the loans? ____________

(Items 8–13 to be completed by FM)

8. Outline the performance of the franchisee in the following areas:
   Operations:
   Competition:
   Facility/Image:
   P&L Management:
   Other comments:
9. Has franchisee been advised how to improve sales? What was the franchisee's response?
10. Has the franchisee been advised to try to sell the restaurant(s)? What was the franchisee's response?
11. Could another franchisee operate the restaurant(s) more effectively than this franchisee?
12. What could another franchisee do differently to improve the business?
    Operations:
    Competition:

Facility/Image:

Other comments:

13. Is there an existing or new franchisee who might be interested in acquiring this restaurant(s)? Who?

(Items 14–15 to be completed by FM and VP)

14. Would the company be interested in acquiring these restaurants?
15. FM to complete Exhibit A regarding Current Operational Rating. FM and VP to complete Exhibit B regarding potential counterclaims.

PLEASE SIGN BELOW TO AUTHORIZE THE LAW DEPARTMENT TO PLACE THE FRANCHISEE IN DEFAULT AND INSTITUTE LEGAL PROCEEDINGS TO COLLECT AMOUNTS DUE:

_______________________________ _______________________________

XXXXXXXXXXX, Director DATE

Regional Finance

_______________________________ _______________________________

XXXXXXXX, Franchise Mgr. DATE

XXXXXXXX Region

_______________________________ _______________________________

XXXXXXXX, V.P. Operations DATE

XXXXXXXX Region

*****Privileged and Confidential*****

Exhibit A
Detailed Addresses/Sales Information

(To Be Completed by Corporate and FM)

Franchisee

Restaurant(s) to be placed in Default:

Unit	Opening Date	Current Opera-tional Rating*	Last 12 Months' Sales			
			Month/ Year	% of Prior Month/ Year Sales	Month/ Year	% of Prior Month/ Year Sales

* Current Operational Rating to be completed by Franchise Manager

Other Units owned by franchisee:

Privileged and Confidential

Exhibit B
Potential Counterclaims

(To Be Completed by Franchise Manager and VP)

1. Please check the appropriate box and identify any complaints, disputes, or issues that this franchisee has or has had with [Franchisor] that may form the basis for a claim by the franchisee against [Franchisor]:
   - No potential claims known to Franchise Manager
   - No potential claims known to Regional Vice-President
   - Potential claims by franchisee are described below:
2. The following individuals have been involved with Franchisee Name and may be aware of other potential counterclaims:

Name	Current Position	Past Relevant Positions

Commitment to CPR Procedure for Resolution of Franchise Disputes

____

COMPANY

____

ADDRESS

____

CITY, STATE, ZIP

____

TELEPHONE

We recognize that for many franchisor/franchisee disputes there is a less expensive and more efficient means to resolve the issues than litigation. For a two-year period commencing on the date set forth below, we commit to use, at a franchisee's request, the CPR Procedure for Resolution of Franchise Disputes ("Resolution Procedure") in an attempt to resolve any dispute with a franchisee covered by the Resolution Procedure. The two-year commitment does not apply to (i) a request for mediation from a franchisee who has voluntarily withdrawn from a mediation concerning the same issue, or (ii) if there has been a completed mediation or final court decision on the same issue involving the same franchisee. We also hereby confirm that we will not penalize any franchisee or withhold any right or privilege accorded to other similarly situated franchisees by virtue of a franchisee seeking to resolve a dispute in accordance with the Resolution Procedure.

____

Chief Executive Officer

____

Chief Legal Officer

____

Date

(Note: Please send a signed copy of your commitment to Center for Public Resources, Inc., 366 Madison Avenue, New York, NY 10017, Attention Franchise Panel Management Group.)

Chapter 5

Termination, Nonrenewal, and Transfer

Susan Tegt and Jeffery Haff

5-1. Introduction: The Importance of Establishing and Following an Organized Compliance Program

A franchisor's ability to enforce its contractual rights and policies with its franchisees depends, for both legal and practical reasons, upon the development and consistent enforcement of reasonable standards and procedures. Developing and consistently following a compliance program is particularly important in the areas of termination, nonrenewal, and transfer. Decisions in these areas affect who will be presenting the franchisor's concept and image to the public and how it will be presented. Moreover, decisions regarding termination, nonrenewal, and transfer most fundamentally affect the rights and interests of franchisees, and so these decisions constitute the most fertile ground for disputes and litigation.

This chapter provides guidelines to assist a franchisor to develop and implement procedures for termination, nonrenewal, and transfer that are (1) consistent with the defined business objectives of the franchisor; (2) fair and reasonable in the context of the franchisor/franchisee relationship; (3) consistently applied to all similarly situated franchisees; and (4) most likely to avoid litigation concerning the franchisor's decisions in these areas or, if litigation occurs, best position the franchisor to prevail in any such dispute.

The development and implementation of a compliance program involves four fundamental steps. First, the franchisor must decide what forms of dispute resolution to use. Second, the franchisor must determine the issues most important to its particular business and franchise system, and it then must establish its policies and procedures in accordance with and in furtherance of these particular business objectives. Third, the franchisor must communicate its policies, procedures, and standards clearly and regularly to its own personnel as well as to all of its franchisees so that there can be no reasonable dispute over what the particular policy is and whether the franchisee was aware of that policy. Fourth, the franchisor must monitor and apply its policies, procedures, and standards diligently and consistently throughout its franchise system, particularly to similarly situated franchisees.

The obvious goal of a compliance program is to further the business objectives of the franchise system while avoiding, wherever possible, disputes and litigation. If a franchisor finds itself in litigation, however, a well-developed and properly implemented compliance program can serve as both a sword and a shield to protect the franchisor's legitimate business interests. For example, reasonable and consistently applied procedures leading up to the termination of a franchise can be powerful evidence in an injunction action by a franchisor against a franchisee that contests or otherwise refuses to acknowledge the termination. Evidence that a franchisor consistently followed not only the black-letter contractual requirements but also its reasonable policies and procedures can help defeat a franchisee's claim for wrongful termination under most contractual or tort theories. The ultimate goal of establishing and consistently following a reasonable compliance program in these areas is to show that regardless of the legal standard that might be applied, the franchisor acted fairly, reasonably, and consistent with the parties' legitimate contractual expectations.

This chapter is intended to provide practical guidance for franchisors to use in establishing or evaluating their own compliance programs in the areas of termination, nonrenewal, and transfer. It deals first with an overview of dispute resolution procedures. It then moves on to termination, which is probably the most fertile ground for problems and disputes because termination often results in a forfeiture of the franchisee's rights and interests. It then addresses nonrenewal and transfer, respectively. Within each of these subjects, the contractual framework of the parties' relationship, potential statutory restrictions on the franchisor's rights, and common law issues relevant to these situations are addressed. Although case law and statutes are discussed for illustrative purposes, this chapter is not intended to be an exhaustive legal analysis of these issues. The key provisions in each state franchise relationship law dealing with termination and nonrenewal are summarized in the appendix to this chapter. Following the appendix are checklists, exhibits, and forms that should be helpful in illustrating many of the issues discussed in this chapter.

5-2. Dispute Resolution—Forms of Dispute Resolution

Termination, nonrenewal, and transfer decisions often expose the franchisor to potential claims. Termination and nonrenewal decisions, in particular, create a great deal of legal wrangling. When you are deciding on a compliance program for termination, nonrenewal, and transfer issues, it is helpful to understand the available dispute resolution methods and the perceived pros and cons of each. Attorneys and other legal commentators differ significantly on which method or methods are best for any franchise system.

(a) Informal Resolution

The best way to handle disputes is to resolve them without the involvement of third parties and without unnecessary attorney costs. In an ideal world, a franchisor can just settle its disputes with its franchisees informally by speaking directly with the franchisee over the telephone or at an in-person meeting. No third parties need to be involved, and costs can be kept to a minimum.

This method of dispute resolution is often successful when the franchisor has a charismatic, persuasive, and well-informed chief executive officer who is willing to take on the role of negotiator. This approach also works well when the dispute is very fact specific to the franchisee or one of the franchisee's locations and does not involve a systemwide issue where other franchisees are likely to piggyback on the dispute and request the same treatment. As with any dispute resolution process, direct negotiation works best when the parties respect one another and are in a mindset to resolve the dispute.

Some franchisor executives may not be good at resolving individual disputes or may not believe that it is a good use of their time. In these situations, the franchisor might choose to set up a more formal ombudsman system and have a designated problem solver to whom franchisees can bring disputes and concerns. An ombudsman system generally works only when the franchisees believe that (1) the ombudsman has some authority or rapport with the franchisor's executives and (2) the ombudsman is at least somewhat independent and does not consistently take the franchisor's side over the positions taken by franchisees.

Another means of informal dispute resolution is for field employees and lower-level officers of the franchisor to work out disputes as they arise. While this can be successful, it may actually cause additional disputes over what was agreed to and whether the officer or employee had authority to offer the agreed-upon solution. As with the ombudsman, if a lower-level employee is seen as having no real authority and no real ability to effect change, then the system breaks down.

A number of more recent forms of franchise agreement contain formal contract provisions that require the informal dispute resolution process to occur prior to any other dispute resolution process. For example, a fairly typical provision of this sort would require (1) written notice of a claim, (2) a written response to the claim by the franchisor, (3) an in-person meeting with the franchisor at the franchisor's headquarters, and (4) a "cooling off" period if the in-person meeting fails to achieve a resolution. The franchise agreement often sets a minimum period of time for negotiations.

A problem that may occur with any such mandatory procedure is that one or both of the parties may decide not to fully engage in the process. Unless both parties approach the informal dispute resolution process in a serious manner the process is less likely to be successful. To maximize the chances that the informal dispute resolution process will achieve resolution, both parties must appoint representatives with authority to resolve the dispute and must be prepared to listen to the other side and consider potential compromises.

(b) Mediation

Mediation is a formal dispute resolution process in which a neutral third-party facilitator (the "mediator") attempts to assist the parties to reach a resolution of their disputes. During a mediation, neither party is under an obligation to resolve the matter, and the mediator has no authority to make either party settle. Franchisors often choose to use formal dispute resolution organizations such as the National Franchise Mediation Program, which is administered by the International Institute for Conflict Prevention & Resolution. Both the American Arbitration Association and JAMS (formerly known as Judicial Arbitration and Mediation Services, Inc.) offer mediation services as well.

Mediators vary in style. The style of most mediators who have been trained since 2010 is to fill a "facilitator" role. These mediators generally (1) have no session at the beginning of the mediation where everyone meets, (2) do not hear opening statements or arguments of counsel in the presence of the other party, and (3) resist the opportunity to evaluate the strengths or weaknesses of the case. The style of older mediators is generally to try to be more evaluative and educate the parties on the strengths and weaknesses of their cases. These mediators often do like to start with a joint session and allow counsel to address their arguments to the opposing party (in the mediator's presence).

Either method of mediation can be effective so long as the parties respect the chosen mediator and trust that he or she is giving them fair and unbiased input. In general, a mediation can be most effective when (1) the parties have a representative present who has full authority to make a decision, (2) the parties are willing to listen to counsel and the mediator, and (3) the mediator is engaged in the process and builds rapport with both parties.

Mediation is far more expensive than informal dispute resolution procedures. Mediator fees can range anywhere from $150 per hour to $1,000 per hour. The parties generally agree to split the fees of the mediator. Just as with informal dispute resolution procedures, a franchisor may want to include in its franchise agreement a specific requirement that a franchisee participate in mediation before bringing any claim in court or arbitration. The location of the mediation and the required length of any mediation should be included in such a "mandatory mediation" clause. See Exhibit 5-1 for a sample mediation provision for a franchise agreement.

(c) Arbitration

Arbitration and mediation are often confused. Mediation, as stated above, is a non-binding process where a neutral third party attempts to facilitate a voluntary settlement. Unlike mediation, arbitration is a *binding* procedure where the decision maker (the "arbitrator") acts effectively as both judge and jury. The arbitrator makes a decision based upon the law and facts presented to the arbitrator at a hearing. The arbitrator's award may be "confirmed" by a court after it is entered. If confirmed, the award becomes a judgment, and that judgment is enforceable like any other court judgment.

Arbitration generally involves one of three situations—one sole arbitrator, three neutral arbitrators, or three arbitrators where two are party-appointed and the third arbitrator is selected by the other two. Which of these three situations applies to a particular dispute depends upon the arbitration clause in the franchise agreement and the rules of the arbitration association that are chosen to govern the dispute.

As far back as the 1960s, arbitration in franchise cases was promoted as being "quicker and less expensive" than litigation. If that was ever true, it is fairly clear that, at least since the early 2000s, there has been a significant increase in written discovery, depositions, and motion practice in franchise arbitrations. As a result, the claims of "fast and inexpensive" have been all but abandoned by advocates who favor arbitration over litigation. In fact, the filing fees and arbitrator fees incurred in arbitrations often result in arbitration being *more* expensive than litigation.

The primary benefits now being touted for arbitration and the arbitration clause are the franchisor's ability to (1) eliminate class actions, (2) eliminate punitive damages, and (3) control the venue of the proceedings. In addition, many advocates of arbitration believe that arbitrators are less willing to award significant damages than are juries. Arbitration clauses are generally effective at precluding litigation.[1]

For better or for worse, arbitration awards are almost unappealable. The loser of the arbitration generally has no right to appeal a mistake of fact or even obvious

1. *See, e.g.*, Mahnke v. Exec. Tans, No. CIV. 07-1416 DSDJJG, 2007 WL 2340056, at *6 (D. Minn. Aug. 13, 2007); Southland v. Keating, 465 U.S. 1 (1984); Seymour v. Gloria Jean's Coffee Bean Franchising Corp., 732 F. Supp. 988 (Minn. 1990).

misapplication of the law.[2] Generally, an arbitration award may be overturned only if (1) the award was obtained through fraud, corruption, or undue means; (2) there was evident partiality or corruption on behalf of the arbitrators; (3) the arbitrators misbehaved, prejudicing the rights of a party—for example, by refusing to postpone a hearing upon good cause or refusing to permit pertinent evidence; or (4) the arbitrators exceeded their powers or defectively executed them such that a mutual, final, and definite award was not made.[3] In addition, arbitrators (like judges often do in a bench trial) generally allow into evidence that which would not be admissible in a jury trial. Therefore, arbitration proceedings often have the feeling of "rough justice." This impression is bolstered by the perceived tendency of certain arbitrators to "split the baby" and award the prevailing party some, but not all, of the relief it has sought.

(d) Litigation

Litigation is the process of pursuing a matter in a state or federal court. Unlike arbitration, litigation results in orders, rulings, and judgment that are susceptible to appeal if erroneous.

Litigation generally involves discovery processes (document requests, interrogatories, depositions) where the parties expend a great deal of time and money trying to bolster strengths in the party's case and find weaknesses in the opponent's case. One "wild card" in litigation is the use of juries—ordinary citizens who determine the winner and loser and the damages award. Advocates of

---

2. *See* Barranco v. 3D Sys. Corp., 734 F. App'x 885, 887 (4th Cir. 2018) (stating "the scope of judicial review for an arbitrator's decision is among the narrowest known at law. [N]either misinterpretation of a contract nor an error of law constitutes a ground on which an award can be vacated and, as long as the arbitrator is even arguably construing or applying the contract and acting within the scope of his authority, that a court is convinced he committed serious error does not suffice to overturn his decision.") (alteration in original) (internal quotations and citations omitted); Data & Dev., Inc. v. Infokall, Inc., No. 11CIV3372BSJRLE, 2012 WL 12887313, at *2 (S.D.N.Y. May 16, 2012), *aff'd*, 513 F. App'x 117 (2d Cir. 2013); GMS Group, LLC v. Benderson, 326 F.3d 75, 77 (2d Cir. 2003); Apex Plumbing Supply, Inc. v. U.S. Supply Co., Inc., 142 F.3d 188, 194 (4th Cir. 1998).

3. 9 U.S.C.A. § 10(a)(1)–(4). *See also* V5 Investments, LLC v. GoWaiter Bus. Holdings, LLC, 210 F. Supp. 3d 1329 (M.D. Fla. 2016) (franchisor's interception of franchisee's e-mails, including e-mails discussing legal strategies the franchisee was to use at arbitration, did not amount to "undue means" warranting the vacatur of the arbitration award where the arbitrator found that the franchisee was aware of the franchisor's interception of the e-mails prior to the arbitration, and the franchisee had consented to such interception); Choice Hotels Int'l, Inc. v. Felizardo, 278 F. Supp. 2d 590 (D. Md. 2003) (arbitrator did not exceed its authority by finding that no valid contract existed between franchisor and franchise); Statewide Remodeling, Inc. v. Williams, 244 S.W.3d 564, 568 (Tex. Ct. App. 2008) (under Texas common law, arbitration award will be set aside only upon a showing of "fraud, misconduct, or such gross mistake as would imply bad faith, or a failure to exercise honest judgment."); Sheldon v. Vermonty, 269 F.3d 1202, 1206 (10th Cir. 2001) (arbitration award may be vacated when made in violation of public policy, with manifest disregard of the law, or if hearing was fundamentally unfair).

arbitration often point out that arbitration tends to limit the chance of a verdict of the sort that might be awarded by a "runaway jury."

Attorneys who prefer litigation over arbitration often identify the availability of motions to dismiss and motions for summary judgment as key elements of the litigation system. These motions give judges the ability to dismiss cases before they ever reach a jury. Commenters and attorneys who favor litigation over arbitration also point out that, while arbitrators are paid to hear a case (and therefore have an incentive to keep it going), judges are often graded on their ability to dispose of cases. Judges, unlike arbitrators, also do not get paid based upon how many cases they hear or how long the case continues.

In recent years, more franchisors have decided to include "jury waivers" in their franchise agreements and demand that cases only be heard by a judge at a bench trial. Advocates of this approach feel that this gives them the best of both worlds. The judge may throw out the case on a motion to dismiss or a motion for summary judgment, but, in addition, the case never proceeds to a possibly out-of-control jury.

5-3. Termination

(a) How Potential Termination Situations Typically Arise

Although potential termination situations can result from a variety of circumstances, they typically arise from a relatively few common fact patterns. A franchisor's compliance program should anticipate these common scenarios but should be flexible enough to deal with them differently as the particular circumstances might warrant.

(i) Financial Difficulties of the Franchisee

The most straightforward circumstance leading to a potential termination is where the franchisee is in financial difficulty and, therefore, cannot or does not pay the required royalties, fees, or other monetary obligations to the franchisor on a timely basis. Virtually all franchise agreements give the franchisor the right to terminate for failure to pay fees, although most agreements include a notice and cure period for this type of default. The notice and opportunity to cure provisions generally range from as little as 5 days' notice to as much as 30 days' notice.

Before immediately sending out a default notice, a franchisor generally should try to understand the reason for the franchisee's poor financial condition. If a franchisee is running an excellent operation, is working 14 hours a day, and yet is losing $100,000 a month, that situation differs greatly from a franchisee who is taking a $90,000 salary and just forgets to pay his or her royalties once in a while. It is possible that every franchisee in the system might be suffering and struggling to pay its bills. The franchisor's options may range from a system-wide response, such as a reduced royalty rate for a limited period; to an individualized work-out arrangement with the particular problem franchisee, which might involve taking a note for past amounts due (often in exchange for a release by the franchisee of all claims) and establishing a stringent payment schedule; to the more direct response of sending a notice of default and then terminating if the franchisee does not cure within the required time. The proper response by the franchisor obviously will depend upon the circumstances in a particular case.

(ii) Disgruntled Franchisee

Another common problem leading to a potential termination is where a disgruntled franchisee simply refuses to pay the royalties, fees, or other amounts due to the franchisor. This situation might arise where a franchisee is upset with a particular decision by the franchisor and retaliates by refusing to pay fees. The situation can also arise in the context of a breakaway franchisee—a franchisee that, having learned the franchisor's business, seeks to leave the franchisor's system and set up a competing business at the same location or a nearby location. The situation of a franchisee that is not unable but rather is unwilling to pay the required fees presents a clear case for immediate action by the franchisor under the default and termination provisions of the franchise agreement.

(iii) Operational Problems

Potential termination situations also can arise for a variety of operational problems. Perhaps most commonly, a particular franchisee might not be complying or achieving operational standards set by the franchisor, such as quality or cleanliness, required hours of operation, or use of only approved product. It is in the area of enforcement of systems standards that a well-developed and consistently implemented compliance program is vitally important and can be most valuable. Again in this context, the franchisor must be able to understand and evaluate the reasons for the particular operational problems of the franchisee. Was the franchisee unaware of the particular standard involved? Was the franchisee aware of the standard but had difficulty effectively implementing it? Or was the franchisee aware of the standard and simply chose to ignore it? Determining the cause of the problem is necessary to determine the franchisor's appropriate response.

(b) How to Evaluate Potential Termination Situations

Once a potential default or termination situation arises, an effective compliance program should provide for a designated representative of the franchisor to analyze the reasons for the problem and for the franchisee's noncompliance. The franchisee that has legitimately tried to meet its contractual requirements but for some reason has fallen short logically should be dealt with differently than the franchisee that simply refuses to comply with its contractual obligations. In the former situation, the franchisor likely will want to make reasonable efforts to assist or counsel the franchisee regarding how to address and remedy the problems, be they financial or operational. In the latter situation, however, it might be more appropriate to take a more stern approach, advising the franchisee of the particular deficiencies noted and warning the franchisee that its failure to correct these deficiencies may result in termination.

Regardless of the course of action chosen by the franchisor, it is critical that the franchisor communicate the standards or requirements involved, the deficiencies noted in the franchisee's performance, and the specific steps necessary for the franchisee to take in order to become in compliance. For example, in the case of a franchisee's failure to meet required quality, service, or other operational standards, the franchisor's notice should specify the particular standards involved and deficiencies noted, possibly by attaching a copy of the inspection report and relevant sections from the operations manual describing how to achieve compliance. These communications should be documented in writing and given in the precise manner specified in the franchise agreement. Where permissible under the agreement, notice should be communicated in an easily verified method, such as by fax, certified mail, or overnight delivery service. The franchisor's efforts to consult with and/or counsel the franchisee also should be documented, in the form of memos or letters by the appropriate franchise support personnel, which are also provided to the franchisee. The goal of all of this is, first, to provide appropriate and effective assistance and/or warning to the franchisee to correct any deficiencies and, second, to provide a clear paper trail of the franchisor's reasonable efforts in the event the franchisor has to defend a subsequent termination decision.

If the franchisor's efforts to assist or to warn the franchisee do not result in sufficient compliance, the next step likely will be to consider whether termination is appropriate. Because this issue involves both business and legal considerations, appropriate franchisor management personnel as well as counsel for the franchisor (whether inside or outside) should be actively involved at this stage.

On the business side, the franchisor might consider establishing a particular individual or committee to review and approve default and termination decisions. Considerations by this person or committee might include the nature of the franchisee's noncompliance, the nature of the franchisor's response (either assistance or fair warning), and the nature of the franchisee's effort to address and/or cure its deficiencies. This analysis also might include the negotiation of a reasonable "cure" that might include reasonable performance criteria to be met by the franchisee and the franchisee's performance against those criteria.

In certain situations, it might also be appropriate or beneficial to involve a franchisee representative or franchisee committee in the decision-making process or as an advocate for the franchise community. This procedure is particularly appropriate where the enforcement of system standards is involved, because a poorly run or noncomplying franchised unit can have a serious negative impact on the goodwill of the franchisor's concept and therefore on the franchise system generally, a situation that other franchisees obviously have a strong interest in avoiding. If the franchisor has a franchisee representative involved in termination decisions, that franchisee representative may be a good witness in any later dispute regarding the termination.

In addition, the establishment of a person or committee to review all default and termination decisions should help ensure that the franchisor's policies, procedures, and standards are applied consistently throughout the system and that similarly situated franchisees are treated in a consistent manner. Consistent, nondiscriminatory treatment of franchisees is required by law in some states,[4] and it also may be considered as a factor in the application of the implied covenant of good faith and fair dealing.[5] In addition, it is an important intangible factor in most types of termination disputes for the franchisor to be able to show that it acted fairly with respect to the challenged conduct. The decision to have an established committee also can help minimize the chance that a decision concerning default and termination of a franchisee will be driven by inappropriate factors such as, for example, personal animosity between a franchisee and a franchisor representative.

Once the franchisor has decided that it must terminate a particular franchisee, the legal aspects of the compliance program come more sharply into focus. The first, and most obvious, place to start is with the default and termination provisions of the franchise agreement, but that is not the end of the inquiry. The franchisor also must examine any applicable statutory restrictions on its termination rights imposed by state franchise relationship laws or industry-specific statutes. Moreover, the franchisor must examine the course of dealings with the particular franchisee to make sure that its contractual rights have not been modified in any way by the conduct of its agents. Finally, the franchisor must consider potential bases for legal claims by the franchisee that might arise out of termination. These issues are addressed individually below.

---

4. *See, e.g.*, CONN. GEN. STAT. § 42-1331(f)(9) (2019) ("No franchisor, directly or indirectly, through any officer, agent or employee, shall . . . discriminate between franchisees . . . ."); HAW. REV. STAT. § 482E-6(2)(C) (2020) ("[I]t shall be an unfair or deceptive act or practice or an unfair method of competition for a franchisor or subfranchisor to . . . Discriminate between franchisees . . . ."); 815 ILL. COMP. STAT. 705/18 (2020) ("It shall be an unfair franchise practice and a violation of this Act for any franchisor to unreasonably and materially discriminate between franchisees . . . ."); IND. CODE § 23-2-2.7-2(5) (2020) ("It is unlawful for a franchisor . . . to engage in any of the following acts and practices . . . Discriminating unfairly among its franchisees . . . ."); WASH. REV. CODE 19.100.180(2)(c) (2020) ("[I]t shall be an unfair or deceptive act or practice or an unfair method of competition and therefore unlawful and a violation of this chapter for any person to . . . Discriminate between franchisees . . . .").

5. *See, e.g.*, Kumon N. Am., Inc. v. Timban, No. CIV.13-4809 RBK/KMW, 2014 WL 2812122, at *7 (D.N.J. June 23, 2014) (dismissing former franchisee's claim that franchisor violated the implied covenant of good faith and fair dealing and looking at former franchisee's argument that it was not treated "in [a] fair and nondiscriminatory manner.") (alterations in original); Fiore v. McDonald's Corp., Bus. Franchise Guide (CCH) ¶ 10,876 (E.D.N.Y. Feb. 23, 1996) (denying motion to dismiss implied covenant claim where franchisee alleged that franchisor targeted franchisee's restaurants for repeated inspections).

(c) Contractual Bases for Termination of a Franchise Agreement

Once a potential termination situation has arisen, the franchisor should look first to the franchise agreement to identify all potential bases for default and termination under that agreement. Most franchise agreements have very extensive and specific sections addressing the types of franchisee conduct that will constitute a default, thereby potentially entitling the franchisor to terminate. Some of the listed contractual grounds might entitle the franchisor to terminate immediately, without notice or opportunity to cure, but the majority of the default/termination provisions in a typical franchise agreement require the franchisor to give notice and allow for a cure period. The franchisor, of course, should strictly comply with the relevant default and termination provisions of its own agreement to make sure it accomplishes a valid termination.

Examples of conduct that, under many franchise agreements, authorizes the franchisor to terminate a franchisee immediately include the following:

- filing of bankruptcy or becoming insolvent,
- appointment of a receiver of the franchisee's assets or property,
- abandonment of the franchise or cessation of the franchised business for some stated period of time without franchisor permission,
- a conviction of or guilty plea by the franchisee to a felony (or, as sometimes stated, a felony that reflects negatively upon the franchisor or the franchised business),
- a transfer or attempted transfer of the franchisee's rights or interest in the franchise to a third party without the franchisor's consent,
- intentional underreporting of sales or maintaining false records,
- operation of the franchised business in such a manner as to pose an immediate threat or danger to public health or safety, and
- "two strikes and you are out" or "three strikes and you are out" provisions regarding multiple and repeated defaults.

These grounds for termination usually are straightforward, apparent, and incurable, and, thus, are subject generally to reasonably definite verification by the franchisor.

A wide variety of other conduct may constitute a default under the franchise agreement that, if not cured, would authorize termination. Such conduct typically includes breach of or failure to perform other material provisions of the franchise agreement, such as failure to pay royalties, fees, or other amounts owed to the franchisor; failure to comply with the franchisor's operational standards, as set forth either in the agreement itself or in an accompanying operations manual; or failure to comply with related legal obligations such as breach of the lease for the franchised premises or violation of other applicable laws and regulations. Most franchise agreements require the franchisor to provide written notice to the franchisee of the default and to allow the franchisee a specified time (often 30 days for nonmonetary defaults and a shorter period of time for monetary defaults) to cure the specified default. Some franchise agreements state that a "reasonable time" is required to cure certain defaults, but a cure effort must begin immediately and continue until cured.

In addition to the relevant franchise agreement provisions, the franchisor should review its operations manuals and policies relating to the particular default issue to make sure the language of the agreement has not been modified or interpreted by the franchisor in a manner inconsistent with the purported basis for the default. If the franchisor has arguably modified any of its contractual requirements by policy or practice, such modification should be cured before attempting to default and terminate a franchisee on such grounds. Similarly, a franchisor should check its correspondence with the franchisee at issue to make sure that no one at the franchisor has stated either that it is fine that the franchisee is doing what it is doing or that the franchisee can "cure" within some longer period of time than is stated in the franchise agreement.

A written notice of default is the mechanism by which the franchisor should communicate the grounds for the default to the franchisee. It is important for the franchisor to identify all defaults in the default letter that it might use as a basis for termination.[6] As a precaution, the franchisor should include a "non-waiver" sentence in its default letter. At a minimum, a notice of default should identify with specificity the following items:

- the franchise agreement involved (especially in the case of multiunit franchisees),
- the contractual provisions (with any related standards) that have been breached,
- a description of the acts or omissions that the franchisor contends constitute a breach of the agreement,
- the specific actions the franchisee must take to cure the default(s),
- the time within which the franchisee must cure the default(s), and
- the method by which the franchisor will determine whether the franchisee has cured the default(s) (actual receipt of funds owed, passing a follow-up inspection for violation of operational standards, and so on).

A notice of default should be reviewed by counsel for the franchisor before it is sent to the franchisee to make sure that it complies with all contractual and other legal requirements. Many franchisors choose to send out notices of default and termination under counsel's signature. Sample notices of default and termination for different types of defaults are attached as forms 5-1, 5-2, and 5-3.

Once a notice of default has been sent, the franchisor should follow up diligently to determine whether the franchisee plans to cure, whether the default has been cured, whether there is basis to terminate, or whether to consider a work-out

---

6. Failure to list all alleged breaches in the notice letter might preclude the franchisor from later relying upon other reasons not set forth therein. *See, e.g.*, ABA Distribs., Inc. v. Adolph Coors Co., 542 F. Supp. 1272 (W.D. Mo. 1982) ("brewer's notice of termination of beer distributorship could not be supported by subsequently discovered evidence not known by brewer at time of termination.").

arrangement. A franchisor can waive its right to terminate if it fails to act promptly to enforce the termination and the franchisee subsequently cures the default, even if it does so after the expiration of the cure period. A franchisor may also risk losing its entitlement to injunctive relief to enforce the termination if it fails to act promptly and the franchisee continues to be in default.

Once the franchisor has decided to terminate the franchisee, in many cases the franchisor should consider whether to try to negotiate a voluntary termination with the franchisee, accompanied by either a closing of the franchised unit or transfer of the business to the franchisor or another franchisee. A voluntary or acknowledged termination has the obvious benefit of avoiding an acrimonious and potentially expensive legal dispute. It also can benefit the franchisor by assuring an orderly transition during which the unit continues to operate, thereby avoiding the potential loss of customer goodwill and the loss of royalties from a unit closed due to a dispute. If the franchisee refuses to acknowledge the termination immediately, the franchisor might consider negotiating certain concessions (for example, forgiving past due royalties, agreeing to pay for de-identification of the premises, waiving of noncompete provisions, or allowing the franchisee a reasonable time to sell the unit) to induce the franchisee to cooperate. A franchisor should always document such a voluntary or acknowledged termination, although the specific terms will vary according to the particular agreement reached. Samples of different types of voluntary termination agreements are attached as forms 5-4 and 5-5.

Cross-default situations may also arise upon the default or termination of certain multiple-unit franchises, depending on the language of the particular franchise agreement at issue. If the franchisee operates multiple units, the franchise agreement for each unit may provide that a default or termination with respect to one of the units gives the franchisor the right to declare a default or to terminate the agreements for the other franchised units. In addition, the termination of a franchise agreement might constitute grounds for terminating a related development agreement, sublease, or other contract with the franchisor. A franchisor should consider whether it is appropriate to invoke such cross-default provisions where that right exists. Cross-default rights are a very powerful tool in achieving compliance; however, the more units a franchisee has, the less realistic it is from a business perspective that all of his or her units should be terminated at one time.

In certain situations, however, a franchisor may decide that a work-out arrangement and reinstatement rather than a termination are more desirable. The reasons for this alternative to termination are varied. For example, the franchisor may wish to avoid negative public relations, costly litigation, or potentially risky counterclaims by the franchisee. A work-out option can generally be offered to troubled franchisees in exchange for compromises on amounts owed, confidentiality agreements, and/or general or specific releases of claims against the franchisor. The specific terms of any work-out agreement will vary depending on the nature of the franchisee's problems, the particular concessions sought by the franchisee, and the return consideration sought by the franchisor. A sample of one type of work-out agreement is attached as form 5-6.

Once the franchisor has made a final decision on termination and actually sent a termination notice, the franchisor should make sure to follow through on enforcing all of the post-termination provisions contained in the franchise agreement. Two of the most important of these obligations are (1) de-identification of the former franchised unit (assuming that the franchisor is not taking possession of the property under a sublease or assignment) and (2) ensuring the return of all trade secret and proprietary materials provided to the former franchisee. Franchise agreements, as well as federal trademark laws, provide that the former franchisee is responsible for de-identifying the unit once the franchise agreement is terminated and the franchisee no longer has the right to use the franchisor's marks and systems. It may be in the franchisor's best interest, however, to take such steps itself, either by agreement of the franchisee or pursuant to court order, so that the public does not develop a negative impression due to a closed or poorly run location still bearing the franchisor's name.

Ensuring the return of all trade secret and proprietary materials is equally important. The franchisor should immediately demand return of the operations manual, all bulletins or other communications regarding the franchisor's system, and all other proprietary documents or materials bearing the franchisor's name and marks. Additionally, the franchisor should cut off the franchisee's access to any electronic or online materials and stop sending to the franchisee any materials that are generally sent to franchisees either electronically or through the mail. These steps are important both to make sure that the former franchisee does not continue to operate its unit using the franchisor's proprietary system and to preserve whatever trade secret and other proprietary rights the franchisor might have with respect to this information and material. The franchisor should consider legal action to enforce these post-termination rights if the franchisee refuses to comply.

A related issue that arises upon termination in many franchise systems is the enforceability of noncompetition provisions in franchise agreements. This issue is an entire topic unto itself and is the subject of an excellent monograph, *Covenants against Competition in Franchise Agreements*,[7] published by the American Bar Association Forum on Franchising, which contains a state-by-state analysis of statutory and case law on this issue. Without delving too deeply into noncompete issues, it is recommended that the franchisor first consider whether it has a great need to enforce any noncompetition provisions against the terminated franchisee, or whether the franchisor is willing to use those rights to bargain for voluntary termination or some other agreement to avoid a legal battle over the termination. If the franchisor desires to enforce a noncompetition provision, the franchisor should consult its legal counsel to determine the enforceability of the particular contractual language under applicable law, which may include the law chosen in the franchise agreement, the law of the state where the franchised business is located, and the law of the states where the franchisee or its guarantor are

7. Covenants Against Competition in Franchise Agreements (Michael R. Gray & Natalma M. McKnew, 3d ed. 2012).

residents. State law varies greatly on this issue, and what is enforceable in one jurisdiction might not be enforceable (or at least not fully enforceable) in another.

(d) Statutory Restrictions on the Right to Terminate

Although the franchisor must have a basis under the franchise agreement to default and terminate a franchisee, the existence of such a contractual right is not the only factor a franchisor must consider in making a termination decision. Eighteen states have franchise relationship statutes of general applicability, which impose varying degrees of restrictions upon a franchisor's right to terminate.[8] Some of these statutes impose a "good cause" requirement for termination, while others mandate the amount of notice the franchisor must give before terminating. Counsel for the franchisor must consider the applicability of such statutes before termination can be implemented. A summary of the key provisions of these statutes relating to termination is contained in the appendix to this chapter.

In the case of a franchisor and franchisee located in different states, the first question to answer is which state's law applies. Most franchise agreements have choice-of-law clauses that purport to apply the laws of the franchisor's home state to either the parties' "agreement" or the parties' "relationship." If the franchisee is located in a state having a relationship law, however, a court (particularly one sitting in the franchisee's home state) might decline to enforce the choice-of-law clause on the grounds that the franchise relationship law of the franchisee's home represents a significant public policy that cannot be overridden by contract.[9] In

8. These statutes are as follows: Ark. Code §§ 4-72-201 to 4-72-210 (2020); Cal. Bus. & Prof. Code §§ 20000 to 20043 (2017); Conn. Gen. Stat. §§ 42-133e to 42-133h (2019); Del. Code tit. 6, §§ 2551 to 2556 (2021); Haw. Rev. Stat. §§ 482E-1 to 482E-12 (2018); 815 Ill. Comp. Stat. §§ 705-18 to 705-26 (2020); Ind. Code §§ 23-2-2.7-1 to 23-2-2.7-7 (2020); Iowa Code §§ 523H.1 to 523H.17 (2021); Iowa Code § 537A.10 (2021); Mich. Comp. Laws §§ 445:1501 to 445:1546 (2020); Minn. Stat. §§ 80C.01 to 80C.22 (2020); Miss. Code § 75-24-53 (2021); Mo. Stat. §§ 407.400 to 407.420 (2020); Neb. Rev. Stat. §§ 87-401 to 87-410 (2020); N.J. Stat. §§ 56:10-1 to 56:10-12 (2020); R.I. Gen. Laws §§ 6-50-1 to 6-50-9 (2021); Va. Code. §§ 13.1-557 to 13.1-574 (2020); Wash. Rev. Code §§ 19.100.010 to 19.100.940 (2020); Wis. Stat. §§ 135.01 to 135.07 (2020).

9. *See, e.g.*, Minn. Stat. § 80C.21 ("any choice of law provision, purporting to bind any person who, at the time of acquiring a franchise is a resident of this state, or, in the case of a partnership or corporation, organized or incorporated under the laws of this state . . . . is void.") (2020); Cottman Transmission Sys., LLC v. Kershner, 492 F. Supp. 2d 461 (E.D. Pa. 2007); Pinnacle Pizza Co. v. Little Caesar Enters., Inc., 395 F. Supp. 2d 891 (D.S.D. 2005); Cromeens, Holloman, Sibert, Inc. v. AB Volvo, 349 F.3d 376 (7th Cir. 2003); Ticknor v. Choice Hotels Int'l, Inc., 265 F.3d 931 (9th Cir. 2001); Wright-Moore Corp. v. Ricoh Corp., 908 F.2d 128 (7th Cir. 1990); Instructional Sys., Inc. v. Computer Curriculum Corp., 614 A.2d 124 (N.J. 1992). Franchisors, however, have been successful in enforcing choice-of-law clauses in some instances. *See, e.g.*, Hockey Enters., Inc. v. Total Hockey Worldwide, LLC, 762 F. Supp. 2d 1138 (D. Minn. 2011); Cottman Transmission Sys., Inc. v. Melody, 869 F. Supp. 1180 (E.D. Pa. 1994); Banek Inc. v. Yogurt Ventures U.S.A., Inc., 6 F.3d 357 (6th Cir. 1993); Hubbard Auto Ctr., Inc. v. Gen. Motors Corp., 422 F. Supp. 2d 999 (N.D. Ind. 2006).

addition, certain states require a state-specific addendum to be executed, stating that the franchisee will be protected by his or her home state laws. If such an addendum is executed, it becomes part of the franchise agreement and overrides a contrary choice-of-law provision. Counsel for the franchisor should analyze the franchise agreement, any signed addenda, any unsigned addenda provided in the franchise disclosure document, and the relevant case law applying any potentially applicable state relationship statutes before implementing a contemplated termination.

Once it has been determined that a particular relationship law applies, the franchisor must measure its grounds for termination against any requirements of the applicable statute. Many of these relationship statutes define what is required as "good cause" to terminate.[10] The definition of "good cause" under most of these statutes includes a franchisee's failure to substantially comply with material obligations under the franchise agreement, although many require that the franchisee first be given notice and an opportunity to cure. Some of these statutes also allow termination in other circumstances such as bankruptcy of the franchisee, abandonment of the franchised premises, or conduct that materially impairs the goodwill of the franchisor's name or mark.

A few of these state relationship laws do not define "good cause," which makes the franchisor's termination analysis more uncertain.[11] It usually is the case, however, that a franchisee's breach of a material provision of the franchise agreement that remains uncured after reasonable notice will be deemed to constitute good cause even under these less well-defined statutes. Counsel for the franchisor should analyze decisions under these statutes carefully before implementing a termination, however, to make sure that the franchisor's reasons are considered to be legitimate.

Finally, counsel for franchisor should check to make sure that there are no industry-specific statutes that might apply even if there is no relationship statute of general applicability. Among the industries that typically have specific statutes regulating the relationship between franchisors and franchisees or manufacturers and dealers are the automobile industry, the petroleum industry, the farm equipment industry, the heavy equipment industry, the beer industry, and the alcoholic beverage industry. Virtually all of these industry-specific statutes regulate the circumstances under which the franchisor, manufacturer, or supplier (sometimes called the "grantor") may terminate a franchisee or dealer.

---

10. Those states having statutes that define "good cause" in some way include Arkansas, California, Connecticut, Hawaii, Illinois, Indiana, Iowa, Michigan, Minnesota, Missouri, Nebraska, New Jersey, Washington, and Wisconsin.

11. *See, e.g.*, Del. Code tit. 6 § 2552 (2021) (statute provides that termination by franchisor will be deemed unjust if termination is without cause or made in bad faith; however, no definitions are provided); Va. Code § 13.1-564 (2020) (statute lacks definition of "reasonable cause" required for cancellation of franchise).

(e) Has the Contract Been Modified? Examination of the Parties' Course of Dealings and Subsequent Performance

If the franchisor determines that it has an apparent contractual basis for termination, it might not be sufficient if the franchisee can establish that the contractual provision relied upon by the franchisor has been modified or waived through the parties' previous course of dealings. Even if the franchise agreement contains an integration clause, the parol evidence rule generally will not bar evidence of the parties' course of dealings after execution of the franchise agreement, where such evidence is offered to assist in the interpretation of contractual language deemed to be vague or ambiguous.[12] A franchisor thus should include, as part of its compliance program for terminations, a thorough review by legal counsel of the relevant files relating to the franchisee sought to be terminated to make sure that no land mines exist that might defeat its apparent contractual rights. Some of the relevant issues to look for are discussed below.

Waiver and estoppel concerns are paramount in this analysis. The franchisor should make sure that it has engaged in no conduct or communications that could reasonably be construed as having waived strict compliance with the particular contractual provision being relied upon for the termination. For example, if the franchisor has accepted late royalty payments from a particular franchisee repeatedly, the franchisor may be deemed to have waived the franchisee's noncompliance with that provision, at least for the moment, and thus not be able to terminate the franchisee immediately for that reason alone.[13] This problem can also arise in the standards context where the franchisor has tolerated noncompliance with

---

12. *See, e.g.*, Randall v. Lady of Am. Franchise Corp., 532 F. Supp. 2d 1071, 1084–85 (D. Minn. 2007); Hamade v. Sunoco Inc. (R&M), 721 N.W.2d 233, 248 (Mich. Ct. App. 2006) ("Where the parties have included an express integration or merger clause within the agreement, it is conclusive and parol evidence is not admissible to show that the agreement is not integrated except in cases of fraud that invalidate the integration clause or where an agreement is obviously incomplete on its face and, therefore, parol evidence is necessary for the filling of gaps.") (internal quotations omitted); It's Just Lunch Int'l, LLC v. Polar Bear, Inc., No. CIV.03-2485 WQH(JFS), 2004 WL 3406117, at *3 (S.D. Cal. Apr. 29, 2004) (permitting parol evidence to be introduced to establish claim of fraud in the inducement, even though the contract specifically states that all conditions and representations are embodied in the contract); Century Pac., Inc. v. Hilton Hotels Corp., 528 F. Supp. 2d 206, 229 (S.D.N.Y. 2007), *aff'd*, 354 F. App'x 496 (2d Cir. 2009) (holding that a general merger clause does not preclude a party from introducing parol evidence upon which their fraud claims are made); Ponderosa Sys., Inc. v. Brandt, 767 F.2d 668, 672 (10th Cir. 1985) (evidence of promotional material admitted because it was "necessary to an understanding of the contract").

13. *See, e.g.*, Sheldon v. Munford, Inc., 950 F.2d 403 (7th Cir. 1991) (franchisor who had regularly allowed franchisee to be in arrears on royalty payments was not allowed to terminate franchise for late payment). *But see* Dunkin' Donuts Franchised Restaurants LLC v. KEV Enters., Inc., 634 F. Supp. 2d 1324 (M.D. Fla. 2009) (franchisors' acceptance of late payments from franchisees did not establish a waiver of its right to terminate the franchise agreements where the franchisors reserved its rights in the notice letters and the franchisees agreed to the non-waiver provision in the franchise agreements); Clinkscales v. Chevron U.S.A., Inc., 831 F.2d 1565, 1573 n.19 (11th Cir. 1987) (explaining in a footnote that the Petroleum Marketing Practices Act allows termination based on the repeated occurrence of

operational standards, such as quality or cleanliness standards or required hours of operation, for an extended period of time.[14]

Even where the franchisor finds itself in this unfortunate situation, the franchisor can take steps to restore its contractual rights. The best procedure for doing so is to send a firm, clear notice in writing to the franchisee indicating that, starting at a specific date, the franchisor will no longer tolerate deviations from the contractually required procedures and will in the future insist upon strict compliance with the terms of the contract. This type of communication is sometimes referred to as a "New Day" letter.[15] Of course, a franchisor that has tolerated noncompliance must give the franchisee a period of time that is reasonable under the circumstances within which to correct its deficiencies and become in compliance under the contract. In extreme cases, a prior waiver may result in an estoppel; for example, where a franchisor has allowed a franchisee to spend a great deal of money on a poor location and operate for several years, terminating the franchisee for having a subpar location may be impossible.

As mentioned earlier, counsel for the franchisor should also review the relevant documents to confirm that no representative or agent of the franchisor has made any specific representations to the franchisee that might contradict the basis for the franchisor's termination decision. For example, if the franchisor is basing its termination upon the franchisee's failure to carry a required menu item, counsel for the franchisor should make sure that none of its franchise support representatives have told the franchisee that it need not do so for some reason. The franchisor should also make sure that none of its representatives have made any representations that might reasonably have induced the franchisee to incur significant new investment in the franchise business shortly prior to the proposed termination. Such representations could lead to a defense or counterclaim for fraudulent misrepresentation or equitable recoupment.

In addition to the issues of waiver and estoppel concerning the franchisee that is the subject of the termination, the franchisor's conduct with respect to similarly situated franchisees also should be analyzed. Some state relationship statutes impose a requirement of nondiscriminatory treatment of similarly situated franchisees.[16] Even where not required by statute, the franchisor should be

---

a particular event even if the franchisor elected not to seek termination based on the previous occurrences).

14. *See, e.g.*, Terry v. Int'l Dairy Queen, Inc., 554 F. Supp. 1088 (N.D. Ind. 1983) (waiver can be implied where franchisor knows of franchisee's failure to meet standards but takes no action).

15. *See, e.g.*, LaGuardia Assocs. v. Holiday Hosp. Franchising, Inc., 92 F. Supp. 2d 119 (E.D.N.Y. 2000) (holding that equity required that the franchisor notify its franchisees that strict adherence to the contractual payment periods would be required in the future before the franchisor could terminate the agreement for noncompliance with payment timing requirements); Chia-Hsin (Charles) Huang v. Holiday Inns, Inc., 594 F. Supp. 352 (C.D. Cal. 1984) (holding that franchisor's termination of franchisee for violation of quality standards was fair and reasonable where prior to termination franchisor implemented a new evaluation program designed to identify quality deficiencies and communicated this new program to all franchisees).

16. *See, e.g.*, statutes cited *supra* note 8.

prepared, as a practical matter, to defend a termination by showing that it has acted fairly and reasonably with respect to the terminated franchisee. Thus, the franchisor should be prepared to show that it has treated similarly situated franchisees in generally the same way, demonstrate a very good reason why it has not done so in a particular situation, or explain in detail why the franchisees are not, in fact, similarly situated.

Another relevant factor to analyze is evidence of the custom and practice in the industry with respect to the conduct providing the basis for termination. Evidence of custom and practice may in some cases be relevant and admissible in litigation to support a party's interpretation of what a particular provision of the contract means.[17]

In addition to looking for potential land mines, counsel's analysis of the course of dealings and relevant documents should be done with an eye toward documenting the basis and broader justification for the termination as extensively as possible in the event the franchisee challenges the termination decision. Establishing and reviewing a strong paper trail showing consistent warnings and efforts to assist the franchisee allows the franchisor's decision makers to have a higher degree of confidence in the termination decision. The paper trail can also be used to explain and/or negotiate issues with respect to the termination with the franchisee or its counsel. Finally, if litigation is necessary, developing a good paper trail will assist the franchisor greatly to prove or defend the propriety of its conduct.

17. *See, e.g.*, Stuller, Inc. v. Steak N Shake Enters., Inc. 877 F. Supp. 2d 674, 691 (C.D. Ill. 2012) (stating "[r]evelant extrinsic evidence includes the parties' negotiations of the contract, the course of performance, course of dealing, and trade usage in the relevant industry."); City of Tacoma v. City of Bonney Lake, 269 P.3d 1017 (Wash. 2012) (finding that the course of dealings evidence was the most helpful for the court in determining whether the franchise agreements required the city to provide and maintain hydrants); Maintainco, Inc. v. Mitsubishi Caterpillar Forklift Am., Inc., No. A-1485-07T2, 2009 WL 2365960 (N.J. Super. Ct. App. Div. July 30, 2009) (the course of dealings between parties was admitted to support the assertion that the dealership was exclusive); Kaeser Compressors, Inc. v. Compressor & Pump Repair Servs., Inc., No. 09-C-521, 2009 WL 3055341, at *1 (E.D. Wis. Sept. 18, 2009) (evidence of parties' course of conduct is admissible to interpret the contract when agreement is silent on those issues, so long as the interpretation is not contrary to the grantor's manifest intentions); *accord* UCC § 2-202 (even terms of written contract intended as final expression of party's agreement with respect to such terms may be "explained or supplemented by course of performance, course of dealing or usage of trade[.]"); Varni Bros. Corp. v. Wine World, Inc., 41 Cal. Rptr. 2d 740 (Cal. Ct. App. 1995), *as modified on denial of reh'g* (July 7, 1995) (evidence of custom in the industry admitted to supply contract terms); Dunafon v. Taco Bell Corp., Bus. Franchise Guide (CCH) ¶ 10,919 (W.D. Mo. 1996) (finding that an oral agreement could have existed given the course of dealing of the parties over a 20-year period); Ralph's Distrib. Co. v. AMF, Inc., 667 F.2d 670 (8th Cir. 1981) (admitting a party's course of performance and usage of trade evidence in order to determine whether the parties intended to include an exclusivity term in the franchise agreements).

(f) Analyze All Potential Bases for Claims by the Franchisee

The termination of a franchise is a serious matter with long-term consequences. Thus, the franchisor should assume that the terminated franchisee will attempt to challenge or reverse this decision by asserting all available legal claims it might possibly have against the franchisor. A franchisor should analyze and evaluate such potential claims to the extent possible prior to sending a notice of termination. This should include both a factual review by the relevant business and operational personnel and an analysis of the legal bases for any potential claims by the franchisor's counsel. Franchisors should also make every attempt to uniformly apply their statutory and contractual termination rights. The strength of any such potential claims by the franchisee might dictate that the franchisor pursue an alternative course at that time, such as negotiated performance criteria or a work-out arrangement. Some of the more commonly asserted franchisee claims are discussed below.

The terminated franchisee might attempt to challenge the franchisor's basis for the termination and assert a claim for breach of contract or applicable relationship statute. The wrongful termination of a franchisee can provide a basis for a breach of contract claim and allow the franchisee to seek either injunctive relief or damages for loss of the franchised business.[18] Confirming the contractual and, if applicable, statutory bases for a termination, however, should already have been addressed as part of the steps outlined above.

The franchisor should also evaluate potential claims based on the implied covenant of good faith and fair dealing, which, in most states, is usually deemed to be a part of every contract. The implied covenant generally applies where one party is vested with discretion in performing a particular right or obligation under the contract. The doctrine operates to prevent that party from exercising its discretion in bad faith, arbitrarily, or for an improper purpose so as not to defeat the other party's reasonable expectations under the contract.[19]

---

18. *See, e.g.*, JRS Prod., Inc. v. Matsushita Elec. Corp. of Am., 8 Cal. Rptr. 3d 840 (Cal. Ct. App. 2004), *as modified on denial of reh'g* (Feb. 25, 2004) (holding that franchisee was entitled to pursue a breach of contract claim against franchisor for common law damages based on franchisor's wrongful termination of the franchise agreement); Cooper Distrib. Co., Inc. v. Amana Refrigeration, Inc., 63 F.3d 262 (3d Cir. 1995) (affirming judgment for wrongful termination under New Jersey Franchise Practices Act although reversing and remanding damages award); Payless Car Rental Sys., Inc. v. Draayer, 716 P.2d 929 (Wash. Ct. App. 1986) (affirming trial court's award of damages to franchisee for lost profits due to franchisor's wrongful termination).

19. *See, e.g.*, Hopkinton Friendly Serv., Inc. v. Glob. Companies LLC, 384 F. Supp. 3d 179, 188 (D. Mass. 2019) (stating "[u]nder Massachusetts law, a covenant of good faith and fair dealing is implied in every contract.") (internal quotations omitted); Lukoil N. Am. LLC v. Turnersville Petroleum Inc., No. CIV.A 14-3810 RMB, 2015 WL 1735369, at *9 (D.N.J. Apr. 16, 2015) (stating "[t]he party claiming a breach of the covenant of good faith and fair dealing must provide evidence sufficient to support a conclusion that the party alleged to have acted in bad faith has engaged in some conduct that denied the benefit of the bargain originally intended by the parties.") (internal quotations omitted); Mercedes-Benz USA

Depending upon what state law is applicable, however, the implied covenant cannot override or negate express contractual terms, so many courts give full effect to contractual provisions setting forth grounds for termination.[20] Further,

LLC v. Concours Motors, Inc., No. 07-C-0389, 2010 WL 55473, at *14 (E.D. Wis. Jan. 4, 2010) (stating that the implied covenant of good faith and fair dealing is breached "where one party attempts to intentionally deprive the other party of the benefits it reasonably expects to receive under the contract."); 7-Eleven, Inc. v. McEvoy, 300 F. Supp. 2d 352, 360 (D. Md. 2004) (stating "[t]he implied duty of good faith and fair dealing generally does little more than prevent one party from affirmatively frustrating the other's performance, it does not create new contract terms."); Cromeens, Holloman, Sibert, Inc. v. AB Volvo, 349 F.3d 376, 395 (7th Cir. 2003) (stating "[t]he covenant requires a party vested with broad discretion to act reasonably and not arbitrarily or in a manner inconsistent with the reasonable expectations of the parties."); Town & Country Equip., Inc. v. Deere & Co., Inc., 133 F. Supp. 2d 665, 668 (W.D. Tenn. 2000) (stating "[u]nder Tennessee law, [e]very contract imposes upon each party a duty of good faith and fair dealing in its performance and enforcement.") (internal quotations omitted); Juliano v. Sun Co. Inc., 166 F.3d 1205 (3d Cir. 1998); Taylor Equip., Inc. v. John Deere Co., 98 F.3d 1028, 1031 (8th Cir. 1996) (stating "South Dakota law implies a covenant of good faith and fair dealing into every contract."); Traumann v. Southland Corp., 842 F. Supp. 386, 392 (N.D. Cal. 1993) (stating "[a]lthough [franchisor] had complete discretion to terminate the [franchisee's] application, it was still bound to exercise this discretionary power in good faith."); Original Great Am. Chocolate Chip Cookie Co., Inc. v. River Valley Cookies, Ltd., 970 F.2d 273, 279 (7th Cir. 1992) (stating "Illinois like other states requires, as a matter of common law, that each party to a contract act with good faith[.]"); Carvel Corp. v. Diversified Mgmt. Group, Inc., 930 F.2d 228, 230 (2d Cir. 1991) (stating that the covenant of good faith "includes an implied undertaking on the part of each party that he will not intentionally and purposely do anything to prevent the other party from carrying out the agreement on his part.") (internal quotations omitted); Anchorage Chrysler Ctr., Inc. v. DaimlerChrysler Motors Corp., 221 P.3d 977, 994 (Ala. 2009) (stating that there is an objective and subjective element to the implied covenant of good faith and fair dealing); Dayan v. McDonald's Corp., 466 N.E.2d 958, 971 (Ill. App. Ct. 1984) (stating "[p]roblems relating to good faith performance typically arise where one party to the contract is given broad discretion in performance. The dependent party must then rely on the party in control to exercise that discretion fairly.").

20. *See, e.g.*, Fleetwood v. Stanley Steemer Int'l, Inc., 725 F. Supp. 2d 1258 (E.D. Wash. 2010), *aff'd sub nom.* Fleetwood v. Stanley Steemer Int'l, 446 F. App'x 868 (9th Cir. 2011); Volvo Const. Equip. N. Am., Inc. v. CLE Equip. Co., Inc., 386 F.3d 581, 599 (4th Cir. 2004) (stating that the Dealer Agreements gave the franchisor the right to terminate without cause; therefore, in terminating the Dealer Agreements, the franchisor "could not have breached its duty of good faith and fair dealing."); Cromeens, Holloman, Sibert, Inc. v. AB Volvo, 349 F.3d 376 (7th Cir. 2003); Taylor Equip., Inc. v. John Deere Co., 98 F.3d 1028, 1032 (8th Cir. 1996) (stating "many courts have held that the implied covenant may not be applied to limit a clear contractual provision allowing termination of the contract without cause."); Chang v. McDonald's Corp., Bus. Franchise Guide (CCH) ¶ 10,677 (N.D. Cal. 1995); Sons of Thunder, Inc. v. Borden, Inc., 690 A.2d 575 (N.J. 1997); Davis v. Sears, Roebuck & Co., 873 F.2d 888 (6th Cir. 1989) (implied covenant held not to override language in contract allowing either party to terminate upon specified notice); Grand Light & Supply Co., Inc. v. Honeywell, Inc., 771 F.2d 672 (2d Cir. 1985) (same). *But see* Wilson v. Amerada Hess Corp., 773 A.2d 1121 (N.J. 2001) (stating that "[u]nlike many other states, in New Jersey a party to a contract may breach the implied covenant of good faith and fair dealing in performing its obligations even when it exercises an express and unconditional right to terminate.") (internal quotations omitted).

certain courts have held that good cause for termination will defeat a claim for breach of the implied covenant based upon the franchisor's allegedly improper motive in taking the challenged action.[21] The doctrine of good faith and fair dealing has been applied to a broad array of franchisor conduct (such as encroachment, advertising, and provision of franchise support services), and the law in this area is constantly evolving. Counsel for the franchisor therefore should be careful to analyze how this doctrine might be used in any aspect of the franchise relationship that might be open to challenge by the franchisee.

In addition to contract-based issues, the franchisor should look for potential claims, such as statutory fraud under state franchise acts, common law fraud, and/or tortious interference with business relations. Particularly in the context of a short-term franchisee that has not performed well financially, counsel for the franchisor should pay careful attention to potential fraudulent inducement claims based on alleged presale misrepresentations. A claim for tortious interference may be anticipated where the franchisor intends to take for itself the territory or group of customers previously served by the terminated franchisee.

Potential federal or state antitrust claims also must be considered. Generally, a franchisor acting unilaterally can terminate a franchisee without violating the antitrust laws, but a franchisor may incur liability by terminating a franchisee pursuant to an agreement with other franchisees that have complained about price-cutting by the terminated franchisee.[22] Claims based upon illegal "tying" arrangements, preferred supplier programs, and horizontal price fixing also are potentially applicable in the franchise context.[23] Counsel for the franchisor must not overlook potentially applicable state antitrust statutes, which may provide different or additional remedies to those available under federal law.

---

21. *See* Volvo Const. Equip. N. Am., Inc. v. CLM Equip. Co., Inc., 386 F.3d 581 (4th Cir. 2004) (there is no breach of the implied covenant of good faith and fair dealing when termination occurred in accordance with the contract); Haynes Trane Serv. Agency, Inc. v. Am. Standard, Inc., 51 Fed. App'x. 786 (10th Cir. 2002) (same); McDonald's Corp. v. Robertson, 147 F.3d 1301 (11th Cir. 1998); *In re* Sizzler Rests. Int'l, Inc., 225 B.R. 466 (Bankr. C.D. Cal. 1998); Wilson v. Amerada Hess Corp., 733 A.2d 1121 (N.J. 2001); Wausau Med. Ctr., S.C. v. Asplund, 514 N.W.2d 34 (Wis. Ct. App. 1994).

22. *See generally* Monsanto Co. v. Spray-Rite Serv. Corp., 465 U.S. 752 (1984).

23. *See generally* Shamrock Mktg., Inc. v. Bridgestone Bandag, LLC, 775 F. Supp. 2d 972 (W.D. Ky. 2011) (tying claim); Little Caesar Enters., Inc. v. Smith, 34 F. Supp. 2d 513 (E.D. Mich. 1998) (tying claim); Ryko Mfg. Co. v. Eden Servs., 832 F.2d 1215 (8th Cir. 1987) (resale price maintenance claim); McCabe's Furniture, Inc. v. La-Z-Boy Chair Co., 798 F.2d 323 (8th Cir. 1986) (resale price maintenance claim); KFC Corp. v. Marion-Kay Co., 620 F. Supp. 1160 (S.D. Ind. 1985) (preferred supplier program); Midwestern Waffles, Inc. v. Waffle House, Inc., 734 F.2d 705 (11th Cir. 1984) (tying claim); Ky. Fried Chicken Corp. v. Diversified Packaging Corp., 549 F.2d 368 (5th Cir. 1977) (preferred supplier program); Chavez v. Whirlpool Corp., 113 Cal. Rptr. 2d 175 (Cal. Ct. App. 2001) (resale price maintenance claim).

Further, while there is no private right of action under the Federal Trade Commission Act,[24] state "Little FTC Acts" or deceptive trade practices acts must be considered. Some state Little FTC Acts provide that any violation of the federal Act constitutes a violation of the state counterpart.[25] Many states also have enacted versions of the Uniform Deceptive Trade Practices Act.[26] Some of these statutes provide for injunctive relief only, not damages.[27] Others permit only the recovery of actual damages.[28] Some provide for recovery of treble damages.[29] Some provide for the recovery of attorneys' fees.[30]

---

24. *See, e.g.*, Kerr v. Am. Home Mortg. Servicing, Inc., No. 10-CV-1612 BEN AJB, 2010 WL 3743879, at *1 (S.D. Cal. Sept. 23, 2010); Fraker v. Bayer Corp., No. CVF08-1564 AWI GSA, 2009 WL 5865687, at *7 (E.D. Cal. Oct. 6, 2009); Am. Airlines v. Christensen, 967 F.2d 410 (10th Cir. 1992); Days Inn of Am. Franchising, Inc. v. Windham, 699 F. Supp. 1581 (N.D. Ga. 1988); Akers v. Bonifasi, 629 F. Supp. 1212 (M.D. Tenn. 1984).

25. *See, e.g.*, Tuckish v. Pompano Motor Co., 337 F. Supp. 2d 1313 (S.D. Fla. 2004); Nieman v. Dryclean U.S.A. Franchise Co., Inc., 178 F.3d 1126 (11th Cir. 1999); Rodopoulos v. Sam Piki Enters., Inc., 570 So. 2d 661 (Ala. 1990), *as modified on denial of reh'g* (Nov. 21, 1990). *But see* Symes v. Bahama Joe's, Inc., Bus. Franchise Guide (CCH) ¶ 9192 (D. Mass. 1988).

26. As of February 2021, 48 states have adopted the Uniform Trade Secrets Act. Michelle Evans, *Proof of Facts to Establish Information as Trade Secret Under Uniform Trade Secrets Act*, 139 Am. Jur. Proof of Facts 3d 241, n.1 (originally published in 2014; February 2021 Update).

27. *See, e.g.*, Minn. Stat. § 325D.45, Subd. 1 (2020); Superior Edge, Inc. v. Monsanto Co., 964 F. Supp. 2d 1017, 1041 (D. Minn. 2013) (stating "[u]nder Minnesota law, the sole statutory remedy for deceptive trade practices is injunctive relief.") (internal quotations omitted).

28. Ariz. Rev. Stat. § 44.1522 (2020); Fla. Stat. § 501.207 (2020); Ind. Code § 24-5-0.5-4 (2020); Kan. Stat. § 50-634 (2019); Me. Rev. Stat. tit. 5, § 213 (2020); Md. Code, Com. Law § 13-408 (2020); Miss. Code § 75-24-15 (2021); Neb. Rev. Stat. § 59-1609 (2020); Okla. Stat. tit. 78, § 54 (2020); S.D. Codified Laws § 37-24-31 (2020); Wyo. Stat. § 40-12-113 (2020). *See also* Mich. Comp. Laws § 445.911 (2020) (greater of $250 or actual); W. Va. Code § 46A-6-106 (2020) (greater of $200 or actual). Some permit the recovery of punitive damages. Cal. Civ. Code § 1780 (2020); Conn. Gen. Stat. § 42-110g (2019); Ga. Code § 10-1-373 (2020); Idaho Code § 48-608 (2020); Ky. Rev. Stat. § 367.220 (2020); Mo. Stat. § 407.025 (2020); Or. Rev. Stat. § 646.638 (2020); 6 R.I. Gen. Laws § 6-13.1-5.2 (2021). *See also* Vt. Stat. tit. 9, § 2461 (2020) (providing punitive damage award not to exceed three times the value given).

29. Ala. Code § 8-19-10 (2016); Alaska Stat. § 45.50.531 (2020); Del. Code tit. 6, § 2533 (2020); La. Stat. § 51:1409 (2020); Mont. Code § 30-14-133 (2019); Nev. Rev. Stat. § 598A.210 (2020); N.H. Rev. Stat. § 358-A:10 (2020); N.J. Stat. § 56:8-19 (2020); N.Y. Gen. Bus. Law § 349 (2020); N.C. Gen. Stat. § 75-16 (2020); N.D. Cent. Code § 51-15-09 (2020); 73 Pa. Stat. and Cons. Stat. § 201-9.2 (2020); S.C. Code § 39-5-140 (2020); Tenn. Code § 47-18-109 (2020); Tex. Bus. & Comm. Code § 17.50 (2020); Wis. Stat. § 100.201 (2020). *See also* Colo. Rev. Stat. § 6-1-113 (2017) (providing greater of $500 or three times actual damages); Haw. Rev. Stat. § 480-13 (2020) (providing greater of $1,000 or three times actual damages); N.M. Stat. § 57-12-10 (2020) (providing greater of $300 or three times actual damages); Utah Code § 13-5-14 (2020) (providing greater of $2,000 or three times actual damages).

30. Del. Code tit. 6, § 2533 (2021); Ind. Code § 24-5-0.5-4 (2020); Kan. Stat. § 50-634 (2019); Md. Code Com. Law. § 13-408 (2020); Mich. Comp. Laws § 445.911 (2020); Minn. Stat. § 325D.45 (2020); Mo. Stat. § 407.025 (2020); Mont. Code § 30-14-133 (2019); Nev. Rev. Stat. § 598A.210 (2020); N.Y. Gen. Bus. Law § 349 (McKinney 2020); N.D. Cent. Code

5-4. Nonrenewal

(a) Differences between Expiration, Nonrenewal, and Termination

Most franchise agreements are contracts for a fixed term running from as little as 5 years to 20 or more years. Many changes can occur during the term of a franchise agreement, with respect to the franchisor's system, the franchisee's performance, and market or competitive conditions. The decision whether and on what terms to renew a franchise agreement, therefore, involves many factors and requires careful business and legal analysis.

Often overlooked in the analysis of "nonrenewal" is the issue of what exactly is a "renewal," what is an "expiration," what is a "rewrite," and what is a "refranchising." Generally, someone who says he or she wants to "renew" something (like a prescription for medicine or his or her wedding vows) generally understands a "renewal" to be a continuance on the same exact terms as before. That person is going to get the exact same medicine and the exact same spouse. In franchising, however, the issue of "renewal" is a more complicated one.

If a franchise agreement has a 20-year term and no renewal rights, the franchisor in most states (New Jersey and Delaware being exceptions) has no obligation to offer another term.[31] This decision is not a "nonrenewal." This is a franchisor allowing an "expiration" and not offering a "new agreement" or a "rewrite." In franchising, for a true nonrenewal decision to occur, there must be a right to a renewal. The franchisee above, unless located in New Jersey or Delaware, has no right to renew. A franchisee with a 10-year initial term and eleven 5-year renewal rights faces the chance of "nonrenewal" every 5 years.

Nonrenewal differs from termination. If a franchise relationship is not renewed, the relationship ends at the expiration of the term specified in the agreement. Nonrenewal occurs pursuant to express contractual language where the franchisee does not have an automatic right to renew the agreement. Termination, on the other hand, involves ending the relationship prior to the end of the bargained-for term and, thus, evokes a forfeiture of the franchisee's contractual rights. Because most modern franchise agreements specify that the franchisee does not have an automatic right to renew, the renewal decision may require the exercise of business discretion by the franchisor. This renewal decision right is often used by the franchisor to require that the franchisee update its franchise with respect to image, method of operation, and competitive circumstances. Assuming

---

§ 51-15-09 (2020); OHIO REV. CODE § 1345.09 (2021); S.C. CODE § 39-5-140 (2020); VT. STAT. tit. 9, § 2461 (2020); W. VA. CODE § 46A-6-106 (2020); WIS. STAT. § 100.201 (2020).

31. *See generally* N.J. STAT. § 56:10-5 (2020); DEL. CODE tit. 6, § 2552 (2021). *See also* Dunkin' Donuts of Am., Inc. v. Middletown Donut Corp., 495 A.2d 66, 76 (N.J. 1985) ("[w]ith the advent of the New Jersey Franchise Practices Act, once a franchise relationship begins, all that a franchisee must do is comply substantially with the terms of the agreement, in return for which he receives the benefit of an 'infinite' franchise—he cannot be terminated or refused renewal.").

that neither the franchise agreement nor any applicable statute requires automatic renewal, the franchisor may have greater flexibility in deciding whether a particular franchisee should be granted another franchise term than it does in deciding whether to end a franchise relationship before the contractual term expires.

The franchisor should begin thinking about its renewal options with respect to its franchisees long before particular franchise agreements begin to expire. This planning process has both "macro" and "micro" elements. From a macro, or system-wide, perspective, the franchisor must decide whether any global changes are appropriate for its agreements or system operation, such as changes in royalty fees or providing for alternative methods of product distribution. From a micro, or particular franchisee, perspective, the franchisor should continually monitor each franchisee's performance throughout the term of the agreement and decide upon what requirements, such as facility upgrades or operational changes, must be met before the franchisor agrees to renew a particular franchisee.

As discussed above with respect to termination decisions, a good practice for the franchisor to establish is a centralized person or committee to review and approve renewal decisions. The factors this person or group might consider would be more business oriented, such as current demographic patterns, current competitive circumstances, long-term business strategies for the franchised system, the franchisee's past performance, and how the particular franchisee fits with the franchisor's future plans for its system. As with termination decisions, the franchisor should make sure that its policies, procedures, and standards are applied consistently throughout the system and that similarly situated franchisees are treated in a consistent manner.

Although termination and nonrenewal are different in many ways, once the franchisor has decided that it does not want to renew a particular franchisee, the franchisor should follow many of the same steps as part of its compliance program before finalizing and acting upon its nonrenewal decision. The place to start is, again, with the franchise agreement to determine what rights and obligations exist with respect to the renewal decision. As with termination, there are also statutory restrictions on the franchisor's nonrenewal rights that must be considered and complied with, where applicable. Further, the franchisor must consider certain common law issues as well as potential legal claims by the franchisee. These issues are discussed below.

(b) Contractual Framework

The most fundamental question in any renewal decision is what rights, if any, the franchisee has under the franchise agreement for an additional term. Most franchise agreements do not grant the franchisee an automatic right to renew, although most contracts might call for renewal provided the franchisee meets certain specified criteria (such as compliance with the franchise agreement and minimum purchase or sales objectives). If the franchise agreement grants a right to renew, either generally or under certain circumstances, the franchisor obviously will have to honor that right absent some material default or failure by the franchisee to meet the required conditions. Failure to do so would subject the franchisor to potential liability for breach of contract.

Some franchise agreements grant the franchisor very broad discretion to make renewal decisions. Agreements often, however, have time frames within which such decisions must be communicated to the franchisee—for example, a certain number of months or years prior to the expiration date. Such a notice requirement allows the franchisee to take appropriate steps to plan for the expiration of the franchise and wind down the relationship; it also gives the franchisor time to evaluate the need for and find a replacement franchisee if appropriate. If a franchise agreement contains a notice requirement, the franchisor must notify the franchisee within the contractually required time, or at least as soon thereafter as any disqualifying event might occur.[32]

Assuming the franchise agreement grants the franchisor discretion to make the renewal decision, the question then arises: what, if any, limits apply to the exercise of that discretion? Where the contract specifically addresses the extent of the franchisor's discretion, courts generally will respect and enforce the terms of the party's bargain. For example, if the agreement provides that the franchisor can decide whether to renew, in its sole and absolute discretion, with or without cause, the franchisor should be able to decide not to renew for any good faith business reason.[33] However, where the franchise agreement provides that consent to renewal by the franchisor cannot be "unreasonably withheld" (or similar qualifying language), the franchisor generally must have a stronger business reason not to renew the particular franchisee. A material default under the franchise agreement most likely would meet this standard, although business reasons solely outside the control of the franchisee might not.

---

32. *See, e.g.*, Burger King Corp. v. Agad, 941 F. Supp. 1217 (N.D. Ga. 1996) (rejecting breach of contract claim by franchisee where the franchisor gave notice of nonrenewal after general contractual notification date but promptly upon disqualifying events by franchisee). *See also* N.I. Petroleum Ventures Corp. v. GLeS, Inc., 333 F. Supp. 2d 251, 257 (D. Del. 2004) (stating that a service station "franchisor seeking to terminate or not to renew a franchise agreement must provide notice to the franchisee in strict compliance with the PMPA.").

33. *See, e.g.*, Gen. Aviation, Inc. v. Cessna Aircraft Co., 915 F.2d 1038 (6th Cir. 1990) (rejecting challenge to nonrenewal where distributorship agreement expressly allowed for nonrenewal without cause); *accord* Hubbard Chevrolet Co. v. Gen. Motors Corp., 873 F.2d 873, 878 (5th Cir. 1989) (reversing jury award to dealer holding that, where contract provided that franchisor had unrestricted authority to approve or disapprove franchise relocation for its own reasons, court could not "reevaluate the wisdom of the parties' decision to leave relocation decisions to GM"). *But cf.* Goldwell of New Jersey, Inc. v. KPSS, Inc., 622 F. Supp. 2d 168, 195 (D.N.J. 2009) (despite language in distributor agreement providing manufacturer with "sole and absolute discretion" to renew or not renew the parties' relationship, "[a] franchisor can in all respects comply with the terms of a franchise agreement, yet violate the NJFPA when it permits a franchise agreement to expire without good cause[.]"); Carvel Corp. v. Baker, 79 F. Supp. 2d 53 (D. Conn. 1997) (despite language in agreement that franchisor had sole discretion to sell through other distribution channels, franchisor had to exercise this discretion reasonably and in good faith).

Whenever a franchise agreement grants discretionary rights to a franchisor in a renewal situation, the implied covenant of good faith and fair dealing comes into play, and counsel for the franchisor must analyze its applicability in a particular situation carefully. As discussed above, the implied covenant applies where one party is vested with discretion in exercising a particular right under the contract, and the doctrine operates to prevent that party from exercising its discretion in bad faith, arbitrarily, or from improper purpose so as not to defeat the other party's reasonable expectations under the contract. This doctrine has been applied to impose liability on a franchisor for refusal to renew a franchisee.[34]

Some courts construe the implied covenant to require that the franchisor's exercise of discretion must be reasonable under the circumstances, which can be an amorphous and uncertain standard.[35] Certainly, the franchisor should not act in subjective bad faith or with an improper motive in exercising its discretion to renew, as to do so would be contrary to the franchisee's reasonable expectations under the contract. In all events, this doctrine is highly fact specific, and counsel for the franchisor should analyze how it has been interpreted in any applicable jurisdictions before making the final renewal decision.

Finally, franchisors should be aware of any specific rights that the franchise agreement provides in connection with the renewal process. Many franchise agreements allow the franchisor to require a new form of agreement (generally an agreement with material changes from the initial agreement) upon renewal, as well as other modifications from the prior relationship, such as upgrades to the franchisee's facility. The franchisor might also consider imposing other requirements on a case-by-case basis, where appropriate, for valid business reasons, such as requiring additional training for marginal operators or relocation of the franchised premises to enhance competitive positioning. In addition, if the franchise agreement's renewal language and applicable law permit, the franchisor should require as part of the renewal application the execution of a release by the franchisee or at least require the franchisee to list all known claims it might have against the franchisor as of that time. Assuming that renewal is at the franchisor's option, and not a matter of right, the franchisor should use this process as an opportunity to update the relationship to the standards required of new franchisees and provide both parties with a fresh start for the renewal term.

(c) Statutory Restrictions on Nonrenewal

As with termination, the franchise agreement is not the only source of rights and duties with respect to the renewal of a franchise. State franchise relationship laws may require a particular form and timing of notice of nonrenewal, and some states

34. *See Payne v. McDonald's Corp., 957 F. Supp. 749 (D. Md. 1997); In re* Vylene Enters., Inc., 90 F.3d 1472 (9th Cir. 1996), *as amended on denial of reh'g and reh'g en banc* (Sept. 12, 1996).

35. *See, e.g.*, 7-Eleven, Inc. v. Dar., 757 N.E.2d 515 (Ill. Ct. App. 2001); *Carvel Corp.*, 79 F. Supp. 2d 53; Infomax Office Sys., Inc. v. MBO Binder & Co. of Am., 976 F. Supp. 1247 (S.D. Iowa 1997); Dayan v. McDonald's Corp., 466 N.E.2d 958 (Ill. App. Ct. 1984).

go so far as to require good cause for the franchisor not to renew the relationship. As discussed in the section regarding termination, the question of which state's law applies to a particular nonrenewal situation is an important, and often dispositive, issue that must be carefully analyzed by counsel for the franchisor.

Some state relationship laws impose only minimum notice requirements for nonrenewal.[36] The length of these notice periods ranges from 60 days to one year. The franchisor must be careful to continue to deal with a nonrenewal franchisee on the same terms and conditions during this notice period or risk liability under contract and/or statute.[37]

At the other end of this spectrum are relationship laws that prohibit the franchisor from not renewing a franchisee absent "good cause." Most of these statutes define "good cause" to be conduct imputable solely to the franchisee, such as failure to comply with a material provision of the franchise agreement.[38] Counsel for the franchisor should also review case law under all potentially applicable statutes to analyze any judicial gloss placed on these general definitions of "good cause." Even when a statute states that it prohibits nonrenewal without good cause, at least one court has determined that an expiration is not a nonrenewal (even though the practical result is the same). See *Betsy-Len Motor Hotel Corp. v. Holiday Inns, Inc.*,[39] where the court held that there was no existing renewal right and, therefore, no nonrenewal, and the "good cause" statute did not apply.

In addition to notice and good cause restrictions, some relationship statutes impose other conditions in the nonrenewal context. For example, some states require that the franchisor repurchase the franchise or its assets where there is a noncompetition provision.[40] Other statutes prohibit the enforcement of noncompetition provisions altogether, at least in certain circumstances.[41] These divergent restrictions underscore the importance of careful review by counsel for the franchisor in connection with any nonrenewal decision. The appendix to this chapter

---

36. States containing minimum notice requirements include Arkansas (90 days), California (180 days), Connecticut (60 days), Delaware (90 days), Illinois (6 months), Indiana (90 days), Iowa (6 months), Minnesota (180 days), Mississippi (90 days), Missouri (90 days), Nebraska (60 days), New Jersey (60 days), Washington (1 year), and Wisconsin (90 days).

37. *See* Am. Bus. Interiors, Inc. v. Haworth, Inc., 798 F.2d 1135 (8th Cir. 1986) (refusal to provide product and pricing information to franchisee during notice period held to be violation of Missouri relationship law).

38. *See, e.g.*, Iowa Code § 523H.7(1) (2021) ("failure of the franchisee to comply with any material lawful requirement of the franchise agreement[.]"); Minn. Stat. § 80C.14, subd. 3(b) (2020) ("failure by the franchisee to substantially comply with the material and reasonable franchise requirements imposed by the franchisor[.]"); N.J. Stat. § 56:10-5 (2020) ("failure by the franchisee to substantially comply with those requirements imposed upon him by the franchise."); Wash. Rev. Code § 19.100.180(2)(j) (2020) ("failure of the franchisee to comply with lawful material provisions of the franchise or other agreement between the franchisor and the franchisee[.]"); Wis. Stat. § 135.02(4)(a) (2020) ("[f]ailure . . . to comply substantially with essential and reasonable requirements[.]").

39. 385 S.E.2d 559 (Va. 1989).

40. *See, e.g.*, Mich. Comp. Laws § 445.1527(d) (2020).

41. *See, e.g.*, Iowa Code § 523H.8.1(b)(3) (2021).

contains a summary of the key renewal provisions of state relationship laws of general applicability to franchising.

Finally, industry-specific statutes almost always contain restrictions on nonrenewal and, generally, expiration or "cancellation" of dealer or distributor agreements. These statutes are generally even more onerous than general franchise relationship laws because contracts in the affected industries are often for very short terms (often one to three years), therefore creating a greater perceived risk of franchisor abuse. Such industry-specific statutes must also be analyzed by franchisor counsel for implementing a nonrenewal decision.

(d) Additional Legal Considerations

A franchisor that has decided that it does not want to renew a franchisee must scrutinize its franchise files and other evidence of past dealings with the franchisee carefully to make sure that its contractual rights have not been waived or modified through the franchisor's conduct or representations. The same type of review discussed earlier with respect to termination decisions should be conducted by counsel for the franchisor to make sure that no such land mines exist.

One significant risk is the possibility of waiver based on the franchisor's failure to insist upon compliance with particular requirements until the time of the renewal decision. Similarly, another risk includes estoppel based upon affirmative representations or failure to take action by the franchisor with respect to particular issues. Of course, the franchisor should be sure to treat similarly situated franchisees consistently. Failure to do so may subject the franchisor to liability by statute in some states or under the implied covenant of good faith and fair dealing in other jurisdictions.

(e) Analyze All Bases for Potential Claims by the Franchisee

Nonrenewal of a franchise, like termination, in most cases takes away the franchisee's current business and livelihood; therefore, it often results in a major dispute and sometimes results in arbitration or litigation. A franchisor should evaluate all potential claims by the nonrenewed franchisee, both factually and legally, before implementing the nonrenewal decision. Understanding the strength of any potential claims by the franchisee is crucial to the negotiating process if a dispute arises. If there is any realistic possibility of exposure, the franchisor can consider whether to negotiate issues such as a buyout, consent to transfer to another franchisee, or a waiver of enforcement of noncompetes to resolve the dispute and avoid litigation. Any settled dispute should come with a full and final release of claims.

The potential claims by a nonrenewed franchisee are generally the same as those discussed earlier with respect to termination. An analysis of contractual and statutory rights and duties should already have been performed prior to reaching this point, and the implied covenant of good faith and fair dealing should also be a part of that analysis. Potential tort claims such as fraud and tortious interference with business relations should also be analyzed. Counsel for the franchisor should also evaluate potential claims under federal or state antitrust statutes, state Little FTC Acts, deceptive trade practices acts, federal or state RICO statutes, and any other potentially applicable federal or state statutes. Franchisors also should consider any mandatory or appropriate voluntary alternative dispute resolution processes as a way to avoid or resolve legal disputes relating to a nonrenewal decision.

In addition, counsel for the franchisor should be aware that some states recognize the common law concept of recoupment, which provides that a franchisee whose agreement is not being renewed must be allowed a reasonable period of time to run its business in order to recoup its investment.[42] Sufficient notice of nonrenewal should avoid this issue, particularly in the case of a long-term franchise agreement where the franchisor can argue that the franchisee has already recouped its investment and obtained the benefit of its bargain.

Finally, the goal of a compliance program for nonrenewal decisions should be the same as it is for terminations—to confirm the validity of the franchisor's grounds for nonrenewal and then to put the franchisor in the best position to defend those grounds or any other claims that might be raised by the franchisee. The nonrenewal analysis should also be conducted with an eye toward whether an objective third party would conclude that the franchisor has acted "fairly" or "reasonably" in reaching and implementing the nonrenewal decision. Meeting the "fairness" or "reasonableness" test will help ensure that the nonrenewal decision both is in the best interest of the franchisor's system and will be upheld against any potential challenge.

5-5. Transfer

The legal parameters of the relationship between a franchisor and a franchisee are defined by the franchise agreement and applicable law. The franchisor's initial decision to grant a franchise to a particular franchisee, however, is based on numerous criteria such as the franchisee's personal characteristics, particular business skills, and financial capabilities. At the inception of the franchise relationship, the franchisor and franchisee envision entering into a long-term contractual relationship with one another for the mutual benefit of both parties. However, many foreseeable and unforeseeable events can occur that make the possibility of a long-term contractual relationship no longer desirable or feasible. Some of these events are discussed in the preceding sections on termination and nonrenewal. This section addresses issues surrounding the proposed transfer of a franchise agreement.

---

42. *See, e.g.*, Ramada Franchise Sys., Inc. v. Capitol View II Ltd. P'ship Venture, 132 F. Supp. 2d 358 (D. Md. 2001); Sofa Gallery, Inc. v. Stratford Co., 872 F.2d 259 (8th Cir. 1989); Schultz v. Onan Corp., 737 F.2d 339 (3d Cir. 1984).

(a) Transfer by the Franchisor

Most franchise agreements provide that a franchisor may transfer or assign a franchise agreement without the franchisee's consent. The granting of such broad authority to the franchisor is reasonable considering that during the term of any given franchise agreement, a franchisor may go through transactions such as corporate restructuring, refinancing, recapitalization, merger, or buy-out that will not materially affect what the franchisee bargained for when entering into the franchise agreement. In most situations, it would be unduly burdensome and impractical to require the franchisor to obtain each franchisee's consent. Therefore, to avoid delaying and/or jeopardizing the franchisor's corporate actions designed for the benefit of the entire system, the franchise agreements generally provide that the franchisor may freely transfer or assign the franchise agreement.[43]

(b) Transfer by the Franchisee

Disillusionment with the system, inability to manage and/or operate the franchise, necessity, and retirement are some of the numerous reasons franchisees may desire to transfer their franchise agreements or franchise businesses. The following outlines some examples of situations that constitute a "transfer" under most franchise agreements, as well as reasons franchisees might want to transfer their franchise agreements or franchise businesses.

(i) Transfer for the Convenience of Ownership

Frequently, an individual enters into a franchise agreement and subsequently seeks to transfer ownership of the franchise to a corporation, limited liability company, or other entity for reasons such as minimizing the individual's potential liability to third parties. The franchisor, on the other hand, may be concerned that the franchise may be transferred to a "shell" entity and may require proof that the proposed entity is adequately funded and that transfers of interests in the entity are subject to the transfer provisions of the franchise agreement. Most franchisors also require the original franchisee/owners to guarantee the entity's performance of the obligations under the franchise agreement, including payment of all amounts owed.

(ii) Transfer as a Work-Out Option

A financially or operationally troubled franchisee may view a transfer of the franchise agreement as a last chance to salvage part of its initial and ongoing investment in a franchise. This option is usually preferable for a franchisor because it allows a franchisor to transition out a troubled franchisee without having to

---

43. Courts have held that franchisors generally have the legal right to transfer franchise agreements. *See generally* Marc's Big Boy Corp. v. Marriott Corp., Bus. Franchise Guide (CCH) ¶ 9100 (E.D. Wis. 1988). *See also* May-Som Gulf, Inc. v. Chevron U.S.A., Inc., 869 F.2d 917 (6th. Cir. 1989).

terminate a franchise agreement and create a risk of litigation. Another advantage to the franchisor is that a transfer under this scenario usually provides for the uninterrupted transition of the franchise business and continuation of the revenue stream.

(iii) Transfer as an Early Exit Option

A franchisee may desire to exit a system before the expiration of the franchise agreement term. The reasons for the premature departure vary and include, but are not limited to, a franchisee's illness, retirement, or desire for a career change. A transfer of the franchise agreement allows a franchisee to avoid breaching the franchise agreement and provides the franchisee the opportunity to recoup some or all of its investment in the system and, in many cases, earn a profit on the sale. The franchisor benefits by acquiring a more engaged business partner and avoiding the business interruption that would otherwise be experienced should the franchisee merely walk away from the franchise agreement and cease operation of the franchise.

(iv) Transfer Due to Changes in the Effective Control of an Entity Franchisee

Any change in the effective control of an entity franchisee due to the sale of assets, shares, and so on can result in a transfer situation. Some franchise agreements define a transfer as the sale or transfer of a certain percentage or more of the ownership interests in the entity franchisee.

(v) Transfer as a Business Strategy

Occasionally, a franchisee may enter into a franchise agreement that, for whatever reason, did not make good business sense. It might be that the franchisee was undercapitalized for an additional franchise, or that an additional franchise spread the franchisee over too many markets. The transfer of the franchise agreement can be a viable business strategy in these instances for both the franchisee and the franchisor.

(vi) Transfer Due to Death or Disability

Most franchise agreements provide that upon the death or disability of a franchisee or principal owner of an entity franchisee, the executor, administrator, or personal representative of the franchisee is required to transfer the franchise agreement. Such transfers must be to a transferee that is qualified to operate the franchise or completes appropriate training.

(vii) Transfer Due to Offering by Franchisee

Much like changes in effective control, a public or private offering of stock in an entity franchisee may result in a transfer situation. Some franchise agreements prohibit public offerings and, alternatively, if they are permitted, require that the franchisee pay a nonrefundable fee to the franchisor to defray the franchisor's costs and expenses associated with reviewing the proposed offering.

(viii) Transfer to a Family Member

Often a franchisee seeks to transfer a franchise agreement to a family member for purposes of estate planning, inheritance, or otherwise. Generally, the franchisor will reserve the right to request that the family member be capable of performing the duties and obligations of the original franchisee and complete the required training.

(ix) Transfers Due to Offers by Third Parties

A franchisee that receives an offer to sell its interest in the franchise to a third party may seek to transfer the franchise agreement. Frequently, franchisors will include a "right of first refusal" provision, or at least a review and approval requirement, in the franchise agreement to address these situations.

(c) Contractual Framework

Most franchise agreements include contractual provisions similar to the following relating to transfer rights.

(i) Personal Relationships

Most franchise agreements contain provisions acknowledging that the initial decision of the franchisor to sell a franchise to the original franchisee was based upon the personal characteristics of the franchisee, including the franchisee's business skill and financial capabilities. For example, the agreement might provide that "Franchisee and Franchisee's Principals understand and acknowledge that the right and duties set forth in this Agreement are personal to Franchisee and that the [Franchisor] has granted this franchise in reliance on the business skill, financial capacity, and personal character of Franchisee and Franchisee's Principals," or that "Franchisor intends to rely upon the personal leadership and financial commitment of the Franchisee to the business of the Unit, and may require the Franchisee to retain absolute control over the decisions relating thereto." These types of provisions are important to show that the franchisor is entitled to, and in fact does, exercise discretion to ensure that only properly qualified persons or entities are allowed to become franchisees.

(ii) Transfers Defined

Most franchise agreements provide a very broad definition of what constitutes a transfer of the franchise. For example, consider the following provision:

> *Assignment.* Franchisee will not sublicense, sell, assign, transfer, convey, or encumber its rights and obligations hereunder or suffer or permit any such assignment, transfer, or encumbrance to occur by operation of law without the prior express written consent of Franchisor. In the event Franchisee is a corporation, limited partnership, business trust, partnership,

or similar association, the shareholder, limited partners, beneficiaries, partners, or investors, as the case may be, may not sell, assign, or otherwise transfer their shares or interests in such corporation, limited partnership, business trust, partnership, or similar association, without the prior written consent of Franchisor. Furthermore, in the event that any shareholder or partner of Franchisee (the "Shareholder") is a corporation, limited partnership, business trust, partnership, or similar association, the interests of the shareholders, limited partners, trustees, beneficiaries, partners, or investors, as the case may be, in such Shareholder, may not be sold, assigned, or otherwise transferred, without the prior written consent of Franchisor. In the event Franchisee (or a Shareholder) is a corporation, all stock certificates of Franchisee or Shareholder, as the case may be, shall have conspicuously endorsed upon them a legend in substantially the following form:

> A transfer of this stock is subject to the terms and conditions of [Franchisor's] Franchise Agreement dated the ______ day of _______________, 20____.

Provisions addressing death and disability, third-party offers, and so on are usually set forth in separate provisions in the transfer section of a franchise agreement. Of course, such contractual definitions of a transfer also could be subject to the definition of and other restrictions imposed upon transfer by applicable state franchise relationship laws.

(iii) Transfer Subject to Franchisor's Prior Written Consent

It would be hard to find a franchise agreement that does not provide that all transfers are subject to the franchisor's prior written consent. In fact, most franchise agreements provide that a transfer without the prior written consent of the franchisor is both invalid and grounds for the default or immediate termination of the franchise agreement, using language such as "[a]ny purported assignment or transfer, by operation of law or otherwise, not having the written consent of Franchisor, will be null and void, and constitutes a material breach of this Agreement, for which Franchisor may then terminate without opportunity to cure."

Most franchise agreements grant broad discretion to the franchisor to approve or refuse its consent to a transfer request. This broad discretion sometimes runs afoul of the statutory and common law restrictions on the franchisor's discretion to approve or disapprove a transfer. Further, some franchise agreements provide that the franchisor will not unreasonably withhold its consent to a transfer, which can also effectively limit the bases on which a franchisor can refuse a transfer request. Some franchise agreements go even further and do not permit any assignment or transfer of the franchise agreement. Consider, for example, the following provision: "The Unit Operator may not assign this Agreement to any person or entity and the Unit Operator further may not assign his estate or interest in or sublet the Sites, or mortgage, pledge, or otherwise encumber his interest in this Agreement or the Sites." These restrictions are also subject to applicable state relationship laws, which are discussed below.

(iv) Conditions for Consent

Franchise agreements generally include the requirements that must be met as a condition for franchisor's approval of a transfer. These requirements serve to protect the franchisor's rights and interests by fully and finally concluding the relationship with its existing franchisee and setting the most appropriate terms for the relationship with its new franchisee. The franchisor might require some or all of the following:

- The franchisee must be current on all accrued monetary obligations owed to the franchisor.
- The transferee must execute the franchisor's then-current form of franchise agreement, the term of which may expire on the date of the original franchise agreement or may include a new term.
- The transferee must meet the franchisor's then-current criteria for new franchisees, including capital and liquidity requirements.
- The franchisee must agree to remain bound by the post-termination covenants of the franchise agreement.
- The franchisee must sign a general release of the franchisor.
- The transferee must agree to complete facility upgrades, reimage requirements, and/or renovations.
- The transferee must complete the required training then in effect for new franchises.
- The transferee or transferor must pay the training fee or other payment to reimburse the franchisor for its reasonable costs and fees associated with training the transferee and reviewing the request to transfer, including, but not limited to, legal and accounting fees.
- The franchisee must pay a transfer fee to the franchisor, which may be in lieu of a new initial franchise fee.
- The transferee must be of good moral character and reputation and must have a business background satisfactory to the franchisor, including but not limited to a good credit rating.
- The transferee must assume all the obligations of the franchisee under the franchise agreement.
- The franchisor may require that the franchisee execute a written guarantee of the transferee's obligations under the franchise agreement, which may be for the life of the franchise agreement or for a limited period of time.
- The franchisee must not be in default of any of the material terms and conditions of the franchise agreement.

The franchisor should consider requiring that a franchisee seeking to transfer the franchise agreement enter into some sort of formal agreement that documents compliance with the franchisor's requirements. A sample transfer and release agreement is attached as form 5-7. These requirements are also subject to the provisions of the applicable state relationship laws, which are discussed below.

(v) Miscellaneous Provisions

Some franchise agreements also include the following miscellaneous provisions that address specific issues relating to transfers.

Nonwaiver. In order to avoid claims that the franchisor has granted its approval of a transfer by accepting payment of royalty or other fees from the proposed transferee, some franchise agreements include express nonwaiver provisions, such as "[a]cceptance by Franchisor of any royalty fee, advertising fee, or any other amount accruing hereunder from any third party, including, but not limited to, any proposed transferee, does not constitute franchisor's approval of such party as a transferee or the transfer of this Franchise Agreement to such party."

Right of first refusal. Many franchise agreements provide that before a franchisee may accept a bona fide offer from a third party to purchase the franchisee's interest in the franchise agreement or the assets used in the operation of the franchise business, the franchisee must provide the franchisor with a right of first refusal. For example, one franchisor's agreement provides as follows:

> If Franchisee or any owner of an interest in Franchisee receives and desires to accept any bona fide offer to Transfer all or any part of his, her, or its Interest in this Agreement or in Franchisee, and the intended Transfer is not a gift to a spouse or a direct descendant, Franchisee or the proposed transferor will submit to [Franchisor] an executed copy of the agreement for Transfer (which will be conditioned on this right of first refusal). [Franchisor] may, within 30 days after receipt of a signed copy of the agreement and all necessary supporting documentation (including financial statements), send written notice to the transferor that [Franchisor] (or a person designated by [Franchisor]) intends to purchase the Interest which is proposed to be Transferred on the same terms and conditions (or, at [Franchisor]'s election, the reasonable cash equivalent, not including the value of any tax benefits, of any noncash consideration) offered by the third party. Any material change in the terms of an agreement before closing will constitute a new agreement, subject to the same right of first refusal by [Franchisor] (or its designee) as in the case of the initial agreement. [Franchisor]'s failure to exercise its right of first refusal will not constitute a waiver of any other provision of this Agreement, including any of the requirements of this Section with respect to approval of the proposed transferee.

Deal terms between franchisee and proposed transferee subject to franchisor's approval. To assure that a proposed transferee is not undercapitalized or otherwise financially disadvantaged at the outset, a franchise agreement may provide that the terms and conditions of the deal between the franchisee and the proposed transferee are subject to the franchisor's approval. For example, as a prerequisite to transfer, a franchisor's agreement may provide as follows:

> We must not have disapproved the material terms and conditions of such transfer (including the price and terms of payment and the amount to be financed by the transferee in connection with such transfer, which will not, in any event, exceed 75 percent of the purchase price of the assets or stock to be transferred) on the basis that they are so burdensome as to be likely, in our judgment, to adversely affect the transferee's operation of your [unit] or its compliance with its franchise agreements, any area development agreements, and any other agreements being transferred.

Death or disability of the franchisee. The death or disability of a franchisee presents a unique transfer situation. Frequently, the death or disability of the franchisee is sudden and/or unexpected, thereby complicating the transfer dynamics. A franchise agreement ordinarily will provide a specified period of time within which the executor, administrator, or personal representative of the franchisee must transfer the franchisee's interest in the franchise agreement and/or assets used in the operation of the franchise business. Some franchise agreements provide that if the proposed transfer is to a descendent, heir, or legatee of the franchisee, the proposed transferee must be capable of performing the duties and obligations of the franchise agreement. In some instances, the franchise agreement will provide for the uninterrupted operation of the unit, such as the following:

> Until such transfer has been consummated in accordance with the provisions of this Article [XX], Franchisor shall have the right, but not the obligation, to assume direct management control of the Restaurant on an interim basis, including, without limitation, installing representatives of Franchisor, at Franchisee's expense.

(d) Statutory Restrictions on the Franchisor's Right to Approve or Disapprove a Transfer

Many of the same state relationship laws that impose restrictions on the franchisor's rights regarding termination and nonrenewal also impose certain limitations on the franchisor's right to approve or disapprove a transfer request. Some states have included such restrictions on the franchisor's transfer rights in their franchise relationship statutes.[44] These statutes contain a variety of different provisions that a franchisor must comply with to process a transfer request, ranging from the requirement of "good cause" for disapproval to merely requiring written notice of approval or disapproval within a specified period. As with termination and nonrenewal, counsel for the franchisor must be fully familiar with the

44. The statutes are as follows: Ark. Code § 4-72-205 (2020); Cal. Bus. & Prof. Code § 20027 (2017); Haw. Rev. Stat. § 482E-6(2)(I) (2020); Ind. Code § 23-2-2.7-2(3) (2020); Iowa Code § 523H.5 (2021); Mich. Comp. Laws § 445.1527 (2020); Minn. Stat. § 80C.14(5) (2020); Neb. Rev. Stat. § 87-405 (2020); N.J. Stat. § 56:10-6 (2020); Wash. Rev. Code § 19.100.180(1), 2(h) (2020).

requirements of these statutes and evaluate their applicability as part of its compliance program regarding transfers.

Hawaii and Michigan's franchise statutes contain explicit provisions prohibiting a franchisor from refusing to permit a transfer of ownership of a franchise except for good cause. Both of these statutes define good cause to include:

- failure of a proposed transferee to meet any of the franchisor's reasonable qualifications or standards then in effect for franchisees,
- the fact that a proposed transferee or affiliate is a competitor of the franchisor,
- the unwillingness of the proposed transferee to agree in writing to comply with all lawful obligations imposed by the franchise, and
- failure of the transferor franchisee or proposed transferee to pay all sums owing to the franchisor and to cure any default under the franchise agreement or other agreements with the franchisor existing at the time of the proposed transfer.[45]

Both of these statutes provide that good cause is not limited to these factors, although a franchisor would put itself at significant risk in these states by rejecting a proposed transferee under circumstances where none of the statutory factors apply.

While they do not contain the words "good cause," the relationship laws of Minnesota and Washington reach substantially the same result by requiring that the franchisor must not "unreasonably withhold consent" to any transfer where the proposed transferee meets the current qualifications and standards required by the franchisor of its other franchisees. This more nebulous standard is subject to greater interpretation and is somewhat analogous to the general commercial reasonableness standard applied by some courts to claims based on the implied covenant of good faith and fair dealing.[46] Some courts have construed the term "unreasonably" to require a legitimate business reason before the franchisor can disapprove a transfer.[47] Thus, as a practical matter, under these statutes a franchisor

---

45. *See, e.g.*, Haw. Rev. Stat. § 482e-6(2)(I) (2020); Mich. Comp. Laws § 445.1527(g) (2020). *See also* Franchise Mgmt. Unlimited v. Am.'s Favorite Chicken, 561 N.W.2d 123, 242 (Mich. Ct. App. 1997) (noting that the list of examples of good cause in the statute are not exhaustive and "[t]he good cause requirement centers on commercial reasonability.").

46. *See, e.g.*, Dayan v. McDonald's Corp., 466 N.E. 2d 958 (Ill. App. Ct. 1984). *See also* VW Credit, Inc. v. Coast Auto. Grp., Ltd., 787 A.2d 951, 958 (N.J. Super. Ct. App. Div. 2002) (stating that the New Jersey courts "have previously interpreted [the New Jersey Franchise Practices Act] to impose a requirement of reasonableness on a franchisor's decision to disapprove a transfer."); Sun Refining & Mktg. Co. v. Brooks-Maupin Car Ctrs. Inc., Bus. Franchise Guide (CCH) ¶ 9325 (E.D. Mich. 1998) (upholding franchisor's transfer refusal based on transferee's lack of experience in the industry where the franchise agreement allowed the franchisor to refuse an assignment for "reasonable and objective business practices and standards.").

47. *Compare, e.g.,* Dunkin' Donuts Inc. v. Sharif, Inc., 177 Fed. Appx. 809 (10th Cir. 2006) (holding the franchisor acted reasonably in withholding consent to transfer when the proposed transferee is a franchisee currently in default of its existing franchise agreement) *and* Zuckerman v. McDonald's Corp., 35 F. Supp. 2d 135 (D. Mass. 1999) (requiring

should have a strong business reason, similar to the good cause factors referenced above, to support disapproval of a transfer request.

The relationship statutes in California, Indiana, and Iowa expressly provide that the surviving spouse or heirs of a franchisee (or sometimes the majority shareholder of the franchisee) must be allowed to continue operating the franchise for a reasonable time after the death of the franchisee, provided that the acquiring party meets the franchisor's then-current standards.[48]

The relationship laws of Arkansas, Nebraska, and New Jersey take a different approach. These statutes require the franchisor to respond to a written request for a transfer within 60 days, and if not, approval is deemed granted. If the franchisor rejects the proposed transfer, the franchisor must state in writing the material reasons relating to the character, financial ability, or business experience of the proposed transferee that form the basis for the denial.[49]

Finally, it should be noted that the relationship laws in Iowa and California are by far the most detailed and restrictive statutes of any state.[50] The Iowa statute incorporates to some degree each of the restrictions discussed above, including that the franchisor must approve a transferee that satisfies the reasonable current qualifications of the franchisor for its new franchisees. These qualifications must be based upon legitimate business reasons. The Iowa statute also includes a written notice requirement, an express nondiscrimination provision, and a limitation on enforcement of restrictive covenants. Significantly, the Iowa law defines a transfer as *not* including, among other things, succession of ownership upon death of a franchisee, incorporation of a franchisee, public offering or transfer to an employee stock ownership plan of less than a 50 percent interest in the franchise, and the granting of a security interest in the franchised business or assets under certain circumstances. Franchisors dealing with Iowa-based franchisees obviously must carefully review the provisions of this statute in evaluating any transfer request.

Perhaps the most significant change in franchise law over the last few years with regard to terminations, nonrenewals, and transfers has occurred in California. In 2016, the California Franchise Relations Act was amended and, among other things, now places significant restrictions upon a franchisor's ability to prevent a franchisee from selling or transferring the franchise provided the purchaser is qualified under the franchisor's standards for the approval of new or renewing franchisees and the franchisee and transferee are not in violation of the transfer conditions specified in the transfer agreement. This does not affect the franchisor's right of first refusal as outlined in the franchise agreement. The

---

transferee to make updates to restaurant were not unreasonable) *with* Richter v. Dairy Queen of S. Arizona, Inc., 643 P.2d 508 (Ariz. Ct. App. 1982) (holding that franchisor's refusal to approve transfer was unreasonable where proposed transferees were experienced businesspersons qualified to operate franchise).

48. Cal. Bus. & Prof. Code § 20027 (2017); Ind. Code § 23-2-2.7-2(3) (2020); Iowa Code § 523H.5(12)(a) (2021).

49. Ark. Code § 4-72-205(b) (2020); Neb. Rev. Stat. § 87-405 (2020); N.J. Stat. § 56:10-6 (2020).

50. Iowa Code § 523H.5 (2021); Cal. Bus. & Prof. Code § 20027 (2017).

amended law is applicable to franchise agreements (1) entered into or renewed on or after January 1, 2016, and (2) to franchises of an indefinite duration that may be terminated by the franchisee or franchisor without cause.

(e) Common Law Restrictions on a Franchisor's Approval or Disapproval of a Transfer Request

Even in the absence of statutory restrictions, a franchisor must be aware of potential common law limitations on its discretion to approve or disapprove a transfer request. Where the franchise agreement requires that the franchisor must not unreasonably withhold its consent, the franchisor generally must have a legitimate business reason to disapprove a transfer. Courts have held the following to constitute legitimate business reasons to disapprove a proposed transferee:

- lack of business experience,[51]
- lack of adequate capitalization,[52]
- too many existing franchise locations to service adequately the prospective new location,[53]
- poor performance by the prospective transferee in the same or similar business,[54]
- sale by the proposed transferee of a competitive product or service,[55] and
- a proposed transferee's criminal record.[56]

Franchisees sometimes also attempt to assert claims for tortious interference with actual or prospective contractual relations in response to a franchisor's disapproval of a prospective transferee.[57] These claims usually are unsuccessful, however, because to be unlawful the interference must be by "improper means," and the franchisor generally has a legal privilege to act to protect its own business interests.[58] Courts also have rejected tortious interference claims on the theory that because the franchisor had the contractual right to approve any transfer request, the franchisor could not have been a "stranger" or third party to the actual or pro-

---

51. *See* Amoco Oil Co. v. Luehrs, 465 A.2d 1192 (Md. Ct. Spec. App. 1983); Sun Refining & Mktg. Co. v. Brooks-Maupin Car Ctrs. Inc., Bus. Franchise Guide (CCH) ¶ 9325 (E.D. Mich. 1998); *Town & Country Ford, Inc.*, Bus. Franchise Guide (CCH) ¶ 8660 (N.D. Ga. 1985).

52. *See In re Pioneer Ford Sales, Inc., 729 F.2d 27 (1st Cir. 1984); Town & Country Ford, Inc.*, Bus. Franchise Guide (CCH) ¶ 8660.

53. *See* Carter Equip. Co. v. John Deere Indus. Equip. Co., 681 F.2d 386 (5th Cir. 1982).

54. *See* Dunkin' Donuts Inc., 177 Fed. Appx. 809; Phila. Fast Foods, Inc. v. Popeye's Famous Fried Chicken, Inc., 647 F. Supp. 216 (E.D. Pa. 1986).

55. *See* Brittain v. Stroh Brewery Co., 991 F.2d 787 (4th Cir. 1993); Hawkins v. Holiday Inns, Inc., 634 F.2d 342 (6th Cir. 1980); Bishay v. Foreign Motors, Inc., 616 N.E.2d 96 (Mass. 1993); Rickel v. Schwinn Bicycle Co., 192 Cal. Rptr. 732 (Cal. Ct. App. 1983).

56. *See* Burger King Corp. v. H&H Rests., LLC, No. 99-2855, 2001 WL 1850888 (S.D. Fla. Nov. 30, 2001); Carrozza v. Webber Chevrolet Co., No. 75-0009, 1978 WL 1328, at *1 (D.R.I. Mar. 1, 1978); Horn v. Mazda Motors of Am., Inc., 265 N.J. Super. 47 (N.J. Sup. Ct. 1993).

57. *See, e.g.*, KMS Rest. Corp. v. Wendy's Int'l, Inc., 362 F.3d 1321 (11th Cir. 2004).

58. *See, e.g.*, Enfield Equip. Co. v. John Deere Co., 64 F. Supp. 2d 483 (D. Md. 1999).

spective contract between the franchisee and the proposed transferee.[59] Thus, if the franchisor has a legitimate business justification for disapproving the requested transfer, a tortious interference claim generally should not be successful.

Further, courts have generally held that a proposed transferee (for example, the buyer in a proposed sale transaction) does *not* have standing to challenge a franchisor's refusal to approve a proposed transfer.[60] Generally only the transferor (the seller) has a contractual claim against the franchisor for such a refusal to permit a transfer.

Finally, absent a contrary relationship statute, courts generally uphold reasonable contractual conditions and requirements relating to approval of transfers. For example, courts have upheld contractual provisions stating that the franchisor may withhold its consent to a transfer with or without cause.[61] In addition, a franchisor may generally require the transferring franchisee to execute a general release of the franchisor as a condition to approval of the transfer.[62] Where a relationship law might restrict the ability to require such a release, the franchisor should make sure that it does not release the transferring franchisee as part of approving the transaction. A franchisor also generally will be allowed to require the transferee to execute a new agreement in the franchisor's then-current form, although some state relationship laws also may contain restrictions on this contractual right as well. Where it is not prohibited from doing so, a franchisor should take advantage of these and other reasonable terms and conditions in order to update and upgrade its franchise systems in connection with approving transfer requests.

---

59. *See, e.g.*, K.P Foods, Inc. v. McDonald's Corp., 420 F. Supp. 2d 966, 968 (E.D. Ark. 2006) (finding that because any transfer was subject to the franchisor's approval, the franchisor was a necessary party to the contract, and a party to the contract cannot be held liable for interference); Hall v. Burger King Corp., 912 F. Supp. 1509, Bus. Franchise Guide (CCH) ¶ 10,799 (S.D. Fla. 1995). *See also* Pasqualetti v. Kia Motors Am., Inc., 663 F. Supp. 2d 586 (N.D. Ohio 2009); Cook v. Little Caesar Enters., Inc., 210 F.3d 653 (6th Cir. 2000).

60. *See, e.g.*, Horn v. Mazda Motor of Am., Inc., 625 A.2d 548 (N.J. Super. Ct. App. Div. 1993); Superlease Rent-A-Car, Inc. v. Budget Rent-A-Car of Md., No. CIV.A. 89-0300 (RCL), 1989 WL 39393, at *1 (D.D.C. Apr. 13, 1989); Genet Co. v. Anheuser-Busch, Inc., 498 So. 2d 683 (Fla. Dist. Ct. App. 1986). *But see* VW Credit, Inc. v. Coast Auto. Grp., Ltd., 787 A.2d 951 (N.J. Super. Ct. App. Div. 2002) (proposed transferee had standing to compel transfer under the New Jersey Franchise Practices Act); Don Rose Oil Co. v. Lindsley, 206 Cal. Rptr. 670 (Cal. Ct. App. 1984).

61. *See, e.g.*, Larese v. Creamland Dairies, Inc., 767 F.2d 716, 718 (10th Cir. 1985) (stating "[w]e do not hold that a provision which expressly grants to the franchisor an absolute right to refuse to consent is unenforceable when such an agreement was freely negotiated.").

62. *See, e.g.*, Am.'s Favorite Chicken Co. v. Suryoutomo, 889 F. Supp. 916 (E.D. La. 1995); Brock v. Entre Computer Ctrs., Inc., 933 F.2d 1253 (4th Cir. 1991); Wells v. Entre Computer Ctrs., Inc., 915 F.2d 1566 (4th Cir. 1990).

5-6. Conclusion

Termination, nonrenewal, and transfer decisions often give rise to disputes and litigation within franchise systems. Where properly monitored and consistently enforced, policies and procedures addressing such issues will help minimize the risk of liability. To develop a solid compliance program, franchisors must identify their business objectives and establish policies and procedures accordingly; effectively communicate those policies and procedures throughout the system; and, finally, consistently monitor and enforce those standards throughout the franchise system. While it is important to remember that no system is immune to problems stemming from terminations, nonrenewals, and transfer decisions, franchisors that have developed a sound compliance program will reduce the risk of disputes and will be more likely to prevail in the event of litigation.

Appendix 5-1
Summary of State Franchise Relationship Laws regarding Termination and Nonrenewal

[Editor's note: This appendix presents only a summary of the laws. In practice, reference to the actual statute is necessary, as these laws may be industry-specific, contain exceptions, have been modified, or be otherwise inapplicable to a particular transaction.]

Arkansas: Arkansas Franchise Practices Act

(ARK. CODE ANN. §§ 4-72-201 to 4-72-210 (2020).)

Termination—Good cause required.

Definition of "good cause":

(i) Franchisee fails to comply substantially with nondiscriminatory standards imposed or sought to be imposed;

(ii) Franchisee fails to act in good faith and commercially reasonable manner;

(iii) Voluntary abandonment by Franchisee;

(iv) Criminal conviction of Franchisee;

(v) Franchisee impairment of trademark or trade name;

(vi) Insolvency or bankruptcy of Franchisee;

(vii) Either party's loss of right to occupy franchise property; *OR*

(viii) Outstanding debt to Franchisor not paid within ten days of past due notice.

Nonrenewal—Franchisor must renew, unless:

(i) Has good cause, *OR*

(ii) Refusal is in accordance with its current policies, practices, and standards that in their establishment, operation, or application are not arbitrary or capricious.

Notice

When Required—90 days for termination or nonrenewal, including 30 days to cure before termination. If reason for termination or nonrenewal is repeated deficiencies within 12-month period giving rise to good cause, only 10 days' notice need be given.

When Not Required—If reason for termination is "good cause" items (iii)–(viii) above.

Franchisee's Remedies

(i) *Treble Damages for Fraud*—If Franchisee is harmed by a misleading or fraudulent scheme, Franchisee may recover treble damages, reasonable attorneys' fees, costs of litigation, and injunctive relief.

(ii) *Actual Damages for Other Violations*—For other harms to Franchisee due to Franchisor's violations, Franchisee may recover damages, including costs and attorneys' fees and/or obtain injunctive relief.

(iii) *Repurchase Obligation*—For termination without good cause, Franchisor must, at Franchisee's option, repurchase inventory, supplies, equipment, and furnishings purchased from Franchisor or supplier designated by Franchisor.

Other

Criminal Penalties—Fraud by Franchisor punishable as a "Class B" felony.

California: California Franchise Relations Act

(CAL. BUS. & PROF. CODE §§ 20000 to 20043 (2017).)

Termination—Termination may be on either:

(i) Good cause; *OR*

Definition of "good cause"—Includes Franchisee's failure to comply with any lawful requirement of the Franchise Agreement, after being given notice thereof and a reasonable opportunity to cure.

For Franchise Agreements entered into or renewed on or after January 1, 2016, or to franchises of an indefinite duration, "good cause" is limited to Franchisee's failure to substantially comply with any lawful requirement of the Franchise Agreement, after being given at least 60 days' notice and at least 60 days to cure.

(ii) Reasonable grounds.

Definition of "reasonable grounds"—If any of the following occur and is relevant to the franchise, Franchisor has "reasonable grounds" to give notice of immediate termination without a cure period: Franchisee insolvency, abandonment by Franchisee, mutual agreement, material misrepresentation or conduct by Franchisee that reflects unfavorably on franchise system, noncompliance with law following 10 days' notice, repeated noncompliance with Franchise Agreement, foreclosure on Franchisee or premises, criminal conviction, failure to pay franchise fees after five days' notice that fees are overdue, or danger to public health or safety.

Nonrenewal—Franchisor must renew, *UNLESS* gives 180 days' notice *AND* one of the following:

(i) Franchisee is permitted during 180 days' notice period to sell to a purchaser that meets Franchisor's then-current requirements for granting new or renewal franchises;

(ii) Refusal to renew is not for conversion of premises for operation by Franchisor *AND* noncompetition covenant is not enforced;

(iii) Termination would be permitted under "good cause" or "reasonable grounds" above;

(iv) Mutual agreement;

(v) Franchisor is withdrawing from geographic market *AND* does not enforce noncompetition covenant *AND* refusal to renew is not for conversion of premises for operation by Franchisor *AND* if Franchisor owns interest in premises, it either offers Franchisee a right of first refusal on such interest or its assignee offers Franchisee a franchise on substantially similar terms; *OR*

(vi) Franchisor offers renewal on substantially the same terms as it customarily offers renewal franchises (or new franchises if it is not then granting a significant number of renewals) AND Franchisor and Franchisee cannot agree on the terms of renewal AND Franchisor gives 30 days' notice that if its renewal offer is not accepted, the franchise will not be renewed.

Notice

(i) Termination—Termination for good cause requires sufficient notice to give Franchisee a reasonable opportunity to cure. Termination on reasonable grounds may be immediate.

(ii) Nonrenewal—180 days.

Franchisee's Remedies

(i) *Repurchase Obligation*—For termination or nonrenewal in violation of law, Franchisor must offer to repurchase current inventory that is required by Franchise Agreement or commercial practice.

(ii) For Franchise Agreements entered into or renewed on or after January 1, 2016, or to franchises of an indefinite duration that may be terminated by the franchisee or franchisor without cause:

(a) *Repurchase Obligation on Lawful Termination or Nonrenewal*—For termination or nonrenewal in violation of law, Franchisor must offer to repurchase Franchisee's inventory, supplies, equipment, and fixtures purchased under Franchise Agreement for value of price paid minus depreciation current inventory that is required by Franchise Agreement or commercial practice.

(b) *Repurchase Obligation on Unlawful Termination or Nonrenewal*—Franchisee entitled to the fair market value of the franchised business and its assets, and Franchisee may be entitled to other damages.

(iii) *Other Rights*—Franchisee not precluded from exercising other legal rights.

Dispute Settlement

Arbitration—Agreements to arbitrate are enforceable as long as standards applied in arbitration are not less than required by California Franchise Relations Act and arbitrators are chosen from list of an impartial body.

Venue—Provision in Franchise Agreement restricting venue to forum outside California is void. This particular provision was determined to be preempted by the Federal Arbitration Act in *Bradley v. Harris Research, Inc.*, 275 F.3d 884 (9th Cir. 2001). It remains enforceable in the federal and state courts.

Connecticut: Franchise Act

(Conn. Gen. Stat. Ann. §§ 42-133e to 42-133h (2019).)

Termination—Requires either:

(i) Good cause;

Definition of "good cause"—Includes Franchisee's failure to comply with material and reasonable obligations of Franchise Agreement.

(ii) Voluntary abandonment; *OR*

(iii) Criminal conviction of Franchisee.

Nonrenewal—Requires either:

(i) Good cause (as defined above);

(ii) Voluntary abandonment,

(iii) Criminal conviction of Franchisee; *OR*

(iv) If Franchisor leases premises to Franchisee, Franchisor may choose not to renew if either:

(a) Franchisor sells or leases premises to other than an affiliate for any use;

(b) Franchisor sells or leases the premises to an affiliate that will not use the premises for the franchise business;

(c) Franchisor converts premises to a new use; *OR*

(d) Franchisor's underlying lease is terminated.

Notice

When Required—With good cause, 60 days for termination or nonrenewal. If reason is voluntary abandonment, 30 days. In case of nonrenewal under item (iv) above, six months.

When Not Required—In event of criminal conviction of Franchisee, notice of termination or nonrenewal is effective immediately.

Note: Notice of termination or nonrenewal that also involves termination of lease to Franchisee must be served by sheriff or other third person and meet certain requirements of Connecticut law.

Franchisee's Remedies

(i) *Repurchase Obligation*—Regardless of reason for termination, Franchisor must, at option of Franchisee, repurchase inventory, supplies, equipment, and furnishings purchased from Franchisor or supplier designated by Franchisor. This remedy appears not to be available for nonrenewal.

(ii) Actual damages, including costs and attorneys' fees.

(iii) Injunctive relief.

Other

Duration—The original and any successive terms of all franchises must be for no less than 3 years.

Delaware: Delaware Franchise Security Law

(Del. Code Ann. tit. 6, §§ 2551 to 2556 (2021).)

Termination—May not be done unjustly.

Definition of "unjustly"—"Without good cause" or "in bad faith" (neither of which are defined).

Nonrenewal—May not be done unjustly (as defined above).

Notice—90 days for termination or nonrenewal.

Franchisee's Remedies—If Franchisor threatens, attempts to, or actually unjustly terminates or fails to renew, Franchisee may seek:

(i) *Assets, Goodwill and Lost Profits*—Damages, including value of assets, lost goodwill, lost profits (at least 5 times profit in most recent fiscal year), and attorneys' fees.

(ii) Injunctive relief.

Other

Refusal to Deal—Franchisor may not "unjustly" refuse to deal with a Franchisee with whom it has been dealing for at least two years.

Rental of Real and Personal Property—Franchisor may not charge Franchisee rent for real or personal property that is unreasonable or excessive.

Hawaii: Franchise Investment Act

(Haw. Rev. Stat. §§ 482E-1 to 482E-12 (2018).)

Termination—Requires either:

(i) Good cause; *OR*

Definition of "good cause"—Includes failure of Franchisee to comply with lawful, material provision of Franchise Agreement, after given notice and a chance to cure.

(ii) In accordance with current nondiscriminatory terms and standards established by the Franchisor, after notice and a reasonable opportunity to cure.

Nonrenewal—Requires either:

(i) Good cause (as defined above); *OR*

(ii) In accordance with current nondiscriminatory terms and standards established by Franchisor.

Notice—Reasonable period of time to cure upon written notice of termination.

Franchisee's Remedies

(i) *Repurchase Obligation*—Upon termination or nonrenewal (even with good cause), Franchisor must, at Franchisee's option, repurchase inventory, supplies, equipment, and furnishings purchased from Franchisor or supplier designated by Franchisor.

(ii) *Goodwill upon Conversion*—If Franchisor refuses renewal in order to convert to Franchisor operation, Franchisee must also be compensated for goodwill.

(iii) *Unfair Competition*—Violations concerning termination and nonrenewal entitle Franchisee to recovery under Hawaii unfair competition and deceptive acts statute.

Other

Nondiscrimination—Unreasonable discrimination between franchises is prohibited.

Civil and Criminal Penalties—Violations subject to civil penalties of up to $100,000 and felony convictions resulting in *minimum* imprisonment of one year.

Illinois: Franchise Disclosure Act

(815 Ill. Rev. Comp. Stat. §§ 705/18 to 705/26 (2020).)

Termination—Good cause required.

Definition of "good cause"—Includes failure to comply with lawful provisions of Franchise Agreement, after notice and 30 days to cure, *OR* assignment for benefit of creditors, voluntary abandonment, criminal misconduct of Franchisee that impairs goodwill of Franchisor's name or mark, or repeated failure to comply with Franchise Agreement.

Nonrenewal—If Franchisor does not renew, it must compensate Franchisee for diminution in value of the franchise business, *UNLESS:*

(i) Noncompetition covenant is waived; *AND*

(ii) Franchisee is given at least six months' notice of nonrenewal.

Notice

When Required—

Termination—30 days' notice and chance to cure.

Nonrenewal—Six months' notice for nonrenewal (plus waiver of any noncompetition agreement) in order to avoid obligation to compensate Franchisee.

When Not Required—No notice required if reason for termination is: assignment for benefit of creditors, voluntary abandonment, criminal conviction, or repeated failure to comply with Franchise Agreement.

Franchisee's Remedies

(i) *Nonrenewal Obligation*—See "Nonrenewal" above.

(ii) Actual damages, including costs and attorneys' fees.

Other

Nondiscrimination—Unreasonable and material discrimination between franchises is prohibited.

Civil and Criminal Penalties—Violations subject to civil penalties of up to $50,000 per violation.

Indiana: Deceptive Franchise Practices Act

(Ind. Code Ann. §§ 23-2-2.7-1 to 23-2-2.7-7 (2020).)

Termination—Requires either:

(i) Good cause; *OR*

Definition of "good cause"—Includes material violation of the Franchise Agreement.

(ii) Bad faith on part of Franchisee.

Note: Impermissible to threaten termination in order to gain any agreement with Franchisee.

Nonrenewal—Unless Franchise Agreement provides that it is not renewable or provides that Franchisee must meet certain conditions specified in Franchise Agreement in order to renew, not renewing requires either:

(i) Good cause (as defined above); *OR*

(ii) Bad faith on part of Franchisee.

Note: Impermissible to threaten nonrenewal in order to gain any agreement with Franchisee.

Notice—Unless otherwise provided in Franchise Agreement, 90 days for termination or nonrenewal.

Franchisee's Remedies—Franchisee may recover damages or seek reformation of the Franchise Agreement.

Dispute Resolution—Not permissible for Franchise Agreement to limit in any manner whatsoever.

Other

Nondiscrimination—Unfair discrimination between franchises is prohibited.

Noncompetition Covenants—Covenants not to compete after termination or nonrenewal must be for no more than three years *AND* not encompass an area greater than exclusive area granted in Franchise Agreement or reasonable area if no exclusive area was granted.

Iowa

(Iowa Code § 537A.10 (2021).)

Termination—Requires either:

(i) Good cause;

Definition of "good cause"—A legitimate business reason, including failure to comply with any material lawful requirement of the Franchise Agreement, after notice and a reasonable opportunity to cure.

(ii) Bankruptcy or insolvency of Franchisee;

(iii) Voluntary abandonment for at least five days;

(iv) Mutual agreement;

(v) Material misrepresentation by Franchisee;

(vi) Repeated material violations by Franchisee;

(vii) Seizure of Franchisee's premises;

(viii) Criminal conviction of Franchisee; OR

(ix) Endangerment to public health and safety.

Nonrenewal—In order not to renew, Franchisor must:

(i) Give at least six months' notice; AND

(ii) One of the following:

(a) Have good cause (as defined above);

(b) Mutual agreement, with waiver of noncompetition covenant; OR

(c) Franchisor completely withdraws from geographic market, with waiver of noncompetition covenant.

Notice

When Required—

Termination—For good cause termination, a reasonable period of time to cure (at least 30 days but no need to be more than 90 days).

Nonrenewal—Six months' notice is required.

When Not Required—Notice, but no time to cure, is required if the reason for termination is items (ii)–(ix) of "Termination" above.

Franchisee's Remedies

(i) *Repurchase Obligation*—If Franchisee terminated or not renewed, Franchisor must offer to purchase franchise for fair market value (minus goodwill value of trademark), UNLESS either noncompetition covenant not enforced or Franchisee will continue in a business with a substantially similar marketing program. (*Note:* This provision only applies to franchises entered into prior to July 1, 2000.)

(ii) Actual damages, including costs and attorneys' and experts' fees.

(iii) Injunctive relief.

Dispute Settlement—Franchise Agreement may not restrict forum to venue outside Iowa, but may provide for arbitration or mediation.

Other

Noncompetition Agreement—Franchisor cannot enforce a noncompetition covenant unless it offers in writing, no later than 10 days before expiration of the franchise, to purchase the assets of the franchised business for its fair market value as a going concern. After a transfer, Franchisor may not enforce noncompetition agreement against former Franchisee.

Michigan: Franchise Investment Law Act

(MICH. COMP. LAWS §§ 445.1527 &445.1535 (2020).)

Termination—Good cause required.

Definition of "good cause"—Includes failure to comply with any lawful provision of Franchise Agreement, after being given notice and reasonable opportunity to cure.

Nonrenewal—If renewal terms generally available to other franchisees, Franchisor must offer such terms to Franchisee. If Franchisor does not renew for any reason, Franchisor must repurchase inventory, supplies, equipment, fixtures, and furnishings if:

(i) Term of the Franchise Agreement is less than 5 years; *AND*

(ii) (a) noncompetition covenant prevents Franchisee from operating under a different name after nonrenewal; *OR*

(b) less than 6 months' notice given.

Notice

Termination—Must give notice and a reasonable opportunity to cure before terminating.

Nonrenewal—Six months' notice for nonrenewal (or no enforcement of noncompetition covenant), in order to avoid repurchase obligation.

Franchisee's Remedies

(i) *Repurchase Obligation*—See "Nonrenewal" above.

(ii) Restitution to Franchisee.

(iii) Injunctive relief.

Dispute Settlement—Franchise Agreement provision requiring litigation or arbitration to be conducted outside of Michigan is unenforceable.

Minnesota: Minnesota Franchise Act

(MINN. STAT. § 80C.14 (2019) and MINN. R. § 2860.4400 (2020).)

Termination—Good cause required.

Definition of "good cause"—Includes failure to comply substantially with material and reasonable requirements imposed by Franchisor, including requirements concerning bankruptcy or insolvency, assignment for benefit of creditors, voluntary abandonment, criminal conviction or plea of guilty or no contest, or material impairment of Franchisor's mark or name.

Nonrenewal—Franchisor may not refuse to renew in order to convert to Franchisor operation. In order otherwise not to renew, Franchisor must either:

(i) Have good cause (as defined above); *OR*

(ii) (a) give at least 180 days' notice; AND

(b) have given Franchisee sufficient time from the date of nonrenewal to enable Franchisee to recover fair market value of the franchise as a going concern.

Notice

When Required—90 days, including 60 days to cure, prior to termination or nonrenewal for good cause. One hundred eighty days prior to nonrenewal if not for good cause.

When Not Required—Notice is effective immediately if reason for termination is for voluntary abandonment, criminal conviction, or failure to cure material impairment of goodwill, after being given at least 24 hours' notice.

Franchisee's Remedies

(i) Actual damages, including costs and attorneys' fees.

(ii) Injunctive relief.

Other

Civil and Criminal Penalties—Violations subject to civil fines of up to $2,000 per violation and criminal penalties of up to $10,000 and/or five years' imprisonment.

Nondiscrimination—Unreasonable discrimination between franchises is prohibited.

Mississippi: Pyramid Sales Scheme Act

(Miss. Code Ann. § 75-24-51 to 75-24-63 (2021).)

Termination—No substantive requirement.

Nonrenewal—No substantive requirement.

Notice

When Required—90 days for termination or nonrenewal.

When Not Required—Notice period not required if reason for termination or nonrenewal is criminal misconduct, fraud, abandonment, bankruptcy, insolvency, or an insufficient funds check.

Franchisee's Remedies

(i) Damages resulting from not being given proper notice, including loss of goodwill and costs of suit.

(ii) Equitable relief.

Other

Criminal Penalties—Violation of notice requirement is a misdemeanor punishable by a fine of not more than $500.00 and/or imprisonment of not more than 6 months.

Missouri: Pyramid Sales Scheme Act

(Mo. Rev. Stat. §§ 407.400 to 407.420 (2020).)

Termination—No substantive requirement.

Nonrenewal—No substantive requirement.

Notice

When Required—90 days' notice for termination or nonrenewal.

When Not Required—Notice period not required if reason for termination or nonrenewal is criminal misconduct, fraud, abandonment, bankruptcy, insolvency, or an insufficient funds check.

Franchisee's Remedies

(i) Damages resulting from not being given proper notice, including lost goodwill and costs of suit.

(ii) Equitable relief.

Nebraska: Franchise Practices Act

(Neb. Rev. Stat. §§ 87-401 to 87-410 (2020).)

Note: Nebraska statute applies only if gross sales between Franchisor and Franchisee for 12 months preceding a suit exceed $35,000.

Termination—Good cause required.

Definition of "good cause"—Limited to failure by the Franchisee to comply substantially with the requirements imposed upon it by the franchise.

Nonrenewal—Good cause (as defined above) required, *UNLESS* Franchise Agreement provides that franchise is not renewable or only renewable if Franchisee meets certain reasonable requirements.

Notice

When Required—60 days for termination or nonrenewal. If reason for termination or nonrenewal is voluntary abandonment, 15 days.

When Not Required—Notice effective immediately if the reason for termination or nonrenewal is criminal conviction, insolvency, default in payment, fraud, danger to public health and safety, or loss of right to occupy premises.

Franchisee's Remedies

(i) Damages, including costs and attorneys' fees.

(ii) Injunctive relief.

New Jersey: Franchise Practices Act

(N.J. Rev. Stat. §§ 56:10-1 to 56:10-12 (2020).)

Note: New Jersey's statute applies only if gross sales between Franchisor and Franchisee for 12 months preceding a suit exceed $35,000 and more than 20 percent of Franchisee's gross sales are intended to be derived from the franchise.

Termination—Good cause required.

Definition of "good cause"—Limited to failure of Franchise to substantially comply with requirements imposed by the franchise.

Nonrenewal—Good cause required (as defined above).

Notice

When Required—60 days for termination or nonrenewal. If reason for termination or nonrenewal is voluntary abandonment, 15 days.

When Not Required—Notice effective immediately if reason for termination or nonrenewal is criminal conviction.

Franchisee's Remedies

(i) Damages, including costs and attorneys' fees.

(ii) Injunctive relief.

North Carolina

(N.C. GEN. STAT. ch. 22B, § 3 (2020).)

Note: No statute of general applicability to franchises.

Other

Dispute Settlement—North Carolina has a statute of general application prohibiting contracts that require litigation outside of North Carolina.

Rhode Island: Fair Dealership Act

(R.I. GEN. LAWS §§ 6-50-1 to 6-50-9 (2021).)

Termination—Good cause required.

Definition of "good cause"—Includes failure to comply with the reasonable requirements of grantor or reasons listed below under "*When Not Required.*"

Nonrenewal—Good cause required (as defined above).

Notice

When Required—60 days, including 30 days to cure, for termination or nonrenewal. If reason for termination or nonrenewal is nonpayment of sums due, 10 days. If reason for termination is violation of law or standard related to public health or safety, 24 hours.

When Not Required—No notice required if reason for termination or nonrenewal is voluntary abandonment by franchisee, conviction of felony related to business, material impairment of goodwill of trademark, material misrepresentation in grant of franchise, unauthorized transfer, insolvency, assignment for the benefit of creditors, or bankruptcy.

Franchisee's Remedies

(i) *Termination Repurchase Obligation*—Upon termination (even if for good cause), Franchisor must, at option of Franchisee, repurchase all merchandise with Franchisor's name or marks on it.

(ii) *Damages*—For termination without good cause, Franchisor liable for damages, including costs and attorneys' fees.

(iii) Injunctive relief.

Virginia: Retail Franchising Act

(VA. CODE ANN. §§ 13.1-557 to 13.1-574 (2020).)

Termination—"Reasonable cause" required (but not defined).

Note: Franchisor also may not use undue influence to induce Franchisee to surrender any right given to it by the Franchise Agreement.

Franchisee's Remedies

(i) Damages, including costs and attorneys' fees.

(ii) Injunctive relief.

Dispute Resolution—Permissible to agree to binding arbitration.

Other

Civil and Criminal Penalties—Violations subject to civil penalties of up to $25,000. Violations can also be prosecuted criminally and are subject to the following:

(i) Class 4 felony, if crime knowingly and willfully committed with intent to defraud Franchisee.

(ii) Fine of $100 to $5,000 and/or imprisonment of 30 days to one year, if knowingly committed.

Washington: Franchise Investment Protection Act

(WASH. REV. CODE §§ 19.100.180 to 19.100.190 (2020).)

Termination—Good cause required.

Definition of "good cause"—Includes failure to comply with lawful material provisions of Franchise Agreement, after given notice and a reasonable opportunity to cure. See repurchase obligation under "Franchisee's Remedies."

Nonrenewal—No substantive requirements except for repurchase obligation under "Franchisee's Remedies."

Notice

When Required—

Termination—Notice and a reasonable opportunity to cure.

Nonrenewal—One year (plus no enforcement of noncompete covenant) in order to avoid obligation to compensate Franchisee for lost goodwill.

When Not Required—No notice required if reason for termination is violation of same provision in Franchise Agreement for fourth time in one year, insolvency, assignment for the benefit of creditors, voluntary abandonment, or criminal conviction or no contest or guilty plea.

Franchisee's Remedies

(i) *Termination Repurchase Obligation*—For termination upon good cause, Franchisor must repurchase inventory and supplies.

(ii) *Nonrenewal Repurchase Obligation*—If Franchisor does not renew, Franchisor must repurchase inventory, supplies, equipment, and furnishings purchased from Franchisor. Franchisor must also compensate Franchisee for goodwill, *UNLESS:*

  (a) gives notice of one year; AND

  (b) waives noncompetition covenant.

(iii) *Unfair or Deceptive Acts*—Violations concerning termination and nonrenewal entitle Franchisee to recovery under Washington unfair or deceptive acts statutes.

Other

Discrimination—Unreasonable discrimination between Franchisees prohibited.

Civil and Criminal Penalties—Violations subject to civil penalties of up to $2,000 and, for willful violations, criminal penalties of up to $5,000 or imprisonment of up to 10 years.

Wisconsin: Fair Dealership Law

(Wis. Stat. §§ 135.01 to 135.07 (2020).)

Termination—Good cause required.

Definition of "good cause"—Includes failure to comply substantially with essential, reasonable, and nondiscriminatory requirements imposed by Franchisor *OR* bad faith by Franchisee.

Nonrenewal—Good cause required (as defined above).

Note: "Good cause" requirement also applies to "substantially chang[ing] the competitive circumstances" of the Franchise Agreement.

Notice

When Required—90 days, including 60 days to cure, for termination or nonrenewal. If reason for termination or nonrenewal is nonpayment of sums due, 10 days.

When Not Required—No notice required if reason for termination or nonrenewal is insolvency, assignment for the benefit of creditors, or bankruptcy.

Franchisee's Remedies

(i) *Termination Repurchase Obligation*—Upon termination (even if for good cause), Franchisor must, at option of Franchisee, repurchase all merchandise with Franchisor's name or marks on it.

(ii) *Damages*—For termination without good cause, Franchisor liable for damages, including costs and attorneys' fees.

(iii) Injunctive relief.

Checklist 5-1
Default and Termination

1. Name of franchise
2. Unit(s) involved
3. Other units operated by or agreements with franchisee
   a. Franchisee's standing under other agreements
   b. Potential for cross-default/termination
4. Franchisor's basis for default/termination
   a. Factual cause/event
   b. Specific contractual basis
5. Communications with or efforts to counsel franchisee regarding basis for default/termination
   a. Specific communications by franchisor
   b. Franchisee's response
6. Whether franchisor/franchisee desires to try to negotiate work-out arrangement to avoid termination
7. Analysis of applicable statutory restrictions on termination
8. Analysis of relevant course of dealings with franchisee
9. Any inconsistency with treatment of other similarly situated franchisees and, if so, reasons for deviation
10. Potential legal claims by franchisee
11. Potential for obtaining negotiated, voluntary termination, and release by franchisee
12. Internal approvals required for default/termination
    a. Business/operational approval
    b. Legal approval
13. Required notice and cure period
    a. Written notice of default
    b. Follow-up by franchisor to determine if cured
    c. Written notice of termination
14. Follow-up by franchisor to confirm compliance with post-termination obligations
    a. De-identification
    b. Return of all manuals and other proprietary materials
    c. Enforcement of noncompetition agreements

Checklist 5-2
Nonrenewal

1. Name of franchisee
2. Unit(s) involved
3. Other units operated by or agreements with franchisee
4. Franchisor's business decision whether it desires to renew franchisee
   a. Operational history
   b. Payment history
   c. Facility image status
   d. Facility location status
   e. Conditions for renewal (for example, release, facility upgrade, new agreement, additional training, and so on)
5. Franchisee's contractual rights regarding renewal
   a. Specific contractual basis
   b. Prerequisites for franchisee to obtain renewal
   c. Good cause for franchisor not to renew
   d. What form of agreement for renewal
   e. Ability of franchisor to impose conditions for renewal (see 4.e. above)
   f. Notice requirements regarding renewal
6. Analysis of applicable statutory restrictions on nonrenewal
   a. Good cause requirement
   b. Notice requirement
   c. Other conditions
7. Analysis of relevant course of dealings with franchisee
8. Any inconsistency with treatment of other similarly situated franchisees and, if so, reasons for deviation
9. Potential legal claims by franchisee
10. Potential for obtaining negotiated, voluntary nonrenewal, and release by franchisee
11. Internal approvals required for nonrenewal
    a. Business/operational approval
    b. Legal approval
12. Communication of required notice
13. Follow up by franchisor to confirm compliance with post-termination obligations
    a. De-identification
    b. Return of all manuals and other proprietary materials
    c. Enforcement of noncompetition agreements

Checklist 5-3
Transfer

1. Name of franchisee
2. Unit(s) involved
3. Other units operated by or agreements with franchisee
4. Analysis of whether proposed transferee meets franchisor's current criteria
    a. Financial resources
    b. Operational experience
    c. Other business interests
5. Franchisor's business decision whether it desires to consent to transfer
    a. Is franchisee current on all obligations?
    b. Conditions for consent to transfer (for example, release, facility upgrade, new agreement, and so on)
    c. Transfer fee
6. Franchisee's contractual rights regarding transfer
    a. Specific contractual provisions
    b. Prerequisites for franchisee to obtain consent
    c. Good cause for franchisor to refuse consent
    d. What form of agreement for transferee
    e. Ability of franchisor to impose conditions for consent (see 5.b above)
7. Analysis of applicable statutory restrictions regarding transfer
    a. Good cause requirement
    b. Notice requirement
8. Potential legal claims by franchisee and proposed transferee
9. Internal approvals required for transfer decisions
    a. Business/operational approval
    b. Legal approval
10. Communication of notice to franchisee and proposed transferee
11. Proper documentation of transfer transaction
    a. Conclusion of relationship with transferor franchisee (for example, payment offers, release, noncompetition agreements, and so on)
    b. New franchisee relationship with transferee (for example, franchise agreement, guaranty, facility upgrade, and so on)

Exhibit 5-1
Sample Mediation Provision

Except where it is necessary for either of the parties to obtain equitable relief, including but not limited to the enforcement of covenants not to compete or the protection of the goodwill of either party's respective businesses, the parties hereby pledge and agree that before resorting to litigation or arbitration, they will first attempt in good faith to resolve any dispute, claim, or controversy arising out of or relating to this Agreement or any alleged breach hereof, including any claim that this Agreement or any part hereof is invalid, illegal, or otherwise voidable or void (collectively, "Dispute"), by mediating the Dispute before a mediator mutually agreed upon by the parties. Mediation will take place in [County, State] and will be conducted and completed within 45 days following the date either party first gives notice of mediation. The fees and expenses of the mediator will be shared equally by the parties. The mediator will be disqualified as a witness, expert, or counsel for any party with respect to the Dispute and any related matter. Mediation is a compromise negotiation and will constitute privileged communications under the law governing this Agreement. The entire mediation process will be confidential and the conduct, statements, promises, offers, views, and opinions of the mediator and the parties will not be discoverable or admissible in any legal proceeding for any purpose; provided, however, that evidence which is otherwise discoverable or admissible will not be excluded from discovery or admission as a result of its use in the mediation.

Form 5-1
Notice of Termination for Financial Default

DATE

CERTIFIED MAIL XXX

Return Receipt Requested and U.S. Mail

Franchisee	Guarantors
XXX	XXX
XXX	XXX

Re: **FRANCHISE AGREEMENT:** XXX
FRANCHISEE: XXX
FRANCHISED RESTAURANT:
Unit No. XXX *Location: XXX*
CONTRACT NO: XXX

Notice of Termination for Financial Default

Dear Franchisee and Guarantors:

On XXX, Franchisee entered into a Franchise Agreement for Unit No. XXX (hereinafter referred to as the "Franchise Agreement") with Franchisor. Further, on or about XXX Franchisee's principals, individually, executed a Guaranty and Subordination Agreement agreeing to be bound jointly and severally with Franchisee for any indebtedness and obligations to Franchisor arising under the Franchise Agreement.

Notice is hereby given that Franchisee is in DEFAULT under the terms and conditions of Paragraph XXX. ("**Fees**") of the above-referenced Franchise Agreement for failure to pay Royalty Fees, Advertising Fund Fees, Finance Charges, and other financial obligations to the Franchisor, in the amounts set forth on EXHIBIT "A" which is attached hereto and incorporated herein by reference (hereinafter referred to as the "Financial Default").

Please be advised that this letter constitutes a formal "NOTICE OF TERMINATION" pursuant to Paragraph XXX of the Franchise Agreement. In the event the foregoing Financial Default is not cured within ten (10) days of Franchisee's receipt of this Notice, the Franchise Agreement shall terminate without further notice, effective immediately upon the expiration of such ten (10) day period, or such longer period as applicable law may require.

Please be further advised that upon termination of the Franchise Agreement, Franchisee will be expected to comply with the provisions of Paragraph XXX of the Franchise Agreement, which sets forth the Franchisee's obligations upon termination. Franchisee's post-termination obligations include the following:

1. Franchisee must immediately cease and forever discontinue any and all operations at that location under the name of Franchisor or any name confusingly similar thereto;

2. Franchisee must immediately and forever cease to use any proprietary materials, information, equipment, procedures, and techniques associated with the Franchisor's System, including any and all trademarks and service marks associated with this Company;
3. Franchisee must immediately de-image the restaurant premises to completely disassociate those premises from the Franchisor's System, including, without limitation, the removal of all signs bearing the Franchisor's name;
4. Franchisee must immediately surrender the Confidential Operations Manual, and all copies thereof, together with all records, files, instructions, correspondence, and any and all other materials relating to the operation of the Franchised Restaurant; and
5. Franchisee must immediately pay any and all sums which are owed to this Company as a result of the operation of the Franchised Restaurant.

Franchisor waives no other defaults under the above-referenced Franchise Agreement and reserves all rights and remedies it may have under the Franchise Agreement or otherwise. Please feel free to contact me in the event you have any questions regarding this matter.

Sincerely,

FRANCHISOR

By: ______________________________

Form 5-2
Notice of Termination for Operational Default

DATE

CERTIFIED MAIL XXX

Return Receipt Requested and U.S. Mail

Franchisee

XXX

XXX

Re: **FRANCHISE AGREEMENT:** XXX
FRANCHISEE: XXX
FRANCHISED RESTAURANT:
Unit No. XXX *Location: XXX*
CONTRACT NO: XXX

Notice of Termination for Operational Default

Dear Franchisee:

On ____, Franchisee entered into a certain Franchise Agreement for Unit No. XXX (hereinafter referred to as the "Franchise Agreement") with Franchisor.

On _____, Franchisor conducted operational assessments of Unit No. XXX (copies of the assessment forms are attached hereto as EXHIBIT "A"). Notice is hereby given that Franchisee is currently in DEFAULT under the terms and conditions of Paragraph XXX. ("Duties of the Franchisee") of the above-referenced Franchise Agreement for failure to operate the Franchised Unit and/or maintain the premises of the Franchised Unit in conformity with Franchisor's standards and specifications for the operation of a restaurant (hereinafter referred to as the "Operational Default"). The foregoing Operational Default includes, but is not limited to, Franchisee's failure to maintain the premises, equipment, etc., in conformity with Franchisor's high standards and public image and failure to make repairs and replacement thereto.

Please be advised that this Notice constitutes a formal "NOTICE OF TERMINATION" pursuant to Paragraph XXX ("Termination") of the Franchise Agreement. In the event the foregoing Operational Default is not cured within thirty (30) days of Franchisee's receipt of this Notice, or such longer period as applicable law may require, the Franchise Agreement shall terminate upon the expiration of the thirty (30) day period or such longer period as applicable law may require.

Please be further advised that upon termination of the above-referenced Franchise Agreement, Franchisee will be expected to comply with the provisions of Paragraph XXX of the Franchise Agreement which set forth the Franchisee's obligations upon termination. Franchisee's post-termination obligations include the following:

1. Franchisee must immediately cease and forever discontinue any and all operations at that location shown on EXHIBIT "A" operating under the name of Franchisor or any name confusingly similar thereto;
2. Franchisee must immediately and forever cease to use any proprietary materials, information, equipment, procedures, and techniques associated with the Franchisor's System, including any and all trademarks and service marks associated with this Company;
3. Franchisee must immediately de-image the restaurant premises to completely disassociate those premises from the Franchisor's System, including, without limitation, the removal of all signs bearing the Franchisor's name and logo;
4. Franchisee must immediately surrender the Confidential Operations Manual, and all copies thereof, together with all records, files, instructions, correspondence, and any and all other materials relating to the operation of the Franchised Restaurant; and
5. Franchisee must immediately pay any and all sums which are owed to this Company as a result of the operation of the Franchised Restaurant.

Franchisor waives no other defaults under the above-referenced Franchise Agreement and reserves all rights and remedies it may have under the Franchise Agreement or otherwise.

Please feel free to contact me in the event you have any further questions regarding this matter.

Sincerely,

FRANCHISOR

By: ______________________________

Form 5-3
Notice of Termination

DATE

CERTIFIED MAIL XXX

RETURN RECEIPT REQUESTED and U.S. Mail

Franchisee

XXX

XXX

Re: **FRANCHISE AGREEMENT:** XXX
FRANCHISEE: XXX
FRANCHISED RESTAURANT:
Unit No. XXX *Location: XXX*
CONTRACT NO: XXX

Notice of Termination

Dear Franchisee:

On XXX, Franchisor entered into a certain Franchise Agreement for Unit No. XXX at the above-referenced location (hereinafter referred to as the "Franchise Agreement for Unit No. XXX") with XXX Franchisee. Further, on or about XXX, by Guaranty and Subordination Agreement, Franchisee's principals, individually, agreed to be bound jointly and severally with Franchisee for any such indebtedness and obligations to Franchisor arising under the Franchise Agreement.

It has come to Franchisor's attention that the above-referenced Franchised Restaurant was permanently closed for business on XXX by Franchisee without the consent of Franchisor. Pursuant to Paragraph XXX ("Termination") of the Franchise Agreement, Franchisor hereby elects to terminate the Franchise Agreement and all rights granted thereunder, effective immediately upon Franchisee's receipt of this Notice of Termination.

Post-termination Obligations of Franchisee

Accordingly, you must **IMMEDIATELY** comply with the post-termination provisions of Paragraph XXX of the Franchise Agreement, which include but are not limited to the following:

1. Franchisee must immediately cease and forever discontinue any and all operations at this location under the name of XXX or any name confusingly similar thereto; Franchisee must immediately and forever cease to use any proprietary materials, information, equipment, procedures, and techniques associated with the XXX System, including any and all trademarks and service marks associated with this Company;

2. Franchisee must immediately de-image the restaurant premises to completely disassociate those premises from the XXX System, including, without limitation, the removal of all signs bearing the XXX name and logo;
3. Franchisee must immediately surrender the Confidential Operations Manual, and all copies thereof, together with all records, files, instructions, correspondence, and any and all other materials relating to the operation of the Franchised Restaurant; and
4. Franchisee must immediately pay any and all sums which are owed to this Company as a result of the operation of the Franchised Restaurant. A Statement of Account for Franchised Restaurant No. XXX indicating a total amount due by Franchisee to Franchisor of $XXX, is attached hereto as EXHIBIT "A" and incorporated herein by reference.

Franchisor waives no other defaults under the above-referenced Franchise Agreement and reserves all rights and remedies it may have under the Franchise Agreement or otherwise.

Please contact me to discuss the immediate de-identification of the premises formerly occupied by the Franchised Restaurant. In the event Franchisee fails to voluntarily comply with all post-termination obligations, the Franchisor will institute legal proceedings to enforce these obligations and seek all damages, costs, and expenses, including reasonable attorneys' fees incurred by Franchisor in seeking damages and/or in obtaining injunctive relief for the enforcement of the Post-termination Obligations set forth in Paragraph XXX of the Franchise Agreement.

Please feel free to contact me in the event you have any further questions regarding this matter.

Sincerely,

FRANCHISOR

By: ______________________________

Form 5-4
Voluntary Termination of Franchise Agreement between [Franchisor] and [Franchisee]

Dated: ___________, 20__

Voluntary Termination of Franchise Agreement

THIS AGREEMENT is made this ____ day of ____, 20__, by and between___________ (hereinafter referred to as "**FRANCHISOR**") and__________ (hereinafter referred to as "**FRANCHISEE**").

Recitals:

WHEREAS, FRANCHISOR, and **FRANCHISEE** are parties to that certain Franchise Agreement dated (hereinafter referred to as the "Franchise Agreement") pursuant to which **FRANCHISOR** granted **FRANCHISEE** the right to operate a [Name and Location of Unit] (hereinafter referred to as "Unit No. ___ or the "Franchised Unit"); and

WHEREAS, on ___, ___, [TITLE] of [FRANCHISEE] executed a Guaranty Agreement agreeing to be bound by all of the terms and conditions of the provisions of the Franchise Agreement for the Franchise Restaurant (hereinafter referred to as the "**GUARANTOR**").

WHEREAS, FRANCHISOR, FRANCHISEE, and **GUARANTOR** have determined that it would be in their mutual best interests and in the best interests of the [FRANCHISOR'S] System to terminate the Franchise Agreement and Guaranty Agreement as of the effective date of this agreement, upon the following terms and conditions:

Agreement:

NOW THEREFORE, and in consideration of the terms, conditions, and covenants contained herein, and for the mutual benefit of the parties hereto, **FRANCHISOR, FRANCHISEE,** and **GUARANTOR** hereby agree as follows:

1. *Termination.* **FRANCHISOR, FRANCHISEE,** and **GUARANTOR** agree that upon execution of this Agreement, the aforesaid Franchise Agreement and Guaranty Agreement shall be terminated in its entirety, and all rights and obligations of the parties flowing from said Franchise Agreement and Guaranty Agreement shall immediately terminate and cease. **FRANCHISEE** and **GUARANTOR** agree to immediately pay one-half (1/2) of any and all sums which are owed to **FRANCHISOR** as a result of the operation of the Franchised Unit. A Statement of Account for the Franchised Unit indicating the total amount due by **FRANCHISEE** and **GUARANTOR** to **FRANCHISOR** of $ _____ is attached hereto as **EXHIBIT "A"** and incorporated herein by reference.
2. *Post-termination Obligations.* **FRANCHISEE** and **GUARANTOR** acknowledge and agree that notwithstanding the terms of this Agreement, **FRANCHISEE** and **GUARANTOR** will continue to be bound by and will comply with all of the requirements of the Franchise Agreement, which, by their nature, are intended to survive the termination or expiration of said Franchise Agreement, including, but

not limited to, the covenants against competition and against disclosure of confidential information as specified therein.

3. *General and Specific Releases Executed by **FRANCHISEE** and **GUARANTOR**.*

   a. **FRANCHISEE** and **GUARANTOR**, as further consideration for the execution of this Agreement, on behalf of **FRANCHISEE** and **GUARANTOR** and **FRANCHISEE'S** and/or **GUARANTOR'S** heirs, executors, assigns, and agents, do hereby release, relieve, acquit, and forever discharge [FRANCHISOR], and any and all of [FRANCHISOR'S] predecessors, successors, present and former officers, directors, affiliates, parent and subsidiary companies, shareholders, employees, agents, and attorneys (collectively the "[FRANCHISOR] Released Parties"), of and from all claims, demands, actions, liabilities, causes of action, and damages of whatever kind or nature, known or unknown, vested or contingent, suspected or unsuspected, dependent in any way on any fact or event occurring on or prior to the date of this Agreement, that **FRANCHISEE** and **GUARANTOR** has, or ever had against the [FRANCHISOR] Released Parties.

   b. Without limiting the foregoing, **FRANCHISEE** and **GUARANTOR** specifically release and forever discharge the [FRANCHISOR] Released Parties of and from all claims, demands, actions, liabilities, and causes of action of whatever kind or nature, known or unknown, vested or contingent, suspected or unsuspected, arising at any time, which **FRANCHISEE** and/or **GUARANTOR** have now, may have in the future, or ever had pertaining to, or arising from the Franchise Agreement and/or Guaranty Agreement.

4. By executing this Agreement, **FRANCHISEE**, **GUARANTOR**, and **FRANCHISOR**, for themselves and their respective successors, represent and warrant that their representations herein are true and correct and that each of them has the right and authority to enter into and to accept the terms and conditions of this Agreement.

5. **FRANCHISEE** and **GUARANTOR** further acknowledge and represent that **FRANCHISEE** and/or **GUARANTOR** have not transferred or assigned the Franchise Agreement, any of the rights licensed therein, the Guaranty Agreement, or any claims, demands, or causes of action which they have or may have against **FRANCHISOR** under any or all of said Franchise Agreement and Guaranty Agreement. **FRANCHISEE** and **GUARANTOR** agree to defend, indemnify, and hold **FRANCHISOR**, its officers, directors, employees, and agents harmless from any claims of any such transferee or assigns.

6. **FRANCHISEE** and **GUARANTOR** shall cooperate fully with **FRANCHISOR** and do all things necessary, including execution of appropriate documents in forms satisfactory in all respects to counsel from **FRANCHISOR**, to satisfy **FRANCHISEE'S** and/or **GUARANTOR'S** obligations under this Agreement.

7. This Agreement represents the complete, integrated, and entire agreement between the parties, and shall not be modified except in writing signed by the parties.

8. This Agreement shall take effect upon its execution and dating by **FRANCHISOR**, and shall be governed by the laws of the State of ______________________________, which laws shall be controlling in the event of any conflict of law.

9. The provisions of this Agreement are severable, and in the event that any of them are held void and unenforceable as a matter of law, the remainder shall continue in full force and effect.
10. Each of the undersigned, if a corporation, hereby represents and warrants that, as of the date of execution of this Agreement, it is in good standing in the state of its incorporation, has the power to enter into this Agreement, has duly authorized the execution of this Agreement, and that such execution does not violate any other agreement to which it is a party.

IN WITNESS WHEREOF, the parties hereto have duly executed, sealed, and delivered this Agreement in duplicate on the day and year first above written;

WITNESS:	**FRANCHISOR:**
______________________________	By: ______________________________
	Its:_________________________
WITNESS:	**FRANCHISEE:**
______________________________	By: ______________________________
	Its:_________________________
WITNESS:	**GUARANTOR:**
______________________________	By: ______________________________
	Its:_________________________

[Signature Page of Voluntary Termination]

Form 5-5
Letter Agreement of Termination

[Date]

VIA FEDERAL EXPRESS

[Franchisee]

RE: Former Unit Nos. _______

Dear [Franchisee]:

On ____________, [Franchisor] sent a Notice of Termination letter to you notifying you of the termination of the Franchise Agreements for the above referenced Units. On _______________, you telephoned me to inform me that you had received my _________ Notice of Termination letter. During that telephone conversation you acknowledged that your account was once again past due and that you understood the _________ __, 20__ Notice of Termination letter to be placing you on notice of the termination of the Franchise Agreements for the above referenced Units.

On or about ___________, [representative of Franchisor] received a letter from you requesting a reconsideration of the termination of the Franchise Agreements for the above-referenced Units. [Representative of Franchisor] has referred your letter to me for a response. Contrary to the statements in your recent letter, the Franchisee (*see* Exhibit "A") has been a chronic credit problem which resulted in the Franchisee being repeatedly placed in financial default. [Franchisor] repeatedly attempted to work with the Franchisee to resolve its payment problems, but to no avail. Prior to sending the ______________ Notice of Termination letter, various [Franchisor] personnel met with you in __________ to discuss several outstanding financial and operational issues between the Franchisee and [Franchisor]. Time and time again, the Franchisee has failed to exhibit a willingness to be a true partner with [Franchisor] and as a result, [Franchisor] will not consider reinstating its Franchise Agreements. However, in the spirit of cooperation, [Franchisor] is prepared to reach the following agreement with you and the Franchisee:

1. By signing this Letter Agreement, Franchisee acknowledges that the Franchise Agreements for the above-referenced Units are terminated effective ____________.
2. By signing this Letter Agreement, Franchisee and you, individually, acknowledge that the Promissory Note dated ____________ was accelerated on ____________. As of this date, Franchisee and you owe $______ to [Franchisor]. (See Exhibit "B").
3. Contingent upon payment of all applicable fees as referenced below and agreement to the payment terms for the accelerated promissory note as set forth in Paragraph 6 below, Franchisee will be allowed to continue to operate the Units for a period not to exceed one hundred twenty (120) days in order to close the sale of the Units to a prospective purchaser(s) who is satisfactory to [Franchisor], provided that the Franchisee pay to [Franchisor] during such one hundred twenty (120) day period, all obligations that would otherwise have come due under the Franchise Agreements, including, but not limited to, royalties and advertising fund contributions (which past due amount currently totals $) (see Exhibit "C") and provided that the Franchisee is in full compliance with [Franchisor's]

operational standards and insurance requirements from the date of this Letter Agreement and continuing throughout the one hundred twenty (120) day period. If requested by the Franchisee, [Franchisor] will provide Franchisee with assistance in attempting to sell the Units by way of providing the Franchisee with the names of any prospective purchaser(s) of which it may become aware.

4. In no event shall the payment or obligation of payment of such amounts or the permission to operate for the one hundred twenty (120) day period be construed to be a reinstatement of the Franchise Agreements.

5. If Franchisee is unable to close the sale of the Units to a purchaser(s) satisfactory to [Franchisor] within the one hundred twenty (120) day period or Franchisee does not pay all obligations on a current basis, or if Franchisee fails to comply with [Franchisor's] operational standards and insurance requirements, Franchisee shall immediately, upon written notice from [Franchisor], de-identify the restaurants by removal of all signs utilizing the [Franchisor's] trademark or otherwise identifying the restaurants as [Franchisor's] Restaurants and will remove all other indicia that the restaurants are [Franchisor's] Restaurants, including any decor items, menu boards, trade dress, paper products, or the like as more fully set forth in the post-termination provisions of the Franchise Agreements for the above-referenced Units.

6. From the date this Letter Agreement is executed by Franchisee and you, individually, until the close of the sale of the Units to a purchaser(s) satisfactory to [Franchisor], Franchisee and you shall continue to pay the current $____ monthly payment towards reducing the balance of the accelerated promissory note which currently totals $____. (See Exhibit "B"). Upon close of the sale of the Units to a purchaser(s) satisfactory to [Franchisor], [Franchisor] will agree to waive the interest on the principal amount of the accelerated promissory note (currently $_____), the interest on the past due installments (currently $_____), and the default payment portion of the accelerated promissory note ($_____) which currently totals $____. (See Exhibit "B"). In exchange, Franchisee and/or you will pay the principal balance of the accelerated promissory note (which currently totals $_____) out of the proceeds of any sale of the Units. Said numbers will be adjusted accordingly at the date of closing. If no sale is consummated at the end of the one hundred twenty (120) day period, [Franchisor] will waive the default payment portion of the accelerated promissory note ($) and [Franchisor] will agree to issue a new promissory note for the principal amount of the promissory note plus all accrued interest, payable in ___ equal monthly installments, at prime plus 2.5%. Finally, if the Franchisee and/or you should become delinquent on any promissory note payment, then the default payment of $_____ will be added to the promissory note balance and the promissory note will be immediately accelerated.

7. By 5:00 p.m. E.S.T. on ______________, Franchisee must wire transfer to [Franchisor's] account or [Franchisor] must receive a cashier's check in the amount of all the past due fees, which currently totals $_______ (as set forth in Paragraph 3 above and Exhibit "C"). [Franchisor's] wire transfer instructions are as follows:

   Wire to: [wiring instructions]

8. Franchisee and you hereby relinquish all rights, interests, and claims of whatever nature to, in or under the Franchise Agreements, the parties thereof, and the relationships created thereby, and do hereby forever release and forever discharge

> [Franchisor], its predecessors, heirs, successors, representatives, assigns, agents, employees, attorneys, officers, and directors, and each of them, of and from any claims, debts, liabilities, demands, obligations, costs, expenses, actions, and causes of action of every nature, character, and description, known or unknown, vested or contingent, which Franchisee and/or you now owns or holds, or had at any time heretofore owned or held, or may at any time own or hold against [Franchisor], arising pursuant to the Franchise Agreements or as a result of or arising out of the course of dealing prior to and including the date of this Letter Agreement.

This offer is final, not subject to further negotiation and is valid until 5:00 p.m. E.S.T. on ______________. If these terms are acceptable to you and the Franchisee, please sign and date this letter on the signature and date lines provided below and return to me via facsimile, by 5:00 p.m. E.S.T. on ______________ and return the original signed document to me via overnight mail.

If you have any questions regarding this matter, please do not hesitate to contact me.

Sincerely,

[Corporate Counsel]

SO AGREED:

____

[Franchisee]

By: ___________________________

Its: ___________________________

____

Date

____

[Franchisee's Principal], Individually

____

Date

Form 5-6
Reinstatement of Franchise Agreement between [Franchisor] and [Franchisee]

THIS REINSTATEMENT AGREEMENT (the "Reinstatement") is made this ____ day of_____, by and between ______________ (hereinafter referred to as "Franchisor") and ______________ (hereinafter referred to as "Franchisee").

WHEREAS, Franchisor and Franchisee entered into a Franchise Agreement dated ______________ (hereinafter the "Franchise Agreement") for the operation of a Unit located at (hereinafter "Unit No. ___" or the "Franchised Unit"); and

WHEREAS, pursuant to a Notice of Termination letter dated ____ Franchisor terminated the Franchise Agreement due to Franchisee's failure to pay Advertising Fund Fees, Service Fees, and other financial obligations due to the Franchisor pursuant to the terms of the Franchise Agreement; and

WHEREAS, Franchisee has requested that Franchisor reinstate the Franchise Agreement, subject to the terms and conditions hereof, and Franchisor has agreed to such request upon the terms and conditions set forth herein.

NOW THEREFORE, in consideration of the mutual covenants and conditions herein contained, and other good and valuable consideration, receipt of which is hereby acknowledged by each of the parties hereto, the parties agree as follows:

1. The Franchise Agreement which was terminated pursuant to the Notice of Termination letter dated ____ is hereby reinstated under the same terms and conditions as set forth therein, except as otherwise provided herein.
2. Franchisee agrees that upon the reinstatement of the Franchise Agreement for Unit No. ___, all accrued monetary obligations owed to Franchisor, including, but not limited to, all obligations arising pursuant to the Franchise Agreement shall be paid in full or a satisfactory arrangement for payment of said fees must be made between Franchisee and Franchisor.
3. This Reinstatement shall be attached to and become a part of the Franchise Agreement. The terms and conditions stated in this Reinstatement, to the extent they are inconsistent with the terms and conditions of the Franchise Agreement, shall prevail over the terms and conditions of the Franchise Agreement.
4. In further consideration of the obligations of the parties undertaken herein, Franchisee hereby releases and forever discharges Franchisor and Franchisor's predecessors, successors, and its present and future representatives, assigns, agents, employees, officers, and directors (hereinafter collectively referred to as "Designees"), and each of them, of and from any claims, debts, liabilities, demands, obligations, costs, expenses, actions, and causes of action of every nature, character, and description, known or unknown, vested or contingent, which Franchisee now owns or holds, or has at any time heretofore, owned or held, or may at any time own or hold against Franchisor, or its Designees (hereinafter collectively referred to as "Claims"). Notwithstanding the foregoing, nothing herein shall release the continuing obligations of Franchisor and Franchisee which are set forth in this Reinstatement, and/or in the Franchise Agreement, the terms of which are hereby ratified by the parties hereto, and which shall remain in full force and effect, except as specifically amended herein. As further consideration

for the execution of this Agreement by Franchisor, Franchisee does hereby forever discharge and release Franchisor, its predecessors, its successors, and its present and former officers, directors, agents, and employees from any and all claims, causes of action, obligations, and liabilities arising prior to the date hereof, it being the intent of Franchisee to grant in favor of the Franchisor a general release of any claims Franchisee might have against Franchisor as a result of or arising out of their course of dealing through the effective date of this Agreement.

5. This Reinstatement, and the documents referred to herein, constitute the entire, full, and complete agreement between Franchisor and Franchisee, concerning the subject matter hereof and supersede any and all prior agreements. No other representations have induced Franchisee to execute this Reinstatement; and there are no representations, inducements, promises, or agreements, oral or otherwise, between the parties not embodied herein which are of any force or effect with reference to this Reinstatement or otherwise. No amendment, charge, or variance from this Reinstatement shall be binding on either party unless executed in writing.
6. The parties hereto agree that this Agreement constitutes the full and complete understanding and agreement among the parties regarding the subject matter hereof, and no representations, agreements, warranties, or statements, oral or in writing, not contained therein, shall be of any force or effect against Franchisor and this Agreement shall not be modified, except in writing, signed by all parties. The parties intend for this Reinstatement to be construed and interpreted under the laws of the State of _______, without regard to its choice of law or conflict of law rules. All parties further waive any right to a jury trial and all defenses of personal jurisdiction and/or venue and agree that any litigation or other legal proceeding pertaining to or arising from the execution of this Agreement shall be brought in a court of competent jurisdiction within the State of_______________ _________________.
7. Franchisee acknowledges that it has received, read, and understood this Reinstatement, that Franchisor has fully and adequately explained its provisions to Franchisee's satisfaction, and that Franchisor has accorded Franchisee ample time and opportunity to consult with advisors of its own choosing, including Franchisee's attorneys, about the potential benefits and risks of entering into this Reinstatement.
8. The Franchise Agreement shall remain in full force and effect except as otherwise provided herein.

Franchisee hereby agrees not to disclose the terms and/or conditions of this Reinstatement to any party, other than to Franchisee's attorneys. Violation of this confidentiality provision shall be deemed a material default of the Franchise Agreement.

IN WITNESS WHEREOF, the parties hereto, intending to be legally bound hereby, have executed this Reinstatement, in duplicate on the day and year first above-written.

WITNESS:	**FRANCHISOR:**
______________________________	By: ______________________________
	Its: ______________________
WITNESS:	**FRANCHISEE:**
______________________________	By: ______________________________
	Its: ______________________

Form 5-7
Transfer and Release Agreement

This **TRANSFER AND RELEASE AGREEMENT** (the "Agreement") is made and entered into on this _____ day of_______________, 20___, by and among **Franchisor**, a XXX corporation, having its principal place of business at XXX, ___________________, a XXX corporation (hereinafter "Franchisee"); and _________________, a XXX company (hereinafter "Transferee").

Witnesseth

WHEREAS, a Franchise Agreement dated ________ was executed by and between Franchisee and Franchisor for the operation of a franchised unit located at (the "Franchised Restaurant"); and

WHEREAS, Franchisor has been notified of Franchisee's desire to transfer to Transferee all right, title, and interest held by Franchisee, in and to the Franchise Agreement and, therefore, has requested that Franchisor consent to the transfer thereof to Transferee pursuant to Section ____ of said Franchise Agreement; and

WHEREAS, Franchisor is willing to grant its consent to the proposed transfer of the Franchise Agreement, subject to the terms and conditions set forth herein.

Agreement

NOW, THEREFORE, in consideration of the mutual covenants and conditions herein contained, and other good and valuable consideration, receipt of which is hereby acknowledged by each of the parties hereto, the parties agree as follows:

1. Franchisor hereby consents to and waives its right of first refusal in connection with the transfer by Franchisee to Transferee of all of Franchisee's right, title, and interest in and to the Franchise Agreement. The foregoing consent and waiver is subject to and made in reliance upon the following terms, conditions, representations, and warranties:

   A. Franchisee and Transferee represent, warrant, and agree that, subject to Franchisor's consent, Franchisee has transferred to Transferee all of Franchisee's right, title, and interest in and to the Franchise Agreement, and that all legal actions necessary to effect such transfer have been accomplished.

   B. Transferee must execute Franchisor's current form Franchise Agreement.

   C. Payment by Franchisee to Franchisor, in a manner satisfactory to Franchisor, of all accrued monetary obligations, including, but not limited to, all obligations pursuant to the Franchise Agreement, and any Lease and/or Sublease Agreement.

   D. Payment by Franchisee, in a manner satisfactory to Franchisor, of all other outstanding statements for equipment and/or merchandise purchased by Franchisee from Franchisor, or any other subsidiary or affiliate of Franchisor.

   E. Franchisee and Transferee acknowledge and agree that all obligations owed by either of them to Franchisor, its subsidiaries and affiliates, must be resolved to Franchisor's satisfaction as a condition of Franchisor's execution of this Agreement.

F. Franchisee acknowledges and agrees that, notwithstanding the terms of this Agreement, Franchisee will comply with all of the requirements of the Franchise Agreement, which, by their nature, are intended to survive the termination or expiration of said Franchise Agreement, including, but not limited to, the covenants against competition and against disclosure of confidential information as specified therein.

G. Transferee shall be and shall remain liable for all obligations under the Franchise Agreement and shall perform all unperformed or partially performed terms and conditions of said Franchise Agreement as though Transferee were the original Franchisee thereunder as of the effective date of this Agreement.

H. For a period of thirty-six (36) months from the date hereof, Franchisee (hereinafter referred to as "Guarantor") shall remain liable, as guarantor, and hereby guaranties all performance, operations, and financial obligations of the Transferee under the Franchise Agreement and the current form franchise agreement to be executed by Transferee. Guarantor acknowledges that, during the effective period of the guaranty, Franchisor may look first to Guarantor for all such unperformed obligations, without being required to first seek recourse against Transferee, the intention of this Paragraph being to render Guarantor and Transferee jointly and severally liable during the effective period of the guaranty. Guarantor shall execute the guaranty in the form attached hereto as Exhibit 1.

I. Transferee must pay to Franchisor a Transfer Fee which is due and payable upon execution of this Agreement.

J. Transferee agrees to satisfy the work requirements for the repair and maintenance items listed on the Scope of Work Schedule attached hereto as Exhibit 2, and to complete such work in accordance with the time periods specified in the attached Exhibit 2. Failure to complete such scope of work in accordance with the time periods specified in the attached Exhibit 2 will be considered a material default of the Franchise Agreement and may result in termination.

2. As further consideration for the execution of this Agreement by Franchisor, Franchisee hereby relinquishes all rights, interests, and claims of whatever nature to, in, or under the Franchise Agreement, and the relationships created thereby, and does hereby forever discharge and release Franchisor, its predecessors, its successors, and its present and former officers, directors, agents, and employees from any and all claims, causes of action, obligations, and liability arising from, under, or out of the Franchise Agreement, or any other act or occurrence of any kind whatsoever, it being the intent of Franchisee to grant in favor of the Franchisor a general release of any claims Franchisee might have against Franchisor as a result of or arising out of their course of dealing through the effective date of this Agreement.

3. Franchisee and Transferee acknowledge and agree that, except for the preparation and execution of this Agreement, Franchisor has not participated in the transaction between them and, therefore, has no knowledge of, and does not attest to, the accuracy of any representations or warranties made by or between Franchisee and Transferee in connection with this transfer. Franchisor assumes no obligations in that regard.

4. All parties understand and acknowledge that Franchisor may, in the future, approve offerings and transfers under different terms, conditions, and policies. Franchisor's consent and waiver in this instance shall not be relied upon in future transactions as indicative of Franchisor's position or the conditions which might be attached to future consents or waivers of its right of first refusal.
5. Franchisee and Transferee acknowledge and agree that Franchisor's execution of this Agreement is not intended to provide, and shall not be construed as providing, Franchisor's consent with regard to a transfer of any right or interest under any other agreement not specifically identified herein. Such consent must be separately obtained.
6. If any material provision or restriction contained herein shall be declared void or unenforceable under applicable law, the parties agree that such provision or restriction will be stricken, and this Agreement will continue in full force and effect. Notwithstanding this Paragraph, however, the parties agree that, to the extent Franchisor suffers harm as a consequence of the striking of such provision or restriction, the other parties to this Agreement shall exercise best efforts to make Franchisor whole.
7. Franchisor and Transferee agree that, until further written notice has been provided in accordance with the terms of the current form franchise agreement to be executed by Transferee, the official mailing address of Transferee shall be:______
____.
8. The parties hereto agree that this Agreement constitutes, as of the date of execution by Franchisor, the complete understanding between the parties regarding the subject matter hereof, and no representation, agreement, warranties, or statement, oral or in writing, not contained herein, shall be of any force and effect against Franchisor and this Agreement shall not be modified, altered, or amended except in writing signed by all parties. The parties intend for this Agreement to be construed and interpreted under the laws of the State of ____________, without regard to its choice of law or conflict of law rules. All parties further waive rights to a jury trial and all defenses of personal jurisdiction and/or venue and agree that any litigation or other legal proceeding pertaining to or arising from the execution of this Agreement shall be brought in a court of competent jurisdiction within the State of _________.

IN WITNESS WHEREOF, this Agreement has been duly signed by the parties hereto as indicated and shall be effective as of the date it is executed by Franchisor.

WITNESS:	**FRANCHISEE:**
______________________________	By:______________________________
WITNESS:	**TRANSFEREE:**
______________________________	By:______________________________
WITNESS:	**FRANCHISOR:**
______________________________	By:______________________________

[Signature Page of Transfer & Release Agreement]

Form 5-7A
Guaranty and Subordination

The Undersigned, for and in consideration of, and as an inducement to, the grant by Franchisor ("Franchisor") of its consent to the transfer of franchise rights to ______________ ("Transferee") for the operation of a restaurant at the location described in the Franchise Agreement establishing said rights, and other good and valuable consideration, receipt, and sufficiency of which are hereby acknowledged, hereby guaranties payments of any and all indebtedness and performance of any and all obligations for which Transferee is now or may hereafter become responsible for a period of thirty-six (36) months from the date of the Transfer and Release Agreement by and among Franchisor, ______________ ("Franchisee") and Transferee. The Undersigned agrees to be bound by, and liable for the breach of, each and every provision (both monetary obligations and obligations to take or refrain from taking specific actions or to engage or refrain from engaging in specific activities) under and pursuant to a certain Franchise Agreement by and between Franchisor and Transferee dated __________________, covering Store No. XXX located at ____________.

The Undersigned hereby agrees to be bound jointly and severally with the Transferee for any such indebtedness and obligations to Franchisor arising under the Franchisee Agreement; and the Undersigned hereby waives (a) acceptance and notice of the acceptance of this Guaranty and Subordination, (b) notice of any and all indebtedness or obligations of Transferee to Franchisor, now existing or which may hereafter exist, (c) notice of default of payment, demand, and diligence, and all other notices of any kind whatsoever, and (d) all legal and equitable defenses to which the undersigned might be entitled under the Franchise Agreement or under this Guaranty and Subordination.

The Undersigned also agrees that the written acknowledgment of the Transferee or the judgment of any court establishing the amount due from the Transferee shall be conclusive and binding on the Undersigned and the Undersigned's successors and assigns, and that any extension of time for payment shall not affect the Undersigned's liability hereunder.

The Undersigned agrees to pay reasonable attorneys' fees and all costs incurred by Franchisor in attempting to collect, or in collecting, any sums owed by the Transferee, as described in the Franchise Agreement (unless attorneys' fees and costs are included in the indebtedness of Transferee for which the Undersigned is liable thereunder), or owed by the Undersigned as a result of or in connection with this Guaranty and Subordination.

The undersigned understands that this Guaranty and Subordination is irrevocable and is independent of any and all other guarantees that may be made by any other parties with respect to the indebtedness or obligations covered hereby.

The Undersigned hereby subordinates to the rights of Franchisor any and all rights to repayment of loans, or any claims associated therewith, made by the Undersigned to Transferee, whether now existing or hereafter arising while this Guaranty and Subordination is in effect.

This Guaranty and Subordination is for the benefit of Franchisor, which may, without any notice whatsoever to anyone, sell, assign, or transfer any part of the indebtedness guaranteed herein, and in that event, each and every successive assignee, transferee, or holder of all or any part of the indebtedness shall have the right to enforce this Guaranty and Subordination, by suit or otherwise, for the benefit of such assignee, transferee, or holder, as fully as though such assignee, transferee, or holder were herein by name given such rights, superior to that of any such assignee, transferee, or holder, to enforce this Guaranty and Subordination for its benefit as to such of said indebtedness that it has not sold, assigned, or transferred.

The Undersigned acknowledge that, during the effective period of this Guaranty and Subordination, Franchisor may look first to the Undersigned for all such unperformed obligations, without being required to first seek recourse or exhaust all remedies against Transferee.

The foregoing is the entire agreement affecting the Undersigned's liability for the obligations described herein. The parties intend for this Guaranty and Subordination to be construed and interpreted under the laws of the State of ____________, without regard to its choice of law or conflict of law rules. The parties further waive rights to a jury trial and all defenses of personal jurisdiction and/or venue and agree that any litigation or other legal proceeding pertaining to or arising from the execution of this Guaranty and Subordination shall be brought in a court of competent jurisdiction within the State of _______.

EXECUTED in multiple originals this _____________ day of _____________, 19___.

WITNESS: GUARANTOR:

_______________________________ _______________________________

Form 5-7B
Scope of Work

[Work requests for repairs and maintenance, along with deadlines for completion of work, to be set forth here.]

CHAPTER 6

Mergers and Acquisitions of Franchise Systems

Kevin P. Hein and Ted Pearce

Contents

6-1. Introduction to Mergers and Acquisitions

Over the past 20 years the franchising ecosystem has changed dramatically. Where the franchise landscape was once populated by nascent individual franchise systems owned by their founders, today there are many franchise systems that have been consolidated or are now owned by strategic operators as well as private equity groups. As organic expansion of franchise systems becomes more challenging, growth through acquisition or consolidation has become the norm.

This chapter addresses the core issues that form the basis for a merger and/or acquisition of one franchise system by another or the acquisition of a franchise system by outside investors or a combination of both. In addressing this issue, the topics explored in this chapter include the motivations that drive franchisors to acquire other systems or to be acquired, factors a purchaser should consider when finding a target, how transactions are commonly structured, due diligence strategies and considerations, the issues that generally arise during a transaction, and topics that should be considered when governing a franchise system after an acquisition. These issues are all interrelated and should be considered together when determining whether a system-wide transaction is viable for both the purchaser and the seller.

Three sample documents are provided in the exhibits section of this chapter. Exhibit 6-1 contains a sample letter of intent that outlines a number of the issues that should generally be agreed upon prior to entering into negotiations for a definitive purchase agreement. Checklist 6-1 outlines many of the issues that should be reviewed as part of the due diligence process in a franchise company merger and acquisition transaction. Checklist 6-2 is a sample closing checklist for use in the acquisition or sale of a franchise company.

6-2. Identifying the Acquisition Target

(a) The Reasons Sellers Seek to Sell and Purchasers Seek to Purchase Franchise Systems

There can be many reasons that precipitate a desire to sell or purchase a franchise system. A primary motivation for the founders seeking to sell their system is the ability to realize a significant return on their initial investment in the franchise concept. Additionally, as the franchise system evolves, often the founders come to understand that they are not suited to take the system to the next level, whether that means accelerated growth domestically or internationally or growing the product or service offerings. Conversely, a purchaser may determine that a purchase of another franchise system, competitive or otherwise, may be the solution for in-filling markets where the purchasing company has not been able to grow organically. A purchaser also may determine that its franchise structure presents management with a platform to operate multiple systems, either in the same or a different product or service category. The reasons supporting an acquisition of a franchise system are legion. These decisions are often driven by the immediate needs of the particular system, which will in turn dictate what a purchaser or seller will seek from its sale and how it will seek and identify the proper acquisition candidate.

The opportunity to complete an acquisition or the sale of a franchise company will be viewed from different sides of the same prism based on whether one is the purchaser or the seller. Will the franchise system that the purchaser wishes to acquire provide it with a sufficient return on its investment? Conversely, for the seller, is in fact the franchise system truly marketable? While the purchaser and seller will conduct different analyses, they both will analyze the health and future prospects of the target franchise system.

(b) Identifying a Seller or Purchaser

In identifying a target, the first thing that a purchaser will do is examine the market for the products and services for the franchise system it seeks to acquire. How will the market change and how fast will this occur? If a purchaser acquires a particular franchise system, it will be critical for the purchaser to understand the future of the market for the products and services that are at the core of the system it intends to purchase. Additionally, understanding the specific market will enable the purchaser to determine the level of investment necessary to be able to realize a specific return on its investment. A purchaser may seek to purchase a heritage brand, which is to say a brand that has a powerful and historically recognizable trademark, but the system may need to be materially refreshed. In that situation the purchaser should understand that substantial investment will need to be made to the basic infrastructure of the system and will, therefore, likely need to account for those costs when setting or evaluating the proposed purchase price.

Alternatively, a purchaser may seek to acquire an emerging franchise system that has growth opportunities and a strong track record. The price may then be dictated more by the growth potential of the particular system. By the same token, a purchaser may seek to add multiple young brands to its stable of brands to balance its portfolio of older and more established brands. Identifying the target will be dictated by the purchaser's business strategy. Whatever the identity of the target, there will be some common characteristics in all targets. For example, in the context of automotive repair franchise systems, as services offered to consumers become more consolidated into a brand that offers an array of services, franchisors have incorporated multiple brands offering different services so that the combined system of multiple brands can realize synergies in attracting and maintaining customers through coordinated advertising, training, and cross-promotion opportunities. By the same token, fast food franchise systems look to capitalize on the myriad tastes of the consuming public. Consequently, a franchisor that owns multiple restaurant brands with different offerings has a greater possibility of capturing customers for more of their weekly restaurant meals.

After making a determination that the state of the industry for a particular franchise concept meets the purchaser's threshold, in most cases the purchaser will identify and evaluate the particular franchise systems that may be available. Whether a prospective purchaser shops using an investment banker or through its own search, the characteristics are the same.

(c) Evaluating a Franchise System

The first thing that a purchaser should examine is the number of units and their geographic location. Are the units primarily old or new? Do they maintain a similar look and size throughout the chain? A review of the franchisor's franchise disclosure document (FDD) will help the purchaser understand the franchise system and offering. A purchaser should review the FDD in many of the same ways that a franchisee prospect would look at the document before deciding to join a franchise chain. What is the age of the system? How many units does the system operate? What are the ages of the individual units? How many franchises were sold and opened during the last three years? Are multi-unit developers opening new locations or in default of their development obligations? How many franchises left the system, and for what reasons? What is the renewal rate over the past five years?

The purchaser also will want to review the franchisor's financial statements carefully. The accountants will review those earnings to verify their quality and to ensure that what is reported on the statements is, in fact, accurate and correct. But a purchaser also will want to look at the character of those earnings. What is the major source of the target's income? Do the vast majority of the revenues come from royalties, initial franchise fees, or product sales? The question for the purchaser will be whether these income streams are sustainable after the purchase. A close examination of the financial health of the target is paramount, especially if the purchaser requires financing to complete the purchase of the target franchise system. What amount of leverage can the target handle and at the same time continue to achieve its business plan or financial model? In some cases, this may be the first time that the franchise system has been leveraged and, therefore, the target must be able to generate cash flow sufficient to sustain both operations and the debt service. Any financing will be accompanied by a substantial credit agreement that will require the franchisor, among other obligations, to maintain its financial operations within certain financial ratios, and to sustain certain target earnings or EBITDA (earnings before interest, taxes, depreciation, and amortization).

In ascertaining whether a target is financeable, a potential lender will assess a number of components of the franchise system to determine if the system can support long-term financing. If the franchisor is involved in maintaining a leasehold position on the various unit locations, a lender will want to review and analyze the terms of the various leases. One of the specific issues to review is the assignability of each lease. Are they self-executing, meaning a change of control will not trigger landlord approval, or will any transfer or change of control of the management or ownership require landlord approval? Another question often asked by lenders is whether there are any environmental issues. Certain types of franchise systems, such as automotive repair facilities, may require a more in-depth environmental analysis. With respect to these leases, the purchaser, as well as its banker, will want to understand the lease turnover rate. A lease that shows significant churning will be viewed negatively for financing purposes. The leased locations also will be examined to determine if the locations are in healthy or declining markets. The buyer will also need to analyze how the target's financial statements will appear to lenders under the revenue recognition changes mandated by ASC 606 in 2019.[1] Does the franchisor's revenue mix permit the buyer to leverage the transaction and remain compliant with the lender's EBITDA covenants under the new revenue recognition rules? The considerations raised by ASC 606 are new to the franchise landscape, and the impact these new rules will

---

1. *See* ASC 606/IFRS 15. Prior to this accounting rule change, Generally Accepted Accounting Principles (GAAP) permitted franchisors to recognize the full value of the initial franchise fee as revenue on the company's income statement when the location opened for business. In its simplest terms, the new accounting rule requires that franchisors recognize all or part of the initial franchise fee as revenue over the term of the franchise agreement. As an example, assume a new franchisee signed a 10-year franchise agreement and paid a $50,000 initial franchise fee. Under the new rule, the franchisor will be allowed to recognize only $5,000 in revenue in each year. More importantly, the unrecognized balance is recorded on the franchisor's balance sheet as a combination of short-term and long-term liabilities. Franchisors who continue to successfully sell franchises will see these liabilities accrue much faster over the years, while the revenue they can recognize will be significantly depressed as a result of this accounting change. The net effect is that most, if not all, new and emerging brands will appear to be money-losing enterprises at least until they get to the stage in which they are royalty self-sufficient.

create on the mergers and acquisitions environment remains to be seen. All of these issues will go into determining whether the target is financeable and, specifically, to determine the interest rate, the term of the financing, and how much of the purchase price a lender will be willing to finance.

The acquiring company, as well as its potential lender, will also want to examine the health of the relationship between the target and its franchisees. A purchaser will want to know how many franchised units have been terminated over the past three to five years and the franchisee renewal rate. A chain that shows a high turnover or churn rate may not be as attractive to a purchaser that is looking to replicate and increase the then-current cash flow. If the purchaser is looking to rejuvenate a heritage brand, management may be more willing to purchase the chain with a less stable franchisee base believing that it will be able to reverse the turnover with a newer business model. Of course, the ultimate purchase price will, in most cases, reflect this instability.

Another important analysis to be undertaken by a potential purchaser is the company's ability to leverage its existing infrastructure to integrate the target. In other words, what synergies will the purchaser be able to realize from the acquisition and, in particular, what duplicate costs will management be able to eliminate from the existing system after the acquisition? The easy cost-cutting measures likely will come from combining much of the back-office operations, such as legal, accounting, and corporate administration. In addition, there may be a certain amount of value in combining real estate, training functions, franchise development, and possibly advertising. The caveat to taking advantage of these synergies is to ensure that they do not dilute the operations of the target. The purchaser's management team will need to take a hard look at whether, for example, combining the advertising functions of two competitive chains will result in a reduction of meaningful advertising costs for one or both of the systems. If the franchise sales departments for two franchise systems are combined, this could result in sales personnel focusing their efforts on the franchise system where it is either easier or more profitable to sell franchise opportunities, thus potentially harming the "less favored" franchise system. In essence, while focusing on synergies as a means to increase the ultimate net cash flow for the purchaser, these synergies must be analyzed from a long-term perspective in the context of the purchaser's goals when deciding to make the acquisition. As discussed in section 6-7(b), once the purchaser acquires the target, management will have to manage it for the ultimate benefit of the franchise system, lest they risk destruction of the assets that they purchased. It is not uncommon for an acquisition to be driven by the financial benefits to be realized by each party resulting from the actual sale; what sometimes gets lost in the transaction is the realization or attention to the details of running the target on a post-acquisition basis.

Another key analysis in identifying a potential target is to review the location of the company's existing company-owned and franchised units. This becomes especially important if the purchaser is acquiring a system that offers products or services that compete with the purchaser's current system. In reviewing the target's FDD, one thing to pay attention to is the reservation of rights described in

Item 12 of the FDD as well as the companion provisions in the franchise agreement. If the target franchisor has not reserved the right to develop or franchise businesses offering similar services under a different trademark inside a franchisee's protected territory, then integrating the target company into an existing franchise platform could be problematic. With older franchise systems franchisors rarely considered being acquired when they established the territorial rights to granted to their franchisees.

After reviewing the territorial provisions set forth in the target's franchise agreement, the purchaser will need to overlay the location of its centers with the target's locations or areas of protection. Is the purchaser planning to run parallel systems, combine the two systems, or operate cobrands if there are complementary products or services? There are distinct consequences surrounding each of these strategies. If the purchaser seeks to run parallel systems, this may require that it keep the systems separate. In that situation, the purchaser may need to run separate operations for real estate and franchise sales departments post-transaction. Running parallel systems may, in fact, interfere with the synergies that the purchaser hopes to achieve from the transaction. By the same token, if the purchaser wants to combine both systems, then management will have to address how this combination affects the territorial rights granted to the franchisees of both franchise systems. The result of the combination may require the franchisor to buy out existing franchisees in either the target or the acquiring chain to maintain the territorial rights of the franchisees.

Likewise, the target may offer complementary products or services to the existing chain that would result in being able to capture more customers who would ordinarily go to two different establishments to obtain the different products or services. A "combo unit" may be a great way for existing franchisees to increase their revenues by not only attracting customers for the new products or services they can offer but also enabling the franchisees to realize synergies of their own, such as having a single unit to offer the products and services instead of two. As part of the overall due diligence that is conducted in the transaction, which is discussed in section 6-5 of this chapter, close attention will need to be paid to the governing documents of each franchise system including the FDDs and the franchise agreements.

Identifying a target will be a direct function of the purchaser's business strategies. In some cases, the purchaser may look for another source of EBITDA to satisfy its investors. Another reason may be to fill in a geographic area that a franchisor has been unable to penetrate for various reasons. In addition, a specific acquisition may be found opportunistically, which is to say that the transaction appears to be too good to pass up. By the same token the selling franchisor will market its system by playing into the needs of the potential suitor and, therefore, emphasizing its particular advantages to meet the needs of the acquiring company. The strategy for marketing a franchise system may best be left to the investment bankers, who have experience in how to emphasize the strengths of a particular franchise system. As just one example, an investment banker may help the potential suitor understand the significance of the cash flow of a franchisor that employs very few assets. That cash flow may be more valuable than a similar cash flow of a manufacturer, which likely must regularly reinvest a portion of its cash flow in its plant and equipment to remain competitive. In the end, almost every franchise system can be made marketable to a potential suitor depending on the goals and needs of that prospective buyer. It goes without saying that a franchise system with an established and growing cash flow from the receipt of ongoing royalties is one of the most attractive targets for any would-be suitor.

6-3. Preparing the Confidential Interest Memorandum and Negotiating the Letter of Intent

When engaging in a purchase or sale of a franchise system, the seller will likely prepare, and the purchaser will want to see, a confidential interest memorandum that describes the target and the target's industry and includes a financial statement and financial model of the selling company. These memoranda or marketing pieces, which can be over 100 pages, are meant to provide an overview of the target and to give the purchaser an ability to "kick the tires" of the target. Be mindful that before the purchaser will be able to view the confidential interest memorandum, and sometimes before the target is identified, the purchaser's management will need to execute with the seller, or the representative investment banker, a nondisclosure and confidentiality agreement. Most of these documents are similar in substance, if not form. The confidentiality agreement will require the recipient to agree that the information being received is confidential and also will likely require the recipient to agree to keep the name and financial data of the target confidential. This last point is extremely important because the seller does not want to reveal, until absolutely necessary, the fact that its franchise system may be up for sale. Of course, this fact is greatly important if the seller is a public company, but even if it is privately held, a premature disclosure of the target may cause great commotion and anxieties within the franchise system—which includes not only the franchisees but also the franchisor's employees, suppliers, and creditors who are not aware that the franchisor may be sold. Whether the fact that a franchise system is up for sale triggers an FDD disclosure requirement must be considered and is addressed in more detail later in this chapter. See section 6-7(a) of this chapter for a more detailed analysis of franchise disclosures during a sale of a franchise system.

While not every sale of a franchise system will call for a letter of intent, the document can be a valuable tool for both the purchaser and seller. The seller may wish to go right to a binding purchase agreement, since its primary concern is receiving the purchase price from the sale, However, from the purchaser's standpoint, the letter of intent can do more than describe the terms of the sale. The purchaser will want to include a provision granting it a period of exclusivity. While an exclusivity agreement may be a separate document or agreement, it is very common to see an exclusivity provision in a letter of intent. Even if the letter of intent is written as a nonbinding document, there are likely to be certain binding provisions within the letter, including the exclusivity period. In addition to the exclusivity provision, any confidential information referred to in the letter of intent will survive the termination of the letter even if no deal is consummated. Likewise, any costs that are incurred during this phase of the transaction and that are discussed in the letter of intent will likely survive the letter of intent.

The due diligence phase may take anywhere from 15 to 90 days and could go beyond. The time frame will be determined by the complexity of the transaction, the size of the system, and the level of interest the purchaser shows in completing the transaction. As discussed in section 6-5, conducting due diligence is a daunting task that requires the purchaser to assemble a sizable legal, operational, and accounting team to review all aspects of the company or assets being purchased. Consequently, time, effort, and money will be expended by the purchaser. From its standpoint, the purchaser does not want to undertake this aspect of the transaction if it knows that the seller is continuing to market and take offers from competitive bidders.

The time and scope of the exclusivity provision may be hotly negotiated in this phase of the transaction. As would be expected, the purchaser will want a longer time while the seller will seek the most abbreviated time frame that it can obtain. The exclusivity provision may require the seller to cease marketing as well as taking bids from others to give the purchaser a solid chance to complete the transaction without interference and without the seller playing the purchaser's preliminary bid against other suitors.

While the purchaser will want the letter of intent to contain an exclusivity provision, the seller is not likely to agree to one without receiving something in return. The quid pro quo likely will be an agreed-upon sales price. The process for establishing the price could consume its own chapter. There are numerous methods of determining a sales price, including taking an appraisal of the assets being sold. The most common method is to agree on a multiple of the EBITDA. The multiple will depend on many things, not least of which is the availability of credit to purchase the target. The multiple could be based in part on the percentage of annual earnings that a creditor will lend the purchaser to purchase the target. The price multiple will also be driven by the market and the history of sale and post-sale performance of other franchise systems in general, with a special focus on franchise systems that are in the same industry as the target.

If the purchaser is purchasing the target for cash without the need for third-party financing, the purchaser will be in a better bargaining position. A well-financed purchaser will have greater leverage to dictate the term and structure of the exclusivity clause in the letter of intent. In establishing the sales price for the purchase of a franchise system, the quality of the earnings used will be of great importance to the purchaser. As discussed earlier, the purchaser will want to understand the nature of the earnings generated by the target franchise system. Are these earning loaded with initial franchise fees because the target has undergone tremendous growth, which may not be available to the purchaser? On the other hand, are the earnings dependent on continuing franchise fees from a mature system with fewer years left on the franchise contracts and a spotty history of renewing franchisees? There are countless questions that the purchaser will ask the target and will need to include in its due diligence examination. Suffice it to say, the purchaser and its investment bank will be put to the highest business judgment in establishing the sales price.

It is not uncommon for the sales price to contain language regarding post-sale adjustment to take into account the working capital at the time of the closing of the sale. In essence, this post-closing calculation will take into consideration many short-term working capital components such as the payment of accounts receivable, accounts payable, refunds of initial franchise fees, and other adjustments to short-term assets and liabilities. The letter of intent may contain an agreed-upon working capital target post-closing, which if not met will require a post-closing adjustment to the purchase price originally agreed upon. The post-closing adjustment will usually extend up to 90 days after the closing of the transaction.

In evaluating the purchase of a target, the purchaser will examine the synergies that it may be able to realize post-closing. From the purchaser's standpoint, it will not wish to include these money-saving possibilities in the calculation of the sales price. Conversely, the seller may try to factor into the sales price cost savings for the purchaser, which is likely to result in an adjusted EBITDA number that translates to a higher sales price when multiplying it by the agreed-upon earnings multiple. The identified synergies could encompass a whole host of annual expenditures, including saving the salaries of certain corporate officers, as well as eliminating expenditures for cars, airplanes, boats, and other personal items that likely will remain with the seller or its owners and not continue post-sale.

As part of establishing the sales price, the parties often agree upon a holdback provision. This holdback is intended to ensure that money is available to the purchaser to cover indemnification items resulting from third-party claims or from breaches of representations and warranties by the seller in the purchase agreement. The need for a holdback will be obvious to the purchaser who believes that after closing, the seller is not likely to keep the money in one bank account that will be available to the purchaser as is necessary. Instead, there may be multiple selling shareholders who will doubtless have plans for their proceeds other than to keep them available for a purchaser seeking to recover a post-closing indemnification claim. The length and time frame for a holdback will be specifically negotiated between the purchaser and seller. In addition, the parties will also have to agree whether the money set aside for the holdback is to be kept with a third-party escrow agent, necessitating a third-party escrow agreement. It is not uncommon to see holdback amounts equal as much as 10 percent of the sales price and the holdback period to last as long as 18 months after the closing.

Other components of the letter of intent will contain the structure of the sale, including whether it will be a stock or asset purchase; the time frame for negotiating the binding purchase agreement; how and when the purchase price is to be paid; and any other financing or other contingencies relevant to the sale. If a confidentiality agreement covering the confidential information that inevitably will be exchanged during the sales process has not already been negotiated, the letter of intent will contain a detailed description of what constitutes confidential information. The confidentiality provision also will outline how the information is to be handled and what happens to the information either post-sale or post-negotiation if there is no sale consummated. A confidentiality provision likely will survive the letter of intent even if a sale is not consummated.

A provision that may be included in a letter of intent is a breakup fee. This fee represents compensation for the damages that either a seller or purchaser would suffer if the other party does not carry through with the contemplated purchase. A breakup fee may be triggered by a number of reasons, including failure of the purchaser to obtain financing or discovery of issues in due diligence that prove problematic for the seller or purchaser. While breakup fees are not always included in the sale of a franchise system, they constitute a provision that either party may want to consider.

As mentioned above, one provision that will always be in a letter of intent is a confidentiality clause requiring both parties to keep the terms of the letter of intent, as well as the existence of the letter of intent, confidential. The parties will also need to agree on how long the confidentiality provisions will extend beyond the termination of the letter of intent or the execution of a purchase agreement.

Another provision that will be important in a letter of intent to purchase a franchise system is the availability of visiting or interviewing representatives of the franchise system. Without a doubt, the purchaser needs to investigate or analyze the health of the franchise system. How much access will be granted to the franchisees of the target will be of concern to the seller who will fear that too much access may cause unnecessary disruption and also could signal to the franchisees that a sale of the system is afoot. Undoubtedly the health of a franchise system is of paramount importance to the purchaser. The principal asset that it is purchasing is the collection of franchise contracts. So understanding whether it is purchasing a contented or malcontented system is of great importance to the purchaser. By the same token, the seller will be concerned that if the franchisees learn of a pending sale, they may inject themselves into the sales process to exact concessions from the selling franchisor in consideration for their cooperation in the sales process. These concessions could include a reduction in their future franchise fees or royalties, which would affect the sales price since this reduction could result in lower future earnings for the purchaser.

The letter of intent is an important element of a franchise system sale. It not only covers certain very important matters that cannot wait to be addressed until there is a binding agreement of sale but also provides both parties with a road map defining how to proceed with the complexities of the sale of the target franchise system.

6-4. Stock versus Asset Acquisition

One of the first decisions that an acquiring company must make when examining a potential acquisition is whether to acquire the stock of the target company or to acquire the assets of the company instead. This issue should be considered even before an initial offer is made to acquire the target company because the structure of the proposed transaction will be a critical element to address in the letter of intent. Each approach has benefits, risks, and significant tax consequences to the purchaser and the seller. This section examines each option, and the attendant tax consequences to the parties, in more detail.

(a) Stock Acquisition

In most cases, the easiest and the cleanest approach to structuring the acquisition of a franchise company is for the purchaser to acquire all of the stock or other forms of equity ownership interest of the target company. To purchase the capital stock of a company is the equivalent of purchasing all of its assets and liabilities, unless specifically excluded. In essence, by purchasing the stock of a company the purchaser will stand in the shoes of the seller as if the purchaser had always owned the company. Accordingly, by purchasing all of the capital stock of a company, the purchaser is acquiring the existing company intact. This enables the purchaser to continue to utilize the franchise company's existing audited financial statements and continue offering and selling franchises through the transaction and after the acquisition is complete. This approach also avoids the requirement that the franchisor "go dark" after the acquisition is complete while audited financial statements are prepared for the new entity and the new franchise entity secures initial registrations of its FDD in the relevant registration states. Instead, in a stock purchase, the target company's disclosure document and state registrations merely need to be amended to reflect the new owner of the entity, as well as the change of its financial circumstances, if any. If the stock acquisition occurs at the parent company or stockholder level, the franchisor may not be required to make any changes to the FDD or to amend its registration filings. Finally, because a stock sale effectively leaves the existing entity in place, this strategy enables the franchise company to take advantage of any registration exemptions available to large franchisors. Most of these exemptions are based on the history[2] and financial condition of the franchise system. With a stock purchase, the history of the franchise system is not disturbed because the legal entity owning the franchise contracts remains the same. Conversely, in an asset pur-

2. The history of a franchise system for purposes of obtaining a franchise registration exemption is based on the number of units a franchise system maintains for a period of years. For example, the California Franchise Investment Law, Cal. Corp. Code § 3101, provides that a franchisor with a specified net worth and a franchise operation history of five years with at least 25 franchises in operation will be exempted from having to register its FDD with the state regulatory authorities.

chase, the franchise contracts are transferred to a new entity, which may create a gap in the history of the franchise system that may result in the franchise system being treated as a new franchise system for purposes of franchise registration.

A stock acquisition is not without some risk. The acquiring company takes control of the assets of the target company but also generally assumes all of the liabilities and contractual obligations owed by the acquired entity to creditors existing as of the closing date, except for those that are expressly excluded in the purchase agreement. Some of these liabilities may not have been fully disclosed to the purchaser. In some cases, they may not have been known by the management of the acquired company at the time of the acquisition; in other cases, the liabilities may be contingent, but the contingency could be significant if the liability matures. In a stock acquisition, the purchaser cannot avoid taking on both the known and unknown liabilities of the target company. The best way for the purchaser to be protected from the financial consequences of unknown or undisclosed liabilities is to negotiate a strong indemnification provision into the purchase agreement, and to ensure that the indemnifying party retains sufficient assets or carries adequate insurance to be able to cover its indemnification obligations in the event the purchaser needs to make a claim. Of course, the risk is that the seller will have exhausted its assets or transferred its assets beyond the reach of the purchaser prior to the time the purchaser has to make a claim for indemnification. In such instances, the purchaser may find that it is saddled with liabilities that infringe on its ability to execute its growth plan for the acquired entity. In a worst-case scenario, the liabilities may be so significant that the acquired company is forced to reorganize its debts under Chapter 11 of the Bankruptcy Code, or even to liquidate its assets. For example, if the purchaser acquires a restive franchise system where there are underlying claims brewing against the former franchisor, the dissatisfaction of the franchisees could ignite into a full-fledged class action that not only would risk the royalty income stream for the purchaser but also could undermine its principal asset, that being the collection of franchise contracts.

(b) Asset Acquisition

On balance, many purchasers prefer to acquire the assets of a target company, rather than its stock. The primary reason is that in an asset acquisition, the purchaser can pick and choose the assets it wants to acquire and the liabilities it is willing to assume. Most asset purchase agreements include a provision stating that any asset not transferred or liability not expressly assumed in the agreement is retained by the seller. This generally allows the purchaser to avoid assuming any undisclosed or contingent liabilities from the seller. See section 6-4(c), Tax Issues.

The downside for the purchaser is that an asset acquisition usually requires the purchaser to place the assets into a newly formed entity. Because the entity is new, state and federal franchise laws require that the entity have a new opening balance sheet audit prepared and that the entity obtain new original registrations.

This means that the new franchisor entity will be prevented from offering or selling franchises in all states until the audit is complete and from offering or selling franchises in registration states until the state registration permits are issued. The new entity will also not be able to take advantage of any state-level large franchisor exemptions because such exemptions require an extended period of operating history.

(c) Tax Issues

Tax ramifications of the sale are some of the primary concerns of both purchasers and sellers in determining whether to structure the acquisition as a stock or an asset acquisition. In this respect, the primary goal of the seller is to minimize the tax it or its shareholders must pay on the gains received from the sale. The primary goal of the purchaser is to structure the transaction to step up the basis of assets acquired in the transaction, so the buyer can depreciate or amortize a greater portion of the purchase price and thereby reduce its future income tax liability. These goals are often in conflict and generally are mutually exclusive. In other words, if one side receives favorable tax treatment, the other side often pays more in taxes.

These tax issues can be particularly acute in the acquisition of a franchise system. Most franchise companies do not acquire and maintain a significant amount of tangible assets. Instead, the heart and soul of a franchise company is its intangible assets—its trademarks and other intellectual property, the system, customer lists, and franchise agreements. In most cases, franchise companies do not have to spend or capitalize significant dollars to build this asset base and, as a result, the basis in these assets is generally fairly low. However, because these assets can generate significant net cash flow in the operation of a franchise system, a purchaser is often willing to pay a hefty premium or goodwill over the net asset value of the company to acquire the franchise company.

In the case of a company stock sale, the selling company does not pay tax as a result of the sale, but the shareholders pay income tax on the difference between their basis in the company's stock and the net proceeds they receive from the sale. Most sellers prefer to sell stock because they are able to take advantage of long-term capital gains tax rates, which are generally lower than the income tax rates for ordinary income for most taxpayers. This long-term capital gains tax rate is available to any selling shareholder who held shares longer than one year.[3]

For the purchaser, a stock acquisition generally does not have as many beneficial tax attributes as an asset purchase. In a stock sale, the value of the assets is generally not adjusted for tax purposes after the sale because the sale of the shares, per se, does not affect the underlying assets of the acquired company,

3. Under current law, the U.S. federal long-term capital gains rate is 15 percent. (Short-term capital gains are generally taxable as ordinary income.) Ordinary income rates for individuals, on the other hand, currently are 35 percent at the highest marginal rate. State income taxes (and county/local taxes, as appropriate) on the stock sale may be payable in addition to federal taxes.

which remains a separate taxpaying entity. Instead, any premium paid by the purchaser becomes part of the purchaser's basis in the acquired shares and is thus treated as part of the purchaser's investment in the franchise company. While this means that the acquiring purchaser/company will have a basis in its stock equal to the price it paid for the franchise company, it will not generally receive any tax benefit for stepping up the value of the assets. In other words, the "inside" relatively low basis of the various assets owned by the franchise company generally is not stepped up (absent a so-called section 338 election, discussed below), so the premium paid for the acquired company's stock is merely reflected in the purchaser's basis in that stock.[4]

The opposite is generally true for the purchaser in the case of an asset acquisition. Because an existing acquiring entity acquires, or a new taxpaying entity is formed to acquire, the assets, the purchaser can step up the basis of the assets in accordance with the price paid to acquire those assets. Allocation of the purchase price among the assets is necessary to establish their respective tax bases, and this allocation is ordinarily best reflected in the purchase and sale agreement itself.[5] This enables the purchaser to begin new depreciation and amortization periods for the assets, and to depreciate or amortize the assets at the higher, stepped-up value. As a result, the tax benefits to the purchaser can be significant.

The selling shareholders in an asset sale situation ultimately pay the price for an asset acquisition. After the sale of all or substantially all of its assets, the selling entity could be left with a significant amount of cash, but also gain or income to report based on the allocated selling price of each such asset. If the entity is a C corporation, it must pay income tax at the entity level (at the ordinary corporate income rate, which is currently 21 percent)[6] on the difference between the basis of each asset sold and the proceeds received for the sale of each asset. The selling company usually then distributes the remaining cash to its shareholders. This distribution is considered a liquidating dividend for tax purposes, and it is taxable to the recipient shareholders, a second level of tax. Whether the shareholders will be able to pay taxes on the distribution at the long-term capital gains rate (or at ordinary rates) depends on their personal tax positions and the length of time they held the shares. Regardless, the shareholders end up paying double tax when

---

4. Book treatment of the purchase, according to U.S. GAAP, may differ from the tax treatment described.

5. As may be evident, the buyer may want to allocate the purchase price to assets that will produce the fastest recovery of that investment in the future, such as to faster depreciation or higher amortization assets, while the seller may want to allocate the purchase price to assets that produce the lowest overall taxable gain in the year of sale. Thus, there is an inherent tension in the allocation process. However, in the end, it is certainly a product of negotiation between the parties and their advisors. Best practice, however, clearly is to have the parties come to an agreement as to the allocation and not to take inconsistent tax reporting positions.

6. Assuming that there is a profit of more than $18,500,000.

the assets of the franchise entity are sold and the proceeds are distributed to them by the selling entity.[7]

Given the differences in tax treatment described above between stock and asset acquisitions, it is not surprising that purchasers may want to acquire the stock of the target and, at the same time, receive the step-up in basis and other tax benefits of an asset acquisition. In such cases, the acquiring company may elect to have the stock acquisition treated like an asset acquisition for tax purposes under section 338 of the Internal Revenue Code. There are actually two different elections under section 338. The rules are specific and precise, but the end result of a proper election is a step-up in tax basis for the assets of the acquired company. In general, the tax effects of making a proper election are as follows: "the acquired corporation is treated as though it sold all of its assets for a price equal to the price paid by the purchaser for the stock and simultaneously repurchased the assets for the same price."[8] However, the electing entity *must* recognize any gain from the deemed sale of the assets and itself pay income tax on the difference between the newly increased value of the assets and the adjusted basis of the assets before the sale. This inherent tax liability in the acquired company becomes an economic issue to the acquiring company, which without reduction of or indemnity against the purchase price of the stock for such liability will essentially have paid more for the acquired franchise company. One of the section 338 elections is available only if the selling shareholder is a company in a consolidated group, a subchapter S corporation, or subchapter S shareholders.[9]

---

7. Some franchise companies are set up as flow-through entities, such as an LLC or subchapter S corporation. In these cases, the selling entity would not be required to pay tax on the sale, since its flow-through character for tax purposes means that only the shareholders ultimately pay tax (a single level of tax) when the sale is finalized and they receive the proceeds, as differentiated from a C corporation structure requiring a second level of tax when the sale and distribution of proceeds processes are both complete. If both the acquiring and acquired entities are C corporations, it may also be possible to structure the acquisition of the franchise company as a tax-free acquisition, pursuant to very specific federal tax rules. These arrangements generally require, however, that the acquired franchise company shareholders remain substantial owners of the acquiring company for a while thereafter, and that the existing tax basis of the assets of the acquired company may transfer over to the acquired company without a possible step up. Either or both of these oversimplified consequences may not be acceptable to the parties, even if they can otherwise structure the acquisition technically to comply with the tax-free-acquisition rules.

8. Mergers & Acquisitions of Franchise Companies 192 (Leonard D. Vines ed., ABA Forum on Franchising 1996).

9. *See* I.R.C. § 338(h)(10). Obviously, if the sellers are individuals and the franchise company is not itself a subchapter S corporation, this type of section 338 election is unavailable. If the franchise company to be acquired is a foreign corporation without any U.S. tax liabilities or nexus, then having it make the other type of section 338 election (the section 338(g) election) may be possible since the deemed gain at the electing entity level would not have any actual U.S. tax consequences. In these situations, care must be taken to properly document and time the election if agreed by the parties and attention paid to possible indemnity or post-acquisition audit issues that may arise. Lastly, if a U.S. company or shareholder group is acquiring a foreign franchise company, the purchasers should consult

Even though a tax on the gain is payable for the tax year in which the election is made, some companies make this election because an amount greater than the tax can be recovered in future years through increased depreciation and amortization deductions. This is particularly true if the purchaser anticipates that tax rates will increase over time or Congress has amended the tax code to provide for accelerated depreciation of certain asset classes that are included within the franchise company.

As noted previously, the Internal Revenue Code requires that a number of conditions must be satisfied before an acquiring company can make a section 338 election,[10] and therefore this approach may not be available under all circumstances. Another issue to bear in mind is that the target corporation is treated as a new taxpaying entity after the deemed sale. As a result, all of its former (pre-election) tax attributes, including "its earnings and profits, net operating losses, tax credits, or other carryovers, are lost forever."[11]

6-5. Acquisition through Bankruptcy and Liquidation[12]

On occasion the opportunity arises to acquire the assets of a struggling or failed franchise company out of the bankruptcy process. As a general rule, an acquirer can purchase such assets by relying on Section 363 of the U.S. Bankruptcy Code or by waiting for the trustee to abandon the assets in the liquidation process. In the case of liquidation, surviving franchisees also have the opportunity to preserve their operating rights or to acquire other franchise agreements and step into the shoes of the franchisor. Each approach is discussed in more detail below.

(a) Acquisition through Section 363 of the U.S. Bankruptcy Code

A sale of assets in a bankruptcy proceeding other than in the ordinary course of business is commonly referred to as a 363 sale.[13] Such sales are more common in Chapter 11 reorganization cases than in Chapter 7 liquidation cases. The debtor or trustee may sell the debtor's assets in a 363 sale more quickly and with less scrutiny than assuming or assigning them as part of a reorganization plan. In a 363 sale, a debtor must prove that (1) the sale, assumption, and assignment is undertaken in the sound exercise of the debtor's business judgment;[14] (2) the

---

with knowledgeable U.S. tax counsel to ensure they understand the potential applicability and U.S, reporting requirements relevant to "controlled foreign corporations."

10. Mergers & Acquisitions of Franchise Companies, *supra* note 8, at 193.

11. Mergers & Acquisitions of Franchise Companies, *supra* note 8, at 193

12. The authors would like to thank Mark Lichtenstein, bankruptcy partner in Akerman's New York office, for his contributions to this section of the chapter.

13. These sales are commonly referred to as 363 sales because they are governed by § 363 of the Bankruptcy Code (11 U.S.C. § 363).

14. *In re* Montgomery Ward Holding Corp., 242 B.R. 147 (D. Del. 1999); *In re* Orion Pictures Corp., 4 F.3d 1095, 1095 (2d Cir. 1993).

debtor will cure or provide adequate assurance of the prompt cure payment and payment of all pecuniary losses;[15] and (3) the proposed purchaser can "provide 'adequate assurance of future performance'" under each agreement.[16]

The purpose of the 363 sale is to obtain the highest and best offer for the assets. Although the Bankruptcy Code does not define *highest* and *best*, bankruptcy courts will often approve a 363 sale after applying a business judgment test to determine that a "sound business reason" exists in support of the 363 sale and that the sale is in the best interest of the bankruptcy estate and the creditors.[17] The courts further require that the debtor's use of the property be proposed in good faith.[18] The good faith element has focused primarily on whether the proposed use or sale would benefit a debtor's insiders to the detriment of its estate and its creditors.[19] This debate has played out over time in various franchisor bankruptcy cases.

For example, in opposition to a potential 363 sale of the franchise system assets to a third party for $6.5 million, franchisees of The Ground Round argued that their offer for the franchise system was higher and better. In that case, franchisees asserted claims for damages in excess of $40 million for lost sales and profits resulting from (1) negative goodwill to the franchise system due to the closure of corporate-owned units, (2) the franchisor's failure to spend monies collected from franchisees on advertising and marketing, and (3) the franchisor's failure to provide operating support to franchisees.[20] The offer submitted by the franchisees included a purchase price of $4.85 million and a waiver of all of their claims. The bankruptcy court determined that the franchisees' offer constituted the highest and best offer to the estate because it prevented the estate from incurring significant litigation expenses, netted the estate $4.85 million, and included a waiver of the franchisees' claims, which the court noted could have resulted in damages of several million dollars.

In another franchisor 363 sale, Opal Concepts, Inc. sold the assets of Fantastic Sams, including franchise agreements, to Cheveux Acquisition, LLC, a regional franchisor in New England.[21] Cheveux Acquisition, LLC outbid a consortium of other Fantastic Sams regional franchisees.[22] The bankruptcy court determined that the sale reflected sound business judgment and a proper exercise of the debt-

15. *In re* Martin Paint Stores, 199 B.R. 258 (Bankr. S.D.N.Y. 1996).

16. *Id.* (quoting 11 U.S.C. §§ 365(b)(1), (f)(2)).

17. *See, e.g.*, *In re* Lionel Corp., 722 F.2d 1063, 1070–71 (2d Cir. 1983); *In re* Phoenix Steel Corp., 82 B.R. 334 (Bankr. D. Del. 1987).

18. *In re* Abbotts Dairies, Inc., 788 F.2d 143, 149–50 (3d Cir. 1986); *In re Lionel*, 722 F.2d at 1070–71.

19. *See, e.g.*, *In re* Indus. Valley Refrigeration & Air Conditioning Supplies, Inc., 77 B.R. 15, 21 (Bankr. E.D. Pa. 1987); *In re Abbotts Dairies*, 788 F.2d at 147–48 ("Typically, the misconduct that would destroy a purchaser's good faith status at a judicial sale involves fraud, collusion between the purchaser and other bidders or the trustee or an attempt to take grossly unfair advantage of other bidders." (quoting *In re* Rock Indus. Mach. Corp., 572 F.2d 1195, 1198 (7th Cir. 1978))).

20. *In re* The Ground Round, 316 B.R. 423 (Bankr. D. Mass. 2004).

21. *In re* Opal Concepts, Inc., No. SA 02-15441 JR (Bankr. C.D. Ca. July 16, 2002).

22. *Id.*

ors' fiduciary duties, thereby protecting the interests of the debtors, their creditors, and their estates.[23]

Section 363 of the Bankruptcy Code is not *intended* to be utilized to sell all or substantially all of the debtor's assets.[24] However, a 363 sale is often used to do exactly that. In some jurisdictions, a proposed 363 sale is sometimes deemed to be an illegal "sub rosa plan," and the sale is denied on that basis.[25] A sub rosa plan is a transaction that has the effect of preempting or dictating the terms of a debtor's ultimate reorganization plan absent the statutory protections required by a reorganization plan.[26] Accordingly, a competing franchisor or a franchisee may want to object to the 363 sale on this basis. However, denial of a 363 sale based on a sub rosa plan objection is rare: many courts that have heard sub rosa–based objections and yet ultimately approved the sale.[27]

The Fifth Circuit in *In re Continental Air Lines, Inc.* determined that 363 sales require an "articulated business" reason to be approved.[28] The Fifth Circuit in *In re Braniff Airways, Inc.* set out other factors that a court is to consider in approving a 363 sale.[29] The factors include consideration of the following questions:

1. Has the debtor used good business judgment?
2. Will the proposed sale further the . . . interests of the debtor, creditors and equity holders?
3. Are the assets increasing or decreasing in value?
4. Does the proposed sale specify terms for adopting . . . a reorganization plan?
5. Will approval of the proposed sale effectuate a *de facto* reorganization plan as to render creditors' rights under . . .chapter 11 meaningless?[30]

Where a proposed 363 sale of real estate reduced secured debt, did not interfere with the debtor's ability to reorganize, and did not impose conditions on the debtor's reorganization, the proposed 363 sale was approved.[31]

Relying on section 363 to purchase the assets of a struggling or failed franchise system is the best way for a buyer to ensure that the assets are being acquired free and clear of all claims by any other creditor. Prospective buyers

---

23. *Id.*
24. 11 U.S.C. § 363(b).
25. *In re* Braniff Airways, Inc., 700 F.2d 935 (5th Cir. 1983); *In re* Copy Crafters Quickprint, Inc., 92 B.R. 973 (Bankr. N.D.N.Y. 1988); *In re* Grant Broad. of Phila., Inc., 71 B.R. 390 (Bankr. E.D. Pa. 1987).
26. *In re Braniff Airways, Inc.*, 700 F.2d 935; *In re Copy Crafters Quickprint, Inc.*, 92 B.R. 973; *In re Grant Broad. of Phila., Inc.*, 71 B.R. 390.
27. *In re* Work Recovery, Inc., 202 B.R. 301 (Bankr. D. Ariz. 1996); *In re* Brethren Care of S. Bend, Inc., 98 B.R. 927 (Bankr. N.D. Ind. 1989); *In re* Terrace Gardens Park P'ship, 96 B.R. 707 (Bankr. W.D. Tex. 1989); *In re* Naron & Wagner, Chartered, 88 B.R. 85, 89 (Bankr. D. Md. 1988).
28. *In re* Cont'l Air Lines, Inc., 780 F.2d 1223 (5th Cir. 1986).
29. *In re Work Recovery*, 202 B.R. at 301 (citing *In re Braniff Airways*, 700 F.2d 935).
30. *Id.*
31. *Id.*

should pay close attention to the docket of the U.S. Bankruptcy Court to look for opportunities to make acquisitions under these circumstances.

(b) Acquisition through the Liquidation Process

When a franchisor files for bankruptcy protection under Chapter 7, the Chapter 7 trustee is empowered to liquidate the debtor's assets to maximize returns. Among the assets that could be sold are the franchisor's trademarks and franchise agreements. When a trustee is able to sell all of the franchisor's assets to a single party, the franchise system will generally be left intact but under new ownership. This could result in a favorable outcome for franchisees depending on the purchaser's franchise experience, business acumen, and financial capability. If the trustee is unable to sell all or some of the franchisor's assets, the unsold assets may be abandoned. Assets of the estate may be abandoned under the Bankruptcy Code either by the trustee during the bankruptcy case or upon the conclusion of the case if the trustee does not administer the property during the bankruptcy case. Upon abandonment, the abandoned asset reverts back to a party with a possessory interest, and the bankruptcy court is divested of jurisdiction over the asset. [32]

If a trustee is able to sell only some of the franchisor's assets, such as the franchisor's real estate, company-owned units, equipment, and other hard assets, the franchise agreements and trademarks may be left unsold. In that case, the franchise agreements may be rejected. A franchisee would then have no rights to use the trademarks and no support for its business. If the trademarks are not sold but are instead abandoned, there may be no party with a possessory interest in the trademarks to assert control over their use and force a franchisee to stop using them. This creates an opportunity for a franchisee whose franchise agreement had been rejected to (1) continue to use those trademarks despite rejection and the accompanying loss of trademark rights and (2) gain independent rights to the trademarks because the franchisor's marks may be deemed abandoned.

Abandonment under trademark law occurs when the owner of a trademark ceases to use that trademark and shows no intention of reinstituting use of that trademark in the future.[33] According to the Lanham Act, three consecutive years of non-use constitutes "prima facie evidence of abandonment."[34] Once a trademark has been abandoned, the previous owner has no rights to the trademark nor can it prevent a third party from using that trademark, and any third party may use that trademark or register it as its own.[35] Of course, the franchisee may not be

32. *In re* S. Int'l Co., L.P., 165 B.R. 815, 819 (Bankr. E.D. Va. 1994) (citing *In re* Wilson, 94 B.R. 886, 888 (Bankr. E.D. Va. 1989); *In re* Reed, 94 B.R. 48, 52 (E.D. Pa. 1988)).

33. 15 U.S.C. § 1127 (45); *see* Cerveceria Centroamericana, S.A. v. Cerveceria India, Inc., 892 F.2d 1021, 1023 (Fed. Cir. 1989) (citing Lanham Act, 15 U.S.C. § 1127).

34. 15 U.S.C. § 1127.

35. Seattle Endeavors, Inc. v. Mastro, 868 P.2d 120 (1994) ("'A trade name may be abandoned or given up by the original appropriator, and, when it is so abandoned or given up, any other person has the right to seize upon it immediately, and make use of it, and thus acquire a right to it superior not only to the right of the original user, but of all the world.'" (quoting Holmes v. Border Brokerage Co., 321 P.2d 898 (Wis. 1958) (internal quotations

able to stop other users of the mark. However, rather than waiting for the trademarks to become abandoned, it is advisable for an interested franchisee to offer to purchase the debtor's trademarks in order to protect its interests in continuing to operate its business under the same trademarks and to avoid any uncertainty over the ownership of the trademarks. A franchisee may also consider purchasing some or all of the franchise agreements and becoming the operator of the franchise system. If, on the other hand, the franchise agreement is sold, a franchisee will be concerned about which other assets have been acquired by the purchaser. If the franchisor's trademarks have also been acquired, a franchisee may be able to continue to use those trademarks instead of rebranding.

6-6. Conducting Due Diligence

A critical part of any acquisition of a franchise company is the due diligence process. Most failed franchise acquisitions die in the due diligence phase, often because the acquiring company learns one or more facts about the target that were not readily apparent from outside of the organization. The due diligence process is the one time that a purchaser can get a free look "under the hood" of a franchise organization. The time period for due diligence is often limited by the terms of the letter of intent or the purchase agreement, so it is critical that the acquisition team and the team's lawyers are as efficient and effective as possible. This section addresses some of the key aspects of a franchise acquisition that should be given particular attention during the due diligence process. This section is intended to highlight some of the most common due diligence issues addressed in the acquisition of a franchise system. It is by no means exhaustive, and there are many other issues that should be reviewed in the sales process. A sample due diligence request list is attached as checklist 6-1.

(a) Franchise Disclosure Documents and Franchise Agreements

A prospective purchaser can learn a lot about the target entity by reviewing the company's FDD and franchise agreement. Of greater importance in the due diligence process is the need to review carefully how the document has evolved over time. In that context, the purchaser should request blacklined versions of the beginning and ending versions of the FDD for each year to be examined during the due diligence period. The purchaser should also request a blacklined version highlighting the changes made to the FDD during each fiscal year being examined. Purchaser's counsel should review the various blacklined versions carefully

omitted))]; Defiance Button Mach. Co. v. C&C Metal Prods. Corp., 759 F.2d 1053 (2d Cir. 1985) ("[I]f the owner expressly abandons his mark, such as by cancelling it, or discontinues using it with the intent not to resume use, others are no longer restrained from using it because it ceases to be associated in the public's mind with the owner's goods or services." (citing Manhattan Indus., Inc. v. Sweater Bee by Banff, Ltd., 627 F.2d 628, 630 (2d Cir. 1980))).

to determine what changes were made to the FDD, when the changes were made, and why the changes were required.

The purchaser should also conduct a fairly exhaustive review of the files for current and former franchisees. This review should confirm that all required documents are included in each file, identify any documents that are not available or are incomplete, and analyze any disclosure or other potential legal violations. In the case of potential violations, the purchaser should assess the nature of the violation and determine the risk that the system might face as the result of each violation. In some cases, the purchaser may want to insist that the current owner resolve outstanding issues with the franchisee prior to consummating the transaction. This may include offering rescission to the franchisee, agreeing to a mutual termination and the waiver of the franchisee's noncompete agreement, or reaching a monetary settlement in exchange for a full release. If this cannot be done prior to consummating the transaction, the purchase agreement can include a specific indemnification for the possible consequences of the violation. This allows the purchaser to resolve the issue with the franchisee and be reimbursed for the consequences through a postclosing adjustment to the purchase price or draw on any holdback.

The analysis of the current franchise files should also include examining the state of relationships with existing franchisees, paying particular attention to any disputes that currently exist or may be brewing. It is critical that the purchaser understand the nature of any disputes and that the purchaser and current owner work together to resolve as many outstanding issues as possible prior to closing. It is never good for a franchise system to be acquired while the state of franchise relations is in turmoil. The best time to address franchisee concerns is before the acquisition is complete because all parties have the greatest incentive to negotiate prior to closing.

In reviewing the files of former franchisees, purchaser's counsel should concentrate on understanding why and how each franchisee left the system. The analysis should confirm that the seller complied with state franchise relationship laws in cases of franchise terminations or nonrenewals. If the franchisee left the system as the result of a transfer, the file should include documentation verifying that the new owner was properly disclosed and that all transfer paperwork was completed. Each file should also have contact information for the former franchise owners to ensure that the franchisor can comply with its disclosure requirements. Finally, to the greatest extent possible, each file should contain a release signed by the former franchisee and all guarantors.

(b) Franchisees in Renewal Pipeline

The purchaser should also review the renewal pipeline for the franchise system. The fact that franchisees are looking to renew their agreements is always a positive sign in a franchise system. If franchisees are up for renewal but are choosing not to remain in the system, this may signal significant issues in the system. More importantly, the purchaser should evaluate whether it will be faced with the prospect of having to enforce the franchise agreement's post-termination covenant against competition against one or a series of former franchisees that have chosen not to renew their agreements. Finally, the purchaser should review the franchisor's process for managing the renewal process to ensure that all required renewal dates are docketed, that all franchisees with upcoming renewal dates are contacted and given the opportunity to renew, and that applicable state relationship laws affecting renewal have been followed. The purchaser should ensure that no franchisee is operating under the terms of an expired franchise agreement. If such circumstances are unearthed during the due diligence process, the purchaser should insist that all such franchisees be required to sign current franchise agreements prior to closing.

(c) Trends in Franchise Sales and Unit Counts

The purchaser should examine franchise sales trends for at least the prior three years. It should ask where franchise leads were coming from, what the conversion ratio was, what the costs per closed lead were, and how the lead flow changed during that period. Most purchasers looking to complete transactions in recent years may observe significant changes in the number and quality of franchise leads and closings compared to a decade ago as the result of the recession of 2008–2009, but the purchasers must look beyond the relatively short-term impact of the recession to determine whether the franchise sales model has shifted fundamentally over these years. Was there a material increase or decrease in the experience and financial resources of such candidates? Did existing operators open more units? What was the primary driver of unit growth? All of these questions will help the purchaser analyze the short-term and long-term prospects of the target.

A purchaser should also carefully analyze the trends in unit count during the past five years. Did the system grow on a net basis or contract during that period? Were some regions affected more than others? Does the brand have strong resonance in some parts of the country but struggle in others? Is the product offered by franchisees subject to environmental factors, such as winter weather in the northern part of the country, that affect its year-round demand? Has growth been limited in certain markets as the result? In the alternative, is there opportunity for unit growth in untapped parts of the country or in other countries? If so, what level of investment and market penetration will be required by the franchisor to expand into those markets successfully? Like the analysis outlined above, determining answers to these questions will enable the purchaser to evaluate future cash flow and growth opportunities available to the target.

(d) Franchise Registration and Financial Assurance Issues

A thorough due diligence process needs to include careful attention to requirements being imposed on the franchisor target as a condition of registration by one or more registration states. State examiners have become more aggressive in recent years in requiring franchisors to make additional disclosures or agree to other requirements before registration rights are granted by the state. These steps include posting new risk factors on the state cover page and revising or restructuring the Item 19 disclosure. Any prospective buyer needs to understand the types and nature of restrictions being imposed on the target company by the various registration states.

In addition to operational and informational restrictions, buyers need to understand requirements imposed on the franchisor target related to financial assurance requirements. These requirements are placed on franchisors when a state examiner has concerns over the capitalization or financial viability of the franchise company at the time of registration. These requirements generally come in three "flavors": (1) deferral of all fees to be paid to the franchisor or its affiliates at the time the franchise agreement is signed until the franchisor has completed all of its pre-opening obligations and the franchisee is ready to open for business, (2) the required purchase of a surety bond to ensure the franchisee can recover its investment in the in initial franchise fee in the event that the franchisor fails to provide all promised pre-opening services before the franchisee is able to open for business, and (3) the requirement that all initial franchise fees be placed in a restricted impound account at a bank until the franchisor has completed all of its pre-opening obligations and the franchisee is ready to open for business.

Fee deferral is a tricky proposition for most franchisors because the franchisee gets to keep the initial franchise fee until opening and therefore literally has no "skin in the game" with regard to complying with its obligations under the franchise agreement. As a result, should the franchisee become disenchanted with the franchise system or experience a degree of buyer's remorse, he or she has very little to lose by walking away from his or her obligations. Because initial franchise fees generally range between $30,000 and $50,000, most franchisees assume that such amounts are too low to justify a lawsuit, and therefore they do not fear that the franchisor will pursue them in court to recover the fee. The risk that a number of "fee deferral" franchisees may walk away may be enhanced by the prospect of an acquisition of the franchisor. In many cases, franchisees are drawn to the personnel of the franchisor, and they often fear an acquisition because the team members they have built relationships with may leave or be forced out by the new ownership. Even though the fee deferral option caries a significant amount of risk to the franchisor, many companies choose this option at registration because it is the "easiest" of the three choices and there is no cost associated with choosing this option. A buyer looking to acquire a brand with franchisees that have had their initial fees deferred needs to understand the status of each of these franchise agreements and make an assessment of the likelihood that the franchisees will actually open. In addition, the seller may seek to be paid some or all of these deferred fees under the theory that the seller actually provided the services necessary to sell and support these franchisees through the opening process. In this case, some provision will need to be made to transfer payments to the seller as these units are opened. Finally, the buyer should also determine whether there are any broker fees or sales commissions that have been deferred and make arrangements to pay the appropriate parties as these fees are collected.

The market for surety bonds in the franchise space is limited and appears to be shrinking. A buyer looking to acquire a system that is reliant upon securing surety bonds in order to get the franchise offering registered needs to identify the company underwriting the bonds and understand the likelihood that such bonds will continue to be available if needed. In addition, the buyer needs to understand the interplay between the liabilities created before the sale and the expectation of the surety bond underwriter after the franchisor's assets have been transferred. Will the surety company continue to provide coverage for claims that arose before the sale but are asserted after the assets have transferred? The buyer may need to negotiate with the surety bond company over these issues or risk finding itself on the hook for liability it believed was covered by the bonding company.

Bank impound accounts also can be tricky for buyers. If the acquiring enterprise is looking to purchase a company that has one or more impound accounts open and is holding franchise fees, it needs to understand exactly where those accounts are held and arrange to have title transferred to the acquiring entity at the time of closing. The various registration states will also need to be notified of the change in ownership of the franchisor so their records reflect the new owner of the accounts. If this step is not taken, the buyer will likely find it challenging to get the bank or the state to release the escrowed funds when a franchisee whose funds have been impounded is ready to open for business. Finally, similar to the fee deferral scenario described above, the buyer should also determine whether there are any broker fees or sales commissions that have been deferred pending release of the impounded funds and make arrangements to pay the appropriate parties as these fees are delivered to the new owner of the franchise company.

Lawyers advising franchisors regarding regulatory compliance issues have seen a significant increase in the number of financial assurance requirements imposed upon their clients since about 2016. With the revenue recognition changes imposed on franchisors by ASC 606 becoming a part of the franchise landscape in 2019, it is reasonable to anticipate that even more new and emerging franchise brands will be forced to accept financial assurance requirements as a condition of franchise registration. Therefore, it will become even more critical for the acquisition team to focus on understanding these requirements and developing a plan for addressing these obligations as they become relevant in the acquisition process.

(e) Franchise Financing Issues

Perhaps no aspect of the franchise ecosystem affects franchising more than access to capital by franchisees. Franchisors can sell as many franchises as they like, but if franchisees cannot secure financing, most locations do not ever open. This is particularly true for those franchisees that signed multi-unit development agreements at the start of the franchise relationship. This makes it imperative that the prospective purchaser investigate and understand how available credit is for franchisees in the target brand.

To better understand this issue, a short-term historical perspective is helpful. Perhaps no aspect of the Great Recession of 2008 and 2009 affected franchising and the growth of franchise companies as much as the significant reduction in available financing for new franchisees and existing franchisees that wanted to expand. Starting in the latter part of 2008, many franchise lenders left the industry or considerably reduced the amount of loan dollars they made available to franchisees. Those lenders that were making loans significantly increased the amount of capital a franchise prospect had to have available to invest in the franchise.[36] While the financial market for the franchise community improved during the past decade, it is critical that any prospective buyer remember the lessons from the past. Historically speaking, the United States experiences a recession once every eight to ten years, so companies looking to buy at the end of the cycle have a duty to their investors to understand the risks the franchisee credit markets can present to the ultimate success of the acquired brand.

The key inquiry for a prospective purchaser of the franchisor in this environment is, "Can we be reasonably certain that we can assist our prospective franchisees in securing the financing they require to open more units?" If the answer is anything other than a solid yes, the purchaser must assess what steps it will be required to take to improve the financing opportunities for new and existing franchisees. In some cases, franchisors have begun offering credit enhancements to induce lenders to finance franchise growth. These programs, however, generally necessitate creative structuring and require that the franchisor make real dollars available to lenders. Specifically, what this means is that with less financing available, franchisors may be called on to give third-party lenders limited or full guaranties of the franchisee's loans. If such steps are required to make a franchise acquisition viable, the purchaser must factor the additional resources required into its working capital needs. In other cases, traditional commercial financing may simply not be available at all. In those instances, the prospective purchaser should consider whether it can source alternative financing from nontraditional sources, including hedge funds, mezzanine funds, and even "strategic" investors, and evaluate the costs to the franchisor and franchisees as it pursues such options. To that end, access to capital is critical for franchisees and franchisors to facilitate growth. If the purchaser cannot satisfy itself that capital will be available, it may be best to walk away from the opportunity until the lending market improves.

(f) Supplier Contracts

Any purchaser of a franchise system should spend time reviewing agreements and relationships with key designated and approved suppliers to the system. The purchaser should pay particular attention to any exclusive arrangements that

36. Jonathan Maze, *More Please*, Franchise Times, Mar. 2010, at 26.

could interfere with agreements or objectives that the purchaser intends to implement after the closing. As part of this review, the purchaser should

- Confirm that any special pricing or delivery terms currently being offered to the system under such agreements will continue to be available after the transaction is complete.
- Require the seller to obtain any advanced consents required to transfer such contracts prior to closing.
- Confirm that all rebates, marketing fees, and other forms of consideration have been disclosed and accounted for properly over the years.
- Prepare a summary of all special deals and obligations contained in these contracts and evaluate how the revenue flow and corresponding obligations affect the projected profitability of the system after the transaction is completed.
- Check to see if any of the supplier contracts contain "change of control" provisions that require the parties to a transaction to obtain the supplier's approval of the proposed sale. In some cases, a change of control provision may trigger a supplier's right to terminate an existing contract. Accordingly, these contracts should be reviewed very closely to ascertain what types of disruptions can occur in the event of a change of control.

(g) Leases

Depending on the makeup of the system, a purchaser should focus on two distinct areas when conducting due diligence on location leases. First, the purchaser should review and evaluate all leases related to "company-owned store" operations of the franchisor or any affiliate that will be acquired as part of the transaction. Can each lease be assigned to the new entity? If so, what requirements does each landlord impose prior to assignment? Is there a possibility that a landlord will request additional consideration or attempt to renegotiate the lease prior to approving the assignment to the purchaser? Most importantly, in cases in which the lease requires the landlord's consent prior to transfer, it is critical to begin the process of securing consent well before the projected closing date. Depending on the size of the landlord's organization, this process can occasionally take significant time, and no one wants to hold up a closing because one or more landlord consents remain outstanding.

Second, the purchaser should also conduct a cursory review of leases for franchisee locations. A transaction undertaken by the franchisor will, generally, not affect an individual franchisee's lease, because the franchisor is not a party to that lease. It is important to get a general understanding of the lease requirements imposed on franchise locations. In addition, if franchisees' leases provide the franchisor with notice and cure rights and the opportunity to assume the lease from a franchisee, then the purchaser will likely need to be made a party to such leases to be able to maintain such rights. Finally, the purchaser should review any relevant radius clauses in franchisees' leases to ensure that the acquisition does not somehow negatively affect the rent to be paid by franchisees, cause a lease default due to operations the purchaser has directly or through franchisees of other systems it owns, or interfere with other plans the purchaser has for the system. Depending on how a franchise agreement is structured, a franchisor purchasing a competitive chain with a different trademark could still find itself violating a franchisee's territorial provision if, for example, the territorial provision prohibited the franchisor from franchising any competitive business in a franchisee's exclusive territory, whether or not it carries the franchisor's trademark.

(h) Franchisee Satisfaction

No franchise acquisition due diligence project can be considered complete until the purchaser has had the opportunity to spend time interviewing some or all of the existing franchisees in the system. The extent of the number of interviews will be determined in large part by the size of the system. Obviously, the greater the number of franchisees, the harder it is for the purchaser to speak with everyone within the time frame necessary to complete the due diligence. In addition, the purchaser's right to interview franchisees in advance of the sale is dependent on the confidentiality provisions of a letter of intent or other agreement entered into prior to the transaction.[37] During the interview process, the purchaser should focus on the level of the franchisees' satisfaction with the system and identify areas that franchisees believe should be changed or improved. The purchaser should also use these discussions to discern whether the proposed acquisition will create legal issues with any franchisees for either the purchaser or the seller after the sale closes. In addition to avoiding unnecessary legal problems, this process will also provide the purchaser with insight into how current franchisees will validate with prospective franchisees. Understanding this aspect of the franchise relationship will provide the purchaser with some additional insight regarding its prospective growth plans.

(i) Franchisee Litigation

An important corollary to the franchise interview process is the review of current and previous franchise litigation. These files will often reveal any history of franchise law violations or contract breaches by the seller that were significant enough to lead to litigation and, at the same time, the review will help the purchaser assess any precedents set by the franchisor in the process of settling litigation.[38] The purchaser will also want to establish a reserve for any potential liability that may accrue to the franchise organization from pending litigation. This process will also enable the purchaser to adjust the value of the transaction, if necessary, or to establish appropriate indemnification thresholds and the size of the required purchase price escrow, to cover litigation contingencies.

---

37. Mark Robertson & Charles Modell, *Anatomy of the Sale of a Brand*, 31st ABA Forum on Franchising (2008).

38. *Id.* at 18.

(j) Management of the Advertising Fund

Since most franchise agreements expressly state that the advertising fund is managed by the franchisor for the benefit of the franchisees, it is important that the purchaser review the manner in which the fund has actually been managed. For example, if the franchise agreements require that the advertising fund be held in an account separate from the franchisor's operating funds, the purchaser should confirm that the fund has been handled in that mariner. The purchaser should also determine if fund collections have exceeded expenditures and whether the purchaser will therefore be assuming a liability. "Even if the purchaser does not specifically assume the liability, the purchaser is acquiring the obligations of the franchisor under the franchise agreements and franchisees will not likely sit quietly when the seller disappears into the night with the franchisees' advertising payments."[39] In the alternative, the franchisor may have spent more funds than collected from franchisees and may therefore be looking for some additional contribution from the purchaser to compensate it for this expenditure. Finally, the purchaser should review the expenditures planned or committed from the fund in the coming year to ensure that sufficient funds will be available to meet the projected expenses. If it turns out that the fund may not have sufficient money to cover the planned expenses, the purchaser will likely seek an adjustment to the purchase price to compensate for the shortfall.

(k) Special Deals Given to Franchisees

"Special deals" given to franchisees can be one of the most complicated issues when acquiring a franchise system. It is critical that the purchaser review each franchisee's file, talk to current and sometimes former management personnel, and talk to each affected franchisee to discern whether the franchisee believes he or she has some special arrangement with the franchisor, These "deals" can include (1) reduced royalties or advertising contributions; (2) special territorial, expansion, or development rights; (3) the right to sell different products or services; (4) different operating hours or other standards; (5) special pricing on goods sold by the franchisor or suppliers; (6) rights of first refusal; and (7) the right to renew using the franchisee's existing contract, to name just a few. It is imperative to ferret out these deals because they can wreak havoc on the purchaser's expansion or development plans. In ascertaining whether a special deal exists, the buyer sometimes needs to go no further than the franchise agreement of the specific franchisee. However, this raises the question of whether there are other deals lingering about the franchise system. Accordingly, a full investigation of each franchisee's file is generally in order. Oftentimes these special deals are found in contract addenda, letter agreements, written correspondence, and sometimes oral representations. In addition to searching through franchise files, it is a good idea to speak with one of the seller's representative historians, often someone who has been with the company for a considerable period of time and knows the inner

39. *Id.* at 13.

workings of the company. Special deals can also create animosity with other franchisees if they are discovered. Most importantly, however, these deals can become potential mine fields for the new owner if they are not honored after the sale is complete. It is critical, therefore, that a purchaser identifies and develops a plan for addressing each of these "deals" before completing the transaction.

(l) Territorial Issues

Some of the more vexing "special deals" granted to franchisees come in the form of territorial grants or protections provided to franchisees. Many of these deals are granted when the franchisor is in its early development years, and they are often the product of the efforts the franchisor had to take to "get the deal done." In the days when territory seemed unlimited and the franchisor was more interested in collecting a check for the initial franchise fee than protecting the integrity of the system, the franchisor's management team may have made deals that come back to haunt the system. It is essential for the purchaser to learn of and build a strategy regarding these deals prior to closing the sale.

Territorial deals come in a variety of forms. The franchisor could have agreed to provide a larger protected territory than initially delineated in the franchise agreement. In some cases, the territorial protection comes in the form of limits on the products the franchisor can offer directly in the territory or rights granted to the franchisee to sell in different channels of distribution. In other cases, the franchisee may have been granted "rights of first refusal" to acquire additional territory if the franchisor finds a prospective franchisee for such territory. Finally, franchisees may have (or claim to have) the right to market to and service customers living or working outside of their territorial boundaries. In these situations, the franchisor may have granted express or implied rights to sell the franchisor's goods or services to such customers. These types of "rights" become an issue when the franchisor attempts to sell a territory adjacent to an existing franchisee or wants to offer new or different products or services in the franchisees' territories. It is critical that a purchaser learn of these "special deals" prior to completing the acquisition, or the purchaser may find that its expansion plans in an area are unduly limited after the sale closes.

Additional territorial issues must be explored when the purchaser is a competitor of or in a similar line of business as the franchisor. When this occurs, the purchaser must review the reservation of rights clauses in each of the existing franchise agreements to ensure that none of these agreements prohibit the franchisor from selling to a competitor. In addition, the purchaser should confirm that it has the right to operate a competing brand using different trademarks and systems in each franchisee's territory. This is particularly critical in situations in which the purchaser is a competitor and knows that it has existing company-owned or franchise-owned stores in a target franchisee's territory.

If the purchaser determines that one or more franchise agreements presents a problem based on the location of the purchaser's existing company-owned stores or franchisees, it is best to address this issue before closing to avoid a protracted legal battle after the sale has been consummated. In some cases, the issue can be resolved by reaching an economic settlement with the affected franchisees. In other situations, more drastic steps must be taken, including reaching an agreement to terminate the affected franchisee and to let the owner continue to compete as an independent operator. Sometimes, the issues are too significant to overcome, and the purchaser may decide the best course is to walk away.

(m) Franchisee Associations

In most franchise companies, franchisee associations come in two forms—an association organized and approved by the franchisor and one or more "unofficial" associations organized by franchisees or third parties. Due diligence on the franchisor-sponsored association should include a review of the minutes of meetings, initiatives undertaken by the association, and the process associated with selecting the organization's governing body.

It is often harder to conduct due diligence on the unofficial associations because the franchisor does not have control of the records of this type of association. When possible, the purchaser should endeavor to have conversations with the leaders of the association to discern the issues that led to the creation of the outside organization and its relationship with the franchisor. The purchaser should also review all correspondence between the franchisor and such organization. This due diligence will often reveal latent issues and simmering disputes inside the system that might not otherwise be detectable in the due diligence process.

(n) Privacy Issues

One of the issues that should be on any prospective purchaser's radar screen is the target company's compliance with various privacy laws and regulations, as both data security through Payment Card Industry Data Security Standards (PCI DSS) and the more general standards found in the GDPR and CCPA discussed below. PCI DSS standards were developed by the payment card industry. The purpose of instituting these standards is to protect the integrity of customer credit card data, including account numbers, name, and validity date of a customer's credit card. Since PCI DSS applies to every company that stores, processes, or transmits cardholder information, including point-of-sale systems, these regulations will affect most franchise systems. The prospective purchaser will want to know whether the franchisor and/or its franchisees have entered into contracts with the various payment card brands to implement these standards. In addition, the prospective purchaser will want to know whether the target company and/or its franchisees have entered into contracts with the payor banks that handle credit transactions. These standards apply to both those that store and those that handle customer credit card information. The prospective purchaser should find out whether the target or its franchisees have been fined for noncompliance of the PCI DSS. In addition, the prospective purchaser should determine what type of secure network the franchisor and/or its franchisees have constructed or caused to be constructed from third parties. In addition, how does the franchisor and/or its franchisees go about protecting cardholder data?

In addition to credit card security issues, the European Union passed the General Data Protection Regulation (GDPR) that took effect in 2018. The regulations are intended to protect an individual's personal data, which is defined as information relating to an identifiable person who can be directly or indirectly identified by reference to an identifier. In essence, an individual will have the right to know how a company is collecting his or her information and how is it to be used. From the purchaser's perspective, if a target company comes under the purview of the GDPR, in addition to understanding how a target protects that information, the purchaser must also determine the character of the privacy notices disseminated to individuals that have interacted with the target company or its affiliates. In addition, the purchaser will want to know whether the target company has collected and maintained opt-in notices from the affected individuals. Not only will the GDPR apply to franchisors that have locations or franchises in the European Union, but also the regulations will apply to customers that are from the EU.

In addition to GDPR, a prospective purchaser also will need to be aware of the newly passed California Consumer Privacy Act (CCPA),[40] which took effect January 1, 2020. Businesses are expected to be in full compliance with the act by that date. The CCPA applies to any for-profit entity that does business in California, has more than $25 million in annual gross sales, and receives personal information relating to more than 50,000 or more California residents. The CCPA applies only to businesses that collect personal information. The law requires the collector of information to disclose to the consumer the categories of personal information being collected and its purpose. As the collector of the information must supply notice to all affected consumers, a potential purchaser of the franchise system will want to know whether notices have been sent out to the affected California consumers. In addition, the consumer has the right to request from the business collecting the information the categories and specific pieces of personal information the business has collected. Other states are expected to pass similar laws. Accordingly, a prospective purchaser will want to know how the target has protected applicable consumer information and how it has handled consumer requests for such information. A prospective purchaser also will want to review a target's customer relationship management (CRM) system to determine how customer information is treated.

(o) Trademark Issues

The backbone of any franchise system is its proprietary marks. A prospective purchaser should pay close attention to the franchisor's portfolio of trademarks. Questions that it should ask and documents it will want to see include the

40. *See* General Data Protection Regulation, OLJ 119 04.05.2016

following: (1) Who is the owner of the various marks, the franchisor or an affiliate? (2) If it is an affiliate that owns the proprietary marks, is there a license agreement running between that affiliate and the franchisor? (3) Are the proprietary marks listed on the principal or supplemental register? (4) Are there any claims of opposition or claims of infringement against the franchisor or the owners of the proprietary marks? (5) Have all trademark applications been renewed as applicable? (6) What international trademark registrations have been undertaken? (7) Are there any countries outside of the United States where the target's proprietary marks are used but not yet registered? (8) Are there any infringers of the target company's proprietary marks outside of the United States? (9) Are there any cancellation proceedings filed against the target company on an international basis? (10) Have all registered user agreements been properly obtained and filed? (11) In what categories are the proprietary marks registered? (12) Do the target's registrations match the services that are being rendered to the customer or to the franchisee? A prospective purchaser will most likely want to match the trademark portfolio provided by the target company with the actual registrations appearing on the USPTO website.

6-7. Negotiating the Purchase Agreement and the Credit Agreement

(a) The Purchase Agreement

After the letter of intent has been completed, and in some cases during or after the due diligence period, the parties will work together to negotiate the form of purchase agreement. In most instances, counsel for the purchaser prepares the initial draft of the purchase agreement. The purchase agreement should incorporate the previously agreed-upon provisions of the letter of intent. The purchase agreement will also go into significantly more detail regarding such topics as closing timing and related obligations, payment and financing terms, disclosure schedules, indemnification, the terms for the holdback, and the length of time that the seller's representations and warranties survive the closing. After the initial draft of the purchase agreement has been prepared, counsel for the seller will generally have an opportunity to review and prepare comments to the document. In most cases, the final form of purchase agreement will be the product of several drafts and much negotiation between the parties. In many cases, it can take weeks or even months to complete these negotiations and come to a final agreement on the form of the document.

One major consideration the parties must address at the outset of negotiations is whether the document will be signed and the transaction will be closed at a later date or the purchase agreement will be signed at the closing table. Some purchasers like to have the purchase agreement negotiated and signed in advance of the commencement of due diligence in order to ensure that the parties have completely agreed upon all of the business and legal issues prior to investing the time and money required by the due diligence process. In these instances, the purchase agreement will include provisions allowing one or both parties to terminate or renegotiate the agreement upon the occurrence of certain specific circumstances. For example, if the purchaser discovers significant and material undisclosed liabilities during the due diligence process, the purchaser would be entitled to either terminate the purchase agreement or seek a reduction in the purchase price. These provisions may also include an obligation to compensate the nonterminating party as the result of the termination of the contract.

If the parties agree to delay signing the purchase agreement until closing, the issues addressing early termination will not need to be incorporated into the purchase agreement. However, this approach tends to put the purchaser at risk because none of the representations and warranties or other key preclosing provisions will be binding on the seller until the purchase agreement is signed by all parties. Consequently, the purchaser has little recourse against the seller if the purchaser discovers undisclosed issues during the due diligence process. Nevertheless, the parties may elect to take on this risk in order to permit the due diligence process and the negotiation process to occur simultaneously.

Another issue in negotiating purchase agreements that has come to the forefront in recent years is the use of representation (reps) and warranties insurance. Reps and warranties insurance is essentially breach of contract insurance designed to enhance or replace indemnification provisions in a purchase agreement. The insurance, subject to disclaimers, will cover breaches of representations and warranties set forth in the purchase agreement. While such insurance is available to both the seller and the buyer, it is most often used by the buyer. In determining the insurability of a target company, the underwriters will look at the nature of the terms of the purchase agreement and the quality of the due diligence that was conducted. Premiums for this type of coverage can range between 1 and 3 percent of the amount of coverage sought. The underwriters will determine what reps and warranties will be excluded in the coverage. In essence underwriters will be doing due diligence on the due diligence to determine what are the unknown contingencies.

(b) The Credit Agreement

Parallel with the negotiation of the purchase agreement will be the preparation of the credit agreement. The target franchisor will want to pay close attention to the terms of this document because this agreement will dictate the operating parameters of the franchisor after the sale in a way that is far more significant than any of the provisions contained in the purchase agreement. Specifically, the credit agreement may set limits on the franchisor's ability to take promissory notes from its franchisees for the financing of initial franchise fees or delinquent fees. In addition, the credit agreement may limit the franchisor's ability to enter into real estate leases, which it may use to control a unit's location. Likewise, the credit agreement may restrict the franchisor's ability to guaranty leases on behalf of its franchisees or any part of a franchisee's financing of a particular unit. It is important that the bank or other creditor understand the operations of the franchise system so that the credit agreement does not function as an impediment to how the franchisor operates for the benefit of the system. The franchisor must make sure that it still retains enough ongoing cash to continue to grow and manage the system.

6-8. Ongoing Operations during Sale Process

(a) Effect on the Franchise Sales Process

As the sales process continues, the sales target faces some fundamental questions relative to its operations during what should be seen as the transition period. During this period, which could extend from the start of negotiations until closing, will the target franchisor be required to alter its business operations? For example, should it curtail its franchise sales efforts? The answer to this question is very tricky since it will require the franchisor to make a business judgment as to whether prospective franchisees have a right to know that the target is involved in a sale. The first question in making this analysis is what effect the transaction will have on the target. For example, after the closing of the transaction, will management change, or will there be a fundamental change to the target's financial condition? If the stock of the target is being purchased for cash with no appreciable change to the target's financial condition, an argument can be made that other than a change in ownership, there has not been a material change until the sale is complete. With respect to corporate parent of a franchisor, unless the parent serves as the franchisor of another concept, furnishes products and services to the franchisee, or guarantees the obligations of the franchisor, only the name and the principal address of the parent need be disclosed in the FDD.[41] The judgment process becomes more difficult if there is an asset purchase, the purchase involves financing, and/or the transaction will result in a change in the management of the target. Any of these components could trigger a material change in the franchise system necessitating that the franchisor amend its FDD.

Assuming that the transaction will result in a material change to the target's franchise offering, at what point in the acquisition process must the target franchisor halt its sales process until the transaction is concluded and new financials and other amendments are made to the FDD? While there is no black-letter law dictating when the transaction must be disclosed and franchise sales temporarily suspended, the benchmark that a target franchisor should use is: at what point does the sale become a certainty?[42] Certainly, it could be argued that until there is a signed purchase agreement, there is no certainty of sale, and therefore there has been no material change to the target franchise system. The trickier question is whether a material change to the franchise system has occurred at the time of an executed letter of intent. As discussed earlier in this chapter, a letter of intent

41. *See* requirements to Item 1 of the FTC Franchise Rule, 16 C.F.R. § 436.3.

42. *See* David J. Kaufmann & Carolyn G. Nussbaum, *Franchise Acquisitions: Duty to Disclose Purchase or Sale Activity*, 18 ABA Franchise L.J. 39 (Fall 1998).

does not rise to the level of a binding agreement of sale; it likely will be subject to a material number of contingencies including the negotiation of a binding purchase agreement. The purchase agreement could also be subject to substantial due diligence or contingencies, which may allow a potential purchaser to terminate the agreement. Accordingly, the franchisor's legal advisor must use his or her best judgment to advise the franchisor when the advisor believes that the sale has progressed to the point that a prospective franchisee would want to know or has a legitimate right to know that there is a likely sale pending for the target franchise system.

In addition to the impact on prospective franchise sales, a pending transaction could affect a target franchisor's ability to process resales and renewals. For each of those transactions, the existing franchisee in a renewal and the incoming franchisee in a resale will be entitled to a new form of FDD if the franchisee is being required to sign the franchisor's then-current form of franchise agreement. Under these circumstances, when the sale transaction has reached the point where a material change occurs triggering an amendment to the FDD, the renewals and franchise resales processes will be affected. On the other hand, if the renewal or resale involves the extension of an existing agreement or the assignment of the existing franchise agreement, then it can be argued that the franchisor would not be required to provide those franchisees with a current FDD.

(b) Preservation of Filing Exemptions

An interesting issue to address with the FDD filed after the transaction is whether previous franchise registration exemptions will be affected by the structure of the sale. Many of the registration states exempt an experienced franchisor from the registration process (some states still require a submission of the FDD in addition to the exemption application).[43] These exemptions are predicated on a threshold net worth of the franchisor as well as an experience threshold determined by the number of open units in existence, which generally ranges between 20 and 25 for at least five years, depending on state law.

If the transaction involving the target is a stock purchase, the target franchisor remains intact with all of its history, assets, and liabilities—subject to the terms of the transaction. In that case it is not likely that the experienced-franchisor exemption would be affected, unless the transaction results in a deterioration of the franchisor's net worth below the threshold level required by the state statute or regulation. Conversely, if the sale of the target franchisor is structured as an asset sale, which would involve a transfer of all or substantially all of the franchisor's assets, including their franchise agreements, to a new entity, the target's ability to retain its previous experienced-franchisor exemption could be affected. Some of the registration states take the position that since the franchise agreements, and thus the franchises themselves, have been transferred to a new entity, their prior history—the threshold number of years with the previous entity—is

43. For a more detailed discussion of this issue, see chapter 2.

broken. Thus, the clock for determining the franchisor's experience begins to run anew. This strict constructionist position taken by some state franchise examiners will often prove to be frustrating to the franchisor that will be required to make a first-time filing of its FDD in states in which it was previously exempt. As an example, the examiners in the state of Maryland have taken the position that notwithstanding the fact that the assets of a franchise system are purchased intact with the same management team, the franchise system loses its history when the assets are placed into a new operating entity.

(c) Notifying Existing and Prospective Franchisees

The precise moment to advise the franchisees of a pending sale is when the franchisor determines it to be the right time. While this seems circular, it means exactly what it says. The target franchisor must know the temperament of its franchisee constituency. There is no black-letter law to assist the franchisor in this part of the sale process. There are many different considerations that will need to be reviewed and discussed with members of the management team and the purchaser and seller.

If the target is a public company, then there will be securities law considerations. If franchisees are advised or otherwise become aware of a pending transaction too soon, this could constitute a violation of state or federal securities laws. Likewise, waiting too long could trigger both securities laws and franchise disclosure issues.

Beyond the legal ramifications, there are practical considerations that can change the dynamics of the transaction. For example, informing franchisees that a sale is pending may give them the unwelcomed opportunity to inject themselves into the sale process. The change of ownership is an opportune time for the franchise body to seek concessions or changes to the franchise relationship. With this type of leverage, they may attempt to exact financial changes to the franchise relationship that can have significant effects on the pending transaction, causing a revision to the transaction; a change, for example, in the future royalty rate will result in a change in future earnings that may require the seller to agree to a discount on the previously agreed-upon sales price.

A premature disclosure of a pending sale also may result in the existing franchisees becoming nervous about the system's future and concerned that the change of ownership may also result in a change of management. As a result, some franchisees may seek to sell their franchises or otherwise try to exit the system prematurely. More importantly, if franchisees begin speculating about a change of ownership, they will no doubt lose focus on their own businesses to their detriment and to the detriment of the target franchise system. What the franchisor wants more than anything during the sale process is a continuation of the status quo and the ability to control the situation. Therefore, from a practical standpoint, keeping knowledge of the pending sale to a limited number of people likely will be the best strategy for the franchisor until it decides that the time is right for a broader disclosure. What this means is that the franchisor will need to be careful not to leak news of the pending sale to any member of the corporate staff that does not have a need to know. Management should also issue a strict warning to those who are within the inner circle of knowledge to keep the information confidential. The only thing faster than a rumor mill is the speed of light.

Once the franchisor determines that the time is right for disclosure, management must determine the best way to notify all interested parties. The franchisor should plan the disclosure well in advance of the actual date planned for the disclosure. While every target franchisor that has been sold has its own step-by-step procedure, the procedure that the authors have found successful is to start from the top of the franchise chain. If the chain has a well-functioning franchisee association, the information should be shared with the association first. The disclosure should announce that the sale has just closed, identify the new owner, describe any changes to management that will occur, and reassure all franchisees that the sale is good for the company and that the management is confident that the sale will enhance the value proposition for the franchise system.

Immediately thereafter, the franchisor should, in person where possible, announce the same to members of the corporate staff, providing them with the same assurances. If possible, management should avoid announcing that there will be immediate synergistic cuts. To the extent that such cuts are inevitable, the franchisor should put together a program that will ease any unnecessary exit of any member of the corporate staff. To keep everyone in place until the optimal time to make these cuts, the franchisor should design a bonus plan that incentivizes employees or managers to stay until the franchisor deems it necessary to make the synergistic change.

Almost simultaneously with the disclosure of the sale to the corporate staff, the franchisor should send out a prerecorded phone or video message to the franchise chain at large. The method of communication can be varied and depends in part on the sophistication of the franchisor's communication system with its franchisees. Certainly, if the franchisor maintains a franchise system intranet, then the message can be communicated through the website. Otherwise, webinars or face-to-face visits can serve this function. The talking points in the video message should be similar to the message provided to the franchise leadership. The message should provide the franchisees with a toll-free number or website location in which there will have been prepared for their review a "frequently asked questions" section designated to answer their most immediate questions regarding how the sale of the franchise system will affect them. These answers should be vetted among management and its legal advisors well in advance of the closing date. It is interesting to note that with many franchise sales, franchisees may become fearful or anxious simply because they do not know what is happening. Once they are informed, understand the reasons for the transaction, and know what will happen to them and the system in the future, they likely, after calling some of their colleagues in the franchise system, will go back to business as usual.

This rather simplistic approach can serve as an outline for the target franchisor. Of course, it may not be as simple as presented in this chapter, given the very particular circumstances of the sale. Merging similar franchise systems will raise a whole host of questions beyond the simplistic approach presented here. However, the key goal for any change of control is to try to maintain the status quo as much as possible and to let the franchisees absorb the news without overreacting.

(d) Managing the System after the Transaction

The nature of the transaction will influence the type of challenges that the target franchisor and the purchaser will face. If the purchaser acquires a franchise system that offers products and services similar to another franchise system owned by the purchaser, then the purchaser must decide if it will operate both systems in parallel or merge one of the systems into the other. Within these strategies, there are numerous subplots that will arise. The issues are almost endless, but at the heart will be how the franchisees within both systems will react. The less dominant franchise system will be very sensitive to the ultimate mission that the purchasing entity pursues. As a means of illustrating some of these issues, the purchaser will need to consider several questions: How will advertising and marketing be conducted? Will each brand have its own managing executive? Will any of the less dominant brand members be invited to join the more dominant brand's system? If the intended strategy is a full integration of one of the brands into the other, are there territorial issues that will prevent this from occurring? The purchaser must be cognizant that both franchise systems will be governed by their own specific franchise agreements; any integration will be subject to the terms of those agreements. If the strategy is to combine these systems, what incentives will the dominant franchisor provide to the franchisees of the less dominant franchise system to induce them to switch brands and modify or terminate their existing agreements? It is likely that those franchisees that cannot or will not subscribe to the dominant franchisor's strategy will either force the franchisor to continue to run parallel systems or negotiate a buyout of their franchises.

If the purchasing franchisor acquired a system with unrelated products and services, the absorption of that franchise system may have fewer integration issues. At the same time that the newly configured franchise system is beginning its operation, many of the planned synergies that the purchaser and target franchisor have agreed to implement will begin to take effect. Doubtless the change in corporate governance will cause the newly combined brands some growing pains as management attempts to meld different corporate cultures. While the synergies are often found in the supporting functions of the franchise system, such as accounting and legal, the franchisees in all of the operating systems will look to the franchisor to provide the same or enhanced services. Often, holding frequent status meetings with the franchisee leadership in an effort to explain to them the changes and progress that the system plans to make and is making post-transaction will be of great benefit to the franchisor and the members of the system. These meetings will help to instill confidence in the franchisees, which will pay countless dividends to the franchisor and the franchise system.

6-9. Post-Transaction Legal Issues

While the mechanics of every purchase agreement will have their own unique characteristics, one thing will be certain in each one of the various purchase documents: the purchase agreement will contain a detailed indemnification provision, which may be tied to a holdback of a portion of the purchase price (unless the parties purchased representation and warranty insurance). (See the discussion on this point in section 6-3 of this chapter.) The holdback or escrowed amount will be retained for a period of time after the transaction is closed to take care of either unresolved legal issues, such as outstanding litigation, or to compensate the purchaser for the breach of the seller's representations and warranties. As has been detailed earlier in this chapter (see section 6-6(a)), most purchase agreements contain a very in-depth representation and warranty section that will address numerous issues from both a general corporate and a franchise perspective. During the holdback period, management of the target franchise system will be obliged to pay attention to the operation of the system to determine whether there are any claims that arise that would be covered by the indemnification.

In addition to the representation and warranty provisions, the post-termination period will give the parties an opportunity to "true-up" the balance sheet of the target franchise system to ascertain if the working capital targets placed in the purchase agreement have been met. If they are over or under target, then post-transaction adjustments will be made to the purchase price requiring either the seller to forfeit a portion of the holdback or the purchaser to pay to the seller an adjustment to the purchase price greater than what is contained in the holdback. An audit of the working capital amount usually takes place between 60 and 90 days after the sale and will contain a wide array of mechanics to assist the purchaser and seller in resolving any disputes that they have regarding the ultimate working capital amount.

6-10. Conclusion

As a lawyer, working on the sale or acquisition of a franchise company can be an exciting and challenging assignment. Because of the ongoing relationship between the franchisor and its franchisees, these deals are often more complex than most merger and acquisition projects. It is critical to take each step in the acquisition process in the proper sequence, and to ensure that the due diligence process is thorough, in order to provide the purchaser and the seller with proper assurances that neither party will face any unanticipated surprises after the transaction is completed. In the end, a well-orchestrated sales process will result in a satisfied purchaser, a fairly compensated seller, and a franchise system poised for growth or renewal under the direction of its new management team.

Exhibit 6-1
Sample Letter of Intent

ABC Corporation
123 17th Street
Denver, Colorado 80202

July 14, 2011

STRICTLY PRIVATE AND CONFIDENTIAL

Target, Inc.
456 Elm Street, Suite 200
Englewood, CO 80112

Dear John, Bob, and George:

This letter ("***Letter Agreement***") sets forth the current understanding between Target, Inc. (the "***Company***") and ABC Corporation ("***ABC Corp.***") pursuant to which ABC Corp. proposes to acquire the Company, on the terms and conditions set forth in this Letter Agreement (the "***Acquisition***").

1. **The Acquisition.** The Acquisition will be structured as a transaction in which ABC Corp. would acquire 100 percent of the outstanding capital stock of the Company. The Acquisition will be governed by a definitive agreement (the "***Definitive Agreement***") to be entered into by the Company, the Company's shareholders (the "***Shareholders***"), and ABC Corp.
2. **Purchase Price.** The purchase price payable at the closing of the Acquisition (the "***Closing***") will be XXX Million Dollars (USD $XXX,000,000) (the "***Purchase Price***"), subject to adjustment and holdback described below. The Purchase Price has been determined on the basis that, as of the closing of the Acquisition: (a) there will not be any outstanding options, warrants, or other rights to purchase any equity interest in the Company, (b) the Company will have no outstanding debt or encumbrances (other than encumbrances relating to real property and equipment leased by the Company), and (c) the Company will not have any cash holdings. The Purchase Price also assumes that the Company's financial statements provided to ABC Corp. have been prepared in accordance with U.S. GAAP, consistently applied, and accurately reflect the financial state of the Company in all material respects.
3. **Adjustment to Purchase Price.** The Purchase Price will be subject to adjustment in the event that the Net Working Capital reflected on the Company's balance sheet as of June 30, 2010, differs from the Net Working Capital reflected on the agreed-upon balance sheet of the Company as at the Closing. "***Net Working Capital***" will be defined as total current assets (excluding cash) minus total current liabilities (excluding debt), each as determined in accordance with U.S. GAAP, applied on a consistent basis. The adjustment, if any, will be made by either reducing or increasing the Purchase Price by the full amount of the difference in Net Working Capital.

   Additionally, the Purchase Price will be: (a) increased by the amount of cash held by Company, if any, as of the Closing, and (b) decreased by any Company debt as of the Closing.

4. **Holdback and Indemnification.** There will be a holdback of eighteen percent (18%) of the Purchase Price (the "***Holdback Amount***") to address any claims that may arise from a breach of the Company's and the Shareholders' representations, warranties, and indemnification obligations contained in the Definitive Agreement. One half of the Holdback Amount would be released after the first anniversary of the Closing, subject to any claims, and the remainder would be released after the second anniversary of the Closing, subject to any claims. No interest shall be payable on the Holdback Amount. The Shareholders will indemnify ABC Corp. in the event that the Holdback Amount is not sufficient to satisfy in full any claim for damages by ABC Corp., up to the full amount of the Acquisition consideration. No claim against the holdback will be brought until such claim or aggregated claims are at least $500,000, at which time the entire amount of the claims will be recoverable.
5. **Definitive Agreement.** The parties agree to use their best efforts to expeditiously negotiate in good faith and to execute and deliver the Definitive Agreement, consistent with the terms of this Letter Agreement. Among other things, the Definitive Agreement will:
   (a) contain comprehensive representations and warranties (which would survive the Closing) relating to Company and its business, operations, assets, liabilities, contracts, intellectual property rights, books, records, legal affairs, financial statements, and employees. The representations and warranties made in the Definitive Agreement with respect to: (i) capitalization of the Company and intellectual property will survive indefinitely, (ii) tax matters will terminate on the expiration of the relevant statute of limitations, and (iii) other representations and warranties will be determined in the Definitive Agreement;

   (b) provide that ABC Corp. and its affiliates will be indemnified by the Shareholders against any damages, liabilities, or expenses arising from a breach by the Company or the Shareholders of any representation, warranty, or covenant contained in the Definitive Agreement; and

   (c) contain other customary provisions mutually agreed upon.

   The execution of the Definitive Agreement is conditioned upon (x) the satisfactory completion by ABC Corp. of its business, financial, regulatory, technical, accounting, and legal due diligence, the results of which will be satisfactory to ABC Corp. in its sole and absolute discretion, and (y) approval by the respective Boards of Directors of the Company and ABC Corp.
6. **Conditions to Closing.** The Closing will be conditioned upon (a) the negotiation, execution, and delivery of the Definitive Agreement and ancillary definitive contracts customary for transactions of this type; (b) any governmental or other third-party consents or waivers (including all necessary consents to a change of control under the Company's agreements); (c) approval by the respective Boards of Directors of the Company and ABC Corp., and all of the Shareholders; (d) completion by ABC Corp. of its due diligence review of the Company to ABC Corp.'s satisfaction; and (e) other customary closing conditions.
7. **Noncompetition Agreements.** At the Closing, the Shareholders and certain other Company key management personnel identified by ABC Corp. will enter into Noncompetition Agreements with ABC Corp. pursuant to which each such indi-

vidual would agree, for a period of five (5) years, to refrain from directly or indirectly engaging in, participating, in, providing services to, or otherwise dealing with any business that competes directly or indirectly with, or is similar to, the business conducted by the Company.

8. **Employees.** As a condition to the Closing, key employees of the Company identified by ABC Corp. shall have accepted offer letters of employment from ABC Corp., with employment becoming effective subsequent to the Closing. Such offers of employment shall be in accordance with ABC Corp.'s standard employment policies and procedures and be consistent with ABC Corp.'s standard compensation and benefits arrangements.
9. **Exclusivity.** From and after the date hereof and until the earlier to occur of the termination of this Letter Agreement or the execution of the Definitive Agreement, Company and Shareholders shall not, and shall not permit their respective officers, directors, employees, advisors, representatives, or agents (collectively, "***Representatives***") to (i) directly or indirectly solicit, initiate, encourage (including by way of furnishing information), or take any other action to facilitate any inquiry or the making of any proposal which constitutes, or could reasonably be expected to lead to, any acquisition or purchase of a substantial amount of the assets or securities of the Company or any tender offer or exchange offer, merger, consolidation, business combination, sale of substantially all assets, sale of securities, recapitalization, spin-off, liquidation, dissolution, or similar transaction involving the Company, or any other transaction the consummation of which would or could reasonably be expected to prevent or materially delay the closing of the Acquisition (collectively, a "***Transaction Proposal***") or agree to or endorse any Transaction Proposal or (ii) propose, enter into, or participate in any discussions or negotiations regarding any Transaction Proposal, or furnish to any other person any information with respect to the business or assets of the Company in connection with a Transaction Proposal, or otherwise cooperate in any way with, or assist or participate in, facilitate, or encourage, any effort or attempt by any other person to do or seek any of the foregoing. The Company shall promptly notify ABC Corp. in the event that it receives any unsolicited indication of interest or proposal regarding the acquisition of the Company or its material assets, including the identity of the person indicating such interest or making such proposal and a copy thereof.
10. **Expenses.** Each of the Company, the Shareholders, and ABC Corp. will bear their own Transaction Expenses. "***Transaction Expenses***" means the expenses (whether or not incurred prior to the date hereof) arising out of, relating to, or incidental to the discussion, evaluation, negotiation, and documentation of this Letter Agreement and the transactions contemplated hereby.
11. **Conduct of Business.** During the term of this Letter Agreement, the Company will conduct its business in a reasonable and prudent manner in accordance with past practices, to preserve its existing business organizations and relations with its employees, customers, suppliers, and others with whom it has a business relationship, to preserve and protect its properties, and to conduct its businesses in compliance with all applicable laws and regulations. During the term of this Letter Agreement, the Company will not (a) issue, or agree to issue, any capital stock or other securities of the Company (except for the issuance of stock options or restricted stock awards to employees in the ordinary course of

business under existing plans) or repurchase or cancel any of its capital stock; (b) incur any debt other than in the ordinary course of business or otherwise encumber its assets, (c) declare or make any dividends or other distributions to, or enter into any agreement with, its shareholders, (d) dispose of or encumber any material assets, or (e) materially increase the compensation of its employees or establish any new compensation plan, or (f) take any action which would be likely to result in a material adverse change to the net asset position or financial status of the Company. During the term of this Letter Agreement, the Company will notify ABC Corp. before (i) entering into any contracts or commitments (including the issuance or acceptance of purchase orders) with a value in excess of $100,000, or (ii) before making any personnel changes.

12. **Access.** The Company will permit ABC Corp., its agents, and representatives to have reasonable access to premises in which it conducts its business and to all of its books, records, patent application files, and personnel and will furnish such financial data, operating data, and other information as each of them may reasonably request.

13. **Confidentiality; Publicity.** The mutual nondisclosure agreement between the Company and ABC Corp., dated May 20, 2011, shall govern the provision and use of all Confidential Information (as defined therein) in connection with this Letter Agreement and the Acquisition. Except as required by law or regulation, in no event shall the Company and its Shareholders on the one side, or ABC Corp. on the other, disclose the existence or terms of this Letter Agreement or the Acquisition contemplated hereunder to third parties or make any public announcement or issue any press release with respect to this Letter Agreement or the Acquisition without (a) first consulting with the other side as to the form and substance thereof and (b) obtaining the prior written consent of the other side.

14. **Amendment.** Any amendment, supplement, modification, or waiver of or to any provision of this Letter Agreement will be effective only if it is made and given in writing signed by the Company and ABC Corp. and only in the specific instance and for the specific purpose for which made or given.

15. **Governing Law.** This Letter Agreement will be governed by, and construed in accordance with, the laws of the State of Colorado without regard to the conflicts of law principles thereof.

16. **Counterparts.** This Letter Agreement may be executed in any number of counterparts, each of which when so executed will be deemed to be an original and all of which taken together will constitute one and the same agreement.

17. **Enforceability.** Except for Section 9 (Exclusivity), Section 10 (Expenses), and Sections 13–17, this Letter Agreement is an expression of intent only and is not legally binding upon any of the parties hereto. This Letter Agreement does not set forth all of the matters upon which agreement must be reached in order for the proposed transaction to be consummated. If the parties have not entered into the Definitive Agreement by September 1, 2011, this Letter Agreement and the obligations of the parties hereunder shall terminate, except for the provisions of Section 13 (Confidentiality; Publicity), which shall be legally binding and enforceable against each of the parties hereto. Notwithstanding the foregoing, the parties may mutually agree to extend the date of execution of the Definitive Agreement.

Please indicate your acceptance and agreement by signing and returning the enclosed copy of this Letter Agreement to the attention of Jane Johnson at ABC Corp. via fax (720-607-3600) no later than July 21, 2011. Upon your acceptance, ABC Corp. will proceed with due diligence and the preparation of a draft of the Definitive Agreement.
ABC Corporation

By:______________________________

James Lee

Vice President, Strategy and Business Development

ACCEPTED AND AGREED TO THIS __________ DAY OF JULY, 2011:

Target, Inc.

By:______________________________

(signature)

____

(print name)

Checklist 6-1
Sample Due Diligence Checklist

Preliminary Due Diligence Request

Set forth below is a preliminary list of documents and information that we wish to review in connection with the proposed acquisition of ____________________ (the "Company"). Please arrange for originals or exact copies of the documents and records described below, including all amendments, schedules, exhibits, supplements, side-agreements, addenda, appendices, attachments, and restatements thereto, to be compiled and furnished for our review.

Where not otherwise indicated, and to the extent appropriate, documents requested should be made available for all periods commencing on and after the date of the Company's formation to the most recent date reasonably feasible. If no document or information exists for which a request is made, please so advise us. If a section of this Preliminary Due Diligence Request would require the production of the same documents and information provided under another section hereof, please provide a statement to that effect and reference the section number pursuant to which such documents and information have been provided. For purposes of this Preliminary Due Diligence Request, "person" includes any natural person or entity and "including" means "including without limitation."

We anticipate that some documents will not be available for review at this time, and new documents within certain of the categories listed below may be created prior to the execution of the definitive purchase agreement. Please furnish us with copies of all such documents as soon as they become available.

Delivered	N/A	
		Company Records
		Articles of Organization and/or other charter document(s) of the Company.
		Bylaws, operating agreements, partnership agreements, shareholder agreements, voting trusts, proxy agreements, or other agreements relating to (a) the voting, issuance, or transfer of capital stock, limited liability company interests or membership interests, partnership interests, or other equity interests (collectively, "Equity Interests," and the holders thereof shall hereinafter be referred to as "Owners") of the Company or (b) options, warrants, convertible debt instruments, or other rights to purchase Equity Interests and any phantom stock, stock appreciation rights, or similar plan or program (collectively, "Equity Rights," and the holders thereof shall hereinafter be referred to as "Equity Rights Holders") in the Company.
		Any agreements relating to registration rights of the Owners or Equity Rights Holders.

Delivered	N/A	
		All stock books and similar records relating to the issuance, transfer, and repurchase of the Equity Interests and/or Equity Rights of the Company.
		All minutes of meetings of Owners, directors, managers, and board of managers or similar management authority of the Company and of all committees thereof.
		Company structure and management organization chart indicating organization of the Company and the titles, functions, and responsibilities of the Company's Owners, directors, managers, members of the board of managers or other similar management authority, officers, and key employees.
		List of full names of the current officers, directors, managers, members of the board of managers or other similar management authority, and all other key employees of the Company, together with, if material, the annual rate of compensation (including bonuses) of each.
		Any reports addressed to the Company's directors, managers, board of managers, or similar management authority in the past 5 years.
		All agreements, memoranda and other documents relating to any bankruptcy, insolvency, or foreclosure proceedings involving the Company or any of its assets.
		List of jurisdictions (other than the jurisdiction of its incorporation or organization) where the Company is qualified to do business and a certificate of authority or similar document evidencing authority to do business in each such jurisdiction.
		Documentation for, and description of, each transaction in which Equity Interests of the Company were issued, recapitalized, or repurchased by the Company, including documentation with respect to any Employee Stock Ownership Plan of the Company.
		Documentation for, and description of, each transaction in which Equity Rights of the Company were issued, canceled, or repurchased by the Company.
		List of all current Owners and Equity Rights Holders of the Company, including a description of the Equity Interests and Equity Rights held by each. If an Owner is an entity, describe the nature of the entity and identify its Owners and Equity Rights Holders.
		Privacy Matters
		Provide copies of Company's written information security and privacy policies and procedures.
		Provide copies of the Company's current and former website privacy policies.
		Provide the results from any vulnerability assessments or security testing the Company has performed on its IT systems or online products.

Delivered	N/A	
		Provide the details of any actual or suspected data security incidents or breaches at the Company.
		Provide the steps the Company has taken to comply with the Payment Card Industry Data Security Standards.
		Provide the steps, if any, that the Company has taken to comply with California's Consumer Protection Act (CCPA).
		Financial Matters and Liabilities
		All of the Company's audited and unaudited financial statements (including interim financial statements) for the past 2 years.
		All material correspondence to the Company from, or by the Company to, the Company's independent public accountants for the past 2 years.
		Any written analyses of the Company or the Company's operations prepared by management consultants, accountants, or other persons, including performance studies, credit reports, and other types of reports, financial or otherwise, for the past 2 years.
		Schedule of all present indebtedness (short- or long-term) for borrowed money, capitalized leases, or purchase money financings, including name of creditor, nature of indebtedness, principal amount, interest rate, repayment schedule, and description of any limitations on optional prepayment.
		Bank letters or agreements confirming lines of credit for all outstanding obligations with the Company.
		All documents and agreements evidencing borrowings, whether secured or unsecured, by the Company that are currently outstanding, including loan and credit agreements, promissory notes and other evidences of indebtedness, and all guarantees with respect to which the Company is a party, beneficiary, surety, guarantor, or maker, and all documents and agreements evidencing any other financing arrangements of the Company, including sale and lease back arrangements, installment purchases, capital leases, etc.
		With respect to currently outstanding obligations, all correspondence with any lender of the Company (including entities that have committed or given preliminary approval to provide financing to the Company), and with any lessor under a capital lease with the Company (including entities committed to lease), including all applications for financing and compliance reports submitted by the Company or the Company's independent public accountants for all outstanding obligations.
		Schedule of aged accounts and notes receivable and accounts and notes payables of the Company at the end of the most recent month and at the end of the last four quarters.

Delivered	N/A	
		Schedule of all the Company's guaranties, indemnities, and commitments that create any actual, potential, or contingent liability or obligation.
		All waivers or agreements canceling claims or rights of material value of the Company and any documents relating to any material write downs or write-offs of notes or accounts receivable of the Company for the past 2 years.
		The Company's projections, forecasts, budgets, and business plans for each of its fiscal years or other accounting period (including future years and periods) for the past 2 years.
		All audit inquiry response letters and all management representation letters provided to the Company's auditors/accountants for the past 2 years.
		All letters from the Company's accountants to management regarding accounting systems, accounting controls, and other "management letter" items for the past 2 years.
		Material Agreements
		Any material contract related to the Company's business to which the Company is a party or beneficiary not otherwise requested herein. For this purpose, a contract is "material" if: It was entered into other than in the ordinary course of business; It has a remaining term of more than one year; It involves payments to or by the Company in excess of $[___]; The Company's cost of performance or contract price materially exceeds the benefits to be derived by the Company under the contract; The termination of the contract would have a material adverse effect on the Company; It calls for the acquisition or sale of any property, plant, or equipment for a consideration exceeding $[___]; It restricts the Company's ability to engage in any line of business or to engage in business with, or sell or purchase goods or services to or from, any other person in any geographic area; or It provides for termination or the payment of money or other penalties or consequences in the event of a change of control of the Company.
		All agreements, contracts, or commitments currently in effect relating only to capital expenditures and a description of all such agreements, contracts, or commitments that have not been memorialized in writing.
		All license agreements currently in effect to which the Company is a party or beneficiary.

Delivered	N/A	
		All management, service, consulting, accountants', attorneys', agency, finder's fee, brokerage, and other service contracts or engagement letters currently in effect to which the Company is a party or beneficiary.
		All joint venture, partnership, participation, cost sharing, and similar agreements currently in effect to which the Company is a party or beneficiary.
		All powers of attorney granted by or to the Company currently in effect.
		All noncompetition and nonsolicitation agreements currently in effect with respect to any director, manager, member of the board of managers or similar management authority, Owner, officer, or other employee of the Company, in which the Company is a party or beneficiary or that relate to the Company's business.
		All documents relating to any acquisition or disposition of assets by the Company other than those made in the ordinary course of the Company's business.
		All material supply or requirements contracts to which the Company is a party or beneficiary that are currently in effect.
		A list and description of all agreements currently in negotiation by the Company that, if entered into, would be an agreement of the type requested under any section of this Preliminary Due Diligence Request.
		Any contract not otherwise requested herein between the Company and any director, manager, member of the board of managers, Owner, or officer of the Company, or any entity in which such director, manager, member of the board of managers, Owner, or officer of the Company or his or her family has any material interest.
		All contracts with distributors, sales agents, or other persons providing marketing, sales, or distribution services to the Company.
		All independent contractor, consulting, commission, agent, service, production, manufacturing, sale, agency, distribution, purchase, marketing, consignment, finder, broker, advertising, and similar contracts to which the Company is a party or beneficiary and where the estimate annual amounts payable thereunder exceed $50,000.
		Real and Tangible Personal Property
		Schedule of all real property, including improvements, owned by the Company.
		Schedule of all real property, including improvements, leased by the Company.
		Schedule of all material equipment and other tangible personal property and fixtures owned by the Company.

Delivered	N/A	
		Schedule of all material equipment and other tangible personal and fixtures leased by the Company.
		All leases of real property and all material leases of any tangible personal property currently in effect, to which the Company is a party or beneficiary, either as lessor or lessee.
		All material correspondence between the Company and any landlord or leasing agent for the past 5 years.
		Deeds to all real property owned in whole or in part by the Company, title reports and title policies relating thereto, and all surveys of any such property.
		Title insurance policies for real property owned or leased by the Company, and documentation for any title exceptions.
		All mortgages (including leasehold mortgages), deeds of trust, or other liens on real property owned or leased by the Company.
		All security agreements covering material machinery, equipment, vehicles, inventory, or other tangible personal property.
		Letter or other documentation from zoning authorities indicating that use of real property complies with zoning requirements for the past 5 years.
		Description of any pending or threatened condemnation proceedings affecting real property owned or leased by the Company.
		Environmental Matters
		All current environmental permits issued by federal, state, and local agencies, including wastewater discharge permits, air emissions permits, and hazardous waste treatment, storage, and disposal permits.
		All correspondence regarding alleged or actual liability under the CERCLA for disposal of hazardous substances on real property owned or leased by the Company or at other locations because of hazardous materials shipped from such properties.
		Statements or reports given by the Company to, and notices, complaints, or similar documents given to the Company by, the federal Environmental Protection Agency or any other federal, state, local, or foreign environmental protection agency relating to the Company's properties or operations, to the extent involving any violation or alleged violation of environmental protection laws or any action required to be taken by the Company to comply with such laws.
		All correspondence from the Company to regulatory agencies regarding failure to comply with environmental permits, violations of permit limitations, and requests for variances from permit requirements.
		All of the most recent applications for all existing environmental permits.

Delivered	N/A	
		All data and reports (including any Phase I or Phase II Environmental Assessments) regarding sampling analyses for contamination of groundwater and soil at or in the vicinity of any real property owned or leased by the Company.
		All environmental audits previously performed at or in the vicinity of any real property currently or formerly owned or occupied by the Company.
		List of facilities with (i) known aboveground and underground storage tanks or injection wells (including a description of the age and condition of each such tank or well, and any known leaking of such tanks or wells), (ii) PCB-containing equipment, or (iii) asbestos-containing structures or materials.
		Intellectual Property
		List all trademarks, service marks, trade names, copyrights, software, and patents that relate to the Company's operations or names, whether or not held or owned by the Company.
		A schedule of all unregistered trademarks and service marks owned by the Company.
		Copies of unregistered trademarks and service marks and any pending applications.
		Schedule of any unregistered trademarks and service marks used by the Company and owned by another person.
		Policies regarding treatment or disclosure of proprietary materials, including all agreements concerning confidentiality and nondisclosure with employees, contractors, visitors, or other parties.
		Documents concerning registration of trademarks and service marks, service providers, and Internet access providers relating to services or date.
		Form (or forms) of end user agreements.
		A list of any exclusive rights (product or geographical) granted by Company with respect to its products or services.
		A list showing where the Company conducts business using any trademark, service mark, trade name, copyright, or patent.
		Licensing, royalty, or similar agreements by which (a) proprietary materials of the Company are used by others or (b) proprietary materials of others are used by the Company.
		Correspondence, pleadings, etc., in the possession of the Company, relating to any claim (a) by the Company for infringement of its intellectual property rights or (b) against the Company for infringement of the intellectual property rights of another person, if the claim was made within the past 5 years or is still pending.

Delivered	N/A	
		Personnel Matters
		All employment contracts between the Company and any of its current or former employees to whom benefits (other than pension benefits) are still owed by the Company, including any contracts relating to special compensation of any employee, severance benefits, "golden parachute" payments, and any contract restricting competition or protecting confidential information.
		All personnel manuals, summary plan descriptions, or similar documentation furnished to employees setting forth personnel policies, procedures, or benefits for the past 5 years.
		Actuarial reports and Form 5500 for employee benefit plans and copies of IRS determination letters for any qualified plans for the past 5 years.
		All collective bargaining or union agreements, and a list of any labor unions or similar organizations that have represented or attempted to organize the Company's employees, if any, and all correspondence relating thereto as well as details of any strikes, organizing activity, grievances filed, hearings held, and any other labor-related problems for the past 5 years.
		Statements or reports given by the Company to, and notices, complaints, or similar documents given to the Company by any federal, state, local, or foreign governmental agency or authority or individual claimant involving any violation or alleged violation of laws or regulations relating to employment discrimination, minimum wages and hours or overtime pay, occupational health and safety, retirement plans or benefits, or other conditions of employment or personnel matters for the past 5 years.
		Details of workers' compensation loss history, reserves, and insurance for the past 5 years.
		Copies of any currently outstanding executive or management compensation plans or programs of the Company, including plans or programs relating to bonuses, phantom stock, Equity Interests, incentive compensation, rights to severance pay, stock options, or other Equity Rights or appreciation rights or any similar compensation plan or program, and the funding arrangements related to each.
		Information regarding retiree medical and life insurance benefits of the Company, including cost figures, any reserve amounts carried on the books of the Company, and any projections for liability under FASB standards for the past 5 years.
		Copies of other personnel policies, including fringe benefits, perquisites, holidays, and vacation, together with copies of all employee handbooks for the past 5 years.
		Copies of any complaints filed in any employment or benefit-related matter (including citations or violations by OSHA or other similar state or local authorities) for the past 5 years.

Delivered	N/A	
		Copies of all contracts for the payment of royalties, licenses, fees, etc. to managers or employees of the Company for the past 5 years.
		All currently outstanding liability insurance policies for directors, managers, members of the board of managers, Owners, and officers of the Company.
		Brochures, information, booklets, policies and procedures manuals, or other written material given to employees or potential employees of the Company to acquaint them with the Company's business and with services, compensation, and benefits offered to employees for the past 5 years.
		All reports concerning compliance of the Company's plans with ERISA requirements for the past 5 years.
		Schedule of all currently outstanding employment, bonus, commission, deferred compensation, severance, contingent compensation, supplemental unemployment compensation plans or programs, insurance coverage, relocation reimbursement (including any commitment to pay any of amount of loss related to the sale of an employee's residence), pension or retirement plans, agreements, arrangements, or practices, all medical, vacation, retiree medical, severance pay plans, programs, or benefits and all other agreements or fringe or other benefit plans, practices, or arrangements (either formal or informal) of the Company and copies of all written documents or other instruments governing or relating to such plans, programs, benefits, arrangements, and practices not otherwise provided in response to other document and information requests hereunder.
		A description of each currently outstanding oral employment, bonus, commission, and other compensation or benefit agreement or understanding.
		Taxes
		All U.S. income tax returns, statements, and reports and any accompanying schedules and attachments and supplements and amendments thereto filed by the Company for the past 5 years.
		All state and local income tax returns, statements, and reports and any accompanying schedules and attachments and supplements and amendments thereto filed by the Company for the past 5 years.
		Any notices, correspondence, reports, and communications, of significance, from or with local, state, U.S., and foreign taxing authorities, including those relating to any tax disputes or proposed or final assessments for the past 5 years.
		Schedule of all statute of limitations waivers or extensions with respect to any U.S., state, local, and foreign tax return or report agreed to by the Company and an explanation of the duration thereof and reasons therefor for the past 5 years.

Delivered	N/A	
		Schedule of states, localities, foreign countries, and other jurisdictions in which income or other taxes were paid by the Company and the nature and amount of taxes paid in each jurisdiction for the past 5 years.
		Schedule of all federal, state, local, or foreign tax audits conducted to which the Company has knowledge (completed or pending) and brief description of all adjustments made as a result of the audits for the past 5 years.
		All tax sharing, tax indemnification, or similar agreements by which the Company allocates tax liabilities or benefits with any other person for the past 5 years.
		Litigation and Compliance Matters
		A list and description of, and the pleadings or similar documents related to, each pending, threatened, and concluded material written claim to the Company threatening to initiate a proceeding unless a dispute is resolved, litigation, arbitration or other proceeding, or investigation relating to the Company, or any of the directors, managers, members of the board of managers, or officers of the Company, of a judicial, regulatory, or administrative nature for the past 5 years (hereinafter collectively referred to as "Litigation"), including the following matters: general civil and commercial Litigation; condemnation; the health and safety of workers, including workers' compensation matters; the health and safety of clients and other persons; employment discrimination; litigation with any of the Company's present or prior franchisees; government contracts and licenses; congressional, administrative, or criminal Litigation; indictments of the Company or any of its directors, managers, members of its board of managers, officers, or employees; alleged violations of environmental laws or regulations or laws or regulations regarding the health and safety of others; and alleged violations of any tax laws, rules, or regulations.
		For each such Litigation, provide a description of the amount of damages or other relief sought, the status of the Litigation, the amount of insurance coverage applicable, whether any insurer has disclaimed coverage with respect thereto, the court or tribunal in which such Litigation is pending, and whether any claim for punitive or exemplary damages has been made.

Delivered	N/A	
		All consent decrees, judgments, other decrees or orders, arbitration awards, settlement agreements, and other agreements to which the Company is a party or beneficiary or is bound, requiring or prohibiting any future activities for the past 5 years.
		All correspondence with, reports of or to, filings with, or other material information with respect to any other administrative or regulatory bodies that regulate a material portion of the business of the Company for the past 5 years.
		All responses by Company counsel to auditors' requests for information concerning contingent liabilities for the past 5 years.
		Statements or reports given by the Company to, and notices, complaints, or similar documents given to the Company by, any federal, state, local, or foreign governmental agency or authority involving any violation or alleged violation of laws or regulations, or any investigation thereof for the past 5 years.
		Governmental Regulations and Filings
		Except as otherwise requested herein, all material reports filed and material correspondence with any U.S., state, local, or foreign regulatory agency, including the Equal Employment Opportunity Commission, Housing and Urban Development, Department of Justice, and Federal Communications Commission relating to the Company and any state, local, or foreign counterparts thereof for the past 5 years.
		All currently existing material governmental, regulatory, and administrative permits and licenses of the Company.
		Material information and documents relating to the Company's compliance with U.S., state, local, and foreign laws and regulations, including actual information requests, and potentially responsible party letters or actual claims addressed to the Company from any governmental or administrative agency for the past 5 years in the Company's possession.
		A chart indicating all applicable effective dates, amendment dates, expiration dates, and renewal dates for all required franchise registration/notice filings, exemption filings, and business opportunity notice filings in each jurisdiction in which Company has offered or sold franchises since January 1, 20__.
		All franchise registration applications (including initial, amendment, or renewal applications) pending or in the process of being prepared for filing.
		Except as otherwise requested herein, a schedule of all material governmental permits, licenses, certificates, consents, approvals, authorizations, and registrations necessary or useful for the current and projected operations and business of the Company, and necessary for the Company to avoid a violation of applicable law.

Delivered	N/A	
		Insurance
		All insurance policies covering the Company or its properties (and all binders and certificates related thereto) and a schedule indicating the insurer, types of coverage (including whether the policy is an "occurrence" or "claims made" policy), limits of liability, annual premiums, amount of premiums prepaid or unpaid from prior years, and the amounts of deductible and/or self-insured retention in effect with respect to the Company.
		All key person life insurance policies relating to any Company employee.
		A description of any self-insurance, fronting, risk retention, or captive insurance program of the Company, and all actuarial studies related thereto.
		A description of the Company's insurance claims history, including the date of claim, nature of loss, and payment or reserve for the past 5 years.
		All correspondence and information relating to any insurer's declining coverage or reserving rights with respect to a pending claim, or aggregating related claims of, or with respect to, the Company for the past 5 years.
		A description of any claims or lawsuits pending or contemplated with respect to the Company's insurance coverage for the past 5 years.
		Any analysis of the Company's insurance program or requirements by an insurance broker, agent, or consultant or by in-house risk management staff for the past 5 years
		Affiliate Transactions
		A brief description of each circumstance where any Owner, director, manager, member of the board of managers, officer, or employee, or affiliated entity or member of the family of same, as applicable, of the Company, owns any property used in or related to the business or operations of the Company or is a party or beneficiary to any contract with the Company or otherwise in respect of the Company.
		A statement of the amounts and other essential terms of any indebtedness or other obligations of or to the Company to or from any Owner, officer, director, manager, member of the board of managers or other managing authority, employee, or other affiliate of the Company.
		Franchise Matters
		A list of all franchise agreements to which the Company is a party (collectively, together with all ancillary agreements related thereto, the "Franchise Agreements"), including for each Franchise Agreement (i) the name, address, and telephone number of each and every subfranchisee, area developer, franchisee, licensee, master licensee, or master franchisee (any of which is hereinafter referred to as a "Franchisee"), and (ii) the effective dates and expiration dates.

Delivered	N/A	
		A copy of the current form Franchise Agreement used by the Company and copies of any and all previous form Franchise Agreements used by the Company.
		All agreements with Franchisees other than on the Company's current or previous form Franchise Agreements.
		All area development agreements or similar agreements.
		All marketing and advertising agreements between the Company and its Franchisees.
		All material correspondence between the Company and its Franchisees relating to any disputes between the parties.
		All FDDs, disclosure documents, or agreements filed in the preceding 3-year period with any foreign or domestic, governmental, administrative, or regulatory agency or otherwise used by the Company in connection with the offer, sale, and operation of Franchises in any jurisdiction (domestic or international).
		All written agreements with independent sales representatives, contractors, brokers, or consultants under which the Company has authorized any person to sell or promote Franchises on behalf of the Company or agreed to rebate or share amounts receivable under any Franchise Agreement.
		A copy of the bylaws, minutes, and other documents relating to any franchisee advisory council or other representative body and any franchisee association, including any documents that create obligations on the part of Company to obtain franchisee approval of standards or policy changes.
		Copies of all transfer, termination, settlement, release, or estoppel agreements with current or former franchisees executed within past 5 years.
		A copy of all advertising and marketing materials used by Company to promote and sell franchises during the past four years, and all related registration filings submitted by or for Company to franchise regulators or governmental agencies during the same period.
		A description of the national advertising or marketing fund Company administers, as well as any other local, regional, national, or international advertising programs Company administers or controls to which franchisees contribute. Include copies of all relevant articles, bylaws, or other governing documents.
		Provide a clean copy of all current (i) manuals distributed to franchisees and (ii) internal policy manuals or other materials prescribing policies relating to franchise sales and administration. In addition, provide any different versions of these manuals Company has used over the past 3 years.

Delivered	N/A	
		A list of manufacturers, suppliers, and distributors designated by Company as an approved source, or as the only or one of the only approved sources, from whom franchisees may or must purchase products and services. Copies of all manufacturing, supply, and distribution agreements, if any, between Company or Company's affiliates and any manufacturers, suppliers, or distributors of products and services to franchisees.
		Describe any commissions, rebates, discounts, or other consideration Company receives from third-party manufacturers, suppliers, and/or distributors as the result of the sale of products and services to franchisees that are not described in the FDDs.
		Provide documentation to show that the Company's and their franchisees' websites are following the Web Content Accessibility Guidelines 2.0 AA standard.
		Describe any proprietary component of the franchise system that is licensed to Company by a third party or otherwise not owned and controlled exclusively by Company.
		Miscellaneous
		Describe all commitments to finders or brokers.
		All closing binders (if any) for any recent significant transactions involving the Company (e.g., financings, reorganizations, recapitalizations, acquisitions, etc.).
		All recent analyses or appraisals of the Company or its business or assets prepared by investment bankers, engineers, management consultants, accountants, appraisers, or others, including marketing studies, financial analyses, appraisals of property, plant, and equipment, and other reports.

Checklist 6-2
Sample Closing Checklist

ABC Corporation Signing and Closing Checklist

Key Information; Defined Terms

Signing Date:	July __, 20__
Stock Purchase Agreement:	STOCK PURCHASE AGREEMENT (the "Purchase Agreement"), dated as of July __, 20__, by and among ABC Corporation, a Delaware corporation ("Purchaser"), Target, Inc., a Colorado corporation (the "Company"), the shareholders of the Company party thereto (collectively, "Sellers"), and Joe Doe, as Sellers' Agent (the "Sellers' Agent"). All section references in this Signing and Closing Checklist are to sections of the Purchase Agreement. All capitalized terms not otherwise defined herein have the meanings ascribed to them in the Purchase Agreement.
Parties & Advisors:	Purchaser: ABC Corporation Company: Target, Inc. F&B: Faegre & Benson LLP, counsel to Purchaser S&S: Smith and Smith, PLLC, counsel to the Company and Sellers Sellers' Agent: Joe Doe as Sellers' Agent JD: Joe Doe BS: Bob Smith GJ: George Jones

Document/Action	**Responsible Party**	**Status**	✓
1. Presigning Actions			
(a) Purchaser			
(i) Due Diligence	Purchaser, F&B		
(ii) Lien Searches	Purchaser, F&B		
(iii) Resolutions of the Board of Purchaser	Purchaser, F&B		
(b) Company			
(i) Resolutions of the Board of the Company	Company, S&S		
2. Signing Documents			
(a) Purchase Agreement and Exhibits/Schedules			
(i) Purchase Agreement	All		
(ii) Exhibit A—Form of Company Counsel Legal Opinion	Company, S&S		

Document/Action	Responsible Party	Status	✓
(iii) Exhibit B—Form of Noncompete Agreement	Purchaser, F&B, Company, S&S, JD, BS, GJ		
(iv) Schedule 1 (Company Capital Stock)	Company		
(v) Schedule 10.1 (Special Indemnification Items)	Purchaser, Company		
(vi) Disclosure Schedule	Company, S&S		
3. Preclosing Items			
(a) Draft Working Capital Statement'	Company, Purchaser		
(b) Working Capital Statement'	Company, Purchaser		
(c) Funds Flow Memorandum	Company, Purchaser, S&S, F&B		
4. Closing Deliveries/Actions of Company			
(a) Transfer of Life Insurance Policies	Company, JD, BS, GJ		
(b) Officer's Certificate of the Company • Fulfillment of Conditions in Section 8.3(A) • Authorizing Resolutions • Company Articles and Company Bylaws • Incumbency	Company, S&S		
(c) Third-Party Consents	Company, S&S		
(d) Payoff Letters	Company, S&S		
(e) Legal Opinion for the Company	S&S		
(f) Good Standing Certificates • Company (CO) • IN • MD • MI • PA • TN • TX • Target Sub (CO)	Company, S&S, F&B		
(g) Resignation Letters from Each Director and Officer of: • Company • Target Sub	Company, S&S		
(h) Evidence of Termination of Company 401(K) Plan • Board Resolutions • Notice to Plan Administrator	Company, S&S		

Document/Action	Responsible Party	Status	✓
(i) FIRPTA Certificate and Authorization Form	Company, S&S		
(j) Landlord Estoppel Certificates • Englewood, CO, Lease • Baltimore City, MD, Lease • Knoxville, TN, Lease • Glen Allen, VA, Lease	Company, S&S		
(k) Noncompete Agreements • JD • BS • GJ	Purchaser, Company, S&S, JD, BS, GJ		
(l) Employment Offer Letters • JD • BS • GJ • Rocco Bognet • John McKay • Diane O'Barr • Andy Ross • David White • Stacy Zerr	Purchaser, Company, JD, BS, GJ, and other employees		
(m) Closing Balance Sheet	Company, Purchaser		
(n) Evidence of Payment of Transaction Expenses by the Company	Company		
(o) List of Employees, if Any, Terminated for Non-compliance with Applicable Law (Immigration)	Company, S&S		
(p) Termination of All Tax-Sharing Agreements	Company, S&S		
5. CLOSING DELIVERIES/ACTIONS OF SELLERS			
(a) Officer's Certificate of Sellers • Fulfillment of Conditions in Section 8.3(a) • Authorizing Resolutions • Company Articles and Company Bylaws • Incumbency	Sellers' Agent, S&S		
(b) Company Certificates, Duly Endorsed or Accompanied by an Assignment Separate from Certificate	JD, BS, GJ, S&S		
6. Closing Deliveries/Actions of Purchaser			
(a) Officer's Certificate of Purchaser Certifying Fulfillment of the Conditions in Section 8.2(a)	Purchaser, F&B		

Document/Action	Responsible Party	Status	✓
(b) Noncompete Agreements • JD • BS • GJ	Purchaser, F&B, Company, S&S, JD, BS, GJ	at Closing	
(c) Employment Offer Letters	Purchaser, Company, JD, BS, GJ, and other employees		
(d) Closing Amount Paid to Sellers	Purchaser		
7. Post Closing			
(a) Release of Indemnification Holdback Amount	Purchaser		
(b) Appointment of Directors and Officers of Company and Target Sub	Purchaser, F&B		
(c) Sun Trust Lien Releases • UCCs • PTO and other IP filings	Purchaser, F&B		

1. To be delivered to Purchaser no fewer than two business days prior to the Closing.
2. To be delivered to Purchaser on the day prior to the Closing.
3. See Section 10.1(c) of the Purchase Agreement for release dates.

CHAPTER 7

International Franchising

Alison C. McElroy and Robert A. Lauer

Contents

7-1. Introduction

U.S.-based franchise systems decide to expand internationally for a number of reasons, ranging from a reasoned determination that the franchise system must supplement U.S. growth to an ad hoc, opportunistic response to an unsolicited inquiry from a potential franchisee with money or a passion for the brand. Whatever the reason for going international, the decision to expand a U.S.-based franchise system internationally should never be taken lightly or considered as franchising in a fifty-first state. In most cases, a franchisor that does not understand and address the myriad business, legal, and cultural issues involved with international franchising is doomed to fail. This chapter outlines the key initial and continuing legal considerations that a franchisor pursuing international expansion must address to protect the franchise system and provide its international franchisees the best opportunity to succeed.[1]

7-2. Initial Considerations for International Expansion

(a) Protection of Intellectual Property

Trademarks, trade secrets, and other intellectual property are the cornerstones of any franchise. A U.S. trademark registration does not automatically provide protection of the trademark in any other country. In addition, the rules governing protection of confidential and trade secret information vary from country to country. Thus, a critical first step in international franchising is the evaluation and protection of the franchise system's intellectual property in foreign countries.

Specifically, before launching an international expansion effort or granting a franchise in a foreign country, one of the first steps a franchisor needs to take is to assess the international status of its intellectual property and apply for registration of its trademark (or find solutions for any potential impediments to registration). A franchisor should create a plan for its international trademark portfolio that takes into account the franchisor's budget, expected timeline, and list of target countries. In setting timelines and target countries, a franchisor should consider factors including (1) whether a country has a first-to-file or first-to-use trademark system, (2) the use requirements and time frames, and (3) whether a country has a history or reputation for trademark piracy or squatters. The details of trademark registration and intellectual property are described in more detail in chapter 1. In addition to registering the trademark and logo in English language

1. For a more expanded discussion of international franchise issues, see FUNDAMENTALS OF INTERNATIONAL FRANCHISING (Richard M. Asbill & Steven M. Goldman eds., ABA Forum on Franchising 2001) [hereinafter INTERNATIONAL FRANCHISING]; INTERNATIONAL FRANCHISE LAW COMPLIANCE MANUAL (William Woods ed., ABA Forum on Franchising 2011); FUNDAMENTALS OF FRANCHISING EUROPE (Robert A. Lauer & John Pratt, eds, ABA Forum on Franchising 2017).

versions, a franchisor should consider registering translations and transliterations of the trademarks and obtaining local domain name registrations, especially in Asian and Middle Eastern markets.

(b) Internal Organizational Structuring and Personnel

In order to control and implement an international franchising program effectively, a franchisor needs the internal organizational structure and personnel to support international franchise development and continuing international operations. International business development must be treated as a long-term, strategic decision and requires commitment at the very top levels of the organization and sufficient resources.

A first step is to put together a project team responsible for evaluating and creating the international expansion strategy. That team should include representatives of senior management from the different functional departments of the organization including sales, operations, marketing, legal, and finance. A sample project plan for evaluating and launching an international franchising effort is attached as exhibit 7-1.

A franchisor's existing organization will need to be modified to shift responsibilities or add personnel who can carry out the expansion plans. Two basic approaches are (1) assign representatives from each functional department of the company responsibility for supporting the international operations and (2) create a new division dedicated to the international operations with its own dedicated staff for each functional area. Depending on the structure chosen for international expansion (see below), the organizational structure may also include hiring personnel in the target country or establishing regional support centers.

The international system should build on the structure and standards already present in the company's franchise program, including training, franchise support, and marketing systems. The domestic systems will need to be modified to account for cultural, language, and other differences in foreign markets, but a strong domestic system provides the critical foundation and base.

(c) Supply Chain Considerations

Supply chain considerations are often overlooked in an initial international expansion plan but are a critical element to a successful international strategy. Key considerations include whether products or services critical to the franchise system are available locally. If not, a franchisor needs to investigate the possibility and cost of exporting the products from the United States or importing the products from another country. In some cases, it may not be possible to import certain items. For example, in the restaurant industry, adequate supply and quality of food ingredients are critical and many countries have restrictions on the importation of certain types of food products (such as dairy products or, during the mad cow disease episode, beef) or limited infrastructure for cold chain supply.

Excellent resources for supply chain considerations are existing suppliers, many of whom may already be doing business in the target international markets.

Initially, a franchisor may choose to ship supplies to a foreign market when a local source of supply is not available or practical. Under this approach, the financial model needs to include the cost of shipping, tax, and customs duty on these supplies. Franchisors may also choose to export certain items for other reasons, such as if a proprietary sauce is required and the market does not protect trade secrets strongly. If the franchisor has an established international presence and a sufficient concentration of franchisees or locations are open in a local market, it may consider establishing a supply chain locally or from nearby countries.

(d) Potential Agreement Structures

Franchising arrangements, particularly in an international context, often involve multiple units, whether through a master franchise, area development, area representative, or other model. Common structures include single or multiple unit franchises, area representatives, master franchising, and joint ventures. A key understanding at the outset is to expect that your international structure and agreement will be more complex than its domestic counterpart and will involve more individual negotiation and adaptation for each deal.

The international development structure that is most appropriate for your organization will depend on many factors, including the unit-level business model, the company's resources and desired results, the desired degree of control, and the characteristics of the foreign markets. Companies may also use a variety of different structures for different regions depending on the size of the market, the sophistication of potential franchisees, the acceptance of the franchise model, and the availability of products and real estate. In evaluating this area, a franchisor may also consider that using different models can add additional administrative and support burdens. Outlined in this section are the most common business models used in international franchising.

(i) Direct Unit Franchises

In a direct unit franchise program, a franchisor enters into individual franchise agreements directly with each foreign franchisee and for each location. Initially, the franchisor may provide service and support from the United States with occasional on-site visits to the franchisee. As the number of units increases in a country or region, the franchisor may establish a local or regional support center. The franchise agreement will usually be similar to a U.S. individual unit franchise agreement with several international provisions added (to address currency exchange, translations, etc.). Sample provisions are attached as exhibit 7-2. The benefits of a unit franchise are that the franchisor has a direct contractual relationship with the franchisee, which gives the franchisor more control over intellectual property, marketing, and operations.

A direct franchise program is generally more capital intensive because it requires a greater level of support from the franchisor, especially if the number of individual franchisees is large. Because of the greater level of support required, a direct franchise program may result in the franchisor being deemed to have a "permanent establishment" in the country and, thus, be required to pay local income taxes or establish a registered presence (such as a branch or subsidiary) in the country. This is particularly likely if the franchisor sets up an in-country office for support and training. This structure is typically used by large, mature franchisors with units that require significant initial investment (for example, hotels).

(ii) Multiple Unit or Area Development Franchise

With a multiple unit or area development structure, the franchisor grants rights to an entire country, a region within a country, and, sometimes, multiple adjacent smaller countries, where the area developer will own and operate all units directly (i.e., no subfranchising rights are granted). Typically, under an area development structure, there will be a development agreement granting one party the right to develop a number of locations according to a development schedule that establishes the number of units to be opened and, sometimes, the general location of the units within the development area over the term of the agreement. The developer may sign individual unit franchise agreements for each location opened pursuant to the development agreement. Alternatively, it may be possible, and preferable, to attach a location or store addendum to the development agreement for each location rather than a complete franchise agreement. With this location addendum approach, the agreement should be drafted carefully to address issues such as the term for each location versus development period, the effect of default as to one location, termination, and any other items to ensure alignment and clarity on the terms that apply. The development schedule and consequences for failure to meet the development schedule raise critical legal issues that should be considered and addressed at the outset. A sample development schedule is attached as exhibit 7-3.

An area development program is generally less capital intensive for the franchisor because all the support for a region is provided to one franchisee that operates multiple units. This structure is common in the restaurant industry and in small countries where the market is not large enough to allow a return on investment in a master franchise structure or justify the franchisor's investment in a direct unit franchise structure.

(iii) Master Franchise

In a master franchise structure, the franchisor grants a master franchisee (or subfranchisor) the right to open—and sublicense others to open—franchises in a defined territory.[2] A master franchise is a three-tiered structure that interposes the

2. *See generally* Jennifer Dolman, Robert A. Lauer & Lawrence M. Weinberg, *Structuring International Master Franchise Relationships for Success and Responding When Things Go Awry*, 30th ABA Forum on Franchising (2007).

master franchisee between the franchisor and the operator of the units (the subfranchisee). The contractual relationship is indirect: the franchisor and master franchisee enter into a master franchise agreement that gives the master franchisee rights to use the system and the marks and to sublicense the system and marks to third parties. The franchisor is generally not a party to the unit franchise agreement, except as a third-party beneficiary for enforcement purposes. Instead, the master franchisee enters the franchise agreements with the subfranchisees and is responsible for training, support, and enforcement.

Because of the indirect contractual relationship and three-tiered structure, a franchisor gives up more control over the system in a master franchise model. The master franchise agreement should address trademark use, development rights and obligations, the fee splits, division of responsibilities and obligations of franchisor and master franchisee for training and support, and the impact on subfranchisees if the master franchisee agreement is terminated. Master franchising is generally also less capital intensive for the franchisor and is the most common international franchising structure because it can provide for rapid expansion at a lower cost and maximizes the benefits of a local owner familiar with the market. A checklist of terms for a master franchise arrangement is attached as checklist 7-1.

(iv) Area Representative

In the area representative structure, the franchisor grants an area representative the right to recruit and support franchisees in a defined territory in exchange for a percentage of the fees and royalty. The franchisor maintains the direct contractual relationship with both the area representative and the unit franchisees. An area representative program is a three-party structure, but it is a triangular relationship rather than the vertically tiered structure of master franchising. See exhibit 7-8 for a diagram comparing these structures. In the area representative model, the franchisor maintains an intermediate degree of control over the unit franchisees because of the direct contractual relationships with the unit franchisees. The challenge of the area representative structure is that the franchisor is contractually obligated to provide services to the unit franchisees, so if the area representative is not fulfilling its obligations, the franchisor needs to be able to fill the gap. An area representative program may also be likely to result in a permanent establishment for the franchisor. There can also be practical challenges for franchisor legal staff in addressing cost-effective resourcing to administer franchise agreements in multiple countries and languages. Area representative structures are not very common in international franchising, but they can be used successfully in the right markets.

(v) Joint Venture

A joint venture structure can be used where the franchisor wants to own an equity interest in the franchisee entity in the target market but does not want to have all of the responsibilities or investment necessary for a direct unit franchise. A joint venture can be structured in a variety of ways and may also involve one or more of the agreement forms described above. For example, the franchisor and a second party may each own an equity interest in an entity in the target country. That entity in turn enters into the master franchise agreement or area development agreement with the franchisor to develop locations in the country. The form of organization and choice of entity of the joint venture require consideration of local and U.S. law and tax issues.

A joint venture can be less capital intensive than direct franchising because the local joint venture partner also provides capital. The joint venture also provides more control than master franchising because of the franchisor's additional status as an owner (or for a joint venture, the rights granted in the joint venture agreement). A key internal issue is to ensure the franchisor's accounting and tax functions can handle the more sophisticated accounting and tax needs of ongoing management of a joint venture. Key issues to address in the joint venture establishment are the roles of each party, the rights of the parties to terminate and unwind the joint venture, and the consequences of termination. For example, the franchisor will want to control the intellectual property created by the joint venture upon termination. A joint venture typically requires significant additional up-front ongoing legal review, strong financial support, and business negotiations. It is a less common structure for most franchisors expanding internationally.

(e) Market Analysis Considerations

Before launching a new international strategy or expanding into a new geographic area, it is essential to vet development plans with targeted local market research. Even the most experienced companies can run into difficulties if their systems are not properly adapted to the local market. Market research assesses the competitive landscape and helps identify the franchisor's differentiation—the factors that may allow a franchise system to provide products or services more efficiently than the local competition. With that intelligence in hand, a franchisor can go forward deliberately—knowing both what will differentiate it in a particular market and what, if any, internal system modifications will be necessary to bring about that differentiation.

Key steps in conducting market analysis include visiting the target country and places of business, identifying and evaluating the local competitive landscape, and gaining an understanding of the business and cultural norms of the country. A list of sources of information and market analysis resources available to U.S. companies expanding abroad is included as exhibit 7-4.

(f) General International Business Considerations

A number of U.S. laws apply to transnational transactions and affect franchise operations around the world. These include the Foreign Corrupt Practices Act (FCPA), export controls, antiterrorism and sanctions programs, and antiboycott laws.[3]

3. *See generally* Jeffrey A. Brimer, Alison C. McElroy & John H. Pratt, *Going International: What Additional Restraints Will You Face?, Structuring International Master*

(i) FCPA

The FCPA is a U.S. federal law that regulates the way U.S. companies conduct foreign business.[4] The FCPA has two main sections: (1) antibribery provisions and (2) books and records provisions. The antibribery provisions prohibit offering or giving anything of value to a public official or political candidate (directly or indirectly) to obtain or retain business or to obtain an improper advantage in doing business. The books and records provisions require that public companies maintain proper internal books and records that reasonably reflect all transactions and disposition of assets. The books and records provisions also mandate internal accounting controls to assure that expenditures are authorized.

The FCPA does not require proof of actual knowledge. A person may be liable for an FCPA violation if a reasonable person under similar circumstances would know that a violation is highly probable. Red flags that might put a company on notice of prohibited activity include

- a request for an unusual method of payment to any participants in the transaction, particularly through third countries or in third country currency;
- known or suspected family relationship between any participants in the transaction and government officials;
- refusal by any participant to sign affidavits or make representations that they will not violate the FCPA;
- requests of payment disproportionate to the services performed;
- known or suspected misrepresentations by the agent or others in connection with a proposed transaction;
- requests by any participant in the transaction that the company prepare false invoices or any other type of false documentation; and
- any negative information developed as part of an independent investigation into the activities and reputation of the agent or other participants in the transaction.

(ii) OFAC/Sanctions/Antiterrorism/SDN List

The Office of Foreign Assets Control (OFAC) is an agency of the U.S. Department of the Treasury that administers and enforces economic sanctions programs against groups of individuals (such as terrorists and narcotics traffickers) and against countries and governments. These laws apply to U.S. companies and can also apply to affiliates, foreign subsidiaries, employees, and other related persons depending on the circumstances.

The programs administered by OFAC include the Specially Designated Nationals (SDN) list, an ever-expanding list of individuals and organizations with which U.S. companies are prohibited from doing business. A convenient

---

Franchise Relationships for Success and Responding When Things Go Awry, 34rd ABA Forum on Franchising (2011).

4. 15 U.S.C. §§ 78dd-1 *et seq.*

directory of the various lists of prohibited persons—appropriately titled "Lists to Check"—is available on the U.S. Department of Commerce website.[5] The lists are updated periodically.

In addition to the due diligence performed at the outset of a business relationship, franchisors should also establish a compliance program to ensure ongoing compliance with their obligations under the U.S. antiterrorism and sanctions programs. A compliance program should include, at a minimum, representations in the agreement that the franchisee is not listed on any of the prohibited lists, periodic certifications from the franchisee confirming compliance, a right to terminate the agreement should the franchisee ever appear on any prohibited lists, and internal training programs so the franchisor's personnel understand their obligations and responsibilities to comply with the law.

OFAC also administers sanctions programs that target specific countries and governments.[6] The scope of the sanctions and prohibited activities varies depending on the country. One aspect of the prohibited activities is that exports of certain items to some countries are permitted only if the company has a license from OFAC or the Department of Commerce (although most licenses that have been granted have been related to communications, technology, or health-related businesses). Another aspect is that there are different limits on exports to and imports from particular countries. There are also some exceptions for humanitarian relief and other limited situations.

(iii) Export Controls

The U.S. Department of Commerce Bureau of Industry and Security (BIS) is responsible for the enforcement of the federal Export Administration Regulations (EAR) that regulate the export of commercial items. While many exports will not require a license, franchisors operating internationally should be aware of potential licensing requirements and should be aware that a wide range of commercial items are subject to the EAR.[7] The EAR and other agencies' regulations regulate not only particular commercial items that are exported but also the exportation of items to particular countries. Franchisors should be aware that export controls will apply based upon the classification of the particular items in question and the countries in which the franchisor intends to ship the items. Although unlikely to affect most franchisors, who will receive the items and the intended use of the

---

5. Dep't of Commerce, Bureau of Indus. & Sec., Lists to Check, http://www.bis.doc.gov/complianceandenforcement/liststocheck.htm.

6. Details of the various sanctions programs are available on the OFAC website at https://home.treasury.gov/policy-issues/office-of-foreign-assets-control-sanctions-programs-and-information. OFAC also publishes the OFAC Guide for Exporters and Importers, which summarizes the various sanctions programs. It is available on the OFAC website at https://home.treasury.gov/systems/files/126/facei.pdf. A list of key government websites can be found at exhibit 7-4.

7. *See* Dep't of Commerce, Bureau of Indus. & Sec., Introduction to Commerce Department Export Controls, http://www.bis.doc.gov/licensing/exportingbasics.htm. Some exports may be controlled by other U.S. government agencies.

items will affect whether an item may be exported and whether a license from the BIS or another federal agency is necessary.

(iv) Antiboycott

Franchisors operating internationally should also be aware of their obligations under U.S. antiboycotting laws. The U.S. antiboycotting laws discourage, and in some cases prohibit, U.S. companies from participating in or supporting foreign boycotts not sanctioned by the U.S. government.

The antiboycotting laws are of particular importance for any company doing business in the Middle East, since several countries in that region support the Arab League boycott of Israel.[8] This Israeli boycott is not supported by the U.S. government, and compliance with this boycott by U.S. entities or individuals violates U.S. laws or may be penalized under applicable U.S. tax laws. The U.S. Department of the Treasury publishes a quarterly list of boycotting countries. Actions that may be penalized or prohibited under the antiboycott laws include

- agreements to refuse or actual refusal to do business with or in Israel or with blacklisted companies;
- agreements to discriminate or actual discrimination against other persons based on race, religion, sex, national origin, or nationality;
- agreements to provide or actually providing information about business relationships with or in Israel or with blacklisted companies; and
- agreements to provide or actually providing information about the race, religion, sex, national origin, or nationality of another person.

Additional examples of permitted and prohibited activities in connection with boycott requests are included in the EAR.[9]

Any requests made to U.S. entities or individuals to comply with the boycott must be reported to the U.S. Department of Commerce on a quarterly basis and to the Internal Revenue Service on an annual basis. Criminal and civil penalties can be imposed for violations of the antiboycott regulations and failure to file the required reports. In addition, cooperation with or participation in an international boycott may result in a company losing certain tax benefits, such as foreign tax credits or deferral of taxation of earnings of a controlled foreign corporation.

U.S. franchisors operating internationally and foreign franchise systems entering the United States must be aware of the obligations imposed by these U.S. laws. Companies involved in transnational business should implement an internal compliance program including official corporate policies and procedures; training for officers, employees, and agents; written compliance certifications; and provisions in agreements addressing these issues. A sample international franchise application and related franchise agreement provisions are attached as

---

8. For instance, Syria has historically required a statement in support of the boycott as a condition to, among other things, a trademark application. *See* Martin A. Weiss, Cong. Res. Serv., RL 33961, Arab League Boycott of Israel 9 (Aug. 27, 2008).

9. *See* Dep't of Commerce, Export Administration Regulations Database, https://www.bis.doc.gov/index.php/regulations/export-administration-regulations-ear.

exhibit 7-5. A sample international letter of intent is attached as exhibit 7-6. Sample international closing and organizational checklists are attached as checklist 7-2.

(g) Role of Consultants and In-House, Outside, and Foreign Counsel

In addition to a company's internal team, outside advisors may assist a franchisor with its international expansion and operations. The team may include the company's in-house counsel, outside counsel, local counsel in the foreign country, and consultants in various roles and responsibilities.

An important point is that all franchisors offering franchises or operating outside the United States will need to engage qualified counsel in the foreign country. Foreign counsel should speak English, have experience working with U.S. companies, and have experience in franchising. Depending on a legal department's experience and workload, a company may choose to manage the international consultants and lawyers internally or may choose to hire an outside law firm to manage the process. For all outside advisors, in-house counsel should ask for an estimate in advance and agree on a budget and responsibilities of each team member.

Consultants play several roles including market researcher, franchise sales manager, and outsourced international department. It is more common to use outside consultants to assist with developing strategy in launching an international expansion initiative, to identify and qualify franchise candidates, and for consulting on specific operational issues. Implementation of the strategy and ongoing operations is generally then handled by in-house personnel.

When selecting consultants, it is important to understand their specific strengths and not take statements regarding their overarching abilities at face value. Talking to references, making sure that the consultant has specific experience in the underlying business and geographic area of interest, and confirming specific tasks and pricing beforehand is crucial to ensuring the use of a consultant is a positive and rewarding experience.

7-3. International Disclosure and Registration

(a) International Disclosure Laws

There is no generally applicable international franchise disclosure obligation, and franchisors may pursue franchise transactions in many countries throughout the world without any franchise-specific statutory disclosure obligation.[10]

10. Countries whose legal system is based on the civil law, which includes continental Europe, South America, and China, impose a duty of disclosure in all contractual relationships. *See* Luiz Henrique O. do Amaral & John H. Pratt, *Civil Law for Common Law*

However, approximately 29 countries[11] other than the United States have laws or regulations governing the offer and sale of a franchise *and* require some form of pre-sale franchise disclosure or registration. While such laws share some similarities with the U.S. Federal Trade Commission (FTC) Rule,[12] each country's franchise disclosure law presents different requirements, including mandatory formats that differ from the FTC Rule, local language requirements, and in some instances unique mandatory pre-sale filings. This section provides an overview and sampling of the types of disclosure and registration requirements a U.S. franchisor may encounter. Franchisors should always seek current advice from experienced counsel at the time of a potential transaction to make sure they account

Practitioners (Or How to Draft an Agreement for Use Overseas), 25th ABA Forum on Franchising (2002).

11. As of the date this chapter was prepared, these countries include the following: Argentina, Australia (Australia Franchising Code, Bus. Franchise Guide (CCH) ¶ 7001), Belgium (Belgium Franchise Law, unofficial translation, Bus. Franchise Guide (CCH) ¶7008), Brazil (Law 13,966/2019, revoking and replacing prior Law 8,955/94), Canada (specifically the provinces of Alberta (Alberta Franchises Act, Bus. Franchise Guide (CCH) ¶ 7010; Alberta Regulation, Bus. Franchise Guide (CCH) ¶ 7015), British Columbia, Manitoba, New Brunswick (Franchises Act, Bus. Franchise Guide (CCH) ¶ 7045), Ontario (Ontario Franchises Act, Bus. Franchise Guide (CCH) ¶ 7050), and Prince Edward Island (Franchises Act, Bus. Franchise Guide (CCH) ¶ 7058)), China (*see generally* Bus. Franchise Guide (CCH) ¶ 7060, *et seq.*), France (Loi Doubin and Decree of Implementing Regulations, Bus. Franchise Guide (CCH) ¶¶ 7130, 7135, 7136), Indonesia (Government Regulation No. 16, Bus. Franchise Guide (CCH) ¶ 7145; Government Regulation No. 71), Italy (Rules on the Regulation of Franchising, Bus. Franchise Guide (CCH) ¶¶ 7150, 7152), Japan (Medium-Small Retail Business Promotion Law, Act No. 101 of 29 Sept. 1973, as amended in April 2002, Bus. Franchise Guide (CCH) ¶ 7158), Kazakhstan (Bus. Franchise Guide (CCH) ¶ 7160), Malaysia (Franchise Act of 1998 *Act No. 950) Bus. Franchise Guide (CCH) ¶ 7180), Mexico (Franchise Provisions, Law on Industrial Property of June 27, 1991, Bus. Franchise Guide (CCH) ¶ 7210; Regulations Under the Law on Industrial Property of Nov. 23, 1994, Bus. Franchise Guide (CCH) ¶ 7215), Netherlands (Title 16. Franchise of Book 7, Dutch Civil Code), Romania (Ordinance and Law, Bus. Franchise Guide (CCH) ¶ 7372), Russia (Bus. Franchise Guide (CCH) ¶ 7230), South Africa (Bus. Franchise Guide (CCH) ¶ 7244), South Korea (Act on Fairness in Franchise Transactions, Bus. Franchise Guide (CCH) ¶¶ 7170–7174), Spain (Article 62, Bus. Franchise Guide (CCH) ¶ 7250, at 10,051), Saudi Arabia (Royal Decree No. 122, dated October 8, 2019 for Law on Commercial Franchise System and its Commercial Franchise Implementing Regulations in Decision No. (00591) dated May 11, 2020), Sweden (Bus. Franchise Guide (CCH) ¶ 7257), Taiwan (Standards Governing Disclosure of Information by Franchisors, Bus. Franchise Guide (CCH) ¶¶ 7260, 7262), Thailand (Guidelines on Unfair Trade Practices in the Franchise Business (published December 6, 2019; Effective February 4, 2020), Tunisia and Vietnam (Bus. Franchise Guide (CCH) ¶ 7280). Other jurisdictions had pending or expressly formal interest in pursuing franchise legislation as of the date of preparation of this chapter, including Egypt. *See* Zwisler, Fotsch, IFA International Committee Global Regulatory Update; 2020 IFA Convention, Orlando, Florida, February 10, 2020, at 19; Zwisler, Fotsch, IFA International Committee Global Regulation Update, February 2, 2021, at 2–14.

12. See chapter 2 for an explanation of franchise registration and disclosure obligations in the United States.

for updated country-specific requirements.[13] By way of example, Brazil, Saudi Arabia, and Thailand all introduced new or revamped franchise laws in late 2019/early 2020, and Belgium, Cambodia, Indonesia, Malaysia, the Netherlands, Ontario, Canada, and Romania all introduced new or amended franchise-related rules or regulations that took effect in 2020 or early 2021, with Australia, Egypt, and Guatemala all reviewing franchise-related legislation as of early 2021.[14]

(b) International Disclosure Format and Substantive Requirements

Franchisors considering franchising in countries beyond the United States often ask whether a U.S. franchise disclosure document (FDD) may be useful in other countries or should be provided to franchisees in a jurisdiction where no franchise disclosure obligation exists or in jurisdictions with their own franchise disclosure laws.

In nearly all countries, providing a US FDD without any additional disclosure is not recommended. Even in jurisdictions with no express franchise disclosure obligation, common law causes of action may be available to franchisees, including country-specific versions of a breach of a duty of good faith and fair dealing, fraud, fraudulent inducement, misrepresentation, deceptive trade practices, contact of adhesion, and breach of fiduciary duty.[15] While certain of these actions exist internationally, perhaps the most omnipresent, non-statutory international disclosure concept is the concept of culpa in contrahendo, which is Latin for "fault in conclusion of a contract".[16] Many U.S. franchisors may not be aware of this concept, which creates a non-contractual obligation of good faith with respect to the negotiation and execution of contracts where there are particular circumstances of which only the franchisor is aware and which are readily identified to be of importance to the prospective franchisee's business-making process and entry into the franchise agreement.[17] This leads to the rather straightforward idea that the franchisor must refrain from providing misleading information regarding itself and the franchise offering, and correspondingly disclose to the prospective franchisee all relevant information about the franchisor and the franchise offering.[18] This is, of course, an extremely broad and obtuse requirement to satisfy, and at times it is more difficult to measure compliance versus a well-defined specific set of statutory disclosure items.

13. English translations of the franchise statutes of other countries often contain ambiguities. In some cases, the language of the statute itself is unclear. Local counsel can best advise on how to address ambiguities and what the local practice is to address ambiguities and specific requirements. *See* INTERNATIONAL FRANCHISING, *supra* note 1, at 190.

14. Zwisler, Fotsch, *supra* note 11.

15. Forgas, Lauer, Trickey, *Should International Disclosure (Documents) Be the Norm or "Best Practice" for International Franchise Transactions?*, IBA/IFA 33rd Annual Joint Conference, May 9–10, 2017, Washington, D.C. U.S.A, at 2–3.

16. *Id.* at 3.

17. *Id.*

18. *Id.*

In these culpa in contrahendo jurisdictions,[19] a U.S. FDD or even a truncated "international information memorandum" may be a useful tool to provide general information about the offering and agreements, but care must be taken to avoid confusing prospects with information that is not relevant to the local market or, even worse, providing information that is misleading and not applicable in the local jurisdiction. For franchisors with an active international franchise program, an abbreviated franchise information memorandum or similar document may be the best option because it provides information regarding the international program and, if maintained on a current basis, can be the initial basis for mandatory international disclosure documents.[20]

With respect to jurisdictions with a franchise disclosure obligation, there is normally significant overlap between the requirements of these international disclosure laws and, in most instances, the requirements of the FTC Rule, which are typically more comprehensive than international disclosure laws.[21] Therefore, many franchisors have historically been tempted to use a "wrap-around" FDD or international disclosure document in an effort to reduce the cost and time burden of compliance with disclosure laws.[22] A wrap-around disclosure document is in essence a uniform disclosure document for use throughout the world; to address each country's specific requirements in a "wrap-around" disclosure document format, the franchisor's counsel adds an addendum to the standard disclosure document.[23] But for franchisors planning to franchise throughout the world, and given the continuing adoption of new franchise laws and the trend to countries specifying a mandatory format for franchise disclosure, the utility of a wrap-around international disclosure has been almost completely eviscerated in the last five to ten years.[24]

In all cases, as in the United States, franchisors should also always review the franchise disclosure law of each country to determine whether there is an exemption that may apply to the transaction. However, at present, with only a couple key variances (namely the Canadian provinces, including Ontario, which expanded its exemptions in 2020), international disclosure laws do not have the full array of typical exemptions or exclusions that are viable for U.S. franchisors at the federal and/or state level. The most historically significant "single franchise" exemption that was originally available under the first edition of the Australia franchise law was removed in 2008. Most current exemptions relate to extremely low initial fee or initial investment levels, and unfortunately most of

19. Countries with culpa in contrahendo include Germany (German Civil Code Section 242), the United Kingdom, Argentina, and Switzerland.

20. See *supra* note 11.

21. International Franchising, *supra* note 1, at 212.

22. Andrew P. Loewinger & Michael K. Lindsey, *International Franchise Disclosure Laws*, at 3, 25th ABA Forum on Franchising (2002) [hereinafter *International Disclosure Laws*].

23. *Id.* at 4. In jurisdictions, such as the Canadian provinces with disclosure laws and Australia, Korea, and Vietnam, a wrap-around disclosure document is not permitted.

24. *See International Disclosure Laws*, supra note 22, at 4.

the franchise disclosure laws are either silent or vague with respect to disclosures in the context of transfers, renewals, amendments, or extensions.

(i) Mandatory Disclosure Formats

For a number of countries, franchisors may use disclosure documents in a format that is similar to their U.S. FDD, because while the applicable local law may set forth certain topical matters that must be addressed in the disclosure, the law may not specify a format that the franchisor must follow, and no governmental authority will vet the disclosure similar to a U.S. state examiner's review.

There are, of course, numerous exceptions to this general statement that likely thwart a franchisor's plan to use a uniform or wrap-around disclosure document, rather than country- or region-specific disclosure documents. The following countries, among others, require that a franchisor's disclosures be presented in specific format:

Australia—The Australia Franchising Code of Conduct[25] requires that the disclosure document must be "in the form and the order, and under the numbering [set forth in the law]."[26] The format that a franchisor must follow is determined by reviewing the franchisor's expected annual turnover—that is, the amount of business the franchisor expects to do in a year.[27] Most franchisors have enough turnover to mandate the full-length disclosure form, which has actually been modified a number of times, most recently in June 2021.[28]

Brazil—Article 2, Section 1 of the 2019 Franchise Law requires that a Franchise Disclosure Document be written in Portuguese in uncomplicated, non-legal language and contain 23 specific items.

Canada—The provincial franchise disclosure laws in Ontario, Alberta, Prince Edward Island, New Brunswick, Manitoba, and British Columbia[29] require that a franchisor provide disclosure, and the various Acts' implementing regulations set out the specific items that must be included in such disclosure.[30] Case law in the province of Ontario has since confirmed that disclosures should be in the proffered format and that use of a U.S. form FDD with Canadian addenda comes with significant risk.[31] Most U.S. franchisors now use a Canadian Disclosure Document that is adapted to combine the format of the Ontario, Alberta, Prince Edward Island, New Brunswick, Manitoba, and British Columbia franchise disclosure

25. Australia Franchising Code, Bus. Franchise Guide (CCH) ¶ 7001.

26. Australia Franchising Code of Conduct Amendments, pt. 2.1(7.), Bus. Franchise Guide (CCH) ¶ 7001A.

27. *Id.* at 13.

28. *Id.*; *see also* https://www.accc.gov.au/business/industry-codes/franchising-code-of-conduct.

29. Ontario Franchises Act, Alberta Franchises Act, Prince Edward Island Franchises Act, New Brunswick Franchises Act, Manitoba Franchises Act and British Columbia Franchises Act, Bus. Franchise Guide (CCH) ¶ 7020 *et seq.*

30. Regulation 581/00, pt. 2, Bus. Franchise Guide (CCH) ¶ 7055.

31. *See, e.g.*, 1518628 Ontario Inc. v. Tutor Time Learning Centres, LLC, Bus. Franchise Guide (CCH) ¶ 7392. Ontario Superior Court of Justice. Case No. 05-CL-5983. Released July 21, 2006.

laws in something akin to a U.S. FDD that is prepared in accordance with the FTC Rule and NASAA guidelines.

Korea—Historically, South Korea's Fair Franchise Transactions Act[32] did not require a specific disclosure format, but amendments that went into effect in 2007 and 2008 and that were later implemented through regulations in August 2009 require that, among other things, the disclosure statement must be registered with the Korea Fair Trade Commission in the Korean language and modeled on an official form promulgated by the Fair Trade Commission. Importantly, the Commission has materially amended the regulations and their internal practices multiple times over the past 10+ years to require additional or modified disclosures almost every year such that even year-to-year filing may require multiple material changes to the Korea disclosure document irrespective of the franchisor's own updating changes. This continuous tinkering with the Korea franchise disclosure document framework has turned Korea into one or the more time-consuming jurisdictions in terms of compliance.

Malaysia—Malaysia's Franchise Act[33] is supported by implementing regulations that specify the format for the disclosure document.[34] Form 1 of Malaysia's regulations titled "Disclosure Document Franchise System Matters to be stated" sets forth Malaysian disclosure requirements in numbered sections.[35]

South Africa—South Africa's Consumer Protection Act[36] provides extensive protection to franchisees and places extensive contractual and disclosure obligations on the franchisor. Regulations 2 and 3 of the Regulations to the Act set forth additional specific disclosure requirements for franchise agreements as well as mandatory requirements to be contained in each franchise agreement. Interestingly, South Africa is one of only a few country-specific disclosure frameworks that divides mandatory franchise disclosures among a specific franchise disclosure document and the franchise agreement itself.[37] This unique aspect some-

---

32. Act on Fairness in Franchise Transactions, Bus. Franchise Guide (CCH) ¶¶ 7170–7174.

33. Franchise Act of 1998 *(Act No. 950) Bus. Franchise Guide (CCH) ¶ 7180.

34. International Franchising, *supra* note 1, at 202.

35. *International Disclosure Laws*, supra note 22, at 99.

36. Franchising in South Africa is regulated by the Consumer Protection Act 2008 (CPA) and the regulations to the Act that came into force on March 31, 2011.

37. Mexico's 1991 Industrial Property Law (IPL), and its Regulations issued in 1994 (1994 Regulations), also require certain disclosure-based information in the franchise agreement. Specifically, Article 142 Bis. of the IPL "[t]he franchisee agreement shall be in writing and must include, at least, the following requirements: I. Geographical zone where franchisee shall perform the activities which constitute the subject matter of the agreement; II. Location, minimum dimensions and specifications of the investments in infrastructure, in respect to the premises where the franchisee shall perform the activities resulting from the agreement; III. Inventory, marketing and advertising policies, as well as any provisions in connection with merchandise supply and engagement of vendors, if applicable; IV. Policies, procedures and terms in relation to reimbursements, financing and any other considerations in charge of the parties under the terms accorded in the agreement; V. Applicable criteria and methods to determine franchisees' commissions and/or profit margins; VI. Technical and operational training specifications of the franchisee's personnel, as well as

times results in a double-take by U.S. counsel that is not used to included "disclosure"-type information in the franchise agreement itself.

(ii) Mandatory Local Language Requirements

The authors are not aware of any franchisors that always provide disclosure in a language other than English as a matter of course (absent perhaps in the context of master franchising). However, a country's franchise disclosure law may require that the franchisor register or provide disclosure in a native language; if a specific language is not required by the law, the law may require that the disclosure document be clear, comprehensible, or free from legalese.[38] Countries with mandatory local language requirements include the following:

Brazil—Pursuant to Brazilian Franchise Law (Law 13,966/2019) that took effect in March 2020, the now more detailed Brazilian FDD will need to be prepared and delivered in Portuguese, and international franchisors will need to prepare a sworn translation of the franchise agreement if it is to be executed in a foreign language. Interestingly, pursuant Article 7, Section II of the 2019 Franchise Law, translations must be paid by the franchisor and cannot be directly charged to the franchisee, and it is unclear under the Brazilian Franchise Law whether an English translation can control.

Korea—Korea's required disclosure statement must be registered with the Korea Fair Trade Commission in the Korean language and modeled on an official form. In addition, in practice, the agreements must also be translated and submitted in the Korean language.

Indonesia—Indonesia's current franchise law and regulations[39] require that all franchisor prospectus registrations include, among other things, a copy of a franchise prospectus in Indonesian (which for U.S. franchisors is normally

---

the method or manner whereby franchisor will provide technical assistance; VII. Criteria, methods and procedures for supervision, information, evaluation and rating performance, as well as the quality of the services the franchisee and the franchisor will be in charge of; VIII. To establish terms and conditions to sub-franchise, should the parties agree to it; IX. Termination causes under the franchise agreement; X. Assumptions under which the parties may review, and if applicable, may amend, by mutual agreement, any terms or conditions related to the franchise agreement; XI. Unless it is otherwise agreed, the franchisee shall not be obliged to sell its assets to franchisor or to the person the latter appoints, at the termination of the franchise agreement, and XII. Unless otherwise agreed, franchisee shall not be obliged to sell or transfer his company shares to the franchisor, nor to make the latter a partner thereof. This article shall be subject, in all applicable issues, to the provisions set forth in the Regulations of this Law."

38. *See, e.g.*, International Franchising, *supra* note 1, at 199 (stating that while Brazil's prior franchise law did not require the disclosure document to be written in Portuguese, the law states that it must be in "clear and comprehensible" language).

39. The Indonesian franchise law was originally contained in Governmental Regulation No. 16/1997 and Decree of the Minister of Industry and Trade No. 259/MPP/Kep/7/1997, but has since been expanded and modified multiple times via, among other regulations, the Franchise Regulations (Government Regulation No. 42/2007, dated 23 July 2007), the Franchise Operations Regulations dated Aug. 21, 2008 and Franchise Regulation, Number 91 of 2019 (MoTR 17/2019).

accompanied by the U.S. version as well). In 2019, additional regulations were issued that require franchise agreements to be offered in Indonesian language and be governed by Indonesian law.[40]

Vietnam—Vietnam's Commercial Law[41] requires that all franchisor registration documents be prepared and submitted in Vietnamese, including the application, the franchise description document, copies of intellectual property registrations, and franchisor corporate documents. Vietnam also requires annual updates and/or statements of material change on an annual basis for franchisors to maintain their registration status (even if the franchisor only sold one active franchise), and all such annual updates and/or statements of material change must also be submitted in the Vietnamese language.

In-house counsel should be aware that translating disclosure documents and related agreements into a local language can be a tremendous cost and administrative burden, and it can delay transactions as translations are prepared or updated. There tends to always also be a tension between use of third-party translation services that may or may not have attorneys on staff, versus a local firm's in-house translation team, which may be slower and more expensive than a translation service but will in most cases be better equipped to deal with the nuances of legal language. See below regarding other translation issues.

(iii) Mandatory Franchisor Director/Officer Certifications

Franchisors may be required to have their officers or directors sign the disclosure document certifying that it is true and correct, which can be disconcerting to executives who may not otherwise be as familiar with the documents being prepared or fully comprehend the potential ramifications of their signature (even now, more than almost two decades after the introduction of Sarbanes/Oxley).

Countries with mandatory certifications include the following:

Australia—Australia's Franchising Code of Conduct requires that an authorized director or officer must certify that the disclosure document is true and correct.

Canada—The Canadian provinces of Ontario, Alberta,[42] Prince Edward Island, New Brunswick,[43] Manitoba, and British Columbia all have certification requirements pursuant to which two authorized directors or officers must certify that the disclosure document is true and correct.

Saudi Arabia—Saudi Arabia's 2020 franchise law requires that two years of franchisor financial statements be accompanied by "[a] statement of the financial status of the Franchisor at the end of its last fiscal year, signed by the manager or official of the Franchisor or its auditor, with a statement indicating the Franchisor's ability to pay its debts on the due date."

---

40. Franchise Regulation, Number 91 of 2019 (MoTR 17/2019).

41. Commercial Law (Jan. 1, 2006), as implemented by Decree Making Detailed Provisions for Implementation of the Commercial Law with Respect to Franchising Activities and Circular Providing Guidelines on Procedures for Registration of Franchising Activities.

42. Franchises Act (1972).

43. The Franchises Act (2007).

South Africa—South Africa requires that the disclosure document be signed and dated by an authorized officer of the franchisor.

In other countries, franchisors may be required to provide not only biographical information on key officers and directors but also other information or documentation about their directors/officers to foreign officials. For example, Vietnam requires that copies of passports and other identifying information be included as part of the franchisor filing. Most experienced franchise practitioners have had to attempt to allay fears of businesspersons who worry about their passports or other information being available in these countries, particularly in the context of future franchise disputes that may arise.

(c) International Registrations and Filings

(i) Franchisor Filings

Several jurisdictions require a franchisor to register as a "franchisor" in the jurisdiction without specifically including franchise-specific disclosures or agreement forms in the registration. These filings are most akin to U.S. business opportunity notice filings.[44] Countries with initial franchisor filings include the following:

Indonesia—In Indonesia, a franchisor must register with the Ministry of Trade its disclosure document and obtain a registration number and a franchise registration certificate under its name before executing a franchise agreement with an Indonesian franchisee. This is separate from the franchisee's requirement to register the franchise agreement and disclosure statements with the Ministry of Trade.

Malaysia—Malaysia's Franchise Act requires prior registration and approval of a franchisor before a "triggering event," such as the execution of a letter of intent or agreement.[45] This franchisor registration is separate and apart from other filings historically required under the Malaysia franchise law, including an obligation on the franchisee to register the franchise agreement after it has been sold.[46] However, in September 2019, the Malaysian High Court decided that foreign franchisors relying upon the Section 54 foreign franchisor registration may not be in compliance with the law and could subject the franchisor to fines.[47] As of early 2021, Malaysia was in the process of adopting additional clarifications and requirements for foreign franchisor filings.[48]

Spain—Spain historically required a separate franchisor filing that was required to be made in order to offer and sell franchises. The filing did not include a copy of a disclosure document or agreement; instead, it provided general information on the franchisor on a form that is rarely more than a page or two. The 2010 amendments to the Spain franchise law, via Royal Decree 201/2010

44. International Franchising, *supra* note 1, at 224.

45. *Id.*

46. *Id.* at 225.

47. *See* Dr. HK Fong Brainbuilder Pte Ltd v SGMaths Sdn Bhd & Ors (2018); *see also* Zwisler, Fotsch, *supra* note 11, at 25–26.

48. Zwisler, Fotsch, *supra* note 11, at 11.

of the 26th February, later required that a U.S. franchisor that does not have a place of business in Spain or any other European Union member state file information at the Registry within three months from the date that the franchisor commences franchise activities in Spain. Most recently, the franchisor registry was abolished as of December 8, 2018, by Royal Decree 20/2018, which derogates all the articles regarding the franchisors registry—that is, articles 5 to 12 of Royal Decree 201/2010. There is anecdotal evidence that the registry was abolished because the cost to maintain the registry was outweighing its utility.

(ii) Offering Filings

In other jurisdictions, U.S. franchisors may find that if they wish to sell franchises in a particular country, they must register their entire offering with applicable government authorities before doing so, as they must do in the so-called registration states in the United States, or immediately thereafter in the case of China and Saudi Arabia. Countries with overarching franchise offering filings include the following:

China—The Administration Guidelines on Commercial Franchise Filing require that all foreign and domestic franchisors that engage in commercial franchise activities within the territorial scope of a province, autonomous region, or municipality (regional franchising) register with the local commercial administration authority directly under the central government, and that all foreign and domestic franchisors that engage in commercial franchise activities across the territorial scope of a province, autonomous region, or municipality directly under the central government ("cross-province" franchising) file with the competent administrative authority of the State Council. The registration is required within 15 days after the franchisor signs the franchise agreement to sell its first franchise, and the filing is currently just a notice filing made online and not a form of registration filing that will generate substantive government review and comment.

Indonesia—Since 2009, the Indonesian Department of Trade has required that franchisors submit a presale franchisor prospectus registration package that includes an application letter (in a specific form required by rule), a copy of the franchise prospectus, copies of documents evidencing the "legality" of the franchisor, and a power of attorney in favor of the registering attorney. While, in September 2019, Minister of Trade Regulation No. 71 of 2019 on the Implementation of Franchises was introduced with the intention of simplifying the registration process and to facilitate franchise investment, the new Trade Regulation maintains the same initial registration process and only simplifies or streamlines certain parts of the initial filing pre-conditions and certain post-filing restrictions.

Korea—Since February 2008, a Korean disclosure statement must be modeled on an official form and registered with the Korea Fair Trade Commission prior to offering and selling franchises. While a form of franchise agreement was not originally expressly required to be included with the disclosure statement by law, in practice the Korean authorities have always required submission of a translated form of franchise agreement, which is a substantial cost to U.S. franchisors, especially since the Korean authorities are closely reviewing the disclosures and agreements and requiring modifications that each time require a new updated translation. More importantly, with annual updates strictly required and scoured over for review, the initial filing stage is only the first of many filings that a franchisor will encounter in Korea to maintain its franchise offering.

Romania—Although the specific requirements and processes were still in flux as of early 2021, 2019 amendments to the Romanian franchise law provided for franchisors to submit their FDDs to the Romanian Franchise Association, which would then establish a National Franchise Register that compiles information provided by franchisors in their FDDs.[49]

Saudi Arabia—The new Saudi Arabia Franchise Law that took effect in 2020 requires that franchisors file their Arabic language franchise disclosure document with the Ministry of Commerce and Investment within 90 days of signing a franchise agreement, and then must also file the franchise agreement itself.[50]

Vietnam—The registration of foreign franchising activities is conducted by the Ministry of Industry and Trade (MOIT), and franchisors are required to register prior to signing documents or taking monies as part of a franchise transaction. The application file for the registration of a franchise must include (1) an application on a form stipulated by the MOIT, (2) a franchise description document on the form stipulated by the MOIT, (3) notarized copies of certificates of protection of intellectual property rights in Vietnam or overseas if there are any transfers of intellectual property, and (4) legalized copies of documents confirming the legal status of the franchisor. The legalization process entails (1) local U.S. notarization, (2) local U.S. certification at the pertinent Secretary of State (state level), (3) local U.S. certification at the Secretary of State (federal level), and (4) U.S. legalization at the nearest Vietnamese consulate, which can be a time-consuming process. Similar to Indonesia, there is a comprehensive annual update and annual report process in Vietnam that must be completed to maintain a franchisor's status to offer and sell franchises in Vietnam.

(iii) Intellectual Property License Filings

Intellectual property license filings are perhaps the most historically common type of foreign franchise-related filing and government approval requirement.[51] Several countries require that trademark license agreements (which, of course, include franchise agreements) be registered with and/or approved by a national trademark office.[52] Some countries require a substantive review of these documents, while others merely require a filing.[53] Complying with any trademark license filing requirements in a particular country will often be to the franchisee's

49. *Id.* at 10–11.

50. Commercial Franchise Implementing Regulations in Decision No. (00591) dated May 11, 2020.

51. International Franchising, *supra* note 1, at 223.

52. *Id.*

53. *Id.*

primary benefit but can also benefit a franchisor in certain instances. For example, registration of a franchisor's trademarks within a country serves as prima facie evidence that the franchisor owns the marks and reserves the right to use them within the country.[54]

In some countries, a failure to register the trademark license may result in the franchisor having limited ability to enforce the agreement. In others, a franchisor may be precluded from receiving payments from the franchisee if the trademark license filing has not been completed.[55] Generally, a franchisor's compliance with trademark license filing requirements increases the franchisor's ability to resist and fight infringement by third parties, but can be burdensome to cancel if the relationship terminates or expires, especially if the termination is contested.

Countries with intellectual-property-driven license filings include the following:

Mexico—Mexico's Industrial Property Law requires that franchise agreements be registered following execution to give notice to third parties of the franchisee's right to use the franchisor's registered trademarks. Many franchisors choose to utilize an abbreviated license agreement that is created solely for filing purposes. Since the filing is mainly designed to provide notice to third parties of the franchisee's right to use the marks in Mexico, one filing is made per franchisee and not per franchise agreement or unit. Importantly, the filing is based on the trademark and the corporate name of the franchisee such that changes to the franchisor's trademark ownership structure and/or transfers and other name changes to the franchisee can all technically result in necessary amendments and updates to the trademark use agreements and filings.

Philippines—Franchise agreements are considered technology transfer arrangements and are regulated by the Intellectual Property (IP) Code promulgated by Republic Act No. 8293. The IP Code provides that a franchisor does not have to file a technology transfer agreement that complies with its requirements, but if the agreement is not filed with the Documentation, Information, and Technology Transfer Bureau and is later found not compliant, it will not be enforceable. Thus, careful review of compliance with the IP Code is crucial if a franchisor elects to forgo a pre-signing filing.

Russia—Chapter 54 of Russia's Civil Code requires the registration of executed franchise agreements with the Federal Service for Intellectual Property (Rospatent). Failure to register a franchise agreement with Rospatent renders the agreement invalid in the eyes of Rospatent and Russian law. Evidence of the Rospatent filing is also generally a pre-condition to the Russian franchisee being able to pay monies abroad to a foreign franchisor. Accordingly, it is imperative to register a franchise transaction with a Russian element with Rospatent, following execution of the underlying franchise agreement.

---

54. *Id.*
55. *Id.*

(iv) Foreign Investment Filings

In addition to registration of a franchise offering or a franchise sale, as noted above, some countries require that a franchisor record the sale of a franchise by filing a copy of the applicable franchise agreement, license agreement, or other short-form evidence of the franchise agreement with the government. These filings are frequently related to approval of foreign investments within their country.[56] Foreign investment filings were historically considered to be among the most burdensome of government approval requirements.[57] In general, foreign investment laws can apply to a franchisor that grants a franchise to a citizen of the affected country, and countries requiring foreign investment filings often require that franchise agreements be approved by the government to be considered valid.[58] It is important that franchisors realize that in most instances a franchisor franchising in these countries will not receive initial fees that would ordinarily be paid at execution until the post-execution filings are made. While franchisors can and should prepare for the filings pre-execution, there can often be a substantial wait for the necessary approvals or registrations to issue allowing payment of monies abroad.

Countries with foreign-investment-driven filings include the following:

Brazil—Separate and apart from the disclosure obligations under Brazil's new 2020 franchise disclosure law, Brazilian Law No. 13,966/2019, international franchise agreements must be recorded with the Brazilian National Institute of Industrial Property (INPI) and approved by the Central Bank of Brazil pursuant to guidelines established by the INPI's Normative Acts and Resolutions. The franchise agreement needs to be recorded with INPI and the Central Bank to remit monies out of Brazil, and the filing requires a translated franchise agreement. This will cause franchisors delay in receiving monies in connection with the execution of a franchise agreement.

In 2017, INPI sought to simplify and modernize the procedure for recordal of technology transfer agreements in Brazil with Normative Act 70, reducing INPI's scope of analysis and making the entire procedure less bureaucratic. The new ruling also directly limited INPI's control over the terms and conditions of the agreements by clearly stipulating that the Certificate of Recordal should merely reflect the amounts, payment conditions, and term stated by the parties, as the filing party responsible for the validity and lawfulness of the agreement or invoice submitted to the INPI. Still, without the INPI filing in place, foreign franchisors may have difficulty getting paid any amounts under their franchise agreements.

China—Historically, after complying with the franchise-specific disclosure and registration requirements of the Chinese franchise law framework, a franchise agreement or other short form needs to be filed with the Ministry of Commerce in order to obtain the necessary authorizations for the transmission of funds outside

56. *Id.* at 221.
57. *Id.*
58. *Id.* at 222.

of China. In May 2014, however, China adopted the new Trademark Law (3rd Amendment) and its Implementing Regulations, and no longer requires an actual license agreement when recording a trademark license; instead, it simply requires an application, power of attorney, certain corporate documents, and a sublicense authorization letter executed by the trademark registrant or the sub-licensor. This has greatly simplified the process for franchisors, but technical issues such as confirming that the actual registrant of the trademark is licensing the trademark to the franchisee can still cause headaches for franchisors attempting to comply with the trademark licensing filing requirements.

India—Historically, India did not recognize franchise transactions per se, and U.S. franchisors and their franchisees were required to seek a series of authorizations involving the Reserve Bank of India (RBI) as part of the process of obtaining authorization for the franchisee to draw and send monies outside of India for the purchase of trademark or franchise rights in India. However, the Foreign Exchange Management (Current Account Transactions) (Amendment) Rules of 2006 and a Circular dated November 28, 2006, recognized franchising for the first time and authorized certain large banks to draw and send foreign exchange for the purchase of trademark or franchise rights without the approval of the RBI as long as these large banks (commonly referred to as "authorized dealers") first certified to the RBI that the transaction and payments satisfy certain foreign exchange requirements set out for franchises (i.e., they must certify that the transaction is a franchise pursuant to the guidelines set forth in the Circular). Unfortunately, the 2006 Circular has been updated numerous times, and there has continued to be considerable confusion about what payments could be made without any approval. In May 2010, the Ministry of Finance and the RBI removed the requirement to obtain consent for royalties exceeding 5 percent from the Foreign Investment Promotion Board or Project Approval Board, but given the history of near-constant change in this area, vigilance and diligence are key, and obtaining the necessary rights to remit monies abroad remains one of the key components of a franchise transaction in India.

(d) International Sales Issues

(i) Financial Performance Representations/Earnings Claims

Similar to the United States, other countries' franchise sales laws provide whether certain earnings information, specifically a financial performance representation or earnings claim, may be distributed to prospective franchisees. A franchisor should review applicable law to determine whether it is permitted to provide a financial performance representation or earnings claim. If a country permits an earnings claim, a franchisor should also carefully consider whether an earnings claim that is based on the performance of U.S. units is relevant within that country, or whether it could be misleading if operating results will vary substantially.

Countries that expressly regulate earnings claims include the following:

Canada—In Ontario and the other disclosure law provinces, the franchise law echoes U.S. franchise requirements by requiring that if earning claims information is provided, the information must be set forth in the disclosure document and contain a statement specifying the reasonable basis for the information, the assumptions underlying the information, and a location where the backup data is available for inspection. Given the reasonable basis requirement, U.S. franchisors must think long and hard about whether using and sharing a U.S. financial performance representation is prudent, even if reflecting upstate New York units that are within an hour or two of potential locations in Canada. Many Canadian practitioners have taken the position that, due to variances ranging from weather and seasonality to differences in labor costs and costs of goods sold, U.S. numbers are per se misleading and inappropriate, and therefore the franchisor has no reasonable basis to present U.S. numbers to a Canadian prospect.

Korea—Korea's franchise law has financial performance representation requirements and limitations that are roughly akin to U.S. earnings claims/financial performance requirements and limitations. Article 9(2) of the Korea Franchise Act stipulates "in [a] case where franchisor provides information regarding franchisees' past performance and future profit estimation, including sales, profit, revenue, gross profit, net profit, etc[.], the franchisor shall maintain the records prescribed by the Presidential Decree at its headquarters and allow prospective or current franchisees to review such records any time upon their request during business hours."[59] The "records prescribed by the Presidential Decree" include "the information on which the calculation and forecast of current profit or future profit are based, the number and the ratio of franchisees in the concerned territory that . . . [were] considered in estimating current or future profit, and the number and the ratio of franchisees that actually achieve the current profit or estimated profit that franchisor claims."[60] In practice, Korean officials vet and question financial information provided in the Korea disclosure statement and require specific attention to projections related to a unit to be developed in Korea.

Malaysia—Under the express requirements of the Malaysia Franchise Act, a franchisor is required to include in its disclosure document financial forecasts for the business for the next three years. In practice, U.S. franchisors who have no experience in the region face a catch-22: provide no forecasts on the basis that there is no experience in the market and any information that might be provided could be misleading, or provide forecasts based on actual U.S. or other Southeast Asia results and qualify the forecasts with multiple disclaimers, knowing that forecasts for a new region could be misleading at best and outright fraud at worst.

South Africa—South Africa's Consumer Protection Act and Regulations requires written projections regarding potential sales, income, gross or net profits, or other financial projections for the franchised business or franchises of similar nature with particulars of the assumptions upon which those representations are made. Franchisors with no operations in or near South Africa face the same quandary of complying with U.S. or other region numbers and disclaiming relevance,

59. Fair Franchise Transactions Act, [Franchise Act], Law No. 20594, January 31, 2008, art. 9(2) (S. Kor.), translated in CCH Bus. Fran. Guide ¶ 7170.

60. *Id.*

or explain why no financial projections can be reliably provided and risk being found to have failed to provide required information under the Act.

(ii) Operating Information

As with earnings claims, some countries will not regulate what, if any, operating information a franchisor provides, while others will have specific requirements. For instance, most international franchise disclosure laws require the franchisor to provide certain information about its own operations, including, in many instances, its financial statements.

The following are examples of specific country requirements:

Australia—In Australia, franchisors must comply with specific financial reporting requirements, including a statement from a director of the franchisor to the effect that the director has reasonable grounds to believe that the franchisor will be able to pay its debts as they fall due, together with financial statements either unaudited for the last two years, prepared in accordance with the Australian Corporations Act 2001 (Cth) (Corporations Act), or an "audit" for the last fiscal year to support the statement. These rules have been subject to varying interpretations, but many believe an opinion by an auditor reporting on the statement is sufficient and a full audit need not be undertaken. The statements need to conform to a format from the Australian Auditing and Assurance Standards Board. In effect, to comply with the financial statement requirements, foreign franchisors must engage Australian auditors either to audit the franchisor's financial statements under Australian generally accepted accounting principles or to restate them under Australian statutory accounting principles.

Belgium—Belgium law requires certain operating information that includes not only generally initial cost information but also continuing cost information. Under Article X.28, § 1, 2° (k) of the Belgian Economic Code, the disclosure document must provide "the expenses and investments to which the person acquiring the right commits himself at the start and during the term of the commercial cooperation agreement, stating the amounts and their purpose as well as their repayment period, the time at which they will be entered into and their fate upon termination of the agreement."

Canada—In the provinces of Ontario, Alberta, New Brunswick, Prince Edward Island, Manitoba, and British Columbia, a franchisor is required to provide audited financial statements for the franchisor itself (and not the financial statements of the parent, which is common in the United States). This can be a major problem for a U.S. franchisor that does not maintain financial statements for its franchisor entity (and instead relies on the audited financial statements of a parent as is permitted under U.S. federal and state franchise law). The provinces each also require specific information on franchisees, locations, and closures, terminations, and other events by which a franchisee leaves the system, and although similar in structure, the provincial requirements differ as to geographical scope, franchisor and affiliate scope, and brand scope, creating a hodgepodge of requirements for those that desire to maintain a single Canada disclosure document.

Spain—Spain requires that the franchisor disclose the "structure and extension of the network in Spain," information that includes the form of organization of the franchise system, the number of units operated by the franchisor in Spain, and other information similar to Item 20 in a U.S. FDD.[61]

Vietnam—As currently interpreted, the Vietnamese franchise law requires information regarding the total number of franchises sold and closed since inception, information that may not be readily available for an older franchise system.

7-4. International Relationship Laws

(a) Existence and Scope of Franchise Relationship Laws and Regulations

U.S. franchisors are normally well familiar with U.S. state franchise relationship laws that govern various aspects of a franchisor's relationship with franchisees. Such laws often regulate and restrict a franchisor's actions relating to transfer, termination, and nonrenewal of a franchise; provide for the law of the particular state to govern; establish that the covenant of good faith applies to the contract terms; and limit certain other common provisions in franchise agreements, such as restrictions on competition during and after the term of a franchise agreement.

Some countries' franchise laws contain similar requirements, and other countries' laws affect such issues indirectly. Where present, such laws may directly affect the franchisor even more than laws in the United States do; for example, a requirement that a franchisor litigate under non-U.S. law would affect not only the enforceability of its franchise agreement but also its ability to successfully litigate claims in another country.

(i) Restrictions on Termination, Transfer, and Renewal

Several countries regulate or restrict a franchisor's right to terminate or refuse to renew a franchise agreement without good cause and prior notice.[62] For example, such laws may require a franchisor to describe the conditions governing termination in the agreement, provide opportunity to cure breaches of the franchise agreement, and have good cause to terminate the franchise agreement.[63]

In addition, franchisors often place significant restrictions on transfer in their U.S. franchise agreements. When franchising in a foreign country, it is often difficult for a U.S. franchisor to enforce such restrictions and prevent an unauthorized transfer.[64] But in most jurisdictions, franchisors are free to impose reasonable conditions and restrictions upon transfer of the franchise.

61. *International Disclosure Laws*, *supra* note 22, at 143.
62. International Franchising, *supra* note 1, at 289.
63. *Id.*
64. *Id.* at 240.

Countries with significant franchise-specific controls over the termination, nonrenewal, and transfer processes include the following:

Australia—The Australian Franchising Code of Conduct expressly states that a franchisor has the right to impose reasonable transfer restrictions and provides that a franchisor may refuse to consent to a transfer if the transferee does not meet the franchisor's standards, if the existing franchisee has not paid all debts to the franchisor or has otherwise breached the franchise agreement, or if the transferee does not meet a reasonable requirement contained in a franchise agreement.[65] A franchisor must be aware of any law of the applicable country so that it can be certain its transfer restrictions will not be viewed as heavy-handed and therefore unenforceable. In addition, amendments to the Australian Franchising Code of Conduct that were announced in June 2021 provide a new right for franchisees to request early termination of a franchise agreement for various reasons and require the franchisor to promptly respond in good faith. If the franchisor refuses early termination, the franchisee has recourse through Australia's mediation process.

Korea—Under Korea's Fair Franchise Transactions Act (FFTA), the franchisor may not terminate the franchise agreement for convenience (i.e., without cause). If any terminating events prescribed under the franchise agreement occur, and the franchisor intends to terminate the agreement based thereon, then the FFTA requires the franchisor to provide written notice at least two times over a period of at least two months specifying details of breach and its intent to terminate if not cured. During such time, the franchisee should have the opportunity to remedy the circumstances that constitute the grounds for termination. Failure by the franchisor to follow such notice procedures will render the termination notice null and void. There are only nine specific exceptions to this burdensome cure and notice process. In addition, as to renewal, under the FFTA, the franchisee can request the renewal of the franchise agreement for up to a total of 10 years for the entire term (including the initial term) by giving notice at least 90 days before (but no earlier than 180 days before) the expiration of the agreement. There are only a handful of statutory conditions that a franchisee must fail to meet to "lose" the right to renew. Finally, the Korean franchise laws and regulations state that a transfer restriction that amounts to an abuse of the franchisor's bargaining power is an unfair trade practice.[66] To increase the odds of restricting unauthorized transfers in foreign countries, a franchisor may require restrictions to be placed in a franchisee's articles of incorporation or other formation document, such as bylaws, to limit transfer.[67]

---

65. *Id. See also* Lockhart v. Holden [2008] QSC 257, in which the Supreme Court of Queensland held that (1) franchisees have the burden of proving that a franchisor wrongfully withheld consent, (2) the list of circumstances in the Code for which a franchisor may withhold consent to transfer is not exclusive, and (3) where the franchisor has followed its adopted policies and selection criteria for approving transfers, even where those policies and criteria consider what is beneficial for the franchisor, as well as for the system, withholding consent will be not unreasonable. While the precedent set by this case is not binding throughout Australia, it is likely to be persuasive.

66. *Id.*

67. *Id.*

Importantly, in 2019, Korea implemented amendments to its regulations requiring that franchisors include in their franchise agreement an express statement regarding franchisor compensation to the franchisee for any harm caused by "unlawful acts by the franchisor or its executives, or acts by them that go against the rules of society and that cause damage to the reputation or credit of the franchise business."[68]

Malaysia—Under Malaysia's Franchise Act, a franchisor must provide compensation to the franchisee if the franchisor refuses to renew the franchise agreement without six months' advance notice or if the franchisee will be bound by a noncompetition covenant following the expiration of the franchise agreement.[69]

Puerto Rico—In Puerto Rico, Act No. 75 of June 24, 1964, specifically prohibits the performance of any act that is detrimental to the established relationship created under a distribution agreement without "just cause." These include the termination of the relationship and any act of impairment short of termination such as violating any exclusivity rights, failing to reasonably supply product, or unreasonably modifying the terms of payment. Act No. 75 actually creates presumptions that the franchisor has violated its provisions under certain circumstances. Agreement provisions that provide for termination, nonrenewal, or default will be scrutinized under the "just cause" standard of review. "Just cause" is defined as the "non-performance on the part of the distributor or dealer of any of the essential obligations of the dealer's contract, on the part of the dealer or any action or omission on his part that adversely and substantially affects the interest of the principal or grantor in promoting the marketing or distribution of the merchandiser's service."[70] Termination, event of default, and renewal clauses should be crafted to obtain certain acknowledgments on the part of the franchisees that certain defaults constitute "just cause" insofar as they would substantially and adversely affect development of the market, distribution of the merchandise, rendering of the services, and/or the operation of the franchise.

Saudi Arabia—The new Saudi Arabia franchise law has franchise relationship components regarding transfers, terminations, and renewals, including a requirement that transfers must not be objected to by the franchisor except in certain very limited circumstances such as bankruptcy, lack of licenses, or if the transferring franchisee is in breach.[71]

(ii) Mandatory Choice of Law and Forum

Even if a U.S. franchisor chooses to have U.S. law govern the franchise and other agreements with a foreign franchisee, the law of the jurisdiction in which the franchise will operate will necessarily affect the interpretation of the franchise agreement and the operation of the franchised unit.[72] However, not every jurisdic-

---

68. Zwisler, Fotsch, *supra* note 11, at 10.

69. *Id.*

70. 10 P.R. Laws Ann. tit. 278 *et seq.* (1964).

71. Royal Decree No. 122, dated October 8, 2019 for Law on Commercial Franchise System.

72. International Franchising, *supra* note 1, at 219.

tion will permit a franchisor to select U.S. law as the governing law or resolve disputes in U.S. courts. For such jurisdictions, it is even more important for the franchisor to consult local counsel to determine how a court within the jurisdiction that requires mandatory choice of law and forum is likely to interpret the franchise and other agreements.

Jurisdictions that mandate local governing law or forum include the following:

Brazil—The new Brazilian Franchise Law mandates Brazilian law for domestic franchise agreements, but if a franchise agreement qualifies as an "international franchise agreement" under Article 7, then Article 7(II) provides for the parties' right to select arbitration as the means to resolve disputes and for an arbitration venue outside of Brazil, but Article 7, Section 3 requires that a legal representative or attorney-in-fact with "powers to represent them in the administrative and judicial spheres" be present in the country of legal venue if a party is not domiciled in the country. This will be ripe for interpretation in the coming years, as will the need for clarifications as to whether an "international franchise agreement" may be subject to the law of a country other than Brazil.

Canada—In Ontario and the other Canadian franchise law provinces, any provision that restricts the application of provincial law or restricts venue to any forum outside of the province (or even the city in which the franchisee is located) is void as to any claim that would otherwise be enforceable.[73]

In practice, franchisors may attempt to limit the local law or forum to disputes under the specific provincial franchise law, but the franchisor may find that local courts will not enforce nuanced provisions or other non-franchise-specific provisions (e.g., transfer restrictions or noncompetition covenants) or will view the contract differently. The failure to account for local laws could have devastating consequences for the franchisor.

United Arab Emirates—Under United Arab Emirate (U.A.E.) law, franchise agreements are deemed commercial agency agreements and are therefore governed by U.A.E. Federal Law No. 18 of 1981 Regulating Commercial Agencies as amended. Among a number of franchisee-friendly provisions, the U.A.E. commercial agency law confers mandatory jurisdiction over registered commercial agencies on the U.A.E. courts.

Regardless of the specific law that might mandate governing law or forum for franchise agreements, the parties' selection of arbitration to settle disputes can affect the procedural wrangling and timing for enforcement of choice of law and forum under these mandatory application jurisdictions, and make the parties' initial decisions about where to file, and in which forum to file, all the more important. For example:

Puerto Rico—In Puerto Rico, some franchisors attempt to avoid Act No. 75 by selecting arbitration in the United States to settle disputes. Act No. 75 requires mandatory application of Puerto Rico law, and foreign choice of forum provisions are unenforceable, except those mandating arbitration. In *Outek Caribbean*

73. International Disclosure Laws, *supra* note 22, at 64.

Distributors v. Echo Inc., the U.S. District Court for the District of Puerto Rico upheld a choice of judicial forum clause under federal law governing change of venue, even in the face of Act No. 75's prohibition against such clauses.[74] The underlying basis is that the Federal Arbitration Act trumps Act No. 75.

(iii) Statutory Limitations on Contractual Terms and Conditions

In addition to providing that a franchise or related agreement may not be governed by another country's law, some countries' statutory schemes limit common terms and conditions found in franchise agreements.

Brazil—The new Brazilian Franchise Law that took effect in March 2020 specifically addresses subleases between the franchisor and franchisee, providing that both the franchisor and franchisee can file suit to renew the property lease agreement and that the franchisor can increase the sublease rent beyond what it may pay to its landlord so long as such rent increase is disclosed and not found to be excessively burdensome.

Indonesia—Indonesian Regulations traditionally required several unconventional clauses in franchise agreements, including but not limited to compensation in the event of termination, the use of domestically produced goods or materials produced and supplied by small-scale enterprises, a term of at least five years, and that the franchise agreement must be drawn up and subject to Indonesian law as well as must include provisions on change of ownership. Further, under the Regulations, a franchise agreement may be subject to counsel from the Minister of Trade or other appointed official for improvement of a franchise agreement with the purpose of protecting the interests of the parties and the participation of small- and-medium-scale enterprises as franchisees or subordinate franchisees or as suppliers of goods and services.

However, with the 2019 passage of Regulation 71, certain of these unique aspects were eliminated or tempered, such as while under prior Regulation 53 required the use of at least 80 percent domestic production for materials, business equipment, and trade goods in a franchised business, Regulation 71 now only requires franchisors to prioritize the use of domestic goods and services as long they meet (1) the standards of the franchisor and (2) the requirements under the relevant technical/sectoral regulations (if applicable).[75] In addition, Regulation 71 now requires a franchise to have proven to be a profitable business, according to the experience of the franchisor over a period of at least five years. This means that the franchisor (or master franchisee) should wait for at least five years in order to be able to offer a franchise (or subfranchise) of its business to another party. While still very new and subject to interpretation, Regulation 71 will still require franchisors entering into Indonesia to address some rather unique

74. 206 F. Supp. 2d 263 (D.C.P.R. 2002) (citing 28 U.S.C. §§ 1404, 1406).

75. Note that information about the use of local products is still required in the Annual Report, and it is unclear how the "priority" requirement will be interpreted by the authorities.

franchise relationship control and oversight concepts they are unlikely to have faced in any other jurisdiction.

Korea—The Korea Franchise Law provides for a laundry list of terms and conditions that must be included in franchise agreements. While most seem axiomatic, the list is rather comprehensive, specifying a grant of right to use the trademarks, operational aspects of the franchise, a clearly defined "business region" in which the franchisee may conduct business, and a term of the agreement. Other provisions govern transfer and assignment of the agreement; termination of the agreement, which must include a minimum of two months' notice; and nonrenewal of an agreement, which must provide that if the franchisor does not give the franchisee notice of nonrenewal at least 90 days before the expiration date, the franchise will be deemed renewed. Provisions governing the franchisee's obligations include that a franchisee must maintain uniformity of the franchise and reputation of the franchisor; maintain an inventory and product displays appropriate for the franchisor's supply schedule and consumer needs; abide by the standards of quality for goods and services specified by the franchisor; abide by appearance standards; maintain and produce accounting books and records necessary for the unified management of the franchise and the formulation of sales strategies by the franchisor; and not engage in a business similar to the franchise during the term of the franchise, regardless of requirements in the franchise agreement. There are also provisions for training and management guidance for franchisees and provisions for remedies that may include not only damages to franchisees but also civil penalties and even disgorgement of profits.

Korea's Franchise Law also contains certain requirements and limitations concerning any required remodeling of a franchised unit. Specifically, under the revised Franchise Act, a franchisor may not compel its franchisee to remodel unless there is "just cause" for doing so, which includes when the franchise unit is in the state of deterioration or when sanitary or safety hazards lead to difficulties in maintaining the uniformity of the franchised business or significantly disrupt the normal operation of the franchise unit. When a franchisor is obligated to contribute toward the remodeling costs, the franchisor's share is generally 20 percent of the remodeling. Meanwhile, the franchisor must contribute 40 percent of the remodeling costs if the cost includes expansion or relocation of the franchise unit. In either instance, the franchisor is liable only for the costs related to changing signboards and interior construction, excluding costs related to equipment and furniture. On the other hand, a franchisor is not obligated to share the remodeling costs if the franchisee voluntarily conducts such remodeling without recommendation of or request from the franchisor.

Malaysia—The Franchise Act requires that the term of a franchise agreement cannot be less than five years.[76] This is ostensibly to ensure return on investment, but for franchise systems with shorter terms that make sense for their business model, this minimum requirement may be an intrusive obstacle to the market.

---

76. *International Disclosure Laws*, *supra* note 22, at 110.

(iv) Mandatory Franchisor Experience or Franchisee Safeguard Requirements

Just as U.S. state examiners scrutinize filings from new franchisors more closely, certain jurisdictions regulate new franchisors by requiring a certain level of experience or number of open units. One jurisdiction ostensibly treats all franchisors like new franchisors by mandating an escrow requirement.

China—In 2005, Chinese regulations were issued requiring that any franchisor desiring to franchise in China must have operated two units in China for one year before being permitted to franchise in China (this became the so-called 2/1 requirement). The requirement caused much concern among U.S. franchisors who wished to pursue a more traditional franchise program. In 2007, the regulations were modified to allow cross-border franchising if the franchisor has operated at least two units for one year either in or outside of China, but the requirement has generally been strictly interpreted such that operation by a franchisor's affiliates would not count. This threshold issue continues to be a thorn in the side of more sophisticated U.S. franchisors that have separate franchisor and operating entities.

Indonesia—As noted above, under the Ministry of Trade's recently issued Regulation No. 71 of 2019 on Franchise, a company must have a minimum of five years' experience in the business to apply for the requisite franchise registration certificate.

Korea—Korea introduced a new franchisor experience requirement related to company operation or management of units in April 2021. In addition, for years Korea has had a unique escrow requirement. If the franchisor receives an initial franchise fee from the franchisee prior to the opening of franchisee's store, the initial franchise fee payable by the franchisee must be deposited with a deposit agent for the protection of the franchisee, unless the franchisor subscribes to a franchise damage compensation insurance policy or an equivalent guarantee. Once the initial franchise fee is deposited, the franchisor will be able to receive the deposited fees from the third party only after the franchisee has commenced business operations of the franchise store or two months following the execution of the franchise agreement, whichever is earlier. Deposit agents, which are designated pursuant to the franchise law, provide the escrow service regulated under the franchise law.

South Africa—Section 65 of the Consumer Protection Act and Section 2(3)(x) of the Franchise Regulations protect deposits made in the franchise context. A supplier with possession of, among other things, a deposit, or other money, or any other property belonging to a consumer, (i) must not treat that property as being the property of the supplier; (ii) in the handling, safeguarding and utilization of that property, must exercise the degree of care, diligence, and skill that can reasonably be expected of a person responsible for managing any property belonging to another person; and (iii) is liable to the owner of the property for any loss resulting from a failure to comply with the above. Section 2(3)(x) of the Franchise Regulations further state that if an application fee constitutes a deposit, the franchisor cannot treat it as its own property and franchisor must keep the deposit in a separate dedicated account. However, there is no requirement that the account would have to be kept in South Africa.

Vietnam—In Vietnam, certain preconditions must be satisfied before a franchisor can offer and sell franchises, including that (1) the business system to be franchised has been operating for at least one year (a subfranchisor must operate in Vietnam for one year before subfranchising), (2) the franchisor has registered the franchising activity, and (3) the goods or services to be franchised must be eligible in accordance with the decree for franchising activities.

(v) Good Faith Requirement

As noted above in Section 7.3(b) relating to culpa non contrahendo, many foreign jurisdictions impose a duty of good faith on franchise and other contractual relationships.

For example:

Canada—In Ontario and the other Canadian franchise law provinces, franchise agreements encompass a duty of good faith and fair dealing in performance and enforcement in accordance with reasonable commercial standards.[77] For instance, in Ontario, by law every franchise agreement imposes on each party a duty of fair dealing in its performance and enforcement. A party to a franchise agreement has a right of action for damages against another party to the franchise agreement who breaches the duty of fair dealing. The laws specifically define fair dealing as including the duty to act in good faith and in accordance with reasonable commercial standards. All discretion exercised by franchisors is subject to a requirement that they act in good faith and honor the fair dealing requirement.

Northern Ireland—Franchisees may use the Unfair Contract Terms Act, which imposes good faith and fairness standards, to avoid the application of franchise agreement terms that are one-sided in favor of the franchisor.[78]

(b) Agency Laws

In the United States, a franchise relationship is not considered an agency relationship.[79] However, so-called commercial agency laws commonly apply to franchise relationships outside of the United States, particularly if the franchisee will be located in a Middle Eastern country. If agency laws apply to a franchise relationship, the franchisee will often be granted additional rights and may be entitled to compensation upon termination of the relationship.

(i) Mandatory Filings and Coverage

If agency laws apply to a franchise agreement, a local court—and in some instances, a court devoted exclusively to agency matters—will assume jurisdiction and apply the country's local law instead of permitting the governing law and venue provisions in the franchise agreement to control. Many countries with

---

77. *Id.* at 64.
78. International Franchising, *supra* note 1, at 266.
79. *Id.* at 261.

agency laws require a copy of an agency (i.e., franchise) agreement to be filed with the government to be categorized as an agency agreement.[80]

Saudi Arabia—Historically in Saudi Arabia, until the recent passage of Royal Decree 122, dated October 8, 2019, franchise agreements were deemed commercial agency relationships and are governed by the Commercial Agencies Regulation.[81] Only Saudi nationals and entities wholly owned by Saudi nationals could be commercial agents. By its terms, the Commercial Agencies Regulation required the registration of all commercial agencies, and the underlying agency agreements, with the Saudi Arabian Ministry of Commerce & Industry, but international franchisors routinely attempted to thwart attempts by their franchisees to register. Still, with the passage of the new law, there will be franchisors whose franchisees are registered as commercial agents and not as franchisees under the new franchise law, and to date the ramifications are unclear.

United Arab Emirates—As noted in Section 7.4(a)(ii) above, under U.A.E. law, franchise agreements are deemed commercial agency agreements and are therefore governed by U.A.E. Federal Law No. 18 of 1981 Regulating Commercial Agencies as amended (the CAL). U.A.E. Federal Law No. 18 of 1993 Promulgating the Commercial Code (the Commercial Code) also contains provisions on commercial agencies; certain Commercial Code provisions appear to be inconsistent with the CAL, although the Commercial Code provisions have not been tested in a U.A.E. court.

The CAL requires that all agreements creating commercial agencies be registered with the U.A.E. Federal Ministry of Economy (the Ministry); however, a 2006 ministerial order appears to preclude registration absent evidence of the foreign party's consent. Only U.A.E. nationals, or entities wholly owned by U.A.E. nationals, are eligible to be commercial agents, although many entities that are at least partially owned by foreign nationals routinely act as distributors, franchisees, and in other capacities that fall within the statutory definition of commercial agency. However, such foreign-owned entities are not eligible for registration, which provides certain benefits to the registrant.

The CAL provides certain benefits to a registered commercial agent that may affect the parties' ability to rely on the negotiated terms of their franchise agreements. Amendments enacted in 2006 liberalized the commercial agency sector, but these amendments were never fully implemented and were repealed in 2010. Currently, the CAL provides registered commercial agents with certain statutory rights including (a) protection against termination or non-renewal of the agency, (b) exclusivity within the specified territory, (c) the right to claim compensation if termination of the agency leads to the infliction of harm, and (d) the right to apply for an order blocking imports by a third party of goods that are subject to

80. *Id.* at 262.

81. Royal Decree No. 11, 20/2/1381AH, as amended by Royal Decree No. 5, 11/6/1389AH, and Royal Decree No. 32, 10/8/1400AH, and its implementing rules issued by Ministerial Resolution No. 1897 of 24-5-1401AH, which was formally applied to franchise relationships by Ministerial Resolution No. 1012 on Applicability of Commercial Agencies Regulations to Franchising Agreements (collectively, the Commercial Agencies Regulation).

the registered agency. The CAL also confers mandatory jurisdiction over registered commercial agencies on the U.A.E. courts.

(ii) Avoiding Filings and Coverage

Most U.S. franchisors wish to avoid the application of agency laws to the franchise agreement and relationship, as various difficulties, including an inability to effectively terminate a franchise agreement, arise if agency laws apply. In many countries, there are no express penalties imposed on a foreign principal for failure to register or file an agreement, and the countries also fail to regularly impose penalties on local agents for failure to register.[82] Many U.S. franchisors include in their franchise agreements with franchisees in countries that have agency laws a requirement that the franchisee not register or file the agreement with government authorities.[83] In addition to an outright prohibition on registering the franchise agreement or refusing to cooperate with any efforts a franchisee makes to register the agreement (normally by refusing to notarize or legalize any franchisor signatures on agreements, side letters, or other correspondence reflecting the franchise relationship or grant of rights), there are other ways for a U.S. franchisor to protect itself from the application of commercial agency laws to the franchise relationship. A franchisor may use a letter of credit or bank guaranty or impose other liquidated damages in the amount the franchisor expects would be imposed if an agency law were to apply to the termination of the agreement.[84] Or, if a development agreement is in place, the franchisor may make the registration or filing of a franchise agreement as an agency agreement a default that causes termination of the development agreement and other franchise agreements.[85]

(c) Government or Trade Association Policies

Although they are not legally binding on U.S. franchisors, U.S. franchisors must evaluate the impact of and abide by government and trade association policies in foreign jurisdictions if they desire to become members and take advantage of the potential benefits of membership, which may include access to information and potential franchisees.

England—There are no franchise-specific registration or disclosure requirements under European Union law or English law. However, the European Franchise Federation's Code of Ethics and the British Franchise Association's Code of Ethics provide franchise disclosure frameworks for their members. Compliance with these codes is voluntary, and most members of these associations are domestic franchisors, but U.S. franchisors that might want to gain an edge on competitors by joining these local associations would need to take care to understand the implications of membership, including as to disclosure.

---

82. International Franchising, *supra* note 1, at 262.
83. *Id.*
84. *Id.*
85. *Id.*

New Zealand—While there is no specific law governing franchising, the Ministry of Economic Development recently confirmed that franchise agreements are subject to generic contract law, intellectual property law, consumer law, and competition law. U.S. franchisors must also note that New Zealand franchises are subject to self-regulation through the Franchise Association of New Zealand (FANZ), a nonprofit body that requires members to abide by a code of practice and a code of ethics. Half of the active franchise systems in New Zealand are FANZ members, and the policies of the group influence franchise contracts in New Zealand.

South Africa—The Franchise Association of South Africa (FASA) has long had a code of ethics and business practice guidelines. Although membership is not compulsory, code provisions are contractually binding on all its members. Among other things, the code states that the franchisor must provide the franchisee with a disclosure document at least 10 days prior to the signing of the franchise agreement and that the franchise agreement must also state that the information that has been provided to the franchisee is, to the best of the franchisor's knowledge and belief, true and accurate and that no material information has been withheld. As of early 2020, a South Africa Department of Industry task force was working on a proposal to codify the FASA's code of ethics so that it applies to all franchisors and includes addition of a regulator of franchising.[86]

7-5. Selected Continuing Legal and Operational Considerations

(a) Privacy and Data Protection Issues

American companies doing business abroad are often challenged by compliance with stringent data protection and privacy laws. In the United States, traditionally privacy and data protection are addressed piecemeal, with a patchwork of specific laws and regulations, and on an as-needed basis. For example, the Fair Credit Reporting Act, Family Educational Rights and Privacy Act, Right to Financial Privacy Act, and other laws were enacted to address specific areas where privacy protection was deemed warranted.[87] While certain U.S. states have started regulating privacy to a greater level,[88] international privacy and data protection laws are generally much more stringent. Although many countries have enacted some form of privacy and data protection law—including Australia and New Zealand, countries in South America (for example, Argentina and Brazil), and countries in Asia (such as Taiwan, Korea, and Japan), among others—the EU

86. *See* Zwisler, Fotsch, *supra* note 11, at 23.

87. Fair Credit Reporting Act, 15 U.S.C. §§ 1681 *et seq.*; Family Educational Rights and Privacy Act, 20 U.S.C. §§ 1332 *et seq.*; Right to Financial Privacy Act, 12 U.S.C. §§ 3401 *et seq.*

88. *See, e.g.*, the California Consumer Privacy Act enacted in 2018 and effective January 1, 2020.

has enacted the most stringent and influential privacy and data protection legislation. Many countries have followed the EU's lead when developing privacy and data protection laws.

European Union—The EU Data Privacy Directive[89] directs each of the member states of the EU to enact implementing legislation.[90] The directive provides a far-reaching regulatory framework that is well beyond what can be addressed within the scope of this chapter. Among other things, the directive places restrictions on the collection and use of "personal data" (as defined by the directive), provides that the "data subject" must consent to the processing of personal data (unless one of several exceptions is utilized), and provides data subjects with access and objection rights.[91] Importantly, the EU Data Privacy Directive's oft-criticized extraterritorial reach restricts member states (and companies located in such states) from transmitting personal data to a third country that has not "ensure[d] an adequate level of protection."[92]

In response to the EU Data Privacy Directive, the U.S. Department of Commerce worked with the EU and Switzerland to create a self-certification mechanism to comply with data protection requirements when transferring personal data from the European Union and Switzerland to the United States in support of transatlantic commerce.[93] In July 2020, the privacy shield program was declared invalid by the Court of Justice of the European Union.[94] As of the date of this writing, the U.S. Department of Commerce and the European Commission are in discussion on a future framework in light of that ruling.

(b) Tax and Currency Issues

Cross-border financial issues such as allocating the burden of paying withholding taxes and addressing currency risks require consideration when negotiating a franchise agreement. Foreign withholding taxes subject the franchisor's income from foreign sources to a higher cumulative tax burden than the franchisor pays on its U.S. source income. That is, the amount of tax withheld abroad from foreign source income, plus the U.S. income tax on net foreign source income (with or without the benefit of a foreign tax credit), may exceed the amount of U.S. tax the franchisor would have paid on an identical amount of U.S. source income. Further, a franchisor loses the use of funds that are withheld from its foreign

89. Directive 95/46 of the European Parliament and the Council of 24 October 1995 on the Protection of Individuals with Regard to the Processing of Personal Data and on the Free Movement of Such Data.

90. Steven R. Salbu, *The European Union Data Privacy Directive and International Relations*, William Davidson Working Paper No. 418, at 17 (Dec. 2001) (citing Jeffrey B. Ritter et al., *Emerging Trends in International Privacy Law*, 15 Emory Int'l L. Rev. 87, 94–95 (2001)).

91. *See id.* at 18–25.

92. *Id.* at 26–27 (quoting EU Data Privacy Directive).

93. *See* U.S. Dep't of Commerce, Privacy Shield Framework, https://www.privacyshield.gov/welcome.

94. https://www.privacyshield.gov/article?id=EU-U-S-Privacy-Shield-Program-Update.

source income between the time the taxes are withheld and the time its U.S. taxes are due.

Experienced franchisors often use two techniques to avoid the distortion that foreign withholding taxes can cause. The first is the so-called tax gross-up technique, which involves shifting the burden of foreign withholding taxes to foreign franchisees. Most countries impose their withholding tax on the franchisee, which must withhold and pay the tax on its royalty and other obligations before remitting payment to a foreign franchisor. Through the tax gross-up technique, franchisors pass the withholding tax's economic and cash flow burden to their franchisees by requiring that franchisees both pay the withholding tax and pay royalties at the full contract rate.

Some franchisors buffer the technique's financial impact on franchisees by providing that if and when the franchisor receives the benefit of a tax credit against its U.S. income taxes for the withholding taxes a franchisee paid, the franchisor will refund to the franchisee an amount equal to the tax credit the franchisor received. Of course, a franchisor that owes no U.S. income taxes on account of current or accumulated net losses cannot take advantage of foreign tax credits, so its foreign franchisees may ultimately receive no benefit from the tax refund provision in their franchise agreements.

It is important to remember that international franchise agreements should have payment and currency provisions addressing three principal issues: the -currency in which the franchisee must pay its royalties and other fees, the exchange rate and conversion date the franchisee must use to purchase the required currency, and the consequences of a change in local law or government policy concerning the purchase or remittance of the required currency. Sample tax and currency provisions are set forth in exhibit 7-2.

(c) Language and Translation Issues

A franchisor needs to take into consideration that language may be the greatest barrier to success in an international expansion plan, from cultural differences to logistics such as the costs incurred when agreements and manuals need to be translated. Translation is always expensive, and deciding who is responsible for the trouble, time, and cost can be a challenge. Some countries require franchise registration documents to be filed in a native language.

Brazil—Brazil requires that FDDs and franchise agreements be translated into and filed in Portuguese, and in certain cases the translations must be certified as such concept exists under Brazilian law.

China—China requires that certain registration filings be translated into and filed in Chinese.

Indonesia—Indonesia requires that certain registration filings be drawn up and filed in Indonesian.

Korea—Korea requires that registration filings be translated into and filed in Korean, including the form of franchise agreement.

Saudi Arabia—Saudi Arabia requires that FDDs and franchise agreements be presented in Arabic and later filed in Arabic after disclosure and execution of the franchise agreement.

Vietnam—Vietnam requires that franchise registration documents be prepared and submitted in Vietnamese. In addition, Vietnamese law requires that the franchise agreement be executed in Vietnamese, except where the franchise is outbound from Vietnam to offshore (not the case where a foreign franchisor sells into Vietnam). In practice, foreign franchisors generally prepare their disclosure documents and franchise agreements in English and then have a translation of the disclosure document prepared for the franchise registration and later for use in disclosing to prospective franchisees.

Even though many countries do not require a franchisor to file translated agreements and other registration documents, a franchisor may still face translation costs. Some international courts may require a translated agreement or may look to a translated agreement for interpretation. Many U.S. franchisors include in their form international agreements a provision stating that even if translated copies are created, any disputes will be resolved under interpretation of the English version of the agreement.

(d) Religious and Cultural Issues

Religious and other customary laws that affect the enforceability of franchise agreements or the operation of a franchise business are common in the Middle East and countries with strict religious laws (Malaysia, Indonesia, and other Islamic countries). Additionally, many of the laws regarding religious practices are recommendations as opposed to mandatory practices and are generally applicable to food service franchises. Franchisors need to be cognizant of the existence of religious customs and restrictions to ensure that a franchisee complies with any approvals or certifications necessary to operate the franchise. More importantly, however, franchisors need to be sensitive to religious and customary laws in order to successfully promote the franchise in such country.

Countries with laws governing restaurants and other food service businesses recommend that certain certifications or approvals be obtained once a restaurant is open to the public. Certifications generally require that a government-appointed agency or private agency approve the methods and operations of the kitchen of a restaurant to ensure that (1) the cook is apprised of any requirements for food preparation, (2) certain meat products are prepared in a manner that complies with religious custom, and (3) menu items and descriptions are specific enough to allow customers with religious requirements to understand the methods used in food preparation.

Indonesia—No specific religious or other laws restrict the operations of a franchise. However, for practical purposes, it is advised that in the case of restaurants, clear and precise information should be provided regarding the services provided (especially with respect to food menus). Although not mandatory, as a matter of course, certification of halal foods (foods that are allowed under Islamic dietary guidelines) should be sought for restaurants not serving pork products. Certification is an easy process and is granted by the Indonesian Uelema Counsel. With respect to the hours of operation of a restaurant or other business, the Directorate General of Tourism is responsible for issuing business licenses that, among other things, govern the hours of operation.

Kuwait—During the holy month of Ramadan, it is not permissible to serve food or drinks to customers for consumption on the premises between fajr (approximately one hour before sunrise) and sunset (this provision of the law is not applicable to service restaurants located in hotels). Kuwaiti law also prohibits the sale of all pork products and alcoholic beverages.

Malaysia—If halal food is being served at a restaurant, certification is required. Certification is somewhat more arduous than in Indonesia, requiring the submission of a formal application to Ilham Daya Sdn Bhd, a private company that inspects the restaurant premises to ensure that those in charge of preparing the food are aware of the halal guidelines and that the meat being served is supplied by a certified slaughterhouse (there is a list of approved U.S. slaughterhouses). The inspector's report is sent to the Islamic Development Department of Malaysia for recommendation of approval. If approved, a halal certificate is issued to the restaurant upon the payment of a certification fee. Halal certification can serve to heighten customer awareness and can make a restaurant more appealing to those potential customers who observe such religious practices.

Not all religious laws or customs pertain to the certification of food.

Israel—Religious (Jewish) customs and rabbinate institutions regulate certain industries, including the hotel industry. Hotels in Israel are operated under strict guidelines and supervision of institutions but are excepted from the requirement of being closed on the Sabbath, which is recognized in Israel from sundown on Friday to sundown on Saturday. Special restrictions relate not only to the 52 Sabbath days each year but also to approximately 20 days of religious holidays throughout the year. These rabbinate restrictions provide rules that affect the manner of providing service both to guests of the hotel and to the public (manner of operation of swimming pools, health clubs, stores, restaurants, etc.).

(e) Local Ownership and Real Estate Issues

Certain countries limit and strictly control investment by foreigners. In such countries, franchisors may be limited to granting franchises to either local individuals, locally created entities, or foreign entities that have a certain percentage of local ownership. The practical result for franchisors in these countries is that it may be more difficult to sign a multicounty development agreement with a single individual or entity, or a franchisor may find itself working with or relying on third-party investors or "agents" who serve as surrogate parties for purposes of meeting local ownership requirements. In addition, local ownership requirements limit a franchisor's ability to exercise purchase options and rights of first refusal under their franchise agreements, unless such options are specifically tailored to specific local ownership requirements.

Bahamas—Restaurant franchises owned and operated in the Bahamas are reserved to Bahamians, although specialty, gourmet, or ethnic restaurants, as well as restaurants operated in hotels and resorts, may be owned and operated by non-Bahamians. The Bahamian government will strictly scrutinize any attempt to set up a superficial nominee arrangement (for example, where the Bahamian nominee merely holds the shares of a company and does not accrue the revenue generated from the restaurant) and reject such an arrangement. Presumably, the underlying force behind such distinctions is the desire to protect and safeguard those industries fundamental to a country's economy. However, this policy also obviously prevents the benefits of foreign investment, such as the influx of new money, the creation of employment opportunities, the exchange of ideas, and most importantly the development of franchising.

Philippines—Republic Act No. 1180 (the Retail Trade Law) prohibits persons (both individuals and legal entities) who are not citizens of the Philippines from engaging in the retail business, either directly or indirectly. The retail business is defined as any act, occupation, or calling of habitually selling direct to the general public merchandise, commodities, or goods for consumption. However, with the passage of the Retail Trade Liberalization Act on March 25, 2000, foreign-owned corporations, partnerships, or associations duly organized and existing under laws of the Philippines may, upon registration with the Securities and Exchange Commission and the Department of Trade and Industry, engage in retail trade in the Philippines subject to certain capital and qualification requirements provided under the Act, which are unobtainable for most franchisors.[95]

Vietnam—In October 2006, Vietnam made certain World Trade Organization commitments[96] to open its economy. However, in doing so, Vietnam specifically reserved certain markets for Vietnamese nationals for certain time periods, including in the area of "catering services" (i.e., restaurants). This made franchising in restaurants by non-Vietnamese franchises extremely difficult until January 2015 unless "in parallel with investment in hotel construction, renovation, restoration or acquisition."[97]

Real estate laws and customs also vary widely among international jurisdictions. In some instances, lease terms may be extremely short. For instance, in Hong Kong, it is not uncommon for lease terms to be two to three years long, with fairly vague renewal terms. Franchisors need to be able to adapt accordingly.

In addition, whereas in the United States many franchisees lease real estate, in some foreign jurisdictions it is far more common for land to be owned or controlled by a wealthy family that is loath to consider any type of right of first refusal or purchase right that would encumber the real estate. Along those lines, traditional lease riders may be extremely hard to negotiate, or there may be lower

95. The requirements include, among other things, minimum paid-up capital, minimum net worth, and minimum operational history requirements.

96. Report of the Working Party, *Accession of Viet Nam*, ¶ 528, WT/ACC/VNM/48 (Oct. 13, 2006).

97. *Id.*

ownership restrictions that would make taking assignment of real estate impossible for a foreign franchisor.

(f) Competition Law Issues

Franchisors doing business in the United States are keenly aware of the potential antitrust implications of franchise relationships. Many of the questions that U.S. franchisors must ask themselves concerning the enforcement of price controls, territorial and customer restrictions, covenants restricting competition, monopolies, and fairness are also relevant to international franchise transactions.

Most franchisors agree that it is desirable to prevent franchisees from opening a competing unit in order to maintain the value, identity, integrity, and reputation of the franchise granted. The key questions for determining the viability of these restrictions internationally are similar to a U.S. state law analysis, including analysis of the scope of business covered, geographic scope, time limitations, the nature of competitive interests being protected, and whether a foreign court would reform covenants that are viewed as overly broad in one or more of these contexts.

Another important consideration for any international transaction is protecting the franchisor's confidential information, including manuals and other trade secrets, know-how, and business information. Some foreign jurisdictions are notorious for providing little or no legal protection for confidential information. Increasingly, many jurisdictions have enacted legislation protecting such intellectual property. However, these laws are generally untested, and their practical effect remains questionable.

Competition laws that affect franchising are generally designed to apply to two forms of anticompetitive activities: (1) collusion by two parties that hinders consumers' choices regarding products and services and (2) abuse of a superior bargaining power that causes harm to another contracting party. Franchise agreement provisions that may run afoul of competition laws may include exclusive supplier or purchase requirements, product tying requirements, retail price restrictions, restrictions on the right to contest the trademarks, restrictions on the geographic area in which the franchisee can conduct business, or self-help provisions that enable a franchisor to impose unilateral action upon a breach of the agreement.

EU—Like the United States, the European Union has significant competition (antitrust) law. Article 81 (restrictions on competition) and Article 82 (regarding abuse of a dominant position) of the EC Treaty set forth the general framework for European competition law. The European Commission has recognized that if the parties to a vertical agreement face competition in the marketplace, the enhanced efficiency created by the vertical agreement can outweigh potential anticompetitive effects. In July 2009, the European Commission proposed a revised Block Exemption Regulation and Guidelines on vertical agreements (that is, supply and distribution agreements). In April 2010, the European Commission adopted the new Vertical Restraints Block Exemption Regulation (VBER) and accompanying guidelines. The new VBER and guidelines were effective as of May 2010.

The VBER creates a safe harbor (i.e., exemption) from competition law rules prohibiting restrictive agreements for distribution agreements that are below the stated market share threshold and that do not contain prohibited restrictions. The VBER market share test provides for a safe harbor if a supplier or buyer has less than 30 percent market share. The Commission revised the VBER in 2010 to account for major recent market developments, including (1) an increase in large distributors' market power and large retailers and (2) the evolution of Internet sales since the time that the regulation was adopted in December 1999. The current VBER requires that for a vertical agreement to benefit from the block exemption, both the supplier's and the buyer's market share would not exceed 30 percent. As to Internet sales, the current VBER refines the distinction between active and passive sales and explains how conditions imposed on such sales, such as territorial restrictions, are to be addressed. As of late 2020, the EU is assessing the impact and utility of the VBER and its continuation.[98]

Turkey—Turkey also has an extensive competition law. Franchise agreements are subject to the general provisions of Communiqué No. 2002/2 on Block Exemption Concerning Vertical Agreements, as amended by Communiqués No. 2003/3 and 2007/2. The exemption provided via the communiqué is applicable if the provider's market share does not exceed 40 percent within the relevant market providing goods or services subject to the vertical agreement. Certain agreements are outside the scope of the exemption provided in the communiqué, such as agreements that purport to prevent the purchaser from determining its own selling price (although setting a maximum selling price may be permitted, provided that it does not transform into a fixed or minimum selling price as a result of duress or incentive by another party) and certain agreements that introduce restrictions regarding regions or customers where or to whom the goods or services that are subject of the contract may be sold. Vertical agreements concerning the transfer of use of intellectual property rights are also within the scope of the amended communiqué but generally benefit from the exemption provisions of the communiqué. Draft franchise agreements should be reviewed by local counsel to confirm they comply with the communiqué or to determine if amendments are necessary to comply.

7-6. International Dispute Resolution

(a) Governing Law

A failure to include a choice of law provision in a U.S. franchise agreement leads to uncertainty; even when a choice of law provision is present, the franchisor may find that another state's law governs some or all of the interpretation of the franchise agreement due to overriding law or policy of another state. The failure to address choice of law at the outset of a franchise relationship with a foreign

98. *See* Zwisler, Fotsch, *supra* note 11, at 2.

franchisee can produce uncertainty tenfold that of having to address choice of law as to a domestic franchise agreement.[99] Therefore, U.S. franchisors should be certain to specify what law will govern disputes and then should engage local counsel to investigate the application of the chosen law versus local law in the foreign country to ensure that local law will not override the chosen law.[100]

(b) Forum and Enforcement of Court Judgments

Many U.S. franchisors are ill-equipped to litigate a dispute in a foreign jurisdiction. Moreover, U.S. franchisors cannot, without some predicted success, litigate a dispute in either a U.S. or a foreign jurisdiction if the franchisor cannot foresee being able to enforce the court's judgment following litigation. The franchise agreement with a foreign franchisee should specify the courts or alternative venues in which the franchisor or franchisee may pursue a legal remedy, unless review of applicable law reveals that such a provision would not be enforceable (e.g., under Ontario's franchise law as addressed in Section 7.4(a)(ii) above).[101] If such a clause would not be enforceable, a franchisor may wish to consider alternatives, including the consequences or potential benefits of having the agreement be enforceable in accordance with the laws of the foreign country.[102] For example, a U.S. judgment may not be enforceable while the foreign court's judgment would be enforceable.[103]

(c) Arbitration and Enforcement of Awards

For many years, arbitration has reigned as most U.S. franchisors' preferred method for resolving disputes with international franchisees.[104] The United States and virtually all developed nations are signatories to the New York Convention on Enforcement of Arbitral Awards. As a result, arbitration has become a common method for resolving cross-border disputes, whether franchise or not.[105] The New York Convention provides that if a franchise agreement specifies that arbitration will be the means of dispute resolution, an award granted to the franchisor through arbitration will be recognized by foreign jurisdictions as enforceable in the foreign jurisdiction.[106] Arbitration provides a clear dispute resolution process with which U.S. franchisors are familiar. In addition, arbitration before a neutral third-party arbitrator can decrease the risk—for both the franchisor and the

99. International Franchising, *supra* note 1, at 307.
100. Dolman, Lauer & Weinberg, *supra* note 2, at 43.
101. *Id.*
102. *Id.*
103. International Franchising, *supra* note 1, at 311.
104. *Id.*
105. *Id.* at 312.
106. *Id.*

franchisee—that local preferences and customs will sway the decision in favor of one party or the other.[107]

(d) Enforcement Tools and Practices

Due to the uncertainties that are present when resolving disputes with a foreign franchisee, whether due to questions about the franchisor's ability to collect on or enforce any judgment in its favor or to questions about the law that will be applied, franchisors frequently choose to impose contractual remedies that will permit the franchisor the ability to self-regulate the franchise relationship if needed.

(i) Letter of Credit and Bank Guaranties

One of the most common ways that U.S. franchisors can guarantee payment and other contractual obligations (e.g., a requirement that the franchisee not register the agreement as an agency agreement, as discussed above) is to require a letter of credit or bank guaranty throughout the term of the agreement. A letter of credit or bank guaranty can also be used in lieu of a personal guaranty where the franchisor's ability to enforce the guaranty is dubious.[108] A letter of credit or bank guaranty permits a franchisor to take specific action—that is, draw down on the letter of credit—without having to pursue formal litigation or other dispute resolution activities.[109] In some instances, a letter of credit is tied to liquidated damages amounts for specific breaches that might not otherwise lend themselves to quantifiable damages, including breaches of confidentiality, noncompetition, transfer, and non-solicitation provisions as well as premature termination/lost profit damages or improper post-termination operations. A sample letter of credit requirement is attached in the sample international letter of intent in exhibit 7-6. A sample irrevocable letter of credit is set forth in exhibit 7-7.

(ii) Non-exclusivity or Territorial Alteration Rights

International development is frequently accomplished through development agreements that permit a franchisee to act as the developer or master franchisee for an entire country or region. As a means of regulating the franchisee's activities and deterring defaults, a franchisor may choose to revoke a grant or exclusivity or reduce a franchisee's territory for noncompliance. The agreement itself should provide that the franchisor may reduce the territory or exclusivity upon default.

Alternatively, a franchisor can elect to start slow, with perhaps a single unit franchise deal and, if successful, move forward on a larger deal. This approach requires a lot of trust, but mistrust can be mitigated to some degree through the use of some form of agreed standstill period during which the franchisor will not seek to enter the market themselves or through a third party. The period could be

107. *Id.*
108. *Id.* at 271.
109. *Id.*

anywhere from six months after the unit opening to upward of two years after opening, and the agreed standstill can be coupled with a right of first refusal that could commence immediately after the agreed standstill period ends.

(iii) Auditing

To ensure continued compliance with the franchise agreement, a U.S. franchisor may schedule regular audits or inspections of a foreign franchisee's business and records. This may entail added cost whether records are maintained in another language or in another accounting framework.

(iv) Workouts

Rather than pursue more formal means of dispute resolution and face attendant issues with enforcing a foreign court's judgment, it is often useful for a franchisor to attempt to work out problems with a franchisee before terminating the agreement or taking other action. For instance, if a franchisee's failure to pay royalties and other fees pursuant to a franchise agreement is due to economic circumstance rather than a refusal to pay, a franchisor may wish to propose a plan by which the franchisee pays reduced royalties for a set period of time and pays overdue royalties back to the franchisor at a later date. Or, if a franchisee fails to meet its development schedule, the franchisor may propose extensions or a reduced development obligation (in exchange for reduced territory) rather than pursue formal legal remedies.

7-7. Conclusion

Preparation is key to a successful international franchise program, and generally it is the role of the legal advisors to temper excitement with the reality that developing and successfully implementing a successful international franchise program can be exponentially more difficult than implementing and managing a U.S. franchise program. Obstacles range from the obvious (distance, language, time zones) to the more opaque (cultural differences, consumer preferences, religious requirements, anti-U.S. sentiment), and to be successful a U.S. franchisor must overcome all such obstacles or face likely failure.

Exhibit 7-1
Sample Project Plans for Evaluating and Launching an International Franchising Effort

(Below are two different forms the authors have used with clients)

Sample 1: International Work Plan

Steps	**Items**	**Description**	**Completed**
Step 1:			
Initial Review and Approval	Initial Communications	1. [Franchisor] tracks contacts with [Franchisee] 2. [Franchisor] selects management lead and legal lead	

	Development of Business Deal	1. [Franchisor] receives and reviews development and royalty fee comparisons (if applicable)
		2. [Franchisor] prepares proposed terms of business deal
		• Proposed terms reviewed by Counsel
		• Proposed terms reviewed by Finance and Tax Departments
		  • Determine whether new entity is needed or existing entity will be used
		  • Determine potential tax consequences—application and effect on transaction and documentation
		  • Accounting considerations—application and effect on transaction and documentation
		  • Address repatriation of royalties
		  • Securitization issues—application and effect on transaction and documentation
		• Proposed terms reviewed and approved by President
		• Facilitate any additional internal review and approval of proposed terms
		• Proposed terms conveyed to Counsel to be incorporated into Letter of Intent	

	Application Stage	1. [Franchisor] receives and reviews Initial Questionnaire from [Franchisee] • [Franchisor] determine what information will be initially provided • [Franchisor] begins to gather information	

Steps	Items	Description	Completed
		2. Counsel reviews and approves form of Franchise Application 3. Counsel reviews and approves form of Nondisclosure Agreement 4. Counsel prepares Letter of Intent 5. [Franchisor] sends to [Franchisee] • Franchise Application • Nondisclosure Agreement • Letter of Intent • Initial Information 6. [Franchisee] completes and submits Franchise Application 7. [Franchisee] submits requested background information: • Business Plan • Development Plan • Infrastructure Plan 8. [Franchisor] reviews application and background information to determine the extent of additional background investigations/due diligence	
	Initial Due Diligence	1. Review and evaluate information and materials supplied by [Franchisee] in the Franchise Application 2. Review information about [Franchisee] received from local counsel and/or investigators 3. Determine extent of any additional background checks that may be required 4. OFAC check 5. [Franchisor] gives initial approval for [Franchisee] as potential franchisee	
	Additional Due Diligence	1. Schedule territory visit • Timing—Week of ______ • Length of visit • Participants • Itinerary 2. Identify and retain country-specific investigator or investigative resource 3. Review and validation of ownership and management of [Franchisee] 4. Civil/criminal background checks 5. Financial due diligence 6. Results of due diligence appended to application	

Steps	Items	Description	Completed
	[Franchisor] Infrastructure—Initial	1. Operations Support—policies and procedures developed 2. Restaurant Development—prototype plans developed 3. Consider additional international operations headcount • Timing • Qualifications • Use of current operations personnel 4. Consider additional international marketing headcount • Timing • Qualifications • Use of current international marketing personnel 5. Consider additional international development headcount • Timing • Qualifications • Use of current international development personnel	
Step 2:			
Initial Negotiations and Final Approval	Letter of Intent; Deposit	1. Counsel confirms the status of [Franchisor]'s trademarks in applicable country(ies) 2. Letter of Intent negotiated and executed by all parties 3. [Franchisee] submits deposit with signed Letter of Intent	
	Disclosure	If required, Counsel prepares disclosure for proposed country(ies) and sends to [Franchisor] for delivery to [Franchisee] at an agreed time	
Step 3:			
Prepare Documents	Agreement Preparation; Trademarks	1. [Franchisee] submits any remaining information/background items 2. Counsel prepares an issues checklist for each country and determines, in conjunction with local counsel, whether an update is required 3. Counsel addresses potential enforceability issues in conjunction with local counsel (e.g., impact of agency laws; terms of letter of credit; cross-defaults; translation instructions)	

Steps	Items	Description	Completed
		4. Counsel prepares forms: • Development agreement • Franchise agreement • Letter of credit • Country-specific pre- and postclosing and organizational checklists • Trademark license agreement(s) as needed • Exchange rates considerations—application and effect on transaction and documentation (note: Counsel to include provisions related to exchange rates in draft agreements) 5. Counsel to seek registration and/or prepares for other governmental approval process	
Step 4:			
Negotiations; Prepare Initial Plans	Negotiations	1. Counsel sends: • Draft agreements to [Franchisor] • Updated pre- and postclosing checklists to [Franchisor] • Draft agreements to [Franchisee] 2. [Franchisor] sends to [Franchisee] any additional information requested by [Franchisee] 3. [Franchisor], working with Counsel, [Franchisee] and counsel for [Franchisee], sets a schedule for the exchange of comments 4. Comments and responses exchanged; open points resolved 5. Counsel to conduct periodic meetings to determine and refine status of transaction and strategy towards closing in line with • Time schedule acceptable to [Franchisor] • The monetary investment in the transaction including legal fees and costs • Primary purpose is to permit [Franchisor] to evaluate the value of the transaction versus the tenor of the negotiations	
Step 5:			
Closing	Agreements/ Documents Finalized	1. Counsel revises draft agreements and distributes for final comments in accordance with schedule for comments	

Steps	Items	Description	Completed
		2. Counsel confirms closing schedule 3. Counsel to advise of legal formalities for execution of agreements and related documents	
	Closing	[Franchisor], with assistance from Counsel, coordinates execution, payment of fees, delivery of letter(s) of credit, and exchange of fully executed documents	
Step 6:			
Postclosing; Prepare Final Plans	Legal Postclosing	1. Counsel prepares closing binders 2. Postclosing activities noted on postclosing checklist	
	[Franchisor] Infrastructure—Ongoing	1. Site Approval Process • Develop appropriate new restaurant site approval process • Review and approve/disapprove individual restaurant plans 2. Final Plan Review and Approval • Consider and approve/disapprove proposed [Franchisee] plan modifications 3. Menu/Product/QA • Review and approve/disapprove proposed menu adjustments • Substitute product review/testing—approve/disapprove • Conduct on-site inspections of food processors 4. Distribution/Supply Chain • Review and approve distribution/supply chain plan • Conduct on-site inspections of distribution centers 5. IT Support—preopening, postopening, POS systems 6. Ops Support—preopening, postopening 7. Training Support—preopening, opening, postopening 8. [Franchisor] approves restaurant(s) locations	

Sample 2: Sales "Steps" Procedures

Step 1: Initial Review and Approval

1. **Initial Communications**—Franchisor's personnel will initiate communications with the prospect through various means including Internet, telephone, and facsimile. Contacts with prospects are tracked internally through Franchisor's database.
2. **Application Stage**—Each prospective franchisee ("Prospect") completes an international application that memorializes the Prospect's official request to Franchisor for authorization to enter into a development or franchise relationship in a specific territory ("Application"). By this time the Prospect may have already received a brochure and other promotional materials, which normally accompanies the Application.
3. **Initial Due Diligence**—The information supplied in the Application (e.g., financial statements, bank and business references) will be reviewed and evaluated to determine the extent of additional background future investigations required or desirable.
4. **Franchisor's Key Franchise Sales and Development Team**—Unless otherwise agreed, Franchisor's ________________ ("Salesperson") will be responsible for ensuring that additional background and due diligence investigations are conducted on the Prospect and its principals and for evaluating and updating the information prior to closing. Salesperson is also responsible for explaining the franchise program and negotiation process to the Prospect. Additionally, Salesperson will obtain the names and contact information for the persons who will be part of the negotiations and with whom Franchisor, the Prospect, and the respective legal counsel will communicate. This information will be distributed to all parties, including Franchisor's ________________ ("Franchise Executive"). This information will be recorded in a contact sheet uniformly used by Franchisor ("Contact Sheet"). The Contact Sheet will be periodically updated by Franchisor. No franchise or other agreements should be sent to the Prospect unless the Prospect has identified its legal counsel and provided the requested contact information. At this time, the need for translations of the letter of intent and agreements for negotiation purposes should be ascertained. Outside counsel can obtain the translations and provide an estimate. This amount should be included in the deposit taken under the Letter of Intent.
5. **OFAC Check**—At this time the Prospect will also be checked against the OFAC list. This foregoing activity may be handled by Salesperson.
6. **Discovery Day**—Discovery Day ("D-Day") is held after Franchisor receives and preliminarily approves the international franchise application from the Prospect. D-Day is typically held in Franchisor's corporate offices, but also occasionally takes place at tradeshows or "in-country" (at the Prospect's location). D-Day is set up to provide both Franchisor and the Prospect with additional information on each other.

Step 2: Initial Negotiations and Final Approval

1. **Letter of Intent**—Assuming the information resulting from the Application and D-Day are acceptable, the Prospect will be reviewed for final approval by the franchise approval committee. If approved, instructions will be given to Outside counsel for preparation of the Letter of Intent ("LOI") based on Franchisor's then-current form (including a country-specific organizational checklist), as negotiated. Outside counsel will also confirm the status of Franchisor trademarks in the applicable country and

prepare a draft of the LOI. The LOI will be reviewed and signed off by Franchise Executive and Salesperson before it is delivered to the Prospect. Once it is executed, Franchise Executive or Salesperson will provide the Application, Contact Sheet, and LOI to Outside counsel with instructions to prepare a country checklist on the pertinent laws applicable to the transaction and a draft of the initial development agreement and form of franchise, as applicable ("Agreements").

2. **Additional Due Diligence**—Additional background and due diligence investigations will be conducted on all Prospects who apply for a franchise and are preliminarily approved, subject to the results of the investigations. At a minimum, the investigations should include the review and validation of the ownership and management of the Prospect. Civil and criminal background investigations should also be conducted. Due to monetary considerations, these investigations will not be conducted until after the Prospect passes the D-Day stage and a LOI has been sent. These investigations will be initiated when International Development makes a request to Franchise Executive to retain a country-specific investigator or investigative resource. All information obtained from the initial background investigation described in Step 1, paragraph 3 (above) and as described in this paragraph will be reported in a supplement to the Application ("Background Report").
3. **Disclosure**—If a country's law requires disclosure, Outside counsel ("Outside counsel") prepares the appropriate stand-alone disclosure document and sends it to the Franchise Executive and Salesperson for delivery to the Prospect at an agreed time.

   The time required to complete the foregoing ranges from a few days to a week depending upon the country selected.

Step 3: Prepare Documents

Outside counsel's work will then include the following:

1. Outside counsel prepares an issues checklist for the country and/or determines whether an update is required based on prior transactions. A copy of this issues checklist will be provided to Franchise Executive and to Salesperson.
2. Foreign legal counsel is selected from Outside counsel's network. A foreign counsel conflicts letter with instructions related to the checklist issues and the Agreements is sent, along with an initial budget, time schedule, and billing instructions.
3. Outside counsel prepares country-specific and deal-specific forms of development agreement and franchise agreement, with all country-specific agreement changes.
4. Outside counsel prepares/updates a country-specific closing and organizational checklist.
5. Outside counsel also prepares any country-specific disclosure document and/or seeks registration and/or prepares for any other applicable governmental approval process. This includes any separate trademark license agreement that is required.
6. Redlines (drafts) to Franchisor's current forms will be provided to Salesperson and Franchise Executive for review and upon approval sent by Outside counsel, Salesperson, or Franchise Executive to the Prospect (and its legal counsel, if applicable). The updated closing and organizational checklist will also be sent at that time.
7. Outside counsel will update preclosing and postclosing checklists so all outstanding points are monitored. These will be provided to Salesperson and Franchise Executive.

8. Salesperson sets a schedule for receipt of initial comments with the Prospect. Once comments to the draft Agreements are received, Salesperson will review the comments and brief Franchise Executive and Outside counsel. This process will continue if no face-to-face negotiating session is conducted as noted below.

Step 4: Negotiations; Prepare Initial Plans

1. In response to the comments received from the Prospect, a determination will be made whether additional telephone or electronic communications should be initiated to resolve open points.
2. Following such negotiations, Outside counsel will redraft the Agreements during and after the negotiation sessions and distribute for final comments. A "comment" schedule will be determined by the Salesperson and the Prospect. Outside counsel will confirm a closing schedule and advise of legal formalities for execution of the Agreements and related documents.
3. Throughout the time that negotiations are proceeding Salesperson and/or Franchise Executive and Outside counsel will conduct periodic meetings (usually bimonthly or quarterly) to determine and continually refine the status of the transaction, the strategy toward closing that should be implemented, the time schedule acceptable to Franchisor, and the monetary investment in the transaction, including legal fees and costs. The primary purpose of this meeting is to permit Franchisor to continually evaluate the value of the transaction versus the tenor of the negotiations.

Step 5: Closing

Franchise Executive or Salesperson will determine whether the closing will occur in person or by paper exchange. In either case, Outside counsel will provide an instruction letter outlining the process for execution and redelivery of the documents.

Step 6: Postclosing; Prepare Final Plans

Outside counsel will prepare hardcopy and electronic closing binders with all appropriate materials, including, as applicable, the Agreements and any letter of credit. Outside counsel will work with Franchise Executive and Salesperson regarding the postclosing activities noted on the postclosing checklist.

Exhibit 7-2
Sample International Franchise Agreement Provisions

Sample Adverse Change of Law Definition and Provision

Adverse Change of Law means the adoption, promulgation, modification, or reinterpretation after the Effective Date, by any governmental or judicial authority in the Country, of any law, regulation, policy, order, circular, or similar directive which action materially and adversely affects Franchisor's ability to enjoy the economic benefits of this Agreement or to enforce its rights hereunder. An Adverse Change of Law does not constitute an event of Force Majeure.

***

Franchisee and the Principals acknowledge that the rights contemplated under this Agreement are granted on the assumption that there will be no Adverse Change of Law during the Term. If, at any time during the Term, there occurs an Adverse Change of Law, the parties agree to use their best efforts and to cooperate with each other to amend this Agreement either to bring it into conformity with the requirements of the Adverse Change of Law or to seek an alternative way to comply with the Adverse Change of Law. If, in Franchisor's judgment, this Agreement cannot be modified to comply with the Adverse Change of Law without undermining material elements of the relationship, Franchisor may, at its option, without liability for such action or any further obligation to Franchisee, terminate this Agreement and the rights granted hereby upon thirty (30) days' written notice to Franchisee.

Sample Withholding Tax Provision

"<u>Tax</u>" means all taxes, charges, fees, levies, or other assessments, including without limitation all net income, gross income, gross receipts, sales, use, ad valorem, value added, turnover, transfer, franchise, profits, license, withholding, payroll, employment, excise, estimated, severance, stamp, occupation, property, or other taxes, customs duties, fees, assessments, or charges of any kind whatsoever, together with any interest and any penalties, additions to tax or additional amounts imposed by any taxing authority and any political subdivision, instrumentality, agency, or similar body of any taxing authority.

"<u>Taxable Payment</u>" means any deduction or withholding from any sum paid or payable to Franchisor as a result of a Tax.

If Franchisee or any other Person associated with Franchisee is required by law to make a Taxable Payment, (1) Franchisee shall notify Franchisor of any such requirement or any change in any such requirement as soon as Franchisee becomes aware of it; (2) Franchisee shall pay such Tax before the date on which penalties attach thereto; such payment is to be made if the liability to pay is imposed on Franchisee for its own account, or if that liability is imposed on Franchisor, on behalf of and in the name of Franchisor; (3) the Taxable Payment will be increased to the extent necessary to ensure that, after the making of that deduction, withholding, or payment, Franchisor receives on the due date a net sum equal to what it would have received if no such deduction, withholding, or payment was required or made; (4) within 30 days after the earlier of (i) the date of Taxable Payment; or (ii) the due date for payment of any Tax which it is required to pay as a result of the Taxable

Payment, Franchisee shall deliver to Franchisor evidence satisfactory to Franchisor of such deduction or withholding and of the remittance of such deduction or withholding to the relevant taxing or other authority; and (5) Franchisee shall set forth in the regular monthly remittance report required by Franchisor pursuant to Section __, the amount of such Tax and the payments to which they relate. [Notwithstanding, if Franchisor or its Affiliates are able to utilize a foreign tax credit (regardless of the terminology used to refer to such credit) to reduce Franchisor's or its Affiliates' U.S. federal income tax liability based on the increase of payments described herein, Franchisor will refund to Franchisee an amount representing the amount of the foreign tax credit so utilized solely as a result thereof within a reasonable period of time following the application of the credit.]

Sample Currency and Currency Legal Restrictions Provision

All amounts payable to Franchisor under this Agreement will be payable in Dollars, and calculated according to the exchange rate on the appropriate date set forth below (as reported by an authorized foreign exchange bank in the Country acceptable to Franchisor). If Dollars are not available in the Country's currency market, payment to Franchisor will be made in another currency to be designated by Franchisor and calculated according to the exchange rate on the appropriate date set forth below, as reported by an authorized foreign exchange bank in the Country designated by Franchisor. The conversion of amounts due under this Agreement will be conducted as follows:

1. When calculating the Monthly Royalty Fee and any other monthly fee due hereunder, this amount will be converted using the exchange rate on the day of the month on which payment is required to be made under Section __ (unless this date is not a Business Day in the Country, in which case the applicable date will be the next Business Day).
2. When calculating the amount due in connection with the reimbursement of expenses paid in a currency other than Dollars, the amount will be converted using the exchange rate in effect either (i) on the date the expenses were originally incurred or (ii) the date of demand or billing by Franchisor, as designated by Franchisor in its discretion.
3. When calculating any other payments due under this Agreement, these payments will, to the extent necessary, be converted using the exchange rate in effect on the date of Franchisor's invoice or such other date as Franchisor reasonably designates.
4. When calculating overdue payments and related interest payable under this Agreement, these amounts will be converted using the exchange rate in effect either (i) in accordance with the calculation time(s) specified for such amounts in Sections __, __, and ___, or (ii) at the time of payment, at Franchisor's direction.

All costs of currency exchange and electronic transfers of funds will be borne by Franchisee.

If any legal restrictions are imposed on the purchase of Dollars, the removal of Dollars from the Country, or the transfer or credit of Dollars by Franchisee to Franchisor, such restrictions shall constitute an Adverse Change of Law and Franchisee shall notify Franchisor immediately. In such a case, Franchisor may direct Franchisee to make payment to Franchisor in such other currency and in such other country or jurisdiction as Franchisor may select. The acceptance by Franchisor of payment in a currency other than Dollars shall not release Franchisee from its obligations to make future payments in Dollars, to the extent permitted by applicable law and if, for any reason, an amount is received in a currency other than Dollars, Franchisee's obligations under this Agreement shall be discharged only if Franchisor may purchase Dollars with such other currency in accordance with normal banking procedures and this Section. If the amount in Dollars which may be so purchased, after deducting any costs of exchange and any other related costs, is less than the relevant sum payable under this Agreement, Franchisee shall immediately pay Franchisor the shortfall. If Franchisee fails to make payments to Franchisor under this Agreement for 60 days or more in a currency acceptable to Franchisor, then Franchisor shall have the right to terminate this Agreement immediately upon written notice to Franchisee.

Sample Commercial Agency Law Definition and Provision

Agency Laws means the agency law(s) set forth in the Summary Pages and any regulations promulgated under such law(s), and any other similar laws, rules, or regulations governing commercial agency relationships in the Country that may exist from time to time.

***

Franchisee and the Principals acknowledge and agree that the Agency Laws shall not at any time during or subsequent to the Term apply to this Agreement or to the relationship established herein and that Franchisor would not have entered into this Agreement if the Agency Laws were applicable to this relationship. Without limiting the foregoing, in consideration of the rights granted herein: (i) Franchisee and the Principals hereby agree to release and waive any rights of Franchisee and the Principals and any obligations of Franchisor, if any, under the Agency Laws, including the payment of any compensation to Franchisee and the Principals upon the expiration or earlier termination of this Agreement and shall defend and indemnify the Indemnified Parties with respect thereto; (ii) Franchisee represents, warrants, and covenants that neither it, any Principal, nor any Affiliate or any principals thereof shall bring or attempt to bring an action under the Agency Laws in any court, arbitration proceeding, or before any other tribunal; and (iii) Franchisee and the Principals acknowledge and agree that any attempt to bring an action under the Agency Laws shall be an event of default under this Agreement, any development agreement, any other franchise agreement, or any other agreement between Franchisor and Franchisee. Franchisee and the Principals agree to take any actions required by Franchisor to give effect to this Section __.

Sample Governmental Approval Provision

Franchisee's right to develop and operate the Unit shall be subject to any required governmental approval, registration, or recordation of this Agreement; provided that Franchisee shall make no attempt to obtain any approval, registration, or recordation of this Agreement without Franchisor's prior written consent. Franchisor and Franchisee agree to cooperate with each other in connection with any dealings with governmental authorities relating to this Agreement. Franchisee will not submit any information to governmental authorities with respect to this Agreement without Franchisor's prior written approval; provided that the foregoing restriction will not apply if formal or informal proceedings are instituted against a party or if a dispute between the parties is submitted to any court or tribunal having jurisdiction over such matters. Franchisee shall bear the expense, either directly or through reimbursement to Franchisor, of obtaining approval of, and/or registering or recording this

Agreement and any amendment with the appropriate governmental authorities (including all legal and other professional expenses) that are consented to by Franchisor.

Sample Language Provision

This Agreement and its exhibits shall be executed in English only. Franchisee shall not translate or allow any translation, in whole or in part, of this Agreement, including any attachments or documents related to the agreements, or the Manuals, without Franchisor's prior written consent, and Franchisee shall not attempt to have this Agreement or any related documents notarized or otherwise authenticated, without Franchisor's prior written consent. Franchisee shall pay for any approved translation of this Agreement, the Manuals, or any other written procedures, policies, manuals, and all costs that may be incurred by Franchisor to review translated material. Notwithstanding, if any translation of this Agreement is required by any court, arbitration panel, or other tribunal, Franchisor will appoint a translator to make the translation, and Franchisor and Franchisee shall share equally the costs and expenses associated with the translation. Franchisee acknowledges that any translation of this Agreement and any documents or other materials related to this Agreement, whether commissioned or paid for by Franchisee or Franchisor, shall be the property of Franchisor and constitute a part of the Confidential Information. Upon Franchisor's request, Franchisee shall execute any assignments or other documents necessary to effect Franchisor's ownership of such translations. If this Agreement or the Manual is translated into any language other than English, and any dispute or question of interpretation arises concerning this Agreement or the Manual, the provisions of the English version(s) shall control.

Sample Data Protection Provision

"Data Protection Laws" means all applicable data protection and privacy laws and regulations in any relevant jurisdiction.

During the Term, Franchisee and Franchisee's Principals shall (i) comply with the Data Protection Laws; (ii) comply with all of Franchisor's requirements regarding the Data Protection Laws if and as set forth in the Standards; (iii) refrain from putting Franchisor or its Affiliates in breach of any of the Data Protection Laws; (iv) do and execute, or arrange to be done and executed, each act, document, and thing necessary or desirable to keep Franchisor and its Affiliates in compliance with any of the Data Protection Laws; and (v) permit Franchisor and its Affiliates to use, in compliance with the Data Protection Laws, any data or other information they gather concerning Franchisee, its Affiliates, and the Franchisee's Principals in connection with the establishment, operation, and franchising of Units under the System by Franchisor and its Affiliates.

Exhibit 7-3
Sample Development Schedule

The parties have tentatively agreed on the following Development Schedule for the development of [Units] in the Development Territory:

Development Period Number/ (Duration)	**Date of Execution of Franchise Agreements**	**Date of Commence-ment of Construction**	**Date of Opening**	**Total Number of [Units] That Must Be Open and in Operation at the End of the Development Period**
1 (__ months)	______, 20__	______, 20__	______, 20__	1
2 (__ months)	______,______ ______,______	______,______ ______,______	______,___ ______,___	2
3 (__ months)	______,______ ______,______	______,______ ______,______	______,___ ______,___	3
4 (__ months)	______,______ ______,______	______,______ ______,______	______,___ ______,___	4

Checklist 7-1
Checklist of Terms for Master Franchise Agreement

The Master Franchise Agreement

1. The Grant
   a. Limiting the Geographic Scope of the Territory
   b. Permitting Offer of Development Agreements to Unit Franchisees
   c. Providing for Specific Reserved Rights in the Territory
2. The Term
3. The Fees
   a. Providing for a Reasonable Initial and Continuing Fees
   b. Reaching Understanding/Agreement on Withholding Tax/Currency Risk Allocation
4. The Manner and Timing for Exercising Development Rights
   a. Requiring One or More Units to be Operated by the Master Franchisee Before Granting/Earning the Right to Offer and Sell to Third Parties
   b. Providing for Consequences for Failure to Timely Develop
   c. Providing for Form Changes Due to Different Countries or Jurisdictions in the Master Franchisee's Territory
5. Franchisor's Contractual Obligations
6. Master Franchisee's Resources/Best Efforts
7. Master Franchisees' Obligations
8. Transfers/Default and Termination

Exhibit 7-4
Resources for U.S. Companies Expanding Abroad (Including Key Government Websites)

World Bank Doing Business Project
http://www.doingbusiness.org

Offers economic and other information on 190 economies.

U.S. Department of Commerce, International Trade Administration
https://www.trade.gov/

Provides resources for companies expanding internationally, including market research, partner due diligence, and matchmaking.

U.S. Department of State, Office of Commercial and Business Affairs
https://www.state.gov/bureaus-offices/under-secretary-for-economic-growth-energy-and-the-environment/bureau-of-economic-and-business-affairs/office-of-commercial-and-business-affairs/

Plays a major role in coordinating trade and investment matters in support of U.S. firms doing business overseas.

Library of Congress Resources, Doing Business Overseas
http://www.loc.gov/rr/business/guide/guide1/sharp9.html

Provides a list of resources for finding business information and for researchers interested in the topic of doing business overseas.

Transparency International, Corruption Perceptions Index
http://www.transparency.org

Transparency International publishes an annual Corruption Perceptions Index that orders the countries of the world according to the degree to which corruption is perceived to exist.

U.S. Small Business Administration, Basic Information on Exporting
https://www.sba.gov/business-guide/grow-your-business/export-products

Provides information on exporting, shipping products overseas, and protecting intellectual property overseas, among other things.

U.S. Department of the Treasury, Office of Foreign Assets Control
http://www.treasury.gov/about/organizational-structure/offices/Pages/Office-of-Foreign-Assets-Control.aspx

Provides list of Specially Designated Nationals, recent OFAC actions, sanctions, and other information.

Exhibit 7-5
Sample International Franchise Application and Compliance Provisions

International Franchise Application

INSTRUCTIONS: Thank you for expressing an interest in obtaining rights from [Franchisor Name] ("we" or "[Franchisor Brand]") to develop and operate franchised [Franchisor Brand] Units ("Units") outside of the United States. This International Franchise Application ("Application") should be completed by each business entity or individual that will hold an interest in the franchise and development rights and/or the Units (referred to as "You" and "Your" in this Application). Please print your responses clearly in the English language, attach all required documents, and then execute this Application in the signature page at the end of the Application.

When completed and signed, please send your Application to [Franchisor Brand] at the following address:

[Franchisor Name]

____

____

Attention: ______________________

Your General Information

*Business Entity applicants must complete and submit the Organizational Information Checklist attached at the end of this Application and may skip questions that are only applicable to individual applicants

Full Name: ______________________________

National Identification Number: ______________________________

Date of Birth: ______________________________

Current Home Address: ______________________________

Telephone Numbers: Home: __________ Business: __________ Mobile: __________

E-Mail Address:______________________________

Mailing Address:______________________________

Your Citizenship and Residency

You are:

☐ A citizen of __________ (Country).

☐ A national of __________ (Country).

☐ A citizen of the United States.

☐ An alien lawfully admitted for permanent residence in the United States (Alien Number A __________).

☐ An alien authorized by the U.S. Citizen and Immigration Service to work in the United States (Alien Number A __________ or Admission Number __________, expiration of employment authorization, if any __________).

Your answers to the above questions will not affect our decision on the merits of your Application.

Please attach to this Application a copy of at least one of the following documents:

☐ Unexpired foreign passport from your country of origin

☐ National Identification Card from your country of origin

☐ Other government-issued identification from your country of origin (describe) ____________________

☐ U.S. Passport or Certificate of U.S. Citizenship

☐ Certificate of Unites States Naturalization or Alien Registration Card with photograph

[Franchisor Brand] reserves the right to ask that you produce original and/or additional documentation verifying your identity.

Your Residency History

How long have you lived at your current residence? __________

If you have lived at your current residence for less than five years, please provide the following information concerning each place where you have lived during the last five years.

Date From	**Date To**	**Number and Street**	**City**	**Country**	**Postal Code**

Your Educational Background

High School: ☐ Diploma
☐ Highest Grade Completed: __________

College: ☐ Degree in __________, __________ (Year)
☐ No. of Years __________

Name and address of College or University: ____________________

Postgraduate: ☐ Degree in __________, __________ (Year)
☐ No. of Years __________

Name and address of College or University: ____________________

Your Recent Employment History

Occupation:

Current Employer:

Employer	Location	Tel. No.

Previous Employer(s) (if not with current employer for past five years)

From	To	Employer	Location	Tel. No.

Your Family

Marital Status: ______________________ Spouse's Name: ______________________

Spouse's Citizenship: ______________________ Spouse's Nationality: ______________________

Spouse's Occupation: ____

Spouse's Employer: ____

Employer	Location	Tel. No.

Number of Children ______________________ Children's Ages ______________________

Children's Citizenship ______________________ Children's Nationality ______________________

Name of Other Dependents ____________ Relation ______________________

Other Background Information

Have you ever been convicted of a felony or other crime involving moral turpitude?
☐ Yes ☐ No

If you answered "yes," please state the name and address of the court, the case number, and the date of conviction, and provide a brief description of the charges for which you were convicted: ____

_____

Are there any civil judgments pending against you that have not been satisfied?
☐ Yes ☐ No

If you answered "yes," please state the name and address of the court, the case number, and the date and amount of the judgment:

Are you currently involved as a defendant in any litigation or arbitration proceeding?
☐ Yes ☐ No

If you answered "yes," please state the name and address of the court and the case number, and provide a brief description of the allegations against you and the amount of the claim:

Have you or any business entity to which you have held a majority ownership interest or exercised control over management ever filed for bankruptcy or sought other similar debt relief?
☐ Yes ☐ No

If you answered "yes," please provide a brief description of the proceedings:

Your Interest in [Franchisor Brand] and Your Food Service Experience

Have you visited an existing [Franchisor Brand] Unit?

☐ Yes ☐ No

If you answered "yes," please identify the location of the unit(s) you have visited:

____

When can you visit _________ to discuss your interest in acquiring a franchise? __________

*You are solely responsible for obtaining visas for you and your employees to travel to the United States for an initial visit and for training. You must provide us a copy of each visa prior to any visit to the United States.

Outline, briefly, the experience(s) that would qualify you to develop and operate a __________operation such as [Franchisor Brand] Units. What specific role would you play in developing the territory?

Describe briefly the experience and qualifications for your organization; including corporate officers, partners, and management who would be responsible for Operations, Human Resources/Recruiting, Real Estate, Construction, Marketing, and Finance. (Please attach additional information.)

Please describe the geographic area (the "territory") in which you are interested in developing and operating Units. __________

How many Units are you interested in developing in the territory?__________

Briefly describe the market for Units in the territory, including existing or known competitors (including, if available, number of units, total sales, and average unit sales): __________

Describe why you believe Units operated in the territory will be successful (include your definition of "success"): __________

Your Anticipated Investment

Please describe range of investment you are interested in making in connection with the development and operation of Units: __________

Please detail the source of funds you plan on investing (including name of financial institution, if applicable, and contact person):__________

Name of Financial Institution:______________________________

Address: ______________________________

DESCRIPTION OF ACCOUNT

City, Country, Zip Code: ______________________________

Phone No.: ______________________________

Account No.: ______________________________

Contact Person: ______________________________

What percentage of the funds will be borrowed? __________

On what terms would you borrow the funds? ___________

Have you ever applied for or obtained credit under another name in the past ten years?

☐ Yes What name(s)? ___________________________

☐ No

Your Partners and Co-Applicants

Please indicate the names of all the business entities and/or individuals (in addition to yourself) who will have a direct, indirect, or beneficial ownership in the franchise or the entity that will own the franchise. All entities or individuals identified below must also complete an Application.

Please describe any additional information you would like [Franchisor Brand] to consider in connection with your Application:

Your Business References

Please provide the requested information concerning five individuals whom you have known for more than three years.

References Brief Description of Affiliation

Name:____

Address: ____

City, Country, Zip Code: __________________________

Phone: ____

Name:____

Address: ____

City, Country, Zip Code: __________________________

Phone: ____

Name:____

Address: ____

City, Country, Zip Code: __________________________

Phone: ____

Name:____

Address: ____

City, Country, Zip Code: __________________________

Phone: ____

Your Financial Information

Current Salary: ___________

Spouse's Income: __________

Bonus and Commission: __________

Dividends and Interest: __________

Total Household Income: __________

Please identify each financial institution (both in your country of origin and within the United States) holding funds or property on your behalf or on behalf of a business entity in which you hold a beneficial ownership interest. Please add additional pages, as necessary.

Name of Financial Institution: ____________________

Address: ____________________

DESCRIPTION OF ACCOUNT

City, Country, Zip Code: ____________________

Phone No.: ____________________

Account No.: ____________________

Name of Financial Institution: ____________________

Address: ____________________

DESCRIPTION OF ACCOUNT

City, Country, Zip Code: ____________________

Phone No.: ____________________

Account No.: ____________________

Name of Financial Institution: ____________________

Address: ____________________

DESCRIPTION OF ACCOUNT

City, Country, Zip Code: ____________________

Phone No.: ____________________

Account No.: ____________________

Name of Financial Institution: ____________________

Address: ____________________

DESCRIPTION OF ACCOUNT

City, Country, Zip Code: ____________________

Phone No.: ____________________

Account No.: ____________________

Name of Financial Institution: ____________________

Address: ____________________

Your Business Interests

Please identify all business enterprises in which you hold a beneficial ownership interest. The term "business enterprise" includes a corporation, association, partnership, business trust, sole proprietorship, or other business, the shares of which are not listed on a securities exchange or otherwise regularly traded.

Under "legal form of business," please describe the type of business entity in which you hold an interest (e.g., corporation, partnership).

Name and Address of Business	Legal Form of Business	Nature of Business	% Ownership	Current Value

Your Financial Statement

Personal and Financial Statement Documentation will be required to support these statements.

Name____________________________________Tax ID/VAT/Passport number #__________

Address ____

Financial Condition as of ______________, 20____

Assets	Dollars	Cents	Liabilities	Dollars	Cents
Cash on Hand			Note Payable to Banks—Unsecured		
Cash in Bank					
Notes Receivable—Secured by Mortgage					
Notes Receivable—Otherwise Secured			Notes Payable—Other than to Banks—Unsecured		
Accounts Receivable—Current			Accounts Payable		
Accounts Receivable—Past Due			Loans on Life Insurance		
U.S. Govt. Obligations			Taxes		
Stocks, Bonds, and other Investments			Mortgages or Liens on Real Estate (Itemize Below)		
Include Funds in Savings & Loan Companies			Any Other Indebtedness—Due within One Year		
(Itemize Page 2)					

Cash value–Life Insurance					
Real Estate (Itemize Below)			Any Other Indebtedness—Due Beyond One Year		
Total Assets			Total Liabilities		
			Net Worth (Total Assets – Total Liabilities = Net Worth)		

Schedule of Real Estate Owned

Legal Description & Location	**Title in Whose Name**	**Improved or Unimproved**	**Appraised Value**	**Mortgage**	**Tax Value**	**Insurance**

Contingent Liability of any Kind (If None, Indicate So)	**Dollars**	**Cents**
Upon Notes or Accounts Receivable Discounted, Sold, or Assigned		
As Guarantor for Other on Notes, Bonds, Contacts, Etc.		
Any Other Contingent Liability—Itemized		
Total Contingent Liabilities		

Your Acknowledgments and Representations Regarding this Application

By completing and submitting this Application to [Franchisor Brand], you acknowledge and/or represent to [Franchisor Brand] that:

- [Franchisor Brand] is relying upon the information provided in this Application and upon the documents you submit in connection with, or in support of, this Application (including all business information, business plans, and/or financial statements you provide).
- All information contained in, and documents submitted in connection with, this Application is true, correct, and complete as of the date submitted and you understand that any misrepresentation or inaccuracy in the information provided by you will be grounds for termination of any franchise or development rights that [Franchisor Brand] may grant to you based on the information in this Application. You will promptly inform [Franchisor Brand] of any material change in any of the information or documents submitted.
- Neither the submission of this Application nor the execution of any definite agreements will violate or conflict with the terms of any other agreement to which you are a party or by which you are bound. You have not been induced by [Franchisor Brand] to terminate or breach any agreement with respect to any opportunity to develop or operate Units.

- [Franchisor Brand] does not enter into, and has not entered into, oral agreements or understandings with respect to (i) the development and operation of Units, or (ii) matters pertaining to the granting of development and franchise rights for Units.
- [Franchisor Brand] has no obligation to grant to you development or franchise rights for Units and no such rights to develop or operate Units shall be granted or obtained unless and until definitive Development and/or Franchise Agreements are signed.
- [Franchisor Brand] reserves the right to approve or reject this Application in its sole discretion, and if [Franchisor Brand] rejects this Application, [Franchisor Brand] shall have no liability to you or any other person or entity.
- Any projections and other financial information you provide [Franchisor Brand] in connection with this Application is voluntarily provided or made by you and has or will have been prepared by you and/or your advisors. [Franchisor Brand] has not, and will not, participate or provide any assistance to you in connection with the preparation of such projections or other financial information prepared by you. You further acknowledge that [Franchisor Brand] has not, and will not, ratify, confirm, approve, or make any other representations concerning the accuracy of such projections and/or information supplied by you, or that you will attain any particular level of financial performance indicated by such projections or other information. You hereby release and forever discharge [Franchisor Brand] and its affiliates from any claims or liability arising from or related to the financial information and/or projections that you provide to [Franchisor Brand].
- You will indemnify [Franchisor Brand] and its affiliates and the directors, employees, agents, representatives, and assignees thereof and will hold them harmless from all liability, costs, damages, and expenses (including legal and accounting fees and expenses) in connection with the breach of any contract or any representation, warranty, or information contained in this Application or in connection with [Franchisor Brand]' reliance on such representations, warranties, and information. [Franchisor Brand] <u>shall have the right independently</u> to take any action it may deem necessary in its sole discretion to protect and defend itself against any threatened action without regard to the expense, forum, or other parties involved. [Franchisor Brand] shall have sole and exclusive control over the defense of any such action (including the right to be represented by counsel of its choosing) and over the settlement, compromise, or other disposition thereof.
- You will keep all oral and written information regarding the [Franchisor Brand] franchise program that you may receive or have access to in strict confidence for an indefinite time period, and will neither use for your own benefit nor disclose or divulge to any other person any part of such information.
- The terms of this Application will survive any approval or rejection of this Application by [Franchisor Brand].

Applicant's Initials ___________

Your Authorizations, Consents, and Releases regarding This Application and Your Personal Information

- You understand that [Franchisor Brand] will be requesting information from various companies, financial and other institutions, universities, credit reporting agencies, professional and academic certification law enforcement agencies, former employers, and/or the military, and you hereby authorize such entities to release any information that they may have about you to [Franchisor Brand] and its agents and designees, and release them from any liability arising out of or related to their release of such information.
- You authorize all financial institutions holding funds or other property on your behalf or on behalf of any business entity in which you hold a beneficial interest, whether or not identified in this Application, to release all records including signature cards, statements, and all documentation reflecting the source of deposited funds, whether the funds were received in the form of cash, credit, electronic fund transfer, or wire transfer.
- You also authorize [Franchisor Brand] and its agents and designees to obtain such credit and other civil and criminal investigative reports as they consider necessary to evaluate this Application, and understand that these reports may contain information about your background, mode of living, character, and personal reputation. This authorization is valid for any current and future reports and updates that may be requested and you agree to execute all additional documents, waivers, or releases that might be necessary for [Franchisor Brand] or its agents and designees to obtain such information or reports.

  ☐ You request a copy of your credit report

  ☐ You do not request a copy of your credit report
- You further authorize [Franchisor Brand] and its agents and designees to contact individuals or entities identified in this Application, or whose names arise in connection with the civil and criminal investigative reports described above for purposes of obtaining character references and verifying the information contained in this Application. You hereby authorize any individual or entity contacted by [Franchisor Brand] or its agent or designee to provide all requested information, and release them from any liability arising out of or related to their release of such information.

APPLICANT:

Sign here if Applicant is an individual:	Sign here if Applicant is a business entity:
Entity Name: ____________________	
Name: ____________________________	By: ____________________________
Date: ____________________________	Name: __________________________
Title: ____________________________	
Date: ____________________________	

Sample Antiterrorism and Anticorruption Provisions

Compliance with Anticorruption and Antiboycott Laws

1. On a joint and several basis, Franchisee and each of its Franchisee's Principals represents and warrants that, as of the date of this Agreement, Franchisee and each Franchisee's Principal is and, during the Term will remain, in full compliance with all applicable U.S. laws and regulations and those of the Country that prohibit unfair, fraudulent, or corrupt business practices in the performance of its obligations under this Agreement and related activities, including the making of any expenditures other than for lawful purposes or directly or indirectly offering, giving, promising to give, or authorizing the payment or the gift of any money, or anything of value, to any Person, while knowing or having reason to know that all or a portion of such money or thing of value will be given or promised, directly or indirectly, to any government official, official of an international organization, officer or employee of any government, or anyone acting in an official capacity for any government, for the purpose of (i) influencing any action, inaction, or decision of such official in a manner contrary to his or her position or creating an improper advantage; or (ii) inducing such official to influence any government or instrumentality thereof to effect or influence any act or decision of such government or instrumentality. FURTHER, FRANCHISEE AND EACH OF ITS FRANCHISEE'S PRINCIPALS REPRESENTS AND WARRANTS THAT: (1) IT/HE IS NOT A "FOREIGN OFFICIAL" UNDER THE UNITED STATES FOREIGN CORRUPT PRACTICES ACT (CURRENTLY LOCATED AT HTTP://WWW.JUSTICE.GOV/CRIMINAL/FRAUD/FCPA), WHICH DEFINES "FOREIGN OFFICIAL" AS ANY OFFICER OR EMPLOYEE OF A FOREIGN GOVERNMENT OR ANY DEPARTMENT, AGENCY, OR INSTRUMENTALITY THEREOF, OR OF A PUBLIC INTERNATIONAL ORGANIZATION, OR ANY PERSON ACTING IN AN OFFICIAL CAPACITY FOR OR ON BEHALF OF ANY SUCH GOVERNMENT OR DEPARTMENT, AGENCY, OR INSTRUMENTALITY, OR FOR OR ON BEHALF OF ANY SUCH PUBLIC INTERNATIONAL ORGANIZATION, (2) NO GOVERNMENT OFFICIAL, OFFICIAL OF AN INTERNATIONAL ORGANIZATION, POLITICAL PARTY OR OFFICIAL THEREOF, OR CANDIDATE HAS ANY DIRECT OR INDIRECT OWNERSHIP OR INVESTMENT INTEREST IN THE REVENUES OR PROFIT OF FRANCHISEE, (3) NEITHER FRANCHISEE NOR ANY OF ITS FRANCHISEE'S PRINCIPALS, AGENTS OR REPRESENTATIVES WILL AT ANY TIME TAKE ANY ACTION IN VIOLATION OF THE U.S. FOREIGN CORRUPT PRACTICES ACT OR SIMILAR LAWS OR MAKE ANY PAYMENT TO, OR EMPLOY, ANY PERSON THEY KNOW, OR HAVE REASON TO BELIEVE, MAY TAKE ANY ACTION IN VIOLATION OF THE U.S. FOREIGN CORRUPT PRACTICES ACT OR SIMILAR LAWS, AND (4) FRANCHISEE WILL CAUSE EACH OF ITS PRINCIPALS AND EMPLOYEES TO SIGN A COPY OF THE STATEMENT ATTACHED HERETO.
2. Franchisee and its Franchisee's Principals represent, covenant, and warrant that they understand and have been advised by legal counsel on the requirements of the applicable laws referred to above, including the U.S. Foreign Corrupt Practices Act, any local foreign corrupt practices laws, and the USA Patriot Act (currently located at http://www.epic.org/privacy/terrorism/hr3162.html), and hereby acknowledge the importance to the System and the parties' relationship of their

respective compliance with the requirements of this section, including any applicable auditing requirements and any requirement to report or provide access to information to Franchisor or any government, that is made part of any applicable law. Franchisee shall take all reasonable steps to require its consultants, agents, and employees to comply with such laws prior to engaging or employing any such persons. Franchisee and each Franchisee's Principal represents, covenants, and warrants that he is not employed by or acting in an official capacity for any government or government agency of any country. Franchisee agrees that it will notify Franchisor in writing immediately of the occurrence of any event that renders the foregoing representations and warranties of this paragraph incorrect.

3. Franchisee and its Franchisee's Principals represent, covenant, and warrant to Franchisor that they shall, and shall cause their employees to, refrain from engaging in any action that may cause Franchisor or its Affiliates to be in violation of any U.S. law or regulation governing or applicable to unsanctioned international boycotts and shall not make or permit the making of any representations to any third party, including any government official in the Country concerning the ownership of Franchisor or its business activities and relationships in any country in the world outside of the Country, without the prior written consent of Franchisor. If Franchisee or any Franchisee's Principal is presented with a request for information about the ownership of Franchisor or its business activities or relationships or receives any other documents or inquiries that would constitute a boycott request under U.S. antiboycott regulations (including, but not limited to, 15 C.F.R. part 760), Franchisee shall promptly notify Franchisor in writing, providing reasonable details related to such request, and shall refrain from responding to such boycott requests or other requests for information unless Franchisor, in writing, directs Franchisee to respond and in such event, Franchisee shall take such steps as Franchisor may require in responding to such requests.
4. Franchisee and its Franchisee's Principals represent, covenant, and warrant to Franchisor that they will not knowingly engage in or facilitate the reexport of any products to Iran, or otherwise take any action that may cause Franchisor or any of its Affiliates to be in violation of any law or regulation applicable to trade involving the United States and Iran. Franchisee shall take all reasonable steps necessary to require its consultants, agents, and employees to comply with such laws. Franchisee agrees that it will notify Franchisor in writing immediately of the occurrence of any event that renders the foregoing representations and warranties of this paragraph incorrect.

Antiterrorism Laws. On a joint and several basis, Franchisee and each Franchisee's Principal represent and warrant to Franchisor that neither Franchisee nor any Franchisee's Principals, nor any executive officer of Franchisee is identified, either by name or an alias, pseudonym, or nickname, on the lists of "Specially Designated Nationals" or "Blocked Persons" maintained by the U.S. Treasury Department's Office of Foreign Assets Control (texts available at http://www.treasury.gov/about/organizational-structure/offices/Pages/Office-of-Foreign-Assets-Control.aspx). Further, Franchisee and each Franchisee's Principal represent and warrant that neither it nor any of Franchisee's Principals or executive officers mentioned above has violated and agrees not to violate any law prohibiting money laundering or the aid or support of Persons who conspire to commit acts of terror against any Person or government, including acts prohibited by the U.S. Patriot Act (text available at http://www.epic.org/privacy/terrorism/hr3162.html), U.S. Executive Order 13,224 (text available at http://www.treasury.gov/resource-center/sanctions/Programs/Documents/terror.pdf), or any similar law. The foregoing constitute continuing representations and warranties, and Franchisee shall immediately notify Franchisor in writing of the occurrence of any event or the development of any circumstance that might render any of the foregoing representations and warranties false, inaccurate, or misleading.

Exhibit 7-6
Sample International Letter of Intent

DRAFT MASTER FORM

FOR REVIEW PURPOSES ONLY

_______, 20__

[INSERT NAME AND ADDRESS]

Re: Letter of Intent—[INSERT COUNTRY]

Dear ____________:

1. Introduction. This Letter of Intent evidences the mutual intention of [INSERT NAME OF FRANCHISOR] ("Franchisor") and ______________ or an entity to be created by ________________ (collectively, "Prospective Developer") to initiate negotiations regarding the development and operation of _______ (__) [Concept X]® [Units] (each individually a "Unit" and collectively, the "[Units]") in ___________ (the "Development Territory"). For the purposes of this Letter of Intent, a Unit is a ____________________ Unit operating under the "[CONCEPT X]®" mark and system. This Letter of Intent outlines certain preliminary terms and conditions, but not all of the essential terms and conditions, of a possible agreement between Franchisor and Prospective Developer (a "Development Agreement"). This Letter of Intent is intended to serve as a guide in the negotiation of a definitive agreement.

2. Development Schedule and Letter of Credit.

   a. Pursuant to a Development Agreement, Prospective Developer will be required to develop and continue to operate no less than _______ (__) [Units] in the Development Territory in accordance with the Development Schedule attached as **Exhibit A** (the "Development Schedule"). Prospective Developer will not be permitted to open [Units] in excess of the number of [Units] set forth in the Development Schedule.

   b. *[In connection with the execution of the Development Agreement, Prospective Developer must obtain (and thereafter must maintain during the term of the Development Agreement and during the term of any then-effective Franchise Agreement executed pursuant to the Development Agreement) a sight draft letter of credit ("Letter of Credit") (including replacements of any expiring Letter of Credit and replenishment of the Letter of Credit to its face amount if any amounts are drawn on the Letter of Credit) in the amounts and upon such terms and conditions as stated in **Exhibit B** and as set forth in the Development Agreement. The Letter of Credit must be maintained for at least one year after the expiration of the last Franchise Agreement executed pursuant to the Development Agreement.]*

3. Grant of Franchise Rights.

   a. In order to exercise its right to operate a Unit in the Development Territory under the Development Agreement, Franchisor and Prospective Developer or an approved affiliated entity controlled by Prospective Developer ("Affiliated Franchisee") will enter into separate [Concept X] franchise agreements (each a "Franchise Agreement" and collectively, the "Franchise Agreements") pursuant to which Prospective Developer or the Affiliated Franchisee will be given the right to operate a Unit. Any right of Prospective Developer or an Affiliated Franchisee to enter into a Franchise Agreement for the operation of a Unit will be subject to, among other things, Franchisor's confirmation that Prospective Developer exercises such degree of control over the Affiliated Franchisee that Franchisor deems necessary, that such Affiliated Franchisee satisfies Franchisor's business, financial, and other standards for [Concept X] franchises, and that Prospective Developer and any Affiliated Franchisees are in full compliance with the development and operating standards of the [Concept X] system. Neither Prospective Developer nor any Affiliated Franchisee shall have any right to license or subfranchise their respective rights to any third party.

b. Prospective Developer acknowledges that the forms of Franchise Agreements will be substantially similar but nevertheless may require certain changes and modifications in order to comply with the business practices, laws, regulations, and customs of a particular region within the Development Territory. Accordingly, Franchisor will have the right, in its sole discretion, to make and require any such changes or modifications as it deems necessary to comply with any laws of any region in which all or a portion of the Development Territory is located.

4. Term/Exclusivity.

a. The term of the Development Agreement will begin on the date Franchisor executes the Development Agreement and will continue until the earlier of the original scheduled opening date of the final Unit to be developed pursuant to the Development Schedule or the actual opening date of such final Unit, unless earlier terminated for cause. The Franchise Agreements will each have a term of 10 years, and will provide for one additional 10-year renewal term.

b. During the term of the Development Agreement, Franchisor will not operate or grant others the right to commence operation of [Units] in the Development Territory, so long as Developer develops and operates [Units] in the Development Territory fully in accordance with the Development Schedule. However, Franchisor or its affiliates may promote and advertise [Units] at any location or in any territory (including the Development Territory), and will retain the exclusive right to establish, alone or in conjunction with others, or license others to establish, [Units] or other food service facilities under other marks at any location other than the approved locations under the respective Franchise Agreements, and to offer collateral products under Franchisor's trademarks, such as clothing, prepackaged food items, and other [CONCEPT X]® memorabilia, at any location other than the approved locations under the respective Franchise Agreements, including, without limitation, at retail, through catalogs, and on the Internet.

c. *[Subject to Prospective Developer's full completion of the Development Schedule, Franchisor will determine if market demand will support additional [Units] in the Development Territory. Franchisor shall have the right in its sole discretion to propose to Prospective Developer an additional Development Schedule and such other conditions precedent to obtaining the additional Development Schedule, which may include, among other things, payment of a new Development Territory Fee, execution of Franchisor's then current form of Development Agreement, execution of a general release to the extent permitted by applicable law, and/or, subject to applicable local ownership requirements, an agreement by which Franchisor and Prospective Developer would jointly develop one or more [Units] to be developed under the additional Development Agreement.]*

5. Services. Under the Franchise Agreement, Franchisor will provide Prospective Developer or Affiliated Franchisee with certain services and assistance as follows: guidelines and specifications for construction; manuals; initial training, field visits, marketing assistance, and ongoing assistance; specifications for uniforms, signs, and related materials; accounting and inventory control methods; approved supplier lists; and access to certain other [Concept X] products and services, if available.

6. Fees. The following fees will be payable to Franchisor:

   a. Holding Fee. Upon the execution of this Letter of Intent, Prospective Developer will pay to Franchisor a nonrefundable holding fee in the amount of ______________ (U.S. __________) (the "Holding Fee").

   b. Development Fee. Upon execution of the Development Agreement, Prospective Developer will pay to Franchisor a nonrefundable Development Fee of ______________ U.S. Dollars (U.S. $_________) (the "Development Fee"); provided that the Holding Fee will be credited in full towards the Development Fee that is payable upon execution of the Development Agreement.

   c. Initial Franchise Fees. Upon execution of each Franchise Agreement, Prospective Developer or its Affiliated Franchisee will pay to Franchisor a nonrefundable initial franchise fee of ______________ U.S. Dollars (U.S. $_______) (the "Initial Franchise Fee").

   d. Royalty Fees. Prospective Developer or Affiliated Franchisee, as applicable, will pay Franchisor each month a royalty fee of ____ percent (__%) of the gross revenues of each Unit in operation, for the preceding calendar month. Gross revenues will include all revenue from the sale of all services and products and other income of every kind related to the Unit, whether for cash or credit and regardless of collection in the case of credit.

   e. Monthly Marketing Expenditure. Prospective Developer or Affiliated Franchisee will be required to spend up to __________percent (___%) of gross revenues per month for marketing purposes for each Unit in operation. Such marketing expenses will be directly expended by Prospective Developer or an Affiliated Franchisee for local marketing. In addition, as requested by Franchisor, Prospective Developer or Affiliated Franchisee must contribute to an international marketing fund to meet the costs of an international marketing campaign that Franchisor will conduct to collectively or regionally promote the [Units] operating under the "[CONCEPT X]®" mark and system. Franchisor may from time to time review and increase the amount of required advertising and promotion expenses.

   The fees in paragraphs (a) to (e) may be recharacterized for tax purposes under applicable law.

7. Payments. The Holding Fee, Development Fee, and Initial Franchise Fee amounts due to Franchisor will be paid in U.S. Dollars. All other fees referenced in paragraph 6 above will be paid and settled in U.S. Dollars at the exchange rate reported by an authorized foreign exchange bank selected by Franchisor on the applicable payment date, and in accordance with any applicable laws in the Development Territory regulating the remittance of U.S. Dollars abroad. All currency exchange costs, withholding taxes, value-added taxes, duties, and other taxes associated with each of the foregoing payments will be paid by, and be for the account of, Prospective Developer or Affiliated Franchisee, as applicable. If Prospective Developer or Affiliated Franchisee is

required to pay or withhold any taxes or duties in connection with a payment to Franchisor under the Development Agreement or any Franchise Agreement, then the payment to Franchisor will be increased to the extent necessary to provide for Franchisor's receipt of a net amount equal to the full amount expressed in such agreement to be payable to Franchisor.

8. Reports. Prospective Developer or Affiliated Franchisee will submit to Franchisor such monthly, quarterly, and annual financial and other information as Franchisor shall require.
9. Individual Obligations. Each officer, director, and key manager of Prospective Developer and Affiliated Franchisee, and certain investors of Prospective Developer and Affiliated Franchisee designated by Franchisor, will be "Franchisee's Principals" for purposes of the Development Agreement and Franchise Agreements and, as such, will be individually bound by certain covenants, including the confidentiality and noncompetition provisions set forth in such Development Agreement and Franchise Agreements. In addition, Prospective Developer and Affiliated Franchisee will designate a "Controlling Principal," "Managing Partner," and "Operating Partner" that will be generally responsible for the supervision of the development and daily operation of each Unit. Each Controlling Principal, Managing Partner, and Operating Partner will be subject to Franchisor's approval. The Controlling Principal, Managing Partner, and Operating Partner and certain other Franchisee's Principals designated by Franchisor will guarantee and be jointly and severally liable for the performance of the obligations of Prospective Developer and Affiliated Franchisee under the Development Agreement and Franchise Agreements.
10. Noncompetition. Prospective Developer, each Affiliated Franchisee, each Franchisee's Principal, and certain employees will agree to not compete directly or indirectly with Franchisor, its affiliates, or any other developer or franchisee of Franchisor or its affiliates, in a geographic area determined by Franchisor, during the term of the Development Agreement, any Franchise Agreements, or other agreements with Franchisor, and will further be prohibited from such competition for a period of two years after the earlier of the termination or expiration of such Development Agreement or Franchise Agreement or termination of such Franchisee's Principal's interest in or employee's association with Prospective Developer or an Affiliated Franchisee.
11. Organizational, Management, and Ownership Information.
    a. Prospective Developer, each Affiliated Franchisee, and each Franchisee's Principal must provide Franchisor with organizational, management, ownership, and financial information regarding each of them, as set forth in the organizational information checklist [see checklist 7-2] and as otherwise requested by Franchisor. Before Franchisor executes the Development Agreement, Prospective Developer must provide Franchisor a list of the names and qualifications of the individuals who will manage Prospective Developer's business and must receive Franchisor approval of Prospective Developer's Operating Principal. Further, receipt of organizational, ownership, and financial information satisfactory to Franchisor will be a condition to any extension of Prospective Developer's rights under this Letter of Intent and the execution of any Development Agreement or Franchise Agreement.
    b. Prospective Developer, each Affiliated Franchisee, and each Franchisee's Principal represent and warrant to Franchisor that none of them: (a) is identified, either

by name or an alias, pseudonym, or nickname, on the list of "Specially Designated Nationals and Blocked Persons" maintained by the U.S. Treasury Department's Office of Foreign Assets Control (texts available at http://www.treasury.gov/about/organizational-structure/offices/Pages/Office-of-Foreign-Assets-Control.aspx; (b) has violated any law prohibiting corrupt business practices, money laundering, or the aid or support of persons or entities who conspire to commit acts of terror against any person, entity, or government, including acts prohibited by the U.S. Patriot Act (text available at http://www.epic.org/privacy/terrorism/hr3162.html), U.S. Executive Order 13,244 (text available at http://www.treasury.gov/resource-center/sanctions/Programs/Documents/terror.pdf), or any similar or successor law, rule, or regulation; (c) has made any expenditures other than for lawful purposes or directly or indirectly offered, gave, promised to give, or authorized the payment or the gift of any money, or anything of value, to any person, while knowing or having reason to know that all or a portion of such money or thing of value would be given or promised, directly or indirectly, to any government official, official of an international organization, officer or employee of a foreign government, or anyone acting in an official capacity for a foreign government, for the purpose of (i) influencing any action, inaction, or decision of such official in a manner contrary to his or her position or creating an improper advantage; or (ii) inducing such official to influence any government or instrumentality thereof to effect or influence any act or decision of such government or instrumentality; (d) is a government official, official of an international organization, political party, or official thereof, or candidate; (e) is directly or indirectly owned or controlled by governmental authorities of any country that is subject to a U.S. embargo; (f) understands and has been advised by legal counsel on the requirements of the U.S. Foreign Corrupt Practices Act (currently located at http://www.justice.gov/criminal/fraud/fcpa/) and any local foreign corrupt practices laws and the Patriot Act (currently located at http://www.epic.org/privacy/terrorism/hr3162.html); and (g) shall not otherwise take any action that would cause Franchisor or its affiliates to violate or potentially violate any applicable laws, rules, or regulations of the United States.

12. Confidentiality. Prospective Developer, each Affiliated Franchisee, each Franchisee's Principal, and certain employees would not at any time communicate, divulge, or use Franchisor's confidential information, knowledge, or know-how other than in connection with the development and operation of any Unit. In the event a definitive Development Agreement and Franchise Agreement for the first Unit are not entered into and this Letter of Intent terminates, Prospective Developer and any Affiliated Franchisee for such first Unit agree to return to Franchisor all tangible confidential information and know-how of Franchisor within five days of the date of termination and agree that the terms of this Section 12 will survive any such termination.

13. Marks. Franchisor has obtained certain rights, title, and interests in and to the "[CONCEPT X]®" mark and certain other trademarks and service marks for use outside of the continental United States of America, including in the country in which the Development Territory is located. A list of the marks that have been registered in the country in which the Development Territory is located, or for which Franchisor or its affiliates have sought registration in the country in which the Development Territory is located, is set forth as **Exhibit C**. Franchisor will be solely responsible for all expenses associated with such registration; however, to the extent that any license agreements or

registered user agreements indicating any Affiliated Franchisee's right to use the Marks described herein are required to be registered, Prospective Developer or such Affiliated Franchisee will be responsible for such costs.

14. Translations and Adaptations. Neither Prospective Developer nor any Affiliated Franchisee may translate the Development Agreement or any Franchise Agreement or related materials into any language without Franchisor's prior written consent. To the extent Franchisor permits in its sole discretion, the Manuals, summary agreements, or other materials or information to be translated or otherwise adapted for use in a language other then English, Prospective Developer shall be solely responsible, at its expense, for translating and otherwise adapting such materials and other information provided by Franchisor to Prospective Developer or any Affiliated Franchisee. Any and all translations and adaptations of any agreements or other materials will be subject to Franchisor's prior consent and approval, and shall be owned by Franchisor.

15. Transfers. Any rights granted to the Prospective Developer under the Development Agreement will not be transferable or assignable. Subject to the foregoing restriction, any transfer by any Franchisee's Principal of any interest in the Prospective Developer or any Affiliated Franchisee, any transfer of the Prospective Developer's or any Affiliated Franchisees' interest in any Franchise Agreement, or any transfer of substantially all of the assets of each Unit or the transfer of any interest in any of Prospective Developer's or any Affiliated Franchisees' Principals will be restricted to transferees approved by Franchisor, in its sole discretion.

16. Termination. If any Franchise Agreement is terminated by Franchisor, Franchisor will have the right to (a) require Prospective Developer or such Affiliated Franchisee to assign all of its rights under any existing leases for any Unit premises and for any Unit equipment to Franchisor or its designee and (b) to purchase any of the Unit's physical assets such as trade fixtures, equipment, and supplies at a price to be determined in accordance with a formula agreed upon by the parties or, failing such agreement, as determined by an appraiser in accordance with the terms of the Franchise Agreement. A material default under a Franchise Agreement will constitute a material default under all other existing Franchise Agreements. A material default under the Development Agreement will not constitute a material default under a Franchise Agreement, except for default of the transfer restrictions under the Development Agreement. Prospective Developer and each Affiliated Franchisee will execute a power of attorney and such other documents that Franchisor deems necessary in order to effect the foregoing.

17. Agency Laws. Prospective Developer and the Franchisee's Principals agree that Franchisor would not consider entering into this Letter of Intent, nor would Franchisor consider entering into any Development Agreement or Franchise Agreement with Prospective Developer or any Affiliated Franchisee were it contemplated by the parties that any laws, rules, or regulations in the Development Territory that apply to agency relationships would apply to the relationships created by a Development Agreement or any Franchise Agreement, including but not limited to _______________ (the "Agency Laws"). Accordingly, Prospective Developer and the Franchisee's Principals agree that the Development Agreement and each Franchise Agreement will require each of them to (a) unconditionally waive any rights that each of them might have under the Agency Laws and any other law of similar import, (b) unconditionally release Franchisor from any liability under the Agency Laws and any other law of similar import, including any obligation to pay Prospective Developer or any Affiliated Franchisee any compensation upon expiration or termination of the Development Agreement or any Franchise Agree-

ment, (c) represent, warrant, and covenant that none of them will seek to file or register themselves as agents under the Agency Laws or bring or attempt to bring any cause of action, suit, proceeding, claim, demand, investigation, or inquiry (whether a formal proceeding or otherwise) under the Agency Laws in any court, arbitration proceeding, or before any other tribunal; and (d) acknowledge and agree that any attempt to register themselves or bring any cause of action, suit, proceeding, claim, demand, investigation, or inquiry (whether a formal proceeding or otherwise) under the Agency Laws will be an event of default under the Development Agreement and any Franchise Agreement between the parties and their respective affiliates.

18. Definitive Agreements.

    a. Upon the complete execution of this Letter of Intent, the undersigned will proceed to negotiate a definitive Development Agreement and Franchise Agreement for the first Unit. Each additional Franchise Agreement will be negotiated in accordance with the time requirements for executing Franchise Agreements described in the Development Agreement.

    b. In the event that a definitive Development Agreement and Franchise Agreement for the first Unit are not executed by Franchisor and Prospective Developer and/or an Affiliated Franchisee on or before ______________ (the "Expiration Date"), this Letter of Intent will expire, and neither of the undersigned shall have any further obligation or liability hereunder with respect to the potential transaction contemplated by this Letter of Intent, including, without limitation, any liability pursuant to any claim of detrimental reliance or promissory estoppel. Except for the agreements expressed in Sections 6.a, 12, 17, 18, 19, 20, 21, and 22, nothing in this Letter of Intent will be deemed to be an offer, representation, warranty, agreement, or legally binding commitment of any kind by the undersigned. Nothing contained in this Letter of Intent shall be interpreted as an agreement to enter into a Development Agreement or Franchise Agreement or to otherwise restrict the nature of negotiations or the freedom of a party to terminate negotiations. Notwithstanding the foregoing, the parties acknowledge and agree that if either party terminates negotiations or this Letter of Intent expires by its terms before the parties have executed definitive agreements, Franchisor shall be entitled to retain the full amount of the Holding Fee described in Section 6.a. Prospective Developer hereby waives any and all claims under applicable law related to any such retention of the Holding Fee by Franchisor.

19. Exclusivity. The undersigned acknowledge that each will expend time, expense, and effort in the negotiations contemplated by this Letter of Intent. Therefore, neither Franchisor nor Prospective Developer will submit any proposal, engage in any negotiation, or enter into any understanding, combination, or agreement with any other person or entity with respect to the establishment of any Unit in the Development Territory until after the Expiration Date of this Letter of Intent, unless otherwise terminated by Franchisor or Prospective Developer upon notice to the other.

20. Cost. Except as provided above and in any definitive Development Agreement or Franchise Agreement, each of the undersigned will bear its own costs and expenses of negotiating and documenting the transactions contemplated herein. Neither of the undersigned has retained nor will retain any broker or finder in connection with the transactions contemplated herein. Any actions taken or costs incurred by either of the undersigned prior to the execution of a definitive agreement are taken and incurred at such person's sole risk, cost, and expense.

21. Public Announcements. Each of the undersigned agrees that it will not make any public announcement or any other disclosure regarding the existence or nature of the negotiations hereunder, the proposed transactions, or any matters contemplated herein unless the other has given its prior written consent to such announcement or disclosure or unless otherwise required by law.

22. Choice of Law and Forum. This Letter of Intent will be interpreted and enforced in accordance with the laws of the United States of America and the State of _________, without giving effect to the conflict of laws principles thereof. The undersigned hereby submit and consent to the jurisdiction of the Courts of the United States of America and the State of ________ in any dispute arising out of the matters contemplated herein. The undersigned agree that all actions initiated or maintained in any dispute arising out of this Letter of Intent shall be brought in the Federal District Court in the ________________. The parties contemplate that the Development Agreement and Franchise Agreements will also be subject to the laws of the United States of America and the State of ________, and that any disputes shall be settled by arbitration to take place in ______________, subject to certain agreed actions that may be litigated in any court of competent jurisdiction. Prior to execution, the terms of this Letter of Intent will remain valid until ________, 20__. Thereafter, unless executed by both parties, this Letter of Intent shall be deemed automatically rescinded.

Please execute in the space provided below to acknowledge that the above described terms accurately reflect your understanding of the proposed franchise program.

Very truly yours,

[INSERT NAME OF FRANCHISOR]

By: ______________________________

Name:_____________________________

Title:_____________________________

Agreed and Accepted this

_____ day of ___________, 20__:

[INSERT NAME OF PROSPECTIVE DEVELOPER]

By: ______________________________

Name:_____________________________

Title:_____________________________

Exhibit A

The parties have tentatively agreed on the following Development Schedule for the development of [Units] in the Development Territory.

Development Period Number/ (Duration)	**Date of Execution of Franchise Agreements**	**Date of Commencement of Construction**	**Date of Opening**	**Total Number of [Units] That Must Be Open and in Operation at the End of the Development Period**
1 (__ months)	______, 20__	______, 20__	______, 20__	1
2 (__ months)	______,______ ______,______	______,______ ______,______	______,___ ______,___	2
3 (__ months)	______,______ ______,______	______,______ ______,______	______,___ ______,___	3
4 (__ months)	______,______ ______,______	______,______ ______,______	______,___ ______,___	4

Exhibit B

The Letter of Credit described in Section 2.b. of the Letter of Intent will at a minimum contain the following provisions and be governed by the following requirements (defined terms not otherwise defined in this Letter of Intent shall have the meaning attributed to them in paragraph 7 below):

1. At least thirty (30) days prior to signing the Development Agreement, Prospective Developer must have provided Franchisor a firm commitment from an Issuing Bank to issue a Letter of Credit in the initial and continuing amounts set forth below in accordance with the Uniform Customs and Practice (UCP) for Documentary Credits. At such time, Prospective Developer must also provide Franchisor a firm commitment from a separate Confirming Bank in accordance with the UCP to confirm the Letter of Credit unconditionally.

Letter of Credit Amount (US$)	**Date**
U.S.$ __________	Upon signing Development Agreement
U.S.$ __________	Upon Opening of the first Unit
U.S.$ __________	Upon Opening of the second Unit
U.S.$ __________	Upon Opening of the third Unit
U.S.$ __________	Upon Opening of the fourth Unit and during such period that any Franchise Agreement remains in full force and effect and for a period of one year thereafter

2. The initial Letter of Credit must be obtained and provided to Franchisor within ten (10) days of the execution of the Development Agreement.
3. The original and each renewal/replacement Letter of Credit shall unconditionally obligate the Issuing Bank and the Confirming Bank to effect payment under the Letter of Credit to Franchisor in the specified amount (in Dollars) upon Franchisor's delivery

of written notice to the Confirming Bank of a breach of any agreement between Franchisor and Prospective Developer or an affiliate that is not cured in accordance with the terms of the applicable agreement. Developer's obligation to provide and maintain the Letter of Credit shall survive termination or expiration of any agreements between Franchisor and Prospective Developer or an affiliate and shall continue until one year following termination or expiration of the last remaining Franchise Agreement entered into pursuant to the Development Agreement.

4. If any breach of any agreements between Franchisor and Prospective Developer or an affiliate remains uncured at the end of any relevant cure period, Franchisor may provide to the Confirming Bank notice of the breach, signed and verified to be true by a senior officer of Franchisor, containing a statement of the amount sought to be drawn under the Letter of Credit and that the amount of damages incurred by Franchisor as a result of the breach equals or exceeds such amount. Such notice shall be deemed conclusive evidence that a breach has occurred and has not been cured in accordance with the terms of the applicable agreement, and of the amount payable to Franchisor under the Letter of Credit. No other form or type of documentation will be required as a condition or predicate of the Confirming Bank's obligation to pay under the Letter of Credit. All payments shall be made in Dollars. If Franchisor draws against the Letter of Credit, within 10 days after the Confirming Bank makes payment to Franchisor, Prospective Developer must arrange for the Issuing Bank to issue and for the Confirming Bank to confirm unconditionally a replacement Letter of Credit in such amount as required above.
5. Not later than 30 days before the scheduled expiration date of the original or any renewal or replacement Letter of Credit, Prospective Developer must provide Franchisor a firm commitment from the Issuing Bank to issue a renewal or replacement Letter of Credit in the required amount as specified above. Within such time period, Prospective Developer must also provide Franchisor a firm commitment from the Confirming Bank to confirm the renewal or replacement Letter of Credit unconditionally. The renewal/replacement Letter of Credit shall be delivered to Franchisor prior to the expiration of the Letter of Credit then in effect.
6. If Prospective Developer fails to provide either commitment within 30 days before the scheduled expiration date of the original or any renewal or replacement Letter of Credit, Franchisor may draw on the letter of Credit as permitted by the parties' agreement. Further, Prospective Developer's failure to provide a renewal or replacement Letter of Credit will constitute a material default under each agreement between Franchisor and Prospective Developer or an Affiliated Franchisee and Franchisor may, at its option, immediately terminate the Development Agreement and any Franchise Agreement entered into between Franchisor and Prospective Developer or an Affiliated Franchisee by written notice to Prospective Developer or such Affiliated Franchisee, as applicable.
7. For purposes of this Letter of Intent, the following terms shall have the below meanings:
   a. **Confirming Bank** means an international bank designated by Franchisor.
   b. **Issuing Bank** means an internationally recognized bank selected by Prospective Developer (i) that has and maintains a net worth in excess of U.S. $1,000,000, (ii) that maintains a correspondent banking relationship with the Confirming Bank, and (iii) that has been identified to and approved by Franchisor.

c. **Letter of Credit** means an irrevocable sight draft letter of credit issued by the Issuing Bank to Franchisor that (i) names Franchisor or its designee as the beneficiary, (ii) is unconditionally confirmed by the Confirming Bank, (iii) is drafted in accordance with and governed by the UCP and incorporates the terms and provisions of the UCP by reference, (iv) provides an expiry (expiration) date not less than 12 months after its date of issuance, (v) is payable in Dollars, (vi) permits both full and partial draws, and (vii) contains the other provisions as Franchisor requires.

d. **UCP** means Uniform Customs and Practice for Documentary Credits, 1993 Revision, ICC Publication No. 500.

Exhibit C
Proprietary Marks

Country	Mark	(Application)/ Registration No.	Class	(Application)/ Registration Date	Status

Checklist 7-2
Sample Closing and Organizational Checklists

Closing Checklist and Organizational Checklist

[INSERT NAME OF FRANCHISOR]

[INSERT NAME OF COUNTRY]

[INSERT NAME OF DEVELOPER/FRANCHISEE]

Updated ______, 20__

Items Required to Be Completed Before Closing

		Status
GENERAL CLOSING OVERVIEW		
1. Need OFAC search on Developer/Franchisee, Guarantors, and Franchisee's Principals		
1. AGREEMENTS		
Actions	**Development Agreement** 1. Incorporate date of last day of Development Schedule into Section 1.B. 2. Letter of Credit (see below) 3. Complete Development Schedule in Section 3.A (to be finalized based on anticipated execution date) 4. Confirm Developer's Principals, including Controlling Principal 5. Confirm Guarantors 6. Provide/Confirm Attachment B information, including e-mail 7. Confirm Attachment D State of Ownership Interests	1. Need 2. Need 3. Need 4. Need 5. Need 6. Need 7. Need
	Franchise Agreement (for first Unit) 1. Confirm City/Region of first Unit for Cover Page/ first Page 2. Confirm Franchisee's Principals, including Controlling Principal, Operating Principal, and Managing Principal 3. Confirm Guarantors 4. Provide/Confirm Attachment A information, including Approved Location, (if known), Managing Partner (if known), and e-mail 5. Confirm Attachment D State of Ownership Interests	1. Need 2. Need 3. Need 4. Need (approved location TBD) 5. Need
2. ORGANIZATIONAL DOCUMENTS		
Actions	See Organizational Checklist (attached) Open Issues:	

		Status
3. EXECUTION FORMALITIES		
Actions	**Development Agreement** 1. **Franchise Agreement** 1.	

Items Required to Be Completed at Closing

	Status
1. Need firm commitment from Issuing Bank and Confirming Bank re Letter of Credit at least 30 days prior to closing (amount below): Letter of Credit Amount (US$) Date U.S.$ ________ Upon signing Development Agreement U.S.$ ________ Upon Opening of the first Unit U.S.$ ________ Upon Opening of the second Unit U.S.$ ________ Upon Opening of the third Unit U.S.$ ________ Upon Opening of the fourth Unit and during such period that any Franchise Agreement remains in full force and effect and for a period of one year thereafter 2. ________	Name/ Commitment of Issuing Bank Need Name/ Commitment of Confirming Bank

Items Required to Be Completed After Closing

	Status
1. Need final Letter of Credit from Issuing Bank and Confirming Bank at least 10 days after closing.	1. Need
2. Need yearly receipt/confirmation of renewal of Letter of Credit (see above amounts).	2. TBD in future

Organizational Information Checklist: Information and Documentation Required to Prepare Documents for Closing

[INSERT NAME OF FRANCHISOR]

FOR USE IN

[INSERT COUNTRY]

[INSERT NAME OF DEVELOPER/FRANCHISEE]

Updated ______, 20__

	Type of Information	**Status**
1.	Identity of Franchisee, Franchisee's Principals, and related parties: a. full legal name of business entity or individual that will be named as the Franchisee in the Franchise Agreement b. form of entity (e.g., corporation, partnership, etc.) and place and date of formation of Franchisee c. principal business address of Franchisee d. list of Franchisee's officers, directors, and equity owners (shareholders, partners, members, etc.), and the ownership interest of each equity owner e. list of officers and directors of any entity that will have a controlling interest in Franchisee	Need
2.	Names of Controlling Principals and Guarantors.	Need
3.	Charter Documents of Franchisee, incorporating restrictions on transfers and restriction on scope of purpose of the Franchisee to the operation of an _________ Unit. See Section 5.X. of the Franchise Agreement.	Need
4.	Name, address, phone number, fax number, and e-mail address of legal counsel for Franchisee.	Need
5.	Proposed Unit Address	Need

Notes: Charter Documents means Franchisee's Articles of Incorporation, Bylaws, Partnership Agreement, Operating Agreement, or equivalent governing document(s).

If a corporate guarantor or a corporate principal will be involved, additional but similar information and documentation as noted above will be required.

Organizational Information Checklist: Documents Required or Action to Be Taken by Prospective Franchisee Prior to Closing

No.	Required Document or Action	Status
1.	Corporate Resolution authorizing Franchisee and its representative on its behalf to execute the Agreements.	Need
2.	Corporate Resolutions authorizing amendment to the Charter Documents of Franchisee to reference the restrictions on transfer set forth in Section 5.X of the Franchise Agreement, unless such limitation is included in the Charter Documents at the time the company is formed.	Need
3.	Corporate Resolutions authorizing amendment to the Charter Documents of Franchisee to limit the scope of the entity's purpose to the operation of an ____________ Unit, pursuant to Section __ of the Franchise Agreement, unless such limitation is included in the Charter Documents at the time the company is formed.	Need
4.	Corporate Certificate verifying that the Charter Documents and Corporate Resolutions of Franchisee are true, correct, and have not been modified.	Need
5.	Stock Certificate specimen of Franchisee with restrictive transfer legend as follows (if applicable): "This certificate is held subject to all restrictions imposed upon assignments or transfers which are set forth in the [Insert name of Franchisor] Unit Franchise Agreement for ________________ between [Insert name of Franchisor] and Franchisee (the "Agreement"). Any assignment or transfer of this certificate which does not fully comply with the restrictions imposed upon assignments and transfers by the Agreements shall be null and void."	Need
6.	Name of Operating Partner.	Need
7.	Identity of Managing Partner.	Need
8.	Certificates of Good Standing and Existence (or their equivalent) for Franchisee.	Need

Note: If a corporate guarantor or a corporate principal will be involved, additional but similar information and documentation as noted above will be required.

Exhibit 7-7
Sample Irrevocable Letter of Credit

Irrevocable Standby Letter of Credit

Date:__________

Letter of Credit Number: __________

Confirming Bank: __________

(as designated by __________)

[INSERT NAME AND ADDRESS OF FRANCHISOR]

Ladies and Gentlemen:

We hereby establish this Irrevocable Letter of Credit in your favor and authorize you to draw on us for the account of our customer [INSERT NAME OF DEVELOPER/FRANCHISEE], a [INSERT TYPE OF ENTITY], for any sum or sums not exceeding in the aggregate [INSERT INITIAL AMOUNT OF LETTER OF CREDIT] U.S. Dollars (U.S. $[__________]) (subject to automatic increase or decrease in accordance with the terms of <u>Exhibit A</u> upon receipt of written notice from you and [INSERT NAME OF DEVELOPER/FRANCHISEE] that an event described in <u>Exhibit A</u> has occurred), or such other amount described (collectively, the "Amount"), payable in U.S. Dollars, available by your draft or drafts at sight drawn on us (or your letter or letters demanding payment under this Letter of Credit), each accompanied by the following:

(1) a statement from you or your transferee, signed by any person described as "authorized," reading as follows:

> The undersigned hereby certifies that the amount drawn is due and owing following a breach and failure to cure under the terms and provisions of a Development Agreement, Unit Franchise Agreement, or other agreement with Franchisor as such agreement(s) may have been amended, modified, supplemented, or assigned from time to time.
>
> ***and***

(2) a copy of the letter by which you made demand for payment of the amount stated in the accompanying draft.

All drafts or demands for payment hereunder must bear the date and number of this Letter of Credit. Partial drawings are permitted.

Drafts or demands for payment of the Amount hereunder must be drawn and presented to us at [INSERT BANK ADDRESS] on or before 5:00 p.m., local time, on [INSERT INITIAL EXPIRATION DATE]; provided, however, that this Letter of Credit shall be automatically renewed within thirty (30) days before each of its expiration dates throughout the term of the Development Agreement and/or Franchise Agreement.

Further, this Letter of Credit shall be restored to the Amount within thirty (30) days after any draw which reduces the amount of the Letter of Credit available for future draws to below fifty percent (50%) of the Amount. All renewals shall be without amendment to this Letter of Credit for successive one (1) year periods from the initial expiration date and each successive expiration date thereafter unless at least sixty (60) days prior to the applicable expiration date we shall notify you by certified mail, return receipt requested, that we elect not to renew this Letter of Credit for any additional period. We will give you at least thirty (30) days' notice if we elect not to restore any amounts available for future draws as described in this paragraph. Such notices shall be deemed to have been given when received by you. Upon your receipt of any such notice, you may draw under this Letter of Credit by draft (or demand for payment), without providing the accompanying statement required above.

We hereby agree with you and the drawers, endorsers, and bona fide holders of all drafts drawn under and in compliance with the terms of this Letter of Credit that such drafts will be duly honored upon presentation to us on or before its expiration date (including any extended expiration date), and we hereby waive any right to defer the immediate honor of any such drafts.

This Letter of Credit is transferable to any beneficiary in the United States upon our receipt of a written notification from you of such a transfer.

This Letter of Credit is subject to the Uniform Customs and Practice for Documentary Credits (1993 Revision), International Chamber of Commerce Publication No. 500.

Very truly yours,

[INSERT NAME OF ISSUING BANK]

By: __________ Authorized Officer

Letter of Credit Amount (US$)	**Triggering Event to Increase or Decrease Amount**
$_____	Upon signing Development Agreement
$_____	Upon Opening of the first Unit
$_____	Upon Opening of the second Unit
$_____	Upon Opening of the third Unit
$_____	Upon Opening of the fourth Unit and during such period that any Franchise Agreement remains in full force and effect and for a period of one year thereafter

Exhibit 7-8

Diagram of Master Franchise Relationship

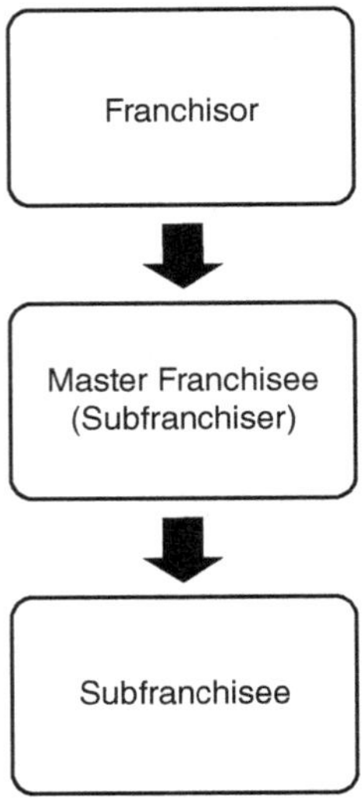

Diagram of Area Represntative Relationship

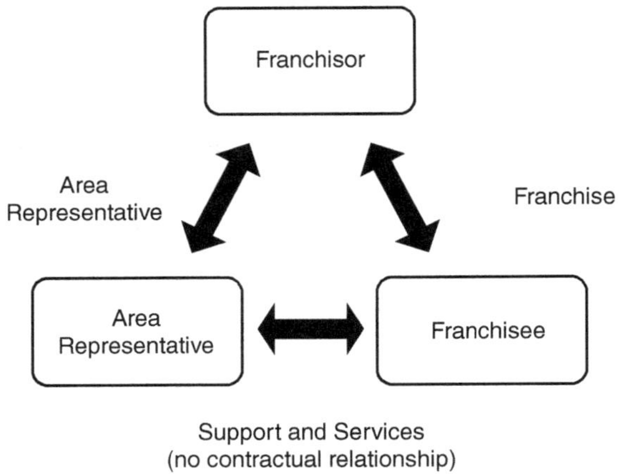

CHAPTER 8

Data Privacy

Brian Hengesbaugh and Mark Melodia[1]

Contents

1. The authors would like to thank the following colleagues for their invaluable assistance in the preparation of this chapter: Paul Bond, Partner, Data Strategy, Security & Privacy at Holland & Knight LLP, and Cristina Messerschmidt, Associate, Privacy and Cybersecurity at Baker McKenzie.

8-1. Introduction: Why Am I, as a Franchisor, in the Data Privacy and Security Business?[2]

In its purest form, "[f]ranchising is a method of expanding a business by licensing independent business men and women to sell the franchisor's products or services or to follow a format and trade style created by the franchisor using the franchisor's trademarks, trade names and other intellectual property."[3]

If the franchise relationship were simply a licensing of intellectual property, the franchisor would have very little to worry about with respect to the franchisee's day-to-day operations. But the reality of a franchise relationship is not so simple. For example, the Federal Trade Commission defines the franchise relationship as involving, in part, an element of franchisor control. To be a franchise means, inter alia, that the franchisor "will exert or has the authority to exert a significant degree of control over the franchisee's method of operation, or provide significant assistance in the franchisee's method of operation."[4] State law is generally in accord that a franchise, by definition, includes a contractual requirement that a franchisee operate "under a marketing plan or system prescribed in substantial part by a franchisor."[5]

At the global level, the amount of control that the franchisor may (and, in some cases, is obligated to) exert over the franchisee varies widely and includes disclosure and registration requirements, tax structure considerations, agreement structures (e.g., restrictions on termination or renewal of the agreement), and safeguard requirements, among others. In Australia, for example, a franchisor-franchisee relationship is defined by the franchisor giving the franchisee the right to distribute goods or services under a plan that is substantially determined by the franchisor.[6] In China, one of the elements is whether the franchisee conducts business under a uniform mode of operation, determined by the franchisor.[7]

Privacy and data security concerns arise most directly where the franchisor is providing "significant control" and/or "significant assistance."[8] For example, franchisor control over site design and operation can touch on issues of physical

2. This introduction and portions of this article draw from "Data Protection and Privacy in Franchising: Who Is Responsible?" presented to the American Bar Association: 36th Annual Forum on Franchising by Mark S. Melodia and Michael K. Lindsey in October 2013.

3. 1 Gladys Glickman, Franchising § 1.01 (2013).

4. Disclosure Requirements and Prohibitions Concerning Franchising and Business Opportunity Ventures, 16 C.F.R. § 463.1(h)(2) (2007).

5. Glickman, supra note 3, § 2.02 n.50 (2013) (surveying state laws on definition of franchise).

6. Australian Competition & Consumer Commission, *Franchising Code of Conduct Compliance Manual*, at 12 (2013), https://www.accc.gov.au/system/files/Franchising%20code%20of%20conduct%20compliance%20manual_0.pdf.

7. China Commercial Franchise Administration Regulation (2007), *available at* http://www.gov.cn/zwgk/2007-02/14/content_527207.htm.

8. Fed. Trade Comm'n, Franchise Rule Compliance Guide 2–4 (May 2008), https://www.ftc.gov/system/files/documents/plain-language/bus70-franchise-rule-compliance-guide.pdf.

security of data. As employees are among the most frequent sources of data loss, theft, or misuse, franchisor control over franchisee personnel policies and practices can impact administrative security. Franchisor control over franchisee participation in promotional campaigns and loyalty programs may require the franchisor to make decisions about how and when to use customer data, and how and when to do consumer outreach. Likewise, franchisor assistance to franchisees in the form of management of locations, personnel advice or training, and providing operating manuals or centralized reservations or credit card systems can involve the franchisor in operational decisions about personal information. Whether couched as franchisor assistance or franchisor control, pervasive franchisor involvement in franchisee activity has been a traditional ground for plaintiffs to seek to hold franchisors liable for alleged franchise-level problems.[9] Indeed, in some jurisdictions, franchisors now fear being deemed employers for their franchisees and the employees of their franchisees.[10]

To the extent that a franchise relationship vests in the franchisor contractual and/or practical control over franchise operations, plaintiffs may seek to impute legal liability for alleged data privacy and security issues at the franchise level to the franchisor. Examples are provided below.

Recently, the role of franchisor in data privacy management has become even more complex. As described below, the California Consumer Protection Act of 2018 has imposed significant obligations on companies that do business in California and process information about California consumers. These obligations include, among other things, honoring access requests, deletion requests, and requests to refrain from the sale of personal data. Functionally, consumers expect these rights to be offered and honored at all levels of the franchise system. Further, the relationship between a franchisor and franchisee raises potentially complicated issues from a data ownership perspective. In the United States, data owners have different obligations in the context of data breaches (see section (c) below) than service providers that maintain data on behalf of corporate customers

---

9. *See, e.g.*, Goodyear Tire & Rubber Co. v. Washington, 719 So. 2d 774, 777 (Ala. 1998) (affirming, in relevant part, decision that a Goodyear service outlet acted as an agent of the manufacturer Goodyear where there was evidence "(1) that Goodyear knowingly allowed and encouraged Tire Pro to use Goodyear signs and to sell Goodyear products; (2) that Goodyear knowingly allowed Tire Pro to represent to customers, through logos on its invoices, that it was a 'Goodyear Certified Auto Service' center; (3) that Goodyear's dealer sales manager testified that Goodyear intended for Tire Pro's customers to believe they were dealing with a Goodyear establishment; (4) that the tires sold to Washington's daughter were 'Goodyear Eagles'; and (5) that the repairs effected on Washington's daughter's car were performed by Tire Pro as a 'Goodyear Certified Auto Service' center"); Nichols v. Arthur Murray, Inc., 248 Cal. App. 2d 610, 614 (Cal. App. 1967) (affirming trial court's determination that "[a] reading of the contract here involved leads me to conclude that rigid effective controls over almost every aspect of the operation were retained by the licensor to the extent that for all intents and purposes it should be regarded as the operator of the business"); 11 Federal Trade Commission Act, 15 U.S.C.A. § 45.

10. *See, e.g.*, Vazquez v. Jan-Pro, 923 F.3d 575 (9th Cir. May 2, 2019), opinion withdrawn, 2019 US App. Lexis 21687 (July 22, 2019), opinion reinstated, 2019 BL 357978 (9th Cir. Sept. 24, 2019).

(called data maintainers), whose obligations are generally limited to notifying the owner of the information about a data breach "immediately following discovery."[11] In the European Union, the General Data Protection Regulation (GDPR) also imposes different obligations on data controllers than on data processors, with the processor being required to "notify the controller without undue delay after becoming aware of a personal data breach."[12] Thus, establishing clear ownership obligations and responsibilities with respect to the data collected, both from franchisee personnel, such as employees or temporary workers, and from business customers and end users, is essential to protect both the franchisee and the franchisor with respect to data privacy obligations worldwide.

Also, as mentioned below, the role of artificial intelligence in retail is expanding as a tool. This poses its own set of risks and rewards. Franchisors must guide deployment of these powerful, and sometime controversial, tools in a manner that limits system-wide exposure.

8-2. Data Ownership and Control

The concept of data ownership centers around control or legal rights over a specific data set. Under the CCPA, for example, primary responsibility for the obligations of the statute rests with the "business" that determines the purposes and means of processing the data. In contrast, an organization that acts as a "service provider" and processes personal information on behalf of the "business" has fewer direct regulatory duties.[13] In contrast, the GDPR employs the concept of the "data controller," defined as "the natural or legal person, public authority, agency or other body which, alone or jointly with others, determines the purposes and means of the processing of personal data."[14] Similar concepts recognizing a distinction between those that control data and those that process data on behalf of another without acquiring ownership or control exist in many jurisdictions, including in countries with relatively strict data privacy regimes such as Brazil, South Korea, and Russia. However, the concept of data ownership is not only limited to general data privacy considerations, but must also require consideration of, among other concepts, intellectual property rights, sector-specific rules and regulations, and contractual provisions.

(a) Franchisor and Franchisee as Independent Data Owners/Controllers

When determining the rights and obligations of the parties to a franchise relationship with respect to data ownership and controllership, one option is for both

11. Cal. Civ. Code § 1798.82
12. EU General Data Protection Regulation (2016/679) Art. 33.
13. *See generally* Cal. Civ. Code § 1798.140(ag)(1)(D).
14. EU General Data Protection Regulation (2016/679) Art. 4.

franchisors and franchisees to be independent owners or controllers of the data. In many cases, the data at issue will include data of the franchisee's personnel (i.e., employees, contractors, job applicants), vendors/suppliers, business partners or corporate customers, and—perhaps most importantly—traditional customers or end users. When the parties choose to act as independent controllers of data, both parties retain independent rights but also have independent obligations with respect to the data.

(b) Franchisor/Franchisee as Data Processor/Maintainer or Data Owner/Controller

Alternatively, the parties could choose a controller/processor relationship, with the franchisee acting as the controller of the data, and the franchisor acting as the processor of the data. Under this arrangement, the franchisor would not have independent rights to the data and would be required act at the direction of the franchisee with respect to the data. However, the franchisor also would not have independent obligations with respect to the data, such as notifying persons to whom the data is a concern in the event of a data breach. A third alternative would be the franchisor being the controller of the data and the franchisee being deemed the processor of the data with the respective obligations in the event of a data breach then being reversed, although we have not seen this often in practice.

8-3. Data Breaches

The primary and still most substantial focus of data privacy and security risk arises from the potential for loss, theft, or misuse of personal information, known as data breaches. Data breaches pose so significant a risk to businesses that the Securities and Exchange Commission issued specific guidance detailing factors to be considered. The SEC warns: "Companies that fall victim to successful cyber-attacks or experience other cybersecurity incidents may incur substantial costs and suffer other negative consequences," which may include the following:

- remediation costs, such as liability for stolen assets or information, repairs of system damage, and incentives to customers or business partners in an effort to maintain relationships after an attack;
- increased cybersecurity protection costs, which may include the costs of making organizational changes, deploying additional personnel and protection technologies, training employees, and engaging third party experts and consultant lost revenues resulting from the unauthorized use of proprietary information or the failure to retain or attract customers following an attack;
- litigation and legal risks, including regulatory actions by state and federal governmental authorities and non-U.S. authorities;
- increased insurance premiums;

- reputational damage that adversely affects customer or investor confidence; and damage to the company's competitiveness, stock price, and long-term shareholder value.[15]

Given a franchisee's greater propensity to directly interact with the public, a franchisor might be lulled into thinking that data security breaches are primarily the franchisee's problem. However, the FTC's action against Wyndham disproved that assumption. In 2012, the FTC filed an action pursuant to its authority under Section 5 of the Federal Trade Commission Act[16] against Wyndham Worldwide Corporation (Wyndham Worldwide), Wyndham Hotel Group (Hotel Group), Wyndham Hotels and Resorts (Hotels and Resorts), and Wyndham Hotel Management (Hotel Management).[17] In its complaint, the FTC alleged that defendants'

> failure to maintain reasonable security allowed intruders to obtain unauthorized access to the computer networks of Wyndham Hotels and Resorts, LLC, and several hotels franchised and managed by Defendants on three separate occasions in less than two years. Defendants' security failures led to fraudulent charges on consumers' accounts, more than $10.6 million in fraud loss and the export of hundreds of thousands of consumers' payment card account information to a domain registered in Russia.

The FTC's complaint made specific allegations about the defendants' control of franchise-level operations. For example, the FTC alleged that

- the franchise agreements "require each Wyndham-branded hotel to purchase, and configure to their specifications, a designated computer system, known as a property management system";
- these property management systems "store personal information about consumers, including names, addresses, email addresses, telephone numbers, payment card, account numbers, expiration dates and security codes";
- all of these property management systems "are part of Hotels and Resorts' computer network, and are linked to its corporate network";
- "[o]nly Defendants, and not the owners of the Wyndham-branded hotels, have administrator access that allows Defendants to control the property management systems at the hotels";
- "Defendants set the rules, including all password requirements, that allow the Wyndham-branded hotels' employees to access their property management systems"; and

15. Securities and Exchange Commission, Commission Statement and Guidance on Public Company Cybersecurity Disclosures, 17 C.F.R. Parts 229 and 249 [Release Nos. 33-10459; 34-82746].

16. 1 Federal Trade Commission Act, 15 U.S.C.A. § 45.

17. Complaint for Injunctive and Equitable Relief, FTC v. Wyndham Worldwide Corp., No. 2:12-cv-1365, 2013 WL 1222491 (D. Ariz. Aug. 9, 2012).

- for those hotels that Hotel Management directly operates under management agreements, Hotel Management controls "information technology and security functions and the hiring of employees to administer the hotels' computer networks."

The FTC also cited to the privacy policy of the central reservation website allegedly operated by Hotel and Resorts as allegedly being deceptive.

The defendants moved to dismiss the action. The defendants' motion asserted that the FTC did not have authority to prescribe or enforce data security standards; that it had not done so with sufficiently fair notice; that the FTC specifically had no enforcement authority with respect to the security of payment card information; and that, in any event, the complaint (as amended) did not sufficiently allege any facts that would make plausible the defendants' liabilities for franchisee-level failures. The trial court rejected these arguments, as did the Third Circuit Court of Appeals, finding that a sufficient claim was stated against the franchisor for data breaches at the franchisee level.[18] Wyndham ultimately settled the case with the FTC, agreeing to a consent order that required, among other things annual certification of its information security posture for the next 20 years.[19]

The FTC has brought dozens of such actions, in the process illustrating that the Commission sees data privacy lapses as unfair and deceptive acts and practices with respect to consumer information. These actions include the following:

- *Guess?* and *Life is good, Inc.*: In each case, the FTC alleged that the payment card information collected on the company's respective website was not as secure as claimed by its online disclosures.[20]
- *Toysmart*: The company had promised in its privacy policy never to resell consumer information, but then it attempted to sell its consumer database as a standalone asset in the context of its bankruptcy.[21]
- *Google*: It was alleged that Google was misrepresenting how registration information for its Google Buzz program would be used, failing to adequately explain options for opting out, and falsely claiming compliance with the European Union–United States Safe Harbor Program.[22]
- *Liberty Financial Companies*: The company's website, which provided financial literacy information for young investors, was alleged to claim

18. FTC v. Wyndham Worldwide Corp., 799 F.3d 236 (3d Cir. 2015).

19. https://www.ftc.gov/news-events/press-releases/2015/12/wyndham-settles-ftc-charges-it-unfairly-placed-consumers-payment.

20. In the Matter of Guess?, Inc., and Guess.com, Inc., Complaint and Decision and Order, FTC File No. 022 3260 (Jul. 30, 2003); In the Matter of Life is good, Inc. and Life is good Retail, Inc., Complaint and Decision and Order, FTC Matter No. 072-3046 (Apr. 18, 2008).

21. FTC v. Toysmart.com, LLC, Stipulated Consent Agreement and Final Order, No. 00-11341-RGS (D. Mass. Jul. 10, 2000).

22. In the Matter of Google, Inc., Decision and Order, FTC File No. 10231236 (Oct. 13, 2011).

that information about minor users would be stored anonymously when the company actually maintained access to identifying information.[23]

- *GeoCities*: This action resolved claims that the company provided registration information about website users to third parties, including for marketing purposes, in contravention of its posted privacy policy.[24]

Although any false statement a company makes concerning privacy and data security potentially can be held against that company by the FTC, the FTC also has prosecuted allegedly unfair practices actions against companies even where no such statements have been made.

For example:

- *BJ's Wholesale Club*: The FTC alleged that the chain had failed to encrypt credit card information in transit throughout its stores, resulting in millions of dollars of credit card fraud.[25] While there was no allegation that the company had promised to encrypt the card information, the FTC stated that failure to do so still constituted an unfair trade practice.
- *DSW, Inc.*: The FTC alleged failure to adequately secure its database of payment card information from unauthorized access.[26] Again, the FTC alleged that unfair trade practices had occurred even though no allegation was made that any consumer disclosure made by the retailer was inaccurate or misleading.

Because preemption is rare in the privacy and data security area (more than one federal agency may have jurisdiction to investigate and prosecute data security infractions, alongside states and privately prosecuted class actions), State Attorneys General began wading into the data breach enforcement waters early on. For example, after a data security breach at the data broker ChoicePoint compromised Social Security numbers and consumer credit reports, ChoicePoint notified California residents who were affected by the data breach, but, because California was the only state in 2005 to have a law mandating such notification, failed to notify residents in other states. In February 2005, 19 State Attorneys General sent a letter to ChoicePoint demanding notification to residents in their states as well. The State Attorneys General then commenced an investigation into ChoicePoint, which culminated in a settlement agreement that was announced in May 2007.[27] The state settlement, which included injunctive relief against ChoicePoint and a civil penalty in the amount of $500,000, was in addition to an

---

23. In the Matter of Liberty Financial Companies, Inc., Decision and Order, FTC File No. 982 3522 (Aug. 12, 1999).

24. In the Matter of Geocities, Decision and Order, FTC File No. 982 3015 (Feb. 5, 1999).

25. In the Matter of BJ's Wholesale Club Inc., Decision and Order, FTC File No. 0423160 (Sept. 20, 2005).

26. In the Matter of DSW, Inc., Decision and Order, FTC File No. 052 3096 (Mar. 7, 2006).

27. *See* Press Release, Illinois Attorney General, Attorney General Madigan Reaches Agreement With Choicepoint (May 31, 2007), https://illinoisattorneygeneral.gov/pressroom/2007_05/20070531.html.

independent FTC settlement that included $5 million in consumer redress and a $10 million civil penalty for alleged violations of the FCRA.[28]

Since 2007, there has been a rollout of security breach notification laws in state after state across the nation. At this time, every state and multiple other U.S. jurisdictions have laws requiring some form of notification to persons whose personal data was subject to loss, theft, or misuse. These laws share certain core characteristics but differ from one another in material ways, such that compliance in a data breach situation involving multiple jurisdictions remains extremely complex. For example, all such state statutes consider Social Security numbers information within the scope of their concern, but some can also be triggered by other personal information identifiers, such as tribal identification numbers, biometrics, mother's maiden name, and so on. Some state statutes cover paper records, while many others relate only to electronic records. Some state statutes require a risk of actual harm before compelling companies to send notices while others do not. In addition, many of the statutes now require notice to specific state officials prior to, or at the same time as, notice is provided to the affected individuals. The states routinely follow up on these notices with additional questions, investigations or even enforcement actions. As an example, in 2017 Hilton "agreed to pay $700,000 and obtain annual assessments of its compliance with the payment card industry's data security standard to resolve claims mounted by the New York and Vermont attorneys general that the hotel chain lacked reasonable data security and waited too long to report a pair of 2015 hacks."[29]

In addition, data breaches can, and often do, give rise to private litigation. Few of the data security breach statutes directly provide such a private right of action. However, under the CCPA, consumers can now sue businesses when their "non-encrypted or non-redacted personal information . . . is subject to unauthorized access and ex-filtration, theft, or disclosure as a result of the business's violation of the duty to implement and maintain reasonable security procedures and practices appropriate to the nature of the information."[30] Under the CCPA, plaintiffs' lawyers and their consumer clients who are the victims of a data breach can now seek statutory damages of between $100 and $750 per consumer, per incident, actual damages, and injunctive relief. In addition, there is no need to demonstrate actual harm to the consumer. Hundreds of class actions have been filed against companies, including franchises, under other theories of federal law, state law, contract law, and common law.[31] For example:

---

28. *See* Press Release, Fed. Trade Comm'n, ChoicePoint Settles Data Security Breach Charges; to Pay $10 Million in Civil Penalties, $5 Million for Consumer Redress (Jan. 26, 2006), https://www.ftc.gov/news-events/press-releases/2006/01/choicepoint-settles-data-security-breach-charges-pay-10-million.

29. https://www.law360.com/articles/980219/ny-vt-ags-strike-deal-to-resolve-hilton-data-breach-probe.

30. Cal. Civ. Code § 1798.150(a).

31. These federal class action lawsuits may be limited after the Supreme Court's decision in *Transunion v. Ramirez*, No. 20-297, 594 U.S. __ (2021), which held that only plaintiffs concretely harmed by a statutory violation have Article III standing to seek damages in federal court.

- Sonic Drive-In reached a $4.3 million settlement with its customers over the chain's data security breach in 2017 that exposed customer credit and debit card information at 325 Sonic Drive-In locations.[32]
- Wendy's agreed to pay $3.4 million to settle the class action lawsuit against them alleging that they failed to protect consumer information in a 2016 data breach.[33]
- Noodles spent $3.4 million just investigating their data security breach.[34]

Even if a franchisor is not legally liable for a data privacy or security failure that occurred at the franchisee level, the risk of franchisee bankruptcy may prompt the franchisor to take action.

A franchise system's obligations and exposure related to data breach are not limited to domestic enforcement actions. In the European Union, the GDPR requires data controllers to "without undue delay and, where feasible, not later than 72 hours after having become aware of it, notify the personal data breach to the supervisory authority competent in accordance with Article 55, unless the personal data breach is unlikely to result in a risk to the rights and freedoms of natural persons."[35] From a practical standpoint, it is rarely possible to determine with certainty—within 72 hours—whether there has been a personal data breach. For franchisors who are under an obligation to report a personal data breach resulting from the accidental or unlawful destruction, loss, alteration, unauthorized disclosure of, or access to, franchisee or customer personal data, the determination of whether there has actually been a personal data breach is likely to take even longer. The franchisor's lack of familiarity with the data collection practices of its Master Franchisees and sub-franchisees could result in further complications when investigating such data breaches, making the timing of the required notification to supervisory authorities even more uncertain.

In addition, the GDPR also requires notification to affected individuals "without undue delay" "when the personal data breach is likely to result in a high risk to the rights and freedoms of natural persons."[36] Although this obligation is imposed on the data controller and not on the data processor, the ability to notify the affected individuals—in a franchisor-franchisee relationship—will often depend on how diligently records have been maintained by the franchisor or franchisee (e.g., Can the e-mail or mailing addresses for business customers be efficiently located?). As such, the data controller's ability to fulfill its legal obligations may depend heavily on the data management practices of other stakeholders in the franchise system.

---

32. Settlement Agmt. and Release, In Re: Sonic Corp. Customer Data Security Breach, No. 1:17-md-02807 (N.D. Ohio), Dkt. No. 132-2.

33. Torres, et al. v. Wendy's International LLC, Case No. 6:16-cv-210-PGB-DCI, in the U.S. District Court for the Middle District of Florida

34. https://www.mashed.com/149178/the-real-reason-why-noodles-and-company-is-struggling/.

35. EU General Data Protection Regulation (2016/679) Art. 33.

36. EU General Data Protection Regulation (2016/679) Art. 34.

Companies can be heftily fined for GDPR violations, with potential fines of up to €20 million or up to 4 percent of annual turnover, whichever is higher. In addition, reporting a personal data breach to EU supervisory authorities may elicit further scrutiny into companies' general data privacy practices.

Although much of the international focus on data privacy regulation has been concentrated on the GDPR, many other jurisdictions around the world have begun imposing strict data breach reporting requirements. Notably, countries where data privacy laws and regulations have increased in strictness over the past few years, such as South Korea and Thailand, also have imposed short time period requirements for reporting breached, ranging from "immediately upon discovery" to 24 to 72 hours from the time of discovery. As in the EU, reporting such breaches to authorities often prompts regulators to further scrutinize companies' data privacy compliance, particularly with respect to local operations. These types of inquiries may be limited to data breach and security incident policies and procedures but are often expanded to include companies' data retention and general data management practices, cross-border transfer of data, training of employees, and other aspects of general compliance.

Lastly, aside from the monetary consequences of data breaches, franchisors will most often be impacted by the reputational harm that can come following a mishandled—or even properly handled—data breach.

Franchisors can take action to reduce their risks. These steps include:

- *Records Retention and Destructions Plan.* Implementing and putting into practice a schedule by which records will be inventoried and consciously kept or deleted.
  - Formulating generic data retention and destruction policy
  - Conducting high-level inventory/business process interviews to customize data deletion practices
  - Drafting and revising written policies concerning data retention and deletion
  - Conducting training in data security best practices
  - Establishing schedules for audits to document enforcement
  - Implementing special policies for FCRA-covered applicant and employee data
- *Incident Response Plan.* Drafting and implementing a written action plan to be followed in the event of the loss, theft, or misuse of personal information and/or compromise of information systems (e.g., by ransomware).
  - Formulating a generic incident response plan
  - Conducting fact-finding and holding discussions to customize plan to the business
  - Conducting training to familiarize employees with the requirements of the incident response plan
  - Holding a tabletop exercise
  - Consider employing third parties to conduct an "ethical hack" of business systems to test for potential weaknesses

- *Review of Cyber Risk Insurance.* Evaluating the coverage options that make sense given the data security profile of the business.
  - Reviewing existing coverage
  - Noting any problematic substantive limits, exclusions, or amounts
  - Suggesting the consideration of alternative coverage, declarations, and endorsements
  - Obtaining broker assistance through the underwriting and binding process

While planning for the potential of a data breach, the franchisor should also consider the potential for facing a ransomware demand. For example, in 2014 a criminal stole personal data for more than 60,000 customers of Domino's franchisees in Belgium and France.[37] The criminal threatened to release the data unless it was paid $40,000. The franchisees informed the franchisor, who made the decision not to pay the ransom demand.

8-4. Additional Privacy Concerns

There does not have to be a data security breach for the franchisor to face serious liability. Liability can also arise from franchisees' improper collection or misuse of consumer information. For example, the FTC investigated and entered into a consent order with Aaron's, Inc., a national, Atlanta-based rent-to-own retailer, "to settle FTC charges that it knowingly played a direct and vital role in its franchisees' installation and use of software on rental computers that secretly monitored consumers including by taking webcam pictures of them in their homes."[38] The tool in question was PC Rental Agent, which allows IT support to remotely access PCs and help fix them. However, certain franchisees misused the tool and used it to improperly spy on consumers. Although the tool was created and provided to franchisees for a legitimate purpose, the FTC held Aaron's responsible because Aaron's was aware of the potential for the tool's abuse by franchisees to engage in privacy invasions. The FTC also noted that Aaron's "stored data collected by the software for its franchisees and also transmitted messages from the software to its franchisees." Under the consent order, Aaron's was "required to conduct annual monitoring and oversight of its franchisees and hold them to the requirements in the agreement that apply to Aaron's and its corporate stores, and to terminate the franchise agreements of franchises that do not meet those requirements."[39]

In May 2010, a putative class action was filed against Papa John's International, as well as several Papa John's franchisees, for violations of the Telephone

37. https://www.law360.com/articles/548383/domino-s-rebuffs-hackers-threat-to-publish-customer-data.

38. *Aaron's Rent-To-Own Chain Settles FTC Charges That it Enabled Computer Spying by Franchisees*, Federal Trade Commission (Oct. 22, 2013), https://www.ftc.gov/news-events/press-releases/2013/10/aarons-rent-own-chain-settles-ftc-charges-it-enabled-computer.

39. *Id.*

Consumer Protection Act (TCPA) and the Washington Consumer Protection Act.[40] Statutory damages under the TCPA are $500 per violation or $1,500 per willful violation.[41] The plaintiffs alleged that they had received commercial text messages sent from Papa John's without the recipient's prior express consent, actions that violate the TCPA and the state consumer protection law. Plaintiffs argued that the franchisor and franchisees, as well as their third-party vendor who actually sent the messages, acted in concert to approve, ratify, and further direct the illegal marketing campaign. Although the defendants argued, among other things, that the franchisor was not liable for the acts of the franchisee, the case dragged on for three years before settling. The nationwide litigation class that was certified in November 2012 included all persons who had received at least one unsolicited text message that marketed a Papa John's branded product, good, or service. The brand mattered, not an individual defendant's status as a franchisor or franchisee. In May 2013, the court approved a proposed class action settlement valued at $16.5 million. The proposed settlement included a free pizza coupon for all class members notified of the settlement and $50 for each class member who filed a claim, as well as administrative costs and plaintiffs' attorney's fees.

The Papa John's plaintiffs arguably did not understand the difference between Papa John's the franchisor and each Papa John's franchisee. All plaintiffs apparently understood was that they received text messages advertising Papa John's pizza deals, and that was enough for them to try to pin liability on all named defendants. Statutory damages for TCPA violations add up quickly, as the calls or texts at issue can sometime be part of a large-scale marketing campaign. Even if a franchisor successfully shows that a franchisee engaged in its own marketing campaign without direction or authority from the franchisor, and the franchisor is thus not liable, the franchisor and brand can suffer. The franchisee may not be able to remain solvent when faced with statutory damages or a settlement. Public perception of the entity at "fault" may not change with a franchisor "win" in court—the public may still view the brand as having acted badly in the marketplace. A more recent TCPA class action that resulted in a $6 million settlement ensnared not only the franchisees who sent the messages but also Pizza Hut itself.[42]

Franchisors can take action to reduce their risks. These steps include:

- *Knowing what franchisees are doing with technology.* Many technologies pose some risk to consumer privacy. At a franchise level there should be some general awareness of what technology is being deployed by franchisees and how it is being used.

---

40. Agne v. Rock City Pizza, LLC, Case No. 10-2-19384-1, Kings County Superior Court (WA) (May 28, 2010). The action was subsequently removed July 14, 2010. Agne v. Rock City Pizza, LLC, Case No. 2:10-cv-01139-JCC (W.D. Wash.).

41. Telephone Consumer Protection Act, 47 U.S.C. § 227(b)(3).

42. Keim v. ADF MidAtlantic LLC et al., case number 9:12-cv-80577 (S.D Fla 2012). https://www.law360.com/articles/1215360/pizza-hut-franchisees-to-pay-6m-to-end-tcpa-class-action.

- *Require training on special uses of technology.* Focusing in on potential use cases that have been the subject of litigation, or that government agencies or the plaintiff's bar have identified as priorities, and then train employees and franchisees and document that the training has occurred.
- *Audit special uses of technology.* Get a real-world sense of how technology is used and abused; consider disciplinary action against franchisees posing harm to the brand.

8-5. The California Consumer Privacy Act of 2018

The California Consumer Privacy Act of 2018 (the CCPA)[43] was signed into law by California Governor Jerry Brown on June 28, 2018, after being introduced and passed in a hurry by the California Legislature. The final bill reflected the rushed circumstances under which it was passed. The CCPA went into effect on January 1, 2020. A number of amendments were passed, including the introduction of a six-month enforcement grace period to July 1, 2020. The recent passage of the Consumer Privacy Rights Act (CPRA) by state referendum in November 2020 has added further amendments to the CCPA;[44] changes will go into effect on January 1, 2023, with enforcement actions commencing on July 1, 2023.[45] The California State Attorney General has issued supporting regulations further specifying compliance with the CCPA.[46] Although the California Attorney General has provided some guidance concerning how the CCPA is to be enforced, it continues to pose challenges to businesses that want to be sure they are doing everything they need to do to ensure CCPA compliance. In turn, the CCPA also creates opportunities for companies to step up and distinguish themselves through strong data privacy and cybersecurity practices. As such, CCPA compliance will help companies bolster their commitments to consumer choice and demonstrate transparency and trust.

---

43. Cal. Civ. Code § 1798.100, *et seq.*

44. Shortly after California's passage of the CPRA, Virginia introduced its own privacy legislation, the Consumer Data Protection Act, granting Virginia residents certain detailed privacy rights. An influx of state-specific privacy laws could add pressure at the federal level to pass a form of overarching privacy legislation to avoid state-by-state inconsistencies. Ashley Shively, *Silver Medal in Consumer Privacy Race Goes to . . . Virginia?* JD Supra (Feb. 5, 2021), https://www.jdsupra.com/legalnews/silver-medal-in-consumer-privacy-race-5939243. Colorado also passed its own privacy legislation, the Colorado Privacy Act. Colorado Privacy Act, Senate Bill 21-190, 73d Leg., 2021 Regular Sess. (Colo. 2021), to be codified in Colo. Rev. Stat. (C.R.S.) Title 6.

45. Wynter Deagle et al., *Californians Pass CPRA, Expanding Consumer Privacy Protections*, JD Supra (Nov. 11, 2020), https://www.jdsupra.com/legalnews/californians-pass-cpra-expanding-36350/.

46. Cal. Code Regs. tit. 11, §§ 999.300–.337.

(a) What Is the CCPA?

The California Consumer Privacy Act is the most comprehensive privacy law in the country. Targeted at companies that collect and/or sell personal information, the CCPA is designed to give "consumers" (defined as natural persons who are California residents) more control over their own data.

The intent of the CCPA is to put consumers in control of their personal information and grant them new statutory rights to learn what personal information a covered business has collected, sold, and disclosed. The CCPA creates four core individual rights for consumers: (1) right to know, (2) right to "opt-out," (3) right to deletion, and (4) right to not be discriminated against for exercising privacy rights under the CCPA. In addition, the CPRA enumerates two new consumer rights to the CCPA: the right to limit use[47] and the right to rectification.[48]

The CCPA defines "personal information" broadly to include any information that "identifies, relates to, describes, references, is capable of being associated with, or could reasonably be linked, directly or indirectly with a particular consumer or household."[49] The definition of personal information in the CCPA includes but is not limited to 11 enumerated categories of information relating to consumers. The CCPA retains the legislature's broad approach defining "personal information" to include categories of personal information that are not typically referenced expressly in U.S. privacy laws, such as commercial information (consumer purchasing history/tendencies) and Internet activity/interactions with websites, advertisements, or applications. Notably, the legislative intent initially was to be applied to consumers and *devices* rather than consumers and *households.* While the CCPA defines personal information in detail, the definition references information linked to a particular household, which could theoretically include any child, spouse, or even roommate residing the household. Additionally, the CPRA adds a new category of "sensitive" personal information that consumers may choose to opt-out from. This category covers information not traditionally included in the definition of "personal information," including race, ethnicity, religion, union membership, private personal communications, and sex life or sexual orientation.[50]

Many of the provisions of the CCPA include complying with consumer requests for their personal information. Others require businesses to make certain disclosures upfront and to retain data they collect in certain instances. The CPRA requires privacy disclosures to describe the retention period for each category of information collected, details regarding the processing of sensitive personal information, the new consumer right to correct information, and whether the personal information is sold or shared.[51] It also requires businesses whose processing

---

47. Cal. Civ. Code § 1798.121 (effective Dec. 16, 2020; operative Jan. 1, 2023, pursuant to Sec. 31 of Proposition 24).

48. Cal. Civ. Code § 1798.106.

49. Cal. Civ. Code § 1798.140(o).

50. Cal. Civ. Code § 1798.140(ae).

51. Cal. Civ. Code § 1798.100(a).

"presents a significant risk to consumers' privacy of security" to perform a cybersecurity audit and submit a risk assessment on a regular basis.[52]

Businesses collecting data from California residents must also be ready to wipe out that data upon request (i.e., right to deletion). Under the CCPA, consumers have a right to request that a business delete any personal information which the business has collected from the consumer. Not only must businesses comply with the consumer's request to delete personal information from its records, but also in many cases it must also direct any service providers to delete the consumer's personal information from their records.

(b) Who Must Comply with the CCPA?

The CCPA imposes obligations on any business that collects and/or processes personal information about California residents (and meets certain additional criteria). Service providers and contractors are also subject to regulation under the CCPA.[53]

The term "business" is broad and includes "a sole proprietorship, partnership, limited liability company, corporation, association, or other legal entity that is organized or operated for the profit or financial benefit of its shareholders or other owners, that collects consumers' personal information . . . alone . . . or jointly with others[.]"[54]

A covered business under the CCPA must satisfy one or more of the following thresholds:

- Annual gross revenues over $25 million;[55]
- Annually buys, receives, sells, or shares personal information of over 100,000 consumers, households, or devices;[56] or
- Derives at least 50 percent of annual revenue from selling or sharing consumers' personal information.

The Act also applies to an entity that controls or is controlled by such a *business* that shares their common branding.

Businesses do have some protections under the CCPA. A business does not have to delete consumer information if it needs the consumer's personal

52. Cal. Civ. Code § 1798.185(a)(15).

53. *See* Cal. Civ. Code § 1798.140(ag)(1)(D) (service provider contracts must be amended to prohibit the sharing of personal information and must also prohibit "combining" personal information received from a given business with any personal information received from others); *see also* Cal. Civ. Code § 1798.140(j) (enumerating required contract terms and requiring contractors to provide a certification that they will comply with restrictions regarding personal information).

54. Cal. Civ. Code § 1798.140(d)(1).

55. Revenues are calculated according to the preceding calendar year. Cal. Civ. Code § 1798.140(d) (effective Dec. 16, 2020; operative Jan. 1, 2023, pursuant to Sec. 31 of Proposition 24).

56. Cal. Civ. Code § 1798.140(d) (effective Dec. 16, 2020; operative Jan. 1, 2023, pursuant to Sec. 31 of Proposition 24).

information in order to complete a transaction for which the personal information was collected or provide a good or service requested by the consumer. The business also does not have to delete the consumer information if it proves to be valuable in detecting security incidents' protecting against malicious, deceptive, fraudulent, or illegal activity or prosecuting those responsible for that activity.

In contrast, "service provider" means a sole proprietorship, partnership, limited liability company, corporation, association, or other legal entity that is organized or operated for the profit or financial benefit of its shareholders or other owners, that processes information on behalf of a business and to which the business discloses a consumer's personal information for a business purpose pursuant to a written contract, provided that the contract prohibits the entity receiving the information from retaining, using, or disclosing the personal information for any purpose other than for the specific purpose of performing the services specified in the contract for the business, or as otherwise permitted by this title, including retaining, using, or disclosing the personal information for a commercial purpose other than providing the services specified in the contract with the business.[57]

(c) The Right to Know

The CCPA grants a California consumer the right to know and request from a business the categories and specific pieces of personal information a business has collected about the consumer, the categories of sources from which that information is collected, the business purpose for collecting or selling the information, and the categories of third parties with whom the personal information is sold or otherwise shared.

The CCPA requires businesses to comply with "verifiable requests" from consumers about the collection, sale, and disclosure of their personal information and outlines specific procedures and timelines that businesses must follow.[58] Businesses will have to disclose the requested information free of charge within 45 days of the receipt of a consumer's request, subject to possible extensions of this time frame. Companies therefore will need to determine how they can monitor their data sharing practices and marshal the requested information within a short period of time pursuant to a data subject's request.

(d) The Right to "Opt-Out"

Under the CCPA, California consumers are afforded the right to "opt-out" of the "sale" (which is broadly defined) or "sharing"[59] of their personal information.

57. CAL. CIV. CODE § 1798.140(v).

58. Whereas previously, consumers were subject to a 12-month "look-back period," consumers now have the right to make requests for disclosures that extend beyond the 12 months preceding the request. CAL. CIV. CODE § 1798.130(a)(2)(B).

59. The CPRA introduces "sharing" as a new term, defined as disclosing personal information to third parties for cross-contextual behavioral advertising purposes, whether or not for monetary or other valuable consideration. CAL. CIV. CODE § 1798.140(ah)(1).

Companies that sell or share consumer data with third parties will need to disclose that practice and give consumers the ability to opt-out of the sale by providing a clear and conspicuous link on the business's home page titled "Do Not Sell My Personal Information." Businesses must implement designated methods for consumers to opt-out (including a toll-free number and website address for opting-out). This is known as the right to opt-out. The CCPA further provides the personal information of minors under the age of 16 may only be sold or shared if the consumer's parent or guardian has affirmatively authorized (opted-in to) the sale. For minors aged 13 to 16, affirmative authorization is also required, but the consumer may provide the authorization. This is known as the right to "opt-in."

(e) The Right to Delete

Under the CCPA, California consumers have a right to request a business delete any personal information about the consumer that the business has collected, with some exceptions.[60] Businesses must honor a "verifiable" request to delete consumer personal information, subject to several notable exceptions, including that a business need not delete personal information if maintaining the information is required to complete a transaction or provide a good or service.[61] A business may deny a deletion request where retaining personal information is reasonably necessary to fulfill the terms of a written warranty or product recall conducted in accordance with federal law. It may also deny a request if it proves to be valuable in detecting security incidents; protecting against malicious, deceptive, fraudulent, or illegal activity; or prosecuting those responsible for that activity.

(f) The Right to Limit Use

Under the CPRA, consumers now have the right to direct a business to limit its use of their personal information to what is necessary to perform services or provide goods reasonably expected by an average consumer who requests those goods or services.[62]

(g) The Right to Rectification

Consumers may also request that a business correct any inaccurate personal information about the consumer, and the business must use "commercially reasonable efforts to correct the inaccurate personal information as directed by the consumer."[63]

60. Cal. Civ. Code § 1798.105(a).

61. Cal. Civ. Code § 1798.105(d)(1).

62. Cal. Civ. Code § 1798.121 (effective Dec. 16, 2020; operative Jan. 1, 2023, pursuant to Sec. 31 of Proposition 24).

63. Cal. Civ. Code § 1798.120.

(h) The Right against Discrimination

The CCPA also prohibits businesses from "discriminating" against consumers for exercising their privacy rights under the statute. More specifically, that means businesses cannot deny goods or services, charge different prices for goods or services, or provide a different quality of goods or services to those consumers who exercise their privacy rights. However, under the CCPA, businesses may charge a different price, or provide a different level of service, to a customer "if that difference is reasonably related to the value provided to the consumer by the consumer's data."[64] It also is worth noting that businesses are permitted to offer financial incentives to consumers for the collection, sale, or deletion of personal information, subject to specific conditions and notice requirements.

8-6. The Regulations Add Confusion around "Discrimination" and the Future of Loyalty Programs

Under the CCPA, discrimination can include denying goods or services to the consumer, charging different prices or rates for goods or services, and providing a different level or quality of goods or services to the consumer.[65] The CCPA includes an exception, however: a business may offer a financial incentive or price or service difference in exchange for retention or sale of a consumer's personal information, so long as the incentive or price or service difference is *reasonably related to the value of the consumer's data.*[66]

The Regulations offer two examples to demonstrate permissible discrimination:[67]

1. A music streaming business offers a free service and a premium service that costs $5 per month. If only the consumers who pay for the music streaming service are allowed to opt-out of the sale of their personal information, then the practice is discriminatory, unless the $5 per month payment is reasonably related to the value of the consumer's data to the business.
2. A retail store offers discounted prices to consumers who sign up to be on their mailing list. If the consumers on the mailing list can continue to receive discounted prices even after they have made a request to know, request to delete, and/or request to opt-out, the differing price level is not discriminatory.

64. Cal. Civ. Code § 1798.125(a)(2).
65. Cal. Civ. Code § 1798.125.
66. Cal. Civ. Code § 1798.125(a)(2) (as amended); Cal Code Regs. § 999.336(a)–(b).
67. Cal. Code Regs. § 999.336(c).

Calculating "the value of the consumer's data" presents its own challenge. The Regulations provide eight methods for calculating the value of data,[68] but they do not provide much needed clarity. The broadest permissible method—"any other practical and reliable method of calculation used in good-faith"—seems to offer businesses significant flexibility, but it also gives the Attorney General significant authority to interpret terms. A franchisor should select a "permissible method" that aligns best with its business model.

8-7. Enforcement

The newly enacted CPRA creates the California Privacy Protection Agency and vests in it the administrative power to implement and enforce the CCPA.[69] The current rulemaking authority held by the Attorney General will transfer to the Agency six months after the Agency provides notice to the Attorney General that it is prepared to begin rulemaking, and the Agency will have until July 1, 2022, to adopt final regulations.[70] The state may not begin any enforcement of most CPRA provisions until July 1, 2023.[71] Consumers, on the other hand, can bring a private right of action for violations of the statute's data breach provision. Complicating businesses' efforts to operationalize the new provisions is the fact that the CPRA no longer contains the one-year, look-back window. In response to consumers' verifiable requests, starting in 2023, businesses must provide personal information that extends beyond 12 months preceding the request.[72] The obligation to provide more than one year of information applies only to personal information collected on or after January 1, 2022.[73]

8-8. What Should a Franchisor Do?

- Review CCPA requirements (both the statute and regulation).
- Determine data bases and data types that are within scope for CCPA.
- Determine how, as a practical matter, the franchise system is able to process data subject requests (using what information, through what queries) for requests to know, requests to delete, and if needed, requests to opt-out.
- Determine whether franchise is a "seller" of information who has to offer an opt-out under CCPA.
- Analyze CCPA requirements flowing from loyalty programs.
- Send a letter to service providers imposing/explaining CCPA requirements.
- Prepare a response to franchisees asking about CCPA.
- Draft and revise CCPA disclosures.

---

68. Cal. Code Regs. § 999.337(b).
69. Cal. Civ. Code § 1798.199.10(a).
70. Cal. Civ. Code § 1798.185(d).
71. Cal. Civ. Code § 1798.185(d).
72. Cal. Civ. Code § 1798.130(a)(2)(B).
73. Cal. Civ. Code § 1798.130(a)(2)(B).

- Do several dry runs of data subject requests of various types.
- Apply lessons learned from dry run.
- Brief CCPA training for relevant employees.
- Make 1-800 number and CCPA disclosures live.

8-9. European Union: GDPR Overview

(a) General Overview

The EU General Data Protection Regulation (GDPR) came into effect on May 25, 2018. At a high level, the GDPR applies to the processing of personal data by data controllers and processors established in the EU, as well as by controllers and processors outside the EU where their processing activities relate to the offering of goods or services (even for free) to data subjects within the EU, or to the monitoring of their behavior.

(b) Data Subject Rights

The GDPR includes a wide range of existing and new rights for data subjects. Among these are the right to data portability (right to obtain a copy of one's personal data from the controller and have it transferred to another controller), right to erasure (or "right to be forgotten"), right to restriction of processing, and right to object to certain processing activities (profiling) and to automated processing decisions. Controllers are also required to provide significantly more information to data subjects about their processing activities.

(c) Data Controllers under GDPR

Controllers are principally responsible for GDPR compliance, including providing notice to and obtaining consent from (where appropriate) from data subjects. They must maintain a record of processing activities and be ready to provide detailed information regarding the same to supervisory authorities upon request. Further, controllers are required to perform a Data Protection Impact Assessment (DPIA) where the processing of personal data (particularly when using new technologies) is likely to result in a high risk to the rights and freedoms of the individuals.

(d) Data Processors under GDPR

The GDPR also imposes compliance obligations directly on processors, such as implementing security measures, notifying the data controller of data breaches, appointing a DPO (if applicable), maintaining records of processing activities, and so on. Processors are directly liable in case of non-compliance and may be subject to direct enforcement action. Controllers and processors will be required to enter into detailed processing agreements or renegotiate existing ones.

(e) Cross-Border Transfers of Data

The mark of a large and well-established franchise system often is its international presence. Large franchises headquartered in the United States will have to contend with putting in place proper mechanisms for the cross-border transfer of data.

- *Transfers from the EU.* Under GDPR, data may be transferred out of the EU/EEA only to countries that have been recognized as providing an adequate level of data protection, unless the transferor can rely on specific derogations or adduces specific additional safeguards ensuring an adequate level of data protection. Such safeguards include the EU Standard Contractual Clauses, Binding Corporate Rules. In the absence of an adequacy decision or appropriate safeguards, personal data may also be transferred out of the EU pursuant to specific derogations.
- Until recently, transfers from the EU to the US were also covered by the EU-US Privacy Shield Framework (Privacy Shield). However, in July 2020, the European Court of Justice (ECJ) declared the European Commission's Privacy Shield decision invalid, largely due to invasive U.S. surveillance practices such as Foreign Intelligence Surveillance Act Orders and National Security Letters, thereby making transfers of personal data on the basis of the Privacy Shield illegal. Although companies in the United States may no longer use Privacy Shield as their sole mechanism for cross-border transfers of data from the EU to the United States, companies that have self-certified to Privacy Shield must still comply with Privacy Shield principles, unless they formally withdraw. Further, companies should also consider ancillary obligations, such as contractual agreements with their affiliates and customers, as well as other representations with respect to Privacy Shield compliance.
- Aside from invalidating the Privacy Shield, the ECJ's decision in *Data Protection Commissioner v. Facebook Ireland and Maximillian Schrems*, Case C-311/18 (Schrems II) affirmed that the SCCs are an adequate mechanism for the cross-border transfer of personal data from the EU to the United States, with the caveat that additional safeguards should be put in place to mitigate the U.S. surveillance concerns mentioned above. The European Data Protection Board (EDPB) subsequently issued draft guidance on this point, which outlines several potential mitigating measures while simultaneously emphasizing the need for a data protection impact assessment for each transfer in part. As of the date of this publication, the EDPB's guidelines are still in draft form.
- Furthermore, almost concurrently with the EDPB's guidelines, the European Commission has also published new draft SCCs, which—once finalized—will replace the existing SCCs that are currently used by many organizations for cross-border transfers from the EU. Importantly, the new draft SCCs include two new "flavors" in addition to the standard

controller-to-controller and controller-to-processor, specifically accounting for processor-to-processor and processor-to-controller transfers.

- *Transfers from other international jurisdictions.* Many other international jurisdictions have put in place requirements for the cross-border transfer of personal data. For example, in China, the Cyberspace Administration of China (CAC) recently published the draft Measures for Security Assessment of Export of Personal Information (Draft Security Assessment Measures). The general proposed rule under the Draft Security Assessment Measures is that in order to transfer any personal information overseas, a network operator (broadly defined under applicable law) must conduct a security self-assessment and then file the self-assessment report with the provincial counterpart of the CAC, for its security assessment review. In Brazil, the Lei Geral de Proteção de Dados Pessoais (LGPD) went into effect in August 2020. Much like the GDPR, the LGPD allows for the cross-border transfer of personal data to countries with adequate data protection laws in place, based upon safeguards (e.g., Standard Contractual Clauses), or based upon the prior, specific consent of the data subject.

Table of Cases

Index

About the Editors

Elizabeth Dillon

Elizabeth (Liz) Dillon is a partner at Lathrop GPM and serves as the leader of the firm's Franchise & Distribution Practice Group. Liz counsels growing and experienced franchisors to expand and maintain their franchise systems. She also assists startup franchisors to develop and position their franchise systems for growth both domestically and internationally. Liz manages the franchise registration process for many well-known and emerging brands every year and has worked with numerous startup franchisors. She has helped franchisors expand into Latin America, the Caribbean, Asia, Europe, and the Middle East. She brings extensive knowledge and experience in preparing and registering disclosure documents, as well as franchise, development, and supply agreements. Liz also assists clients through mergers and acquisitions, providing franchise, licensing, and distribution expertise for transactions. In addition to representing franchisors, Liz represents other companies in the myriad legal issues involved with the distribution of goods. She advises on matters including dealer/distribution agreements, international sale of goods, and avoiding franchise and business opportunity laws (accidental franchise). Liz has been recognized by Chambers USA and Chambers Global for her work in franchising.

James Goniea

James (Jim) Goniea has been practicing franchise law for over 30 years during which time he has had the opportunity to represent many of the most prominent brands in franchising. Jim has repeatedly been recognized as a leader in the field of franchise law. Currently, he is the General Counsel of Self Esteem Brands, LLC, whose brands include Anytime Fitness, Waxing the City, Basecamp Fitness, The Bar Method, and Stronger U. Jim is a frequent presenter at both the ABA Forum on Franchising Annual Conference and the IFA Legal Symposium. Jim previously served two terms on the Forum Governing Committee where, among other things, he served as Chair of the Publications Committee and Chair of the Technology Committee. Jim is the co-author of *Annual Franchise and Distribution Law Developments*, 2012, and is a previous chapter author of *The Franchise Compliance Manual*, 2d ed.

About the Authors

Brian H. Cole

Brian Cole has been practicing law for 40 years. He is currently a sole practitioner in Manhattan Beach, California, as well as Of Counsel to the Chase Law Group in the same city. For more than 30 years, Brian has devoted the bulk of his time to franchise law and related matters, including as an in-house attorney for one of the nation's largest franchisors, with two large law firms, and as a sole practitioner. Currently, Brian represents both franchisors and franchisees in transactional and regulatory matters and has also testified as an expert witness on franchise law. He has spoken over a dozen times to the Forum on Franchising or other bar-related groups and has authored or co-authored articles, papers, and chapters of books on a wide variety of franchise-related topics. Brian has served on the Franchise Law Committee of the State Bar of California (now known as the California Lawyers Association), including three terms as Chair of that Committee, and has also served (including as Chair) on the Franchise and Distribution Law Advisory committee to the California Board of Legal Specialization. Brian received his J.D. degree (with honors) from the University of Texas at Austin after completing his undergraduate education at Rice University in Houston. He is admitted to the Bars in California, Colorado (inactive), and Hawaii (inactive), and has been certified by the California Board of Legal Specialization as a Certified Specialist in Franchise and Distribution Law. Brian has been recognized as a Legal Eagle by *Franchise Times* magazine and as a Super Lawyer in Franchise and Distribution Law. His is rated AV Preeminent by Martindale-Hubbell.

Leslie D. Curran

Leslie D. Curran is a partner in the law firm Plave Koch PLC in Reston, Virginia. She focuses her practice on representing brand owners in connection with a broad range of domestic and international franchise, intellectual property licensing, and distribution and related legal issues. Leslie was named "Washington DC Franchise Law Lawyer of the Year" by *U.S. News/Best Lawyers* for 2016. She has also been recognized by, among others, Chambers U.S.A., *International Who's Who of Franchise Lawyers*, and *Franchise Times* as a Legal Eagle. Leslie is an active member of the ABA Forum on Franchising and other trade associations and business groups. She is a former member of the Governing Committee of the American Bar Association's Forum on Franchising. Leslie is a frequent author and speaker on franchise law and related topics. She was a co-editor of *Exemptions and Exclusions* (2017), and she has spoken at the ABA Forum on Franchising's annual meeting numerous times including on topics such as Exemption Based Franchising (Intensive) (2017); Art and Science of FDD Drafting (2014), and Crisis and Reputation Management (2013).

Elisa Edlund

Elisa Edlund was born in Colombia and immigrated to the United States at a young age. She received her B.A. from Concordia College in Moorhead, Minnesota, her J.D. from Washington University in St. Louis, and her LL.M. in Taxation from the University of Florida. She studied law abroad at the National University of Singapore and is licensed to practice law in Minnesota and New York. Elisa has worked in-house at various companies for over 18 years, most recently with American Dairy Queen Corporation (ADQ) since 2007. She provides legal counsel for the Dairy Queen® brand worldwide in advertising, privacy, and food law; negotiates a variety of advertising and technology-related contracts; and manages ADQ's global trademark and domain portfolios. In previous roles at ADQ, Elisa managed franchise disclosure document drafting and registration in the United States and Canada, and she oversaw worldwide intellectual property trademark infringement matters. Elisa is a past co-chair of the Minneapolis chapter of the Women's Franchise Network and a former volunteer for Big Brothers Big Sisters Twin Cities and the Immigrant Law Center of Minnesota. In addition to being an attorney, Elisa is a helicopter pilot with a private pilot license.

Jeff S. Haff

Jeff Haff is a franchise attorney in Minneapolis, Minnesota. Jeff has been recognized by numerous national publications as one of the best franchise lawyers in America. As a litigator, he has won, through settlement or trial, tens of millions of dollars for his franchisee clients. A 1989 honors graduate of the Duke University School of Law, Jeff lives with his wife, Carol, in Maple Grove, Minnesota.

Kevin P. Hein

Kevin Hein serves as co-chair of Akerman's Franchise and Licensing Practice, a highly experienced team that handles U.S. and international franchising, licensing, dealership and trademark counseling, registration, and litigation matters for franchisors, licensors, subfranchisors, dealers, and other business clients. For more than two decades, Kevin has focused his practice on counseling companies that rely on franchising as part of their distribution models on a wide range of legal issues, including state and federal disclosure requirements, compliance with state relationship laws, franchise sales compliance, restaurant and retail development, franchising in the health and wellness industries, mergers and acquisitions, corporate counseling, bankruptcy and reorganization, and dispute resolution. Kevin's experience in the restaurant industry includes advising clients regarding corporate formation, real estate acquisition and development, leasing issues, corporate financing activities, mergers and acquisitions, dispute resolution, general corporate matters, and franchise relationship issues. In addition, he regularly counsels established and emerging health care and wellness clients to ensure their franchise systems and licensing programs are structured to comply with federal and state laws regarding corporate practice of medicine, fee-splitting, Stark and physician self-referral regulations, HIPAA compliance, and other health care–related compliance issues.

Brian Hengesbaugh

Brian Hengesbaugh is Chair of Baker Mackenzie's Global Data Privacy and Security Business Unit and a member of the firm's Global IP Tech Steering Committee. Brian is listed in the Legal 500 Hall of Fame and was recognized as a Regulatory & Compliance Trailblazer by the *National Law Journal*. He is also listed as a Leading Lawyer for Cyber law (including data protection and privacy) in *The Legal 500* and is listed in Chambers. Formerly Special Counsel to the General Counsel of the U.S. Department of Commerce, Brian played a key role in the development and implementation of U.S. domestic and international policy in the area of privacy and electronic commerce. In particular, he served on the core team that negotiated the US-EU Safe Harbor Privacy Arrangement (Safe Harbor) and earned a Medal Award from the Department of Commerce for this service. Brian has been quoted in the *Wall Street Journal, New York Times, Forbes, CNET, Slate Magazine, Compliance Weekly, BNA Bloomberg, PCWorld*, and other news publications on global privacy and security issues.

Eric H. Karp

Eric H. Karp serves as counsel to franchisee associations and has represented franchisees throughout the country in myriad franchise issues. He served as Chair of the Governing Committee of the Forum on Franchising from 2017 to 2019. Eric also served as the Editor-in-Chief of *The Franchise Lawyer* from 2008 to 2010, and two terms as a Member at Large of the Governing Committee, during which he served as the Finance Officer of the Forum. He has been a presenter at the ABA Forum on Franchising on 12 occasions. Most recently he served as Chair of the 2020 and 2021 Nominating Committees. Since 1996, Eric has served on the Franchise Project Group of the Franchise and Business Opportunities Committee of the North American Securities Administrators Association.

Robert A. Lauer

Robert A. Lauer is a Partner in the Austin office of Haynes and Boone, LLP, and a member of the firm's Franchise and Distribution Practice Group. His practice focuses on all aspects of domestic and international franchise transactions. Robert was named to Chambers, Global Franchising, Band 3, 2011, Band 4, 2012, and Band 3, 2013 to 2021; Chambers USA, Franchising (Nationwide), Up and Coming, 2012 and Band 4, 2013 to 2020; the International Who's Who of Franchise Lawyers, Law Business Research, 2010 through 2020; The Best Lawyers in America® for Franchise Law in 2008 through 2021; and a "Texas Rising Star" by *Law & Politics Magazine* and *Texas Monthly* for 2005 and 2007 through 2012. He is a member of the ABA Forum on Franchising's Governing Committee through August 2022 and current officer of the International Bar Association's International Franchising Committee through 2022. Robert is a 1997 cum laude graduate of the St. Mary's University School of Law, where he served as an Associate Editor of *St. Mary's Law Journal*, and a 1994 graduate of Trinity University in San Antonio, Texas.

Alison (Ali) C. McElroy

Alison (Ali) McElroy is an experienced business executive and attorney specialized in building and leading high-impact teams for growth-oriented franchise, consumer service, and international businesses. Ali is President, International and Chief Legal Officer with Lift Brands, Inc. based in Minnesota. She is responsible for business development and operations for Lift Brands' international business units including SNAP FITNESS global operations in 20-plus countries and the company's 9ROUND licensed locations in Europe, Australia/New Zealand, and Mexico. Together, SNAP FITNESS and 9ROUND have over 2,000 locations. Ali is also responsible for the legal, franchise administration, and human resources functions for Lift Brands, including the SNAP FITNESS franchise system, franchise investments divisions, and all commercial divisions. She serves on the International Franchise Committee of the International Franchise Association and is also a member of the American Bar Association Forum on Franchising and served as chair of the Corporate Counsel Division Steering Committee from 2014 to 2016. Ali was named one of 100 Influential Women in Franchising in 2020 by *Global Franchise* magazine.

Mark Melodia

Mark Melodia is based in New York City with Holland & Knight LLP and leads its Data Strategy, Security & Privacy practice. Mark has defended clients facing privacy and data security class actions in state and federal courts throughout the country. Over the past 15 years, he has been lead defense counsel in over 100 putative class actions (and three MDLs) arising from either a data security incident (breach, exposed vulnerability, or ransomware) or allegations of data misuse, over sharing or over collection. Most recently, he has defended a series of cases making claims that data sharing on websites and IoT devices are violating federal and state wiretap statutes. He also represents clients on privacy and data security issues before the FTC, OCR, and State AGs. Mark helps companies in a wide range of industries prepare for and respond to significant cyber events and is called upon by their boards and senior management teams to help realize the potential and minimize the risk of their data. He is recognized by Chambers U.S. and Chambers Global as one of the top five privacy litigators, and he is an Elected Member of the American Law Institute. He is an honors graduate of both Princeton University and New York University School of Law.

David W. Oppenheim

David W. Oppenheim is a Principal Shareholder at Greenberg Traurig, LLP. He concentrates his practice on domestic and international franchising, licensing, and distribution matters. He advises both emerging and mature companies with respect to planning, structuring, and implementing national and international franchise, distribution, and licensing programs. David also represents private equity firms and public and private companies in the acquisition of franchise, licensing, and distribution systems. He is recognized by Chambers USA as a leading, national franchise attorney. He served as a member of the ABA Forum on Franchising Governing Committee (2013-2019) and as Co-Chair of the 39th Annual Forum on Franchising in Miami Beach, Florida. David is a Past Chair of the New York State Bar Association Business Law Section, and he is a Past Chair of the New York State Bar's Franchise, Licensing and Distribution Committee. He has been featured in Best Lawyers in America annually since 2009 and was named its "Franchise Lawyer of the Year" in New York for 2013, 2017, and 2019. David has been repeatedly selected as a New York Super Lawyer and has been featured in *The International Who's Who of Franchise Lawyers* annually since 2010 and in *Franchise Times* as a "Legal Eagle" annually since 2006. He is a frequent author and speaker on the topic of franchising and related legal issues.

Ted Pearce

Ted Pearce is counsel with the law firm of Bradley Arant Boult Cummings in Charlotte, North Carolina. Prior to Bradley, Ted was the Vice President and General Counsel for Driven Brands, which owns Meineke Car Care Centers, Maaco Auto Painting, Econo Lube and Tune, and other notable auto-aftermarket brands. Ted has been a frequent speaker at the ABA forum meetings and the International Franchise Association. He is the author of numerous articles on franchising chapters of various ABA Forum franchise treatises.

Sherin Sakr

Sherin Sakr was born in Cairo, Egypt, and lived in Germany and Puerto Rico before settling in the United States. She is fluent in Arabic, German, Spanish, and English. Sherin received her B.S. from the University of Cincinnati in 1996 and her J.D. and LL.M. in Taxation from the University of Denver in 1999 and 2001, respectively. Before leaving Denver, she worked for the regional law firm of Snell & Wilmer LLP, during which time she assisted in the drafting of disclosure documents and franchise agreements for Cold Stone Creamery's development into Taiwan, China, and South Korea. Immediately prior to joining Kahala Brands, Sherin was a Senior in the International Tax Services group of Ernst & Young LLP in Irvine, CA. In her various roles at Kahala Brands, she drafted and negotiated international franchise agreements, managed the international trademark portfolio for all brands franchised by Kahala Brands, prosecuted trademark infringers around the globe, and was actively involved in the negotiation and purchase of America's Taco Shop, Planet Smoothie, Tasty D'Lite, Pinkberry, Maui Wowi, Baja Fresh, and La Salsa; the integration of those brands into Kahala's systems, including the drafting of franchise disclosure documents and re-negotiation of supplier agreements; and the ultimate sale of Kahala Brands to MTY Group in Canada. As VP Legal at Realogy Franchise Group, she was brand counsel for Century 21 Real Estate and Coldwell Banker Real Estate, supporting their sales, operations, and marketing functions, as well as being involved in various company-wide strategic projects impacting all brands franchised by Realogy. Sherin is now General Counsel for WellBiz Brands, the franchisor of Amazing Lash Studio, Elements Massage, Fitness Together, and most recently, Drybar.

Max J. Schott, II

Max J. Schott, II, is a shareholder in the Minneapolis office of Larkin Hoffman. He represents franchisors, manufacturers, distributors, and suppliers in the areas of franchise and distribution law. His clients range from startups to nationally recognized companies with multiple brands. With a practice that has spanned over 25 years, Max has a unique understanding of the business challenges facing his clients. He assists and counsels them on issues of disclosure and registration, domestic and international program structuring, relationship matters, supply chain maintenance, advertising, licensing, and acquisitions. Max frequently writes and speaks on franchise-related topics and is a co-author of the chapter "Structuring the Franchise Relationship" in the ABA Forum's *Fundamentals of Franchising*, Fourth Edition. As an active member of the ABA Forum, he previously served as Editor-in-Chief of *The Franchise Lawyer* and currently serves on the Marketing Committee. Throughout his career, Max has been recognized by Chambers USA as one of the country's leading franchise lawyers for business (2011–2020), The International Who's Who of Franchise Lawyers (2011–2020), Franchise Times as a Legal Eagle (2007–2019, 2021), "North Star Lawyers," Minnesota State Bar Association (2012, 2014–2018), and The Best Lawyers in America© (2016–2021). Max received a B.A. in political science from Grinnell College in 1990 and a J.D., with distinction, from the University of Iowa College of Law in 1993.

Susan Sheely

Susan Sheely is VP and Deputy General Counsel for Self Esteem Brands, LLC, where she provides legal advice and support to compliance, operations, franchise administration, and franchise sales teams for the company's four franchise brands: Anytime Fitness®, Waxing the City®, Basecamp® Fitness, and The Bar Method®. Prior to joining Self Esteem Brands, Susan was in-house litigation counsel for Ameriprise Financial, providing legal support to multiple business lines as well as representing franchisee financial advisors in arbitration actions nationwide. In private practice, Susan represented clients in state and federal courts throughout Minnesota and assisted clients in resolving business disputes through negotiation, mediation, and litigation. She is a 2005 graduate of Mitchell Hamline School of Law.

Susan Tegt

Susan Tegt is a partner at Larkin Hoffman in Minneapolis, Minnesota, and is co-chair of the firm's franchise and distribution practice group. Susan's practice focuses on representing franchisors across a broad range of industries in litigation and arbitration involving franchise sales and terminations, navigating state disclosure and relationship laws, covenants not to compete, unfair competition, and protecting trademark and trade secret rights. She also defends manufacturers and other putative franchisors facing claims brought under state franchise laws. Susan also worked as in-house counsel for an international franchisor, providing her with a unique skill set and familiarity with the issues commonly faced by her clients. She is a former member of the Forum on Franchising's Women's Caucus and a repeat author of the Forum's *Franchise Lawyer*. She has been recognized since 2018 as one of the Best Lawyers in America® for franchise law and is consistently recognized as a "Rising Star" by Super Lawyers® and a "Legal Eagle" by Franchise Times.